Toward
New Interior

Toward a New Interior

—

An Anthology of Interior Design Theory

Lois Weinthal, editor

Princeton Architectural Press · New York

Published by
Princeton Architectural Press
A McEvoy Group company
202 Warren Street, Hudson, NY 12534

Visit our website at www.papress.com

Editor: Dan Simon

Special thanks to: Bree Anne Apperley, Sara Bader, Nicola Bednarek Brower,
Janet Behning, Fannie Bushin, Megan Carey, Carina Cha, Tom Cho,
Russell Fernandez, Jan Haux, Linda Lee, Jennifer Lippert, John Myers,
Katharine Myers, Margaret Rogalski, Paul Wagner, Joseph Weston,
and Deb Wood of Princeton Architectural Press
—Kevin C. Lippert, publisher

Library of Congress
Cataloging-in-Publication Data
Toward a new interior / [edited by] Lois Weinthal. — 1st ed.
648 p. : ill. ; 23 cm.
Includes bibliographical references and index.
ISBN 978-1-61689-030-8 (alk. paper)
1. Interior architecture—Philosophy. I. Weinthal, Lois.
NA2850.T69 2011
729—dc23

2011021280

Table of Contents

Chapter 4: Color and Surfaces

Chapter 5: Mapping the Interior

Chapter 6: Private Chambers

Acknowledgments

It would not have been possible to bring together this collection of essays and frame them into a new vision for interiors without the assistance and guidance of former students, colleagues, and those dearest to me who have provided feedback and support along the way. Encouragement first came from students who had passed through my seminar suggesting I publish the course reader. One former student, Allison Hsiao Gaskins, provided insightful feedback during the seminar and I thank her for assisting me early in the transformation of the theory reader into this publication. Christine Cantwell, a colleague and friend who has traveled with me to many of the sites explored in this reader, offered guidance in organizing ideas that she has heard me speak about for years. She gave me words when I was at a loss for them. I would like to thank her for her editing, critiquing, and most important, encouraging me to include personal anecdotes, thereby breaking one of the conventions of architectural theory.

The process of locating text and images put me in contact with many of the authors and artists represented in these essays whom I would like to thank for their contribution to this reader. I am appreciative of funding for this publication made possible by a University Co-operative Society Subvention Grant awarded by The University of Texas at Austin. A generous thank you goes to Dean Frederick Steiner and Dr. Nancy Kwallek from the School of Architecture at The University of Texas at Austin for support of this project. A special thank you goes to my editors, Jennifer Thompson and Dan Simon at Princeton Architectural Press, for recognizing the need for an interior design theory reader. I would like to thank my siblings, mother, and late father for being the actors that brought life to our family home. I am in gratitude for my husband, Jeff, who provided unconditional support in the undertaking of this project and to whom this book is dedicated. His patience over the years, especially in the final year of coordinating this book, made this publication a reality. Without him, it would have been impossible. And finally to our daughter, Sophia, who I hope will always explore interiors.

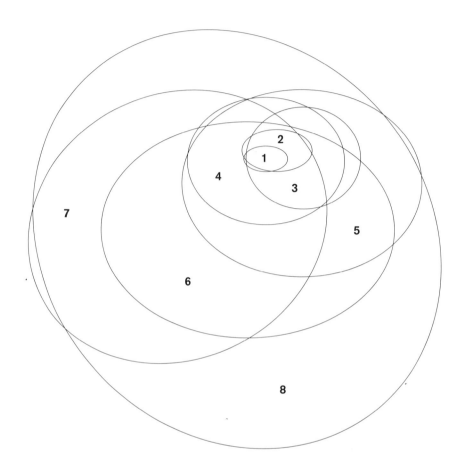

1: Body and Perception
2: Clothing and Identity
3: Furniture and Objects
4: Color and Surfaces
5: Mapping the Interior
6: Private Chambers
7: Public Performace
8: Bridging the Interior and Exterior

Preface

Interior design literature is in need of theoretical framing. While mentioned briefly in narrative histories or in an architectural context, there is more available knowledge and analysis about interior space to which design students and practitioners might otherwise have access. Architectural theory identifies major themes and ideas in the history of architecture, but an equivalent framework for interiors—one that references design history and simultaneously builds upon its interdisciplinary relationships—is missing and needs to be written.

Designers act upon interiors through multiple entry points that include atmospheric conditions like color and light, understanding the client's needs, giving form and shape to materials, and unifying these elements into a captivating design. These entry points have yet to be rationally organized to allow the development of interior design theory. This reader presents a structure for interior theory that considers physical construction and its resulting phenomenal experiences that constitute the interior. Its framework does not stem from any preexisting structure found in architecture; rather it comes from what is inherent to producing interiors.

A diagram of this anthology's organizational strategy and hypothesis imagines the interior viewed in eight concentric nested layers. Each layer (corresponding to the book's sections) comprises selected essays that relate to a broader set of concerns in interior design. The diagram's (and the book's) theoretical core begins with the body, which is surrounded by rings representing clothing, furniture, and architecture. These rings represent layers that organize the physical world so that emotionally charged themes, some left unspoken like nostalgia and memory, are allowed to emerge.

This reader places emphasis on a collection of artifacts within these layers in order to draw out themes. These artifacts represent interior design's interdisciplinary nature: a dialogue formed by architecture, art, fashion, film, engineering, history, literature, photography, philosophy, product design, and textiles. Some sources not directly based in interior design history, theory, or design studio offer a critique from alternate perspectives that reference the interior. This should give interior designers common points of intersection, resulting in a reader that richly explores the intangible in order to productively shape the tangible. As a result, this collection of sources looks to the interdisciplinary nature of the interior as a reflection of its evolution.

The book's organizational structure is intended to give interior design theory an origin. A look at theory in related disciplines, such as fine art and architecture, reveals that future interior design literature could reveal and increase the depth of the discipline by systematically exploring themes inherent to the interior.

My curiosity about how interior design history and theory could influence design was put into practice in a seminar that I first taught in 2001 at The University of Texas at Austin's School of Architecture and later continued at Parsons The New School for Design. I hoped to find source material that proposed alternative strategies for designing interiors. I eventually ventured into other disciplines, seeking to offer focus in a discipline rarely unified in an anthology.

Absorbing these sources and situating them within the realm of interiors requires patience. It requires stopping and thinking about the subtle nuances that people experience in interior space. The process of collecting essays and images for this reader has also been a patient search that put me in contact with many authors, artists, and publishers. This book gave me the opportunity to reach out to them, and they added more voice and authority to essays that had already spoken to me. Undertaking the research to locate these works and images in museums, galleries, libraries, and archives has been a journey that has allowed me to step into the shoes of many authors and better understand their intentions. Archivists who are privy to significant drawings that the public rarely sees escorted me into their worlds.

My journey to attain permission to republish images for an essay by the architectural historian and theorist Robin Evans reached a high point when, having followed a trail of clues in his writings, I landed in London, where his research drawings materialized. Despite Evans's passing in 1994, in London I felt his presence, viewing images in the Architectural Association Library that allowed me to learn one more lesson from him about the importance and pleasure of looking—really looking—at drawings, not just for techniques, but for underlying ideas that led to their construction.

In the case of receiving a still image from the Alfred Hitchcock film *Rear Window* from the Royal Film Archive in Brussels, I was amazed by the previously unnoticed details of the film that were revealed through a high-resolution photograph of the film's set design. Like Evan's sketches, the

Archive's photographs allowed me to see the set as if I were in the presence of James Stewart, Alfred Hitchcock, and cinematographer Robert Burks.

This reader developed out of my quest for theory, shared by many of my students. Because they found elegant points of entry into their work through related fields, this book is intended for undergraduate and graduate students studying interior design. The interdisciplinary nature of this collection also offers access for students in other design disciplines, such as art, film, and product design. Students of architecture can look to this reader for a magnified view of interiors, often represented as voids in architectural models.

My vision for shaping interior design theory begins with this sourcebook. I hope that these selected authors' ideas will help contribute to a proliferation of interior design theory.

Lois Weinthal
Austin, Texas, 2011

Introduction

"There is no such thing as a simple room."[1]

At first glance, interiors are composed of objects, color, light, and people, but this is an oversimplified, flattened image, as if it were a photograph of a stage set. It's only the beginning of what constitutes an interior. Latent and less visible intersections of these elements and their effect upon the interior come to the foreground when, for example, one tries to transform a static photograph into an animated film. An interior requires a designer's finely tuned eye in order to comprehend major and minor adjustments. These turn everyday interiors into a filmic space, changing hour by hour and day by day, according to the interior's setting and peoples' actions. At a certain point, the interior designer has set the stage and leaves the alterations and actions to the occupants.

The contemporary interior designer plays a multifaceted role in shaping interior space, at times acting as a coordinator of color, furniture, textile, lighting, and product design, while at others, the designer is an architect, re-shaping spaces, apertures, and thresholds. Interior design is a discipline within which practitioners must have knowledge of ornament and decoration at the small scale in order to affect the architectural space at a large scale. He or she must respond to projects with environmental strategies that exist at the scale of global issues. Interior design synthesizes a vast array of elements, from architecture to decoration, yet it is never clearly defined as either, because each has its own distinct, traditional histories, tools, and practices. Rather, contemporary interior design, as a newly emerging discipline, seeks to reconcile these different identities so that they can coexist.

"It was the room, the set, that obsessed me."[2]

The house I grew up in was a 1960s suburban track model home. The exterior was traditional with brick and wood siding and the interior had clean

15

white walls and wood floors. In the mid-1970s, my mother hired an interior decorator and the house exploded. The beautiful wood floors were covered in three-tone shag carpet and the white walls were covered in wallpaper. In some rooms, two intense wallpaper patterns met at a corner producing a dizzying effect. Our quiet suburban home was now loud. I tried to push the loud color and patterns into the background as I longed for the wood floors lying underneath the shag carpet. At ten, I was already nostalgic.

My longing for these underlying surfaces speaks to an aesthetic that Le Corbusier coined as *type-objects*—objects that are "well made, neat and clean, pure and healthy."[3] The interior decorator turned our type-object house into the opposite, described by Le Corbusier as "the personal, the arbitrary, the fantastic, the eccentric."[4] Unlike architecture, the interior can arbitrarily be personalized at every detail and can easily cross the threshold between the two opposing identities in Le Corbusier's statement.

In the cacophonic interior, there was one corner in the front foyer that always drew my attention. Sunlight entered through the front door window and faded an area of wallpaper that I saw change over the next thirty years on my return visits. Early on I only subconsciously registered the fading wallpaper until later when I consciously learned about the movement of the sun's path. In architecture school we were taught about the sun's movement mostly to understand its effect for shadows, but I could not stop thinking about the eroding effect the sun had on that patch of yellow wallpaper. It reminded me of a novella I had read years earlier called *The Yellow Wallpaper,* by Charlotte Perkins Gilman, a story where the wallpaper played a central role. Gilman animated the wallpaper when she wrote, "This paper looks to me as if it *knew* what a vicious influence it had! There is a recurrent spot where the pattern lolls like a broken neck and two bulbous eyes stare at you upside down."[5] Gilman's intention was for the wallpaper to be a symbol of women's oppression in the domestic realm, but I viewed it as an interior layer that became animated with life, regardless of its intended symbolism by Gilman.

Architecture school offered moments where narratives entered into the design process, such as essays by Jorge Luis Borges and Italo Calvino, but *The Yellow Wallpaper* is a story that should be required reading for anyone interested in interiors. Gilman reveals the profound effect that wallpaper can have, when it is seen as an animated character in the politically charged narrative and drama of the house. Repositioning this narrative and the role of wallpaper in the discipline of interior design offers a non-traditional view of wallpaper and a closer look at the subtleties that pattern design can have on a space. Like Gilman's character who literally tears down the wallpaper, I too figuratively tried to pull down the wallpaper and rip up the shag carpet. I longed for our house to return to the type-object interior.

"A room within a room, a private interior space."[6]

Walking down the hallway of my parents' house to my bedroom, there was a small door in the wall that gave access to the laundry chute. I knew its point of origin and destination, but the route between the two was a source of a mystery. Where there should have been a void, a poché of some thickness running vertically through the house, I would lose sight of our falling laundry on its way down to the basement. Architecture history courses taught me about poché through Beaux-Arts drawings with thick heavy lines in plan and section to represent the thickness of walls, floors and ceilings. Sectional drawings provide the clearest view of poché, and with it, curiosity about the space inside the wall is raised. The purpose of thick black lines on these drawings is to represent boundaries between rooms, but their thickness also claims an imaginary space that I want to see into as if I had x-ray vision. This opaque unknown leaves me with a lingering desire to understand the thickness of a wall without cutting into it. The architectural poché, much like its French root definition—pocket—is the location of enveloping interiors that hold the potential for wonder to reside.

Pockets of space can sometimes get lost over time. In an architecture office where I once worked, in the Carnegie Hall studios on 57th Street in Manhattan, a small room, sealed off for forty years, was discovered in the course of some repairs. After the repairs the small room was absorbed into the closet as an extension. Shouldn't someone have questioned earlier why the poché of that area did not seem right? That perhaps, the wall was too thick, when there appeared to be no structural or mechanical systems running through it? After so many years, the pocket of space within another pocket of space was opened and allowed to breathe. Discoveries like this invite the projection of anthropomorphic qualities onto architecture and interiors. Poché does not reveal inner workings; instead, it masks them so that emphasis can be placed on the interior, similar to the way in which the skin wraps the body, hiding bones, muscles, and organs.

If there was a simple lapse of updating a drawing with the sealed room, it resulted in the misalignment of interiors waiting to be realigned in the minds of architects. It was no surprise that when I read a children's book about a house that was anthropomorphized, with the attic as the head, and the basement as the bowels, my experience of the childhood house was transformed when I viewed myself living in a body inside of another body. The anthropomorphized house suggested that the house knew and possibly hurt when a door was slammed or a nail was hammered into the wall. Wondering whether or not that body could act intelligently on the house would lead me to develop an anthropomorphic compassion for the inner working of interiors.

The philosopher Michel Serres understands the anthropomorphized house when he describes windows as eyes that look out to the landscape. Like the body, Serres also implies that the house has skins with "strata and partitions from rough concrete to bed linen, the number of skins until we reach our real skin."[7] It is not often that an architect writes specifications for bed linens, yet linens often come up in conversations with interior designers since they are expected to have knowledge of textiles and weaves, and understand what materials lie next to the body as well as those upholstered over furniture (with clothing as an interstitial layer). The installation of linens is a demarcation that distinguishes the temporary nature of interior design. Because linens and laundry are part of daily rituals that accumulate traces of the body, materials that follow the figure are set apart from the permanent nature of architecture. These details of everyday life are visible in the lived-in interior.

"It seems that the boudoir was much more than a room."[8]

There are few opportunities to explore the intimate details of another's domestic interior. When my grandmother passed away, I went with my mother to her apartment to decide what would be kept, given away, or thrown out. Until then, I had only known her apartment based upon a few areas of interest to me, such as a round cookie tin on top of the refrigerator, the ceramic candy holder on the coffee table, the kitchen table where we ate cherry soup, the box of toys in the corner of the guest bedroom and the two single beds in her bedroom. This last image told me a lot about her, even though when it was formed I was too young to understand what sleeping in a bed next to a lover meant. I never met my grandfather—he passed away before I was born—but the two beds separated by a night table told me that even when he was alive, intimacy and sleep were separate, as was probably normal for their post-Victorian generation. The simple placement of the night table between the two beds revealed the proximity of another era. A historical study using the proximity of furniture pieces to one another reveals degrees of social engagement in Robin Evans' essay "The Developed Surface: An Inquiry into the Brief Life of an Eighteenth-Century Drawing Technique." Interior design is responsible for constructing proximities that account for multiple levels of intimacy. The interior realm is a rich reality precisely because of its architectures of intimacy.

My recollection of these personal experiences draws out underlying themes inherent in the interior. It is often taboo to make reference to personal anecdotes when writing about architecture, but in writing about interiors the personal should not always be avoided. The interior decoration of the house I grew up in stands in contrast to Le Corbusier's type-object because of its similarity to "the personal, the arbitrary, the fantastic, the eccentric."[9] Nothing could have been more eccentric than two mismatched wallpaper patterns lining the same room. Architecture—according to Adolf Loos and Le Corbusier—was meant to be non-personal and certainly not arbitrary. Yet the interiors of our experience are associated with things both personal and casual. Even in residences designed by architects, it is the interior where personalization begins and the architect leaves.

> "Interiors are experienced as the real containers of the immediately adjacent living space."[10]

Nostalgia, anthropomorphism, the animated secrets of poché, and intimacy provide a lens through which interiors reveal themes often found outside their technical terminology. These themes suggest to designers and theorists that reflecting upon meaningful experiences embedded in the interior has a critical and analytical aspect.

For me, the interior begins with the elements that are closest to the body, forming concentric and more complex layers as it progresses from the body into spaces where larger scales are accommodated without losing their relatedness to the body and emotion. Architecture, for instance, is often described as having layers like an onion that peel away to reveal layer after of layer of detail. In that analogy, the layers of the onion represent distinct entities. Applying this same analogy to interiors, the layers are stretched and skewed to overlap and share spatial relationships, as well as details of objects, such as the body that wears clothing but also occupies furniture, or private rooms that spill into public spaces.

The process of writing about the making of space is guided by layers that do not follow any conventional chronological order like that used in most art and architectural history or theory literature. The interior is experienced from elements closest to us in scale and intimacy, such as clothing, to those farther away, such as perimeter walls that divide interior from exterior, and their interrelatedness at different scales and atmospheres. If literature is to move toward a new interior, thinking that stems from how we integrally experience the interior realm between these scales acts as a starting point for recognizing the interdisciplinary nature of the interior and extending it to the making and writing of this space.

> "To live means to leave traces."[11]

To work at the interior scale is to work at full-scale. In doing so, we find materials are at their true weight, details comply with gravity, and the scale of the body is always present. Once these natural elements activate the interior, living within it becomes real. But before this point is reached, the designer employs tools to help visualize the making of space. Small-scale architectural models and drawings provide traditional foundations for design, while design strategies range from determining aesthetic decisions to employing analytical studies to materialize desired phenomena. The interior designer can look to strategies employed by related disciplines, such as architecture, art, and industrial design. The interior has traits embedded within it that are not always explored strategically, for example the presence of wear and dust signals the actions of nature upon structure and with it, material and artistic opportunity.

A full-scale interior shows the marks of wear and tear that appear over time. Architecture accepts this and poeticizes it with words like weathering. The interior has these moments too, such as the marks of foot traffic over floors, but less poetic is the accumulation of dust. It is left unspoken and unrendered in architectural models and drawings, although it too announces the passing of time. Filmmakers like the Quay Brothers and photographer James Casebere construct interior models as a component of their work and integrate the impression of time by articulating surfaces with wear and tear and dust. The result produces a kind of atmosphere that is missing from architectural models; they romanticize dust. Without it, their interior models would look compositionally incomplete.

When architecture and interiors transition from small-scale representation to full-scale occupation, dust requires maintenance, so much so that this by-product of living employs people to attend to making it disappear. Janitors and maintenance workers intimately know interiors in ways that the architect and interior designer never experience. Dust is not a romantic topic to consider in the design process, but it does ask the interior designer to bear in mind the lived-in outcome of a built project over time. Writing about dust as a critical subject in the discipline of interior theory is largely absent but it should be an element of interest for the discipline to claim and develop.

The architectural model fulfills a different set of roles rather than representing the microscopic scale of dust. Architecture relies upon models to mediate between the small-scale conceptual design process and full-scale construction, and to serve as a tool for exploring ideas. Students and practitioners are accustomed to seeing models made from basswood, chipboard, foam core, and Plexiglas. Both the Quay Brothers and Casebere integrate scaled-down dust in their models, as well as details that only a closely focused eye can see. The Quay Brothers's animated films, among other things, are a checklist of details found on the interior—similarly to the organizing layers of this reader. When architectural models have exhausted their use in exploring spatial elements, they pick up on the design of clothes to support the narratives that are integrated into their set designs. Clothes that are tailored to puppets contain an aura of nostalgia because of their type-object nature. Interior designers can look to these models as a seductive aide memoire of the marks that appear in the everyday but often go unnoticed in the design process. By description, these models can be confused with doll-houses that try to mimic reality, but when viewed, they mimic dreams.

Building three-dimensionally at both full-scale and in miniature allows for insights on measurement, fashion, and making to emerge. These themes, like the previous set introduced through the anecdotes, reappear through-out the layers we inhabit, revealing that they cannot be limited to one layer since they transcend multiples. Although these layers are not discrete, they reappear throughout this reader in partial defiance of exact definition and categorization, in full view of studio practice and its concomitant reflection. They invite their inscription as a set of fundamental imperatives for writing and theoretical analysis of interior design in a distinct and integral whole, separate from architecture.

Notes

1   Mark Wigley, "Inside the Inside," in *The Architectural Unconscious: James Casebere + Glen Seator*, ed. Joseph N. Newland (Andover: Addison Gallery of American Art, Phillips Academy, 2000), 23.

2   Rachel Lichtenstein and Iain Sinclair, *Rodinsky's Room* (London: Granta Book, 1999), 256.

3   Le Corbusier, "The Decorative Art of Today," in *The Decorative Art of Today*, trans. James I. Dunnet (Cambridge, MA: MIT Press, 1987), 87.

4   Ibid., 84–5.

5   Charlotte Perkins Gilman, "The Yellow Wallpaper," originally appeared in *The New England Magazine*, 1892. Page number for this quote from the original publication is unknown.

6   Diana Fuss and Joel Sanders, "Berggasse 19: Inside Freud's Office," in *Stud: Architectures of Masculinity*, ed. Joel Sanders (New York: Princeton Architectural Press, 1996), 124.

7   Michel Serres, "The Five Senses: Boxes," in *The Five Senses: A Philosophy of Mingled Bodies*, trans. Margaret Sankey and Peter Cowley (London: Continuum, 2008), 148.

8   Ed Lilley, "The Name of the Boudoir," in *Journal of the Society of Architectural Historians* 53, no. 2 (June 1994): 193.

9   Le Corbusier, 84–5.

10   Meisenheimer, Wolfgang. "Of the Hollow Spaces in the Skin of the Architectural Body." *Daidalos* 13 (1984): 103.

11   Walter Benjamin, "Paris, Capital of the Nineteenth Century," in *Reflections*, trans. Edmund Jephcott, (New York: Schocken Books, 1986), 155.

1

Body and Perception

Introduction:
Body and Perception

The body comprehends the world through senses and physical grasp. The senses of sight and sound are internally registered through eyes and ears while the physical grasp of materials relies upon the body's outward engagement of touch. Together, these inward and outward perceptions contribute to an overall understanding of the built environment. Essays in this first section explore these two forms of perception and how they influence the projection of the body's measurement in shaping interiors.

Architectural historian and theorist Christian Norberg-Schulz conveys ideas of the senses in his essay "The Phenomenon of Place" that people understand the built world through concrete and phenomenal modalities.[1] For him concrete modalities are tangible objects that people engage on a daily basis, such as the material touch of a chair or height of a window; phenomena are sensory perceptions of the world, such as the way light enters through a window. Together these senses and measure of the body guide how we read and shape the architectural interior realm. The body's ability to comprehend the senses is crucial to the study of the interior in architecture, in part because crafting interior spaces ultimately relies on the senses for perceiving elements inherent to the interior, such as color, light, and darkness, sound and silence, and the texture of materials.

The selected readings in Body and Perception draw upon art, classic literature, and architecture to reveal ways that the body perceives the built environment. Originating from Leonardo da Vinci's *Vitruvian Man*, referencing classical order, the famous drawing of a man's body and its placement in measured space provides a foundation for design theory and its interpretations of space. The human figure is located within a constructed geometry that measures the body, while projecting measurement outward as a means of generating architectural space.

Architecture has a long-standing tradition of analyzing the measure of man that can be seen in historical reference to the writings of Vitruvius,

Leonardo da Vinci, Le Corbusier, and more recently, Joseph Rykwert. These writings situate the body in systems of measurement that in some cases are generative of architecture. The interior builds upon these analyses but has further need for representation specific to furniture and products. These types of diagrams and proportional systems can be found in the research on ergonomics, largely undertaken by the industrial designer Henry Dreyfuss in the early twentieth century. By applying bodily proportions to interiors, Dreyfuss influenced human factors on the engineering of products and spaces. The essays that constitute this first section reference the measured body alongside concrete and phenomenal modalities, parallel to the physical and perceptual.

Chapter 1 begins with a reading that offers an alternative example of bodily measurement and representation. Doris von Drathen frames the artist Rebecca Horn's work in intrinsic forms of measurement in her essay, "Places at the Zero Point." Horn, whose body projects *Measure Box* and *White Body Fan* focus on the body and its ability to be measured and to project measurement, repositioned da Vinci's classical figure to allow for later critical interpretations that focus on a feminized version of the drawing. Where the *Vitruvian Man* is static, contained, and inscribed within a circle, Horn's *White Body Fan* is dynamic—she can inscribe or un-scribe the circle around her.

The body continuously establishes a relationship to the scale of interior space by projecting its measurements onto the physical world. An excerpt from Kobo Abé's *Box Man* provides an immediate example of how occupants project their bodies onto neutral space by giving it scale. *Box Man* is the story of a homeless man (the Box Man) who personalizes the interior of his cardboard box based upon basic needs: sight, sound, and shelter. Like the Vitruvian Man inscribed within a circle, the Box Man's perception of geometric boundaries is a projection of his measurements. He creates openings to take in light and sound. His box mimics architecture with visible and audible thresholds that mark a distinction between interior and exterior. The limited flexibility of altering architectural materials to reflect the body is not the case with the Box Man, where the temporary nature of cardboard easily allows for alterations. In this narrative, cardboard acts as both exterior shell and interior wallpaper.

Abé focuses on comprehending the internal senses of sight, sound, and smell. The outward sense of touch is the focus of Juhani Pallasmaa's essay, "An Architecture of the Seven Senses." Pallasmaa conveys how interior space can be used to gauge the physical body. He focuses on architectural details that measure the body with interior elements such as the rise and run of stairs. Like Abé, he explores occupied space using the senses of sound and smell. They are revealed through architectural techniques that strike a balance between tangible, everyday elements and how we perceive them. These range from a door handle to a finish material, which absorbs our use, accumulating a patina over time. Pallasmaa manifests a poetic description of the built environment through the senses.

In the last essay of this section, "Body Troubles," Robert McAnulty looks to the interior as a site for re-thinking these modes of perception as they rely upon the interior as an occupied site. There, an indecipherable zone emerges where architecture, body, and object cross paths. They meet at the scale of the interior, where external forces find their way into the representation of the architectural interior through comparisons of body and world, objective and subjective, natural and artificial.

This chapter defines the properties of the body. It inhabits architecture, creates scale, and engages objects within a space. It is a recurring theme in this chapter that demonstrates the interior as a meeting between the intimate scale of the senses and the larger scale of interior architecture they shape. As later chapters build upon environments' and objects' increasing scales, the body stands as a basis for comparison.

1 Christian Norberg-Schulz, "The Phenomenon of Place," *Architectural Association Quarterly*, 4 (1976): 3–10.

Places at the Zero Point

Doris von Drathen

INTRODUCTION

The body interprets the constructed world through unconscious calculations of orientation and measurement. We find these calculations represented in the dimensions of the human body in the writings of Vitruvius and in Leonardo da Vinci's Vitruvius-inspired drawing, the Vitruvian Man. *These systems define how human measurement and proportion establish an equivalent foundation for architectural representation relative to the body. In the following essay, Doris von Drathen repositions artist Rebecca Horn's work from its context of measurement and orientation, to offer an alternative image of the body, and in doing so, forming the space of interiors.*

Horn's early works focused on using body extensions to measure and gauge the world. Unlike static Renaissance drawings of the body, Horn's tools are dynamic, set in motion by human interaction. The body is just as important as the work itself. Without it, her art does not truly convey its intent.

Horn's White Body Fan *shares a similar approach to da Vinci's static male figure, but omits a confining perimeter; instead it is animated with geometric forms. A sequence of photographs depict Horn's movement with large, white fans, opening and closing, subtly implying horizontal and vertical relationships to the body and the ground, while opening up limitless possibilities for making space, using the edges of the wings as if they were drawing tools. Von Drathen draws a distinction between the architect and artist, the former limited by a set of rules, the latter open to infinite possibilities. Although Horn's work can certainly be called an artistic endeavor, the body's central location in the mechanisms that activate it suggests interiority.*

Interior design, as a recent discipline, has fewer references to anthropomorphized structures. If classical drawings of the body are a foundation of architecture that guided later interpretations, such as Le Corbusier's Modulor Man, *what are the analogues to interior design? Classical architectural*

Originally appeared in *Rebecca Horn: Moon Mirror* (Ostfildern-Ruit, Germany: Hatje Cantz Verlag, 2005), 41–46.

drawings represent the body two-dimensionally, often drafted with lines gen-erating measurement and proportion, while Horn's representation is three-dimensional. In one photograph of White Body Fan, *Horn wraps herself within the fans, transforming her body inscribed in a circle, as it were, into an enclosure that implies spatiality.*

———

IS THERE SPACE: before or behind space? Is there time beneath shaped time, when a crack opens up in the seamless sequence of no-longer and not-yet moments? The awe that seizes us in the face of such questions stems from a primeval phenomenon that permeates all cultures: the premonition of a chasm of nothingness. "The depths of the vast chasm are filled with shape-less forces," we are told by the ancient scriptures; only the processual devel-opment of the world can lend them form and create something from them. Until this has happened, this chasm or "primal space" remains the pre-serve of darkness.[1] Time and space have more in common than the fact that anyone who seeks to penetrate their inner mystery becomes even further embroiled in their unfathomableness: they are also characterized by this chasm of nothingness. It is the crack that opens up when we venture beyond our well-defined and measurable notion of space or our familiar framework of time.

Anything that defies definition immediately invokes a sense of limit-lessness; it is impossible for us in our limited condition to conceive of, let alone create, infinity. It suffices to go just one step beyond the reassuringly measurable units of time or space for us to experience this staggering rift that opens up an indeterminate field of possibilities.

So one might logically assume that artistic creativity would go in search of such an opening, however daunting this might seem, in order to proceed further into new realms. How astonishing it then is that so few art-ists possess the courage to face this challenge. In the work of Rebecca Horn, however, the crack appears to be transformed into a primeval moment of creativity, into a dynamic core of space- and timelessness, into the zero point of a new beginning.

Being the World Axis Oneself

It is precisely from this zero point that Rebecca Horn begins to reinvent her universe, by establishing her very own measuring system as a means of com-prehending and creating space. She proceeds empirically, using the human body, its movements, and its proportions as her yardstick to measure the uni-verse. As if her aim were to dispense with all timeworn, accustomed parame-ters, she first founds a world axis that she herself determines.

In archaic traditions, when a new community was being founded, a tall wooden stake would be driven into the ground at a chosen spot. This stake was to connect heaven and earth; it was declared the *axis mundi* and was thus considered the center around which all the other buildings would be oriented. Without consciously alluding to such traditions, Rebecca Horn creates an image in one of her first performances[2] that can be understood as an *axis mundi*. Characteristically, however, the artist invents a wandering, mobile world axis: in the performance *Unicorn* (1970) a woman bears on her head a long, upright pole, thus using her own body to establish a connection between heaven and earth. She paces freely through the field and forest, measuring herself "against every tree and cloud."[3] The length of the vertical pole, which transforms the woman into a creature from another world, is not some arbitrary number of centimeters but precisely half the length of the woman's body. In all of the performances from this period these sculptural body extensions are calculated in exact proportion to the performers' stature. For example, a horizontal pole that a man awkwardly balances on his head is three times as long as he is tall (*Balance Pole*, 1972). In these first performances Rebecca Horn is thus in fact concentrating on the vertical and horizontal measurement of space. She works purely functionally and experimentally, using extensions of the body to venture a direct physical transgression of her own dimensions and her own spatial reach.

In order to determine more simply the physical proportions of the various participants in her performances, the artist built a metal construction in the early 1970s that she called *Measure Box* (1970). [Figs. 1.1 + 1.2] It was nothing more than an open steel frame whose four upright struts were perforated at regular intervals so that slender horizontal rods could be slid in and out. Each participant in a performance would stand in this measuring box and be palpated by the metal rods; on stepping out, the shape of his or her body would remain behind as an empty form in outline. In this manner, the artist was able to produce individually proportioned body extensions for each participant.

Characteristic of these early performances is Rebecca Horn's experimentation with a kind of dialogic experience of space. From the very outset she worked within correlational systems. After a long period of isolation due to a lung infection, this collaboration with other participants (recruited from among her friends and fellow students) represented for her the first major step towards re-establishing contact with others. Experimenting with space thus also became a way of measuring others, of being concerned and assuming responsibility. She herself tailored the body extensions and made sure that no one came to harm when risk was involved. In her first *documenta* piece in 1972, a man's head was inserted inside the *Head Extension*, a towering mask-like object that was twice as tall as the man and tapered to

a point at the top. Four people, including the artist, positioned themselves around the man along the axes of the four points of the compass, each holding a rope that was connected to the pinnacle of the obelisk-like object. The man's balance could only be safeguarded by maintaining equal and constant tension on all four ropes, enabling him to move about very carefully with the rest of the group. Even the slightest disturbance in the group's focused sense of balance would have pulled the man, whose sight was obstructed by the head extension, crashing to the ground. Frequently, the risk involved in such performances was not restricted to the physical experience of spatial boundaries, bur also verged on the extremes of physical danger. These were precarious situations witnessed only by the participants themselves; at this juncture the performances still took place without an audience.

Certain critics have filed away these first works by Rebecca Horn under "physical experience," failing to explore them further in terms of their pictorial function and power. But if one considers the spatially expansive imagery of these performances, it becomes immediately clear that through a highly original procedure they evolve their own spatial parameters and that, seen now with hindsight, they already schematically form the basis for the artist's entire later oeuvre in the realm of spatial composition. For, from the very start, these acts of gauging and measuring the crossed vertical and horizontal axes open up the greatest degree of freedom within unlimited space.

In these terms, far greater significance should be attached to the frequently underestimated *Measure Box* than has previously been the case: even if this sculpture ostensibly served a technical purpose, it was also the first of many spaces Rebecca Horn was to create. It says a great deal about the extreme precision of her later spatial compositions that her early performances and sculptures possess, for all their astonishing beauty, the technical and functional character of an architecture completely of her own making.

Measure Box recalls the theory of proportions put forward by the Roman architect Vitruvius, who started out from the "measurements of nature" and calculated thus: "4 fingers make 1 palm, and 4 palms make 1 foot, 6 palms make 1 cubit; 4 cubits make a man's height. And 4 cubits make one pace and 24 palms make a man." Vitruvius matter-of-factly postulated man as the only possible model for his architecture.[4]

Although Rebecca Horn has herself never directly referred to Vitruvius, her first *axis mundi* can nonetheless be seen very clearly within this broad tradition of gauging space by means of human proportions. Yet in this the artist differs in one crucial aspect: from the very start she demonstrates that her notion of space is also determined by experience and movement. The woman who moves through open countryside as a mobile world axis, establishing a new center for determining space with each step, is herself spanning a field between heaven and earth, is the embodiment of this spatial axis. The Hebrew word for earth, *adamah,* was traditionally read as *adammah,* meaning: "Adam-What?" The earthbound universe was called *mah* ("What?"), while the character for the heavenly universe is called *mi,* meaning: "Who?" Resonating in the image of the *Unicorn* is not only the sense that enquiry is fundamentally inscribed into human nature, but also that the human condition intrinsically causes man to move back and forth between these two questions.

Building Spaces with Living Determinants

The large *Body Fans* (1972), in which Rebecca Horn explores the substantiality of air, represent another context where she measures space on her own terms. [Figs. 1.3–1.5] The fans tower over the artist, half as tall again as she is. They are strapped to her body at regular intervals from her ankles to her shoulders. When the artist sets the giant semicircular sails in motion against the resistance of the air, it is as if the wings of a giant butterfly were opening and closing around her body; this is the first mobile space in the artist's oeuvre, a space that—initially—only the artist can experience.

The silent deployment of individuals in the artist's early experiments, in which she measured and created space with her own body or the bodies of invited participants, is reminiscent of the "monads" or "living determinants"[5] Giordano Bruno described as a means of explaining spatial relationships in terms of human experience. As if these bodies were merely being substituted, the later walk-in spatial compositions introduce kinetic sculptures that seem no less alive and no less corporeal. The viewers, who

Figs. 1.3–1.5: Rebecca Horn, *Weißer Körperfächer (White Body Fan)*, 1972. Copyright 2011, Rebecca Horn: VG Bild Kunst Bonn: ARS. Photo credit: Achim Thode (1.4)

were absent in the early performances, are ultimately also drawn into the equation as "living determinants" and over the course of the years become increasingly visible as components of such spaces.

Each of the elements with which Rebecca Horn works is itself an excerpt from reality; none of the objects is invented. What makes them seem so unfamiliar is the way in which their reality is isolated and inserted into new contexts. Like the protagonists of a world theater, each time they step onto the stage they perform new roles; their movements and pictorial power are dependent on the respective space and the new sculptures they encounter. On each occasion they develop new relations to one another and to the new space in which they occur. They occupy floors, ceilings, and walls, and erupt through windows and skylights. It is through the dialogue between the various sculptures that each spatial composition becomes an overall, dynamic work of art. At the same time, however, they are also acts of naming. It often seems as if reality taken literally is precisely what constitutes the poetry of her composed visual spaces. Rebecca Horn's oeuvre thus evolves like a stream of images that swells progressively in volume, and in which old and new constructional elements create unexpected spatial events. Simply enumerating these elements says little about their roles or about the visual spaces they create; the ladder, small hammers, styli, conductors' batons, metronomes, violins, cellos, pianos, spring wheels, flashes of light, mirrors, water baths, towers of beds, funnels, typewriters, butterflies, mercury pumps, pistols, copper tubes, water drops, suitcases, shoes, umbrellas, thermometers, beehives, boulders, skulls, ostrich eggs, pyramids of pigment, and walls of ash become units for measuring an energy of things and spaces that goes far beyond the material presence of these "determinants," an energy whose movement utterly surpasses such materiality. Thus, for example, a rod from an old Chinese scale balance, once used to measure weight, is transformed into a baton that floats freely in the air. With its conducting motions it connects spaces that are temporally and spatially distant from one another to create a single, large spatial composition.[6]

In our attempt to understand the distinctive way in which Rebecca Horn conceives her spaces, the spatial terminology of architecture will not offer much help. Unless, that is, we enlist the sort of architects who always try to incorporate infinity, and who see in every building "a unique place in this infinity."[7] Can art history offer other possibilities for comparison? Max Raphael teaches us that space is not "form alone—at least not abstract form alone, completely independent of content—because things insist on appearing that cannot have a reality in our surroundings, that cannot be represented by means of the surrounding space; because space and time may be different, but they cannot be separated." Cutting across the history of art, Max Raphael defines the range of such spatial contents: noting, for example the "space of the dream world" in Frans Hals and Velázquez; the "space of the unconscious" in Vermeer; the "space of transition from this world to the beyond" in Hugo van der Goes and Tintoretto; the "space of the infinitely empty" in Egypt; the "space of infinite fullness or fulfillment," the "space of mood within the soul," or the "space of contemplation" in India; the "space of physical and spiritual action, of charges of energy between this world and the one beyond" in El Greco; or the "space of the dissolution of existence" in Hieronymus Bosch.[8]

Yet any attempt to use Max Raphael's method to analyze Rebecca Horn's spaces would immediately raise fundamental doubts: to speak of contents suggests some kind of spatial shell containing them. But it is precisely such delimiting barriers that the artist breaches. The unique thing about her spaces is that they generate openness. The constructional elements she employs burst through the boundaries of their spatial surroundings, creating conditions for a space that manifestly lies outside architectural parameters and maintains a precarious balance between the definition and the dissolution of space. Each of her compositions establishes a specific relationship to the preexisting space and site for which it was developed. The point of reference here, however, is not the site's physical architecture but its historical and ethical significance: the lost place. This, ultimately, is the essence of the spatial and temporal autonomy embodied in her places.

But let us not forget that the fundamental precondition for all metaphysical experience of these spaces is an extremely precise calculation of the mathematics and physics of angles, proportions, and light reflections. The world of physical phenomena and our ability to perceive them symbolically or spiritually stand in close proximity.

Notes

1   See Gershom Scholem, *Die jüdische Mystik in ihren Hauptströmungen* (Frankfurt am Main, 1980), p. 325.

2   In most of her performances in the 1970s Rebecca Horn worked with fellow students or artist colleagues. For *Unicorn* she invited a fellow female student whose height made her a suitable choice.

3   Rebecca Horn, poem on the work *Unicorn,* in *Rebecca Horn: The Glance of Infinity,* exh. cat. Kestner Gesellschaft, Hanover (Zurich, 1997), p. 56.

4   Leonardo da Vinci, *The Literary Works of Leonardo da Vinci,* ed. Jean Paul Richter and Irma A. Richter, trans. R. C. Bell, 2nd ed. (London, 1939), p. 255; Leonardo is paraphrasing *De architectura* by Vitruvius (first century BC).

5   Jochen Kirchhoff uses this term to summarize Giordano Bruno's theory of monads in his *Giordano Bruno in Selbstzeugnissen und Bilddokumenten* (Reinbek bei Hamburg, 1980), p. 74.

6   See pp. 52–3 in [von Drathen, *Rebecca Horn,* 2005]. *Concert for Buchenwald, Part 1 Tram Depot,* and *Part 2 Schloss Ettersburg, White Salon* (1999).

7   Peter Zumthor, "Composing in Space," *a+u* (architecture and urbanism), special issue (Tokyo, 1989), p. 20. "When we as architects are concerned with space we are concerned with but a tiny part of the infinity that surrounds the earth, each and every building marks a unique place in this infinity."

8   Max Raphael, *Raumgestaltungen: Der Beginn der modernen Kunst im Kubismus und im Werk von Georges Braque* (Frankfurt am Main and New York, 1986), p. 63. Max Raphael (1889–1952) wrote this study during the 1940s, living in exile in New York, where he committed suicide.

The Box Man

Kobo Abé

INTRODUCTION

The layers that wrap the body include a range of scales that span from clothing to architecture. This excerpt from Kobo Abé's existential novel The Box Man *focuses on one of the more unconventional of these layers—a box that houses the body, like architecture, but is worn like clothing.*

In the book, Abé's title character, Box Man, seeks anonymity and refuge from a Japanese culture that is changing around him. The Box Man seeks solitude in an anonymous cardboard box and guides us through his instructions to convert it into a personal shelter unit. Step by step the measurements projected onto the box represent the dimensions of the Box Man and alterations to the inside reflect the personalization of space intrinsic to the interior.

The Box Man's simple act of cutting into a box reveals his vision for creating liveable space. His cuts are guided by fundamental needs: for the body to breathe, see, hear, and be sheltered. He cuts, for example, a window in front for the eyes and small holes on two sides for hearing. Additonal layers of function are added, such as a curtain over the eye window, which Abé treats with an anthropomorphic quality, as in "expression of the eyes."* The openings are referenced by different names: apertures, windows, openings, or peepholes. They reveal the multitude of form interpretations an opening can have.

Abé's selection of a standard cardboard box for its anonymity recalls Adolf Loos's article on men's fashion that appeared in the Neue Freie Presse *in 1898. Loos called for architecture—like the exterior of a man's dinner jacket—to be styled anonymous and inconspicuously.† For Loos and Abé, the interior realm is where we should be allowed to demonstrate individuality. The Box Man arranges his personal effects (consisting only of essentials that include a radio, mug, thermos, flashlight, towel, and small miscellaneous bag) around the inside of the box.‡ In doing so, he addresses issues of construction, material properties, and programming for an unconventional but instructive solution. The neutrality of the Box Man's tone and his desire for an anonymous*

---

exterior and personalized interior forms an analogy to architectural and inte-
rior design. Like Loos' writings, the difference of identity on the interior and
exterior play out in the cardboard box sharing the same aesthetic issues that
accompany the outward appearance of the body.

——

My Case

This is the record of a box man.

I am beginning this account in a box. A cardboard box that reaches just
to my hips when I put it on over my head.

That is to say, at this juncture the box man is me. A box man, in his box,
is recording the chronicle of a box man.

Instructions for Making a Box

MATERIALS:
- 1 empty box of corrugated cardboard
- Vinyl sheet (semitransparent)—twenty inches square
- Rubber tape (water-resistant)—about eight yards
- Wire—about two yards
- Small pointed knife (a tool)

(*To have on hand, if necessary: Three pieces of worn canvas and one pair of*
work boots in addition to regular work clothes for streetwear.)

Any empty box a yard long by a yard wide and about four feet deep will do.
However, in practice, one of the standard forms commonly called a "quarto"
is desirable. Standard items are easy to find, and most commercial articles
that use standard-sized boxes are generally of irregular shape—various types
of foodstuffs precisely adaptable to the container—so that the construction
is sturdier than others. The most important reason to use the standardized
form is that it is hard to distinguish one box from another. As far as I know,
most box men utilize this quarto box. For if the box has any striking features
to it, its special anonymity will suffer.

Even the common variety of corrugated cardboard has recently been
strengthened, and since it is semiwaterproof there is no need to select any
special kind unless you are going through the rainy season. Ordinary cardboard has better ventilation and is lighter and easier to use. For those who
wish to occupy one box over a period of time, regardless of the season, I rec-
ommend the Frog Box, especially good in wet weather. This box has a vinyl
finish, and as the name suggests, it is exceedingly strong in water. When new

it has a sheen as if oiled, but apparently it produces static electricity easily, quickly absorbs dirt, and gets covered with dust; then the edge is thicker than the ordinary one and looks wavy. You can tell it at once from the common box.

To construct your box there is no particular procedure to follow. First decide what is to be the bottom and the top of the box—decide according to whatever design there may be or make the top the side with the least wear or just decide arbitrarily—and cut out the bottom part. In cases where one has numerous personal effects to carry, the bottom part can be folded inward without cutting, and, with wire and tape, the two ends can be made into a baggage rack. Tape the exposed part of the edges at the three points on the ceiling and at the one on the side where they come together.

The greatest care must be taken when making the observation window. First decide on its size and location; since there will be individual variations, the following figures are purely for the sake of reference. Ideally, the upper edge of the window will be six inches from the top of the box, and the lower edge eleven inches below that; the width will be seventeen inches. After you have subtracted the thickness of the base to stabilize the box when in place (I put a magazine on my head), the upper edge of the window comes to the eyebrows. You may perhaps consider this to be too low, but one seldom gets the opportunity to look up, while the lower edge is used frequently. When you are in an upright position, it will be difficult to walk if a stretch of at least five feet is not visible in front. There are no special grounds for computing the width. These parts should be adjusted to the required ventilation and the lateral strength of the box. At any rate since you can see right down to the ground, the window should be as small as possible.

Next comes the installation of the frosted vinyl curtain over the window. There's a little trick here too. That is, the upper edge is taped to the outside of the opening and the rest left to hang free, but please do not forget to anticipate a lengthwise slit. This simple device is useful beyond all expectations. The slit should be in the center, and the two flaps should overlap a fraction of an inch. As long as the box is held vertical, they will serve as screens, and no one will be able to see in. When the box is tilted slightly, an opening appears, permitting you to see out. It is a simple but extremely subtle contrivance, so be very careful when selecting the vinyl. Something rather heavy yet flexible is desirable. Anything cheap that immediately stiffens with temperature changes will be a problem. Anything flimsy is even worse. You need something flexible yet heavy enough not to have to worry about every little draft; the breadth of the opening can be easily regulated by tilting the box. For a box man the slit in the vinyl is comparable, as it were, to the expression of the eyes. It is wrong to consider this aperture as being on the same level as a peephole. With very slight adjustments it is easy to express yourself. Of course, this is not a look of kindness. The worst threatening glare is not so offensive as this slit. Without exaggeration, this is one of the few self-defenses an unprotected box man has. I should like to see the man capable of returning this look with composure.

In case you're in crowds a lot, I suppose you might as well puncture holes in the right and left walls while you're about it. Using a thickish nail, bore as many openings as possible in an area of about six inches in diameter, leaving enough space between them so the strength of the cardboard isn't affected. These apertures will serve as both supplementary peepholes and be convenient for distinguishing the direction of sounds. However unsightly, it will be more advantageous in case of rain to open the holes from the inside out and have the flaps facing out.

Last of all, cut the remaining wire into one-, two-, four-, and six-inch lengths, bend back both ends, and prepare them as hooks for hanging things on the wall. You should restrict your personal effects to a minimum; as it is, it's quite exhausting to arrange the indispensable items: radio, mug, thermos, flashlight, towel, and small miscellaneous bag.

As for the rubber boots, there's nothing particular to add. Just as long as they don't have any holes. If the canvas is wrapped around the waist, it is excellent for filling the space between oneself and the box and for holding the box in place. With three layers, divided in front, it is easy to move in all ways as well as being most convenient for defecation and urinating and for sundry other purposes.

Notes

*   Kobo Abé, *The Box Man* (New York: Alfred A. Knopf, 1974), 6.

†   Adolf Loos, "Men's Fashion," *Neue Freie Presse*, May 22, 1898.

‡   Abé, 7.

An Architecture of the Seven Senses

Juhani Pallasmaa

INTRODUCTION

In the following essay, Juhani Pallasmaa probes the sensual nature of architecture and interiors by examining places that present their accumulated history, such as his grandfather's barn, with a distinct patina made visible to the senses. By describing these places and their pasts, Pallasmaa uncovers embedded senses of sight, sound, smell, taste, touch and a sense of movement he describes as skeleton and muscle. By looking at the materials, details, and events that have occurred inside these structures, Pallasmaa poetically uncovers the sense-based qualities that contribute to the particularity of architecture.

Referring to personal experiences allows Pallasmaa to focus on the interiors, what he considers to be collections of sensory experiences that were realized through emphasis on materials. For example, different qualities of sound are heard in a vacant room than in one filled with furniture, textiles, and personal possessions. The former room reflects sound while the latter's solid volumes and soft materials absorb it.

The atmospheric qualities Pallasmaa brings to his description of interiors are material characteristics that develop with time and use, and cannot be forced into new construction. The properties of such materials, those that accumulate an authentic patina through use, create a condition of mutual dependence. These interior details embody a collection of stories. When Pallasmaa describes the narratives of place in romantic, anthropomorphic observations like the "door handle is the handshake of the building…we shake the hands of countless generations…" he nurtures the notion that we are humbled by a simple detail such as a door handle that has received the hands of people before us. *He reminds us of our body's temporary occupation and stewardship in architecture and interiors.*

Pallasmaa's closely read details reveal an appreciation for the scalar relationship between body and construction. The body's cadence as it moves

From *Questions of Perception: Phenomenology of Architecture*, edited by Steven Holl, Juhani Pallasmaa, and Alberto Pérez-Gómez (Tokyo: a+u Publishing Co., Ltd., 1994), 29–37.

up and down stairs or the force needed to open a door relies upon muscles and their resistance to materials. Repetitive use inscribes the body onto interior elements and they record the body's presence over time.

Manufactured and crafted parts of the interior are experienced at the scale of 1:1, and as they are normally situated in rooms, the interior becomes the repository for memories of fully embodied sensory experiences. Pallasmaa draws out familiar senses—memories of the interior that are rarely expressed in architectural literature.

———

Retinal Architecture and Loss of Plasticity

The architecture of our time is turning into the retinal art of the eye. Architecture at large has become an art of the printed image fixed by the hurried eye of the camera. The gaze itself tends to flatten into a picture and lose its plasticity; instead of experiencing our being in the world, we behold it from outside as spectators of images projected on the surface of the retina.

As buildings lose their plasticity and their connection with the language and wisdom of the body, they become isolated in the cool and distant realm of vision. With the loss of tactility and the scale and details crafted for the human body and hand, our structures become repulsively flat, sharp-edged, immaterial, and unreal. The detachment of construction from the realities of matter and craft turns architecture into stage sets for the eye, devoid of the authenticity of material and tectonic logic.

Natural materials—stone, brick and wood—allow the gaze to penetrate their surfaces and they enable us to become convinced of the veracity of matter. Natural material expresses its age and history as well as the tale of its birth and human use. The patina of wear adds the enriching experience of time; matter exists in the continuum of time. But the materials of today—sheets of glass, enameled metal and synthetic materials—present their unyielding surfaces to the eye without conveying anything of their material essence or age.

Beyond architecture, our culture at large seems to drift toward a distancing, a kind of chilling, de-sensualization and de-eroticization of the human relation to reality. Painting and sculpture have also lost their sensuality, and instead of inviting sensory intimacy, contemporary works of art frequently signal a distancing rejection of sensuous curiosity.

The current over-emphasis on the intellectual and conceptual dimensions of architecture further contributes to a disappearance of the physical, sensual and embodied essence of architecture.

Architecture of the Senses

In Renaissance times, the five senses were understood to form a hierarchical system from the highest sense of vision down to the lowest sense, touch. The system of the senses was related to the image of the cosmic body; vision was correlated to fire and light, hearing to air, smell to vapor, taste to water, touch to earth.

Man has not always been isolated in the realm of vision; a primordial dominance of hearing has gradually been replaced by that of vision. In his book *Orality & Literacy* Walter J. Ong points out that "The shift from oral to written speech is essentially a shift from sound to visual space...print replaced the lingering hearing-dominance in the world of thought and expression with the sight-dominance which had its beginning in writing.... This is an insistent world of cold, non-human facts."

Every touching experience of architecture is multi-sensory; qualities of matter, space and scale are measured equally by the eye, ear, nose, skin, tongue, skeleton and muscle. Architecture involves seven realms of sensory experience which interact and infuse each other.

In the words of Merleau-Ponty, "We see the depth, speed, softness and hardness of objects—Cezanne says we see even their odor. If a painter wishes to express the world, his system of color must generate this indivisible complex of impressions, otherwise his painting only hints at possibilities without producing the unity, presence and unsurpassable diversity that governs the experience and which is the definition of reality for us."

A walk through a forest or a Japanese garden is invigorating and healing because of the essential interaction of all sense modalities reinforcing each other; our sense of reality is thus strengthened and articulated.

Images of one sensory realm feed further imagery in another modality. In *The Book of Tea* Kakuzo Okakura gives a fine description of the multi-sensory imagery evoked by the extremely simple situation of the tea ceremony, "...quiet reigns with nothing to break the silence save the note of the boiling water in the iron kettle. The kettle sings well, for pieces of iron are so arranged in the bottom as to produce a peculiar melody in which one may hear the echoes of a cataract muffled by clouds, of a distant sea breaking among the rocks, a rainstorm sweeping through a bamboo forest, or of the soughing of pines on some faraway hill."

The senses do not only mediate information for the judgment of the intellect; they are also a means of articulating sensory thought.

Acoustic Intimacy

One who has half-risen to the sound of a distant train at night and, through his sleep, experienced the space of the city with its countless inhabitants scattered around its structures, knows the power of sound to the imagination;

the nocturnal whistle of a train makes one conscious of the entire sleeping city. Anyone who has become entranced by the sound of water drops in the darkness of a ruin can attest to the extraordinary capacity of the ear to carve a volume into the void of darkness. The space traced by the ear becomes a cavity sculpted in the interior of the mind.

We can recall the acoustic harshness of an uninhabited and unfurnished house as compared to the affability of a lived home in which sound is refracted and softened by the surfaces of numerous objects of personal life. Every building or space has its characteristic sound of intimacy or monumentality, rejection or invitation, hospitality or hostility.

Sight makes us solitary, whereas hearing creates a sense of connection and solidarity; the gaze wanders lonesomely in the dark depths of a cathedral, but the sound of the organ makes us realize our affinity with the space. We stare alone at the suspense of the circus, but the burst of applause after the relaxation of suspense unites us to the crowd. The sound of church bells through the streets makes us aware of our citizenship. The echo of steps on a paved street has an emotional charge because the sound bouncing off the surrounding walls puts us in direct interaction with space; the sound measures space and makes its scale comprehensible. We stroke the edges of the space with our ears. But, the contemporary city has lost its echo.

Silence, Time and Solitude

However, the most essential auditory experience created by architecture is tranquility. Architecture presents the drama of construction silenced into matter and space; architecture is the art of petrified silence. After the clutter of building has ceased and the shouting of workers has died away, the building becomes a museum of a waiting, patient silence. In Egyptian temples we encounter the silence of the pharaohs, in the silence of a Gothic cathedral we are reminded of the last dying note of a Gregorian chant, and echo of Roman footsteps has just faded on the walls of the Pantheon.

An architectural experience silences all external noise; it focuses attention on one's very existence. Architecture, as all art, makes us aware of our fundamental solitude. At the same time, architecture detaches us from the present and allows us to experience the slow, firm flow of time and tradition. Buildings and cities are instruments and museums of time. They enable us to see and understand the passing of history.

Architecture connects us with the dead; through buildings we are able to imagine the bustle of the medieval street and fancy a solemn procession approaching the cathedral. The time of architecture is a detained time; in the greatest of buildings time stands firmly still. Time in the Great Peristyle at Karnak has petrified into a timeless present.

Experiencing a work of art is a private dialogue between the work and the viewer that excludes other interactions. "Art is made by the alone felt the alone," as Cyrille Connolly writes in *The Unquiet Grave*. Melancholy lies beneath moving experiences of art; this is the tragedy of beauty's immaterial temporality. Art projects an unattainable ideal.

Space of Scent

The strongest memory of a space is often its odor; I cannot remember the appearance of the door to my grandfather's farm-house from my early childhood, but I do remember the resistance of its weight, the patina of its wood surface scarred by a half century of use, and I recall especially the scent of home that hit my face as an invisible wall behind the door.

A particular smell may make us secretly re-enter a space that has been completely erased from the retinal memory; the nostrils project a forgotten image and we are enticed to enter a vivid daydream.

"…Memory and imagination remain associated," Gaston Bachelard writes. "I alone in my memories of another century can open the deep cupboard that still retains for me alone that unique odor, the odor of raisins, drying on a wicker tray. The odor of raisins! It is an odor that is beyond description, one that it takes a lot of imagination to smell."

And what a delight to move from one realm of odor to the next in the narrow streets of an old town; the scent sphere of a candy store makes one think of the innocence and curiosity of childhood; the dense smell of a shoemaker's workshop makes one imagine horses and saddles, harness straps and the excitement of riding; the fragrance of a bread shop projects images of health, sustenance and physical strength, whereas the perfume of a pastry shop makes one think of bourgeois felicity.

Why do abandoned houses always have the same hollow smell; is it because the particular smell is caused by the visual emptiness observed by the eye?

In his *Notebooks of Malte Laurids Brigge*, Rainer Maria Rilke gives a dramatic description of images of past life in an already demolished house conveyed by traces imprinted on the wall of its neighboring house. "There were the midday meals and sicknesses and the exhalations and the smoke of years, and the sweat that breaks out under the armpits and makes the garments heavy, and the stale breath of mouths, and the oily odour of perspiring feet. There were the pungent tang of urine and the stench of burning soot and the grey reek of potatoes, and the heavy, sickly fumes of rancid grease. The sweetish, lingering smell of neglected infants was there, and the smell of frightened children who go to school and the stuffiness of the beds of nubile youths."

Contemporary images of architecture appear sterile and lifeless as compared to the emotional and associative power of Rilke's olfactory imagery.

The Shape of Touch

The skin reads the texture, weight, density and temperature of matter. The surface of an old object, polished to perfection by the tool of the craftsman and the assiduous hands of its users, seduces the stroking of our hand. It is pleasurable to press a door handle shining from the thousand hands that have entered the door before us; the clean shimmer of ageless wear has turned into an image of welcome and hospitality. The door handle is the handshake of the building. The tactile sense connects us with time and tradition; through marks of touch we shake the hands of countless generations.

The skin traces spaces of temperature with unerring precision; the cool and invigorating shadow under a tree or the caressing sphere of warmth in a spot of sun. In my childhood-images of the countryside, I can vividly recall walls against the angle of the sun, walls which intensified the heat of radiation and melted the snow, allowing the first smell of pregnant soil to announce the approach of summer. These pockets of spring were identified by the skin and the nose as much as by the eye.

We trace the density and texture of the ground through our soles. Standing barefoot on a smooth glacial rock by the sea at sunset and sensing through one's soles the warmth of the stone heated by the sun is a healing experience; it makes one part of the eternal cycle of nature. One senses the slow breathing of the earth.

There is a strong identity between the skin and the sensation of home. The experience of home is essentially an experience of warmth. The space of warmth around a fireplace is the space of ultimate intimacy and comfort. A sense of homecoming is never stronger than seeing a light in the window of a house in a snow-covered landscape at dusk; the remembrance of its warm interior gently warms one's frozen limbs. Home and skin turn into a single sensation.

But the eye also touches; the gaze implies an unconscious bodily mimesis, identification. Perhaps, we should think of touch as the unconscious of vision. Our gaze strokes distant surfaces, contours and edges, and the unconscious tactile sensation determines the agreeableness or unpleasantness of the experience. The distant and the near are experienced with the same intensity.

Great architecture offers shapes and surfaces molded for the pleasurable touch of the eye.

The eye is the sense of separation and distance, whereas touch is the sense of nearness, intimacy and affection. During overpowering emotional states we tend to close off the distancing sense of vision; we close our eyes when caressing our loved ones. Deep shadows and darkness are essential, because they dim the sharpness of vision and invite unconscious peripheral vision and tactile fantasy. Homogeneous light paralyzes the imagination in the same way that homogenization eliminates the experience of place.

In his *In Praise of Shadows*, Jun'ichiro Tanizaki points out that even Japanese cooking depends upon shadows and is inseparable from darkness. "And when yokan is served in a lacquer dish, it is as if the darkness of the room were melting on your tongue." In olden times the blackened teeth of the geisha and her green-black lips and white face were also intended to emphasize the darkness and shadows of the room. In Luis Barragan's view most of contemporary houses would be more pleasant with only half of their window surface.

In emotional states, sense stimuli seem to shift from the more refined senses toward the more archaic, from vision down to touch and smell. A culture that seeks to control its citizens is likely to value the opposite direction of interface; away from the intimate identification toward the publicly distant detachment. A society of surveillance is necessarily a society of a voyeurist eye.

Images of Muscle and Bone

Primitive man used his body, the dimensioning and proportioning system of his constructions. The builders of traditional societies shaped their buildings with their own bodies in the same way that a bird molds its nest by its body. The essence of a tradition is the wisdom of the body stored in the haptic memory. The essential knowledge of the ancient hunter, fisherman and farmer, as well as of the mason and stone cutter, was an imitation of an embodied tradition of the trade, stored in the muscular and tactile senses.

"The word habit is too worn a word to express this passionate liaison of our bodies, which do not forget, with an unforgettable house," writes Bachelard of the strength of bodily memory.

There is an inherent suggestion of action in images of architecture, the moment of active encounter or a promise of use and purpose. A bodily reaction is an inseparable aspect of the experience of architecture as a consequence of this implied action. A real architectural experience is not simply a series of retinal images; a building is encountered—it is approached, confronted, encountered, related to one's body, moved about, utilized as a condition for other things, etc.

Stepping stones set in the grass of a garden are images and imprints of human steps.

As we open a door, our body weight meets the weight of the door; our legs measure the steps as we ascend a stair, our hand strokes the handrail and our entire body moves diagonally and dramatically through space.

A building is not an end to itself; it frames, articulates, restructures, gives significance, relates, separates and unites, facilitates and prohibits. Consequently, elements of an architectural experience seem to have a verb form rather than being nouns. Authentic architectural experiences consist then of approaching, or confronting a building rather than the facade; of the act of entering and not simply the frame of the door, of looking in or out of a window, rather than the window itself.

In the analysis of Fra Angelico's *Annunciation* in his essay "From the Doorstep to the Common Room" (1926), Alvar Aalto recognizes the verb essence of architectural experience; he speaks of entering a room, not of the porch or the door, for instance.

The authenticity of architectural experience is grounded in the tectonic language of building and the comprehensibility of the act of construction to the senses. We behold, touch, listen and measure the world with our entire bodily existence and the experiential world is organized and articulated around the center of the body. Our domicile is the refuge of our body, memory and identity. We are in constant dialogue and interaction with the environment, to the degree that it is impossible to detach the image of the Self from its spatial and situational existence. "I am the space, where I am," as the poet Noel Arnaud established.

Bodily Identification

Henry Moore wrote perceptively of the necessity of a bodily identification in art, "This is what the sculptor must do. He must strive continually to think of, and use, form in its full spatial completeness. He gets the solid shape, as it were, inside his head—he thinks of it, whatever its size, as if he were holding it completely enclosed in the hollow of his hand. He mentally visualizes a complex form from all round itself; he knows while he looks at one side what the other side is like; he identifies himself with its center of gravity, its mass, its weight; he realizes its volume, and the space that the shape displaces in the air."

The encounter of any work of art implies a bodily interaction. A work of art functions as another person, with whom we converse. Melanie Klein's notion of projective identification suggests that, in fact, all human interaction implies projection of fragments of the Self to the other person. The painter Graham Sutherland expresses the same view in regards to his own work, "In a sense the landscape painter must almost look at the landscape as if it were himself—himself as a human being." In Paul Cézanne's view the landscape thinks through him and he is the consciousness of the landscape.

Similarly, an architect internalizes a building in his body; movement, balance, distance and scale are felt unconsciously through the body as tension in the muscular system and in the positions of the skeleton and inner organs. As the work interacts with the body of the observer the experience mirrors these bodily sensations of the maker. Consequently, architecture is communication from the body of the architect directly to the body of the inhabitant.

Understanding architectural scale implies the unconscious measuring of an object or a building with one's body, and projecting one's bodily scheme on the space in question. We feel pleasure and protection when the body discovers its resonance in space.

When experiencing a structure, we unconsciously mimic its configuration with bones and muscles; the pleasurably animated flow of a piece of music is subconsciously transformed into bodily sensations, the composition of an abstract painting is experienced as tensions to the muscular system. The structures of a building are unconsciously imitated and comprehended through the skeletal system unknowingly, as we perform the task of the column or the vault with our body. The brick wants to become a vault, as Louis Kahn has said, but this metamorphosis takes place through the mimesis of our own body.

The sense of gravity is the essence of all architectonic structures and great architecture makes us conscious of gravity and earth. Architecture strengthens verticality of our experience of the world. At the same time architecture makes us aware of the depth of earth, it makes us dream of levitation and flight.

Taste of Architecture

Adrian Stokes writes about the "oral invitation of Veronese marble." There is a subtle transference between tactile and taste experiences. Vision also becomes transferred to taste; certain colors as well as delicate details evoke oral sensations. A delicately colored polished stone surface is subliminally sensed by the tongue. Many years ago I felt compelled to kneel and touch the white marble threshold of the James residence in Carmel, California, designed by Charles and Henry Greene. Carlo Scarpa's architecture also frequently presents similar experiences of taste.

Tanizaki gives an impressive description of the subtle interaction of the senses,

"With lacquerware there is a beauty in that moment between removing the lid and lifting the bowl to the mouth when one gazes at the still, silent liquid in the dark depths of the bowl, its colour hardly differing from the bowl itself. What lies within the darkness one cannot distinguish, but the palm senses the gentle movements of the liquid, vapor rises from within forming droplets on the rim, and a fragrance carried upon the vapor brings a delicate anticipation."

The Task of Architecture

The timeless task of architecture is to create embodied existential metaphors that concretize and structure man's being in the world. Images of architecture reflect and externalize ideas and images of life; architecture materializes our images of ideal life. Buildings and towns enable us to structure, understand and remember who we are. Architecture enables us to place ourselves in the continuum of culture.

All experience implies the acts of recollecting, remembering and comparing. An embodied memory has an essential role as the basis of remembering a space or a place. Our home and domicile are integrated with our self-identity; they become part of our own body and being.

In memorable experiences of architecture, space, matter and time fuse into one single dimension, into the basic substance of being, that penetrates the consciousness. We identify ourselves with this space, this place, this moment and these dimensions as they become ingredients of our very existence. Architecture is the art of mediation and reconciliation.

Notes

*   Juhani Pallasmaa, "An Architecture of the Seven Senses," in *a+u Architecture and Urbanism: Questions of Perception*, ed. Steven Holl, Juhani Pallasmaa, and Alberto Pérez-Gómez (Tokyo: a+u Publishing Co., Ltd., 1994), 33.

Body Troubles

Robert McAnulty

INTRODUCTION

Architectural history reveals the relationship between the dimensions of the human body and the creation of architectural form. In "Body Troubles," Robert McAnulty takes us through four examples of representational and conceptual reflections on thinking and technology that contribute to interior form making. While this essay is situated in the discourse of architecture because of references to Peter Eisenman, John Hejduk, and Diller and Scofidio, McAnulty's framing of their work uncovers influences at the scale of the body and interior.

As this section seeks to advance the study of the body's measure, McAnulty's essay emphasizes the dynamic relationship between the body and interior space. Objects, surfaces, and the role of proximity contribute to this relationship. When McAnulty focuses his sights beyond the classical representation of the body (see Geoffrey Scott's Architecture of Humanism*), he offers new perspectives on the interior. He continues by adding three new readings to the classical dimensions of the body. First, he expands Eisenman's so-called "objectified" approach. Eisenman, according to McAnulty, renders the body as an objective representation of communal agreement, dismissing individualism. In order to situate the body in Eisenman's work, McAnulty references Michel Foucault's representation of the body as an abstracted, communal body influenced by political and societal rules.*

McAnulty's second reading takes Hejduk's animated characters and reads them as body/architecture hybrids. Hejduk allows the body to inscribe animations onto the architectural object, which in turn mirrors physical being. The body's ability to see, reach, and move in synthesis with architecture creates scale between body and building.

The works of Diller and Scofidio stem from Hejduk's oeuvre into new territory that addresses social realms within constructed space. Architecture becomes subordinate to the role of the social norms that construct it and that conflict is ultimately played out in interior space. McAnulty references Diller + Scofidio's Body Building *experiment, which manipulated the social*

Originally appeared in *Strategies in Architectural Thinking*, edited by John Whiteman, Jeffrey Kipnis, and Richard Burdett (Cambridge, MA: The MIT Press, 1992), 180–97.

norms/physical body dichotomy, making architecture that was closer to the body: somewhere between clothing and room. Diller and Scofidio referenced the domestic social structure as a vehicle that exposed domestic data typically hidden in full-scale occupation visible here in the language of architectural drawing. Only traces of the body are present, discernable through spatial mechanics and inscription.

———

WHAT ARE THE consequences for architecture of the "death of Man," the revered subject of humanism? More importantly perhaps for architecture, what became of his body? All around us, everywhere we turn, the mechanisms of criticism are abuzz with talk of "the post-structuralist body," "body invaders," "bodybuildings," and so on. Clearly the issue of rewriting the classical body is a hot topic these days. And an important topic for an architectural discourse whose very foundations, we have been taught to believe, rest on its relation to the human figure. Once "man" has gone, and presumably taken his body along with him, what are we architects left with? Who do we serve? Where do we look for our formal models? Must we abandon ourselves to the "procession of simulacra," reveling in an apocalyptic fin-de-millennium free fall?[1] Must we resuscitate our fallen man phenomenologically or psychoanalytically so as to re-ground our "destabilized" foundations? Or can we begin to imagine other ways of traversing the horns of this dilemma, routes which map the site of the body and multiply the possibilities for architectural action?

This paper is organized into four sections: the first three dealing with issues of body and architecture of Michel Foucault, Alberto Pérez-Gómez, and Anthony Vidler respectively. Finally I will turn my attention briefly to the work of two of our contemporaries, Elizabeth Diller and Ricardo Scofidio, who are themselves attempting to rewrite the body in their projects.[2]

The numerous recent attempts to refocus attention on the body all share in their questioning of humanist theories of the subject. Such humanist theories have served indirectly to emphasize the hierarchical centrality of the human figure. Although they have been under attack for some time now, it is worth briefly recapitulating the issues at hand in architectural terms. We are all familiar with the famous drawing by Leonardo da Vinci of the Vitruvian Man, the male body standing upright with arms extended, inscribed within a circle and a square with the centers of both geometrical figures at the body's navel. Two formal issues are worth noting here. First, the body is presented frontally, as a statically balanced, symmetrical figure with well-defined limbs and orderly musculature, thus prompting an understanding of the human body as a figural unity: compositionally complete, confidently stable, and hierarchically ordered. Second, a mathematical unity pervades the image in which both the natural figure (the body) and the geometrical figures (the circle and the square) share a point of origin in the body's navel. We find a body that is presented as embodying the harmonic order of a divinely inspired network of Euclidian geometry, thus empowering it in its claim to the pivotal position in an anthropocentric world.

The unified body of the Vitruvian image was taken as the model for classical architecture; buildings were to mimic the order, harmony, and proportions of the Vitruvian body. This mimetic relationship to the human figure dominated architecture through the sixteenth century and continues to have significant impact even today. As a graduate student I was assigned to read Geoffrey Scott's *Architecture of Humanism,* published in 1914. Nostalgically recalling a bygone era, Scott exhorted us that,

> The center of that architecture was the human body; its method, to transcribe in stone the body's favorite states; and the moods of the spirit took visible shape along its borders, power and laughter, strength and terror and calm.[3]

Scott's so-called architectural "transcription" can be questioned in formal terms that inquire about the body's position relative to the building. If the body is to transcribe or project itself onto the building, then it must be operating at some distance from that which it is being projected upon. This distance is formalized in Euclidean geometry and perspectival models, which provide the conceptual framework for a relationship of division or alienation between the body/subject and its world/object. This dichotomy between subject and object is fundamental to a model of perception in which the body is seen as projecting its favorite *interior* "states" onto the *exterior* world. The body is understood as necessarily being independent, complete and constituted prior to the world, a world that takes form only insofar as it is embodied. The terms underlying the very possibility of the body's figural self-sufficiency and its projection onto a presumably undifferentiated world are those which I would like to call into question.

Recent architectural discourse has grappled with questions about the centrality of the humanist subject, as raised by theoretical developments in other fields. In this country, Peter Eisenman has led the attack on anthropomorphism, describing it as a "dangerous illusion" that has needed a "reexamination [in all human endeavors] of the repressive effects of this illusion." Eisenman prefers to couch his own reexamination in the language of psychoanalysis; yet, it is also clear that he has been influenced by the early writings of Michel Foucault.[4] Although Eisenman and other architectural theorists have typically focused on Foucault's critique of discursive structures and the appearance in history of discontinuities or "ruptures," it is my sense that we would all benefit from a rereading of his seminal work on the body.

Foucault describes his research as an "archeology of knowledge." In the study of the history of such institutions as the prison, the clinic, and the school, the archeologist attends to the cultural play of discourse: discursive practices that constitute the channels in which we necessarily speak and think. Abandoning the kind of inquiry into the origin of subjectivity prior to its situation in a political field that marks the other disciplines, such an archeological approach avoids the shortcomings of histories of the body, which consider it biologically, psychologically, or historically. Such histories tend to overlook the fact that, "…the body is also directly involved in a political field; power relations have an immediate hold on it; they mark it, train it, force it to carry out its tasks, to perform ceremonies, to emit signs."[5] Foucault considers the political technology of the body at some length in *Discipline and Punish*.[6] Focusing his inquiry on the systems of punishment that came to supplant public executions and torture, he formulates the model of a body that finds itself inscribed by its political situation. Foucault describes the formation of these newly subjected "docile bodies" as follows:

> Through this technique of subjection a new object was being formed; slowly, it superseded the mechanical body—the body composed of solids and assigned movements, the image of which had for so long haunted those who dream of disciplinary perfection. This new object is the natural body, the bearer of forces and the seat of duration; it is the body susceptible to specified operations, which have their order, their stages, their internal conditions, their constituent elements.…It is the body of exercise rather than speculative physics; a body manipulated by authority, rather than imbued with animal spirits; a body of useful training and not of rational mechanics…[7]

This newly formed natural body found its purest expression in the figure of the soldier. His body was instrumentally coded at the most minute levels. The articulation of his every gesture, from his marching posture to his penmanship, was broken down into its component parts, each of which was assigned a duration and an order of appearance. The Vitruvian body, subject to metaphysical analysis, was replaced by the manipulable body, inscribed through training and control.

In *Discipline and Punish,* Foucault traces the change in disciplinary practices that accompanied the demise of sovereign power. The popular public executions and torture used prior to the eighteenth century allowed the power of the king to be publicly demonstrated through its marking of the body of the condemned. As political structures changed and were no longer associated solely with the figure of the sovereign, the nature of power changed as well. No longer perceived as the property of an individual or a dominant class, power came to be observable only by way of its exercise or activity. Consequently, Foucault argues that power must now be seen as "investing" subjugated bodies within its structure, "it is transmitted by them and through them, it exerts pressure upon them, just as they themselves, in their struggle against it, resist the grip it has on them."[8] Such complete dispersion of the effects of power throughout political structures eliminates the necessity for an overt inscription of the condemned body wherein the exercise of power is observed directly in its graphic markings. The machine of Kafka's *The Penal Colony*,[9] which punishes the body of the condemned colonist by means of a system of vibrating needles inscribing such maxims as "Honor Thy Superiors" is no longer necessary in a society that is itself inscribed by a network of socially accepted codes. Such overt inscription has been replaced by a system of constant surveillance that underwrites self-colonization. Foucault describes the insidious effect of surveillance as follows:

> He who is subjected to a field of visibility, and who knows it, assumes responsibility for the constraints of power; he makes them play spontaneously upon himself; *he inscribes in himself* the power relation in which he simultaneously plays both roles; he becomes the principle of his own subjection.[10]

The structures of power inevitably become so pervasive that the body monitors itself, inscribes on itself the disciplinary exercises to which it is exposed and subjected. Conformance to social codes or norms becomes a matter of self-discipline.

As I have already noted, the primary mechanism whereby disciplinary societies exercise power over bodies is surveillance. An architecture that facilitated visual observation was the natural outcome of the new disciplinary procedures for controlling bodies. The institutionalization of visual control was made manifest in an architecture that was

> ...no longer built to be seen (as with ostentatious palaces), or to observe the external space, but to permit an internal, articulated and detailed control—to render visible those who are inside it; in more general terms, an architecture that operates to transform individuals; to act on those it shelters, to provide a hold on their conduct, to carry the effects of power right to them, to make it possible to know them, to alter them.[11]

Although he traces the effects of this architecture of visibility in such institutions as schools, factories, and clinics, Foucault is especially interested in Jeremy Bentham's Panopticon as a "compact model of the disciplinary mechanism." Since his analysis of the formal characteristics of the Panopticon is by now well known among architectural theorists, its recapitulation is no longer necessary. Suffice it to say that for Foucault, architecture is clearly complicitous with the disciplinary structures of power. Rather than finding evidence of a divine harmony between an idealized body and its world in the circular, symmetrical form of the Panopticon, Foucault finds evidence of institutionalized subjection of the prisoner's pliable body. And the architect, caught within the intricate relations of power, subjects him/herself to the disciplinary procedures that confine practice to the socially inscribed norms of power.

By now I hope it is clear that Foucault has almost completely inverted the body-world problematic originally posed in the humanist model. In place of the autonomous figure shaping objects in its own image, Foucault inserts the figure of an individual fabricated by power. This new social body is formed from the exterior by its inscription within a network of complex and constantly changing cultural relationships and discursive practises. The web of power is always already active prior to the body, the social precedes the individual. Insofar as the body becomes autonomous and individuated at all, it is as the result of the actions of power. Although I find Foucault's critique of architecture's complicity with power to be somewhat rhetorical, it seems clear that his understanding of the body in terms of its *exteriority* (versus the interiority of humanism) and its position of engagement *within* the world (versus a position of perspectival distance) is one that contemporary architecture must confront, however uncomfortable such a confrontation may be. The body's struggle to inscribe the structures of social power requires a geometrical or relational model that is far more subtle than the Vitruvian circle. And although the ways in which architectural practice can proceed in its attempts to re-inscribe the body are not at all clear as yet, we should recognize our indebtedness to Foucault's insights before condemning his political impotence.

In recent architectural discourse, one response to the dilemma posed by Foucault's analysis has been what I consider to be a metaphysics of the mysterious, which, somewhat paradoxically, seems to draw its inspiration from existentialism. Insistently calling attention to the plight of the modern individual as estranged and isolated from any sense of community, much recent architectural theory seeks a means of redressing such alienation. For Alberto Pérez-Gómez, the abject condition of contemporary society has been caused for the most part by the growing importance of science and technology in our lives and the instrumentality that accompanies such growth. For architecture this instrumentality has meant a loss of focus on what is understood to be fundamental to human experience: the body and its life-world. For this reason, in Pérez-Gómez' eyes, the body has fallen into disrepair and requires immediate attention if we are to find our way back to a "meaningful reality." As he has written in an article on the work of John Hejduk, entitled "The Renovation of the Body,"[12] "an authentic interest in architectural meaning in our times must be accompanied by a conscious or unconscious renovation of the body."[13] Continuing on the theme of authenticity, he writes, "Authentic architecture has always enabled man to come to terms with his mortality and transcend it."[14] Pérez-Gómez goes on to argue that Hejduk's later work, in particular the Masque projects, is representative of such authenticity at work. These themes are also embodied in such modernist monuments as Le Corbusier's La Tourette, Aalto's Paimio Sanatorium, Mies' Barcelona Pavilion, and Gaudí's Sagrada Familia. What these works share, in the "physiognomic" terms of the renovated body, is not at all clear from Pérez-Gómez' argument, but that is a subject for another time.

One thing these works apparently do share, in Pérez-Gómez' eyes, is a repudiation of what Foucault also refers to as the "classical" tradition that came to supplant Renaissance theories of the cosmos in the eighteenth century. Alternatively, Pérez-Gómez valorizes what he terms the Homeric (preclassical) tradition, which does not distinguish between the body and its way of engaging the world. Sight, in this model, does not recognize the distinction between the subject who sees and the object seen, focusing rather on the immediacy of the act of seeing, which is necessarily prior to the body-world (subject-object) distinction. Pérez-Gómez believes that the continuity between the body and its lived world has been obscured by classical metaphysics and modern science, both founded on a Cartesian dualism that finds the body as unitary and distinct from the world.

By his own admission, Pérez-Gómez' proposed body renovation is heavily reliant on his reading of existential phenomenology, in particular, Heidegger and Merleau-Ponty. In this reading, the body and world must be understood as acting in concert, as a "continuum." Such a continuum reverses the hierarchical division of the rationalist, Cartesian model of the sciences:

> In spite of our rationalist prejudices, body and world remain mysteriously related. The world is endowed with meaning in the immediacy of perception, and it is given a physiognomy which derives from the projection of our body image on to it.[15]

In this model, the world achieves some measure of significance only inso-far as it is embodied by the body's projection of its own image. The world as a projected, mimetic embodiment of the subject's interior is reminiscent of its humanist forebears and is subject to the same critiques. What is differ-ent in the phenomenological model is the site of the projection. Where for Renaissance theorists the body and world are formally linked in a divine nat-uralism based in geometry, for Pérez-Gómez, following Heidegger, the body finds the site for its projection onto the world in the figure of the "clearing."[16] This clearing is the place where a sort of primordial communion with nature occurs. It is the place where man "dwells" in the recognition of his essen-tially non-instrumental unity with the world. This "face-to-face" encounter must necessarily take place prior to any subsequent instrumentalization, any move to establish perspective distance between the body and its objects, any formal projection of its image by the subject.

As we can imagine, the trick here is to find the site where the "ground of being" reveals itself, where the body's continuity with the world is exposed. Pérez-Gómez describes the primordial experience of the clear-ing in the metaphysical-religious term: transcendence. In the experience of transcendence, the body somehow comes to terms with its own mortality, presumably by recognizing its essential identity with some aspect of nature that it sees as immortal. Authentic architecture facilitates transcendence by constructing places or clearings where the body "dwells." Unfortunately for all those seeking the transcendental experience, the modern world is domi-nated by inauthentic architecture that stands as evidence of the architect's growing interest in maintaining little more than "efficient technological control."

What then does all this have to do with Hejduk? How is he implicated in this argument? Not surprisingly, for Pérez-Gómez, Hejduk's work ren-ovates the body and in doing so, it renovates architecture. His reading of Hejduk's work goes as follows:

> The participants in Hejduk's Masques are more like bodily skins than skins of buildings. They refer in a direct way to the body, but they are not anthropomorphic in the classical tradition. Rather they take on the qualities of the flesh, as described by Merleau-Ponty....The protagonists of the Masques have a mysterious emanation of being, a seductive power that can create dangerous illusions. Rather than representing that which is alive, pre-classical *daidala* allowed inanimate matter to become magi-cally alive. Like Hejduk's architecture, they were *thaumata,* marvelously animated machines with brilliant suits of armour and scintillating eyes. This architecture is the mimesis of a transcendental emotion. It discloses the possible totality through the fragment.[17]

Hejduk's Masque projects abound with small-scale, totemic, solitary (typically upright) figures, each of which is frequently accompanied by a name for the construction, a name for its inhabitant, and occasionally by a short, enigmatic text describing the inhabitant's history and his function within a fictional community or tribe. The figures are quite literally animal-like with scales, fins, and spikes. Since we understand the renovated body to be that body capable of experiencing transcendence, somehow that transcendence is to be achieved by the body's experience of these mysterious objects that seem alive, although not "anthropomorphic in the classical tradition." But, in the terms of Pérez-Gómez' argument, is it not true that the animism we ascribe to Hejduk's figures is directly attributable to the body's projection of its own image onto the world *subsequent* to the originary transcendental encounter? And isn't it the case that such animistic projection onto the world inevitably initiates a certain distance between the body and its objects, thus instrumentally undermining the sense of their essential continuity?

Whatever the answers to these questions may be, Pérez-Gómez identifies architecture's essential character with that of "poetic naming":

> Through poetic naming, the architecture attains an unfathomable concreteness. The word allows the architect to reveal the ground of the "thing," of the products of *poesis*, and to attain archetypal meanings, thus the abstract becomes concrete and the figural is regained....Poetry speaks in images in order to let us dwell, states Heidegger.[18]

This, then, represents Pérez-Gómez' prescription for the renovation of the body. Future generations of architects, seeking authenticity, should turn their attention to the peculiarly personal task of poetic naming through the construction of enigmatic, animistic figures that allow the body to "apprehend [its] place in the face of destiny." This task is as "rigorously introspective" as it is a-political, as self-absorbed as it is disconnected to its cultural situation, and as timeless and universal as it is a-historical. What starts as an attempt to outline a strategy for retrieving, resuscitating, and renovating the body in phenomenological terms becomes a prescriptive ideal with a very specific formal analogue. My sense is that the degeneration into animism marks the difficulty of translating the Heideggerian concept of dwelling, which is essentially non-volitional, into an architectural pragmatics, which is unavoidably instrumental.

A much more provocative attempt to reformulate the issue of the body in architectural terms comes from Anthony Vidler in a lecture entitled "The Building in Pain"[19] (a play on the recently published *The Body in Pain* by Elaine Scarry[20]). Following a discussion of a "gradual erosion of confidence" in the classical model of the unified body, Vidler raises the question, How does the perception that a building is a body manage to survive the various attacks on the classical model of the body? Has the notion that a building is a body disappeared? Has the body really disappeared? If not, how does it appear and what kind of presence might it have? These questions prefigure Vidler's response—no, the body has not disappeared, it continues to animate our experience of artifacts and buildings, although after Freud the body (and the self) has undergone some changes.

Like Pérez-Gómez, Vidler locates the beginning of what he is later to call the "poststructuralist" body in existentialism. His lecture began with a recapitulation of Jean-Paul Sartre's questioning of the body in *Being and Nothingness*.[21] In Sartre's reformulation of the classic analogical model, the body is seen as a participant in an instrumental complex of tools awaiting action. The body comes to know itself only insofar as it is active in the instrumental world. It can never achieve sufficient distance from itself or its tools so as to be capable of understanding itself independent of its world. The body and the man-made object have a reciprocal relationship—each needs the other in order to recognize itself. And the body that is "lived, not thought," recognizes its contingency by virtue of its dependence on objects. The Sartre passage quoted by Vidler goes as follows:

> I live my body in danger as regards menacing machines for manageable instruments. My body is everywhere: the bomb which destroys my house also damages my body insofar as my house was already an indication of my body…my body always extends across the tool which it utilizes: it is at the end of the telescope which shows me the stars…it is my adaptation to those tools.[22]

This is a somewhat familiar critique of the humanist model: the dualistic model of the body-world relationship, which claims mimetic analogy as its formal operation, must be replaced by a "post-structuralist" model whose initial insight recognizes a fundamental reciprocity (inter-relatedness) between body and world.

Having located in Sartre's work the possibility of rewriting the body in "post-structuralist" terms, Vidler now returns to his initial questions. How can buildings be like bodies if the body has disappeared? Has the body really disappeared? If not, how does it manifest itself, how is it present in the objects of the world? This portion of Vidler's thesis relies heavily on Scarry. Sounding a note that has familiar overtones, Scarry argues that, "…artifacts are (in spite of their inertness) perhaps most accurately perceived as 'a making sentient of the external world.'"[23] Such sentience is achieved by any man-made object as a projection of the human body. Scarry reformulates the phenomenon of projection in three different ways, each progressively more interior than the previous one. We move from bodily projections that are formally mimetic (lens, pumps), to the projection of bodily attributes (seeing, desiring), to the projection of an animistic sense of aliveness. Of animistic projection, she writes, "'Aliveness' or 'awareness of aliveness' is in some very qualified sense projected out onto the object world."[24] Here then we have the answer to the question of whether the body is really missing at all. Since all artifacts bear the mark of the bodies that made/projected them, then the preeminent status of the body in the very structure of perception is restored. Once again buildings can be like bodies.

How then, we must ask, do the exteriorized embodiments/projections of the so-called "post-structuralist" body differ from those of the classical body? If in both cases, the formal model is projection, then we can only account for the differences between the forms projected by reformulating the interior conditions of the post-structuralist body. For this reformulation Vidler turns to Jacques Lacan. To briefly recount Lacan's famous essay on the "mirror stage," he describes the moment an infant sees himself for the first time in the mirror and concomitantly identifies himself as a totality or integrated self. Prior to the mirror stage, the infant perceives himself only as "morselated" or fragmented. Following the encounter with the mirror, this fragmentary condition is repressed in the unconscious. The subsequent unexpected reappearance of the repressed material returns through a pathological network of dreams and psychoses. The form of this repressed material is marked, in Lacan's words, "by disjointed members and organs figured in exoscopy…"[25] which is presumably the formal character of "morselation." Vidler identifies the renewed contact with those experiences previously repressed or hidden from consciousness as the experience of the "uncanny," about which he has written at length elsewhere.[26] To summarize the argument, we are led to understand that a building, as one of the man-made artifacts of the world, stands as the result of the projection of the body. Endowed with an animism that results from the exteriorization of the sentient qualities of the post-Freudian body, certain buildings cause us to lose our sense of grounding by revealing the presence of something that we had believed to be absent, but in fact had only been repressed.

Here again the language of animism has replaced that of anthropomorphism. Whereas Pérez-Gómez describes the animistic in Hejduk's work by reference to the "marvelously animated machines with brilliant suits of armour," Vidler cites the work of Alvaro Siza, Silvetti and Machado, and Coop Himmelblau. I have reason to believe that Vidler is unhappy with this portion of his lecture, so I won't dwell on his examples. Briefly, however, Coop Himmelblau's Red Angel Cafe is cited for its play on Melville's description of the wind in *Moby Dick* as being "bodiless as object but not as agent."

Presumably Vidler reads the project's formal play of cutting and fragmentation as evidence of the "animal-like" play of some bodiless agent (the mythic Red Angel), a presence that cannot be understood in the conventional terms of finite self-closure that characterize the body as a static, figural object. In Vidler's eyes, Siza's architecture school for Porta displays a similar animistic awareness in its fractional composition. It is not clear from Vidler's description of these projects how they serve to reveal the presence of some absent experience that has been repressed. Notwithstanding his detailed development of Scarry's thesis, Vidler's animistic readings of architectural projects are peculiarly limited in their scope. Since we come away from the lecture with a somewhat unsatisfying image of Coop Himmelblau's "panther in the urban jungle" (whose formal counterpart turns out to be nothing more than a simple beam characterized as spinelike), we continue to wonder how the panther figures in our unconscious, how the animistic presence of its figural absence is representative of some presocial mirror stage. In deference to Vidler, perhaps we should assume that there is more analysis yet to come.

In noting the brevity of Vidler's account of the way in which animism or the body's animistic projection informs buildings, my reading is that he is less concerned with the "poststructuralist" body in figural terms than he is with the psychological or psychoanalytic readings of the projects he has chosen to describe. Near the end of the lecture, his account shrewdly changes its focus from the question of the body's projection of its interior states to *our* body's experience of the products of such projection. In his description of our experience of such projects as the Red Angel Cafe, we are variously "contorted, racked, cut, wounded, impaled, and dissected." And the effect of all this pain is to make us lose our sense of "grounding," to force us to question the apparent stability of our psychological foundations. In short, we experience the "uncanny" and in so doing we initiate a movement wherein we will "overcome the mirror stage" in our return to the "stage before the mirror." In summoning the experience of the "uncanny," these buildings make possible our recognition that the apparent autonomy of consciousness and the unity of our bodies are never more than fictive social constructions. So far, so good, we say, such a critique appears to be leading toward identifying the social inscription of the body in terms similar to Foucault's. But here we encounter a difficulty. For now, having described the frightening return of previously repressed materials, the so-called "presence of absence," Vidler proceeds to speak of the importance of a *return* to a pre-mirror condition. The clever translation into spatial terms of the pre-mirror stage to the "stage before the mirror" serves to mask the temporal condition in which the subject appears prior to the mirror rather than in front of it. This is precisely the sort of appeal to a primordial lost origin that characterized Pérez-Gómez' argument. We are to go back in search of the presocial body that is understood as being constituted prior to its experience of the world. Although this body is now described in formal terms that differ from those of the humanist figure, i.e., morselated versus whole, nonetheless we are once again faced with a model of a unified subject that precedes its object-making activities in the world. So once again, buildings can be like bodies because they are the exteriorized result of the body's projection of its interiorized condition, be they fragmented or otherwise. In spatial terms, this model regenerates the perspectival distance between the body and its objects that Heidegger and Sartre worked so hard to disperse.

Now isn't it curious that both Pérez-Gómez and Vidler arrive at the issue of animism in their search for the missing body? All the more curious because of the body's reactions to its own image projected animistically. For Pérez-Gómez, the body's experience of itself in the form of "marvelously animated machines with brilliant suits of armour and scintillating eyes" is akin to an act of ritualized transcendence; its essence is revelatory and emancipatory. For Vidler, on the other hand, the experience is also revelatory, but this revelation is a frightening and uncomfortable one because it reveals to the body the instability of its egocentric unity. Whereas for Pérez-Gómez the body's concern for transcendence is natural and healthy, Vidler's body is in pain, its experience of its own animistic projections is necessary, but difficult.

Both, however, must be seen as reformulating the issue of the body and architecture in terms fundamentally unchanged from those of Geoffrey Scott. Both insist on a model that finds the body as an interiorized subject projecting itself onto an exterior world. As such, both fail to answer the challenges posed by Foucault's formulation of the subject as pure exteriority, the product of the inscription of the relations of power in culture. And in failing to answer Foucault's critique, the psychoanalytic and phenomenological models fail us in two ways. First, in their unwillingness to propose an alternative to a model based on analogic projection, they fail to dislocate the preeminent position of the humanist subject within architectural discourse. Second, and perhaps more important, in their refusal to formulate the body-architecture question in *relational* terms, they fail to offer us the possibility of responding to it in anything other than *figural* terms. Having concluded that the body *figures* architecture, one finds little choice but to explore the languages of renovation or return; hardly the most fertile terrain in a culture whose *relational* structures remain to be mapped.

How does the work of Elizabeth Diller and Ricardo Scofidio manage to satisfy all the criticisms of the first three models? Very simply, it doesn't. I choose to focus on them because I find their work to be amongst the most aggressive and provocative being done in architecture today. This is not to posit it as a new formal model (although that has clearly already happened in the schools) or to suggest that a comprehensive new way of figuring the body is immanent in the work and susceptible to analysis. On the contrary, I bring their work to your attention in hopes of sparking a dialogue about the multiple possibilities for rewriting the body and about how we architects might best remain open to these possibilities.

To start with, we must get beyond Diller and Scofidio's own stated intentions. Due at least in part to the insatiable appetites of the media machinery, Diller and Scofidio have produced textual materials that do not always do justice to the projects themselves. One such text clearly locates Diller and Scofidio in the mainstream of body-world dualism:

> Leonardo da Vinci and Schlemmer constructed two fundamentally different models for the relationship between man and this world. As we slip further away from the model of Leonardo and past that of Schlemmer, into a time of revered artifice and spatial implosion, the relation of man to his world has become a subject of renewed interest. What could a new model of this relationship be? *Could there be one?*[27]

Only the final sentence suggests the possibility of moving beyond the self-projecting subject of humanism. Given the remarkably exploratory character of their projects, this inability to formulate the question in terms other than figural, those of a projected interiority, is testament to the success of the phenomenological and psychoanalytic models in suppressing the alternative possibilities for formulating (versus reformulating) the question. As long as the question is marked by figural terminology, our answers will be inevitably prefigured.

From the outset, I should note that although Diller and Scofidio have somewhat disingenuously attempted to unify their projects to date by identifying them as "bodybuildings," I find the work lacking the unitary character of a "body" of work. Hence, whether consciously or subconsciously, there is already a questioning of architecture's traditional insistence on identifying the body with the self-enclosed figure. My reading, prompted by Deleuze and Artaud, is that Diller and Scofidio are attempting to make themselves a "body without organs." Lacking a fixed hierarchy of ideas/organs organized by an internal logic of function and circulation, the projects indicate multiple directions for reformulating the body; as such, these so-called "probes" are intended to ignite our desire to engage the body anew. This body is not to be understood either as a corpse awaiting our autopsy, inert and static, nor as a figure to gaze upon, upright and complete. The readings of Diller and Scofidio work that follow attempt to map their body (of work) as a multiplicity of simultaneous trajectories sharing neither originary source, nor similar speed, nor parallel direction.[28] Such reading does not aspire to the synthetic

Fig. 1.6: Diller and Scofidio, *the withDrawing room* installation at 65 Capp Street, San Francisco, 1987. Image courtesy of Diller Scofidio + Renfro

completion or organic fullness of the historian's exegesis, but prefers instead to project possibilities for further investigatory work.

First, their writings notwithstanding, Diller and Scofidio's projects do not attempt to replace the Vitruvian figure with another figure. There is no attempt at renovation nor resuscitation here, no return to figural origins. By confining their focus to a limited number of peculiar *spatial* relationships, Diller and Scofidio shift attention from the figural presence of the body acting within a world of objects, to the conditions under which the body comes to embody certain social definitions. For instance, the remarkable emptiness of projects like the installations for Capp Street and Gallery Nature Morte is due to an unusual absence of figural bodies. This absence is not intended to nostalgically recall a time of figural presence, but to reveal the necessarily fictive identity of the body fabricated by social structures. Capp Street's floating "dining room," less its floor, the "living room" cut by the reflected property line, the "bed room" with its hinged bed, all speak to the absence of the bodies whose ritualized domesticity is inscribed in their workings. [Figs. 1.6–1.8] The domesticated body is no longer present in this project, replaced by Diller and Scofidio's concretization of the social practices that precede and prefigure the body. Here then we are not confined to the twin figures of figural "presence" and "presence of absence," which haunt Vidler's psychoanalytic readings of architecture. Instead Diller and Scofidio call to our attention a third possibility, that of the presence of something nonfigural—the spatial structures that order our bodies. If this is so, then the effect of the emptiness to which I referred to earlier need not be frightening discomfort so

Figs. 1.7 + 1.8: Diller and Scofidio, *the withDrawing room* installation at 65 Capp Street, San Francisco, 1987. Images courtesy of Diller Scofidio + Renfro

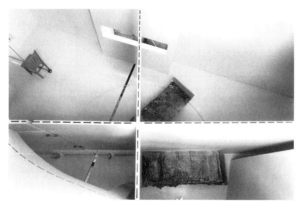

much as startling disclosure. And by confining their attention to these non-figural structures, Diller and Scofidio resist the temptation to substitute some new "postmodern" figure for the models written by Vitruvius, Leonardo, and Schlemmer. Alternatively, Diller and Scofidio actively engage the social practices that give form to our lives by cutting them open, laying them bare for our inspection, independent of our use. Their method is descriptive rather than prescriptive, culturally analytical rather than psychoanalytical.

Given the media's obsession with the bodily appendages, which appear in so many Diller and Scofidio projects, it may be difficult to find reason for my suggestion that the work be read as a spatial (versus figural) critique. But attention to such figures as the *Bride in Her Corset* and the *Automarionette* should be directed to their bondage rather than to their figural unity. The physicality of the human figure is the basis for the addition of the mechanisms of control. Reminiscent of Kleist's puppet figures, the apparatus of the *Automarionette* shapes the body's engagement with the world by limiting its sight (with a mask), its touch (with gloves), and its movement (with a system of counterweights). The *Bride's* sexuality is held firmly in place

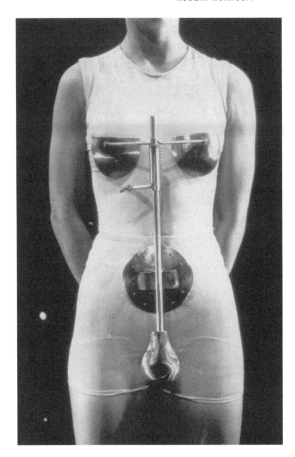

Fig. 1.9: Diller and Scofidio, "The Bride's Armor," from *The Notary Rotary and His Hot Plate*, 1987.

Image courtesy of Diller Scofidio + Renfro

(and protected) by her metal corset. [Fig. 1.9] In neither case does the body seem comfortable in its bondage, that is, this is not an argument for some new form of biomechanical naturalism. These bodies are capable of action and reaction, but their movements are defined within a network of forces, both political and gravitational. And this network is important to us because it inscribes our bodies through our constructions, our spaces. Here again we are confronted with a model of space wherein the body's significance is not as a figural source of mimetic projection, but as site for the inscriptions of power.

Finally, we cannot fail to note the explicitly sexual character of Diller and Scofidio's body (of work), as opposed to the body's spiritualized asexuality in the models, which claim animism as their starting point. In their investigations of the social structures that assign sexual roles, Diller and Scofidio take on the issue at the level of gender difference. The performance apparatus for "A Delay in Glass" (based on Duchamp's *Large Glass)* represents,

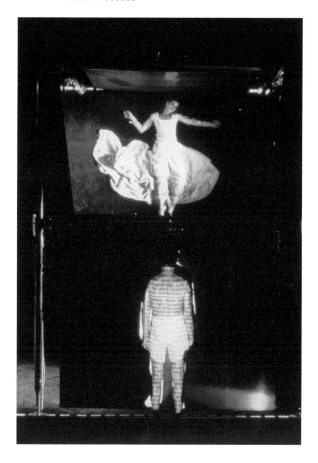

Fig. 1.10: Diller and
Scofidio, "The Chase,"
from *The Notary Rotary
and His Hot Plate*, 1987.
Image courtesy of Diller
Scofidio + Renfro

in Diller and Scofidio's words, the "irreconcilability between male and female."[29] Despite tendencies to androgyny in the *Bachelor*, the classical sexual differences between male and female remain intact and unreconciled. The masks, the armor, the rope all are signs of a sexual struggle that resists easy conciliation. The stereotypical division of sexual roles, which is marked by the horizontal line in Duchamp's *Glass*, is dislocated from the vertical plane of the window to the horizontal plane of the floor. [Figs. 1.10–1.11] No longer pure and detached, this *Bride* is dominated by the same sexual energies as her suitor, yet their bodies are always separated by the social apparatus of the metallic door. The painful desire to reconcile, to become one, is only consummated virtually, in the reflection of the mirror mounted diagonally overhead. Neither the body of the *Bride* nor of the *Bachelor* can be understood independent of its sexuality, but the social roles inscribed by terms like masculinity and femininity are assigned by social conventions and institutions. Diller and Scofidio acknowledge architecture's complicity in prescribing

Fig. 1.11: Diller and Scofidio, "The Chase," from *The Notary Rotary and His Hot Plate*, 1987.
Image courtesy of Diller Scofidio + Renfro

sexual difference in the figure of the pivoting door, while simultaneously reflecting on the inscriptive power of convention through the figure of the mirror.

In the briefest outline this paper marks the beginnings of a map that reformulates the body in spatial (versus figural), inscriptive (versus projective), and sexual (versus animistic) terms. And as beginnings, it serves only to point the way for further exploration. One last thing should be said: we must be wary of all attempts to confine our mapping to areas already explored. No matter how cleverly the naturalistic terrain of humanism is newly refigured by phenomenology or psychoanalysis, we should not allow ourselves to be tricked into retracing our steps.

Notes

1   A. Kraker and D. Cook, *The Postmodern Scene* (New York, 1986), p. 12.

2   For a more extensive review of the work of Diller and Scofidio, see my essay in the Philadelphia Institute of Contemporary Art, *Investigations* 23 (Philadelphia, 1988), n.p.

3   G. Scott, *The Architecture of Humanism* (Gloucester, 1914), p. 177.

4   M. Foucault, *The Order of Things* (New York, 1970).

5   Ibid., p. 25.

6   M. Foucault, *Discipline and Punish,* tr. A. Sheridan (New York, 1979), passim.

7   Ibid., p. 155.

8   Ibid., p. 27.

9   F. Kafka, *The Penal Colony,* tr. W. and E. Muir (New York, 1961), pp. 191–230.

10   M. Foucault, *Discipline and Punish,* pp. 202 –203. Emphasis added.

11   Ibid., p. 172.

12   A. Pérez-Gómez, "The Renovation of the Body: John Hejduk and the Cultural Relevance of Theoretical Project," *AA Files* 13, pp. 26–29.

13   Ibid., p. 27.

14   Ibid., p. 28.

15   Ibid., p. 26.

16   M. Heidegger, "The Origin of the Work of Art," in *Poetry, Language, Thought,* tr. A. Hofstadter (New York, 1971), p. 53.

17   A. Pérez-Gómez, "The Renovation of the Body," p. 26.

18   Ibid., p. 28.

19   A. Vidler, "The Building in Pain: The Body and Architecture in Post-Urban Culture," unpublished lecture delivered at the Cooper Union, Spring 1988. Since this paper was delivered in September of 1988, I understand that Vidler has taken steps to develop and refine the arguments presented in the lecture to which I refer herein.

20   E. Scarry, *The Body in Pain* (New York, 1985).

21   J.-P. Sartre, *Being and Nothingness* (New York, 1959).

22   Ibid., p. 428.

23   E. Scarry, *The Body in Pain,* p. 281.

24   Ibid., p. 286.

25   J. Lacan, "The Mirror Stage," *Écrits,* tr. A. Sheridan (New York, 1977), pp. 1–7.

26   A. Vidler, "The Architecture of the Uncanny," *Assemblage* 3, pp. 7–30.

27   Diller and Scofidio, unpublished teaching text.

28   I am indebted to G. Deleuze and F. Guattari, *A Thousand Plateaus,* tr. B. Massumi (Minneapolis, 1987) for this formulation.

29   Diller and Scofidio, unpublished teaching text.

Clothing and Identity

Introduction:
Clothing and Identity

Clothing, immediately next to the body, can be seen as the first layer that forms an interior. So it is not surprising that textiles, a flexible medium that clothes both the body and the interior, enable us to see bodies and interiors in a visual and tactile dialogue. Clothing is a significant bridge between body and interior, sharing characteristics of the body with its representational form, yet its material and construction methods allow comparison with upholstery and drapery.

The previous chapter, Body and Perception, concluded with how sensory perception, imagery, and technology represent the body. In Clothing and Identity, those two elements are materialized through representation, fabrication, and fashion—the common foundations of clothing and interiors. In a sense, bodies wear furniture just the same as clothing, suggesting that they can share relative characteristics. An empty chair, for instance, reflects the shape of a reclined body as much as clothing on a hanger mimics the figure; even in its absence, traces of the the body are still present.

Different tools and methodologies are used for shaping clothes and interior textiles. Clothing employs patterns, mannequins, and materials at full-scale, while interiors work with multiple architectural scales, transitioning from small- to full-scale models. Although there are differences in their fabrication, clothing and furniture share sensibilities in terms of fashion. Clothing designer Hussein Chalayan, for example, explores these relationships, testing fashion conventions in his hybrid clothing and furniture, demonstrating that the relationship between clothing and furniture is sometimes so intimate that they embody the same object.

Clothing patterns have a more obvious resemblance to the body than furniture patterns because the body's silhouette is defined in the outline of the pattern; furniture patterns, on the other hand, reference linear geometric forms, more closely represented in architectural orthographic views (plan, section, elevation). Chalayan's clothing patterns double as upholstery patterns and reinforce a less-visible connection to furniture. He makes it possible for these hybrid garments to be fitted to each because of the attention to construction processes unique to clothing and upholstered furniture.

A specific form of textile, drapery, allows for a comparison of clothing and the interior. Kerstin Kraft analyzes the history of clothing patterns in her essay "Cutting Patterns" to show the evolution from draping to tailoring using tools and measurement, arguing that historically, "fashion was not sewn or woven, but cut [from cloth]," thereby situating tailors as "the early forerunners of *Vogue* and *Elle*." Designing fashion, whether as clothing or interior reveals stylistic preference and projects an identity. Because we surround ourselves with clothing and interiors, there is no escape from this projection. In "Drapery," Anne Hollander brings visual reference to these techniques through a sampling of historical portrait and scenic paintings.

Jacques Herzog speaks of fashion as an expression of time and place in his interview with Jeffrey Kipnis. Architectural discourse typically does not use the term fashion when describing styles, possibly because of the temporary nature it invokes, or that the term implies a less rigorous way of making. Herzog believes that fashion is part of the language of architecture because of the public role it plays. Clothing, interiors, and architecture all respond to fashion. Architectural styles reflect transient modes of thought that leave one movement behind to move forward with another. Clothing and interiors register these changes more quickly than architecture because of influences from art, graphics, materials, and technology.

But current and fashion are not necessarily synonymous. Nostalgia often creeps in, and figures and interiors can both be dressed in styles from any era. Often clothing and interiors have a shorter life span than architecture before being repspectively discarded or renovated. Architectural construction has higher costs, both in terms of funds and its mark on the landscape, compared to fashion and interiors that thrive on the immediacy of change. Perhaps beacuse of this, they are sometimes considered subordinate to architecture, as if lack of permanence consigns them to a superfluous existence. This ephemeral nature contributes to the identity of interior space as frivolous, excessive, and without content.

Filmmaker Wim Wenders develops a personal dialogue on what constitutes identity in his essay "Notebook on Clothes and Cities," written while filming clothing designer Yohji Yamamoto. To explore how identity is understood from one's country and clothing, Wenders addresses the concepts of original and copy. That dialogue is echoed in Susan Sontag's essay "On Photography," where she discusses the differences between paintings and photographs. Like paintings, clothing and interiors can be produced as originals, like photography, they can also be made in multiples by hand or mass-produced. The one-of-a-kind quality that handcrafts represent offers a new form of intrinsic value.

The essays in this chapter help dismantle current preconceptions about materialism through a broader set of underlying issues embedded in fabric construction. Measure, craft, technology, culture, and nostalgia all emerge from a designer's intentions and the identity they choose to project onto their clothing. Although clothing design collections change seasonally, and interiors lag behind, change re-designs identities to respond to the speed with which art and graphics evolve. The permanent nature of architecture grounds it in an identity that responds to structure. By contrast, interior design has the freedom to integrate structure when needed and the potential to operate at the speed of technology.

Cutting Patterns

Kerstin Kraft

INTRODUCTION

Measuring the body and shaping cloth are the focus of Kerstin Kraft's essay. After first defining the word "cut," Kraft weaves together a history and theory of clothing and tailoring that connects the cut of cloth to the cut of the body, situated in fashion, philosophy, economics, anatomy, architecture, and folklore. In doing so, she develops a greater understanding of clothing construction and its evolution. The techniques and methods presented here recall similar tools and drawings employed in the making of interiors.

The shift from clothing worn as drapery to that sewn from cut patterns created new ways to represent the body. Because the seam allowed parts to contribute to a whole garment, the body's dimensions changed. The economics of cloth and the technological and social implications of cutting versus draping, measurable versus immeasurable, are explored as ideological contingencies. The overall shift to constructed clothing resulted in more manufacturing waste. To save money, excess material was made into ornamental details, such as collars. Pattern making allowed for "mass coordination of body and clothing," an enormous shift from the hand-tailored to the mass-produced.*

Kraft refers to tools for measuring the body that are similar to those for drawing and constructing architectural and interior elements. An image from the System of Dress Cutting *(1885) shows a body measuring device caught between the rigid tools for measuring architecture and those bent to measure the body's curves. The device conforms to the body but also projects an image of being encaged. Despite its stiffness, its goal is to produce a two-dimensional map of the curved body for pattern making. Kraft notes how tools such as these, and the drawings they produce, recall views of the body in anatomical studies. Common tools like tape measures are precursors to the modern-day full-scale body scanners that produce a perfect fit without traditional fittings.*

The traditional fitting spanned separate discourses, giving identity to the bourgeois recipients and prompting a dialogue between mathematicians, who

---

From *form + zweck*, no. 15 (1998): 66–69. Originally published in Gabriele Mentges and Heide Nixdorff, *zeit.schnitte. Kulturelle Konstruktionen von Kleidung und Mode* (Dortmund, Germany: Editions Eberbach, 2001).

sought out solutions to aid in cutting patterns, and tailors. These same discourses are applicable to the interior—issues of style and detailing are inherent to the discipline. The 1:1 scale places clothing and furniture in the same interior sphere because of the direct translation from concept to construction.[†] Clothing's and furniture's proximity and similarly curved forms suggest that the concepts behind the tools of their trades may also be shared.

———

THERE IS SOMETHING FINAL, something irreversible about the notion of "cutting." It was with a cut that Thanatos put an end to his life; the surgeon—perhaps—puts an end to suffering; and today's cineast is confronted with a fictive reality which has been cut down by the film cutter.

Cutting has always been a feature of life. Nevertheless, this procedure is not as natural as it would at first seem. There is a difference between cutting off and cutting to fit, between cutting with a knife, with a laser, or with hinged scissors. The cutting, the tools, the processes determine the cut and the cut determines the forms. It is remarkable that in the classical cutting sector, that is the clothing sector, hardly anybody has so far asked what consequences the technical development of cutting has for form. The reason might be that this is not a simple, not a purely aesthetic question. This is because in the clothing sector the three-dimensional human body is wrapped in cutting surfaces, the double curvature of which is based on special surface ends which are the result of cutting patterns. Although it is obvious that different cuts lead to different styles of clothing, the history of the cut and its significance for the history of clothing has so far largely been neglected.

History and its Protagonists

The process of measuring and cutting some given material in order to put it back together and give it a different form, the process of transforming what is two dimensional into a spatial object according to a spatial plan, this procedure only began to become widespread in European clothing manufacture during the late Middle Ages. It had a philosophical correspondence in the emergence of the modern Cartesian conception of the world. The notion of the cut is the precondition for the modeling of the human body at the end of industrial society.

The following text is an attempt to outline the history of this cut, this cutting to fit, this tailoring, in western European clothing. This narrative is based on the interaction of a number of protagonists: the central figure is the tailor, who first cuts textiles and then puts them back together, and his tools—scissors, sewing needles, thread, cloth, ell.

Scissors are a "tool for dividing or cutting into materials." The simplicity of their construction and handling as well as the fact that they have become such an everyday object—everybody knows what they are, everybody has their own—have condemned this tool to scientific invisibility.

In the history of their development, the knife preceded scissors and in linguistic history this manifests itself in the transition from Old High German to Middle High German: the singular *schoere* is derived from the Old High German plural *scari*.

Hinged scissors begin to appear in illustrations of tailor's workshops from the 14th century. They are the basis for modern tailoring; scissors as a tool represent mastery, they have a symbolic function in the workshop signs, and they are part of the coat of arms of the tailors' guild.

The development of the clothing industry only really began with the emergence of independent towns in the 12th century. It is interesting that the manufacturers of clothing came together as tailors, those who cut the material, and not as sewers or seamstresses, and that therefore from the very start the tailor, the cutter, was at the center of the manufacture of clothing. It is cutting/dividing which is to be found at the beginning of European clothing and not the activity of joining. Although the sewing needle, the tool which combines two working processes—pressing through material and passing through the thread—had existed since ancient times, it was not until the 14th century that the wielders of the needle came together to form a guild.

In contrast to scissors, which divide, and the needle and thread, which join together, the ell is an economic tool. It was used for measuring, for calculating how much material was needed and therefore had to be paid for. Prior to the mass production of textiles, this material, cloth, was a valuable commodity, a cultural asset, often with its origins in far-away regions: material which must not be destroyed, which always had to be recycled.

The Incision

We should assume that the clothing of the Middle Ages was based on the circular form.[1] The circle as the basic cut in clothing represented a whole which enclosed the people of the Middle Ages and made them part of the Christian world. What is modern is that tailors have cut up this whole, have dissected it, piece for piece.

The breaking down, the dividing into pieces, of this circular clothing of human existence allowed the form which enclosed and encased the human body to be adapted more logically. This cutting to fit served to emphasize the specific features of the body, its individuality. Individual parts are slowly removed from the circle, which holds the person wearing it in its midst. An independent collar is developed out of the trimmings around the neck line. The sleeve liberates itself from the rest of the body—which was to have cultural consequences: the sleeve becomes the object of courtly love. Lovers would tear off the sleeves of their beloved and keep them as a sentimental memory.

Man's breaking out of the restricted circle of his existence is mirrored in the reduction of the circle in the basic cut of clothing: the initial basic form of the circle is reduced to a segment.

The practice, which began to emerge in the Middle Ages, of cutting into the basic circle form in order to consign the body into it, to insert the body, is the beginning of the tendency toward subjectivisation and individualization which was also beginning to be felt in many other areas of design at that time. It is visible in the development of the central perspective in painting, and it is readable in the use of the first person singular. As far as clothing is concerned, it is of interest that the individualization of man begins with the cutting up, the dissection, of material; that it is a parallel development.

The German *Schneiden*, the verb *to cut*, leads back to the very beginning. It is only in Middle High German—that is in the time after 1100—that the Old German word *snit* is used to signify "the cutting to fit of clothes." Before this time, cutting with a knife, saw and sickle (not with scissors!) were only employed in relation to the harvest and wounds.[2] The case governed by the verb "Schneiden" in Middle High German shows that from the very beginning the tailoring of clothes, cutting to fit, was based on the body of the person who would wear the clothes: the clothes were cut to the shape this person's body. In a more extensive sense than the present day, the cut of clothes signified what is today characterized by line or fashion. Fashion was not sewn or woven, but cut. By the 12th century the French style was already dictating this cut.[3] It should also be mentioned that there was a specific epic form for communicating about the form of the cut: the so-called tailor's verses in courtly epics bear witness to this and are, therefore, the early forerunners of *Vogue* and *Elle*.

There are many reasons for this tendency toward subjectivisation and individualization, at the heart of which are certainly the spatial intermingling of different social and human groups at court and in the cities. This coming together of people who knew nothing of each other made a clearer and more visible differentiation necessary, or at least, led to such a process. Clothing—the superficial expression of these groups—became a carrier of signals expressing social differences, social standing. In the present age of ready-to-wear clothes we have little understanding for the fact that dress codes not only dictate what one should wear, but that dress codes represent regulations that affect the very production of clothing. It was in this way that the first sumptuary laws, which date back to circa 1250, relate not only to the colour and quality of clothing but also to the cut.[4] The cut of cloth was connoted with wealth. Because it was so expensive to manufacture, cloth was a valuable commodity in the Middle Ages. Wearing cut clothing was thus a public demonstration of waste. In the late Middle Ages it was not the effective use of cloth that was the center of attention, although it was hardly of merely peripheral interest: an unusual cut meant that material could not be recycled. This statement that the material would not be re-employed in a different context must have seemed entirely scandalous to contemporaries accustomed to recycling everything not just once but several times. The high point of this ostentatious cut, designed to indicate wealth, was what was know as "Zaddelung," the ornate cutting and shaping of hems.[5] It was just a short time later that the cutting to fit of clothes became the central element in the manufacture of clothing and superseded what had simply been draping—the gathering and arranging of material.

The Ideal of the Corporeal

From today's perspective, links between architecture and clothing become visible; links which reach well beyond the mere demonstration of the social differences and property rights of the Middle Ages. The upward-reaching dynamism which was characteristic of Gothic architecture and script were also visible in clothing. It is assumed that there are religious reasons for this dynamism and vertical drive and that it is based on constructive design. What is certain is that the drawn-out silhouettes of Gothic clothing could only be achieved through the way they were cut. This cut represented a constructive approach and also brought with it the opening and closing of items of clothing. Rows of buttons, head clothing such as the Hennin, footwear like the Schnabelschuh (a shoe with a turned-up toe) and hanging sleeves with ornamented hems all emphasized the verticality and linearity of the Gothic age. The tailoring of the period, however, must have fallen short of the workmanship involved in the art of the stone-masons. The desired elongated figure was achieved by cutting the material "nach sínem líbe wol" (intuitively) and then using belts and cords to fix it to the body.[6] This method later resulted in a specific item of clothing, the laced stomacher, the corset. Emphasizing the vertical by enveloping, indeed by constraining, is also to be found in what was know as "sewing in the girl," that is sewing directly on the body of the wearer.[7] It is conceivable that the subsequent dismantling of the garment, which was part of this process and which amounted to de-robing, was of especial significance in acquiring knowledge of where best to place seam lines. Cutting methods were also influenced by impulses of a more martial nature from the manufacture of armour. The exigencies of battle required maximum freedom of movement without diminishing protection. Armourers responded to this challenge by creating armour of bizarre beauty.[8] The use of rigid material made it necessary to consider in advance the body and its mobility. Unlike civilian clothing, the fitting and functionality of armour were existential qualities. Technical innovations such as the kneecap led to the shortening of the tasse, which was reflected in the gradual shortening of frock coats—the predecessors of the modern sports.

Anatomy—Dissection and Making Visible

Through the development of cutting methods in tailoring it became possible to make the body visible by creating clothes that fitted tightly. To this end individual items of clothing detached themselves from the core. Closed structures in clothing were broken up, deconstructed. This dissolution of wholes is especially apparent in the genesis of the sleeve. Before the sleeve began its independent existence it was firmly attached to the body of the item of clothing, that is it was cut out of the main part of the material. However, the body-emphasizing fashion of the time required a different solution. Whether this was a result of the fact that too many tight-fitting sleeves had been torn off at the same point, or whether the armourer served as a model, is unclear. Whatever the answer, sleeves were divided off from the main body, were cut off from the torso, cut to fit and then (temporarily) sewn back on. From the 14th century on, the inserted sleeve, firmly attached to the rump through a durable seam, becomes standard practice.

The separation of the sleeve enabled it to be studied anatomically in relation to the anatomy of the arm. The freedom of movement of the shoulder had to be guaranteed by providing added width in the upper arm, the extra breadth for the elbow was reduced through a tuck toward the wrist. This led to the development of what was called the sleeve ball and the two-seam sleeve. Precise observation of the forms of the body led to a distinction between right and left sleeves, a development which took place three hundred years before that in shoes.[9]

The tailor shared this precision of analysis of the human body with the surgeon. The idea of cutting based on precise investigation is also the basis for anatomy.[10] However, while the tailors of the 12th century were already coming to terms with the arm and the body it was not until the sixteenth century that Andreas Vesal was to lay the foundations for modern anatomy. It can certainly be said that it was tailors who cut open a path for later anatomical investigation: when tailors dissected the body into its individual parts before putting them back together again the church charged them with irreverence and pride, but did not ban such activities outright, as had been the case with surgery and medical dissection. It was in this way that tailors developed solution to problems which were later adopted by surgeons: the "quilting seam" as a method of back stitching was used for wounds, "turning up" was used on ulcers and the "stretch stitch" for sewing over perforations.

In the close proximity to the natural sciences of modern times two principles of tailoring become evident. The first is the making visible, the second dissection. The clothing industry took advantage of both principles and in terms of practical utilization left the natural sciences a long way behind.

The body is dissected in order to render visible what is within, to achieve greater understanding. Today's diagnostic procedures (computer and nuclear spin tomography) have perfected and dematerialized dissection. Other medical advances have led to so much progress in the research of individual body parts that it is now conceivable for them to be creatively reconstituted. That which has long been practiced by tailors is now becoming possible in the world of science: the "making to measure" of a child or the mass cloning of living creatures.

The concepts of cutting open, cutting into and dissecting the body also had an effect on cutting methods in tailoring. While cutting had enabled clothes to be adapted to fit the body, the notion of the body being dissected into various different parts became the basis for the reproduction of the form of these parts, their modification and combination. Furthermore, the composition of the parts—sleeve, collar, waist, etc.—also led to new possibilities in terms of the making visible of the body, for example through cuts which produced an internal structuring which trace or idealize the body.

Thinking is Cutting

The possibilities of re-composition could be increased still further though the use of aids. The flexible material, cloth, had to be padded out, reinforced and supported in order to create forms which had no immediate relationship to the body. The clothed body of the sixteenth century seemed to be a collection of triangles, cones and circles, the modeling of the body had led to its artificiality, a development which reached its peak in the eighteenth century. Each individual body part could be exaggerated and highlighted. The manipulation of the individual body parts also served to produce an overall silhouette as its sum. The body was dissected in order to be recomposed in geometrical form. Tailors were apparently fully aware that they were contributing to this development.

The origins of this geometrization go back a long way. The oldest surviving books of clothing patterns, which date from sixteenth-century Spain, all already included the term geometry in their titles.[11] This idea of the geometrical body is also well known from the drawings of Leonardo and Dürer. The rationalization of the body using the methods of geometry makes it measurable, and therefore calculable, comprehensible and therefore manageable. Thus the human body becomes part of a materialistic and mechanical view of the world, reflecting a new way of seeing the mechanics of heavenly bodies, which had replaced the traditional cosmologies. In 'Discours de la méthode' Decartes describes the procedure which has produced the new systematic ordering of the world: it is the principle of analysis, the dissection of the whole into elementary parts. Descartes' philosophy idealized a geometry in which cutting methods are also discussed. Taken together the mechanistic image of the body and the principle of dissection as well as the use of the coordinate system in cutting methods make Descartes a theoretician of the cut: the rules of his "Discourse" include dissection—the cutting of cloth—and the order in which the parts are to be sewn together, constructed according to a previously defined expedience—sewing together according to the stipulations of a design.

The tailor puts these theories into practice by acting, by cutting, by ignoring them. He visualizes them, he is the illustrator of philosophical ideas avant la lettre. The tailor attains the distance to the material, a precondition for such abstraction, through the use of certain tools: scissors and ell help him to distance himself from the sensory reality of the naked hand and—as Vilem Flusser believed—introduce the dimension of a value. The interface between tailoring and philosophy manifests itself as an interface between action and thought. The action, in this case the act of cutting, corresponds with a certain kind of thought—categorial, structural thought. Are we indebted to the act of cutting to fit for the analytical philosophy, the rationalistic idea that "thought is cutting"?

The Systematization of Cutting

While cutting led to analysis at the beginning of the modern age, cutting methods were themselves systematized and ordered in the nineteenth century. It was from this time on that they were dominated by a geometry and mathematics which reflected their processes. And it was here that the century of cutting methods began. Previously the practice of handicrafts, based on values handed down from generation to generation, had led to highly varied developments and levels of perfection from region to region, all of which depended more on accident and experiment rather than single-minded purpose.

The introduction of the meter gave cutting methods a unified reference system. Together with the invention of the tape measure, the preconditions had been created for precisely measuring the human body and employing these measurements for cutting clothes. In an immaterial sense the metric system opened up the capacity for abstraction (the use of body-based units of measurement such as the ell, foot or span could be grasped, were comprehensible) and, as far as cutting methods were concerned, encouraged the conception of the geometrical dimensional leap: the two-dimensional representation of three-dimensional bodies in individual parts. In 1815 the French

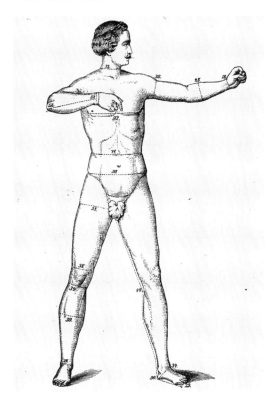

Fig. 2.1: Drawing of the male
figure after the statue of
Apollo in The Louvre, Paris.
Reprinted from Heinrich Klemm,
*Heinrich Klemm's neuestes
illustriertes Handbuch der höheren
Bekleidungskunst.* Dresden: 1894.

master tailor F. A. Barde invented the tape measure, an unspectacular object
by today's standards. But the tape measure enabled precision through notation when it came to measuring the human body. The ell, which tailors had
used to indicate the width of pieces of material, was not a pliable measurement and therefore unsuitable for measuring the curves of the body. What is
more, the dimensions of the body were transferred directly to the measuring instrument, carried away and not noted in the metric system: because
the tape measure had not yet been invented strips of paper or parchment
were used, marked with notches indicating the breadth of the customer's
body. Practical measurement and the drawing of cutting patterns therefore
involved lines and lengths, but not numbers. The noting down of measurements, which became necessary with the introduction of the tape measure,
enabled certain proportions to become arithmetically visible. Cutting methods profited from advances in art and the natural sciences where thorough
investigation of the proportions of the human body had been carried out (for
example, Lavater with his physiognomic studies, Zeising's demonstration
of the golden mean as a morphological law). Taking up the fascination with
classical art, classical sculptures were presented as the ideal representation

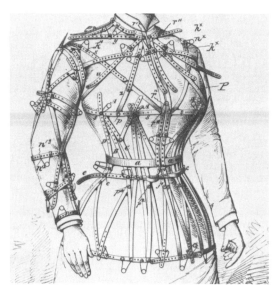

Fig. 2.2: In 1885 William Bloomer Pollock of Philadelphia was granted patents in the United States (320,496) and Britain for this conforming device, which could be taken apart and laid flat. (US Patent Office). Reprinted from Claudia B. Kidwell, *Cutting a Fashionable Fit*. City of Washington: Smithsonian Institution Press, 1979, figure 46.

of the human body and the basis for measurement and proportions. Greek perfection and bourgeois precision entered into a symbiosis: Apollo with a moustache. [Fig. 2.1] The knowledge that the precise calculation of the proportions of the body would have to be the basis for any cutting method led to a number of other inventions which did not, however, receive wide acceptance. For example, a machine for measuring proportions, developed in 1885, which, however, pointed the way to the solution of problems which have only today come to light. [Fig. 2.2] Body scanners generate information presented by a computer as a grid model. Efforts to shape clothes to fit the body exactly are, therefore, not only based on technical breakthroughs, on possibilities. The distinctions of fashion are seismographically more profound movements. Both the perfect fit and the exclusive manufacture of clothing became signs of luxury in the bourgeois nineteenth century. The upper middle classes, the haute bourgeoisie, replaced the aristocracy as the class which set fashion standards and created its own new system of signs: the *Paßform*— clothes tailored to fit. This term requires explanation. In the history of clothing the Paßform has been a variable measure. Until the nineteenth century, clothes had a distinct silhouette independent of the body of the wearer. The Paßform, the perfect fit, of the bourgeois age was designed to constrain and repress the body: the accent was on deportment. Today whether or not clothes fit is more a question of standard size than of the clothes themselves. In order to fulfill some abstract ideal of beauty, modern men and women, believers in the magic of numbers, allow themselves to be squeezed into an imaginary corset, expressed in the figures 90–60–90 (centimeters).

This pattern of fold-less respectability—and with it the social image of the bourgeois—was produced by the tailor. He created clothing which required no additional decoration to identify the social standing of its wearer. What followed was a "process of miniaturization" which cut across the postulated post-revolutionary equality.[12]

This function of demonstrating social rank through well-fitting clothes boosted the self-esteem of tailors and was reflected in a number of publications with titles drawing attention to tailors as representatives of the worlds of the arts and the sciences.[13] As was customary in the sciences, the authors began their argumentation in the preface before either declaring their support for certain methods or defining their own and waxing polemical against those of others. Putting aside a degree of overlapping, it is possible to identify two main methods of cutting to fit which were developed within a short period of time: the proportional method and corporismetrie. The tried-and-tested elements of both methods were later utilized in combined methods. The proportional method was based on certain proportions deemed fundamental to the body. The circumference of the chest was, for example, made up, in three equal parts, of the breadth of the chest, the breadth of the armhole, and the width of the back. The standard chest measurement used for calculating the proportions was stipulated to be 96 centimeters. The chest measurement was then take as a basis for calculating the other constructional measurements proportionally. However, it quickly proved a mistake to view all deviations in size as proportional reductions or enlargements. The system had to be extended to include further units of measurement, above all units of length. From the its very beginnings, corporismetrie—F. A. Barde, the inventor of the tape measure, is generally viewed as its founder—had put dimensions derived from the human body at the forefront of cutting methods. To this end Barde also developed new instruments for measuring physical bearing. [Fig. 2.3] As the illustration shows, the proportions were measured above the clothing, which showed due respect for the prudery of

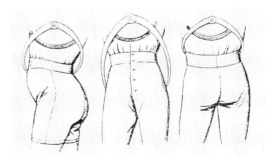

Fig. 2.3: One of the measuring instruments to determine the "design and posture" of the body: *Corporismetrie*. Reprinted from Fulerand Antoine Barde, *Traité encyclopédique de l'Art du Tailleur*. Paris: 1850.

the customers and saved them from a good deal of embarrassment. This system of measurement, with its high number of measurement lines and complicated construction, was a source of many errors. Michael Müller brought the two systems together when he created the so-called "system of the future." This description proved visionary to the extent that the system was the only one that has survived: it is still taught in Germany today under the title 'Müller & Son.' The difficulties experienced by tailors when it comes to measuring the human body and utilizing these measurements to make an item of clothing are easier to understand when one transfers the point of view from that of the craftsman, the hand-worker, to that of the mathematician. In the middle of the last [nineteenth] century the mathematics professor Dr. Henry Wampen, who had previously studied both anatomy and anthropometry, wrote two books on the construction of clothes. He developed a system for measuring the human body based on geometrical principles. However, contemporary tailors found the process of transposing this system into a cutting method too difficult, complaining that they found it difficult to understand, that there was too much mathematical terminology: that it was all simply too abstruse: "It can be said that Dr. Wampen pulls back the skin from the body, divides the surface into sections which he measures, and then transfers their contents onto paper."[14] But when cutting problems are expressed in mathematical termini it is not only tailors who can no longer follow. The English geometry professor Christopher Zeemann investigated the problem of cutting constructions from a topological and geometrical perspective.[15] The result: the back had a negative curvature and the tuck was given a tangential end line. But simply putting a name to the problem, that is, producing negative curvatures on a flat surface, does not solve it. Mathematicians like Schneider are also helpless when confronted with the catastrophic character of a tuck end. In mathematical terms, the most difficult problem which Zeemann set himself is padding a piece of clothing with several openings such as a sleeveless dress. [Fig. 2.4] Probably no tailor has ever tried to answer the question why it is not possible to turn out all openings (arm and neck lines) at the same time and then pull the lining inside. The fact that this is indeed not possible is something that tailors have learnt through bitter experience and has meant that many a seam has had to be undone. One look at

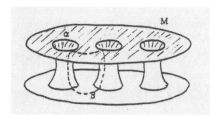

Fig. 2.4: Professor Sir Christopher Zeeman, "Mathematics applied to Dressmaking."
Reprinted from *Costume: The Journal of the Costume Society*. Nr. 28. London, 1994, fig. 7. www.maney.co.uk/journals/cos and www.ingentaconnect.com/content/maney/cos

the formula for solving this problem shows why tailors should remain cautious: "Let M be an unknotted orientable surface in R3 of genus 3 with two boundary components. Then there is an isotopy of M back onto itself that interchanges the two sides of M."[16]

The Cut of the Body

There are certain production methods which can be used to disguise insufficiencies concerning either the cut itself or the body to be clothed—in the sense of a deviation from the postulated ideal body at any given. Ironing, steaming, reinforcing and wadding all help through shaping to counteract the main problem involved in tailoring—covering a three-dimensional body with tailored parts that are two-dimensional. In the nineteenth century these methods were employed to achieve two goals. On the one hand it was intended that "the external form of the customer should be presented as refined and, where possible, proportioned."[17] On the other, the aim was to achieve an upright comportment which would both underline the perfect fit of the clothes and be underlined by it. Balzac finds the correspondence of social bearing in the way it is clothed: the translation makes the analogy all the more obvious.[18] The "roideur," the stiffness, which he describes made itself apparent in all social spheres, in art, in social mores, in literature. This stiffness also had its effect on clothing, in the form of bougran, buckram. This yearning to achieve the perfect body and perfect clothing reached its high point in gimp buttons and so-called sleeve fish—two techniques employed in bespoke tailoring.

It was only with the spread of off-the-peg clothing that the process of cutting to fit led to the mass coordination of body and clothing.

The forerunner of this ready-to-wear clothing was the provision of uniforms for the standing armies which began in the seventeenth century. Rudimentary measurements were undertaken before the soldiers were given their uniforms: they were divided into three or four categories according to body size. Guild-affiliated master tailors were then charged with the production of the uniforms.

Off-the-peg production became more significant outside military confines with the growth of large-scale trading houses and department stores, with the mass demand of the larger cities. Among the preconditions for this development were technical improvements in spinning and weaving mills which guaranteed an unbroken flow of material as well as a significant acceleration in the processing of the material sparked by the introduction of the sewing machine. Initially only broad-fitting outer garments, which were easier to fit, were mass-produced.

Paper patterns significantly alleviated the process of cutting to fit. The American Ebenezer Butterick invented and first used paper cuts in a range of standardized sizes in 1863. Cutting methods, above all the proportional method, provided a lot of both practical and theoretical information concerning the "normal body." Such categories of sizes were, however, only applicable in cases of regular physical growth—the cut prescribed a specific ideal body. But setting such norms for physical proportions also had consequences for tailors themselves: by using simplifications of this kind they were, perhaps unknowingly, paving the way for their competitors—a development which would lead to the demise of their own guilds.

The Seam

The mass production of clothes is based on the principle of isolated actions, reduced gestures. This resulted from the dismantling of the body, the isolation of the arm due to the sleeve. It was the seam which first brought the individual pieces back together in a new form. The cut determines the form of the dress and it determines the line of the seam. However, it is not until the pieces have been sewn together to produce an item of clothing that what is new becomes visible.

It is the seam that first realizes the cut, that first allows the cut to have an effect on the body, that transfers the cut surfaces into three dimensions. In contrast to draped clothes, which can in a certain sense be an extension of the body or—in the words of Gilles Deleuze—can draw it out to infinity, clothes which are cut to fit constrain the body. The rational principle of cutting methods together with certain production techniques, which in a broad sense include all supporting structures such as crinoline, hip padding, collar stiffeners, etc., enabled the differentiated control of human emotions, subsumed clothing under the process of civilization. The cutting into the circle and the dividing up of the body, which at the very beginning of the process of cutting had promised the body greater freedom, became in the nineteenth century the very facilitator of discipline and control. The cut form of clothing showed (revealed) the individuality of the body, made it visible, public and vulnerable.

The dissection of the clothing of the body opened the way for the exclusive handling, the exclusive treatment, of specific parts of the body. The most obvious expressions of control and physical force exercised in this way through clothing are of course the chastity belt, the straight jacket and the reins sometimes used by parents to restrain toddlers. A more subtle form of restriction of movement was sewn into the clothing itself and is at first sight invisible. Women's skirts prevent them from striding out, from asserting themselves, and consign them to a passive role. Hats, collars and bonnets prevent the wearer from looking around and tend to reduce and restrict the field of vision. Sleeve forms especially, whether especially tight or especially loose fitting, condemn the wearer to immobility, demonstrating leisure or un-freedom. However, as the sleeve became shorter the hand was "uncovered," man, the "hand-ler," the actor, was dissevered. Clothing can become both a prison and a stage for freedom.

Clothing is made up of soft or, as scientists would put it, malleable surfaces. They require a body which wears them and thus gives them shape and form. The mutual dependence of clothing and wearer, of the shape of clothing and the shape of the body, has so far been a barrier to the kind of three-dimensional design and cutting activities which are, for example, practiced in the iron and steel industry. The complicated nature, the complexity, of the interaction of surface and body in the cutting of clothes mean that computer assisted design can only be used in a very restricted way, such as in the production of the basic cut and in adapting models.

Cutting remains a human activity and it is man who alters the dimensions. He uses tools to take control of the world and re-shape it. The development of cutting methods is intimately linked with the increased influence of technology and the emergence of a scientific worldview. The prevalence of western styles of dress—for example in contrast to un-cut Asian clothing—is evidence that the energy generated by cutting and sewing back together is far from exhausted.

Although in today's clothing industry cuts are constructed which involved full circles, semicircles and quarter circles, the circle no longer has any symbolic function and the human body is imagined as a geometrical and mathematical body.

This explains why in the manufacture of, for example, a dress it is the waist measurement, idealized as a circle, which is used as the basic measurement. By way of contrast, flat circular surfaces were at the heart of the thinking of the people of the Middle Ages and they inscribed themselves into these surfaces—flatly, without perspective. This form of insertion allowed man to become the bearer of symbolic images. Today such symbolic application of basic cutting forms can only be found in liturgical garments and the official dress of high office. The round form protects those who wear it, provides them with distance, and has a territorial affect. In this way the body steps behind the purpose it is serving, the body of the judge wears the function of justice, the priest is the servant of God, for the university professor the robe guarantees the inviolability of knowledge.

Notes

*   Kerstin Kraft, "Cutting Patterns," *form + zweck* 15 (1998): 69.

†   This phrase references Robin Evans's essay "Translations from Drawing to Building," *AA Files* 12 (1986). Evans describes the use of scale to translate drawing into construction and the differences that arise in art and architecture.

1   See also: Lore Ritgen: "Die Kleidung der Isle de France in der 2. Hälfte des 13. und 14. Jahrhunderts" in: *Waffen- und Kostümkunde* 2 (1962), page 87, and: Adrien Harmand: *Jean d'Arc. Ses Costumes, son armure*, Paris 1929, page 103.

2   Jacob and Wilhelm Grimm. *Deutsches Wörterbuch*, Leipzig 1893, volume 8, column 1259.

3   Joachim Bumke: *Höfische Kultur*, Munich 1983, volume 1, page 177.

4   Liselotte C. Eisenbart: *Kleiderordnungen der deutsche Städte zwischen 1350 und 1700*, Göttingen, Frankfurt, Berlin 1962.

5   Zaddelung was a form of decoration in which the seams were cut in special forms such as leaves.

6   Elke Brüggen: *Kleidung und Mode in der höfischen Epik des 12. und 13. Jahrhunderts*, Heidelberg 1989, page 40.

7   Ibid.

8   Dario Lanzardo (ed.), *Ritter-Rüstungen*, Munich 1990.

9   See: *Deutsches Ledermuseum*, Katalog Heft 6, Deutsches Schuhmuseum, Offenbach 1980, page 6.19.

10   The Greek word *ana-temnein* means "to cut open."

11   Juan de Alcega: *Libro de Geometria practica y traca*; Diego de Freyle: *Geometria y traca para el oficio de los sastres*; Martin Anduxar: *Geometria y trazas pertenencias al oficio de sastres.*

12   Richard Sennett: *Verfall und Ende des öffentlichen Lebens. Die Tyrannei der Intimität*, Frankfurt/Main 1986, page 214.

13   Some examples: Friedrich Borchers Jr.: *Neue Zuschneidekunst für Damenbekleidung*, Hannover 1889; Edward B. Giles: *The Art of Cutting and History of English Costume*, 1896, published by R. L. Shep, Lopez Island 1987; Gustav Adolf Müller and Anton Gunkel: *Zeichnungen und Schnittconstructionen zur gesammten Fach-Wissenschaftlich des Schneiders*, volume 2, Dresden 1860.

14   Wendelin Mottl: *Die Grundlagen und die neusten Fortschritte der Zuschneidekunst*, Dresden 1905 (11th edition), page 62.

15   Christopher Zeemann: "Mathematics Applied to Dressmaking," in: *Costume*, Number 28, London, page 97.

16   Ibid, page 101.

17   Mottl, page 175.

18   Honoré de Balzac: "Physiologie de la Toilette," 1830, page 468 in: *Oeuvres complètes*, Vol. 20, Paris 1870.

Drapery

Anne Hollander

INTRODUCTION

The fold, *a term appropriated by French philosopher Gilles Deleuze, carries a distinct meaning in architecture. Folds are also present in the interior, but are rarely addressed and placed in context. In the following essay, Anne Hollander redefines the fold, a technical term associated with clothing construction and drapery, contextualizing it within the interior—looking at historical characteristics that have underlying meaning for the body and interior.*

Hollander's history of folds starts in the fourteenth century with examples of folded and draped cloth in paintings that integrated the appearance of cloth as banderoles, whose written mottos provide a silent narrative. Later paintings depicted looping fabric, suggesting that the painter anticipated the role of the interior designer by portraying the nuances in spatial experience from flat to textured backgrounds. Color became a focus for cloth in the seventeenth century, while the eighteenth and nineteenth centuries saw a return to an abundance of fabric draped over arches and columns. Paintings with canopied pavilions recall Gottfried Semper's theory of textiles and skins as the first act of architecture, before the supporting structure. These paintings reinforce the dominant role that textiles play in the background of portrait paintings.

Hollander builds on the fold's visual quality in her analysis of François Clouet's Portrait of Pierre Quthe *(1562):*

> *Here the gentleman wears a rather somber tight black suit, but next to him, in the same plane, hangs a glittering green satin drapery, falling from somewhere above and caught up halfway down. It does not frame him or hang over and behind him; instead it seems to accompany him rather like a beautifully dressed wife.**

The contrast between stiff clothing and shimmering, loose folds suggests early on the artist's ability to anthropomorphize the interior, equating the curving drapery with the imaginary female figure. Similarly, the body's proximity to interior surfaces reinforces the idea that textiles can share layers of space between body and interior.

————

CURTAINS ARE PRACTICAL arrangements for achieving a number of purposes. They may divide large spaces into small sections, shut out drafts and light, and conceal the presence of anything that does not smell or make a noise. They can do all this in a conveniently temporary way, and then be folded back and made to reverse the same functions by permitting the passage of light and air, opening up large spaces, and revealing what has been hidden. All this may be accomplished without the trouble and expense of solid construction or elaborate technical devices other than rods for support. The purest use of curtains thus would appear to be that ancient invention, the tent—a whole building made of cloth. Tents are freighted with all the mythological power of any sudden manifestation: they may appear overnight in huge numbers in the desert wastes, or rise like visions in dark, empty forests, and then just as suddenly vanish. In the Western European imagination tents were associated not only with military camps but also with the exotic customs of the East; and so they lent themselves to visualizations of both biblical scenes and the heroic, legendary events of Classical times.

One important version of the tent is the pavilion, which is a kind of freestanding platform with a roof held up by four corner supports. Such open-sided, canopied structures were part of the interior architecture of churches from early medieval times. They were often honorific settings for tombs, but they had their origins in the *ciborium*, the dwelling place of the Eucharist or Easter Sepulcher. Religious drama often made use of these pavilions in churches for enacting scenes of special importance, and they appear in medieval paintings for the same purpose when emphasis is required for a central group of figures. A curtain across one side of such a structure could form a background; across three sides, a completely enclosed niche. When all four sides were curtained, the result looked like a tent. The closing or opening of hangings around a pavilion was an obvious dramatic as well as a ritualistic device, and the secular theater also made use of it. The drama in many Early Renaissance paintings is emphasized not by the action of the figures but by its occurrence inside a pavilion, with or without curtains.

Tomb sculpture of the fifteenth century, following the Church custom for the Easter Sepulcher, often shows the sarcophagus inside a pavilion, sometimes revealed by angels drawing aside stone hangings. Tents and pavilions are often interchangeable in Renaissance scenes; a hero may legitimately appear in a tent, and a king in an actual pavilion or in a symbolic one surrounding a throne. A canopied throne, with hangings at the back and sides, is an honorific tent, and so is a bed similarly caparisoned when it is used in art as a setting for the birth of the Virgin, for example. Cloth put up as a background or tacked around three sides of an unroofed space, on the other hand, was used in the secular theater simply to symbolize an interior.

When hangings are represented in art in the late Middle Ages and early Renaissance, the drapery is visibly attached to some throne or pavilion logically present in the picture. In actual life, such hangings of thrones and indoor partitions are to be carefully distinguished from any purely decorative drapery. They were ways of using cloth—whether for ritual or honorific or practical purposes—as a movable architectural element similar to a screen; the point is that a flat curtain altered the existing space. In art, folds that occurred when the curtains were drawn back are shown as a necessary result rather than as a specially created, pleasing effect. So, too, in the case of tapestries; although their practical function was to keep out drafts and damp, rather like vertical carpeting, the aesthetic satisfaction came not from folds but basically from the flat expanse of color and pattern.

Hangings obviously date from the earliest uses of cloth; but until the sixteenth century their three-dimensional plastic beauty was a consideration secondary to their function. Purely decorative cloth hangings, distinct from ceremonial and dramatic ones and from the essentially practical tapestries, were indeed used through the Middle Ages and the Renaissance on festival occasions. The arrival of a king in a city would be greeted with a display of cloths hung on buildings, arches, and gates. The stuff, however, was not swagged or bunched but spread out flat to provide color and sometimes painted to show scenes, emblems, and coats of arms. Cloth, as we have seen, was by this time closely associated with luxury and treasure. For garments its excessive use had long been a sign of wealth, and artists had demonstrated the casual beauty of lush folds of clothing or curtains. But real cloth for *decoration* was evidently spread flat. Flags, pennants, and military standards were obvious exceptions, and would have been admired for their flap and flutter.

The whipping of flags and standards is shown in Renaissance art, and the phenomenon is further exploited in the pictorial use of swirling banderoles with names or utterances or mottoes on them that provide useful glosses to the pictures. [Fig. 2.5] They are often held by figures, or they may simply float in the air. They are very frequent in the illustrations for emblem books and in the decorative material surrounding pages of printed text, where they are held by allegorical figures or swagged across arches. These informative strips of cloth or parchment were used in Renaissance theatrical performances and particularly in the *tableaux vivants* set up for state occasions; and when they appear in pictures, as in the case of curtains, their formal elements may be decorative but it is their useful purpose that justifies their presence.

Fig. 2.5: Master of Flémalle (1378/9–1444), *Nativity*. Musee des Beaux-Arts, Dijon, France.
Photo credit: Erich Lessing: Art Resource, NY

Fig. 2.6: Hans Holbein the Younger (1497/8–1543), *Venus and Amor*
(Portrait of Magdalena Offenburg), 1526.
Fig. 2.7: Hans Holbein the Younger (1497/8–1543), *Sir Thomas More*, 1527.
Copyright The Frick Collection, New York
Fig. 2.8: François Clouet (c. 1510–1572), *Portrait of Pierre Quthe*, 1562. The Louvre, Paris.
Photo Musees Nationaux. Photo credit: Scala: Art Resource, NY

Renaissance decorative material in printed books contains no free-floating drapery much before 1550 that is neither a tent flap (pavilion or throne hanging), a banderole with a written message, nor part of a garment. Swagging and swirling for purely ornamental effect is done instead by yards of garlands, leafy motifs, flames, animal and human forms, clouds, or water. Then, about the middle of the century, for the first time ornamental pieces of draped cloth appear, without even vestigial pavilions to account for them. Interior backing or framing for parts of scenes and for portraits had already begun to consist of fancily draped material that seemed to have no practical or formally honorific purpose and often no visible source.

Holbein's portraits of Magdalena Offenburg as Venus and of Sir Thomas More, from 1526 and 1527, have a profusion of sweeping draperies behind the subject that might conceivably hang from a canopy or cover a door, but no specific reference is made to these possibilities. [Figs. 2.6 + 2.7] Another one of many startling examples, this time from the middle of the century, is Clouet's portrait of Pierre Quthe. [Fig. 2.8] Here the gentleman wears a rather somber tight black suit, but next to him, in the same plane, hangs a glittering green satin drapery, falling from somewhere above and caught up halfway down. It does not frame him or hang over and behind him; instead it seems to accompany him rather like a beautifully dressed wife. There are many cases of such living, breathing drapery, like a presence brought into existence to speak a poetic language of its own, in counterpoint to the straightforward diction of a portrait likeness wearing dark and simple clothes.

We have noticed how crushed curtains seemed needed to decorate many portraits of rigidly clad Elizabethans and to back up Bronzino's chic

Fig. 2.9: Agnolo Bronzino (1503–1572), *Portrait*, called Eleonora of Toledo. Galleria Sabauda, Turin, Italy.

Photo credit: Alinari: Art Resource, NY

youths in their form-fitting doublets, but the tight clothes do not entirely count for all the draperies, since they are not invariably worn. Another vivid example from Bronzino is the transparent striped fabric falling behind the likeness of a lady, called Eleonora of Toledo, in the Galleria Sabauda in Turin. [Fig. 2.9] Here the stuff falls down plentifully on the left but then it bunches and billows up again on the right, seemingly heaped on a shelf as if the lady were buying yard goods.

It is striking that during the period of increasing use of drapery with, and not only behind, a portrait subject, the cloth in the painting is often an insistent green in color. The habit appears all over Europe, beginning with Raphael and Holbein, and continues throughout the sixteenth century at the hands of artists good and bad. Green was a color that had, of course, acquired layers of symbolic and literary significance by that time; but so had all the other strong, constant colors in nature. Whatever the reason, the extraordinary prevalence of bright green for the decorative draping of portrait settings did not survive into the seventeenth century, when red, brown, gold, and various grays came to be favored.

The decorative swagging and looping up of stuff seem to have become self-justified in pictorial art during the sixteenth century, but it would be interesting to know whether this artistic practice was reflected in actual interiors of the time. The custom of festooning and bunching up cloth to create gratuitous drapery, for no other purpose than to enjoy the way it looks,

Fig. 2.10: Abraham Bosse (1602–1676), *Allegory of the Sense of Sight*, c. 1630. Domestic interior with flat tapestry, boxlike bed drapery, and no window curtain. Musee des Beaux-Arts, Tours, France. Photo credit: Scala/White Images: Art Resource, NY

seems to have been invented not by interior decorators but by the artists of the sixteenth century, who first used the kinds of pictorial drapery rhetoric so conventionalized in following centuries. Before the seventeenth century, European rooms were apparently furnished with little hung and draped material except for the hangings of beds, which had the purpose of keeping out drafts and light. Curtains covered doorways for the same reason, but windows were evidently not curtained at all for hundreds of years. The swept-up excessive hangings that share the picture frame with so many sixteenth-century likenesses do not appear in any of the pictures of the actual rooms in which such personages lived. Tapestries and cloth coverings for walls were spread out to hang straight; and when fabric did drape, it did so when bed curtains or door hangings had to be pushed aside for convenience, not beauty.

The seventeenth century brought back a fashion for full, loose clothes and with it a love for full, loose drapery to decorate surroundings, probably in imitation of the purely pictorial modes invented during the preceding century. Interior scenes began to show curtains swept back dramatically from doors and beds (though still not near windows) rather than pushed back neatly. Scenes of humble cottage life might include a torn, rough door hanging as elegantly draped as a velvet curtain. Whether it was the artist's idea or actual custom that produced these folds is, of course, difficult to judge. But it is nevertheless clear that in fashionable early Baroque portraits, the dynamically active miles of fabric that invest so many settings have little to do with current schemes of interior decoration. [Fig. 2.10] Later on, the phenomenon of life imitating art may be observed in the elaborately developed art of window draping in the early nineteenth century. Neo-Classic taste required the use of drapery in clothes and for domestic interiors to carry the look of

Fig. 2.11: Thomas Cole (1801–1848), *The Course of Empire: Consummation* (3rd in series), 1836. Oil on canvas, 51-1/4 x 76 inches. Collection of The New-York Historical Society, accession no. 1858.3

antiquity even into the usages of everyday life. The spell of Classical drapery, never entirely broken, was asserting itself yet again in cloth-conscious industrial Europe. Ultimately, in the late nineteenth century, it appeared in the draping of absolutely everything from bustles to banisters.

Evidence for the usage of draped cloth in the interiors of antiquity is sparse. Coverings for seats and beds do constantly appear in all Classical art—spread out, rucked up, and tousled rather than draped to advantage; and lengths of fabric tacked up at regular intervals appear as backgrounds. This room-dividing stuff is clearly meant to spread fairly flat, dipping slightly from point to point of attachment without emphatic swagging. Draperies were similarly tacked up around beds, with knots of fabric to hold them up, and also around couches, presumably for privacy. Specifically for decoration, however, elaborately draped hanging cloth does not seem to have been much used, nor is it painted on for decoration in the Roman houses. The painted or carved swagged cloth, used exactly like garlands, which characterizes Neo-Classic decor, has no source among Classical decorative motifs. But once the High Renaissance convention was inaugurated for using ornamental drapery off the figure, either randomly or formally arranged, without any visible specific function, it became a universally useful element. It lent itself with great accommodation particularly to Neo-Classic artistic ideals, first in the seventeenth century and later in the nineteenth.

Reconstructed Classical scenes in the art of both periods, displaying great efforts at accuracy in costume and architecture, might also include a

Fig. 2.12: Thomas Cole, *The Architect's Dream*, 1840. Oil on canvas, 53 x 84-1/16 in. Toledo Museum of Art, Toledo, Ohio. Purchased with funds from the Florence Scott Libbey Bequest in Memory of her Father, Maurice A. Scott, 1949.162. Photo credit: Image Source, Toledo

profusion of invented drapery to clothe columns and arches. An exaggerated example from early-nineteenth-century Romantic Neo-Classicism is the third panel, *Consummation*, of the set of five paintings entitled *The Course of Empire* (1836) by Thomas Cole. [Fig. 2.11] This shows an imaginary, more-or-less Roman triumph taking place in a harbor city glittering with riches and celebrations. The procession occurs in the foreground under arches decked in huge, unimaginable and unmanageable lengths of bright-colored draped material. Indulging this grandiose fancy, Cole goes further with such colossal curtains in *The Architect's Dream*, in which literally thousands of yards drape the architectural elements in the foreground, dwarfing the tiny figure. [Fig. 2.12]

I have tried to distinguish this specifically decorative stuff, which first appears in the art of the High Renaissance, from the functional drapery intended to represent discarded or disarranged clothing, bed linen, or the conventional hangings of beds, tents, and canopies, which Western artists had always put to ornamental use and, of course, continued to use. But it is also not quite the same thing as the new, expressive pictorial cloth used in the visionary religious art prefigured by Michelangelo on the Sistine Ceiling, a fabric that appears in Mannerist painting, where no decorative or functional trappings can account for it.

The billowing bag in which Michelangelo's God is wrapped and borne forward by his attendant angels is an early example of such visionary cloth. The drapery drawn back from an unsupported heavenly curtain rod to reveal

Raphael's Sistine Madonna is another. This new, proto-Baroque scene drapery shares its unaccountable qualities with the kind of clothing also invented for the religious art of the sixteenth century. The garments first given by Michelangelo to his divine and legendary characters began in his early years with the same conventions everybody else followed: gowns, tunics, armor, and cloaks, all rational in their construction, with visible shapes and seams. Most of the clothed figures on the Sistine Ceiling (1512) wear comprehensible, if fanciful, garments; but in the Pauline Chapel frescoes, painted during the 1540s, the figures are often dressed in bubbles and pockets of fabric, sometimes readable as draped rectangles but more often impossible to interpret except as unpredictable stuff analogous, though not similar, to rays of light or clouds.

Mannerist painters all over Italy were creating such fabric fancies just at the period when the ascendancy of the Counter-Reformation required religious art to generalize the stage properties of sacred scenes. Unspecific drapery, on or off the figure, could serve, like clouds, as an expressive vehicle good for both worldly and spiritual subjects; and now, since Michelangelo, it demanded no clear indication of its structure, the way buildings and furniture do. Furthermore, the magnificent drift of cloth could just as correctly be shown to characterize the lowly garments suitable for shepherds as it might the sumptuous hangings proper to princes. And so it might safely be used to enrich a biblical scene without falling into the error of a too specific, and perhaps canonically incorrect, detail.

Once the visual acceptability of indeterminate swatches of fabric had been well established, they could be called into play whenever needed, for figures as well as for scenes. The floating little bits of pubic drapery added by Daniele da Volterra to Michelangelo's *The Last Judgment* would have been impossible for an earlier public to accept, not because it had different theories about genitalia but because it was accustomed to pictures of clothes and drapery making basic sense. Classical sources, which are responsible for our acceptance of any sort of artistic drapery, never used the smallest amount that was not rational, even if it were very stylized or exaggerated. The same scruple applied to most medieval drapery, with a few exceptions usually arising from a shaky misreading of a clear prototype. And the drapery of the early Renaissance through the fifteenth century, however unnaturally it may flutter, is always nevertheless in perfect essential harmony with fact. Tunics and gowns have comprehensible forms and construction, and cloaks and veils have edges and corners, whether worn by angels or shopkeepers.

By the mid-sixteenth century, however, a distinction appears between such "visionary" cloth exempt from realistic properties, whether on or off figures, and the careful rendering of actual clothing. There was a division in portraits between gaudily draped scenic curtains and severely cut clothes, but there was also a division between vague, baffling, Michelangelesque draped clothing (suitable for high themes and heavenly beings) and ordinary people's cut and sewn garments. One picture might by this time contain both, so as to show common men transported to higher spheres or heaven brought down to earth, all by means of fabric.

Clothing in Mannerist religious scenes in the late sixteenth century might consist, as in El Greco and much Venetian art, of garments from which it would be impossible to draft a pattern or, in portraits, of detailed costumes with no kind of extra fabric in the picture. It also became possible to combine them not just by draping the background but by showing a man in an elegant tailored suit, with a sort of free-floating vague drape worn over it, presumably indicating a cloak. The vagueness itself would invoke all that such yardage had come to suggest during the preceding decades: that it was not ornamental but somehow transfiguring.

By the early seventeenth century cloudlike, flamelike rivers of cloth could billow behind a prosperous citizen or flow over his shoulder and across his lap. Rigid modes in fashionable dress now included such loose accessories—until taste shifted entirely toward billow and the new Baroque sense of cloth asserted itself. Draped cloth per se accumulated an immense expressive visual power, first from its august origins in Classical sculpture, on through its medieval associations with holiness and luxury, and finally through its emergence as a purely artistic basic element, ready for use in any representational convention. During the seventeenth and eighteenth centuries, not only did widely differing Baroque artists invade this visionary fabric warehouse but also profuse draped stuff itself, drawing on its vast pictorial credit, came into its own in interior decoration.

Notes

Interior Drapery: See Praz, *An Illustrated History of Furnishings from the Renaissance to the 20th Century,* passim. This monumental history comprises many pictures of rooms, often without figures, chosen expressly for their lack of symbolic or rhetorical content. Many are not professional works of art, but simple records. They represent a neutral view of detailed interior settings since the early Renaissance, with a few examples from earlier times. They were collected to provide evidence, and the professional artists represented are those committed to precise detail, such as Carpaccio and various Dutch genre painters. Indoor scenes with fanciful or minimal surroundings have been omitted; and so the exact role of real drapery has presumably been reliably recorded in these pictures, however exaggerated its behavior may be in other works of art.

* Anne Hollander, *Seeing through Clothes* (New York: Penguin Group Inc., 1978), 29.

Notebook on Clothes and Cities

Wim Wenders

INTRODUCTION

The word coat *brings to mind what most people would see as a collar, but-tons down the front, perhaps a dark color such as gray. A coat ties German filmmaker Wim Wenders and Japanese clothing designer Yohji Yamamoto together in a documentary film titled* Notebook on Clothes and Cities. *This essay contains the portions of Wenders' script which invokes a set of themes that relate fashion to filmmaking.*

The documentary begins with a question about the original and copy. It argues that "original" implies a level of uniqueness or craft, whereas "copy" implies mass-production. Interior design also grapples with these issues, as design decisions can lead to mass-production-influenced interiors by IKEA and the like, or unique interiors that involve craftsmanship. Wenders dwells on the word craft, *since to him it evokes the essence of a thing: "We spoke of craftsmanship and of a craftsman's morals: to build the true chair, to design the true shirt, in short, to find the essence of a thing in the process of fabri-cating it."* He experiences this in a coat and shirt designed by Yamamoto. Wearing them, he remembers a similar coat owned by his father. Is it the cut and sewing of patterns that contains the memory of his father? Can a coat contain an essence of memory? Yamamoto's ability to create clothing that transcends time and fashion recalls Le Corbusier's notion of designed objects possessing an inherent, reproducible utility and identity.*

Recognizing and explaining essence requires a description that involves a different form of looking. Seeking to uncover the essence of Yamamoto's work, Wenders asks questions about identity and looks to Yamamoto's design process for answers, causing him to reflect on his own filmmaking technique. When he captures the identity of Yamamoto's studio in the film, we are given access to images that influence his work. We discover vintage photographs where the clothes are not Yamamoto's main source of influence; rather it is the faces and setting that portray a complete identity. All of these aspects contrib-ute to the essence of Yamamoto's clothing design.

Originally appeared in *The Act of Seeing: Essays and Conversations* (London: Faber and Faber Ltd, 1997), 81–92.

Wenders' script guides us through the design process for both film and clothing, determining the answer that both possess an essence—it remains a question that can also be directed toward the interior realm.

———

We live in the cities.
The cities live in us…
time passes.
We move from one city to another,
from one country to another.
We change languages,
we change habits,
we change opinions,
we change clothes,
we change everything.
Everything changes. And fast.
Images above all,

change faster and faster, and they have been multiplying
at a hellish rate ever since the explosion that unleashed the
electronic images; the very images which are now replacing
photography.

We have learned to trust the photographic image.
Can we trust the electronic image?
With painting everything was simple:
the original was unique and each copy was a copy,
a forgery.
With photography and then film it began to get complicated:
the original was a negative, without a print it did not
exist, just the opposite…each copy was the original.
But now, with the electronic image and soon the digital,
there is no more negative and no more positive.
The very notion of the 'original' is obsolete. Everything
is copy.
All distinctions have become arbitrary.
No wonder the idea of identity finds itself in such a
feeble state.
Identity is OUT! Out of fashion. Exactly.
Then what is in vogue if not fashion itself?
By definition, fashion is always IN.

1

You live wherever you live,
you do whatever work you do,
you talk however you talk,
you eat whatever you eat,
you wear whatever clothes you wear,
you look at whatever images you see…

YOU'RE LIVING HOWEVER YOU CAN.
YOU ARE WHOEVER YOU ARE.

'Identity'…
of a person,
of a thing,
of a place.

'Identity.'
The word itself gives me shivers.
It rings of calm, comfort, contentedness.
What is it, identity?
To know where you belong?
To know your self worth?
To know who you are?
How do you recognize identity?
We are creating an image of ourselves,
we are attempting to resemble this image…
Is that what we call identity?
The accord
between the image we have created of ourselves
and…ourselves?
Just who is that, 'ourselves'?
'Identity' and 'fashion'; are the two contradictory?
'Fashion. I'll have nothing of it.'
At least that was my first reaction when the Centre Georges
Pompidou in Paris asked me to make a short film 'in the
context of fashion.'
'The world of fashion. I'm interested in the world, not in
fashion…'
But maybe I was too quick to put down fashion.
Why not look at it without prejudice?
Why not examine it like any other industry, like the movies

for example?
Maybe fashion and cinema had something in common.
And something else; this film would give me the opportunity
to meet someone who had already aroused my curiosity,
someone who worked in Tokyo.

2

Film-making…should just remain a way of life sometimes,
like taking a walk, reading a newspaper, eating, writing
notes, driving a car…or shooting this film here, for
instance, made from day to day,
carried along by nothing other than its curiosity;
a notebook on cities and clothes.

3

My first encounter with Yohji Yamamoto was, in a way, an
experience of identity:
I bought a shirt and a jacket.
You know the feeling…you put on new clothes, you look
at yourself in the mirror, you're content, excited about
your new skin.

But with this shirt and this jacket, it was different.
From the beginning they were NEW and OLD at the same time.
In the mirror I saw ME, of course, only better: more 'me'
than before.
And I had the strangest sensation: I was wearing, I had no
other words for it, I was wearing THE SHIRT ITSELF and THE
JACKET ITSELF: And in them, I was MYself…
I felt protected like a knight in his armour.
By what? By a shirt and a jacket?
I was flattered.
The label said 'Yohji Yamamoto.'
Who was he? What secret had he discovered, this Yamamoto?
A shape, a cut, a fabric?
None of these explained what I felt.
It came from further away, from deeper. It came from the past.
This jacket reminded me of my childhood, and of my father,
as if the essence of this memory were tailored into it, not
in the details, rather woven into the cloth itself.

The jacket was a direct translation of this feeling, and it
expressed 'father' better than words.
What did Yamamoto know about me, about everybody?
I went to visit him in Tokyo.

4

Yohji's Tokyo office was brimming with photos and images,
stuck to the walls and scattered about his work table, and
the shelves were crowded with photo books, among which I
discovered one that I knew and treasured as much as he:
Citizens of the Twentieth Century by August Sander.

5

I believe this photo of a young gypsy was Yohji's favourite
in the book.
Not simply for what he was wearing, rather for the forlorn
look in his eyes and the way he stuck his hand into his
pocket.

6

Tokyo is a long way from Europe. European clothing has only
been accepted here for about a century.
If, on my first encounter with Yohji I had been amazed by
the history locked into a shirt and a jacket and the
protection they had offered me, I was indeed more amazed to
see the effect of his work on Solveig.
She had worn dresses by Yohji for some time already and
each time they seemed to have transformed her. As if by
slipping into these dresses she had slipped into a new part
in an altogether new play.
So when I went to Tokyo to film Yohji in his studio as he
was doing the fittings for his new summer collection,
I was most curious about his rapport with women.

7

When you don't understand somebody else's craft the first
questions are usually very simple:

Where does your work begin?
What's the first step you take?

8

Form and material.
Same old dilemma, same ritual as any other craft:
stand back, look, approach again, grasp, feel, hesitate,
then sudden activity, and then, another long pause.
After a while, I began to see a certain paradox in Yohji's work.
What he creates is necessarily ephemeral, victim to the
immediate and voracious consumption, which is the rule of
his game.
After all, fashion is about 'here and now.' It only deals
with 'today' and never yesterday.
By the same token, Yohji was inspired by the photographs of
another time and by the workclothes of an era when people
lived by a different rhythm, and when 'work' had a
different sense of dignity.
So it seemed to me that Yohji expressed himself in two
languages simultaneously. He played two instruments at the
same time:
the fluid and the solid,
the fleeting and the permanent,
the fugitive and the stable.

9

Me too, I felt like some monster making this film,
working like him in two different languages and using two
essentially different systems.
Behind my little 35mm movie camera, I felt as though I were
manipulating something ancient,
or perhaps 'classic.' Yes. That's the word.
Because my camera only takes 50-metre rolls of film, I was
obliged to reload every 60 seconds.
Therefore I found myself more often behind my video camera,
which was always ready and allowed me to capture Yohji's
work in real time.
Its language was not 'classic,' rather practical and
efficient.

The video images even felt more accurate sometimes, as if
they had a better understanding of the phenomena before the
lens, as if they had a certain affinity with fashion.

10

My little old Eyemo. You have to wind her by hand,
and she sounds like a sewing machine. She knows about
waiting, too.
Night fell.
Yohji did not stop working for one second.
One dress followed another.
Later on, most of them would be made of black materials.
I asked what black meant to him.

11

Slowly, and almost in spite of myself, I began to appreciate
working with the video camera.
With the Eyemo, I always felt like an intruder.
She made too much of an impression.
The video camera impressed and disturbed no one.
She was just there.

12

On the way to the courtyard of the Louvre, where the
fashion show would take place the following day,
we happened to encounter this young Japanese woman on the
Pont des Arts, dressed in clothes by Yohji.
In the turmoil of rehearsals, he remained a monument
of calm…

13

The direction, well, nobody seemed to know it except Yohji.
At least that was the impression I got in the chaotic
atmosphere of the Paris studio the night before the show.
Actually it had the mood of an editing room just before
finishing a first cut.
In effect, that is exactly what Yohji did that night:

he established a montage and the proper series of scenes
and images for tomorrow's show.

14

When I visited Yohji in Tokyo for the second time, he was
preparing the reopening of one of his shops that had just
been renovated.
It turned out that the most difficult part of the process
was the signing.
When your signature has become a trademark, then you have
to reproduce, in this one gesture, and each time anew, what
you are all about.

15

In Japanese, the name Yamamoto means:
at the foot of the mountain.

16

All of a sudden, on the turbulent streets of Tokyo,
I realized that a valid image of this city might very well be
an electronic one and not only my 'sacred' celluloid
images…
In its own language, the video camera was capturing this
city in an appropriate way. I was shocked:
a language of images was not the privilege of cinema.
Wasn't it necessary then to re-evaluate everything?
All notions of identity, of language, images, authorship…
Perhaps our future authors were the makers of commercials,
or video clips, or the designers of electronic games and
computer programs…
Holy shit…

17

And movies?
This nineteenth-century invention,
this art of the mechanical age,
this beautiful language of light and movement, of myths
and adventure,

that can speak of love and hate,
of war and peace,
of life and death.
What would become of it?
And all these craftsmen, behind the cameras, behind the
lights, at the editing tables, would they have to unlearn
everything?
Would there ever be an electronic craft, a digital
craftsman?
And would this new electronic language be capable of
showing the *Citizens of the Twentieth Century* like the still
camera of August Sander or the film camera of John
Cassavetes?

18

We spoke of craftsmanship and of a craftsman's morals:
to build the true chair,
to design the true shirt,
in short, to find the essence of a thing in the process of
fabricating it.

19

In a different studio, with other collaborators, Yohji was
doing the fittings for his next Japanese collection, the
'domestic market.'
The atmosphere was different.
This time he was teaching. He was truly the master
surrounded by his students.

20

One day, we spoke of 'style' and how it might present an
enormous difficulty.
Style could become a prison,
a hall of mirrors in which you can only reflect and imitate
yourself.
Yohji knew this problem well.
Of course he had fallen into that trap. He had escaped from
it, he said, the moment he had learned to accept his
own style.

Suddenly the prison had opened up to a great freedom,
he said.
That, for me, is an author.
Someone who has something to say in the first place, who
then knows how to express himself with his own voice, and
who can finally find the strength in himself and the
insolence necessary to become the guardian of his prison
and not to stay its prisoner.

21

The photograph of Jean Paul Sartre that lay on the floor
was by Cartier-Bresson.
What interested Yohji was simply the collar: the collar on
the coat that Sartre wore.

21a

Not only clothes are fashionable,
buildings can be fashionable, too. Or cars, rock music,
Swiss watches, books, movies…
Fashion can make things move.
Yohji was working on several collections simultaneously,
including his next one for men.
Was the approach different than for women?

21b

What was Yohji searching for in these old photographs?
Why did he surround himself with them even when they had no
direct connection to his work?

22

So, their mission was completed.
The show in Paris went well.
Immediately afterwards, the whole team had returned to the
studio to watch the tape of the show together.
This evening they would all go out and celebrate together.
Tomorrow they would all fly back to Tokyo together to begin
work the next day on the new collection.
It was only here, looking at these tired, but content faces

that I understood how Yohji's tender and delicate language
could survive in each of his creations:
these people, his assistants, his company which had
reminded me at times of a monastery, they were his
translators.
With all of their attentiveness, their care, their fervour,
they ensured that the integrity of Yohji's work remained
intact and they watched that the dignity of every dress,
every shirt, every jacket was preserved.
Inside an industrial production process, they were the
guardian angels of an author.

23

So I looked at them like they were a kind of film crew, and
Yohji among them was a director shooting a never-ending
film.
His images were not to be shown on a screen.
If you sat down to watch his film, you found yourself
instead in front of that very private screen which any
mirror that reflects your image can become.
To be able to look at your own reflection in such a way
that you can recognize and more readily accept your body,
your appearance, your history, in short, yourself,
that, it seems to me, is the continuing screenplay of the
friendly film by Yohji Yamamoto.

24

From the notebook of images that I collected over a certain
time as I was observing Yohji at work, I have saved my
favourite for last.
In a privileged moment, an electronic eye caught these
guardian angels on the job.

Notes
*   Wim Wenders, *The Act of Seeing* (London: Faber and Faber Limited,
1997), 89.

A Conversation with Jacques Herzog

Jeffrey Kipnis

INTRODUCTION

Seasonal considerations typically govern fashion in the clothing industry. Interiors on the other hand change at a slower pace. Shifts in architecture occur at the slowest pace because it is the most highly structured. It would seem that the less structural an element—for example, objects, furniture, and clothing—the more ephemeral it is. With that in mind, interior space constitutes both the temporary and the permanent.

In an interview with Jacques Herzog of Herzog & de Meuron (H&dM), Jeffrey Kipnis opens the conversation with a question about fashion. Architects rarely talk about fashion because of its fleeting nature, yet Herzog comfortably discusses fashion as a litmus test of the time we live in. H&dM integrates new technologies and formats to stay current. The firm applies photographic imagery onto interior and exterior skins, giving a new graphic quality to familiar materials. As a result, H&dM's work updates relationships between skin, clothing, fashion, and facade.

For Herzog, the goal is "to use well known forms and materials in a new way so that they become alive again. We would love to do a building that would cause people to say, 'well, this looks like an old traditional house, but at the same time there is something totally new in it.'"* Using the familiar to make something new reveals the importance of foundational forms. They exist not only in architecture but also in the basic shapes found in clothing, products, and furniture. A coat can have many styles, but there is always an underlying cut to the fabric that locates all coats in the same category. These forms provide a base upon which the temporal nature of fashion can attach and detach.

Consider the evolution of fashion from one era to another where clothing patterns provide fundamental forms of the body augmented by the fashion of the time. Without fashion, the patterns are anonymous and familiar at

---

Originally appeared in *El Croquis*, no. 84 (1997): 7–21.

the same time. Herzog's interest in the familiar recalls Le Corbusier's belief in the "type-object" whose familiarity relies on basic functional forms. Herzog believes that fashion can cloak these forms so that they speak of new technologies and fashion yet retain their identity. The dialogue between Kipnis and Herzog explores the balance between past and present and functional and fashion that H&dM bring to their work. At the same time, these dichotomies provide a way of looking at and strategizing for interior design, where interiors are often rooted in these dichotomies.

———

I love your jacket: do you follow fashion?

We think it is interesting. I am personally very attracted by clothes and textiles. My mother, who was a tailor, has always had all that textile stuff around her which attracted me a lot. And scents! Smell is a spatial experience, in some ways stronger than sight....We have always wanted to design a scent, and now we notice that some of our ideas such as hot asphalt, summer rain or wet concrete are beginning to show up in the market....No architect has ever been allowed to design a scent by a major house. Why? An architect's name may be well known in the media, but not in a way that the perfume houses think is valuable. Some day this may change because it makes sense and it is obvious that architecture is related to scents. Scents have a strong spatial and emotional effect on everybody.

It has been said that your work accelerates the degree to which architecture has become fashion.

Is that because we talk about such things as clothes and scents? We do not mind such a comment. If someone says it pejoratively, they underestimate the power of fashion. Why is fashion a bad thing? So many people think that contemporary fashion, music and even art are superficial when compared to the aspirations and responsibilities of architecture. But we disagree. We think it is arrogant to think in such categories. These are practices that shape our sensibilities, they are expressions of our times. It is not the glamorous aspect of fashion which fascinates us. In fact we are more interested in what people are wearing, what they like to wrap around their bodies. We are interested in that aspect of artificial skin which becomes so much of an intimate part of people.

In that respect the human body can be compared to a building. Everybody creates his or her own architecture, which then becomes part of the city. Clothes are a kind of link between the public and the private just like a house. In other words there are quite a few things which architecture and fashion have in common. The good thing about fashion is you can give it away if you don't like it anymore or when you think you need to change your public face. Architecture cannot do that.

Architects spend other people's money, so we should make the work last and be of the highest quality....And we affect the lives of people, so our work should be sensitive. Also, a building may be around for many years, so we must take care not just to express the tastes of a moment, but to capture the eternal aspects of a moment. Nevertheless, desires change over time and architecture must know and respond to these changes. (It is not that we want to bring every vogue to our work, but exploring fashion, music and especially working with artists gives us a sense of the times, outside the field of architecture. All of the desires and tastes of a moment taken together create the spirit of the time, the very notion of *our time*. A lifetime is a walk through the layers and spaces of several such *times*. If you do architecture and you are not involved in your time, in the music of your time, the art of your time, the fashions of your time, you cannot speak the language of your time.) Architects must be able to speak the language of their time because architecture is a public art, it is an art for people. Paradoxically it is only then that architecture can last forever, only then it is more than just a creation for moment.

Let us take the fashion question one step further. Could you conceive of H&dM Architecture boutiques?

That would be difficult. Such an enterprise would take some precise thought....On the other hand, it does not make sense for every project to always attempt to create a new thing. And copying, particularly the bad copying rampant today, is so disheartening and destructive for architecture. The idea that certain buildings or certain techniques, not only ones by us but by others, could become established as standards that others use and develop might be much healthier than the current practice of taking a building by an influential architect and, without actually understanding it, twisting it a little here or there to disguise the copy, only to make it much worse.

We would not mind if some of our works, say for example the *Signal Boxes*, became prototypes. Or perhaps we could develop standards for some of our preferred techniques such as the printing on materials or the copper bands, then catalogue and distribute them. We would like to see how others used these techniques and apply them in their buildings. We could imagine exploring such ideas…, though we would want to avoid at all costs the cynical potential of such a thought. We abhor cynicism.

How does your office work?

We are 50–60 people, a figure which has grown slowly over many years. We work in teams, but the teams are not permanent. We rearrange them as new projects begin. All of the work still comes out of the discussions between Pierre and me, and between us and our partners, Christine Binswanger and Harry Gugger. We work together as a team and the product which results from that is called architecture by H&dM. Many journalists keep asking us who is doing what, or in other words: who is the leader, who is the artist? This is a totally uninteresting issue. Who cares about an author? Who had the idea to bend the copper bands for the *Signal Box*? Who found the path which led us to the concrete printing? Who had the idea to collect stones in the Napa Valley and put them into gabions for our *Dominus Winery*? We all have different talents and we try to bring these different talents into the team in order to get the best result.

We also enjoy collaborations with others, particularly artists. Rémy Zaugg has been involved in several projects like a fifth partner. He is an artist from whom we could learn a lot....We believe we have developed a unique ability to collaborate with others—perhaps because Pierre and I have always had to work together in a partnership since the time we went to kindergarten together. We think it is not a bad strategy to survive in our time.

Let's talk more about your interest in art, in artists.

We prefer art to architecture, and for that matter artists to architects… London has an incredible art scene today. If you compare the young artists' innovative thinking to their architect colleagues': their accomplishments are fantastic. We became aware of this again very recently at the opening of Tracey Emin's show in South London—the young people, their energy was absolutely amazing. Their lives are their work and their work their lives. Architects never bring their life into their work. Architects would never celebrate one of their colleagues in such a way. Architects are more diplomatic, they are more discrete, even uncommunicative. We wonder why they do not pursue the fantastic—at least when they are young, when they are not yet bound to budgets and commissions.

When one considers the vitality and activity of the London art scene, the English architecture scene—just like in other cities—becomes bizarre. Contemporary English architecture is often described as innovative high-tech architecture but in fact it's a kind of neogothic revival. It is very traditional masked with a technical outfit. Nothing but bad neo-gothic. The young architects in London and the United States never get a chance. The older generation sits on them until they suffocate.

We think and of course we hope that our work at least tries to appeal to life, and to liveliness, it appeals to the five senses. There are critics who look at our work and only see tasteful facades and cartesian form and call it conservative. That is something we cannot understand! These are stale judgments. They think in conservative categories, such as: square is boring, or solidity is old fashioned. With such a way of thinking you cannot have access to our architecture which avoids entertainment and spectacular gestures. At the limit we believe that architecture should merge more with life, to merge the artificial and natural the mechanical and biological…

Because it would result in better art…?

Because it would result in better architecture for people to live in. It would help the whole of architecture and building technology. We have done a few projects which attempt to involve natural phenomena, e.g. for the *SUVA* building. We like this building—it does good things and it works well, but we now think that it is a bit too complicated, it is technologically overdone.

There are wonderful advantages to a static building that resists all influences. We should not be too quick to abandon these advantages. On the other hand there is an extraordinary potential for architecture which is technologically more advanced and which adapts—to the sun, to the warm and cold, to the noise—like an organism. There is a new generation of computer designs coming on the market very soon which uses biological material to enhance complexity and speed of communication. We believe that, in the long run, biology will provide better adaptive solutions than mechanical technologies. Our own—very primitive—experiments with algae were undertaken with this idea in mind. We would create a biological sun screen and at the same time it would look amazing, the color, the texture.

Were you after a similar effect with the wash of water on the wall at *Ricola II*?

A day or two after the rain, water still comes down in slow motion almost like a 24-hour video by Douglas Gordon. When it is wet, that wall appears more transparent than the glass wall, an effect we really like because it is not only beautiful but it raises questions about solidity and transparency. When it dries, it gets muddy, but it is still beautiful. And the water layer is a natural protection of the concrete surface.

That building was designed in no time. A first sketch defined the profile and transverse section. Most of the design work on the building involved choosing the right image for printing on the glass facade. We tried many

different motifs and different scales. Believe me, if the image is not exactly
right, the result is horrible.

**I thought at first that the image might be symbolic of the Ricola
production…**

No it was not that at all, it had nothing to do with Ricola's use of herbs
and such…

Then how did you come to that image?

We wanted something that related to the garden outside, but that was not too
naturalistic. We tried many different images, especially leaves and plants. It
is amazing when we work with images; it is impossible to actually say in the
end how we decide. The effect of the image in repetition was crucial; the one
we chose was still recognizable as a plant, but the repetition also turned it
into something different, something entirely new.…This effect of repetition,
its ability to transform the commonplace into something new, is an aspect
you can also find in Andy Warhol's work. Anyway, we cannot tell you how
we knew it. Some of the tests were just horrible—e.g., wrong in scale—but
when we saw the one we used, we knew it was right, absolutely, viscerally.
We did not work with an artist on that facade—we have found Blossfeldt's
photograph in an old book and like the degree of abstraction in his pictures.
[Fig. 2.13]

Comparisons of your work to the art of Warhol are frequent.

Andy Warhol is an artist we would most like to have known. He transcended
categories. It is too simple to call him a Pop artist. His work does not glo-
rify Pop images, it uses common Pop images to say something new. That is
exactly what we are interested in: to use well-known forms and materials in
a new way so that they become alive again. We would love to do a building
that would cause people to say, "well, this looks like an old traditional house,
but at the same time there is something totally new in it."

No one has yet truly accomplished that in contemporary architecture.
Architecture which looks familiar, which does not urge you to look at it,
which is quite normal—but at the same time it has also another dimension,
a dimension of the new, of something unexpected, something questioning,
even disturbing. Gottfried Semper moved along that line and for that reason
we think he was much more interesting and subversive than his classicist
colleague Schinkel. His work is more ambiguous; he used the same classical

above
Fig. 2.13: Factory and Warehouse
for Ricola in Mulhouse-Brunn Statt,
France, 1992–1993.
Photo credit: Hisao Suzuki

left
Fig. 2.14: Gottfried Semper,
The Architecture of the Cuppola.
Kunsthistorisches Museum, Vienna

repertoire as Schinkel, but he used it to produce an unsettling, disturbing result. [Fig. 2.14]

We love to destroy the clichés of architecture. To do this most effectively, it is something useful to work with them. You not only have the fight against the clichés of architecture, but against the clichés of your own ideas. Nothing is more boring or stupid than to wake up in the morning, naively confident in what you already know.

Would you consider there to be any influence of the perceptual artists like James Turrell in your work?

We find his crater project interesting. When we first saw his light-rooms, we were overwhelmed by what we can do with light. The problem with these installations is that you have to first enter a dark room—something which is also a problem for video projections.

I was surprised about your relationship to Beuys. In certain ways, I find your work the opposite of his. Even if both luxuriate in the reality of materials, Beuys' work is full of memory and meaning, while

Fig. 2.15: Joseph Beuys, *Felt Suit*, 1970. Tate Gallery, London, Great Britain. © 2011 Artists Rights Society (ARS), New York: VG Bild-Kunst, Bonn. Photo credit: Tate, London: Art Resource, NY

yours is almost empty. Beuys' materials become real through their saturation with meaning, associations. Yours produce the reality of your materials precisely by detaching them from meaning, from associations. [Fig. 2.15]

Beuys is an exceptional artist and he was a very charismatic man. When we had the chance to work with him on *Feuerstätte II* in 1978 this was certainly a very important moment in our intellectual development. He showed us things we had never seen before: e.g., the way he operated with materials, he didn't use them only in a mono-functional way like architects tend to do—he had a much more sensual approach and he did attribute symbolic meaning to materials. This symbolic side however became part of our own work. That's perhaps what you mean when you talk about emptiness in regard to our work.

At one point, you characterized Zaugg more as a theorist than as a painter. That, for me, would not have been a compliment…

You are right, that would be a terrible and wrong condemnation. Some people are more attracted by his texts than by his paintings because his work is painfully dry. His work is about perception, it asks for a lot of active participation—this is not what many visitors of galleries want to do. They want to be entertained. We think his work is very important and we are lucky to work with him. This is also true for other artists such as Thomas Ruff, Helmut Federle and Dan Graham. They are all not very entertaining. But we don't believe in entertainment in art nor in architecture. In that field of entertainment, art as well as architecture would be lost compared to electronic media, to film or to music. There are many things which are more fun and less boring—at least at first sight!

You mention research often. What constitutes architectural research?

Different things: e.g., research on materials. The materials world is what we deal with—we try to understand what *matter* is. What it means and how we can use it in order to enhance its specific qualities. The methods we use to print on concrete, for example, are a product of our research. The printing method existed, but we started to adapt it to and use it for printing photographs on concrete. It is a very interesting, yet simple process. Chemical treatment in the pattern of the photograph causes the surface of the concrete to cure at different lengths of time.…Another examples is the algae, which we have discussed. We are also interested in the mosses and lichens that grow on the surfaces of stones. They are an indicator of air quality and their color is spectacular, so bright—the oranges, the yellows—so beautiful that it almost blinds you. It would be fantastic to have these as another tool in our work: color, photographic images, transparency, solidity. The *pencil of nature* would also become the pencil of architecture!

We guess our research falls into two areas: *what is life today*—and here we mean art, music, media and other contemporary media activities; and *what techniques* we can discover or invent to bring architecture to life—here we mean what science, what technology, what invention enables us to realize our architectural vision, to cohabit and merge artificial and natural processes in our daily life.

What buildings interest you, influence you?

It is usually anonymous buildings. In Japan we were fascinated by the abrupt disjunctions between old and new, between scales, we like that very much perhaps because it reminded us of our home country. Switzerland also has very attractive, cosy or harmless architecture or landscapes next to horrible and brutal half urban, half rural settlements....There are no models for us, no paradigms of great architecture that we worship. Rather, there are moments in buildings—sometimes great, sometimes terrible—that we pay attention to, that we learn from. I would love to walk with you through Harvard square and look at some buildings and talk about what we see walking and talking. It is an interesting experience because it has some very good unspectacular and a few bad but spectacular buildings.

Looking at buildings—any buildings—and describing what you see is the best way to learn about architecture. For instance when you look at Le Corbusier's Carpenter Centre you wouldn't believe that he always said *"il faut apprendre à voir ce que, l'on voi."* Obviously this means something different for everybody.

Do you consider your work to be Swiss?

Many people still imagine Switzerland as a small, isolated traditional country and perceive our work as coming out of the tradition of the Swiss artisan. Nothing could be further from the truth. Switzerland has lost all these roots. Switzerland is perhaps the most modern, the most technologically advanced country in Europe. Of course it is also a very ambiguous country because it still keeps turning an attitude of peacefulness toward the outside, even if it deals with big money and big industry. This is a conflict which actually dominates more and more the political debates of this country: the awareness of being part of a global culture without any historical privileges left! If our work is in any way Swiss, it is so only in that sense of a country which has no national identity anymore. Our work is not based on any tradition, particularly any Swiss tradition. But it reflects the idea of tradition. It raises the question of tradition.

When we were in school in the early '70s, we were trained in architecture as a form of sociology, a product of the post '68 transformation of the discipline. Our first teacher was Lucius Burckhardt, a very interesting man, who taught us that whatever we do, we should not build; instead, we should think, we should learn about people. It was inspiring, but it was also frustrating....Then Aldo Rossi came to teach us, and he told us the opposite. He said forget sociology, return to architecture....In that regard, Rossi was perhaps our greatest influence. He interested us in images, but we were never interested in his images, never interested in collecting images of architectural memories.

You seem to be more interested in the sensations, the feelings an image generates, rather than the information it communicates.

Feelings sounds a bit too naïve. But you are right, we are more interested in the direct physical and emotional impact, like the sound of music or the scent of a flower. We are not looking for meaning in our buildings. A building cannot be read like a book, it does not have any credits, subtitles or labels like pictures in a gallery. A building is a building. In that sense, we are absolutely anti-representational. The strength of our buildings is the immediate, visceral impact they have on a visitor. For us that is all that is important in architecture.

We want to make a building that can cause sensations, not present this or that idea. Images we use are not narrative, they don't represent only this or that like the narrative glass walls in a gothic cathedral. The leaves in the *Ricola Factory* or the photographic facade of the *Eberswalde Library*, all these images are rather non-representational than representational.

Do you imagine that everyone everywhere would experience your work in the same way or in different ways depending on their differing situations, contexts and their cultural backgrounds? When I talk to students and other architects about your work, I find it fascinating that, while almost everyone, whether they are English, Spanish, Japanese or American, speaks of the same projects, the account they give of their enthusiasm, of why they like *Ricola*, the *Signal Box* or the *Greek Orthodox Church*, varies widely.

We are of course flattered when young people pay attention to our work, no matter which way they look at it. Our ambition, though, is to do work which is basic, comprehensible for everybody, everywhere, so that it cuts through the mind, through layers of contexts and cultures, directly to the sensations.

What do you think of architecture critics, of what they write about your work?

Some texts are certainly very well written by interested and interesting people. But they remain texts *about* something,—they don't stand alone like literature or like architecture. No critic, but also no architect, has ever written a text which has survived more than one generation. What survives, what influences architecture, what makes architecture architecture is the work, the buildings and projects. We do not remember any text that has changed our way of thinking, that has meant anything to our architecture. Words and texts are seductions. Wonderful, but meaningless; they offer no help in any way. There is not one exception to this.

Rossi's "*The Architecture of the City*"?

Did you read it recently—it sounds bizarre today! A beautiful book, wonderful language. And Aldo was such a fascinating man—charming and good looking, we loved him, we really were in love with him. And the way he read from his book at the ETH in the early seventies in broken German, that was really sexy! But what is left from that? OK, maybe it helped him do his work, but no one else. We don't mean this cynically, we just don't think his books will remain important for a future generation of architects.

Le Corbusier's "*Vers une Architecture*"?

It is amazing how old fashioned and also arrogant this sounds today. He wrote with such a blind passion, that in the end he confused everything: writing and architecture, art and architecture....Not only do we believe that architects cannot write, we also believe that they cannot do art.

As much as we love art, as much as we are influenced by it, as much as we try to use it in, on and with our buildings, we do not try to make our buildings art.

"*Complexity and Contradiction*"?

An important book for us as students, but Venturi's work proves that the book is wrong. The phenomena he described are fascinating, but they did not need Venturi, and as soon as he tried to reproduce them in his work, he ruined them and his work. Writers can write about architecture, filmmakers can film architecture, painters—like Hopper for instance—can paint it, but only architects can do it, and that is all that they can do.

Was your presentation to the MoMA board similar to your presentation at the Tate?

We have the impression that both panels were first attracted by the buildings. Only later they discovered the conceptual side of it, which is based on strategies, not styles....We reject the model of the heroic architect with one idea, one strategy for every occasion. We are interested in treating every project, every affair according to its own situation. Of course we are interested in creating something new, something seductive. But we try to convince clients that we do things in the right way for their project, that we understand the particulars, the realities of the project. We like to deal with existing structures, make them more powerful, *expose* them and add some new parts if necessary. We try to enhance the existing qualities to rediscover what is here in front of all of us.

How has your work changed over time?

Earlier, our thought about the image was more literal, and we were more influenced by others, e.g., by Aalto and Scharoun. Scharoun was one of our favorites. We found his work ugly, strange, very real and unreal at the same time. We loved the aluminum gold clad of the philharmonic. The skylights of the *Photo Studio Frei* were originally intended to be clad in gold. We wanted to relate to the sky.

We did that building after we saw the philharmonic. But the gold clad was too expensive and technically too problematic. We still like the walls of that building, the plywood and asphalt boards which look like casual American architecture. The mixture of gold and asphalt intrigued us a lot. It was a kind of start for all our experiments with materials.

For all of your interest in materials, you are cautious with color.

Everything needs caution, especially color. Sill we used some color: the blue for the *Blue House*, our first building, and later, we used brown in the *House for a Veterinary*. We imitated bad wood painting in order to relate to the mediocre Swiss architecture of the 1970s. That building has been criticized because it has so many different themes in it which don't go together very well and probably this is right. I think it has some interesting moments which we further explored in the future work. We used color more often in earlier works and are coming back to that now, e.g., with the printed green glass facade for the *Rossetti Hospital Pharmacy*.

You do not seem to have any interest in the program. You handle it almost as an efficiency expert.

Is that a criticism or a compliment? We seem to be very pragmatic about that. Most of the time in Europe, buildings are so regulated and the budgets so restricted that there is virtually no room for programmatic invention. So we have to be very canny to find room for a new architectural idea. Housing is the worst. Social housing regulations make any idea about plan and interior space impossible. No architect can change this.

Your approach to program seems not only pragmatic, but almost antagonistic. It is as if, wherever possible, you subtract program from the brief.

For some projects that is right. Program specifies the space. We are more interested in the flexibility of flowing, non-representational space and the impact space itself makes. In the same way, we are not very interested in sculptural architecture. It is often too specific. It is interesting when you first see it, but then often it gets boring very fast. This is an old experience in architecture—it was already there in Jugenstil vs. Classicism, late Corb versus Mies.

Today, there are quite a few talented architects working in a sculptural way, but very few who really create relaxed, open space. It seems like it's more difficult to achieve this relaxed quality today than earlier because architects feel themselves in competition with the fascinating electronic media which are so much more fun than architecture. Simplicity and openness are difficult qualities to achieve and even more difficult to communicate to the public—even if nothing were to be more desirable for all of us.

Notes

*   Jeffrey Kipnis, "A Conversation with Jacques Herzog," *Croquis* 84 (1997): 12.

No Man's Land

Caroline Evans

INTRODUCTION

In this essay Caroline Evans focuses on the clothing designer Hussein Chalayan, who steps outside the norms of fashion to address themes of homeland and identity. In doing so, nontraditional themes related to clothing design emerge and can be applied to the interior. Chalayan's core interest lies in the individual's ability to adapt to a new culture by using clothing to fit in socially. Although fashion is not intrinsically linked to a site, Chalayan finds it essential to consider site and nonsite in his work.

Home and homeland provide site, while the transitory state of travel and relocation represent nonsite. Chayalan incorporates cultural forms and patterns into clothing and, when taken out of context, uses them to retain cultural memory, integrating new cultures found in a transitory state. If transitioning from one site to another can be seen as psychological adaptation, then he gives form and shape to transitional states through traditional tailoring techniques altered to respond to memory and transition.

For Chalayan, clothing can have dual identities. He draws on the domestic interior as a site for alteration in a runway performance piece that critiques this duality in fashion design. In his collection Afterwords (Autumn/ Winter 2000), upholstery—which he designs as garments tailored to furniture—slips off and on as a dress. This surprising body-furniture relationship allows the model to carry part of the interior realm with her by walking off literally wearing the furniture. The relationship has personal resonance for Chalayan, who identifies with objects imbued with memories carried across geographical borders and treats them as remedies for homesickness.

In addition to working with cloth, Chalayan incorporates new materials from aircraft research and fabrication to harden clothing patterns and construct a protective shell for the body. His construction techniques apply to the shaping of seamless curved surfaces as in works of the architect Zaha Hadid. Other times his use of plywood recalls the furniture of Charles and Ray Eames.

Originally appeared in *Hussein Chalayan*, edited by Caroline Evans, Suzy Menkes, Ted Polhemus, and Bradley Quinn (Rotterdam, The Netherlands: NAi Publishers, 2005), 8–15.

Transferring material technologies from one discipline to another hints at Le Corbusier's vision of using industrial materials in architecture. Here Chalayan treats clothing as "a machine for living in." Traditional buckles and hardware complete the forms so they attain a familiarity of typical objects found in the home. Evans notes that "Chalayan replaced the tailor with the furniture maker, or made pockets the same shape as possessions, he rethought fashion as a kind of portable architecture."* Chalayan's hybrid clothing looks inward and outward to new and old typologies that offer alternative forms of occupation.

———

Border Crossings

For a person with a passport, travelling through no man's land can induce a sensation of unexpected dread. Twenty years ago, I stepped off a ferry at the Spanish port of Algeciras on the North coast of Africa, from where I had to make my way in the dark a couple of kilometres by road to the Moroccan border. That night-time drive along a stateless, pitch-black stretch of no man's land between Spain and Morocco was one of the most uncanny sensations of my otherwise rooted life, and the memory of it still makes me uneasy.

When Hussein Chalayan sends fashion journalists on a mini-voyage across East London, traversing a Bengali religious festival in the streets outside the fashion show venue, what he does is very similar to sending his audience out into the transitional space that weaves back and forth across the borders between architecture, technology and fashion design. It is also the type of space he himself inhabits as a designer, moving between markets, media, discourses and communities—from fashion to film, from concepts to commerce and from academic anthropology to the experience of exile. No wonder he has a particular affinity with the city of Istanbul, that crucible of cultural criss-crossing and historical layering. Straddling the landmasses of Europe and Asia, and sitting on the sediment of the Byzantine and Ottoman empires, the city spans continents and histories. The blue surrounding seas lap its several shores, thus connecting a watery city whose citizens routinely traverse two continents in their daily comings and goings.

Chalayan graduated in 1993 in fashion from Central Saint Martins in London with *The Tangent Flows*, a collection which included clothing that had been covered in iron filings and buried in a friend's garden for six weeks. Immediately bought by the well-known London retailer Browns, the collection launched him as a significant new designer in a fashion city with a reputation for novelty and innovation.

His first collection after leaving college, shown during London Fashion Week, drew on philosophical and scientific theories, the pattern-cutting involved complex mathematic formulae, and the fabrics were printed with minimal musical scores. It set the tone for Chalayan's subsequent collections and their presentation: cerebral rather than sexy, austere rather than pretty, his designs were shown in plain, modernist stage sets and were often accompanied by boiler-suited experimental musical ensembles. Breaking with the usual protocol of using fashion or pop producers to stage his shows, Chalayan employed the product designer Michael Anastassiades to design the sets for three—*Scent of Tempest*, *Panoramic* and *Between*.

Chalayan's themes were atypical of fashion, encompassing nature, culture and technology. He showed a particular interest in cultural identity, nation states, migration and nomadism. If there was a fashion precedent for the way that he researched, it was in the work of Pierre Cardin and Paco Rabanne who, in the 1960s, looked to architecture, technology and new materials for ideas, rather than to the history and tradition of Parisian fashion. As a precedent for his design practice, he shared with Christobal Balenciaga a monkish and serious dedication to the engineering of garments, constructing an

Fig. 2.16: Hussein Chalayan, *Along False Equator*, Autumn/Winter 1995. Photo credit: Christopher Moore, Catwalking. London

Fig. 2.17: Hussein Chalayan, *Afterwords*, Autumn/Winter 2000.
Photo credit: Christopher Moore, Catwalking. London

architecture of dress through the weight, tailoring, drape and fall of cloth. [Figs. 2.16 + 2.17]

Twice named as British Designer of the Year since setting up his own label in 1994, over the following decade Chalayan consolidated his identity as a thoughtful designer whose work appealed to a significant niche market of tastemakers. While the high seriousness of his work guaranteed that it would never cross over into the luxury goods market (Chalayan is the only high-profile London designer in the 1990s who did not go and work for a Paris couturier), he sells internationally and now shows in Paris. In tandem with designing for his own label, he has produced collections for the New York cashmere company Tse, and for the London high street retailers Top Shop and Marks & Spencer. Unusually for a fashion designer, he has succeeded in working simultaneously in a commercial and a conceptual vein, developing his ideas in film and installation work as well as in the fashion industry. From the mid-1990s he was, with Alexander McQueen and John Galliano, largely responsible for the flowering of London fashion shows.

Chalayan has routinely collaborated across disciplines with industrial designers, musicians, jewellers and textile designers, and most of his showpieces have been made by the Scottish industrial designer Paul Topen. Several have been selected by art curators for international exhibitions, such as the massive *Century City* exhibition at Tate Modern in London in 2001, which featured Chalayan's *Afterwords* (Autumn/Winter 2000) in the London section. His collections have made reference to new technology, engineering and machine aesthetics, as well as to the historical avant gardes and their legacy within 1970s' minimal art. Although his work is popular with constituencies usually inimical to fashion, such as architects, product designers, art historians and curators, he makes no claims for it as fine art and moves comfortably between commercial and conceptual spheres, often exploring the same ideas with differing degrees of intensity in a film or installation, a runway showpiece and a commercial collection. For example, for his research for *Geotropics* (Spring/Summer 1999) Chalayan created a microgeography of the body in a computer animation that morphed together national costumes from different dates and places along the 2,000-year-old Silk Road from China to the West. From the morph, he then drew and designed a series of simple, white, pleated shift dresses for the catwalk, each with slight variations. Chalayan subsequently explored how the idea and catwalk image could mutate again for print media. In an issue of *Visionaire*, art-directed with Marcus Tomlinson, Chalayan layered translucent images of the morphing dress on tracing-paper pages that gradually revealed the naked figure of the model as the reader turned the pages.

Yet despite the copious quantities of research generated by each collection, by the time the clothes are made the concepts have magically mutated: ideas are never literally interpreted or 'illustrated,' but seem to have been absorbed into the formal qualities of cut and construction. His work can be playful too, such as the ruffled dresses in a Hawaiian-style print (Spring/Summer 2004). Only close inspection reveals that the print is of Cyprus (Chalayan's birth place) and features a modern tower-block skyline behind historical battle scenes of the Ottomans and Venetians warring over the island. A customer interested in the way the clothes may embody history and narrative can enjoy the knowledge that for this collection Chalayan worked with a genetic anthropologist, had himself genetically tested and then looked at the genetic patterns of different ethnic groups in Cyprus. It is not, however, a prerequisite.

In the emphasis on the concepts and narratives behind Chalayan's collections, it is easy to write out the haptic element of the worn clothing—the physicality of the garments and the sensory pleasures of wearing them. Often positioned as the philosopher-king of fashion, Chalayan is in fact a more tactile and three-dimensional designer than his concern with abstraction would suggest. The compelling wearability of his clothing—its luxurious and uncompromisingly expensive fabrics, its complex yet unostentatious cut and its interesting details—is one of its strongest features. Despite the conceptual play of the showpieces on the catwalk, such as a 'memory dress' with shape alloy hem, or a remote-control dress with opening and closing panels, the selling collections are free of gimmicks and gizmos. Their design is, on the contrary, quiet, subtle and austere; it can be reflective and even, sometimes, introspective. Stephen Todd pointed out in the magazine *Dutch* that 'the weight of his metaphysical musings, the garments are easy and light. All the work lies within and behind them, programmed in like a code composed by the designer himself.'[1]

In Chalayan's description, being a fashion designer is like being an actor, enabling him to move at will between the conceptual and spectacular registers, according to the demands of the job and the mood of each collection. It is this capacity to work across various registers and modes, as well as across media and markets, that characterizes him as a fashion designer. His work is multivalent, speaking to different audiences in different voices, the ideas more diluted in the commercial collections and more intense in the film and installation pieces.

That Chalayan himself is so agile at border crossings of all kinds may be due in part to his own history. As a child in Nicosia, he experienced at first hand the forcible division of Cyprus into Greek and Turkish parts in 1974. Of living in a partitioned country, Chalayan has said 'you are living in mystery, you don't know what's on the other side,' implying that such painful splitting nevertheless can be a spur to curiosity, generating the inquisitiveness a designer needs. Sent to an English boarding school at the age of 12, he had to accommodate both cultural difference and short-term family separation. His parents divorced, his early youth split between two cultures, it would be easy to make the case for Chalayan's career choice of fashion design as typifying the quintessential modern subject described by the French academic Gilles Lipovetsky who argues that fashion, far from being frivolous, has an important role to play in training us to be flexible, modern citizens, adept at the psychological quick-changes required by today's world.

Yet it would be too glib simply to attribute Chalayan's facility for border-crossings to his personal history. Mobility and cultural flux are part of the modern condition to which we are all subject, whether we travel in real time and space or virtually, through cultures and representations. We are all foot-loose now, habituated to the no man's land between different cultural territories. Heidegger wrote: 'Homelessness is coming to be the destiny of the world.'[2] In fashion, in particular, we are all migrants, and there is no such place as home. The fashionable being is constantly in the process of re-imagining and re-creating him or herself in a rootless world, and this process of self-fashioning may be simultaneously pleasurable and alienating, nowhere more so than in the metaphor of the journey.

Homelessness

An early Hussein Chalayan jacket in paper fabric stamped on the reverse with the *par avion* postmark was redesigned as an envelope sent through the post that unfolded into a wearable dress. *Absence and Presence* (Spring/Summer 2003), his first menswear collection, contained T-shirts that could transform into A3 envelopes and be posted. Several other collections have featured a range of travel motifs. *Along False Equator* (Autumn/Winter 1995) included dresses printed with the flight paths of aeroplanes and paper suits embedded with lights that flashed like aeroplanes at night, tracing flight-path patterns on the paper. *Geotropics* (Spring/Summer 1999) explored the idea of an itinerant existence through the idea of carrying a chair with you, so that you can sit down wherever you are. This concept carried the germ of a later idea, that travel can be a permanent state of being as much as a functional way of arriving at a destination.

In the following collection, *Echoform* (Autumn/Winter 1999), Chalayan looked at the body's natural capacity for speed and the way it can be enhanced by technology, focusing on ergonomics and the interior design of cars in a black leather dress with a padded collar like a car head rest. [Fig. 2.18] In these two collections and the subsequent *Before Minus Now* (Spring/Summer 2000), Chalayan also developed a single concept in three monumental dresses that used technology from the aircraft industry. Made out of a composite of glass fibre and resin, they were cast in specially created moulds. [Fig. 2.19] The second, the white aeroplane dress which Chalayan would subsequently develop into a film and installation project with Marcus Tomlinson, *Echoform*, was fastened with chrome automobile catches. It contained a concealed battery and gears and wheels activated through an internal switch by the model on the runway, so that sections slid down and flapped out like the moving parts of aeroplanes. The third dress, in pale pink, was operated by a small boy using a remote control on the runway.

Marcus Tomlinson's film for *Echoform* made explicit the link between woman and aeroplane, that emblem of modernist progress and mobility. When Chalayan repeated this design motif in three rigid dresses across three collections, like a series of musical variations, he posited a series of experiments in constructing the self. The plane technology is about engineering and suggests that perhaps it is not only the dress but also the self that can be engineered, fine-tuned, technologically adjusted and played with. As Susan Sontag wrote: 'the self is a text [...] a project, something to be built.'[3] Gilles Lipovetsky has proposed an optimistic analysis of the connection between

Fig. 2.18: Hussein Chalayan,
Echoform, Autumn/Winter
1999.
Photo credit: Christopher Moore,
Catwalking. London

Fig. 2.19: Hussein Chalayan,
Geotropics, Spring/Summer
1999.
Photo credit: Christopher Moore,
Catwalking. London

Fig. 2.20–22: Hussein Chalayan, *Afterwords*, Autumn/Winter 2000.

Photo credit: Christopher Moore, Catwalking. London

Figs. 2.23–25:
Hussein Chalayan,
Afterword,
Autumn/Winter
2000.
Photo credit:
Christopher Moore,
Catwalking. London

fashion and psychological flexibility, arguing that modern fashion has produced a new individual, 'the fashion person, who has no deep attachments, a
mobile individual with a fluctuating personality and tastes.'[4] Thus the fashionable person is an avatar of modernity. Such social agents who are open
to change, constitute 'a new type of kinetic, open personality' that societies
undergoing rapid transition depend on.[5]

For Lipovetsky's argument that fashion trains the modern subject to
be flexible, mobile and psychologically adaptable, Chalayan provided the
physical cladding and the metaphysical speculation about identity in the
twenty-first century. In *Afterwords* (Autumn/Winter 2000), a table becomes
a skirt and chair covers turn into dresses, while the chair frames fold up into
suitcases. [Figs. 2.20–25] The blurring of the boundaries between the traditional functions of clothing and dress brought to mind furniture designers
who have thought of furniture as a flexible membrane, possibly an intelligent one, that mediates between the body and the built environment. For
many designers from the late 1990s, thinking about how to live in the modern world involved thinking about how to live flexibly, imagining new forms
of urban nomadism, in which the differences between dress and architecture diminished and cladding and clothing became—equally—flexible membranes that responded to their environment.

When, in *Afterwords*, Chalayan replaced the tailor with the furniture maker, or made pockets the same shape as possessions, he rethought fashion as a kind of portable architecture. Yet the show was about travelling light, about having to leave one's home in time of war and to take all one's possessions with one. The dislocation and rootlessness of enforced migrancy were evoked through the opening scene of a refugee family of five that shuffled offstage, converting pinafores into cloaks as they went. The idea was reiterated in the sparse set design of the living room, the transformation of its furniture into portable possessions as the show unfolded, and the existential bleakness of the harsh, Bulgarian singing that accompanied it. It could not, therefore, by any stretch of the imagination, be understood solely as a paean to the infinite flexibility of the modern subject.

The theme of travel so prevalent in Chalayan's work can be understood, both literally and figuratively, as a journey of alienation and loss, as much as it is one of self-discovery and self-fashioning. Although Chalayan's design motifs in many of his collections were the modernist ones of technological progress (flight, engineering, travel and mobility), they were shadowed by the darker motifs of dislocation, migrancy and exile. For all the modernity and refusal of obvious nostalgia and historicism in his designs, there is a melancholy edge to the great modernist icons which fascinate him, such as the shabby, abandoned aeroplane he photographed at Nicosia International Airport and presented as a fold-out image for the Belgian magazine *No.C* (September 2002).

This Janus-headed quality characterizes his film *Place to Passage* (2003) which follows an androgynous woman travelling in a self-piloted pod, in a state of perfect self-sufficiency, from an underground car park through an anonymous post-industrial wasteland and over the Bosphorus. The pod borrows the utopian design language of 1960s' architectural groups such as Archigram. Constructed with 3-D modelling techniques inspired by a visit to the Formula One car factory (the film was sponsored by Formula One racing team BAR Honda), the pod is something between a car, a plane and a platonic ideal. Travelling light, Chalayan's gnomic model eats and sleeps as she travels in seamless symbiosis with her vehicle, evoking J.G. Ballard's definition of fashion for the twenty-first century: 'A recognition that nature has endowed us with one skin too few, and that a fully sentient being should wear its nervous system externally.'[6]

A sensitive membrane bordering on a home, the pod-vessel of *Place to Passage* begs the redefinition of comfort, familiarity and nostalgia. It is, on the one hand, anti-nostalgic: its inhabitant wears her home like a shell. It suggests that travel itself is a kind of no-place or no man's land, that takes us out of culture and history—the purest expression of 'between-ness.' However, set against any utopian fantasy of self-sufficiency are the claims of nostalgia and home, even if only of an imagined home. Precisely because it is an imagined home, we cannot get back to it: 'You can't go home again. Why? Because you *are* home…'[7] Against Le Corbusier's formulation of the rational 'house-machine' of the future ('the mass-produced house, healthy [...] and beautiful') rises up the idea of 'the house as an object of memory [...] an instrument of a generalised nostalgia.'[8] Chalayan speculates on the consequences:

> Our lives are in a constant state of mobility and [...] in some ways that could affect memory, could affect our attachment to domestic things. What would new comfort zones be in those kinds of situations? You know it's this whole idea of creating a refuge wherever you are. It's quite abstract, in a way it's like meditating on solitude, maybe a bit about nostalgia, how we reminisce, creating a place within a cavity, all those kinds of ideas.[9]

Yoking together domesticity, refuge and the cavity, Chalayan evokes Gaston Bachelard's images of rootedness, such as 'the house, the stomach, the cave.'[10] Bachelard relates these images to the overall theme of the return to the mother, the idea articulated by Sigmund Freud in the saying 'love is homesickness.'[11]

In his 1919 essay on the uncanny, Freud argued that whenever we dream of a place which we think we have visited before, we are in fact dreaming of the maternal body, the place from which we all came and to which we cannot return. The first home, which is lost to us, except as a form of congealed longing, is the womb, and there is something of this nostalgia for the maternal space not only in Chalayan's pod, but in all his melancholy evocations of loss. We are in no man's land in more ways than one. This maternal space is nowhere articulated, but everywhere inflected in Chalayan's work. Commentators focus on the rational, cultural and scientific influences in his thinking, but more rarely on the poetic melancholy that also pervades his designs, a form of melancholy that, for want of a better term, I have categorized as the maternal space. The maternal—and its absence—can be configured in the turn to fashion itself, more especially in the return to the female body as well as in the haptic pleasures of the actual clothes and in the idea of a garment that can be *in*habited, in all senses—simultaneously as refuge and comfort, nostalgia and exploration, living space and space capsule.

A Rendez-Vous of Questions and Question Marks

If alienation produces deracinated modern subjects, it also gives them a certain freedom to reinvent themselves, turning estrangement to their advantage, nowhere more so than through fashion—'an intimate technology which reproduces itself via human intervention.'[12] Fashion's compulsive drive to alteration makes it an emblem of modernity, a means to map the modern through a series of images and ideas triangulated from diverse points across cultures and centuries. The 'story' of fashion is just one of many contemporary narratives of the self, for, as the academic Mark Poster has argued 'in an increasingly hyper-aestheticised everyday life it is through various fictions that we endeavour to come to know ourselves.'[13]

For a designer like Chalayan, these fictions can be played out in a sophisticated interaction between reality and virtuality, two and three dimensions, image and object. In his earlier shows, the compositional trope of confusing image and reality used the simple technologies of mirrors and slide projections, rather than the complex digital effects that came to the fore in later shows. For example, in *Panoramic* (Autumn/Winter 1998), the models gradually became confused with their reflections in the mirrored set, so that their bodies became mere patterns in a moving picture show, while at the same time a slide show on another white wall echoed their disappearance from the narrative in a scene that was gradually reduced to a set of abstract elements.

In *Geotropics* (Spring/Summer 1999), *Echoform* (Autumn/Winter 1999) and *Before Minus Now* (Spring/Summer 2000), Chalayan's three hard resin dresses were mirrored, or repeated, with subtle differences, in a series of equivalents in cloth that followed them a little later onto the catwalk like an echo. The resin dresses were a blueprint for a set of experiments and comments in cloth, experiments which in some cases Chalayan also conducted in film and computer animations, thereby extending his narrative to virtual and real effects. In this context, the use of live music in the shows became a compositional element that marked the show as a real-time performance.

In *Ventriloquy* (Spring/Summer 2001), Chalayan segued between the new technology of digital imagery and the traditions of the catwalk show, opening the show with a computer-generated film of wireframe models in a gridded architectural space. Their pixellated actions prefigured the narrative that was subsequently staged by the real models in the show's stark, white, angular set painted with receding, black, perspectival lines to echo the architectural space of the video. In the video, the wireframe figures interact ruthlessly before fracturing into thousands of pieces, while the real show culminated in three models who produced hammers and smashed the rigid sugar-glass dresses of the models next to them. Here Chalayan played on the contrast between computer model and fashion model, between virtual and actual body, between image and object.

His early fascination with morphing from *Geotropics* (Spring/summer 1999) surfaced again in *Ambimorphous* (Autumn/Winter 2002/03), where the themes of migration and cultural hybridity were pictured as the garments moved in two fluid morphs between Western black, ethnic Turkish and arty deconstruction. In *Kinship Journey* (Autumn/Winter 2003/04), the morph was a continuous jigsaw of plaid, shearling, austere minimalism, technology, engineering and Turkish embroidery of olive trees.

The morph can be in time as well as in space. In *Echoform* (Autumn/Winter 1999), Chalayan scrambled time by imagining a range of denim dresses with memories of other clothes, each with a section omitted, as if only in part remembered. He had the idea of ghostly dresses destroyed by their doubles, so that each dress bore the traces of an earlier one. For *Place/Non-Place*, his first menswear collection (Autumn/Winter 2003/04), he made jackets with dozens of internal pockets in which an object could come to rest, each one a repository for a memory, to reanimate the impersonal, industrially produced jacket as meaningful.

In *Medea* (Spring/Summer 2002), the morph was historical. Chalayan's show notes refer to history's stratification:

> The garment is a ghost of all the multiple lives it may have had. Nothing is shiny and new; everything has a history [...] A '60s dress gets cut away to reveal its past as a medieval dress. A Victorian corset gets cut away to reveal a modern jersey vest. A '30s dress gets cut away to reveal its past as an Edwardian dress. The design is a wish or a curse that casts the garment and its wearer into a time warp through historical periods, like a sudden tumble through the sediment of an archaeological dig.[14]

The resulting shredded and deconstructed garments contained versions of Chalayan's earlier collections that looked as if they had been battered and destroyed by the passage of time. Chalayan raided his own archive to reproduce pieces from past seasons in new combinations, fabrics and colours that were then deconstructed, such as the khaki cotton biker dress that reworked a fluted black cotton and tulle dress from *Afterwords*.

In all these shows and in their associated films and installations, Chalayan the fashion migrant moved between virtual and real worlds, crossing histories, geographies and cultures, negotiating pathways, brokering visual translations. Speculative, critical design is a kind of perpetual departure which obliges a practitioner continually to reinvent the world, and migrancy can be a metaphor for the path taken by the modern designer. She or he picks up what is to hand—history, time and language—and runs with it. Unlike travel, which implies a homecoming, migrancy 'calls for a dwelling in language, in histories, in identities that are constantly subject to mutation.'[15] And it is precisely the homelessness of the cultures of new media and technology that generates the language with which Chalayan goes exploring. There may not yet be a dictionary or even an established lexicon, for this visual language that is being invented as it is spoken, a kind of babble or cultural pidgin, made up as he goes. Neither may there yet be a chart to map his route. Space cannot be mapped the first time it is walked, for one cannot draw the map and explore simultaneously. Cartography comes later.

The talent lies in the ability to lose oneself in over-familiar terrain, to step off the track, to get used to being lost, to cross boundaries and even to confound them. Awarding oneself a *permis de passage* through the jungle, or a *passe-partout* that by-passes ports, throws into crisis the very idea of borders and categories. Rather than solving the riddle of the sphinx, these explorations put its very foundations in doubt: 'Which of us is Oedipus here? Which of us sphinx? It is, it seems, a *rendez-vous* of questions and question-marks.'[16]

Notes

*   Caroline Evans, "No Man's Land," in *Hussein Chalayan*, ed. Caroline Evans, Suzy Menkes, Ted Polhemus, and Bradley Quinn (Rotterdam, NAi Publishers, 2005), 12.

1   Stephen Todd, 'Hussein Chalayan: London's Not Calling,' in: *Dutch* no. 14, 1998, p. 171–172.

2   Martin Heidegger, *Basic Writings,* New York: Harpers & Row, 1977, p. 101.

3   Susan Sontag, introduction to Walter Benjamin, *One Way Street and Other Writings,* London: Verso, 1985, p. 14.

4   Gilles Lipovetsky, *The Empire of Fashion: Dressing Modern Democracy,* New Jersey: Princeton University Press, 1994, p. 149.

5   Lipovetsky, ibid.

6   J. G. Ballard, 'Project for a Glossary of the Twentieth Century,' from: Jonathan Crary & Sanford Kwinter (eds), *Incorporations,* New York: Zone, 1992, p. 275.

7   Marjorie Garber, *Shakespeare's Ghost Writers,* London: Methuen, 1987, p. 159.

8   Anthony Vidler, *The Architectural Uncanny: Essays in the Modern Unhomely,* Cambridge Mass.: MIT Press, 1992, p. 63–64.

9   Marcus Fairs, *Icon,* December 1993, n.p.

10   Gaston Bachelard, *La Terre et les rêveries du repos,* 1948, quoted in Vidler, ibid, p. 64.

11   Sigmund Freud, 'The Uncanny' [1919] in: *Works: the Standard Edition of the Complete Psychological Works of Sigmund Freud,* vol.xvii, London: Hogarth Press, 1955, p. 245.

12   Forecaster Deidre Crowley, quoted in: Martin Raymond, 'Clothes with Meaning,' *Blueprint,* 154, October 1998, p. 28.

13   Mark Poster, 'Postmodern Virtualities' in: Mike Featherstone & Roger Burrows (eds) *Cyberspace/Cyberbodies/Cyberpunk,* London: Sage Publications/ New Delhi: Thousand Oaks, 1995, p. 13.

14   Hussein Chalayan, show notes *Medea,* Spring/Summer 2002.

15   Iain Chambers, *Migrancy, Culture, Identity,* London: Comedia/Routledge, 1994, p. 5.

16   Friedrich Nietzsche, *Beyond Good and Evil,* Harmondsworth: Penguin, 1973, p. 15.

Furniture
and Objects

Introduction:
Furniture and Objects

Like clothing, furniture and objects can also resemble the body. A hand is reflected in such common objects as a door handle, glass, or computer mouse. The interior is full of objects that range from purely functional to aesthetic or decorative. Furniture and Objects addresses these connections and looks at methods of fabrication. These include forms of making (mass produced or hand-crafted), the embedding of memory and nostalgia within objects and furniture, and the collection of objects in the interior that lead to the *Gesamtkunstwerk*, the total work of art, with no detail left undesigned. These methods offer ways to look at furniture and objects as distinct from their aesthetic appearance.

Methods of fabrication vary depending on the materials and the quantity produced. These changes began at the turn of the nineteenth century with the manufacture of small industrial objects like typewriters and sewing machines. The Industrial Revolution ushered in mass production which created an illusion of precision and repetition. The resulting machine-made objects brought a new aesthetic to the interior.

Le Corbusier and Adolf Loos analyzed mass-produced objects to formulate rules for a modern aesthetic. Loos summarized his opinions in his essay "Ornament and Crime," and Le Corbusier, who refers to Loos in "The Decorative Art of Today," shared the same anti-ornament beliefs. For Le Corbusier, mass-production was the measure by which he critically approved or disapproved of design in architectural form, furniture, or objects. Ornament had no place in mass production because it was mainly used to conceal imperfections in production methods. For Loos, ornament was allowable, but only under a specific set of rules.

Decades after Le Corbusier and Loos, the design of household products and the role of ornament are revisited in East German consumer goods by Milena Veenis in her essay "A Battle Against Kitsch." Veenis reveals how the split between ornament and modernism played a pivotal role in expressing political ideology. The essays in this chapter either embrace the aesthetic and ideological positions against ornament or challenge them with examples whose designers emphasize one-of-a-kind, hand-crafted objects. At a time when products have combined do-it-yourself methods with mass production, these two forms of making contribute to our daily experience of the interior. The results of each are explored in essays that lead to a difference between collectibles and a throwaway culture.

Memory and nostalgia find their way into furniture and objects through marks of wear and tear that remind us of personal histories and attachments. Literature transforms nondescript objects into ones that conjure up the past and emanate nostalgia. In "For the Love of Things," Louise Schouwenberg looks at furniture and objects through the lens of sentiment, citing examples by Marcel Proust to reinforce the connection between interiors and nostalgia. Schouwenberg deconstructs a selection of objects to better understand their materials and method of fabrication in relation to technology and market forces. The integration of evolving technologies into contemporary product design has led to a throwaway culture because of materials with a lesser quality and technology with a high turnover rate. At a time when the disposal of digital objects has ramifications in discarding harmful materials, the essays in this chapter are timely in allowing us to believe that a positive side of forming attachments to our objects may be conservation. Though we know the cycle of accumulating and discarding possessions is unsustainable, we have not yet analyzed preserving and maintaining. The essay "Courtney Smith, Tongue and Groove: Moveable Furniture" highlights works by Smith that utilize throwaway furniture, especially its potential for reuse.

If we account for everyday furniture and objects, we would have the beginnings of a list of designed products associated with the Gesamtkunstwerk. Loos mocks this concept in his essay "The Story of a Poor Rich Man." This concept cannot be ignored in interior design because it asks, at what level of detail does the role of the interior designer's influence end? Loos was critical of architects from the Wiener Werkstätte who designed every detail and artifact including furniture, light fixtures, and cutlery in architectural projects. Intimate objects from everyday rituals such as washing, dressing, eating, and sleeping were within the purview of the interior designer's influence. The artist Andrea Zittel produces works that treat her home/studio as the site for experimental design that focuses on these quotidian acts, much like the architect Allan Wexler who materializes daily rituals into architecture. In this regard, Andrew Blauvelt also speaks to this realm in his essay "Strangely Familiar: Design and Everyday Life." He observes the relationship between lifestyles and consumer culture through the lens of the quotidian. In it he represents a lifestyle and responds

145

to myriad issues charged with nostalgia, technology, mass-production, and craft.

This selection of essays offers philosophical positions centered on aesthetics, manufacture, nostalgia, and consumption. The translation of these themes into the built environment can be seen in works of artists and architects who modify what is familiar to us.

The Decorative Art of Today

Le Corbusier

INTRODUCTION

Le Corbusier is a staple of architectural history courses, often introduced as the architect's architect. But the interior played a significant role in forming his beliefs. In this essay Le Corbusier rejects the terminology of the decorative arts and advocates for the merger of design and mass-production, while confidently denigrating the use of ornament. A pivotal element of his logic is the viewer's ability to recognize the "typical-object." Such objects have an underlying common form—no matter how stylistic nuances alter them. Form-based character is timeless in its application, ever present in design, and identified by subtle means. With references to everyday common objects that fill the interior, he constructs an idealized specific image—meant for an ordinary person—consisting of a clean, white interior with flower vase, table, Thonet chair, and lamp. When citing them, he emphasized machine-made objects that expressed functionality. Le Corbusier was fascinated by ships, automobiles, furniture, glassware, and machinery and romanticized them. To further prove his point about the importance of pure form, he devised highly orchestrated photographs of the placement of objects in his interiors and their documentation. The photographs reveal how machine-made products and the translation of functional spaces, such as ships, into shaping interior space influenced Le Corbusier.

Decoration is inherent in the interior. Le Corbusier did not deny the significance of decoration in the home, but proposed renegotiating decorative art forms to integrate the new technologies of his time. He explicitly stated that previous decorative forms are nonapplicable to new forms of mass-production. The change in production method challenged previous paradigms by integrating or eliminating what could be transferred.

To an extent, this supports Le Corbusier's observation of typical-objects, which, despite changing methods of fabrication, retain underlying essential

Originally appeared in *The Decorative Art of Today*, translated by James Dunnett, 2,556 word excerpt from pages 81–101, including image on page 93. © 2011 Artists Rights Society (ARS), New York / ADAGP, Paris / F.L.C. Le Corbusier, © 1987 Massachusetts Institute of Technology, by permission of The MIT Press.

forms consistent with functional needs. His appeal to the public to accept designed objects without excessive decoration was contingent on the excitement of design responding to new forms of fabrication. Although this essay was written in 1925, the nature of design as engagement with the continual evolution and integration of new technologies is current.

––––

THE DECORATIVE ART of today! Am I plunging into paradox?—a paradox that is only apparent. To include under this rubric everything that is free from decoration, whilst making due apology for what is simply banal, indifferent, or void of *artistic intention*, to invite the eye and the spirit to take pleasure in the company of such things and perhaps to rebel against the flourish, the stain, the distracting din of colours and ornaments, to dismiss a whole mass of artefacts, some of which are not without merit, to pass over an activity that has sometimes been disinterested, sometimes idealistic, to disdain the work of so many schools, so many masters, so many pupils, and to think thus of them: 'they are as disagreeable as mosquitoes'; and thence to arrive at this impasse: *modern decorative art is not decorated.* Have we not the right? A moment's thought will confirm it. The paradox lies not in reality, but in the words. Why do the objects that concern us here have to be called *decorative art*? This is the paradox: why should chairs, bottles, baskets, shoes, which are all objects of utility, all *tools*, be called *decorative art*? The paradox of making art out of tools. Let's be clear. I mean, the paradox of making *decorative* art out of tools. To make art out of tools is fair enough, if we hold with Larousse's definition, which is that ART is *the application of knowledge to the realisation of an idea.* Then yes. We are indeed committed to apply all our knowledge to the perfect creation of a tool: know-how, skill, efficiency, economy, precision, the sum of knowledge. A good tool, an excellent tool, the very best tool. This is the world of *manufacture*, of industry; we are looking for a standard and our concerns are far from the personal, the arbitrary, the fantastic, the eccentric; our interest is in the norm, and we are creating type-objects.

So the paradox certainly lies in the terminology.

But we are told that decoration is necessary to our existence. Let us correct that: art is necessary to us; that is to say, a disinterested passion that exalts us. Decoration: baubles, charming entertainment for a savage. (And I do not deny that it is an excellent thing to keep an element of the savage alive in us—a small one.) But in the twentieth century our powers of judgement have developed greatly and we have raised our level of consciousness. Our spiritual needs are different, and higher worlds than those of decoration offer us commensurate experience. It seems justified to affirm: *the more cultivated a people becomes, the more decoration disappears.* (Surely it was Loos who put it so neatly.)

So, to see things clearly, it is sufficient to separate the satisfaction of disinterested emotion from that of utilitarian need. Utilitarian needs call for tools brought in *every respect* to that degree of perfection seen in industry. This then is the magnificent programme for *decorative art* (decidedly, an inappropriate term!).[1]

To provoke elevated sensations is the prerogative of proportion, which is a sensed mathematic; it is afforded most particularly by architecture,[2] painting, and sculpture—works of no immediate utility, disinterested, exceptional, works that are plastic creations invested with passion, the passion of a man—the manifold drama that arrests us, jolts us, rouses us, moves us.[3] Now and always there is a hierarchy. There is a time for work, when one uses oneself up, and also a time for meditation, when one recovers one's bearing and rediscovers harmony. There should be no confusion between them; we are no longer in the age of the dilettante, but at an hour that is harsh and epic, serious and violent, pressured and productive, fertile and economic. Everything has its classification; work and meditation.

The classes too have their classification: those who struggle for their crust of bread have the simple ideal of a decent lodging (and they love to see the fanciest furniture, Henry II or Louis XV, which gives them the feeling of wealth—an elementary ideal). And those well-enough endowed to have the ability and the duty to think (and they aspire to the wisdom of Diogenes). Previously, decorative objects were rare and costly. Today they are commonplace and cheap. Previously, plain objects were commonplace and cheap; today they are rare and expensive. Previously, decorative objects were items for special display: the plate which the peasant family hung on the wall and the embroidered waistcoat for holidays; grist for the propaganda of princes. Today decorative objects flood the shelves of the Department Stores; they sell cheaply to shop-girls. If they sell cheaply, it is because they are badly made and because decoration hides faults in their manufacture and the poor quality of their materials: decoration is disguise. It pays the manufacturer to employ a decorator to disguise the faults in his products, to conceal the poor quality of their materials and to distract the eye from their blemishes by offering it the spiced morsels of glowing gold-plate and strident symphonies. Trash is always abundantly decorated; the luxury object is well made, neat and clean, pure and healthy, and its bareness reveals the quality of its manufacture. It is to industry that we owe this reversal in the state of affairs: a cast-iron stove overflowing with decoration costs less than a plain one; amidst the surging leaf patterns flaws in the casting cannot be seen. And the same applies generally. Take some plain calico and soak it in colour; the printing machine will instantly cover it in the most fashionable patterns (for example, copies of Spanish mantillas, Bulgarian embroidery, Persian silks, etc.) and without incurring much expense one can double the sale price. I quite agree that it can be as charming, as gay, and as shop-girl–like as you could want, and I would want that to continue. What would spring be without it! But this surface elaboration, if extended without discernment over absolutely everything, becomes repugnant and scandalous; it smells of pretence, and the healthy gaiety of the shop-girl in her flower-patterned cretonne dress, becomes rank corruption when surrounded by Renaissance stoves, Turkish smoking tables, Japanese umbrellas, chamber pots and bidets from Lunéville or Rouen, Bichara perfumes, bordello lamp-shades, pumpkin cushions, divans spread with gold and silver *lamé*, black velvets flecked like the Grand Turk, rugs with baskets of flowers and kissing doves, linoleum printed with Louis XVI ribbons. The pretty little shepherdess shop-girl in her flowery cretonne dress, as fresh as spring, seems, in a bazaar such as this, like a sickening apparition from the show-cases of the costume department in the ethnographic museum.

Not only is this accumulation of false richness unsavoury, but above all and before all, this taste for decorating everything around one is a false taste, an abominable little perversion. I reverse the painting; the shepherdess shop-girl is in a pretty room, bright and clear, white walls, a good chair— wickerwork or Thonet; table from the *Bazaar de l'Hotel de Ville* (in the manner of Louis XIII, a very beautiful table) painted with ripolin. A good well-polished lamp, some crockery of white porcelain; and on the table three tulips in a vase can be seen lending a lordly presence. It is healthy, clean, decent. And to make something attractive, as little as that is enough.

Certainly, the modern decorative art of the decorators has different objectives, and it is fair to say that the picture I painted above was no more than the vulgarisation of much worthier intentions. So at this point in our search for a guiding principle, we arrive at the impasse of decorative art: decorative art that is not decorated. And we assert that this art without decoration is made not by artists but by anonymous industry following its airy and limpid path of economy.

The guiding principle of decorators with serious intentions is to cater for the enjoyment of life by a sophisticated clientele. As a result of fashions, the publication of books, and the assiduous efforts of a whole generation of decorators, this clientele has seen its tastes sharply awakened to matters connected with art. Today there is a lively aesthetic awareness and a taste for a contemporary art responding to very much more subtle requirements and to a new spirit. As a result there is a distinct evolution toward ideas reflecting the new spirit; the experience of decoration as art from 1900 to the war has illustrated the impasse of decoration and the fragility of the attempt to make our tools expressive of sentiment and of individual states of mind.

There has been a reaction to this obtrusive presence, and it is being rejected. Day after day, on the other hand, we notice among the products of industry articles of perfect convenience and utility, that soothe our spirits with the luxury afforded by the elegance of their conception, the purity of their execution, and the efficiency of their operation. They are so well thought out that we feel them to be harmonious, and this harmony is sufficient for our gratification.

And so, having opened our eyes and rid ourselves of the romantic and Ruskinian baggage that formed our education, we have to ask ourselves whether these new objects do not suit us very well, and whether this rational perfection and precise formulation in each does not constitute sufficient common ground between them to allow the recognition of a *style*!

We have seen that, freed from all reminiscence and traditional preconception, a rational and reassuring rigour has been applied to their design. Their choice of material, first of all, has been dictated by considerations of strength, lightness, economy, and durability alone; objects for centuries made of wood have been adapted to metal and steel—objects such as office furniture, from which an entirely new precision of operation is demanded. [Fig. 3.1] Thus the 'Voltaire' low armchair has become a totally different machine for sitting in since it was covered in leather.

As a result of this adaptation to new materials, the structure has been transformed, often radically; for a long time these new forms offended us and, by a fatal process of reasoning, provoked a violent *nationalist* (that is to say, regionalist) reaction, an appeal to handicraft as opposed to the machine, seen as a modern hydra. A sterile reaction: one cannot swim back against the current, and the machine which does its work with purity and exactitude is

Fig. 3.1: City-National Bank of Tuscaloosa, USA. © 2011 Artists Rights Society (ARS), New York: ADAGP, Paris: F.L.C. Le Corbusier. Translated by James Dunnett, *The Decorative Art of Today*, image on page 93, © 1987 Massachusetts Institute of Technology, by permission of The MIT Press.

from today dispelling this anachronistic backwash. Let us allow one or two generations brought up in the religion of patina and the 'handmade' to fade away quietly. The young generations are born to the new light and turn naturally and with enthusiasm to the simple truths. When an electric light bulb is at last *weighed*, one fine day, in the design office of a manufacturer of chandeliers, its 50 grams will weigh heavily in the scales that determine the fate of industries doomed to disappearance; the technological firm will replace the artistic: so it is written.

Thus, as new materials and forms were inevitably introduced into the decorative art industries, at the dictate of the all-powerful gods of price and performance, some alert and enquiring minds noted the unvarying laws that were shaping the new products. These laws endowed everything with a common character, and the confidence that they gave to the mind constituted the basis of a new sense of harmony.

If we pause to consider the situation, we are bound to admit that there is no need to wait any longer for objects of utility.

Without a revolution, barricades, or gun-fire, but as a result of simple evolution accelerated by the rapid tempo of our time, we can see decorative art in its decline, and observe that the almost hysterical rush in recent years toward quasi-orgiastic decoration is no more than the final spasm of an already forseeable death.

In face of this unbroken and continuing evidence, good sense has gradually rejected the tendency to luxuriousness as inappropriate to our needs. Its last popular resort has been a devotion to *beautiful materials,* which leads to real byzantinism. The final retreat for ostentation is in polished marbles with restless patterns of veining, in panelling of rare woods as exotic to us as humming-birds, in glass pastes, in lacquers copied from *the excesses* of the Mandarins and thence made the starting point for further elaboration. At the same time, the Prefecture of Police has set about pursuing the pedlars of cocaine. This is all of a piece: feverish pulses and nerves shattered in the aftermath of war like to cool themselves by contact with these inhuman materials that keep us at a distance; in other circumstances they could well offer us a delicate slice of the miracle of nature; but the matrix of amethyst split and polished, or a lump of rock crystal set on my desk is just as expressive, and a great deal more comfortable as an exemplar of the glittering geometries that enthrall us and that we discover with delight in natural phenomena. When we have occasion to enter one of these troubled sanctuaries where so many artful reflections flit about amongst the black or white marbles, the gilt, the red or blue lacquers, we are seized by malaise, by anguish: we long to leave this den, to escape to the open air, and there, reassured and confident, to seat ourselves in a cell such as that in the convent of Fiesole, or better still, to get down to work in the superb office of a modern factory, which is clear and rectilinear and painted with white ripolin and in which healthy activity and industrious optimism reign.

The religion of beautiful materials is now no more than the final spasm of an agony.

During these last years we have witnessed the successive stages of a development: with metallic construction, the *separation of decoration from structure*. Then the fashion for *expressing the construction*, the sign of a new construction. Then the ecstasy before *nature*, showing a desire to rediscover (by however circuitous a path!) the laws of *the organic*. Then the craze for the *simple*, the first contact with the truths of the machine leading us back to good sense, and the instinctive manifestation of an aesthetic for our era.

To tie up the final strand: a triggering of our consciousness, a classification, and a normal perception of the objects in our life will emerge, which distinguishes the highly practical things of work from the intensely free, living, ideal things of the mind.

Notes

1   It has to be said that for thirty years no one has been able to find an accurate term. Is that not because the activity lacks precision, lacks direction, and that as a result it is impossible to define it? The Germans invented the word *Kunstgewerb* (industrial art); that is even more equivocal! I was forgetting that pejorative term *applied art*.

2   Architecture begins where calculation ends.

3   And without doubt furniture can lead us toward architecture, and in place of decoration we shall see the rise of architecture.

A Battle Against Kitsch

Milena Veenis

INTRODUCTION

The rise and fall of the German Democratic Republic (GDR) from 1949 to 1990, as a communist state under the Soviet bloc, was also known as a forty-year political experiment. With the formation of the GDR came a visual identity for the nation that also applied to private domestic interiors. In the GDR the political and economic agenda directly influenced the design of domestic objects. Milena Veenis probes this relationship in her essay, uncovering the rift between a minimalist style representing a one-class society favored by the state and a decorative kitsch that attracted many of its citizens seeking a bourgeois identity.

Personal possessions and objects in the domestic interior reveal the identity of its resident. Citizens of the GDR were no different in their desire to express who they were. Because of the homogeneous cultural identity associated with communism under the Soviet bloc, rules were established for design that focused first on function and utility and eliminated decoration. The design aesthetic that evolved was based on objectivity, whose foundation was geometry and science. The rationale for such a neutral design solution meant that it could not be disputed. Inevitably a split occurred between comrades who accepted the new minimalist forms and those who yearned for decoration and ornament. To dissuade its citizens from displaying the nostalgic objects of former years, the state associated them with proscribed class distinctions: "all those so-called 'romantic-looking' old things are in fact nothing but the silent testimonies of the life of the poor and exploited."* The state took the position that replicating nostalgic and ornamental objects by mass production was false. The GDR's design agenda recalled Le Corbusier's writings on modern methods of fabrication, conveying a predetermined style.

To some extent, the state's propaganda positioned its citizens against the state ideals. Thus furniture and domestic objects symbolic of latent political

Excerpted from "Consumption in East Germany: The Seduction and Betrayal of Things," *Journal of Material Culture* vol. 4, no. 1 (1999): 84–90. © 1999 by Sage Publications. Reprinted by Permission of SAGE.

unrest became central figures in a social and ideological conversion to a new lifestyle. Although politics and economics often exist at an abstract scale far removed from interior design in the West, in the GDR as in other Soviet bloc countries, politics had a tangible, visible effect on the domestic realm.

———

THE INTERESTING THING about the history of socialist ideology in the GDR is that the socialist promise of a golden future was not just attached to the material basis of society (the means and modes of production) as such, but also to concrete material objects. Within the GDR, the design of the material world was dictated by an outspokenly ideological conviction that it was possible to give life a progressive sense, content and meaning, by rearranging its material structure. As for instance the popular women's magazine *Kultur im Heim* (Culture at Home) makes clear: it is important to pay social and public attention to the design and organization of even the most private material affairs, because:

> If our living-room is nothing other than the representation of subjective characteristics, images and tastes, we wouldn't have to pay public attention to it: it would be a matter of mere private concern. But its important constitutive meaning for the development of human nature ('des menschlichen Wesens'), for the richer of socialist reality-coherences, and its fundamental function within social psychology, make the composition of the living-room a public issue concerning the 'res publica.' (KiH, 1977(4): 34)

Time and again, the editors of the journal made it clear that the inhabitants of socialist East Germany ought to have a different relationship toward their material surroundings; their taste concerning things ought to be different from the inhabitants of bourgeois societies. 'Everything that was made within the GDR, was in fact made against the West,' an East German designer told me. Every time she designed an object, she had to explain what an object with the same function looked like in the West, why that was reprehensible and in what (enlightening) way her own design was superior. The so-called romantic frills and supposedly ancient motives which were so popular in the West were 'not wanted in the GDR' she told me. And in the same vein, another designer explained:

> When we designed a glass, we always proceeded from the question of what a glass should be able to do and what its function was, namely: stand straight, be stable and contain liquid. Furthermore, people had to

155

be able to drink from it. And on the basis of these requirements we conceptualized a form. Whereas in the West, they seemed to do it the other way around.

Practical, functional and rational: it fully corresponds to the picture of communism as it is sketched by the sociologist Bauman: 'communism was thoroughly modern in its passionate conviction that good society can only be a society carefully designed, rationally managed and thoroughly industrialized' (1991: 266).

Daily life in the socialist GDR was organized according to 'fundamentally secular and scientific' (Borneman, 1992: 162) principles,[1] and these particularly concerned the material organization of society. Very generally speaking, one could say that East German material culture was as functional, practical and rational as possible. And even at the end of the 1980s, women's magazines, material culture and design journals bulged with incitements toward 'Sachlichkeit' (succinctness), 'Zweckmäßigkeit' (purposiveness), 'Notwendigkeit' (necessity), 'Minimalgestaltung' (minimal-composition) and 'das Wesentliche' (the essential), to which designers, producers and consumers had to restrict themselves.[2]

Although it is impossible (within the limited scope of this article) to do justice to the many changes and more subtle differentiations that characterize the history of design and material culture in the GDR, it is important to know that the principles listed here were not uncontested. On the contrary: from the very beginning up until the ultimate breakdown of the GDR, there was a battle going on between East German designers, producers, politicians and consumers about the question of what (somewhat ironically speaking) 'a socialist coffee-cup' (Hirdina, 1988: 155) should look like. And although this battle was eventually won by the protagonists of a functionalist perspective on material culture and design, this does not mean that the East German material world looked as immaculately functionalist as one would expect. Many East German producers and politicians had a taste different from the functionalist and modernist style that was so characteristic in East German designer-discourse, and they frequently succeeded in adding adornments, reintroducing flowered decorations or different elements of (what was called) *kitsch,* to the modernist plans, ideas and products presented by designers.

But in spite of these 'disturbing' influences, one can nevertheless conclude that the East German material world was extremely monotonous and distinctly functionalist. Everything that was made in the GDR bore the same functionalist family-resemblances: rectangularity, straightness and rationality. The main reason for this was that functionalist principles to a large extent coincided with economic requirements. It is no coincidence that the

East German designer Heinz Hirdina concludes his standard work on East German design with the observation: 'despised by self-conceited people, and renounced as outmoded by those who want to show how fashionable they are, functionalism always manages to survive in factories and construction sites' (1988: 255).

Functionalist principles about the (social-educational) importance of *zeitgemäß*, honest and 'true' present-day, industrial and mass-produced forms and products, turned out to be outspokenly practical as well—that is, economic and cheap—because a straight, rectangular table is of course much easier, cheaper and faster to produce than a table with rounded edges or curved adornments. And both for ideological and economical reasons, East German material culture discourse and practice turned out to be one vast struggle against material 'styles of the past' (KiH, 1973[5]) and 'ornamental desires' (KiH, 1980[3]: 41). It was a struggle against material objects whose power of attraction was condemned as distinctly superficial and banal.

All those Western objects 'adorned with horrible brass-ware, all those wildly dangling lamps…those undulating lines and swarming meanders on table—and book-covers' (KiH, 1982[3]: 31); and all those new, industrially-made objects that were made to look old: they were all equally 'unnatural, meaningless, overloaded, unpractical and profuse' (KiH, 1969[1]: 49); they were all criticized for being 'mushy, untruthful, unreal, counterfeit, bad plagiarism, functionless and falsified' (KiH, 1966[4]: 22). According to East German designers, editors, salesmen and producers, those objects aimed to 'deceive the consumer' (KiH, 1977[2]: 3) and the desire to possess them is expressive of a sad form of 'primitive thinking,' a 'deformation of the aesthetic consciousness,' from which socialist people needed to be 'freed' (KiH, 1968[6]: 4) as soon as possible. The hollow and vacuous power of attraction of these objects had to be unmasked and people had to learn that these things just didn't fit in with actual society and way of life.

> When you prefer a candle-holder or salt-sprinkler that seems to be directly derived from grandmother's days, then please be consistent and…unscrew the safety fuses, hold two pine-chips of about 40 centimeters long between your teeth, and use this precursory 'pocket-lantern' while running your household. (KiH, 1965[3]: 27)

The message that East German journals and magazines time and again tried to impress upon their readers runs something like: 'Former days and former things were different! And we just don't want to go back to them; would you? Don't you know that all those so-called "romantic-looking" old things are in fact nothing but the silent testimonies of the life of the poor and exploited?' And in order to inform people about the 'true nature' of the things that they thought were beautiful, journals and magazines dedicated numerous articles to the historical background of these objects. Because only when they learned to think carefully about what they saw would East Germans be able to correct their 'immature' (KiH, 1968[5]) taste-preferences:

> empirical perception alone is not enough to penetrate reality to such an extent, that the essential truth of the entire historical movement and development…are the result. One needs a higher level of thinking, which is unattainable without a scientifically founded world-view. (Schmidt, 1966: 1436)

'You don't know what you see!,' East Germans were told. Because if they knew what they saw, their taste would be different; then it would be in line with present-day modes and means of (industrial) production, with modern times and modernist taste-preferences.

These convictions formed the basis for a material culture that looked distinctly rectilinear, rather severe and puritan. East German couches, easy-chairs, side-tables and dining-areas were all equally straight and no matter where one looks (in design-journals, popular women's magazines, journals for furniture producers or catalogues of East German material culture and design), the pictures all look alike: they show a material world that first and foremost looked extremely simple, uniform and straight.

Whereas the whole of East German life was fitted in a materialistic ideology, the importance of material objects was at the same time neutralized, in the ongoing efforts to educate people's taste in a more rational, practical and economic direction.

But no matter how forcefully material goods were framed in beautiful educational intentions, their quality left much to be desired. Since timber was scarce,[3] it was imitated in many different ways and most furniture was made from a mixture of saw-dust and glue, which was then covered with plastic foil with a motif of wood on it. And constrained by the increasing scarcity of materials, the East German production motto became 'produce more from less,' that is to say (East German joke): 'do you know how to make more pasta out of less flour? Increase the holes in the macaroni'! Hard couches, bending staples and the need to use ten matches to light a candle: that was the material reality of the GDR. But it all took place within the frame of highly justified ideals. Even as late as 1987, the journal *Kultur im Heim* urges its readers that 'Crammed decorations or the use of ornamental elements out of the past estrange industrially produced objects… Good industrial forms are instead associated with simplicity, straightness of form and proportion.' It is like listening to a strict but patient mother, talking to her children. And at the end of the article the author sighs, just like a mother after a long day during which her children kept on eating out of the sugar basin, despite her repeated warnings that this is bad for their teeth: 'To inform people's individual taste and aesthetic perception is a laborious teaching-process.'

The promotion of functionalist material culture was a civilizing-process against 'the sentimental appeal of the "nice" little things of life' (Bertsch and Hedler, 1990: 19), against the 'fancy tea-pots, bread baskets decorated with christmas-trees, napkin-rings depicting cyclamens' (Bertsch and Hedler, 1990: 19), that kept on dominating West German material supplies.[4]

This is fully in line with the socialist salvation fantasies, in which material progress and striving forward was only useful within the context of the 'wonderful promises of modernity' (Bauman, 1991: 266) and in which every possible connection with the past was taboo: 'it did not trust history to find the way to the millennium. Neither was it prepared to wait till history proved this mistrust wrong. Its war-cry was: "Kingdom of Reason—now!"' (Bauman, 1991: 266).

The past was closed off, salvation was only to be expected in forward-striving movements and the future was the only goal. It must have been an extremely confusing means of orientation for those living in East Germany, given the way in which the socialist promise was realized. Decay and rust, greyness and cracked walls arose where material progress was preached. And although the official East German media kept on proclaiming the same success stories (things are going better, they will ameliorate even further, we are about to reach our goals), for most people it was evident that the contrary was true. It is not necessary to describe them in detail: the shattered roads, the decomposed inner towns, the dreary *Plattenbau* quarters and the paintless, grey and shabby-looking consumer goods, that seem to come straight from the 1950s.

On the basis of that, one would expect East Germans to be only cynical and distrustful vis-a-vis the materialist salvation-ideology that was poured over them. And although they certainly did not believe in the war-cries about their national material 'expressions, that are honest, life-embracing and truthful' (KiH, 1977[4]: 34), it is at the same time clear that daily life in the GDR turned out to be distinctly materialistic. And although materialist ideology was not able to realize its promises at all, 'the material' turned out to be one of the most important guidelines and themes in the everyday life of most East Germans.

This was partly due to the central regulation and continuous scarcity of consumer-goods, which practically forced people to spend an enormous amount of time, attention and energy on the acquisition of basic material goods. But apart from that, in East Germany consumption was a far more encompassing activity than it was in the western part of the country. Here, consumption also entailed social and cultural aspects. Most East Germans were part of social networks in which material exchange, transactions and rumours played an important role. Colleagues helped each other with the acquisition of scarce goods and everybody was always looking out for anything that might be on sale somewhere and for queues (a sign that something scarce, that is, valuable, was for sale). 'The material' therefore included much more than material things as such; it was a social network, a web of meanings, clues, rumours, the right interpretation of meaningful signs and the development of the right social skills.

And as such, part of the socialist message about mutual equality, solidarity and concern, could find its daily confirmation and concrete form in people's continuous striving for material satisfaction. To stand in line for someone else is also to show concern for each other. As Borneman points out:

> people used th(e) romantic emplotment provided by the state to integrate their own experiences into a meaningful and coherent narrative....By socialism they appeal to a working-together, a unity of purpose in a relatively egalitarian group, and a strong sense of belonging to an empirical community. (Borneman, 1992: 120)

Maybe even more so than in West Germany, in the GDR 'the material' could develop into one of the most meaningful symbols of The Good Life and (future) Happiness Together. Objects become the symbols of the aim of Forward Together!

And especially because all beautiful socialist promises about the Good Life were not kept and because the central meaning of the material sphere of life as one of the main sources of self-realization was frustrated almost daily by the necessity to queue for everything and to be bawled at when one dared to ask for unattainable goods like toasters or tights, things could become targets of largely unspecified, but extremely high hopes and expectations. When a well-known West German historian was permitted to do research in the GDR in 1987, he was shocked when he was confronted with the importance people attached to consumption:

> The critique on supplies turned out to be a dominant theme in almost every interview....The criticisms about this [were] extremely stereotyped and they usually concentrated on the supply of consumer goods.... The critique on supplies [seemed to be] an officially licensed valve and, at the same time, an expression of a deep consensus with the system's economistic standards of value....The 'economism'[;] this...very understandable reduction of the fullness of life to the straightforward material,

had become a *lingua franca* in the GDR, *into which all feelings were translated.* (Niethammer et al., 1991: 39)

The material had become a condensation into which all feelings and strivings were translated: things as a source of success and of failure, as goal and means, as social cohesion and individual aspiration, as source of happiness and of misfortune. But internally, it was first and foremost an ongoing source of frustration[5] because the gap between the beautiful words in the official reports and material reality widened every month.

Notes

* Milena Veenis, "Consumption in East Germany: The Seduction and Betrayal of Things," *Journal of Material Culture* vol. 4 no. 1 (1999): 87.

1 Also see Habermas who, in a letter written to Christa Wolf, writes that in the post-war history of both East and West Germany, there is a strong (but according to him just) taboo on all 'seductions of the archaic' (Wolf, 1994:147). In the same letter Habermas pays attention to what he considers to be the worst consequence of the ruined and fraudulent defeat of socialism within the GDR: 'with its political rhetoric (this state has) misused progressive ideas for its legitimation; and through its inhuman praxis it has not only jeeringly repudiated them, but thereby also discredited them fully. I am afraid that these dialectics of invalidation will have more ruinous effects on the spiritual hygiene in Germany, than six generations of *anti-enlightened, anti-Semitic, false romantic, German-gushing obscurantism* have been able to bring about' (143–4). Note especially the (for 'right-thinking' Germans self-evident) relation between anti-enlightened and anti-semitic ideas, which is suggested here!

2 Although the picture about the material composition of daily life in the GDR is more complex and differentiated than I can describe here, terms like 'Sachlichkeit' and 'Minimalgestaltung' are nevertheless characteristic for the East German material world. See also Bertsch (1990), Halter (1991), John (1978), Kelm (1971), Kühne (1981), the volumes of the East German design journal *Form und Zweck*, the women's magazine *Kultur im Heim*, the advertising journal *Neue Werbung*, the journal of the furniture industry *Möbel und Wohnraum* and especially the pictures in the book of the East German designer Heinz Hirdina (1988).

3 Although all the woods in the country were cut down, the timber was exported to Western countries, in exchange for Western currency. The topic 'East German economic relations with capitalist countries' is extremely interesting, because it makes clear that the GDR was willing to deny its own idealist principles, in order to satisfy (at least to a certain extent) the internal material situation. Also see Kleßmann and Wagner (1993: 377).

4 For an elaboration of the role of socialist regimes as (supposed) civilizing forces, see also Mattijs Van de Port (1994).

5 Also see Gries (1991: 327).

References

Bauman, Zygmunt (1991) *Modernity and Ambivalence*. Cambridge: Polity Press.

Bertsch, Georg and Ernst Hedler (1990) *SED Schönes Einheits Design*. Köln: Taschenverlag.

Borneman, John (1992) *Belonging in the Two Berlins: Kin, State, Nation*. Cambridge: Cambridge University Press.

Hirdina, Heinz (1988) *Gestalten für die Serie. Design in der DDR 1949–1985*. Dresden: VEB Verlag der Kunst.

K.i.H. (1965–1989) *Kultur im Heim*.

Niethammer, Lutz, Alexander von Plato and Dorothee Wierling (1991) *Die volkseigene Erfahrung. Eine Archäologie des Lebens in der Industrieprovinz der DDR*. Berlin: Rowohlt.

Schmidt, Jutta (1966) 'Über die Gestaltung des sozialistischen Menschenbildes,' *Einheit*, 21(11): 1434–43.

Strangely Familiar:
Design and Everyday Life

Andrew Blauvelt

INTRODUCTION

Interior design is a discipline whose many roles include designing site-specific elements and crafting a complete interior based on an aggregate of preexisting objects, to achieve a modern version of the Gesamtkunstwerk. Andrew Blauvelt unravels the interior through perspectives both concrete and phenomenal.* Interior design curricula emphasize design strategies, materials, detailing, codes, and history to teach about crafting succinct interiors. Blauvelt takes a step backward to reveal underlying issues inherent in these academic areas by examining the "familiar" and the "everyday" in design.

The quotidian—the everyday—plays a seminal role in the writings of Michel de Certeau, Henri Lefebvre, and Georges Perec, who provide phenomenological readings of spaces people occupy. Blauvelt summarizes their writings to construct a stage for events and rituals that play out in the world of the interior. Happenstance events are not necessarily designed in Blauvelt's play, but the constructed interior guides them into occurring, making it possible for the unpredictable to be sited. The interior designer's role as director attunes to ephemeral events and finds a balance between constructing the physical site and allowing fortuitous events to take place.

Through the quotidian, the familiar in our everyday emerges. Blauvelt focuses on tangible forms of the familiar to complement the phenomenal, leading to commercial and less commercial objects as found in branded "lifestyles" that become a commodity available through Martha Stewart Living *and* Wallpaper, *while the less mainstream elements surface as boutique commodities. Blauvelt invests his interest in the latter, the "strangely familiar," that incorporates alternative design strategies not so easily branded, whose identities emerge after a close look at their role in the everyday. "Strangely Familiar" challenges conventions, which prompts new forms of design, where alterations to the norm reflect subtle influences inherent in utility or by a humor*

Originally appeared in the exhibition catalog *Strangely Familiar: Design and Everyday Life*, edited by Andrew Blauvelt, 14–24. Reprinted with permission and © 2003 Walker Art Center.

embedded in installation. By highlighting a selection of these objects, Blauvelt reminds us that design can reveal latent aspects of the quotidian made visible in our tangible world of interiors.

———

Design in the Age of Design

A paradoxical presence in our lives, design is both invisible and conspicuous, familiar and strange. It surrounds us while fading from view, becoming second nature and yet seemingly unknowable. Broadly conceived as the world of human-made artifacts, design is everywhere: the tools we use, the furnishings we keep, the clothes we wear, the cars we drive, the books we read, the houses where we dwell, the offices where we work, and the cities in which we live. Even nature does not escape the reach of design, whether a park, a new species of plant, or the manipulation of human bodies and genes. In a typical day the average person encounters hundreds of objects and thousands of messages, each designed by someone.

Despite this utter ubiquity, design remains for many people a mysterious force. This is in part because it presents itself through the myriad objects and images it creates—autonomous and mute things, which tend to conceal rather than reveal the process of their making. Thus, the vast majority of people come into contact with design as consumers learning to discern among innumerable offerings. Far fewer individuals have access to designers or are privy to the processes employed by them. While the activity of design is pervasive and the numbers of professionals who engage in it are quite vast in any modern society, most design escapes notice, emerging from the landscape or entering the world rather quietly, often anonymously. The relative invisibility of design is also a matter of perceptual survival. Most new things are quickly absorbed into our immediate surroundings, forming the background against which we go about our everyday lives. Without this ability to integrate objects into our environment, the world would seem a daunting place—an ever-changing visual cacophony.

Just as design populates a familiar world, it can also stand apart from it. Modern societies demand designs that create distinctions by signaling what is different or new. During the 1990s there was a marked increase in design awareness within the media, among businesses, in the government, and most certainly in the culture at large. There are numerous markers for this conspicuousness: Frank Gehry's design of the Guggenheim Bilbao, which inaugurated the phenomenon of spectacle architecture; the introduction of numerous self-consciously designed products, such as Apple Computer's multicolored iMacs and Nike's proliferation of footwear styles; or Prime Minister Tony Blair's rebranding of British heritage as "Cool Britannia." No longer the province of specialty shops with inaccessible prices, mass-market retailers promoted the democratization of design at the international furnishings company IKEA, or in once unthinkable places such as the home of the "bluelight special," K-Mart, whose aisles now stock domestic denizen Martha Stewart's line of housewares. Other retailers such as Target produced signature collections by architect Michael Graves and designers such as Todd Oldham and Philippe Starck. Not content to fill only the pages of specialist journals, design became a subject for newspapers and mainstream magazines, and spawned new publishing genres. The concept of lifestyle coalesced; that elusive but identifiable thing united such disparate patterns as one's preferences in clothing, automobiles, and furniture with tastes in music, movies, travel, and cuisine and packaged it under titles such as *Wallpaper** or *Martha Stewart Living* (to name only two). Today design is expected to perform in an ensemble cast, no longer as a wallflower or mere product feature, but in a starring role in a story where branding, lifestyle, and products form various narratives of consumer experience.

The aforementioned examples belie the invisibility of design in the world at large. Indeed, they map the terrain in which design emerged as a potent force transforming products into lifestyles, companies into brands, and neighborhoods into destinations. Design in the 1990s exemplified the transformation of the economy from its postindustrial condition (which was after all only a symptom) to its more synergistic guise—what economists James Gilmore and Joseph Pine have famously termed the "experience economy."[1] In such an economy, products are merely props in the staging of memorable moments of consumption. In economies of the past, we understood the function of goods in terms of exchange value (worth) or use value (utility). The experience economy represents the systematic development of what philosopher Jean Baudrillard refers to as sign value (meaning). Like a medieval cosmology where objects are imbued with mysterious meanings, nothing represents itself literally in the world of experience economies: sneakers are signs of wellness, competitiveness, and prestige, and coffee is no longer just a drink but the nexus of social conviviality and a barometer of lifestyle. This suggests that objects are merely nodes in a larger web of references and connections in which consumptive desires, patterns, and actions are central.

The design fields responded to the needs of this economy by producing a plethora of new things. The 1990s were the most prolific and important years for design since the 1960s. This vitality could be seen in the massive building boom that demanded more inventive and expressive forms of architecture, or in glitzy new consumer products—mobile phones, digital audio players, other handheld electronics, or even the more pedestrian garbage cans, toothbrushes, and staplers—whose forms were undergoing rapid change. With computer-aided design programs, contemporary culture has been visually transformed by the spline curve, adding sinuous edges to everything from buildings to cars to sneakers in what promoters and detractors have come to call "blobjects" and "blobitecture."[2] It is both tempting and plausible to view the last ten years as an exercise in this new styling, a contemporaneous version of 1930s streamlining. However, despite the increasingly seductive products on offer, it would be misleading to focus solely on this formal aspect of design.

A comparison of the last decade's output to the 1960s is instructive. In many ways, one sensed an air of optimism, even an unbridled enthusiasm, about the possibilities of design—the same attitude that pervaded the youthful exuberance surrounding inflatable furniture, modish environments, and geodesic housing of thirty years prior. In fact, many contemporary designers acknowledge their inspiration from sources such as the visionary architectural proposals of Archigram; the fluid, colorful spaces and mod furniture of Verner Panton; or the social consciousness espoused by design gurus Victor Papenak and Buckminster Fuller. The spirit of social liberation that spawned various possibilities for alternative living in the sixties (communes, bachelor pads, converted school buses, or even imagined colonies in outer space) has its contemporary corollary in the desire for evermore connected but mobile lifestyles and all of the things that go with it. The ecological imperative of the *Whole Earth Catalog* or Fuller's *Operating Manual for Spaceship Earth* finds its 1990s equivalent in "green architecture" with, for instance, its rooftop garden schemes, and in "disassembly lines," by which manufacturers can reclaim the components of their discarded products.

Certainly it would be possible to view many segments of recent design through these perspectives of formal evolution, historical zeitgeist, technological change, or ecological concern. Many books and exhibitions have done precisely that. Instead, the exhibition *Strangely Familiar: Design and Everyday Life* takes a broader approach, examining a range of projects across many areas of design. What connects these disparate works are a strong conceptual basis and a desire to rethink certain assumptions about design by offering us imaginative and often strange solutions. These projects force us to look at our everyday world anew, challenge our own presumptions about what is possible, and reconsider our relationship to things that once seemed so familiar.

If the last decade has been about the special nature of design—its strange and conspicuous presence in our world—then there has been a countervailing need to examine the more mundane and familiar world of daily life. The everyday is an elusive subject, a kind of residual realm encompassing those activities, practices, spaces, and things that exist beyond or beside the reach of society's official dictates and actions. It can be said that the everyday acts as a foil to design's increasingly active presence in the world.

Conversely, design can be the measure by which we gauge our encounter with the everyday.

Thinking about the Everyday

How should we take account of, question, describe what happens every day and recurs every day: the banal, the quotidian, the obvious, the common, the ordinary, the infraordinary, the background noise, the habitual?
—Georges Perec[3]

The quotidian has long been a touchstone for many artists and movements, from scenes of daily life famously detailed in seventeenth-century Dutch paintings or the once-shocking ordinariness of Postimpressionist subject matter. No longer content with depicting daily life, artists soon sought to disrupt it. Duchamp's "readymades" and the Surrealists' oneiric tableaux transformed mundane objects, radically altering their once familiar contexts. As modern artists sought to join art with life, everyday practices became a principle component of their work, from the gamelike strategies of Fluxus to the Situationists' technique of the *dérive* (partially programmed wanderings through the city), to the unflinching recording of banal activities in the Andy Warhol films *Sleep* or *Eat*. In both artistic practice and intellectual inquiry, the everyday as a subject of critical examination developed in the postwar period with the advent of a modern consumer society. In the social sciences, the quotidian has been studied for decades by philosophers such as Henri Lefebvre and Michel de Certeau or writers like Georges Perec. Each of these individuals provides a departure point for understanding the role of everyday life.

Lefebvre, in his pioneering analysis first published in 1947, *Critique de la vie quotidienne (The Critique of Everyday Life)*, argues that the quotidian as the subject of philosophical study had been long neglected, treated as trivial in favor of "higher" or more serious topics. Because everyday life was particular and concrete and had to be lived to be truly understood, he faulted the abstract, systematic theories of then-evolving studies such as structural anthropology and semiotics. Born at the turn of the twentieth century, Lefebvre saw French daily life eroded by the effects of modernization. By suggesting the alienation experienced in modern society, which estranged people from a once holistic conception of life and work through the fragmentation and specialization of industrialized labor, Lefebvre argues against what much of everyday life had been reduced to, namely the drudgery and repetitiveness of work, bureaucratic social control, and empty consumerism. It is difficult to locate in his writings any direction for design to take, because in so many ways it contributes to the very problems he identifies:

the mechanisms of advertising to create desire, the proliferation of identical consumer goods, and the rationalized strictures of modern urban planning. Nevertheless, his 1974 treatise *La production de l'espace (The Production of Space)* has influenced recent thinking in the fields of urbanism and architecture (undoubtedly due in part to its translation into English in 1991). As the title indicates, Lefebvre understands space as neither natural nor abstract, but rather as something that is consciously created, and in turn, produces specific effects. He countered the idea of classical and modernist notions of a universal, abstract space dominated by the visual by proposing instead a social space composed of differences. For him, space is a social product, not a neutral container, one that can encourage or discourage certain practices and behaviors.

Perhaps not surprisingly, his ideas about the ideological nature of space were of interest to those involved in architecture and urban planning during the 1980s and 1990s, a time when such subjects were increasingly examined, no matter how belatedly, through the lenses of gender, race, and class. This also signals a shift away from the modernist preoccupation with formal aspects to a more postmodernist stance considering content or effect. Contained within *The Production of Space* is a fictitious exchange in which Lefebvre answers his critics who would complain that true creativity lies within formal innovation itself. One side contends that "for architects who concern themselves primarily with content, as for 'users,' as for the activity of dwelling itself—all these merely reproduce outdated forms. They are in no sense innovative forces."[4] Lefebvre replies: "Surely there comes a moment when formalism is exhausted, when only a new injection of content into form can destroy it and so open up the way to innovation."[5] In many ways, this passage would epitomize a major shift in design thinking, opening avenues of innovation to other possibilities, other uses, and other contexts.

While Lefebvre articulated more overarching principles governing an understanding of everyday life, de Certeau, a sociologist and historian, took a more specific and ethnographic approach. His investigations into the realm of routine practices, or the "arts of doing" such as walking, talking, reading, dwelling, and cooking, were guided by his belief that despite repressive aspects of modern society, there exists an element of creative resistance to these strictures enacted by ordinary people. In *L'invention du quotidien (The Practice of Everyday Life)*, de Certeau outlines an important critical distinction between strategies and tactics in this battle of repression and expression. According to him, strategies are used by those within organizational power structures, whether small or large, such as the state or municipality, the corporation or the proprietor, a scientific enterprise or the scientist. Strategies are deployed against some external entity to institute a set of relations for official or proper ends, whether adversaries, competitors, clients, customers, or simply subjects. Tactics, on the other hand, are employed by those who are subjugated. By their very nature tactics are defensive and opportunistic, used in more limited ways and seized momentarily within spaces, both physical and psychological, produced and governed by more powerful strategic relations.

Importantly, de Certeau shifts attention to acts of consumption, or use, and away from the historical preoccupation with the means of production. In so doing he focuses, for example, not on authorship but on reading, not on urban design but on walking through the city, not on theories of language but on the provisional and improvisational aspects of conversation. For de Certeau, consumption is not merely empty or passive, as many critics claim, but can contain elements of user resistance—nonconformist, adaptive, appropriative, or otherwise transgressive tactics—that become creative acts of their own fashioning. By locating such creativity in the user and beyond the conventional role assumed by the designer, de Certeau opens the possibilities of a design attuned to its use, context, and life rather than only its material quality, prescribed functionality, or formal expression.

While de Certeau saw the potential for individual acts of imaginative consumption, Perec enthusiastically wrote about a more poetic reimagination of everyday life. He was a member of the literary group OuLiPo, which was an affiliation of mathematicians and writers interested in producing poetry using systematic methods and agreed-upon constraints. One of his most famous literary contributions in this regard was *La Disparition (A Void)*, a three-hundred-page novel that did not use a single word with the letter "e." His embrace of the quotidian can best be gleaned from the work *Espéces d'espaces (Species of Spaces)*, a selection of ruminations on urban and domestic realms. Perec's literary inventiveness and poetic sensibility pervade the texts, which consider subjects such as the space of the page, the functionality inscribed by the rooms of a typical apartment, and the social life of a street or neighborhood. In the essay "Approaches to What?" he coins neologisms such as the "infraordinary" (versus the extraordinary) or the "endotic" (as opposed to the exotic) in order to discuss the specific character of the everyday. Most importantly, he obliges the reader to question the commonplace things that become habitual:

> "What we need to question is bricks, concrete, glass, our table manners, our utensils, our tools, the way we spend our time, our rhythms. To question that which seems to have ceased forever to astonish us. We live, true, we breathe, true; we walk, we open doors, we go down staircases, we sit at a table in order to eat, we lie down on a bed in order to sleep. How? Where? When? Why?"[6]

Perec's lists of possible inquiries and subjects for consideration are the very stuff of everyday life, the objects around us, the places we inhabit, the habits we form, the routines we perform. He asks such seemingly simple questions as "What is there under your wallpaper?"[7] Or he imagines an apartment that is organized around the senses instead of rooms: "We can imagine well enough what a gustatorium might be, or an auditory, but one might wonder what a seeery might look like, or a smellery or a feelery."[8] His poetic inquisition of the everyday affords design an opportunity to reimagine itself and to engage the world in new and inventive ways. Interestingly, two designs appear to respond to Perec's questioning, although not intentionally. Gis Bakker's *Peep Show* wallpaper produced under the auspices of Droog Design in the early 1990s was a blank white surface with large circles cut out, exposing the wall beneath and thereby reversing its conventional function. Architects Annette Gigon and Mike Guyer recently completed the design of a museum for an archaeological site in Germany where in A.D. 9 the Teutons defeated the Romans. Their design also includes three pavilions, "seeing," "hearing," and "questioning," which are devoted to different sensorial experiences. One space functions as a camera obscura and another, through a moveable acoustical pipe much like an ear trumpet, amplifies the sound of the surrounding fields, while a third transmits televised news broadcasts from around the world—stories that too often carry headlines of contemporary armed conflicts. Each space serves to underscore in a distinct way the visitor's perception of the site where an ancient battle once took place.

Design and Everyday Life

While the everyday has played an important role within modern art and the social sciences, it has only recently become central to discussions of design gaining momentum over the last decade. This tardiness seems implausible given that design, in its most basic sense, always already implicates itself in the construction of the everyday world. Yet, it is one thing to be part of the everyday—to help create it—and quite another to make it the subject of analysis or even critique. It is not coincidental that the quotidian should be of interest just as contemporary consumer culture is even more intricately woven into all aspects of daily life.

Among designers, interest in the quotidian is of course varied in its interpretations and responses. The nineties (and millennial) take on the everyday is different from earlier interests in anonymous or vernacular architecture, which saw such efforts as aspirational or inspirational—whether designers were learning from Venturi's Las Vegas or absorbing the lessons of Bernard Rudofsky.[9] These unschooled examples of design held some allure because they represented an untainted world that had existed independently of the discipline's increasing professionalization and before the expansive reach of commercial culture had taken hold. Seen through the professional's eyes, the vernacular attains an exotic status, while the commonplace fades from view. Today's everydayness is not reducible to period styles of the vernacular or the untrained informality of the anonymous. It accepts the bland, the generic, and the ordinary as the predominant context in which design will be situated, and against which the brand name and the spectacular operate.

Within architectural circles, interest in the everyday has taken on a particular meaning borne out of a reaction against the theory-laden 1980s, with its interests in the instruments of textual analysis, poststructuralism, and, in particular, deconstruction, as well as an economic climate favorable to high-profile building in the 1990s.[10] Highly analytical, conceptually abstract, and predominantly textual in their focus, these theories were seen as too removed from actual lived experience, specific contexts, and practical constraints. Whether intended or not, such concepts were elastic enough to be adapted to intensive formal experimentation and innovation, and therefore provided a much-needed antidote to the regressive forms of most postmodernist design of the period. Not surprisingly, the opposing tack of the everyday would emphasize a renewed pragmatism, embracing specific conditions of use and actual social contexts. Following this shift, architecture is real, not abstract; it resists analysis and must be experienced, inhabited, and otherwise occupied. Against the rising cult of celebrity surrounding the architects of the 1990s building boom, the doctrines of everydayness advocate an antiheroic approach, opting to see architecture expressed as moments and cycles of habitation rather than in one-off monuments of expressiveness.[11]

Within the realm of product design, interest in everydayness can trace its development in the reaction to the design of the 1980s, with its elaborate use of materials and finishes and a hyper-styling of forms. Ventures such as Droog Design, a loose collective of initially Dutch designers who gained notoriety and influence in the design world in the early 1990s, typified this shift.[12] Embracing a renewed sobriety in the face of a resplendent materialism, Droog adopted a more straightforward attitude to materials, an inventive approach to fabrication processes and methods, and a resistance to product styling. The attitude of Droog became defined by the latent humor and wit that characterizes so many of its products: a chandelier made from a cluster of eighty-five exposed lightbulbs, a chest of drawers created by strapping together a variety of used drawers, or a polyester-impregnated felt sink.

At the same time, a growing interest in ecology, sustainability, recycling, and product obsolescence fostered a change in attitude among many product designers that required a rethinking of previously held and unquestioned assumptions within the field about resourcefulness and wastefulness in production, the life cycles of products, and the role of use and consumption.[13] If product design was to be more than styling exercises, it needed to expand conceptually, explore new methods of fabrication, and be informed by the use, adaptation, and personalization of objects by users.

Without resorting to orderly definitions, this exhibition offers its own interpretation of everydayness and design. The assembled works are not recessive; they do not fade away into the familiarity of the world around us. Instead, these projects transform the ordinary into the extraordinary, acknowledging that the everyday is a participatory realm where design is essentially incomplete, knowing that people will eventually inhabit and adapt what is given. Collectively, these works are meant to challenge some basic tenets of design accepted in both public perception and professional preconceptions. [Figs. 3.2–3.6]

Fig. 3.2: Gijs Bakker, Peepshow wallpaper for Droog.
Photographer: Gerard van Hees

Fig. 3.3: Maurice Scheltens, Tableau tablecloth for Droog.
Photographer: Droog

Fig. 3.4: Tejo Remy, Rag chair for Droog.

Photographer: Gerard van Hees

Fig. 3.5: 85 Rody Graumans, Lamps for Droog.

Photographer: Gerard van Hees

Fig. 3.6: Joris Laarman, Heat wave electric radiator for Droog.

Photographer: Gerard van Hees

Notes

* The phenomenal and concrete are complimentary terms used by Christian Norberg-Schulz in his essay "The Phenomenology of Place," *Architectural Association Quarterly* 8, no. 4 (1976): 3–10. The concrete specifically applies to the physical environment as opposed to the less tangible phenomenal.

1 B. Joseph Pine II and James H. Gilmore, "Welcome to the Experience Economy," in *Harvard Business Review* (July–August 1998): 97–105.

2 Product designer Karim Rashid claims to have coined the term "blobjects." See his essay "Blobism" in *Karim Rashid: I Want to Change the World* (New York: Universe, 2001). For a discussion of "blobitecture," and other aspects of digitally produced architecture, see *Architecture* 89, no. 9 (September 2000).

3 Georges Perec, "Approaches to What?," in *Species of Spaces and Other Pieces,* ed. John Sturrock (London: Penguin Books, 1997), 210.

4 Henri Lefebvre, *The Production of Space,* trans. Donald Nicholson-Smith (Oxford: Blackwell, 1991), 145.

5 Ibid.

6 Perec, 210.

7 Ibid.

8 Perec, 31.

9 Robert Venturi, Denise Scott Brown, and Steven Izenour, *Learning from Las Vegas* (Cambridge, Massachusetts: The MIT Press, 1972). Bernard Rudofsky, *Architecture without Architects: An Introduction to Non-Pedigreed Architecture* (New York: The Museum of Modern Art, 1964).

10 Steven Harris, "Everyday Architecture" in *Architecture of the Everyday,* eds. Steven Harris and Deborah Berke (New York: Princeton Architectural Press, 1997), 1–8.

11 Deborah Berke, "Thoughts on the Everyday" in *Architecture of the Everyday*, 222–226.

12 For an account of Droog Design, see *Droog Design: Spirit of the Nineties,* eds. Renny Ramakers and Gijs Bakker (Rotterdam: 010 Publishers, 1998).

13 See Ed van Hinte, ed., *Eternally Yours: Visions on Product Endurance* (Rotterdam: 010 Publishers, 1997) for discussions and strategies surrounding issues of product obsolescence and life cycle; and Conny Bakker and Ed van Hinte, eds., *Trespassers: Inspirations for Eco-Efficient Design* (Rotterdam: 010 Publishers, 1999) for a more lighthearted approach to sustainable design.

The Rules of Her Game:
A-Z at Work and Play

Trevor Smith

INTRODUCTION

Layer by layer, designer Andrea Zittel peels away objects and surfaces that surround us and views them under a lens that reveals subtle qualities often passive in design strategies. Her work is not confined to one layer or medium but extends to include fashion, interiors, and architecture. Zittel begins with these disciplines to restructure and fabricate objects based on her observations about how the domestic realm is occupied. Her unique ability to fully embed herself within her work unites work and life. Every component of her lifestyle is designed in a contemporary version of Gesamtkunstwerk. *This collection of her work parallels lifestyle designs commonly used by interior designers inclusive of logos and advertisements. Trevor Smith's essay provides an overview of Zittel's work that reveals its embedded humor which comments on marketing lifestyles.*

Smith's essay emphasizes Zittel's use of the body and its influence on the design of her textiles, clothing, and portable living containers. An identity based on fabrication, including craft, mass production, and customization, emerges from these designs. Her fabrication-based strategies allow for varying degrees of personalization to be expressed in her work; similar to interior designs that go through cycles of styles that emphasize forms of fabrication. The degree of personalization reached in Zittel's work confronts larger social issues like the waste of consumerism. Her ability to control the smallest detail opens up the opportunity to respond to these issues through re-use and repair.

A final theme that surfaces in Zittel's work is anonymity. In one example, she culls through her interior, masking consumer icons, logos, and book titles to achieve a level of neutrality. The anonymous interior fosters intimacy: to identify specific books, for example, she must know their weight and size. The masking of things gives her interiors a new identity: fresh, uncluttered, and organized. At a larger scale, Zittel distinguishes between customized interiors and anonymous exteriors, best seen in her A-Z Escape Vehicles. *The vehicles, intended for retreat, are customized to accommodate her clients'*

Originally appeared in *Andrea Zittel: Critical Space*, edited by Paola Morsiani and Trevor Smith (Munich and New York: Prestel Verlag, 2005), 36–43.

fantasies. She is willing to use materials, no matter how artificial–faux rocks, for example—to privilege motifs. Her customization of vehicle interiors parallels what is commonplace in our domestic culture, a highly personalized interior embedded in an anonymous exterior architecture. This critique of material culture has developed over time, in multiple scales of Zittel's work as a contemporary artist.

———

> *I don't think that you are freer artistically in the desert than you are inside a room.*[1]
> —Robert Smithson, 1970

> *I have never been forced to accept compromises but I have willingly accepted constraints.*[2]
> —Charles Eames, 1969

OVER THE LAST fifteen years, Andrea Zittel has offered a timely and playful critique of the conflation of leisure and freedom in contemporary consumer culture. Her establishment of A-Z Administrative Services in 1991, followed by The A-Z in 1994 (now called A-Z East) and A-Z West in 2000 as a combination of home, studio, and presentation space, has been crucial to this endeavor. Zittel's creative engagement with the physical constraints and social situations at play in each of these sites has consistently evolved new developments in her work. While A-Z West is located on twenty-five acres adjacent to the Joshua Tree National Park in California, the East Coast manifestations, established in the inner-city environment of Williamsburg, Brooklyn, echoed the tradition of the home business or corner shop, a "pre 7-Eleven" quick stop where the owner's family would live above or behind the storefront. Such a model refuses the segregation of work and play so central to consumer marketing of leisure lifestyle as recompense for thankless and unrewarding work.

In 1989 Zittel moved from southern California to the East Coast to earn her master's degree at the Rhode Island School of Design in Providence and eventually to set up her first studio in New York City, renting space in the Fink building at the corner of Berry Street and Broadway on the south side of Williamsburg, Brooklyn, a neighborhood that would be her base of operations for the next decade. While Williamsburg today is a bustling inner-city neighborhood already at the other side of an arts-led recovery, in the early 1990s the local economy was in a recession, and New York's infrastructure was still only just shaking off the effects of the city's late 1970s near-bankruptcy. Although it is just one subway stop out of Manhattan,

Williamsburg was a post-industrial frontier, pockmarked with empty build-ings and boarded-up shops. Filled with underutilized industrial buildings, the neighborhood seemed to be a victim of urban decay, shifting demograph-ics, corporatism, and the franchising of American productivity.

Zittel recalls being "overwhelmed by the decay. In California every-thing had been all about progress and newness, but here in New York build-ings were being abandoned and rents were going down and nothing was being repaired."[3] One response to her shock at this state of affairs was to col-lect and repair badly damaged objects found lying discarded in the street. Most of the *Repair Work* (1991) began with objects damaged beyond any obvi-ous likelihood of restoration: a side table with two missing legs and no cross bracing, a statuette with its facial features completely worn away, or an ordi-nary drinking glass broken in several pieces. By lavishing attention on these most abject of discards, Zittel formulated a reproach to the ease with which society often casually discards objects with changes in style and fashion. Her repairs were minimal and pragmatic: for example, she replaced the missing table legs with unfinished pieces of wood, sawn to length and nailed in place without consideration for style or codes of craftsmanship. The comic visibil-ity of the repair made palpable the difference between the table's use value and its display value: while it had lost its stylistic gestalt, it was once again a supportive surface.

Like the *Repair Work,* which in effect inaugurated Zittel's engagement with the New York environment, one of her earliest projects at A-Z West was inspired by the problem of waste. A diary entry for Thursday, June 21, 2001, reads:

> Trash bags were piling up behind the house, so today I loaded them into the truck and drove to the landfill, which is in the middle of some of the most beautiful rock formations in the area. Whoever decided to turn that area into a dump had a sick sense of humor. Hauling everything away myself makes me realize how much I "consume" and also how much I seem to value visual stimulation over efficiency. I really love great pack-aging, but I wish that I could find a way to reconcile this with the need to be economical. For instance, if there were a way to turn that packaging and other waste into something beautiful and practical like furniture.[4]

The project that resulted after several experiments was *A-Z Paper Pulp Panel* (2002) in which Zittel used a papier-mâché technique to "farm" her household waste in *The Regenerating Field* (2002), a gridlike array of mold-ing trays set out in the desert in front of her home. The molds are made in various low-relief rectangular patterns, and varied materials can be added to the pulp paper to play with different looks for the decorative or architectural panels. Zittel's move to the desert was not unprecedented, art historically speaking. Donald Judd famously decamped from his five-story loft building in New York to Marfa, Texas, in early 1972. Judd's move represented, at least in part, an ideological refusal of the slipshod and ephemeral installation options for the presentation of contemporary art. As he put it in 1983, "If somewhere there were serious and permanent installations, the ephemeral exhibitions of the gallery and the awful environments of the work in public could be criticized and endured."[5] Zittel, on the other hand, described her move as more "logistical than ideological," a search for a place where she could remain in an urban dialogue but "where existence isn't quite so difficult and where more experimental artworks could actually happen."[6] If Judd chose Marfa because its isolation provided the stable environment necessary to produce his large-scale permanent installations, Zittel chose Joshua Tree because it was only relatively isolated. The population density is low, but on a good day it is only a three-hour drive from Los Angeles. It thus held the potential to develop a supportive community where she didn't have to "disappear from the face of the earth."[7]

Looking at Zittel's *sfnwvlei* (*Something for Nothing with Very Little Effort Involved*) gouaches, which document the production of the *A-Z Paper Pulp Panel*, it is possible to see her playing knowingly with the mythic tropes of homesteading and the heroic individualism that led an earlier generation of artists to the desert. Her self-representation echoes, even if obliquely, photographs of Robert Smithson walking on *Spiral Jetty* or Michael Heizer on his motorcycle. Posing in a desert landscape, she depicts her body or hands up close to the picture plane, at once monumentalizing her body and placing it within a vast landscape, with a far distant horizon line both echoed and flattened by parallel bands of color. While these drawings might appear to be a sly feminist retort to visual tropes of masculinity, it is instructive to look at these hallucinatory images of Zittel's back-to-the-earth, do-it-yourself activity in relation to her recent observation that Minimalism and Conceptualism emerged as a reaction against not only:

> the subjectivity of the Abstract Expressionists or the illusionism of spatial representation but also hallucinogenic-drug culture, grassroots political movements, and the era's newfound interest in Eastern religion, which opened new modes of experience and of reading the "self" in relationship to the greater whole.[8]

The exploration of forms of sociability—"the 'self' in relationship to the greater whole"—is central to Zittel's practice. From 1991, art and life, studio practice and public engagement, all commingled to facilitate a working process more closely modeled on workshop critique, design iteration, and prototyping than the traditional professional artistic cycle of long studio isolation and brief public exhibition. Each of the sites presented a very different set of constraints. From 1991 to 1993, A-Z Administrative Services occupied a small 200-square-foot shopfront on South 8th Street. In 1993 she moved to a large raw space on Union Street, and beginning in 1994, she occupied a three-story former boardinghouse at 150 Wythe Avenue. Since 2000 A-Z West has been located in the Mojave Desert just beyond Los Angeles' exurban sprawl.

Even as Zittel extended the visual vocabularies and design strategies of modernism to work with the unique constraints of each of these sites, the environments she created for herself operated in critical contrast to the separation of work and leisure privileged in modern consumer culture. Even if, for a brief moment at the height of the dot-com boom in the 1990s, such blending became the representative cliché of a new media company workspace, it remained the exception rather than the corporate rule. (As such, it was later held up as a sign of the folly and decadence that led to that market bubble's collapse.) Unlike dot-com offices, or even most home offices for that matter, Zittel's studios did not develop from a simple interest in engendering a pleasant and creative work environment. Describing her *A-Z Yard Yacht* (1998), later *A-Z Yard Yacht: Work Station*—a large recreational vehicle that she customized as a home office when she relocated to Los Angeles in 1997—she suggested that one of its most interesting qualities was that it inverted "the function of a recreational vehicle from leisuretime freedoms to labor-based freedoms. Rather than escaping labor, it became more interesting to think about ways to give it more meaning and use it as a means of pleasure."[9] [Figs. 3.7 + 3.8]

The *A-Z Six-Month Personal Uniform* that Zittel produced between 1991 and 1993 similarly used the language of labor—uniforms—to describe

Fig. 3.7: A-Z West, *A-Z Yard Yacht: Work Station*, 1998. Collection of Andy and Karen Stillpass.

Fig. 3.8: A-Z West, *A-Z Yard Yacht: Work Station*, 1998. Andrea Zittel.

Courtesy of Andrea Rosen Gallery, New York

Fig. 3.9: *A-Z Personal Panel Uniform*. Seven uniforms of various fabrics. Emanuel Hoffmann Foundation, permanent loan to the Öffentliche Kunstsammlung, Basel, Switzerland. Installation view, A-Z Uniforms 1991–2002, Andrea Rosen Gallery, New York, 2004. Courtesy of Andrea Rosen Gallery, New York

dresses that she produced to take care of all her clothing needs for a six-month period. [Fig. 3.9] For example, she described the *Spring/Summer 1991 Uniform* as "a simple sleeveless linen design that made an easy transition from an un-air-conditioned Brooklyn studio to a day job in a Soho gallery."[10] The skirt/pant combination for *Spring/Summer 1993* was inspired by the need to take visitors up a ladder to the chicken coop she was keeping on the roof. By contrast *Fall/Winter 1992-93* was:

> something of a fantasy dress mixing heavy leather suspenders and a tailored men's dress shirt with a full black taffeta skirt and a hidden petticoat. The dense petticoat was sewn from layers of wool jersey (for warmth) and black tulle. It was then edged with two shades of pale green satin ribbon and decorated all over with tiny green silk flowers.[11]

The idea of wearing a uniform every day for six months relieved Zittel of the time spent making clothing decisions or shopping for fashions. And the monotony of wearing the same dress each day was relieved by "dreaming up the next season's design."[12]

At A-Z East, Zittel took this drive to customize and produce to the point that it was extremely rare to find a corporate logo anywhere on the premises. Not only did she customize the early Apple Mac computer with black spray paint, but she covered the spines of all the books with green buckram tape, and then shelved them by subject. With neither author names nor publisher logos visible, one could only locate books by familiarity with their subject, shape, and heft.

It is hard not to escape the echo of William Morris, one of the founders of the Arts and Crafts Movement in England in the nineteenth century, in Zittel's individual customizations and her celebration of work-based freedoms. Where Morris posited a celebration of craftsmanship and the handmade as a challenge to the banalities of industrial production, Zittel's do-it-yourself approach to production, and her creation and experimentation with her own rules, offers a challenge to the passivity of consumer culture. Yet where Morris dreamed of a socialist utopia where creativity would be unleashed through the abolition of alienated labor and through democratic control of the means of production, Zittel is more ambivalent about collectivity, proposing instead a socially responsive self-awareness where each person examines "his own talents and options, and then based on these begins to invent new models or roles to fulfill his or her needs."[13] Strategically positioning herself in opposition to the tired cliché of the artist as bohemian rule-breaker, Zittel proposed instead that:

> the formation of rules is more "creative" than the destruction of them. Their creation demands a higher level of reasoning and the drawing of connections between cause and effect. The best rules are never stable or permanent, and they evolve naturally according to context or need. I like to make rules—but I don't really like to impose rules on other people. I guess that is why I am always making rules for myself.[14]

In this regard it is useful to briefly consider Zittel's work in relation to her contemporary Joep van Lieshout, who operates Atelier Van Lieshout—a Rotterdam-based art, architecture, and design collective that develops architectural and design forms examining the dynamics of individual desire in social situations, *Sportopia* (2002) is a sculpture that functions as a primitive exercise studio, bed, and bar, while his most recent installation, *The Technocrat* (2004), feeds, waters, and sleeps 1,000 people for the primary purpose of producing biogas. Many of his sculptures and drawings depict individuals engaged in orgiastic or anarchistic acts that are clear provocations of social conventions. Van Lieshout purposefully flaunts rules of social control—going so far as to declare his studio compound a free state at one point—to reveal the collective id repressed beneath the European social superego. As such his work has much in common with J. G. Ballard's hallucinatory fictions of the near future. While Ballard's writings were an early influence on Zittel, her work evolved in another direction. Unlike Van Lieshout, she designs rules for herself, rather than flaunting society's mandates, in an effort to subvert the conformity produced by the passive consumption of a branded lifestyle in American culture.

While Zittel's use of her initials to name A-Z East and A-Z West could be prosaically understood as a shorthand version of the artist's signature, it is more interesting to consider it as a branding strategy. Beginning as A-Z

Administrative Apparel briefly, which became A-Z Administrative Services in 1991, Zittel's corporate guise was initially a humorous jest. While she was working on her *Breeding Works* (1991–93) however, Zittel's adopted corporate identity lent her correspondence with animal breeders and trainers a form of legitimation that an emerging artist with a "southern California mall-girl accent"[15] simply couldn't muster. Curiously, "A-Z Administrative Services" is not at all suggestive of contemporary corporations, services, and franchises with their wishful evocations of lifestyle and well-being in their names—Starbucks, Target, Blockbuster. Instead the A-Z brand evokes the kinds of small companies from the 1950s and 1960s that engendered customer confidence through the projection of encyclopedic competence—Acme, Paragon, Universal, and so on. As a brand, A-Z Administrative Services evokes the world of the great Chuck Jones Roadrunner and Coyote cartoons in which the Coyote, perched by the side of the road on some distant desert mesa, would take delivery of some implausible scheme from a company whose name always began with ACME.

By today's standards such companies were small operations, sometimes even home businesses; the universalist confidence writ large in their brand names belied their small scale and local nature. Squeezed out by shrinking profit margins and competition from franchise operations as well as the globalization of markets, they were the types of companies that had closed up shop in Williamsburg and elsewhere by the early 1990s, just as Zittel's was taking shape. In an important group of drawings on vellum from the early 1990s, Zittel reproduced animal breeding advertisements drawn from small community newspapers and specialist magazines. As direct appropriations from advertisements, these drawings are singular in her oeuvre, suggestive not only of the parallels she was making at the time between the selection of aesthetic traits through breeding and the art world's promotion of particular movements and aesthetic values, but also of the fact that many such small-scale businesses were themselves becoming endangered species.

The early *Breeding Works* evolved out of Zittel's interest in how the development of domestic breeds corresponded to "the breakdown of traditional class structure in humans. In the late 1800s breeds in animals like dogs were 'designed' possibly as a way to try and create a stable and hierarchical social system which the owners of the animals could identify with."[16] While Zittel worked early on with houseflies and quails, chickens quickly became her species of choice, particularly Bantams. She spoke of how chickens made "perfect sense as a choice of art material": they "hatch from eggs so there is complete authorship of the 'creation,'" and they "have an amazing array of genetic possibilities; they possess many types of physical variations with which to work with." She added, "Bantams are 'miniature' chickens used for 'decoration and for exhibition.'"[17] Moving from aesthetic to social considerations, it is likely that the fact that chickens are subject to industrial production was also significant. Her *Single-Egg Incubator* (1991), for example, establishes an empathetic, quasi-parental relationship to a single egg, something in sharp and deliberate contrast to the factory incubators designed to anonymously hatch thousands of eggs at a time.

Working specifically with breeder chickens in *A-Z Breeding Unit for Reassigning Flight* (1993), Zittel set up a series of four compartments in the window of the New Museum of Contemporary Art in New York. Designed to evolve the capacity of flight back into these birds, each compartment featured nests of different heights, arranged such that only eggs from the highest nest would be channeled into the incubator in the next compartment, where the chicks would:

> hatch, grow up, and then once again be presented with nests of different heights. The chickens could only reach each successive breeding compartment by higher and higher passages. The idea was to bring this recessive gene forward through subsequent generations and so return this bird to flight.[18]

With the *A-Z Breeding Unit for Averaging Eight Breeds* (1993), Zittel turned her attention not to bringing recessive genes forward but to reversing evolution to reinstate a perfectly average bird. This unit takes the ironic form of an upside-down pyramid, inverting the usual progression of breeding refinement. At the top are eight hutches for eight separate breeds that have been bred to draw out highly unusual recessive traits—long silky black feathers or a mottled black-and-white coloring or an enormous comb, and so on. At each successive layer down, the hutches halve in number as the chickens crossbreed. Finally at the bottom, the new breed of chicken emerges whose carefully cultivated recessive genes have once again been submerged.

Zittel carried out her early breeding experiments at the South 8th Street shopfront, where she also began to produce works that dealt productively with the physical constraints of her space: two 100-square-foot rooms with an office in front and private space in back. Although they came slightly later and depict an apartment as opposed to a shopfront space, her *Domestic Models A-E* (1993) test out alternative propositions to subdividing a small space or arranging furniture heights, based on activity, privacy, hygiene, and so on. While such schema address basic human needs, the rationales and functional combinations are often surprising. Model D reads, "Bed and bath are secluded in back as private areas. Kitchen and office are in front as public area," while Model E makes an alternative proposition, reading, "Bed and office are in front as areas associated with the mind. Kitchen and bath in back for processing the body."

Fig. 3.10: *A-Z Management and Maintenance Unit, Model 003*, 1992. Collection of
Andrea Rosen, New York. Courtesy of Andrea Rosen Gallery, New York

Thinking through these kinds of basic needs led Zittel to produce one
of her first signature works: the *A-Z Management and Maintenance Unit,
Model 003* (1992). [Fig. 3.10] Its square channel metal frame and birch plywood
construction evokes the look of mid-century modernism, but unlike one of
Charles and Ray Eames's 1950 Storage Units (ESU), which primarily store
and display objects and books, Zittel's unit had to facilitate all the aspects
of living. Within an extremely constrained footprint of sixty square feet, she
attempted:

> to satisfy the often conflicting needs of security, stability, freedom and
> autonomy. Owning a *Living Unit* created the security and permanence
> of a home which could then be set up inside of homes that other peo-
> ple owned. It provided freedom because whenever the owner wanted to
> move they could collapse it and move the unit to a new location.[19]

When Zittel moved from the small shopfront to a large industrial space
in 1993, the constraints that she was productively channeling in the *A-Z
Management and Maintenance Unit* shifted dramatically. Where previously
the small volume of space was the limitation, here it became the challenges
of a very large space that was impossible to heat, cool, and keep clean. This
new environment gave birth to a series of works that were exhibited in the
Purity exhibition in 1993. These include cabinets that Zittel called *Prototype
for A-Z Warm Chamber* and *Prototype for A-Z Cool Chamber* (both 1993).

These cabinets are big enough for one person to sit in comfortably and either cool off with an air conditioner or warm up under the heat of a light bulb. *Prototype for A-Z Cleansing Chamber* (1993) combines all cleaning functions, from bathing to washing dishes, in a single unit.

While Zittel developed these works in relation to very real needs, her engagement with functionalism is clearly leavened with a sense of humor. *A-Z Body Processing Unit* (1993), another *Purity* work, functions as both kitchen and toilet, and it packs down into a compact and elegant carrying case. Her dry wit comes through in the description:

> although the kitchen and the bathroom are similar to each other, traditional architecture always segregates them in the home. It always seemed that it would be more convenient to create an integrated but well organized hygienic system: the *A-Z Body Processing Unit.* The intake functions are on the top, and the outtake functions are on the bottom.[20]

Another slyly subversive group of works is her *A-Z Carpet Furniture* (1992-93). Inspired by a neighbor who was also living in a very small space, but one without furniture, Zittel produced carpets that were in fact 1:1 scale representations of standard furniture arrangements—initially a living room and later a bedroom and dining room. With their rectangular forms and their rectilinear and angular arrangements, the furniture patterns evoke the visual vocabulary of Russian Constructivism and, more generally speaking, early twentieth-century modernism. [Fig. 3.11] Zittel has wittily proposed that you could use these flat carpets as furniture, but that they would also look elegant hanging on a wall if you needed to move the "furniture" out of the way.[21]

 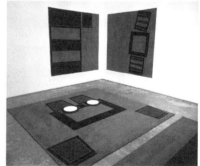

Fig. 3.11: *My Neighbor Charles with His A-Z Carpet Furniture*, 1999. Collection of Martha Moriarty, Madrid. Fig. 3.12: *A-Z Carpet Furniture* (Dining Room Table with Extra Seating), 1993. Collection of Thomas Solomon, Los Angeles. *A-Z Carpet Furniture* (Table with Two Chairs), 1993. *A-Z Carpet Furniture* (Twin Bed with Night Stand), 1993. Collection of Allison and Thomas Daniel, Honolulu. Installation view from Christopher Grimes Gallery, Santa Monica, California, 1993. Images courtesy of Andrea Rosen Gallery, New York.

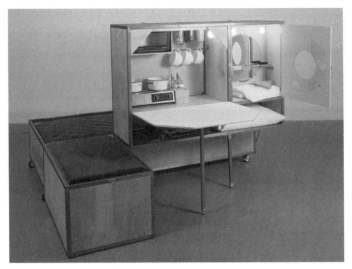

Fig. 3.13: *A-Z 1994 Living Unit*, view of open unit, 1994. Collection of Patrizia Sandretto Re Rebaudengo, Turin, Italy. Courtesy of Andrea Rosen Gallery, New York

[Fig. 3.12] Laid on the floor, the carpets provide a measure of comfort while parodying the idea of decor. Hanging on the wall in a more or less empty room, they also suggest a domestic travesty of the corporate practice of hanging soft, textured modernist tapestries in the lobbies of 1950s and 1960s skyscrapers.

If *A-Z Carpet Furniture* parodies domestic comforts, five years later *A-Z Raugh Furniture* (1998) would refuse domestic space entirely. A series of rock formations carved from high-density foam, *Raugh Furniture* appears more Neolithic than neo-modern. In spite of first appearances, this work continues Zittel's questioning of modernist assumptions—in this instance the conflation of modern design with democracy and ergonomic comfort. Zittel recalled anthropological studies that indicate chairs evolved as a means of elevating certain individuals in a social hierarchy and not as the most comfortable seating position for the body.[22] Both *A-Z Carpet Furniture* and *A-Z Raugh Furniture* refuse such hierarchies by positioning users on the ground where they are, at least metaphorically, equal.

If *A-Z Carpet Furniture* and *A-Z Raugh Furniture* propose a form of democratic primitivism, Zittel's egalitarian tendencies are based on valuing ways in which individuals make up their own rules and fantasies as to how they might interact with broader society. One way in which she explores this practice has been to invite purchasers to individually customize her works. Following the *A-Z Management and Maintenance Unit, Model 003*, which expressed her desire to turn her "limitations into luxuries," she produced a smaller portable exemplar, the first *A-Z 1993 Living Unit*. Closed, it is about

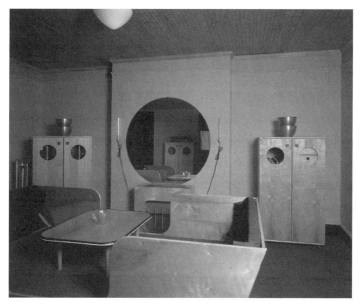

Fig. 3.14: Four *A-Z Chamber Pots*, two *A-Z Cabinets*, *A-Z Warmth Unit*, *A-Z Sofa*, and *A-Z Cover* in *A-Z Comfort Room*, A-Z East, 1998. Courtesy of Andrea Rosen Gallery, New York

the size of a large shipping trunk, but when it is opened, it provides a wardrobe, desk and filing space, and cooking facilities. A folding campstool for sitting and a cot for sleeping can also be stored in the unit. In 1994, the same year that she moved to A-Z East, she devised a slightly larger, more commodious version, the *A-Z 1994 Living Unit,* and invited purchasers of the work to customize it according to their tastes and needs. [Fig. 3.13]

This social aspect of her work was amplified by the incarnation of A-Z East in a converted, three-story former boardinghouse at 150 Wythe Avenue. Of all the locations in Williamsburg where Zittel worked, this was the longest lasting and the site of her most playful social experiments and events. As if to underline these experiments' engagement with consumerism and lifestyle questions, Zittel used the building's storefront as the *A-Z Personal Presentation Room*, where she would present her latest projects and ideas. This room also was the site of loosely themed cocktail parties that she hosted with different artists and friends. During this period she also produced thirteen issues of the *A-Z Personal Profiles Newsletter*, approximately one every month.

While the renovation of the building required a great deal of work, in this more commodious environment, Zittel focused on the ideals and constraints of comfort. In the upstairs *A-Z Comfort Room*, many different furniture sculptures such as the *A-Z Ottoman Furniture* (1994), *A-Z Fled* (1994), *A-Z Pit Bed* (1995), *A-Z Platform Bed* (1995), and *A-Z Bofa* (1996) were prototyped and tested. [Fig. 3.14] Like the *A-Z 1994 Living Unit,* the *A-Z Comfort Unit* (1994) was developed to playfully explore individual fantasies of domestic comforts.

This creative negotiation with the purchasers of her work had already been going on for some time, involving other works such as the *A-Z Jon Tower Life Improvement Project* (1991-92) or the 1993 *A-Z Apparel Commissions,* including *A-Z Uniform for Andy Stillpass* and *A-Z Collector's Coat for Frank Kolodny.* While these earlier projects were about developing a functional product based on the client's needs and desires, the *Living Unit* and *Comfort Unit* were vehicles to test and even contradict her hypotheses and rules for living. Yet because these works were purchased as an "Andrea Zittel" and because she proposed the units as functional objects, Zittel's rules were not subverted or questioned as often as she may have wished.

It was this desire for greater latitude of interpretation that led to the development of the *A-Z Escape Vehicle* (1996, pp. 200-205) in which Zittel shifted ground from the fantasy of function to the function of fantasy. The *Escape Vehicle* is a small, metal-clad trailer structure whose interior can be customized at the whim of the purchaser. [Figs. 3.15 + 16] Like the earlier *Living Unit,* the *Escape Vehicle* operates within an extremely constrained space. At this time Zittel was theorizing her idea that freedom is often exercised through constraint. In the "Limited Universe" issue of her *A-Z Personal Profiles Newsletter* in November 1996 she wrote:

Fig. 3.15 + 16: 1996, *A-Z Escape Vehicle* owned and customized by Dean Valentine.
Collection of Dean Valentine and Amy Adelson, Los Angeles. Courtesy of Andrea Rosen Gallery, New York

Why is it that you find it so much easier to create a totally fantastic environment for yourself in the tiny capsule-like confines of the *EV [Escape Vehicle]*? We feel it is because in some ways limitations actually *liberate* you. Ultimately, it is within defined boundaries that make it easier for us to let go and be creative. We bet that if we gave you an entire room in which to construct your fantasy you would feel pretty overwhelmed. On the other hand, the little capsule-like space of the EV presents one with an intimate and malleable little universe. It is within the security and intimacy created by this structure that many of us feel most comfortable in extending our fantasies to their most exquisite realizations.[23]

Even in the expansive acreage of A-Z West, the recent *A-Z Wagon Station* (2002–present) continues Zittel's hypothesis of the freedom of the intimate universe. The prospect of customizing these units, this time undertaken by friends of the artist, seems to present a greater variety of challenges to Zittel's philosophy of invented constraints. Eighteen simple rectangular structures—approximately six feet long, four feet high, and four feet wide—with a curved hatch at the front, sit in the landscape around A-Z West, each customized by a different person. Hal McFeely's is rustic, while Russell Whitten's draws on the culture of car customization. Jonas Hauptman applied monster truck and camper expansion principles to build out from the original *A-Z Wagon Station* chassis to create a structure that has ended up looking more like the Apollo Lunar Landing Module.

If Zittel's early *A-Z Management and Maintenance Unit, Model 003* stands as an extension of modernism's ironic inversion of industrial materials and luxury, later works such as the *A-Z Cellular Compartment Units* (2001) operate as a parody of functional regimentation in suburban home design: an accumulation of ten cabins, four by four by eight feet, fits into an overall area about the size of a large studio apartment, each unit customized around a single unique function—eating, sleeping, reading, and so on. While the tone and subject of Zittel's art shifts in these two signal works between the poles of constrained urban apartment and exurban sprawl, her critique of consumerism and its effect on our culture and environment has remained consistent. That she leavens her critique with humor and playfulness does not diminish her seriousness. Writing a history of seventeenth-century Dutch painting, an art form ascendant at the birthplace of the stock market, Max J. Friedlander noted:

To play is nothing but the imitative substitution of a pleasurable, superfluous and voluntary action for a serious, necessary, imperative and difficult one. At the cradle of play as well as of artistic activity there stood leisure, tedium entailed by increased spiritual mobility, a horror vacui, the need of letting forms no longer imprisoned move freely, of filling empty time with sequences of notes, empty space with sequences of form.[24]

Zittel's work suggests that consumer culture's promise of leisure-time freedom is inadequate and comes at too heavy a price. Part-time emancipation is no emancipation at all. Instead we each might need to look to our very real social and physical constraints to create new rules for our game: at work and at play.

Notes

1   Robert Smithson, interview with Robert Smithson, Michael Heizer, and Dennis Oppenheim, *Avalanche* (1970), found in Andrea Zittel notebooks.

2   Charles Eames, "What Is Design?" in John Neuhart, Marilyn Neuhart, and Ray Eames, *Eames Design: The Work of the Office of Charles and Ray Eames* (New York: Harry N. Abrams, 1989), p. 15.

3   Andrea Zittel, quoted in Stefano Basilico, "Andrea Zittel," *Bomb,* Spring 2001, p.72.

4   Andrea Zittel, *Diary: Andrea Zittel,* Diary, ed. Simona Vendrame, no. #01 (Milan: Tema Celeste Editions, 2002), p. 14.

5   Donald Judd, "On Installation," in *Donald Judd: Complete Writings 1975–1986* (Eindhoven, Netherlands: Van Abbemuseum, 1987), p. 20.

6   Zittel, quoted in Basilico, p. 76.

7   Zittel, quoted in Basilico, p. 76.

8   Andrea Zittel, "Shabby Clique," *Artforum,* Summer 2004, p. 211.

9   Andrea Zittel, quoted in Zdenek Felix, ed., *Andrea Zittel-Personal Programs* (Ostfildern-Ruit, Germany: Hatje Cantz Verlag, 2000), p. 58.

10   Andrea Zittel, www.zittel.org.

11   Zittel, www.zittel.org.

12   Zittel, *Diary: Andrea Zittel,* p. 76.

13   Zittel, quoted in Basilico, p. 76.

14   Zittel, *Diary: Andrea Zittel,* p. 33.

15   Zittel, quoted in Basilico, p. 72.

16   Zittel, www.zittel.org.

17   Zittel, www.zittel.org, and p. 149 in this book.

18   Zittel, www.zittel.org.

19   Zittel, quoted in Felix, p. 19.

20   Zittel, www.zittel.org.

21   Zittel, quoted in Felix, p. 32.

22   Zittel, www.zittel.org.

23   *A–Z Personal Profiles Newsletter #3, November* 1996, "Limited Universe" issue.

24   Max J. Friedlander, *On Art and Connoisseurship* (Oxford: Bruno Cassirer, 1942), p. 42.

For the Love of Things

Louise Schouwenberg

INTRODUCTION

The interior is a constantly changing realm. Its objects have long or short life spans, from custom-built furniture meant for years of use to the flowers in a vase that live only a handful of days. The quick disposal of objects is the focus of Louise Schouwenberg's essay on the material and technological integration within objects. Interfacing with objects and the attachment we form with them affects our behaviors, concepts that Schouwenberg sees in Proust's writings on teapots and other domestic objects in Remembrance of Things Past. *Her inquiry emphasizes materiality, fabrication, and use—and to what degree design affects how people form sensate and emotional attachments to objects.*

For Proust, an object that collected marks over time, whether a scratch or patina, took on the role of a container representing the past, able to hold memories. The objects of his interest aged well because of the attention to materials and handcrafting, gaining a sense of proprietary ownership with use. As a result, people kept them. In contrast, contemporary objects introduce a questionable level of commitment, because of how easily they are replaced. Schouwenberg demonstrates that the speed of technological change is reflected in the objects people consume, and the desire to stay current has made a culture that readily disposes of things. Schouwenberg proposes a subtle and readily available solution to sustainability that is accessible to all: a commitment to possessions.

Looking at the aesthetics unleashed by the integration of technology (most notably, a plastic aesthetic), reveals that these new materials do not necessarily age well. Technology has affected not only the fabrication of objects but also our lifestyle. Our dependency on technology to make us mobile and fast reinforces our noncommitment to objects, and people no longer need "context-bound objects."

Originally appeared in *Hella Jongerius* (London and New York: Phaidon, 2003).

Interiors that integrate technology have thinned out their realm as manipulable space. Bulky objects have altered their appearance, such as flat-screen televisions. Cords that plug into utility lines gave way to streaming lines of wireless connections. The interior registers these revolutionary changes of technological integration, forming identities with them.

———

MY BRAND NEW mobile phone looks great, nestles snugly in the hand, has a limitless repertoire of polyphonic ringing tones and color display effects, and I can phone people with it just like I could with the last one. By the time I had transferred my phone book and downloaded the life-management tools to the new phone, the old one had practically vanished from my conscious universe.

The trouble with today's useful articles is that they hardly have a chance to worm their way into our lives before it's time to replace them with a new, improved version. What most of these products have in common is a short life span, and none of us expects otherwise. Another thing they share is the way they shamelessly scream for attention, without denying their own complete replaceability. How different things seemed not even a hundred years ago:

> When I awoke like this, and my mind struggled in an unsuccessful attempt to discover where I was, everything would be moving round me through the darkness, things, places, years. My body, still too heavy with sleep to move, would make an effort to construe the form, piece together and to give a name to the house in which it must be living. Its memory, the composite memory of its ribs, knees, and shoulder-blades offered it a whole series of rooms in which it had at one time or another slept: while the unseen walls kept changing, adapting themselves to the shape of each successive room that it remembered, whirling madly through the darkness....My body, the side upon which I was lying, loyally preserving from the past an impression which my mind should never have forgotten, brought back before my eyes the glimmering flame of the night-light in its bowl of Bohemian glass, shaped like an urn and hung by chains from the ceiling, and the chimney-piece of Siena marble in my bedroom at Combray, in my great-aunt's house, in those far-distant days which, at the moment of waking, seemed present without being clearly defined. (Marcel Proust, *Á la recherche u temps perdu*, 1913)

Marcel Proust sought time lost and rediscovered it in trivial, everyday useful objects. Memories of personal experiences were considered in his time, the early twentieth century, as invaluable components of the personality, and these memories seemed intimately connected with the objects with which one surrounded oneself. Functional things, which we normally assume to play no significant role apart from their functionality, were expected to absorb, as it were, one's personal secrets. They were not things one would simply dispose of, for they were a means of access to tender feelings that were at risk of disappearing forever into the mists of memory.

The examples Proust gives sound dated in several respects. Their equivalents of a century later not only look different, but also are no longer designed to have a long, secluded existence—not even in memory. There are several causes for this, among them the increased mobility that leaves us less scope for cherishing context-bound objects, and the dazzling pace of technological innovation, which follows a logic entirely its own. Now, in 2003, do we still long for useful objects that act as carriers for our cherished personal experiences?

The importance of a sensory contact with the world of concrete, tangible things is brilliantly expressed by the philosopher Maurice Merleau-Ponty in *Phénoménologie de la Perception* (1945). He argues that for centuries we have been relying entirely on our vaunted superior rational powers, while rationality is itself inconceivable outside our own physical realm. He therefore identifies the most important human mode of perception as "*Être-au-monde*," or "being in the world." We accord purpose and meaning to the world around us through our bodies. Before we can give a name at a conscious level to what we see, to our perceptions, we have already accumulated by purely somatic means knowledge about space, about the objects in it, and about our relation to those objects. This implies that we may expect things to have properties that make it both possible and worthwhile for us to attach experiences and meanings to them. The commonplace objects of the time of Proust and Merleau-Ponty give rise to different connotations than do the commonplace things of our own day. The night-light in its Bohemian glass and the Siena-marble chimneypiece have their equivalents in the Philippe Starck chairs, the Nokia mobile phone, and the Apple notebook computer.

Many contemporary utilitarian objects are technical in character. They often give us access to experiences that lie far beyond our bodily horizon. But however far these virtual journeys may range, my body remains immobile in the chair facing the computer screen. The mobile phone may well ignore my physical limitations, but I have to hold it in my hand. Consciously or unconsciously, I know at a physical level how the chair feels under me, I recognize the boundary between the computer screen and the background to it, and I know how the mouse slides over the mouse pad until it encounters a sudden resistance at the edge. My perception of the world, whether physical or virtual, is largely dependant on my physical "being in the world."

Designers naturally take the physical desires of future users into account at an early stage of the design process. This produces much user-friendliness in the outcome, ranging from ergonomically correct chairs to incredibly miniaturized electronics, from high-speed food processors to multiaction beds. Things match up seamlessly with the presumed wishes of today's consumer. But does the consumer still know what that the consumer really wants? Is a pure, personal, sensory contact with the world still a crucial determinant of meaning?

Functional Object or Consumer Good?

While furniture and table china were made with much love and precision in Proust's time, the bond between production and the object has been completely sundered in our own. With today's products the much lower cost of the manufacturing process no longer allows us a peek behind the scenes; indeed, those scenes may be far away, somewhere in Taiwan or India. While manufactured goods once had—and were expected to have—a long life-span, those that pervade our modern life aspire neither to a past nor to a future. Their ephemeral nature has even become an important determinant of their quality. This applies above all, of course, to technical gadgets that do not stem from archetypal examples and are subject to a breathtakingly fast aging process. Within the technological universe, terms such as *obsolescence* and *innovation* are magic words that are seldom examined with any critical distance. Yet the same short life and compulsive renewal has infected classes of objects for which ephemerality is anything but an inherent quality. We not only replace a computer that still works perfectly well with the latest model, but we just as readily dispense with our furniture and crockery in favor of new goods.

While a more or less direct relation between the article and its use, between the production process and value, between quality and ticket price, was normal in a preindustrial society, functional objects have, since the latter years of the twentieth century, represented merely consumption values within a complex code system of mass consumption. The philosopher Jean Baudrillard wrote in 1981 about utilitarian objects having a symbolic value that has come to exceed both their use value and their exchange value. He considers these objects to function within an all-dominating consumption system as coded signs we use to distinguish ourselves from others. Paradoxically, this makes us resemble one another to a remarkable degree; we no longer distinguish ourselves by our character but by our possessions. The consequences are fairly predictable: The contemporary consumer is completely open to the manipulation of his or her wishes by external forces. The power of the advertising message is considerable. Clear illustrations include the mobile phone, which has elevated telephoning from a means to a goal in its own right, and the timesaving food processor, which raises but does not answer the question of why we want to shave minutes off a relaxing activity like cooking. It is not the function or the timesaving that matters, but the promise; it is not the use but the status we gain—the sex appeal, happiness, and individuality—the proof that we are up there with the latest trends. In a classless world without conventional status symbols, consumer products prove we are not outsiders. In a throwaway society, we so warmly embrace the idea of being seduced by inflated promises that we find ourselves disillusioned by the actual products and must then go in search of new promises.

The value we ascribe to most goods that are programmed for disposability is, of course, a value which is universal and which is dictated by the consumer society. These products are not good vehicles for the purely personal connotations of love, belonging, or even betrayal.

Consumer Object or Work of Art?

Proust discovered the "stories" embedded in everyday artifacts that reach further than the objects themselves. However, a significance beyond the physical product is traditionally more the preserve of art. We expect works of art, whether in traditional forms such as painting and sculpture or in more evanescent media, to give us sensory access to deeper layers and meanings. In 1936, for example, Meret Oppenheim covered a cup and saucer with fur. The resulting object evokes a wide range of associations: with tea sets, with animals, with fur-coated ladies sipping tea, and with sexuality, with Freudian projection or fetishistic pleasures. Sixty years later, Tracey Emin embroidered colorful quilts with disturbing texts in a work that confronts the complacent museum visitor with his own banal contemplations. Intriguing meanings have taken possession of commonplace utilitarian objects in the work of both artists. But designers of useful objects have never had the same degree of freedom. They can tell a story but must do so within the bounds of functionality. This restricts any story that may be embodied and may also restrict the impact of the eventual object. That functionality can nonetheless be an extremely interesting constraint is convincingly illustrated by the passage from Proust. In the preindustrial society within which his objects existed, it was not difficult to reconcile their functions with "stories" because the objects had labor-intensive production histories, because they were exclusive and expensive, and because they were scarce products designed for a long useful life span. As reliable, aesthetically approved artifacts, they effaced themselves, as it were; their usefulness made them almost invisible, but they stayed with us for a long time. The result was that they evolved unnoticed into carriers of intense personal experiences. With the rise of the consumer society, not only did the durable value of the utilitarian objects disappear, but the story we can link to them became short-lived and general. At the same time, these same objects refuse to veil themselves with their short-lived usefulness but screamingly draw attention to their illusory character. We have surrounded ourselves with products, objects, stuff, and attention-demanding things that have no significant impact on our manner of being.

Designer Products

The contemporary design world has in fact emerged from the consumer system. The success it enjoyed by the late twentieth century not only related to the area of functionality but also reached beyond this "natural" frontier. Ephemeral designer products that comply fully with the rules of the consumer system have since then not only been on sale on every street corner, but their more successful representatives flaunt themselves on pedestals in whitewashed museums and galleries, as though they were autonomous works of art. Several decades later, we can draw a balance. The world is flooded with interchangeable throwaway articles of contemporary design that populate not only the domestic interior magazines and TV programs but also our private and public spaces. At the other end of the spectrum, in the vanguard of the design world, interesting designs emerge, but even before their themes are well and truly crystallized, shameless copies which manage to imitate only the superficial appearance of their better predecessors start appearing on the market. The design rip-offs sully the image of the field, but they are still the best money-spinners. The consumer system has clearly triumphed. But is the victory final? Or will the future bring a more meaningful attitude toward the concrete things of the world? Not only does the design world call for products with more character—more soul, even—but the experienced consumer also is no longer satisfied with empty promises.

Where, then, is the soul that people seek? How can the human longing for immaterial qualities, for sensory experiences that give rise to meaning, be met? By things. By direct physical contact with concrete, tangible things. That is how we give purpose and meaning to the world. We are fond of things, especially of things that are capable of being cherished and of absorbing secrets. There is no need to turn back the clock for that. Most utilitarian goods serve a temporary purpose and give temporary satisfaction; this is certainly true for technical products, by their very nature. But the shortness of useful life cannot be an alibi for a lack of significance—even ephemerality can make some claim to deeper layers. Understandably, the design avant-garde has ventured into the territory of visual art, although it cannot be justified in seeking its primary platform there. The impact of designer products lies primarily in the area of functionality, where everyday objects are eminently capable of surprising us with a sudden sea of experiences and

Fig. 3.17: Shippo Plates, 2007. Material: Copper, enamel. Dimensions: plate #1: 3.5 x 19.5 cm, plate #2: 4 x 19.5 cm, plate #3: 3 x 24 cm, plate #4: 3.5 x 30.5 cm, plate #5: 6 x 42 cm. Category: Unlimited Production. Commission: Cibone. Production: Cibone and Frozen Fountain.
Photo credit: Gerrit Schreurs

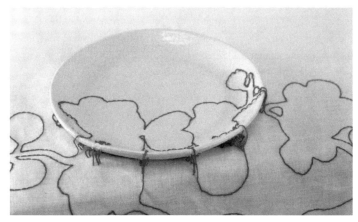

Fig. 3.18: Embroidered Tablecloth, 1999. Material: Linen, cotton, earthenware. Dimensions: 80 x 120 cm. Category: Limited Edition: 2 versions: red flower decoration and grey dragon decoration (10 of each version). Every tablecloth is to a great extent the result of handicraft and therefore unique. Commission: Own initiative. Production: Jongeriuslab. Collection: Textielmuseum Tilburg, Stedelijk Museum's Hertogenbosch, FNAC Puteaux, Musée de Rochechouart, FRAC Nord Dunkerque, Art Institute of Chicago, private collectors, collection of the designer.
Photo credit: Jongeriuslab

sensations. Design will never win the same kind of impact in the art world, and art, conversely, could never launch its visions in the same unexpected way as design. The question is, How much autonomy can a functional object tolerate? How much is needed for it to tell us a story beyond its primary use, without laying claim to artistic status?

The Proustian craftsman has left the field to the designer. The story inspired by scarcity and exclusiveness has made way for a meaning that rubs shoulders with visual art. We eat from the irregular plates of the *B-Set* china and feel a bond with both the designer Hella Jongerius and the factory craftsman who has taken such meticulous pains to ensure that the technical symbols of industrial fabrication remain visible in the fragile porcelain. Jongerius's embroideries, their afterimages in the glaze, the syrupy strands of rubber on archetypal vases, the threads with which the plates are sewn to the tablecloth, are all visual idioms that hint at a world dominated by good manners and old customs. [Figs. 3.17 + 3.18] Her unorthodox and innovative use of decorative patterns demonstrates that the signifier and the signified no longer match. She thereby offers the user every scope to attach his/her own fond and strictly personal memories to everyday objects. Only where contemporary utilitarian objects are bold enough to cross the boundary between usefulness and relative artistic autonomy do they have the potential to simultaneously deny and prove themselves. They fulfill their promise as vehicles of meaning so that:

> As soon as each hour of one's life has died, it embodies itself in some material object, as do the souls of the dead in certain folk-stories, and hides there. There it remains captive, captive forever, unless we should happen on the object, recognize what lies within, call it by its name, and so set it free. (M. Proust, *Contre Sainte-Beuve*, 1954)

Furnishing the Primitive Hut:
Allan Wexler's Experiments
Beyond Buildings

Aaron Betsky

INTRODUCTION

Allan Wexler's works explore the foundations of architecture, furniture, and clothing to find their shared fundamentals. To do this, he learns that he needs to unlearn the conventions of design and makes them evident in experimental projects. With a background in architecture, he starts with drawing, modeling, scale relationships, and details to uncover tools of the discipline. He realizes that using small-scale models to explore ideas becomes confused in full-scale constructions, while drawings have trouble making the transition from two to three dimensions. Wexler's work is established in the realm of experimentation and conceptual development where early design processes grow. Intentional misreading of these basic tools reveals new potential for their reapplication into architecture and an entry point into related design critiques.

To uncover these tools, Aaron Betsky frames Wexler's works in the context of everyday rituals. Wexler chooses programs to work with, often through such basic rituals as preparing a meal or drinking coffee. The dynamics involved in these rituals are translated into dynamic spaces to contain them. One example is a mobile kitchen designed for Parsons The New School for Design that presents itself as an anonymous crate with handles and hinges as the only clue for its opening. The crate resides in a void in the wall and, when pulled out, opens up to reveal all the necessary amenities custom-built into the kitchen crate. Wine glasses, napkins, plates, and so on are all custom fit into specific compartments. This comprehensive interior does not stem from the history of the Gesamtkunstwerk *but from the starting point of exploring how interiors can be altered to include these objects in a mappable location.*

Wexler focuses on details that are often more intricate than those of a conventional kitchen, such as a vertical panel that holds each individual wine glass inserted into a cutout profile of itself. When the vertical plane is opened,

Originally appeared in *Custom Built: A Twenty-Year Survey of Work by Allan Wexler*, edited by Christopher Scoates and Debra Wilbur (Atlanta, GA: Atlanta College of Art Gallery, 1999), 11–31.

it becomes a semitransparent wall. Wexler's curiosity resides in these types of thresholds where walls are treated as permeable surfaces and poché is altered to register activities on both sides. Where a wall is typically passive, Wexler integrates functions normally found in the interior and pushes them into the wall, embedding functional interiors within passive interiors. These works test boundaries, whether they are larger conceptual or more immediate such as poché.

———

ALLAN WEXLER is an artist whose gallery objects bring us back to first things: how we keep the rain off our heads, how we define our space, how we measure our time, how we dress. He elaborates on these simple acts in form. This is the core of his work. It is a type of experimentation with what we think we know; his work confronts us with the unknowability of even the simplest aspects of our daily lives.

Wexler accomplishes this revelation in scale models of our reality. He reduces the complexity of our routines into totemic objects. These activities let us stage a ritual re-enactment of daily practices that it is up to us as viewers to invent. Wexler makes basic shapes that he elaborates into forms beyond function. He represents what is real in reality itself, and then makes it impossible to come to any simple understanding of his work. Eminently simple yet complex in its implications, Wexler's work stands as a paradigm for a practice of making, which is beyond either art or architecture.

I propose a concern with the primitive hut at the core of Wexler's work. This preoccupation is most evident in the series of sukkahs that he designed between 1988 and 1990. The sukkah is a ritualistic object or house Jews erect at harvest time to celebrate their bounty, give thanks, and center themselves in the world. The structures Wexler proposed bring together many of the themes in his other work, and pose a reference point both for our understanding of his activity and for the role of such an artist as Wexler in our society. Rooted in his heritage as a Jew and as an architect, these pieces make remaining solely within that heritage impossible in the same way they confound our attempts to see the structures as the serene shelters we might expect. They are models for Wexler's art.

In designing these pieces, but also in the many reiterations of their basic forms in his later work, Wexler went back to first principles. As architectural historian Joseph Rykwert has pointed out, the sukkah is a version of the primitive hut or aedicula that many architects propose as the core of their discipline, its Rosetta stone and essence.[1] For many architects, the primitive hut is still the beginning point of an investigation of what it means to make architecture and what makes us at home in the world today.

Architects justify their activity through particular foundation myths. They assume that a time came in the evolution of erect apes into a human society that architecture was necessary.[2] Why we might need something called architecture, or what it was in its most primitive form, is open to discussion, and it is all these speculations that we can find in Wexler's work. We can find them in forms that are open, experimental, and uncertain in their status. Starting from architecture and its basic principles, Wexler gives us something that denies the certainty of architecture, its history, and its future.

The most universal assumption architects hold is that the core of their work is the making of some sort of order in the world. The first act of architecture is the creation of a place defined by borders. This enclosed territory has the function of keeping out both nature (wind, rain, snow, sun) and others who might want what one has. In the version promulgated by the abbé Laugier, this primitive hut is four posts that hold up a pyramidal roof.[3] This is an aedicula we can still find reiterated in countless forms of architecture.[4] The aedicula is a three-dimensional form of the mandala: it divides the world into four quadrants that correspond to the four directions of the winds and mark the passing of the sun both through the day and through the seasons.[5] Within the aedicula, man (not, at least until much later, woman), is at the center. From here, everything makes sense.

The temple, the palace, and the home itself are no more than elaborations of this first place of order. The throne room, the altar, the four-poster bed, and the dining table all re-enact this first point. This humanist story of architecture resonates with the child's drawing of a house, with our predilection for enclosed spaces with sloped roofs (such as our safe suburban homes), and with our desire to elaborate that first order in concatenations of rooms.[6]

There is another myth, however. It is one that goes back to Vitruvius and postulates the first gathering of man and woman not in a space of isolation, but around a campfire. Here, according to Vitruvius, language was born, and thus society grew up around a center that we could never occupy.[7] The fire is still at the core of our homes as the hearth, as are, later, those forms of technology that draw us out of the world and into a separate space; heating, plumbing, and television are versions of that original cultural center. The center of the house is not a place that we inhabit through a geometry realized in construction, but a void that we bring alive through the importation of both energy and narrative. Architecture is not an abstract endeavor, but a solidification of the stories we tell to make sense out of the world. Such narratives fix themselves not in one form, but into tools for changing nature into a place of human habitation. Architecture is essentially an enabler of technological importation.[8]

A third myth, best typified by the writing of German art historian Gottfried Semper, places the moveable tent at the core of architecture.[9] In this story, the first places we inhabited as human beings were temporary structures woven together from the twigs and branches around us. The act of building was originally an act of gathering together what already existed into a more and more intricate order. As we stripped the trees of their bark and wove increasingly elaborate structures, we began to develop patterns or rhythms that turned into decorative motifs.[10] Decoration and structure were to Semper not two separate elements, but were intricately and inexorably bound together.

The tent, moreover, was not something that replaces the ground on which it sits. It either decayed (or grew) after we stopped using it, or it became something we took with us when we moved on to the next campsite. Architecture here is no more and no less than an extension of our clothes, our furniture, and our tools into a form that can, if only for a night, enclose us. It is at the same time no more and no less than a conventionalization of the nature we still find all around us.

All three of these myths imply different attitudes about architecture and its role in our society. While the first assumes that we make forms that are abstract, rational, and separate from the world around us, the second implies that architecture is a form of signification that clarifies and actively changes the world. This latter story also displaces human habitation in favor of what man does, i.e., technology. Our ability to create an artificial environment, whether by words or by buildings, is here at the core of architecture. In the third postulated myth, the results of technology and the way in which we weave them together into patterns of everyday life form the elements of architecture.

Wexler has, whether consciously or not, explored all three of these modes of architecture. At the core of much of his work is the primitive hut, the child's drawing of the house turned into a three-dimensional form, and the ordering of reality into simple geometries. His early *Temple Houses* of 1977 and 1978, his *Office Buildings* of 1982 and 1988, and most particularly his stage set for the *Memory Theater of Giulio Camillo* (1986) all indicate this interest in the primitive hut. His studies into *Expandable Building* (1996), the various essays into how to drain rain off a roof (*Building for Water Collection with Buckets*, 1994), his more recent *Floating Roof Building* (1996), and even his attempts to make a simple house form out of a single sheet of material in a day (*8 Hours 15 Minutes*, 1997) are all part of the investigation of the Laugierian hut.

The same investigations into building materials are also a way of looking at architecture, in the second of the three scenarios, as a language. This is an investigation that Wexler continued with his "misreading" of the basic

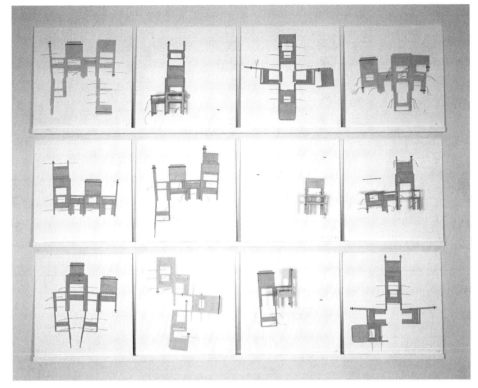

Fig. 3.19: Allan Wexler, *Twelve Unfolding Chairs*, 1998.

building block of American architecture—the wood stud—in paper form. It is one of his current obsessions, and it is leading him to propose forms that are as ephemeral as a painting. In *Twenty-Four Unfolded Houses* (1997) and *Twelve Unfolding Chairs* (1998), the architecture becomes literally just image. [Fig. 3.19] The ghost of construction implies the making of something, but, rather than constructing its reality, tells us a story about this act in its image cut loose from utility. At the same time, technology, and plumbing in particular, has long been central in much of his work. Wexler is telling us stories about what it means to make sense and a space within and outside of the metropolitan environment that surrounds us.

The notion of architecture as something that one weaves together is not as clearly present throughout Wexler's work, but it is evident in some of his earliest pieces, such as the *Forest Houses* (1976) and *Tree Intersecting Plane* (1977). Here Wexler gathered twigs and formed them into the simplest form of a house. Though he later became more and more preoccupied with the abstract form these early essays implied, his interest in architecture as pattern or convention remained strong. Such interest is evident in his hybrids between clothes, furniture, and architecture (*Body Furniture*,

Fig. 3.20: Allan Wexler, *Body Furniture*, 1991.

1991) and his reduction of the primitive hut to a series of multicolored forms (*Color Studies for the House*, 1998). [Fig. 3.20]

Wexler is not content to investigate the potential of these myths. If he did, he might have become a conventional architect who translates her or his investigations in buildings that bury those ideas within forms that shelter or contain us. Instead, Wexler is interested in exploring the inconsistencies, absurdities, and lyrical qualities of all stories of architecture. His house forms come apart, peel away, and lose dimension as he dissects them. What they lose in their potential to represent inhabitation they gain in their ability to highlight the act of architecture. In a sense, Wexler is a rhetorician: he is engaged in making us aware of the urgency of architecture and convincing us of its necessity. To do this, he makes use of metaphors, enlarges details, glosses over the coherence of the story of building, and erects a convincing image of an alternative world.[11]

Thus the buckets that collect rain dangle in mid-air: the gutters that extend from the house in *Houses for Painting* (1994) become an abstract geometric pattern in the landscape (the cross that marks the spot of inhabitation becomes, perhaps ironically, perhaps unconsciously, but to great effect, a swastika); the houses split, come apart, and pose themselves as flayed and naked examples of what it means to make a place of inhabitation. These objects frustrate use not in order to confound us, but to confront us with the true nature of what it is they do.

Unlike a demagogue, however, Wexler does not convince us of anything. He leaves us dangling. Having investigated the basic elements of architecture and highlighted their functions, their associations, and their material, he leaves them in a delicate balance that he resolves only through composition. His work is, after all, not a proposal for the construction of houses that will make us comfortable, or a treatise about architecture, but art. It crystallizes our reality into forms that make us wonder about the world around us. It does so through representation and abstraction, employing both traditional methods of explanation and the twentieth century methodology of collage. These are assemblies that work within the tradition of Schwitters' Merzbau, Malevich's investigations into new forms for a new century and a new society, van Doesburg's elaboration of neo-plastic forms into cafes and houses, and Mario Merz's igloos for postmodern nomads.

What enters into Wexler's work through its place within the art world is an endgame. Modern artists are not only interested in going back to first principles, but they also employ this return to basics to postulate a future in which art will approach reality. In doing so, they surmise, art will corrode both the naked world it has uncovered and its own making into nothing: pure white, an ultimate abstraction, the realm of the spirit, or the black hole that sucks up all the complexity and contradiction of modern art into the liebestod of modern art. Whether one approaches that end point through abstraction, as the De Stijl group and the constructivists did, through narrative, as in the work of some American precisionists or the work of Mark Rothko, or through the gathering of the world into an amalgamation that becomes so dense and enigmatic that we cannot read it, as did Merz and Joseph Beuys, for instance, or whether one employs all three techniques, as Gerhard Richter continues to do, matters little. The result is nothingness.

This is not the point at which Wexler arrives. Though some of his most lyrical pieces so destroy the basis out of which he has developed them ("paintings" in which the shadows of the chairs or houses he has cut out of the canvas become purely minimal ghosts), they always remain eminently real. They hold onto their sense of construction and utility while pulling it apart, because all the work shares one dominant characteristic: it is a model. These are not abstract images that hang on the wall; nor are they objects of use. Instead, they hover between those two extremes in scale, material, and function. They are proposals, miniature versions, or translations of a reality that may not exist and may not be something that could come into being.

The model is of course the basic working tool of the architect. It is what allows her or him the opportunity to reduce reality to a form that we can subject to our gaze and our manipulation. By reducing the real world to something that is smaller than us, we can exert control over it. This means that we can impose our will on the world, but also that we can project our personality onto that artificial realm. This is true not just for those who propose buildings. Dollhouses have the same function. They let us create a version of our world that we can arrange according to our will while letting us imagine a home in which we could have the role that we would like.

The model also serves as a ritualistic giver of order. The mandala and the aedicula are likewise such elements. All three rearrange a world that might be out of order in geometries that balance opposites, weave together complex relations, and propose a new form of order.[12] In a miniature, we can

Figs. 3.21 + 3.22: Allan Wexler, *Vinyl Milford House*, 1994.

see the world as if in a glass: it is removed from us, yet mirrors our reality. By building models, we lay a sense of order over the world that we believe will, through that very act, and if all the rituals are followed with precision (if the contract and the client follow our plans, for instance), come into being.

What is strange about Wexler's models is that they are out of whack. They peel apart at the seams, cannot stand up by themselves, don't present a reality that we would ever want to see realized. The *Series* of 1979 and 1980, for instance, present the primitive hut coming apart into pieces. The *Body Furniture* piece (1991) cannot operate unless we imprison ourselves within the objects, and at that point they lose their compositional integrity. The *Axonometric Chairs* of 1998 exist, like some of Peter Eisenman's buildings, only as projections that translate the modeling tool itself into an unusable and perhaps purposely unsuitable form.[13]

These are, nonetheless, models. They have the scale of something smaller than ourselves. Even when they are "life size," as in *Vinyl Milford House* (1994) or *Home Show II* (1996), they are not structures that have a full sense of life and order to them as they exist. [Figs. 3.21 + 22] They have to be expanded, pulled apart, and elaborated by the user—at least as a proposition—in order for them to escape from their status as art objects. In doing so, they would of course immediately lose their connection to the artist's work as well as their financial value. Some of Vito Acconci's work comes to mind.

It is the status of these objects as both art objects and architectural models, and the tension Wexler manages to maintain between these two states, that gives them their force and originality. As such, they point to the beginnings of architecture and thus to the most fundamental questions about what make us at home in the world. They also refer us to the mundane reality of everyday life. At the same time, they remove these concerns from the environment that engendered them, whether this is the rarefied world of architectural history or the immediacy of our daily routines. As objects that exist in frames or on pedestals, they aspire to our attention. They distance themselves from us and propose something else. Like the Dutch

Fig. 3.23: Allan Wexler, *Parsons Kitchen*, 1994.

artist Constant, who for four decades has been erecting a utopian scenario in a similar mixture of paintings, models, and plans (*New Babylon*, 1958– present),[14] Wexler cannot propose any definite solutions. This makes his work all the more poignant and, in our speculative society, effective.

Wexler is acting as a tinker or mechanic. His working method is a strange combination of the deliberate and the ad hoc, mixing rigid rules for construction (time limits, material choices, geometries, typologies) with a sense that the whole thing is thrown together so that one can see all the pieces that went into its construction. In this sense, Wexler is engaged in explorations of form that mix the rational traditions of architecture with the more intuitive methods of what we consider art. What brings these two together is another, all-American notion—that of the maker, whether artist or architect, as a tinker who operates on a reality that is always new and fresh and transforms it through objects that are meant to be both importations into and condensations of this landscape. From Thomas Jefferson to Frank Lloyd Wright to Frank Gehry, architects have engaged in such forms of making, but one can also find this tradition in the work of such artists as Joseph Cornell and Robert Rauschenberg.

In surveying Wexler's work, it is important to remember that he has moved beyond, or perhaps farther into, modes of inhabitation. Here he is acting as a mechanic of exposition: he exposes and works on *Parsons Kitchen* (1994) as perhaps the anti-model for this aspect of his work. [Fig. 3.23] Here the piece is not a model, but a working implement that serves as an unfolding bar for a school of architecture. The box is simple and dense. Its beauty derives from the arrangement of objects within it. This is a condensation at real scale and of real use. As such, it is a translation of the intention of his very first proposal that went beyond the making of a building—*Proposal for the Manhattan Skyline* (1973) into the forms that are familiar from Wexler's other work. Arrangement here is everything.

Wexler has done several other works of this sort, including the *Crate House* of 1991 and the *Bucket House* of 1997. These are real buildings that we can actually inhabit. Yet all is not well, even in these houses. We engage in them only through ritual, and only in an ordered manner. We have to push and pull at them, deforming them to make them work. Here the work is more like a tea ritual. The house itself, its place in the landscape, the implements it contains, and the actions one performs in it offer an alternative artifice in which a balance between the body, the mind, and the world is finally something one can achieve.[15] The relation to this way of organizing the world becomes evident in such pieces as *Coffee Seeks Its Own Level* (1990), in which the participants must follow the rules the artist has set in order to complete the work.

Hat/Roof (1994) typifies much of this work: here the pyramidal roof no longer tops a building, but rather is a piece of clothing one wears. The furniture one might find inside a dwelling here become planes that cantilever off the wearer. The object can only exist in use, and yet it is not particularly functional. Though one might find precedents for work like this in both folk culture (display racks Asian vendors carry with them, or African hats that act as storage devices) and in architecture (the *Archigram Suitaloon* of 1966), this piece proposes something slightly different: that we cannot separate architecture, functional objects, and the user or observer.

We do know this hybrid between structure of inhabitation, object of use, and user in our daily lives. We call it furniture. Much of Wexler's work indeed has the quality of being like a chair, a table, or a storage device. It resembles such pieces quite literally, to the point that one could call Wexler as much a furniture designer as an architect. He is, of course, neither, but an artist—someone who uses these particular media not in order to affirm their nature, but to explore their potential and make us aware of them. Though this might sound like a reductivist definition of his work, Wexler's capability at activating the simple act of sitting or using a flat surface is immense.

The most extreme example of his art in this case is the *Scaffold Furniture* (1988), in which each aspect of using a piece of furniture is separated into a single object which is then stretched out in a Giacometti-like elongation of an otherwise familiar form. The effect approaches that of a tea ritual, because issues of balance and sequence of use become such a delicate set of considerations. Though pieces such as *Recycle-Conference Room* (1990) and the *Chair A Day* series of the same year might seem to present much more "normal" versions of furniture, they confound our expectations

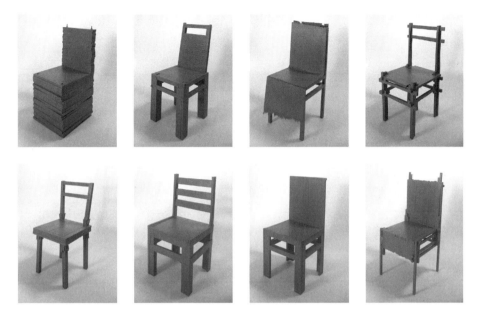

Fig. 3.24: Allan Wexler, *Chair A Day*, 1990.

not in use, but in material. [Fig. 3.24] The former is a collection of pieces Wexler gathered out of cast-off chairs and reassembled for an extremely formal use. The latter falls into the same category as the above-mentioned *8 Hours 15 Minutes* with its interest in serial production using a limited palette in a set period of time.

In more recent work, it is becoming difficult to tell furniture, model, building, and abstract object apart. Wexler seems to be working toward not so much an integration of his various concerns into singular objects, as a resolution of the profound instability of his work into itself. He is now making furniture out of paper, furniture that is painting, furniture that is buildings, and furniture that exists as models. Instead of making houses in miniature form or inhabiting models with accouterments, Wexler is exploring the unstable position between all of these things. He then represents this in materials that mix media, so that a house is made out of the stuff of drawings and drawings are made out of furniture.

We can call the result either art or furniture. Traditionally, furniture is something that exists between the act of making shelter, structure, or order, and the body itself. It exists as a piece of technology that lets us inhabit and be comfortable in a world we have made for ourselves. It stands at the end of a long tradition of honing basic forms down into shapes that are easy to construct and that respond to the shape of the body. It confers status and defines areas of use.

Figs. 3.25–27: Allan Wexler, *Mattress Factory Gallery Residence*, 1988.

In Wexler's hands, furniture becomes something that does none of these things. It constricts or confronts the body. It denies use. Wexler has either removed functionality or has designated the object as something he is willing to sell within the art market (the use of which, therefore, will diminish its value). Wexler's furniture is, therefore, Wexler's art.

If I were to designate Wexler's work in any manner beyond this, I would say that it is experimental. Wexler experiments on and in the real world. He pulls apart the structures of our everyday life, plays with the materials out of which we construct our surroundings and our implements, and opens up new spaces within a world we thought we had defined. Sometimes these are spaces that only the imagination can enter through the portal of the model. Sometimes the proposals seem to indicate a return to basic principles rather than a progression into a bright future. What remains inherent throughout his work is the sense of experimentation—an investigation that operates as an extension of our ability to be at home in the world, to remake our reality, and to question our existence through what we make. [Figs. 3.25–27]

Notes

1   Joseph Rykwert, *On Adam's House in Paradise: The Idea of the Primitive hut in Architectural History* (New York: The Museum of Modern Art, 1972).

2   As Rykwert rightly points out, discussions about the beginnings of architecture dominated much of the thinking at the Ecole des Beaux Arts in the 18th and 19th centuries. For an especially fruitful discussion of the impact of historical meanings on the definition of the language of architecture, see Sylvia Lavin, *Quatremere de Quincy and the Invention of a Modern Language of Architecture* (Cambridge, MA: The MIT Press, 1992).

3   Marc-Antoine Laugier, *Essai sur l'Architecture* (Paris: Michel Lambert, 1753).

4   John Summerson, "Heavenly Mansions," in *Heavenly Mansions and Other Essays on Architecture* (New York: W. W. Norton & Company, 1963), pp. 1–28.

5   Though the mandala was popularized in the west by Jung, it has long been and remains an active part of many Buddhist religions.

6   For a modern speculation on this elaboration, see Kent Bloomer and Charles Moore, *Body, Memory, and Architecture* (New Haven: Yale University Press, 1977).

7   Vitruvius Pollio, *The Ten Books on Architecture*, trans. Morris Hicky Morgan (New York: Dover Publications, 1960), pp. 35ff.

8   Cf. Reyner Banham, *The Architecture of the Well-Tempered Environment* (London: The Architectural Press, 1969) and Siegfried Giedion, *Mechanization Takes Command: A Contribution to Anonymous History* (New York: Oxford University Press, 1948).

9   Gottfried Semper, *The Four Elements of Architecture and Other Writings*, trans. Harry Francis Mallgrave and Wolfgang Herman (Cambridge: Cambridge University Press, 1989).

10   Ornament has, of course, become anathema to most architects. Only recently have theoreticians and practitioners begun to re-examine the possibility of seeing ornament, decoration, and non-structural pattern as an integral part of the body of architecture.

11   Cf. Judith Buber, *Excitable Speech: A Politics of the Performative* (London: Routledge Publishers, 1997).

12   This is the structuralist view of the model as espoused by Claude Levi Strauss in his *The Elementary Structures of Kinship*.

13   Eisenman built an "axonometric model" as the end result of his House X Project in 1979.

14   Cf. Constant, *Schilderijen/Paintings*, trans. James Harte Bell and John Richard Von Sturmer (Amsterdam and Boston: Stedeljik Museum and Beacon Press, 1996).

15   The tea ceremony has long fascinated Western artists and designers for its fusion of ritual, design, and sensory experiences. The classic text on the subject, first published in 1906, is *The Book of Tea* by Uakuzo Okakura (Boston: Charles E. Tuttle Co., 1956).

Courtney Smith, Tongue and Groove: Movable Sculpture

Manon Slome

INTRODUCTION

Courtney Smith animates the interior by deconstructing and reconstructing furniture, whose assemblages form a dialogue with the interior and reference the body that occupies it. Manon Slome brings these constructs to life by situating the furniture in the context of anthropomorphism. Because of animated features that resemble the body, an easy association can be made between them in Smith's work. A similar language is already shared between the two: arms, legs, back, and seat, along with the suggestion of the body in repose implied in the furniture. Further contributing to the animistic nature of Smith's furniture are titles informed by literature that often have dual, slightly tongue-in-cheek meanings.

Smith begins her work with discarded furniture. She gives the pieces life and new identity by projecting a persona onto them and placing them in interior spaces. Doing so virtually taunts the occupants of imaginary interiors by casting them out of their rooms. Her anthropomorphic furniture becomes the substitute inhabitant of the human-scale interior. Smith develops the language of shared limbs to animate furniture to fold and unfold, project outward and inward, and mimic masculine and feminine genders. The analogy of the body provides visual details, for example, the joints of the body and furniture. Slome recognizes this in the "ladylike" or "knocked-kneed fawns" of table legs.* At a larger scale, Smith's alteration of a boudoir ensemble no longer awaits its female occupant. Instead, a series of mechanized hinges enables the ensemble, consisting of a chair, table, and mirror, to unfurl or retract to conceal itself within a larger armoire acting as a skin, providing access or denial. Smith explores the furniture's surface as skin in additional pieces where ornament is carved into wood similar to applying a tattoo. In contrast, Smith integrates smooth formica surfaces with furniture, revealing an evolution of styles from ornamental to minimalist.

From *Tongue and Groove: Movable Sculpture* (New York: Chelsea Art Museum, 2006).

By ascribing anthropomorphic qualities to furniture, Smith and her movable sculpture reveal underlying qualities that reinforce the body-furniture relationship. Elements of furniture design such as ornament, materials, details, and utility are present in Smith's furniture, but they have been reinterpreted to reveal the integration of bodily characteristics.

———

THE TITLE OF the exhibition, Tongue and Groove: Movable Sculpture, was selected by Courtney Smith. Like many of the titles she gives her work, this is a revealing choice both of the work and the artist. It points to both the origins of her work in a love of language, literature and linguistic play as well as her desire to physically perform her theoretical concerns into a material version. Tongue and groove is a technical term from carpentry, which refers to a type of wood joint, the fitting of the "masculine" element into the "feminine." Movable Sculpture refers to the core of her work in furniture based sculpture. Furniture is called "movable" in many languages—as opposed to the "unmovable" architecture which contains it—but "movable" is also descriptive of the pieces which contain within themselves a range and potential for movement, that has parallels to the movement of a body in space. This punning, the sliding from one reference to another, the desire, as it were, to "have it both ways," informs much of the evocative, sensual and conceptually challenging work of Courtney Smith.

Smith's sculptural work with furniture begins for her with the fiction of "feeding off" existing objects. Furniture has a strong appeal for Smith both for its metonymic relationship to the human form that employs it and the architectural form that contains it. A mutable symbol for both the body and its home, it is ripe with narrative associations. It can carry nostalgia for a bygone era, speak of class, gender, taste, craftsmanship or mass production. Smith both allows and discounts any such readings, preferring to let the pieces exist in their own complexity, calling them "more dangerous" when such interpretations are withheld. She works by co-opting information from the original body of furniture usurping its own principles, conceptual or functional, or manipulating its parts to create a new structure. Smith has worked with this essentially collage paradigm of deconstruction and reconstruction in a variety of materials, both the tangible furniture series and the language/text and collage series.

Having studied literature as well as art, Courtney Smith began making paintings based on specific chromatic categories and their general conceptual attributes (an interest that emerges again within her sculpture). Although she continued with the same ideas, and was also exploring them in her work with text, her interest gradually shifted from the painted surface to the material of the surface itself, signaling the beginning of her work in sculpture. Her early three-dimensional work was in cloth, but then the artist describes a "solidifying" process when the work moved from soft to hard as she began her work with furniture. Two installations she completed in the late nineties, in Brazil where she had moved after university, serve as transitional works.

To say that this transitional work was like a butterfly emerging from a chrysalis would normally read as clichéd and artificial. But the reference suits. In Smith's work there exists from this period a sense of the fanciful, the fey, a delight in metaphor and play. Both installations were grounded in Smith's concern with color and were chromatically organized around, respectively, red and white. The first piece, *Rêve Rouge* (1998) consists of a stack of 17 mattresses, each hand dyed a different shade of red. Every mattress was stuffed with a different kind of material—feathers, raw lamb's wool, hay, straw and raw cotton. The vertical stack of sumptuous red, hand crafted mattresses with their pungent aromas tie a rich visual presence to the fantasy and interplay of an easily bruised princess.

The second installation, *Virgem na Torre* (1998), taps even more deeply into those familiar literary constructs that Smith engages again and again. Stacked white furniture, an assemblage of elements from an imaginary room, conveys a sense of repression, of incarceration, the trapped figure—a presence suggested by the vertical, anthropomorphic arrangement of the furniture. The transition between the "fiction" and the chromatic and structural organization of the piece functions as a continual visual pun.

The anthropomorphic content of the furniture interventions to which Smith increasingly turned, was a synthesis of the either/or quality of the two early installations. Furniture for Smith became a perfect medium for her artistic need to "have it both ways." Made for the body and as a dramatic stand in that can play itself and something else at the same time, it serves as metaphor for the human figure. Furniture has legs, back, arms and, in the "vanities" that Smith so favors, can even return the gaze. Furthermore, the movements of the body—sitting, reclining, lying, posing—are all mirrored in the "use value" of the furniture.

In the first phase of "movable sculpture," which she refers to as "articulations," Smith cut up a series of chairs, removing everything (seat, fabric, cane, etc.) except their skeletal structures. Bisecting the skeletal forms through the middle, she installed hinges creating joints which would articulate the body of the structure. Hinged, fanned out or blocked, these reconstructed forms resemble now "ladylike" figures with legs tightly closed, now knocked-kneed fawns—awkward, with a wobbly, learning-to-walk-on-their-own quality. Smith called these works *chair de fée*, fairy flesh, playing with the word "chair"—flesh in French, and the immediate visual connection between the word "chair" and the original object.

Fig. 3.28: Courtney Smith,
Vanité, 2000. Vanity table, hinges
and hooks. APT, New York.
Photo credit: Fausto Fleury

Brazil, where she lived from 1989 to 2000, afforded Smith an enormous amount of discarded furniture with exotic woods, particularly the nostalgic vanity tables whose presence would continue to reappear in her work. As an object/image, the vanity is romantic and feminine; as a contemporary sign, it could evoke an obsession with narcissistic beauty—female furniture as an object of desire. But although her interventions subvert the furniture's original purpose or function, Smith circumvents that reading, preferring to take the furniture at face value and use the material freely, obstinately addressing only its form and structure, against expectations, leaving the viewer in suspense as to the meaning of the recurrent vanity image. [Fig. 3.28]

In the Psychê series[1] such as *Psychê Complex* (2003), Smith began with an armoire, a vanity table with a stool and a pair of twin cabinets—all pieces from early twentieth century Brazilian interpretations and hybridizations of European furniture styles. After dissecting the pieces, Smith reassembled them with an elaborate system of hinging, transforming the furniture into a set of possibilities with collapsible parts that could alternately be absorbed and enclosed into one central body or dispersed in space into an improvisational boudoir. [Fig. 3.29] The resulting work plays between static, though interrupted, use value—the coquettish nature of the boudoir and the stillness of the self-adoring gaze—and the range of sculptural possibilities made both potential and apparent through the intervention. The inherent choreography of the work, its ability to expand and contract like a dancer through space, also suggests the phantom possessors of the boudoir as they went through the elaborate rituals of their "toilette."

As Smith developed these articulated pieces, the operations become more and more elaborate. With the more complex cutting and hinging the transformation results in an increasingly organic, zoomorphic form, abounding with implied behavioral movement, the inward folding of the pieces resembling an animal closing into its shell, or expanding and spilling out like a strutting male. At this stage, Smith applied rosewood veneer to the inside

Fig. 3.29: Courtney Smith, *Psichê Complexo*, 2003. Armoire, vanity, two side-cabinets, stool with cushion, hinges, buckles and hooks. Speyer Family Collection, New York. Photo credit: Fausto Fleury, Vincente de Mello

surfaces so that on opening the exposed interior resembles markings like the underside of a buck's tail raised in alarm.

When Smith returned to the United States in 2000, we can observe a subtle rupture in the work, partly prompted by the different quality of material available to her. She began a new series of sculptural interventions in existing furniture, but this time literally sculpting into the wood furniture. Rather than the additive process of hinging and articulating, Smith began a self-described "obsessive" phase of elaborate carving. As the baroque ornamentation of nonsensical outbreaks of acanthus leaves and S-scrolls began to take over and erase these lowly objects, Smith's intention was less a fable of transformation of the common into the precious; rather, the carving took on the aura of a degenerative affliction in the form of ornamentation, a strange and rampant growth that crept up the sides and legs of the furniture and started to devour the piece. [Fig. 3.30] In such works as *Telephone* (2002) for example, the rash of pseudo-rococo carving, which spreads over the tired surface of the desk and chair, creates a fascinating and somewhat surreal contrast in its sumptuous presence to the crude furniture whose skin looks corroded by the extravagant carving. Taking her cue from an existing characteristic of the piece, like a keyhole or any preexisting decorative element, Smith drew directly onto the furniture in a lavish freestyle, connecting one formation to another, letting the drawing contract and expand as it travels from surface to surface.

Fig. 3.30: Courtney Smith, *Noir*, 2002. Rosewood stool and hand carving. Collection of Igor da Costa, New York. Photo credit: Rodrigo Pereda

Still playing on the idea of contamination of a host body, Smith turned in a subsequent series of work to an inverse operation, to that of implanting a foreign element in the furniture, which in turn, starts to proliferate like a growth or parasite. In *Reis* (2003) or *Santo Antonio* (2003), for example, the chests of drawers are infected with inserted plywood modules that replicate the form, or the function of the original furniture. The baroque or rococo references of the carving now give way to minimalist blocks and modules, spreading in rectilinear construction patterns. Throughout the series, the plywood modules increasingly invade and ultimately replace the original structure, penetrating the surface in a potentially endless relocation of the internal information and logic of each piece. This invasion intensifies from piece to piece until the original body is completely compromised, hardly recognizable as itself. [Fig. 3.31] As in *Tin Tin por Tin Tin* (2003), *Voce e Eu* or *Sim or Nao* (both 2004), the originating chairs are now completely disembodied, their fragments encased within plywood blocks, an inventory of parts arranged on the floor with no logic that refers to the initial function, shape or purpose of the chair. [Fig. 3.32] Similarly, in *Homestar* (2004) and *Dollhouse* (2004), a vanity and a desk are cut up and reconstituted into a set of blocks, becoming a puzzle that cannot be put together.

Polly Blue Pell Mell (2005) functions as a synthesis of Smith's strategies of deconstruction and reorganization. Blue formica, a full declaration of artificiality, and an absolute version of the prosthetic parts that are alien to the original body, have now covered the plywood with a blue plastic skin. With multiple interlocking components that can slide back and forth on their slick surfaces, the resulting work can be stacked or unstacked, compacted or spread out, abstracted or representing its original form, reassembled in a myriad of ways. Invoking the chromatic interest from her early work, the blue of the formica has a rigorous conceptual presence that banishes any residual references to the nostalgic past of the furniture. The blue signifies the parasitical process which is now a clinical, observable fact.

The move to industrially produced formica from the organic references of the exotic woods of earlier work has been called a shift in reference

Fig. 3.31: Courtney Smith, *Reis*, 2003. Chest of drawers and plywood. APT, New York.
Photo credit: Mauro Restiffe
Fig. 3.32: Courtney Smith, *Você e Eu*, 2004. Rosewood chair (Sergio Rodrigues, 1958)
and plywood. Collection of Peter Norton, Santa Monica. Photo credit : Rodrigo Pereda

from the naturally degenerative order of the body to the relentless disorder of social architecture. Again, as discussed in the vanity series, Smith allows these discourses to flow around the work while both formally and conceptually she is following a certain logic of production and its co-relative in a fictional narrative of process. Smith's next series of sculpture moves further into the embrace of artificiality; by employing only new materials, the work contains only the memory of a hypothetical original (or a synthesis of information from several "originals") so that the piece exists now only as a spectacle. Made of plywood or formica units and fused into one unitary or reintegrated body, these works mark the completion of a cycle.

Smith's latest body of work returns to the actual fragment but it is now reconstituted in a drastically homogenized process as a standardized brick-like module. A new work, *Junk House* (2006), contains 1000 such bricks, five surfaces made of plywood and one face containing a remnant of furniture, some from the waste of earlier pieces, others from any wood or material Smith can salvage. This recycling of matter from other sculptures proceeds in a manner as aesthetically detached as possible (although the process itself is voracious in the amount of "waste" it demands). While the plywood blocks impose a modular controlling order, they are yet full of reference, of memory, but only on one surface, which may or not be exposed. Again it is a structure which allows Smith to have it both ways, playing the errant individuality of a single surface against the uniform modality, while the brick units themselves can be installed in an infinite variety of ways, producing when built endless configurations and subdivisions (textural, chromatic, etc.).

Smith's collage-on-paper pieces and her text pieces employ a similar method of deconstruction and reconstruction to the sculpture. In the collage pieces, using do-it-yourself guides to construction with wood, Smith carefully cuts out individual illustrations of the actual "building material," tiny drawings of blocks, bricks and beams, and builds from these a 2D construction of a fictitious and impossible structure. Drawing from a finite set of inflexible pieces, the composition is the result of a challenging game of connecting each individual piece to another by matching angles and flush edges until a complete closed circuit is achieved. Once a perimeter is established, the construction can keep growing in all directions according to the building system.

The texts, as with the sculptures, are constructions made of reconstituted fragments. They are printed as if they were a page taken from an old book, constructions made from different sentences extracted from familiar stories and fairy tales. Like the brick pieces, the set of loose sentences works as a kit, with a fixed number of pieces, from which to build new pseudo-narratives. Each page is a different construction made of the same material, each construction setting up its individual logic, sometimes imitating a traditional narrative structure, or sometimes creating an alternative, labyrinthine structure.

From the less material texts to the complex structures of her sculpture, Smith's hybrid constructions—dysfunctional, complex, conceptually rich and sensuously evocative—embody the possibilities of multiple readings and visual options. What, however, cannot always be apprehended from a museum or gallery installation is what I have referred to as the inherent choreography of the work, the possibilities for movement and manipulation created by the hinging, the fragmentation and multiple configurations. Photographs of the pieces in various stages or positions are included with the exhibition and these contribute somewhat to an understanding. Ultimately, though, it will be the imagination that enables viewers to enter into the fictions of these pieces and participate in their frozen dance.

Notes

* Manon Slome, *Courtney Smith, Tongue and Groove: Moveable Sculpture* (New York: Roebling Hall, 2006), unpaginated.

1 Here again Smith in her titles engages in a linguistic play, psychê being the Brazilian term for the type of vanity Smith favored; it is a term borrowed from the equivalent French word "psyché," which is itself taken from the name of the Greek goddess of love and divine beauty.

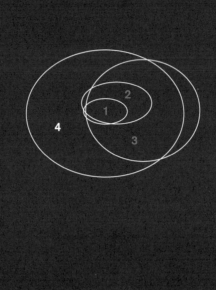

Color and Surfaces

Introduction:
Color and Surfaces

Color palettes, wall coverings, and textiles reflect trends easily replaceable from one season to the next. Color especially plays a significant role in bringing new identity to interiors through a minimal amount of material, for example, a layer of paint can impact an interior as much as the architecture itself. This chapter looks at interior skins through essays that are categorized in two groups. The first is color, which has no beginning or end and relies on the pigment-filled medium it occupies to give it shape.[1] Because color is often the final layer added to an interior, its application reinforces the distinction between skin and structure. The second category is surfaces that line the interior. This category includes traditional tapestries, wallpaper, or those that lie closest to us, such as bed linens, as well as emerging artificial skins influenced by the latest technologies.

Color and surfaces evoke hierarchical relationships, and their application depends on underlying structures. Themes of primary and secondary opposition act as an overarching framework for broad social, political, and technical themes including feminism, ornament, politics, the artificial, and the organic. Each has a semantic reference to color, surface, or both, revealing the subtleties of these properties as they permeate disciplines outside interior design and, in turn, reveal the complexity of the interior realm.

Interior design is traditionally associated with the feminine, perhaps because of its alignment with women and gay men in the interior design profession, or as an intimate association with women's work. In contrast, architecture is viewed as masculine. These perceptions set up a hierarchy that places architecture above the interior. The application of color and surfaces reinforces the secondary role of interiors because without structure (on which to apply it), color would be immaterial.[2] To work with color is to be feminine, an association that architects are willing to dabble in but rarely make central to their professional focus. Color is always present in architecture, though it gets little attention in architecture schools where color decisions

are made by default based on chipboard or basswood, the materials of student model building. David Batchelor in his essay "Chromophobia" observes,
"The minor is always undoing the major."[3] Batchelor recognizes that color
is the minor to drawing (or form), much as interiors are the minor to architecture and the feminine is the minor to masculine.[4] The interior is similar
to color because they both rely on a border to define their realms. Charlotte
Perkins Gilman captures this bias about hierarchal dominance in *The Yellow
Wallpaper*—a story interpreted by psychologists and feminists to be about a
woman repressing her own instincts in deference to a dominating husband—
by writing about the action of the wallpaper color permeating beyond its confined borders. Over a few weeks, the woman believes the wallpaper pattern
holds captive other women behind it. The story concludes with the woman
confronting the wallpaper to release the imaginary women followed by the
woman confronting her husband, with the minor undoing the major.

The second theme, the relationship of skin and structure, appears in
Adolf Loos's essay "The Principle of Cladding." He directly addressed the
relationship of skin to structure and indirectly, perhaps unintentionally, drew
an early distinction between architecture and interior design—in advance of
interior design as a profession. Loos refers to Gottfried Semper by describing
the architect's first and second tasks: to hang carpets to form "a warm and
livable space" and to provide structure behind it for support.[5] Michel Serres
emphasized these layers in his essay "The Five Senses: Boxes" where he
looked to one of the most intimate layers found in the interior—bed sheets. In
a site-specific example, "Introduction to the Amber Room," Catherine Scott-
Clark and Adrian Levy describe a historical moment where political upheaval
uncovered a surface and structure relationship.

By repositioning Loos's essay in present times, the first task falls within
the scope of work by the interior designer and the second, the architect. This
new reading reverses conventions and makes the interior the primary on
which architecture—as secondary—supports. A look at the interior design of
the Casa da Música by Petra Blaisse and her office Inside Outside in "Curtain
as Architecture" reveals the dominance color and surface can have over
architecture. The distinction between skin and structure on the opera house
does not go away but is in fact further reinforced. Textiles and color patterns
dominate the interior. Wood grain is overemphasized by the application of
gold paint, and hand-woven curtains obscure architectural views. The outcome reverses hierarchies and promotes to primary the interior.

Loos's attention to the difference between structure and cladding
is still applicable in looking at substantive advances that demonstrate the
impact material science has on reshaping the properties of skins. Where previously skin and structure remained two materials attached through connections, a revolution in materials from contemporary architectural work

has collapsed the distance between them. Ellen Lupton's essay "Skin: New Design Organics" probes advances made by material science in the discovery and manufacture of artificial skins that can host embedded structure. The dissolution of hierarchy between skin and structure dissolves concerns about the politics of primary and secondary. As skin and structure move toward one integrated system in advanced product design and other architectures that are the subject of museum exhibitions and archive catalogs of materials and design, the hierarchical differences between the professions of interior design and architecture are being renegotiated.

Notes

1   David Batchelor, *Chromophobia* (London: Reaktion Books, 2000), 28.

2   Ibid., 22–3.

3   Ibid., 31.

4   Ibid., 23.

5   Adolf Loos, "The Principle of Cladding," in *Spoken into the Void: Collected Essays, 1897–1900*, trans. Jane O. Newman and John H. Smith (Cambridge, MA: MIT Press, 1982), 66.

Chromophobia

David Batchelor

INTRODUCTION

Color pervades the interior: no matter how subtle, color is visible in furniture, objects, and surfaces. Decisions about color are unavoidable in the discipline of interior design. Architecture and interior design traditionally distinguish themselves from one another in the form of structure and what fills structure, architecture responsible for the former, and interior design the latter, including the application of color. Accompanying this distinction are stereotypes associated with masculine and feminine. David Batchelor, in his essay, expands on these stereotypes through the lens of color, or rather, the fear of color. As a painter, Batchelor is interested in a parallel in painting written about by Charles Blanc in the mid-nineteenth century, whereby the drawn line preceded color to provide a structure for color to fill.

A division and hierarchy emerge from distinguishing between form and fill. Underlying this recognition of difference is a prejudice about and disassociation from color that is still common among architecture practitioners. Color is perceived as secondary, superfluous, and nonspecific, as opposed to the orderly nature of architecture that embodies classical ideals. Interior design grapples with its role in architecture, never quite attaining the latter's iconic stature. Batchelor builds on these oppositions with reference to painting and film to uncover latent fears and prejudices that exist in the reception of color. He draws attention to the early work and writings of Le Corbusier, whose notebooks reveal the judicious and controlled use of color in projects, despite the idealistic rationalism of the philosophical polemic.

To frame an attitude toward color, Batchelor looks to black and white and color in The Wizard of Oz, *as signatory indicators delineating the transition from one to the other as the space of the "Fall." In the film, Dorothy literally falls into color. When Batchelor writes about the Fall in this essay, he marks the threshold between masculine and feminine, order and chaos, primary and secondary. The fear of falling into the unknown is what keeps color at bay.*

Batchelor makes this impact best understood with a quote from Charles Blanc: "Colour is both secondary and dangerous; in fact, it is dangerous

Excerpted from *Chromophobia* (London: Reaktion Books, 2000), 21–24, 27–31, 36–37, 39–49. © David Batchelor 2000.

because it is secondary. Otherwise there would be no Fall." With such simplicity, Batchelor reveals the consequences of falling and provides a reason for the disparity between interior design and architecture.*

———

IF IT STARTED WITH a short visit to an inside-out interior of a colourless whiteness where clarity was confusion, simplicity was complication and art was uniformly grey, then it would be comforting to think that it might also end there. After all, there can't be many places like this interior which was home only to the very few things that had submitted to its harsh regime. And those few things were, in effect, sealed off from the unwanted and uncertain contingencies of the world outside. No exchange, no seepage, no spillage. Rather: isolation, confinement. But this shutting-off began to speak more and more about what it excluded than what it contained. What did this great white hollow make me think about? Not, for long, its whiteness. Rather, its colour.

If colour is unimportant, I began to wonder, why is it so important to exclude it so forcefully? If colour doesn't matter, why does its abolition matter so much? In one sense, it doesn't matter, or it wouldn't if we could say for certain that this inside really was as self-contained and isolated as it looked. But this house was a very *ambitious* inside. It was not a retreat, it was not a monastic emptiness. Its 'voluntary poverty'—that's how its architect likes to talk—was altogether more righteous and evangelical. It looked like it wanted to impose its order upon the disorder around it. Like neo-classicism, like the manifestos of Adolf Loos or Le Corbusier, it wanted to rescue a culture and lead it to salvation. In which case, colour does matter. It mattered to Melville and Conrad, and it mattered to Pater and Winkelmann; it mattered to Le Corbusier, and, it turns out, it has mattered to many others for whom, in one way or another, the fate of Western culture has mattered. It mattered because it got in the way. And it still matters because it still does.

The notion that colour is bound up with the fate of Western culture sounds odd, and not very likely. But this is what I want to argue: that colour has been the object of extreme prejudice in Western culture. For the most part, this prejudice has remained unchecked and passed unnoticed. And yet it is a prejudice that is so all-embracing and generalized that, at one time or another, it has enrolled just about every other prejudice in its service. If its object were a furry animal, it would be protected by international law. But its object is, it is said, almost nothing, even though it is at the same time a part of almost everything and exists almost everywhere. It is, I believe, no exaggeration to say that, in the West, since Antiquity, colour has been systematically marginalized, reviled, diminished and degraded. Generations of philosophers, artists, art historians and cultural theorists of one stripe or another have kept this prejudice alive, warm, fed and groomed. As with all prejudices, its manifest form, its loathing, masks a fear: a fear of contamination and corruption by something that is unknown or appears unknowable. This loathing of colour, this fear of corruption through colour, needs a name: chromophobia.

Chromophobia manifests itself in the many and varied attempts to purge colour from culture, to devalue colour, to diminish its significance, to deny its complexity. More specifically: this purging of colour is usually accomplished in one of two ways. In the first, colour is made out to be the property of some 'foreign' body—usually the feminine, the oriental, the primitive, the infantile, the vulgar, the queer or the pathological. In the second, colour is relegated to the realm of the superficial, the supplementary, the inessential or the cosmetic. In one, colour is regarded as alien and therefore dangerous; in the other, it is perceived merely as a secondary quality of experience, and thus unworthy of serious consideration. Colour is dangerous, or it is trivial, or it is both. (It is typical of prejudices to conflate the sinister and the superficial.) Either way, colour is routinely excluded from the higher concerns of the Mind. It is other to the higher values of Western culture. Or perhaps culture is other to the higher values of colour. Or colour is the corruption of culture.

Here is a near-perfect example of textbook chromophobia: 'The union of design and colour is necessary to beget painting just as is the union of man and woman to beget mankind, but design must maintain its preponderance over colour. Otherwise painting speeds to its ruin: it will fall through colour just as mankind fell through Eve.'[1] This passage was written in the last decade of the nineteenth century by the appropriately named Charles Blanc, critic, colour theorist and sometime Director of the Arts in the 1848 Socialist government in France. It is interesting on a number of counts. Blanc identified colour with the 'feminine' in art; he asserted the need to subordinate colour to the 'masculine' discipline of design or drawing; he exhibited a reaction typical of phobics (a massive overvaluation of the power of that which he feared); and he said nothing particularly original. For Blanc, colour could not simply be ignored or dismissed; it was always there. It had to be contained and subordinated—like a woman. Colour was a permanent internal threat, an ever-present inner other which, if unleashed, would be the ruin of everything, the fall of culture. For our contemporary chromophobic architect, colour also represents a kind of ruination. Colour for him signifies the mythical savage state out of which civilization, the nobility of the human spirit, slowly, heroically, has lifted itself—but back into which it could always slide. For one, colour was coded in the feminine; for the other, it is coded in the primitive. For both, colour is a corruption, a lapse, a Fall.

There are many different accounts of the fall into colour, and many of these—well, several, enough—take the shape of stories. This chapter is, for the most part, a story of a few of those stories.

There are many ways to fall: head first, feet first; like a leaf or a stone; on a banana skin or off a log; in a blaze of glory or in the darkness of despair. A fall can be trivial or dangerous; falls have a place of honour in comedy, in the circus, in tragedy and in melodrama. A fall may be biblical or farcical or, perhaps, both. Many of the different stories of the descent into colour are stories of a fall from grace. That is to say, they have roughly similar beginnings and ends; we know very generally where they are going to finish up. In that sense, they are not mysteries. But the manner and details of the falls are what's interesting: the terms used to describe the descent; the stages and locations; the twists and turns; the costumes and props; and, finally, the place where the falling stops, the place of colour [....]

For Blanc, there were only two ways to avoid the Fall: abandoning colour altogether or *controlling it*. Both had their risks. He is a little vague about the first option; at times, colour is 'essential' to painting, but in the same breath it might be only 'almost indispensable.' Elsewhere, he convinces himself that 'painters can sometimes dispense with colour,' yet a little later on it is reinstated: 'Colour being that which especially distinguishes painting from the other arts, it is indispensable to the painter.' Blanc appears to have been genuinely uncertain about colour; it shifts from being essential to being dispensable, from being low in the order of nature and representation to being the very essence and uniqueness of painting as an art. But for the most part, Blanc accepted that colour cannot be willed away; the job therefore is to master it by learning its laws and harnessing its unpredictable power: '...let the colourist choose in the harmonies of colour those that seem to *conform to his thought.*'

Conform, subordinate, control: we are back with Adam and Eve, back in a universe populated entirely by unequal opposites: male and female, mind and heart, reason and emotion, order and disorder, absolute and relative, structure and appearance, depth and surface, high and low, occident and orient, line and colour... For example: 'Here we recognize the power of colour, and that its role is to tell us what agitates the heart, while drawing shows us what passes in the mind, a new proof...that drawing is the masculine side of art, colour the feminine side.' Or: 'As sentiment is multiple, while reason is one, so colour is a mobile, vague, intangible element, while form, on the contrary, is precise, limited, palpable and constant.' Or: '...colour, which speaks to the senses rather than to the mind' is 'more external, hence, more secondary.' Or: 'There is...in painting, an essential element which does not readily lend itself to emblematic expressions—that is, colour...the artist using

OPPOSITES

colour will particularise what he seeks to generalise, and he will contradict his own grandeur.' Or: 'The predominance of colour at the expense of drawing is a usurpation of the relative over the absolute, of fleeting appearance over permanent form, of physical impression over the empire of the soul.'

Blanc inherited these opposites from an intimidating and ancient tradition of *disegno versus colore:* drawing versus colouring-in. When, in the art room at primary school, I was told to take a line for a walk and then colour it in, I certainly wasn't told that the line I was being asked to draw was in fact the continuation of a much longer one which could be followed almost without interruption back to the philosophical art rooms of ancient Greece. Nor was I told that within this apparently harmless opposition between line and colour, many other oppositions were in fact coded and concealed, all of them far from innocent. As Jacqueline Lichtenstein shows in her brilliant study of painting and rhetoric, *The Eloquence of Color*, evidence of chromophobia in the West can be found as far back as Aristotle, for whom the suppression of colour was the price to be paid for bailing art out from a more general Platonic iconophobia. For Aristotle, the repository of thought in art was line. The rest was ornament, or worse. In his *Poetics*, he wrote: '…a random distribution of the most attractive colours would never yield as much pleasure as a definite image without colour.'[2] It is from here that we inherited a hierarchical ordering within painting which in its polished form describes a descent from 'invention' through 'design' to 'chiaroscuro' and, finally, to 'colour.' But hang on a minute. Since when was 'random' associated with colour and 'definite' with drawing? Since when did drawing and colour become ciphers for order and chaos? Perhaps it doesn't matter: the prejudice is in place.

Since Aristotle's time, the discrimination against colour has taken a number of forms, some technical, some moral, some racial, some sexual, some social. As John Gage notes in his vast historical survey of colour theory, colour has regularly been linked with other better-documented sexual and racial phobias. As far back as Pliny, it was placed at the 'wrong' end of the opposition between the occidental and the oriental, the Attic and the Asian, in a belief that 'the rational traditions of western culture were under threat from insidious non-western sensuality.'[3] In later times, the Academies of the West continued and consolidated this opposition. For Kant, colour could never participate in the grand schemes of the Beautiful or the Sublime. It was at best 'agreeable' and could add 'charm' to a work of art, but it could not have any real bearing on aesthetic judgement. In a similar vein, Rousseau maintained that:

> colours, nicely modulated, give the eye pleasure, but that pleasure is purely sensory. It is the drawing, the imitation that endows these colours with life and soul, it is the passions which they express that succeed in

arousing our own, the objects which they represent that succeed in affecting us. Interest and sentiment do not depend on colours; the lines of a touching painting touch us in etching as well: remove them from the painting, and the colours will cease to have any effect.[4]

Likewise, Joshua Reynolds, founder of the Royal Academy:

Though it might be allowed that elaborate harmony of colouring, a brilliancy of tints, a soft and gradual transition from one to another, present to the eye, what a harmonious concert of musick does to the ear, it must be remembered, that painting is not merely a gratification of the sight. Such excellence, though properly cultivated, where nothing higher than elegance is intended, is weak and unworthy of regard, when the work aspires to grandeur and subliminity.[5]

Or Bernard Berenson, English aesthete and classicist: 'It appears…as if form was the expression of a society where vitality and energy were severely controlled by mind, and as if colour was indulged in by communities where brain was subordinated to muscle. If these suppositions are true,' he added with heavy irony, 'we may cherish the hope that a marvelous outburst of colour is ahead of us.'[6]

So it hadn't ended when many of the Academies collapsed under their own weight during the later nineteenth century. To this day, there remains a belief, often unspoken perhaps but equally often unquestioned, that seriousness in art and culture is a black-and-white issue, that depth is measured only in shades of grey. Forms of chromophobia persist in a diverse range of art from more recent years—in varieties of Realism, for instance, with its unnatural fondness for brown, or in Conceptual art, which often made a fetish of black and white. And it is in much art criticism, the authors of which seem able to maintain an unbroken vow of silence on the subject of colour even when it is quite literally staring them in the face. Likewise, when Hollywood discovered colour, it was deemed suitable mainly for fantasies, musicals and period pieces; drama remained a largely monochrome issue. Then there is the question of architecture, which we have already touched upon. But this is to get ahead of the story…

One thing that becomes clear from Blanc's thesis is that colour is both secondary *and* dangerous; in fact, it is dangerous because it is secondary. Otherwise there would be no Fall. The minor is always the undoing of the major [….]

The theme of colour as a fall from grace—or a fall into grace—can be updated a little. For example: Wim Wenders's 1986–7 film *Wings of Desire,* in which

the viewer is taken to and fro between two worlds: the realm of the spirits and angels, and the sensuous world of embodied beings. We know where
we are only because the latter is shown in full colour, but the spirit world is
shown in black and white. When the angel (played by Bruno Ganz) falls to
earth as the result of another fall—into love—he lands with a thud. Dazed and
amazed, he looks around the Berlin wasteland into which he has dropped.
He feels a small cut on the back of his head and looks at the blood left on his
hand. He approaches a passer-by:

> 'Is this red?'
> 'Yes.'
> 'And the pipes?'
> 'They're yellow.'
> 'And him there?' [pointing at some painted figures on the Berlin Wall]
> 'He's grey-blue.'
> 'Him?'
> 'He's orange…ochre.'
> 'Orange or ochre?'
> 'Ochre.'
> 'Red….Yellow….And him?'
> 'He's green.'
> 'And the bit above the eyes?'
> 'That's blue.'

The first questions the angel asks are the names of the colours he sees.
His fall from grace is a fall into colour, with a thud. It is a fall from the disembodied all-observing spirit world into the world of the particular and the
contingent, a world of sensuous existence, of hot and cold, of taste and touch,
but most of all it is a fall into a world of desire. It is a fall into a world of consciousness and self, or rather a fall from super-consciousness into individual
consciousness, but it is a fall into self made with the explicit purpose of losing the self in desire […]

There are several less terrifying falls into colour in the movies, although in
these too, colour for the most part remains beyond the orderly and the rational, and thus remains dangerous and disruptive. There is, for example, the
recent *Pleasantville*, about two full-colour American '90s teenagers sucked
into a monochrome '50s sitcom. But one film stands out from all the others: the extraordinary, wonderful *The Wizard of Oz*. Made in 1939, this movie's great set piece is a spectacular descent into brilliant Technicolor. Having
been scooped up by the tornado, Dorothy's house, together with Dorothy
herself (Judy Garland) and Toto, falls out of the sky into Munchkinland, a

fall that has a direct impact on the narrative and an especially direct impact on the Wicked Witch of the East. Dorothy's own drift into colour is, as I was devastated to discover when I first saw the film, revealed to be 'only' a dream-state, a result of her fall into unconsciousness. So Dorothy falls, twice. And she does so in a way that Baudelaire, Cézanne and Barthes would have understood. As she lands, she is greeted by the saccharine Glinda, aka the Good Witch of the North, who instructs the Munchkins to:

> …meet the young lady who fell from a star.
> She fell from the sky,
> She fell very far,
> And Kansas she says is the name of the star…
> When she fell out of Kansas,
> A miracle occurred.

Dorothy falls, and also finds herself among Charles Blanc's lower strata of nature: the Emerald City, the Yellow Brick Road and, of course, the Ruby Slippers. And there is talk of a rainbow (but not of God or Newton). Then there is the Horse of a Different Colour You've Heard Tell About. 'Toto, I have a feeling we are not in Kansas anymore,' says Dorothy, observantly, to her dog. No, Kansas was *grey*, so grey that it was ur-grey. As Salman Rushdie notes in his unapologetically Totophobic account of the film and L. Frank Baum's book,

> …everything is grey as far as the eye can see—the prairie is grey and so is the house in which Dorothy lives. As for Auntie Em and Uncle Henry: 'The sun and the wind…had taken the sparkle from her eyes and left them a sober grey; they had taken the red from her cheeks and lips, and they were grey also. She was thin and gaunt, and never smiled now.' Whereas 'Uncle Henry never laughed. He was grey also, from his long beard to his rough boots.' The sky? It was 'even greyer than usual.'[7]

And when Dorothy's release from greyness arrives, it is itself a maelstrom of grey: 'It is out of this greyness—the gathering, cumulative greyness of that bleak world—that calamity comes. The tornado is the greyness gathered together and whirled about and unleashed, so to speak, against itself.'

For Rushdie, we are not so much caught up in a Fall as in an uprooting and displacement into colour. Within the yearning in Judy Garland's voice

> is the human dream of *leaving*, a dream at least as powerful as its countervailing dream of roots. At the heart of *The Wizard of Oz* is a great tension between these two dreams.…In its most potent emotional moment,

this is unarguably a film about the joys of going away, of leaving the grey-ness and entering the colour, of making a new life in the 'place where there isn't any trouble.' 'Over the Rainbow' is, or ought to be, the anthem of all the world's migrants, all those who go in search of the place where 'the dreams that you dare to dream really do come true.' It is a celebra-tion of Escape, a great paean to the Uprooted Self, a hymn—the hymn—to elsewhere.

Falling or leaving: these two metaphors of colour are closely related. Their terminologies—of dreams, of joys, of uprootings or undoings of self—remain more or less the same. More than that, perhaps, the descent into colour often involves lateral as well as vertical displacement; it means being blown sideways at the same time as falling downwards. After all, Blanc's 'impassioned colourist' falls from the rational Academies of the West into the market stalls and bestiaries of the East, and numerous other accounts, chro-mophobic and chromophilic alike, describe something similar. In the end, Dorothy has to return from colour—to Home, Family, Childhood, Kansas and Grey. 'East, West, Home is Best.' So she chants (in the book), albeit with-out a chance of convincing anyone who has taken a moment to compare the land of Oz with the grey-on-grey of Kansas, as Rushdie points out. Perhaps the implications of not returning, of not recovering from the Fall into colour, were too radical for Hollywood to contemplate.

And not just for Hollywood. There is a curious parallel between the dream-journey of Dorothy and travels described by Charles-Edouard Jeanneret, aka the architect Le Corbusier, in his *Journey to the East.* Coming from the man who would later say that colour was 'suited to simple races, peasants and savages,' it's surprising to find that his first published writing is in fact an ecstatic, intoxicated, confusing, delirious, sensuous plunge into colour. Written in 1911 as a series of newspaper articles and only published in 1965 as *Le Voyage d'Orient,* this is a story of leaving and of entering colour, a story of returning and a story told as if it were a dream.

Near the beginning of the narrative, Le Corbusier describes in passing a journey by boat which is vaguely reminiscent in its monochromatic stark-ness of Conrad's journey down the Thames: 'The great white boat had left Budapest at nightfall. Helped by the strong current, it made its way down the immense watercourse that marked out with a black path to the right and the left the two distant riverbanks…'[8] This imagery makes the travel-ler's entry into colour all the more dramatic. Once in his Orient, almost every description becomes tinted; almost every observation becomes a poem to colour. Sometimes, this appears quite innocent: 'There is in the sky, before the night hardens things, a watershed of emerald green and indigo blue.' But more often, in the intense daylight, the descriptions of colours, objects, architecture and people begin to blur, spill or dissolve into each other as if their limits had been lost in a haze of sexual intensity:

> You recognise these joys: to feel the generous belly of a vase, to caress its slender neck, and then to explore the subtleties of its contours. To thrust your hands into the deepest part of your pockets and, with eyes half closed, to give way to the slow intoxication of the fantastic glazes, the bursts of yellows, the velvet tones of the blues…

A little later on: 'Everything is smothered in flowers, and under these ephemeral bouquets, other ephemeral bouquets…young girls, beautiful women, smiling, somewhat depraved, perhaps a little inflamed by their desires. Gentlemen in black play second fiddle in this orchestra of colours…' For Le Corbusier, the Orient becomes an 'explosion of colours,' and inevitably 'The eye becomes confused, a little perturbed by this kaleidoscopic cinema where dance the most dizzying combinations of colours.' His preferred description for this undifferentiated assault on the senses is a dreamy 'intoxication': 'The colour…exists for the caress and intoxication of the eye'; 'the intoxicating embrace of the moist evening, wafting voluptuously from the mountainside'; 'in the drowsiness of everything, in the vague intoxication of feeling space collapse and expand,' You are left helpless: 'You are intoxicated; you cannot react at all.'

Once again, the drug of colour begins to weigh heavily on our eyes; we become drowsy; we begin to lose consciousness as we fall under its narcotic spell; we lose focus; we lose our sense of the distinctions between things; we descend into delirium; we lose ourselves in colour as colour frees itself from the grip of objects and floods over our scrambled senses; we drown in the sexual heat of colour…And the Technicolor dream continues:

> The exterior is as red as iron reaching melting point. There it is, swollen, supple, and so close to the earth on its level shoreline, its pleasing oval forms radiant with clarity like an Egyptian alabaster urn carrying a burning lamp. The urn is strangely protective this evening, as if in mystical abandon outright gifts are torn away from living flesh and offered in painful and bloody oblations to the Beyond, to the Other, to Whomever, to any Other than the self. The overwhelming delirium of this moment and place.

We have no sense of direction. We drift. Hallucination follows hallucination. We are in confusion: '…we others from the centre of civilisation, are savages…' And then, as if by chance—although chance has no particular meaning in our dreamwork—we discover a destination, an awakening, a recovery which puts our dream into an envelope of rationality, like it did for poor Dorothy. But unlike Dorothy's, Le Corbusier's awakening occurs *within* the dream. His dream-awakening dream is the Acropolis: 'To see the Acropolis is a dream one treasures without even dreaming to realise it.' Yet, realized, this dream is no less a dream. Stuck in Athens for weeks because of a cholera outbreak, Le Corbusier reflects: 'Days and weeks passed in this dream and nightmare, in a bright morning, through an intoxicating noon, until evening…' He is entranced, captive to its absolute spell: 'Nothing existed but the temple'; it was 'an ineluctable presence'; 'the Parthenon, the undeniable Master'; 'Admiration, adoration, and then annihilation.'

Annihilation? Of what? There could be several answers to this. On the one hand, Le Corbusier is surrounded by a cholera epidemic; he sees the dead being taken from their houses; perhaps he sees his own death in the dead around him. But I suspect he had a bigger death in mind: self-annihilation in the face of the incomprehensible sublime force that was the Acropolis, and with it the annihilation of all that came before this over-whelming experience: annihilation of the Orient and everything that was the dream-journey that preceded and led to this moment of revelation; anni-hilation of confusion; annihilation, perhaps, of desire. For once he had seen the Acropolis, Le Corbusier immediately decided that he had no further need of the East; the rest of his journey (not described in the book) would be through Italy and back to France: 'I will see neither the Mosque of Omar nor the pyramids. And yet I write with eyes that have seen the Acropolis, and I will leave with joy. Oh! Light! Marbles! Monochromy!'

East, West, Home is Best.

What colour was the Parthenon in Le Corbusier's dream? Not, as one might expect from his later writings, a magnificent, triumphant, all-embracing white. Or not immediately. Rather, in his description of the great temple, next to the form, volume, mass and space of the architecture, colour begins to *give way;* colour no longer appears to be such a significant force; it no longer has the same power to intoxicate; it no longer has quite the same intensity. His description becomes more muted: 'I shall give this entire account an ochre cast'; the marbles adopt the colour of the landscape and 'seem as reddish-brown as terra-cotta.' And yet in this *reflected* colour, there is still something awesome: 'Never in my life have I experienced the subtleties of such monochromy.' Only later, during a storm, does the Parthenon whiten: 'I saw through the large drops of rain the hill becom-ing suddenly white and the temple sparkle like a diadem against the ink-black Hymettus and the Pentilicus ravaged by downpours.' Once again, the Parthenon absorbs and reflects the colours of its surroundings and atmo-sphere, but it does not seem to have colour of its own; the Parthenon is some-how beyond colour.

In Le Corbusier's earlier evocations, just about every object had brilliant local colour, and these intense hues were often intermingled with strong blacks and dazzling whites. White was the precondition for colour; colour was intensified by its proximity to white; there was no sense of opposition between the two; they were co-dependent and co-operative. That was certainly part of the brilliance of Le Corbusier's early writing on colour. The *separation* of whiteness and colour would come later. Le Corbusier in 1925 in *The Decorative Art of Today*:

> What shimmering silks, what fancy, glittering marbles, what opulent bronzes and golds! What fashionable blacks, what striking vermilions, what silver lames from Byzantium and the Orient! Enough. Such stuff founders in a narcotic haze. Let's have done with it…It is time to crusade for whitewash and Diogenes.[9]

The architect was done with drugs. He had been off them since at least 1920; the Great War had seen to that. In their place: Order. Reason. Purity. Truth. Architecture. Whitewash.

In his evangelical *Rappel à l'ordre* tirade against 'the flourish, the stain, the distracting din of colours and ornaments,' and in his campaign for a world shaped by the New Spirit and a new architecture, Le Corbusier aligned himself with the earlier but equally evangelical Adolf Loos: 'We have gone beyond ornament, we have achieved plain, undecorated simplicity. Behold, the time is at hand, fulfilment awaits us. Soon the streets of the city will shine like white walls! Like Zion, the Holy City, Heaven's capital. The fulfilment will be ours.'[10] Heaven is white; that which gets closest to God—the Parthenon, the Idea, Purity, Cleanliness—also sheds its colour. But for Le Corbusier, ornament, clutter, glitter and colour were not so much signs of primitive 'degeneracy,' as they had been for Loos, as they were the particularly modern form of degeneration that we now call kitsch. The difference is important, because at no time did Le Corbusier attack what he saw as the authentic 'simplicity' of the folk cultures of the past, cultures which, he conceded, had their own whiteness: 'Whitewash has been associated with human habitation since the birth of mankind.' The problem was, rather, modern industrialized ornamentation and colouring, a problem which, for Le Corbusier, reeked of confusion, disorder, dishonesty, imbalance, subservience, narcosis and dirt.

Thus, under the chapter title 'A Coat of Whitewash: The Law of Ripolin' (a phrase that is constantly repeated and usually capitalized):

> we would perform a moral act: *to love purity!*
> we would improve our condition: *to have the power of judgement!*

An act which leads to the joy of life: the pursuit of perfection.

Imagine the results of the Law of Ripolin. Every citizen is required to replace his hangings, his damasks, his wall-papers, his stencils, with a plain coat of white ripolin. *His home* is made clean. There are no more dirty, dark corners. *Everything is shown as it is.* Then comes *inner* cleanness, for the course adopted leads to refusal to allow anything which is not correct, authorised, intended, desired, thought-out: no action before thought. When you are surrounded with shadows and dark corners you are at home only as far as the hazy edges of the darkness your eyes cannot penetrate. You are not master in your own house. Once you have put ripolin on your walls you will be *master of your own house.*

White is clean, clear, healthy, moral, rational, masterful....White, it seems, was everywhere, at least in the minds of Le Corbusier's contemporaries and followers. Theo van Doesburg, for example:

> WHITE is the spiritual colour of our times, the clearness which directs all our actions. It is neither grey white nor ivory white, but pure white.
> WHITE is the colour of modern times, the colour which dissipates a whole era; our era is one of perfection, purity and certitude.
> WHITE It includes everything.
> We have superseded both the 'brown' of decadence and classicism and the 'blue' of divisionism, the cult of the blue sky, the gods with green beards and the spectrum.
> WHITE pure white.[11]

In Le Corbusier's intoxicated rationalism, the rhetoric of order, purity and truth is inscribed in a pure, blinding white surface. So blinding, in fact, that the discourse of modern architecture has almost entirely failed to notice that most of his buildings are actually *coloured*. This marvellous paradox in the rhetoric of whiteness has been carefully picked apart by Mark Wigley, who has observed, for example, that Le Corbusier's manifesto building, the Pavilion de l'Esprit Nouveau, built in the same year as *The Decorative Arts of Today* was written, was actually painted in ten different colours: white, black, light grey, dark grey, yellow ochre, pale yellow ochre, burnt sienna, dark burnt sienna and light blue. Wigley has noted that Le Corbusier only ever made one white building. In spite of this, he has argued, there is 'a self-imposed blindness...shared by almost all of the dominant historiographies... Colour is detached from the master narrative' of architecture. Once again, it appears that we are not dealing with something as simple as white things and white surfaces, with white as an empirically verifiable fact or as a colour. Rather, we are in the realm of *whiteness*. White as myth, as an aesthetic fantasy, a fantasy so strong that it summons up negative hallucinations, so intense that it produces a blindness to colour, even when colour is literally in front of your face.

In *Purism,* a manifesto for painting co-written in 1920 with Amedee Ozenfant, Le Corbusier writes of painting as a kind of architecture: 'A painting is an association of purified, related, and architectured elements'; 'Painting is a question of architecture.'[12] In later writing, he often describes architecture as a kind of painting, a process that follows the academic logic from 'composition,' through 'contour,' to 'light and shade.' If this is the case, if architecture is a kind of painting as much as painting is a kind of architecture, then Le Corbusier, like Blanc before him, was forced by his own logic to recognize the presence of colour in a work. This he did, and in a very similar way to Blanc. *Purism* is ultra-rationalist; the text is speckled with terms such as 'logic,' 'order,' 'control,' 'constant,' 'certainty,' 'severe,' 'system,' 'fixed,' 'universal,' 'mathematical' and so on. But, as the authors acknowledge, 'when one says painting, inevitably he says colour.' And in the Purist universe, colour is a problem, a 'perilous agent'; it has the 'properties of shock' and a 'formidable fatality'; it often 'destroys or disorganises' an art which aims to address itself 'to the elevated faculties of the mind.'

Colour, then, must be controlled. It must be ordered and classified; a hierarchy must be established. And so it is. Le Corbusier and Ozenfant come up with three 'scales' for colour: the 'major scale,' the 'dynamic scale' and the 'transitional scale.' The major scale is made up of 'ochre yellows, reds, earths, white, black, ultramarine blue and...certain of their derivatives.' This scale is 'strong' and 'stable'; it gives 'unity' and 'balance'; these colours are 'constructive' and are employed 'in all the great periods.' And they are also almost exactly the colours employed by Le Corbusier in his 1925 Pavilion. The dynamic scale is made up of 'disturbing elements': citron yellow, oranges, vermilions and other 'animated,' 'agitated' colours; the transitional scale, 'the madders, emerald green, and all the lakes,' are simply 'not of construction.' A painting 'cannot be made without colour,' but the painter is advised to stick with the major scale; therein lies the tradition of great painting. The further one drifts down the scale of colour, the further one drifts from the 'architectural aesthetic' to the 'aesthetic of printed cloth'— that is, the further one drifts from art to mere decoration. This, in the end, was Cézanne's 'error,' for he 'accepted without examination the attractive offer of the colour-vendor, in a period marked by a fad for colour-chemistry, a science with no possible effect on great painting.' Such 'sensory jubilations of the paint tube' were best left 'to the clothes-dyers,' because while painting could not be made without colour, 'in a true and durable plastic work, it is *form* which comes first and everything else should be subordinated to it.' The 'architectural' aesthetic of painting was concerned with the unified representation of volumes (whereas the clothes-dyers' aesthetic was limited to flat patterns); colours of the 'major scale' were strong and stable insofar as they served and emphasized this representation of volume. The same logic applies to the 'painterly' aesthetic of Le Corbusier's architecture: the function of coloured planes in a space is to render the volumes and spaces more balanced and coherent, more exact and, in the end, more white: 'To tell the truth, my house does not seem white unless I have disposed the active forces of colours and values in the appropriate places.' White must be whiter than white, and to achieve that, colour must be added.

It doesn't much matter whether this hierarchy of colours is coherent, any more than it matters whether Blanc's cosmology of colour makes any real sense. What matters is the show of force: the rhetorical subordination of colour to the rule of line and the higher concerns of the mind. No longer intoxicating, narcotic or orgasmic, colour is learned, ordered, subordinated and tamed. Broken.

Notes

*   David Batchelor, *Chromophobia* (London: Reaktion Books, 2000), 31.

1   Charles Blanc, quoted in Charles A. Riley II, *Color Codes* (Hanover and London, 1995), p. 6.

2   Aristotle, quoted in Jacqueline Lichtenstein, *The Eloquence of Color: Rhetoric and Painting in the French Classical Age,* trans. E. McVarish (Berkeley, 1993), p. 59.

3   John Gage, *Colour and Culture* (London, 1993), p. 10.

4   Jean-Jacques Rousseau, *Discourses and Essay on the Origins of Language,* trans. Victor Gourevitch (New York, 1986), pp. 239–94, 279.

5   Joshua Reynolds, 'Discourse IV,' in *Discourses,* ed. Pat Rogers (London, 1992), p. 129.

6   Bernard Berenson, *Aesthetics and History* (London, 1950), p. 76.

7   Salman Rushdie, *The Wizard of Oz* (London, 1992), p. 16.

8   Le Corbusier, *Journey to the East,* trans. I. Zaknic (Cambridge, MA, 1987), p. 19. Subsequent quotations are from pp. 14, 16, 20, 24, 25, 26, 36, 110, 140, 177, 203, 207, 209–12, 216, 230.

9   Le Corbusier, *The Decorative Art of Today,* in *Essential Le Corbusier: L'Esprit Nouveau Articles,* trans. J. Dunnett (Oxford, 1998), p. 135.

10   Adolf Loos, 'Ornament and Crime,' in *The Architecture of Adolf Loos,* trans. W. Wang (London, 1985), p. 168.

11   Theo van Doesburg, quoted in Mark Wigley, *White Walls, Designer Dresses: The Fashioning of Modern Architecture* (Cambridge, MA, and London, 1995), p. 239.

12   Le Corbusier and Amédée Ozenfant, 'Purism,' in *Modern Artists on Art: Ten Unabridged Essays,* ed. R. L. Herbert (New Brunswick, NJ, 1964), pp. 67, 70. Subsequent quotations are from pp. 67–71.

The Principle of Cladding

Adolf Loos

INTRODUCTION

In a series of writings to the Viennese newspaper Neue Freie Presse *at the turn of the twentieth century, Adolf Loos addressed architectural styles and laid out rules for constructing architecture and interiors, fabricating furniture and decorative arts, using materials and clothing style. With an overtly passionate voice that still can be confused with sanctimoniousness, he adamantly proselytized his design ideology. By writing for a newspaper, he was able to reach an audience that included the general public, making the dissemination of his ideas more accessible outside of architecture and the arts.*

"The Principle of Cladding" is an essay in which he analyzed the application of finished surfaces. It specifically pertained to architecture and interiors, but he brought in examples from furniture and clothing, and less obvious examples such as tramcars, to prove the objectivity of his rule. Loos developed his arguments on logic and the notion of pure materials and appropriate applications. Looking back to this commitment to rational simplification, including removing all ornamental pretense and critical propriety—and along with his habit of denigrating the artistic Vienna Secession style of the time—has led historians to credit Loos as an early proponent of modernism.

Loos looked to interior specification categories for his rule of cladding. Simply put, a material may not be clad with an imitation of itself. To prove his point, he writes justifications—such as the need for materials to perform functionally rather than artistically—with the argument that function results in good aesthetics. The decision to choose materials, such as enameled tile in bathrooms, reveals how these decisions drive an aesthetic. In one case, Loos supported his argument with an example outside architecture and interiors. By looking at clothing, he concluded that underclothes can be any

Originally appeared in *Spoken into the Void: Collected Essays by Adolf Loos,* 1897–1900, Oppositions Books series, translated by Jane O. Newman and John H. Smith, 2,115 word excerpt from pages 66–69. © 1982 Massachusetts Institute of Technology, by permission of The MIT Press.

color other than that of the color of skin. He used this example to make his point about building materials—that wood should not be clad in an imitation of itself.

Revisiting Loos's essay in contemporary times offers perspective on current materials that contradict Loos's beliefs without questioning current practices. Much of Loos's ideology relied on inhabiting the interior as a starting point. His attention to surface finishes reveals a potential area for articulating the interior.

———

EVEN IF ALL MATERIALS are of equal value to the artist, they are not equally suited to all his purposes. The requisite durability, the necessary construction often demand materials that are not in harmony with the true purpose of the building. The architect's general task is to provide a warm and livable space. Carpets are warm and livable. He decides for this reason to spread out one carpet on the floor and to hang up four to form the four walls. But you cannot build a house out of carpets. Both the carpet on the floor and the tapestry on the wall require a structural frame to hold them in the correct place. To invent this frame is the architect's second task.

This is the correct and logical path to be followed in architecture. It was in this sequence that mankind learned how to build. In the beginning was cladding.[1] Man sought shelter from inclement weather and protection and warmth while he slept. He sought to cover himself. The covering is the oldest architectural detail. Originally it was made out of animal skins or textile products. This meaning of the word is still known today in the Germanic languages.[2] Then the covering had to be put up somewhere if it was to afford enough shelter to a family! Thus the walls were added, which at the same time provided protection on the sides. In this way the idea of architecture developed in the minds of mankind and individual men.

There are architects who do things differently. Their imaginations create not spaces but sections of walls. That which is left over around the walls then forms the rooms. And for these rooms some kind of cladding is subsequently chosen, whatever seems fitting to the architect.

But the artist, the *architect,* first senses the effect that he intends to realize and sees the rooms he wants to create in his mind's eye. He senses the effect that he wishes to exert upon the spectator: fear and horror if it is a dungeon, reverence if a church, respect for the power of the state if a government palace, piety if a tomb, homeyness if a residence, gaiety if a tavern. These effects are produced by both the material and the form of the space.

Every material possesses its own language of forms, and none may lay claim for itself to the forms of another material. For forms have been

constituted out of the applicability and the methods of production of materials. They have come into being with and through materials. No material permits an encroachment into its own circle of forms. Whoever dares to make
such an encroachment notwithstanding this is branded by the world a coun-
terfeiter. Art, however, has nothing to do with counterfeiting or lying. Her
paths are full of thorns, but they are pure.

One could cast St. Stefan's Tower in cement and erect it somewhere,
but then it would not be a work of art. And what goes for the Stefan's Tower
also goes for the Pitti Palace; and what goes for the Pitti Palace goes for the
Farnese Palace. And with this building we have arrived in the midst of our
own Ringstrasse architecture. It was a sad time for art, a sad time for those
few artists among the architects of that time who were forced to prostitute
their art for the sake of the masses. It was granted to only a small number
consistently to find contractors broad-minded enough to let the artist have
his way. Schmidt was probably the luckiest. After him came Hansen, who,
when he was having a rough time, sought solace in terra-cotta buildings.
Poor Ferstel must have endured terrible agonies when they forced him at
the last minute to nail an entire section of facade in poured cement onto his
University.[3] The remaining architects of this period—with a few exceptions—
knew how to keep themselves free of nightmarish agonies like these.

Is it any different now? Allow me to answer this question. Imitation
and surrogate art still dominate architecture. Yes, more than ever. In recent
years people have even appeared who have lent themselves to defending
this tendency (one person, of course, did so anonymously, since the issue did
not seem clear-cut enough to him); so that the surrogate architect no longer
need stand diminutively on the sidelines. Nowadays one nails the structure
to the facade with aplomb and hangs the "keystone" under the main molding
with artistic authority. But come hither, you heralds of imitation, you makers of stenciled inlays, of botch-up-your-home windows and papier-mâché
tankards! There is a new spring awakening for you in Vienna! The earth is
freshly fertilized!

But is the living space that has been constructed entirely of rugs not
an imitation? The walls are not really built out of carpets! Certainly not. But
these carpets are meant only to be carpets and not building stones. They
were never meant to be taken as such, to imitate them in form or color, but
rather to reveal clearly their own meaning as a cladding for the wall surface.
They fulfill their purpose according to the principles of cladding.

As I already mentioned at the outset, cladding is older even than structure. The reasons for cladding things are numerous. At times it is a protection
against bad weather—oil-base paint, for example, on wood, iron, or stone; at
times there are hygienic reasons for it—as in the case of enameled tiles that
cover the wall surfaces in the bathroom; at times it is the means to a specific

effect—as in the color painting of statues, the tapestries on walls, the veneer on wood. The principle of cladding, which was first articulated by Semper, extends to nature as well. Man is covered with skin, the tree with bark.

From the principle of cladding, however, I have derived a very precise law which I call the law of cladding. Do not be alarmed. It is usually said that laws put an end to all progressive development. And indeed, the old masters got along perfectly well without laws. Certainly. It would be idleness to establish laws against thievery in a place where thievery is unknown. When the materials used for cladding had not yet been imitated, there was no need for laws. But now it seems to me to be high time for them.

The law goes like this: we must work in such a way that a confusion of the material clad with its cladding is impossible. That means, for example, that wood may be painted any color except one—the color of wood. In a city where the exhibition committee decided that all of the wood in the Rotunda should be painted "like mahogany," in a city in which wood graining is the exclusive type of painted decoration, this is a very daring law. There seem to be people here who consider this kind of thing elegant. Since the railway and tramway cars—as well as the entire technique of carriage building—come from England, they are the only wooden objects that display pure colors. I now dare to assert that this kind of tramcar—especially one of the electric line—is more pleasing to me with its pure colors than it would be if, according to the principles of beauty set out by the exhibition committee, it had been painted "like mahogany."

But a true feeling for elegance lies dormant, although deep and buried, even in our people. If not, the railway administration could not count on the fact that the brown color of the third-class cars painted to look like wood would call forth a lesser feeling of elegance than the green color of the second- and first-class cars.

I once demonstrated this unconscious feeling to one of my colleagues in a drastic manner. On the first floor of a building there were two apartments. The tenant of the one apartment had had his window bars, which had been stained brown, painted white at his own expense. We made a bet according to which we brought a certain number of people to the front of the building and, without pointing out to them the difference between the window bars, asked them on which side they felt that Herr Pluntzengruber lived and on which side Prince Liechtenstein—these were the two parties that we told them rented the apartments. All of those who were taken to the building unanimously declared that the wood-stained side was Pluntzengruber's. Since then my colleague has only painted things white.

Wood staining is, of course, an invention of our century. The Middle Ages painted wood bright red for the most part, the Renaissance blue; the Baroque and Rococo painted interiors white, exteriors green. Our peasants still retain enough good sense to paint only with pure colors. Don't the green gate and the green fence of the countryside, the green jalousies against the freshly whitewashed wall, have a charming effect? Unfortunately several villages have already adopted the taste of the exhibition commission.

One will still recall the moral indignation that arose in the camp of the surrogate arts and crafts when the first furniture painted with oil-base paint came to Vienna from England. But the rage of these good men was not directed against the paint. They painted with oil-base paints in Vienna too as soon as softwood came into use. But the fact that the English pieces dared to display their colors so openly and freely instead of imitating hardwood provoked these strange fellows. They rolled their eyes and acted as if they had never used oil-base colors at all. These gentlemen presumably thought that everyone hitherto had assumed their stained-wood furniture and buildings were actually made of hardwood.

I trust I can be assured of the Association's gratitude if, after such observations, I name no names among the painters at the exhibition.

Applied to stuccowork, the principle of cladding would run like this: stucco can take any ornament with just one exception—rough brickwork. One would think the declaration of such a self-evident fact to be unnecessary, but just recently someone drew my attention to a building whose plaster walls were painted red and then seamed with white lines. Similarly, the type of decoration so beloved in kitchens—imitation stone squares—belongs in this category. In general, any and all materials used to cover walls—wallpaper, oilcloth, fabric, or tapestries—ought not to aspire to represent squares of brick or stone. It is thus easy to understand why the legs of our dancers when covered with knit stockinets have such an unaesthetic effect. Woven underclothing may be dyed any color at all, just not skin color.

The cladding material can keep its natural color if the area to be covered happens to be of the same color. Thus, I can smear tar on black iron or cover wood with another wood (veneer, marquetry, and so on) without having to color the covering wood; I can coat one metal with another by heating or galvanizing it. But the principle of cladding forbids the cladding material to imitate the coloration of the underlying material. Thus iron can be tarred, painted with oil colors, or galvanized, but it can never be camouflaged with a bronze color or any other metallic color.

Here *chamottes*[4] and artificial stone tiles also deserve mention. The one kind imitates terrazzo (mosaic) paving, the other Persian carpets. Certainly there are people who actually take the tiles for what they are imitating—for the manufacturers must know their customers.

But no, you imitators and surrogate architects, you are mistaken! The human soul is too lofty and sublime for you to be able to dupe it with your tactics and tricks. Of course, our pitiful bodies are in your power. They have only five senses at their disposal to distinguish real from counterfeit. And at that point where the man with his sense organs is no longer adequate begins your true domain. There is your realm. But even here—you are mistaken once more! Paint the best inlays high, high up on the wood ceiling and our poor eyes will have to take it on good faith perhaps. But the divine spirits will not be fooled by your tricks. They sense that even those intarsia decorations most skillfully painted to look "like inlay" are nothing but oil paint.

Notes

1   *Bekleidung.* "*Bekleidung* signifies the external covering of the building materials by other materials, either for technical reasons—for example, weatherproofing—or aesthetic ones.…The problem of so called correctness of materials *[Materialgerechtheit]* is closely related to the question of *Bekleidung*" (*Wasmuths Lexikon der Baukunst* [Leipzig, 1932]). The root *Kleidung* means "clothing."

2   Besides its general meaning of "covering" or "blanket," and its architectural meaning of "ceiling" or "roof," in anatomy *Decke* signifies the skin or coat of an animal.

3   Friedrich Schmidt (1825–1891), Theophil Hansen (1813–1891), and Heinrich von Ferstel (1828–1883) were three of the chief architects of the Vienna Ringstrasse, most of which was built from 1861 to 1865 and from 1868 to 1873. Vienna University, in the Italian Renaissance style, was built by Ferstel from 1873 to 1884. Ferstel also designed and built the Austrian Museum for Art and Industry; it was completed in 1871.

4   Tiles made out of crushed pieces of pottery.

The Amber Room: Introduction

Catherine Scott-Clark and Adrian Levy

INTRODUCTION

Catherine Scott-Clark and Adrian Levy investigated the mystery of the disappearance of the Amber Room during the politically charged atmosphere in the Soviet Union during the German invasion at the start of World War II. A valuable room in the Catherine Palace in Leningrad, the Amber Room was celebrated for the richness and glow of its material. But after the Nazis dismantled the room in 1941, the Amber Room was thrust into a new historical context. Its exemplary interior was no longer its predominant feature, surpassed instead by the perception of the room as a symbol of Russian culture undone by the throes of politics. Interiors are rarely viewed through such a lens, but political events are often played out in interior spaces.

In 1941 the palace's curators knew the room's monetary and political significance, so they developed a plan to hide it. But unlike other treasures and artworks that could be packed away, the room itself posed a challenge because the amber was adhered to the walls and its removal led to crumbling. An initial, hopeful solution—adding a layer of surface wadding over it—was attempted to mask it. When the curators returned to the palace in 1944 they found an empty room and no amber. Scott-Clark and Levy's concise introduction revisits a decades-old mystery and their search worldwide to uncover the story's missing pieces.

Treasures can be hidden at many scales. The Amber Room, at the scale of politics and national identity, recalls the role museums play in keeping cultural treasures secure. An equivalent in terms of personal possessions would be a safe or jewelry box. But a significant difference between the two is the impossibility of removing an interior that is itself the jewel, as in the case of the Amber Room. Its delicate and brittle nature asks, how can a room be preserved when its interior skin is permanently affixed? In contrast, contemporary interiors treat wall surfaces as skins that can easily change by wallpaper or paint color. Interior skins no longer retain the same preciousness as historical examples.

Originally appeared in *The Amber Room: The Untold Story of the Greatest Hoax of the Twentieth Century*, 3–8. Used by permission of Atlantic, an imprint of Atlantic Books, London. © Catherine Scott-Clark and Adrian Levy 2004.

Loos's theme of structure and cladding can be seen in the Amber Room, as both interior space and artifact, but the room moves beyond this dialogue because of the symbolic role the interior played in representing the riches of a country and the pivotal role it played in war and politics. Where rooms are often passive sites in political events, Scott-Clark and Levy cast the Amber Room at the center.

———

AN URGENT ORDER arrived just after midday on 22 June 1941: pack up Leningrad. The Nazis had invaded the Soviet Union at 4 that morning without a declaration of war. So rapid was the advance that the Kremlin calculated Leningrad's southern gateway of Moskovsky Prospekt would be overrun within weeks.

But 22 June was a radiant Sunday, the first in what had been a lousy year. Weekend revellers strolled along the banks of the River Neva, popping bottles of sweet Soviet champagne, or headed out to the suburban estates of the former tsars, their hampers filled with herrings and pickled mushrooms. The scale of the crisis only filtered through the city by 6 p. m. Grinding across the Soviet Union was the greatest invasion force in history: 4 million German soldiers, 207 Wehrmacht divisions, 3,300 tanks.

Evacuate Leningrad's treasures. The order came from LenGorIsPolKom (the city's executive committee). Everyone was listening now. Collections from the city's palaces and museums had to be saved. But there were 2.5 million exhibits in the State Hermitage, and hundreds of thousands more in the Alexander, Catherine and Pavlovsk Palaces as well as the collections housed at Peterhof, Oranienbaum and Gatchina.

A curator at the Catherine Palace in the town of Pushkin scribbled in his diary: '22 June. Flown through the halls this evening, packing what we can.'

But there was too much work: '24 June. Comrades having nosebleeds from leaning over the packing crates. Run out of boxes and paper....Had to use the tsarinas' dress trunks and their clothes to wrap up our treasures.'[1]

And what should they do with the city's most unique treasure, an artefact that was often said to encompass old Russia's imperial might? At the centre of a chain of linked halls on the first floor of the Catherine Palace, where salon opened into salon, stood a gorgeous chamber made of amber, a substance that, at the time of its construction, was twelve times more valuable than gold.

The idea of panelling a room entirely in amber had first been mooted at the Prussian court in 1701. The resulting radical and complex construction came to symbolize the Age of Reason in which it was conceived. Tons of resin, the Gold of the North, had been fished in nuggets from the Baltic Sea, then heated, shaped and coloured before being slotted together on huge backing boards like a gigantic jigsaw puzzle. When, sixty years later, the panels of the Amber Room were gifted to Russia, they were heralded by visitors to the court in St Petersburg as the 'Eighth Wonder of the World.' 'We have now reached one of the most remarkable rarities—I want to tell you about the Amber Room,' wrote a French novelist. 'Only in *The Thousand and One Nights* and in magic fairy tales, where the architecture of palaces is trusted to magicians, spirits and genies, can one read about rooms made of diamonds, rubies, jacinth and other jewels.'[2]

Even after the Revolution, when the estates of the tsars were transformed into Soviet museums, the Amber Room remained Leningrad's most popular exhibit.[3] But by the summer of 1941, the installation of central heating had made the amber brittle and the Catherine Palace staff feared dismantling it. When, eight days after Germany invaded, the first Soviet train loaded with exhibits steamed out of Leningrad and east toward Siberia, the Amber Room was not on board.

The curators left behind had no more time to think about it. They were enlisted to bolster the town's defences. One wrote in her diary: 'We carry out the work of guards, office workers, cleaners. All walls are bare.' Apart from the walls of the Amber Room.

By the end of August, the Nazis had taken Mga, a railway terminal 10 miles south of Leningrad, isolating two million citizens who would not see the outside world for almost 900 days. It was now too late to evacuate anything else. By 1 September a Nazi perimeter bristling with munitions had fenced the city in. The British monitored the advance: '9 September. XVI Panzer Korps is moving to Leningrad.'

On 13 September the town of Pushkin came under fire. 'Koluft Panzer Group Four now in Detskoye Selo [Pushkin].' The following day, the attack came from above. 'Fliegerkorps have landed. Attack on Pushkin has been carried out. All bombs have landed in the target area.'

Inside the Catherine Palace, a handful of curators continued to work, attempting to safeguard what they could, scattering sand on the floors to protect the precious inlaid wood, packing all but the most cumbersome pieces of furniture into storerooms. But there was still one thing that no one had properly secured.

Couriers carried reports from Pushkin back to the city authorities in Leningrad. The last came on 17 September at 5 a.m.: 'The park and north of the town are battling hard. Everyone is moving to the west. We have even taken the typewriters. We will leave nothing for them.'

Apart from the Amber Room, which was hidden in the dark beneath another, plainer room constructed out of muslin and cotton. Rather than evacuate it, Catherine Palace staff had decided to conceal the delicate treasure in situ. The irreplaceable amber walls had been covered over with layers of cloth and padding. If the Nazis managed to force their way into the Catherine Palace, it was hoped they would be deceived into thinking that here was just another ordinary, empty room.

Within hours the palace was overrun. One German officer described how almost immediately crude signs were nailed to the gilded doors, listing them 'reserved for the 1st Company etc., etc....'[4] Everywhere there were 'sleeping [German] soldiers with their muddy boots resting on the precious settees and chairs.' The Nazi advance had been exhaustingly rapid. Then a cheer went up and the German officer raced to see what his men had discovered. On the first floor, in a room in the middle of a long corridor, 'two privates in curiosity toiled in tearing protective...covers off [the walls]. They revealed wonderfully shining amber carvings, the frames of a mosaic picture.'

When Soviet curators returned to the Catherine Palace in March 1944 they entered through the buckled iron gates and across a courtyard strewn with barbed wire and Nazi graves. Up to the first-floor suite of rooms they climbed—not by the marble stairs, as they had been blown to smithereens— and discovered that where they had concealed the 'Eighth Wonder of the World' there was now just a void. The Amber Room had vanished. All the Nazis had left behind were bare boards and a tangled mystery.

In the Autumn of 2001 we pieced together this much of the story about the Amber Room using a handful of published sources and the declassified Enigma files at the Public Records Office in London, in which are recorded some of the 2,000 signals intercepted every day by the Ultra project that eavesdropped on German communications throughout the Second World War.[5]

Our curiosity about the fate of the Amber Room, then a subject of which we knew very little, had been roused by a stream of press releases and news stories coming out of Russia and Germany. In 1999, a German company had stepped in to help the Russians construct a replica of the original Amber Room with a gift of 3.5 million dollars. Now, one and a half years later, the project was almost complete and the stage was set for a grand unveiling.

The St Petersburg and Moscow authorities gushed about their new Amber Room, describing it as a memorial to everything the Soviet Union had lost in the Second World War. Publicity from the German sponsors extolled the rebuilding project as a symbol of the new Europe, without a Wall or Iron Curtain. The Kremlin announced it would invite forty heads of state and government to the opening, which was set to coincide with the three-hundredth anniversary of the founding of St Petersburg on 31 May 2003. The event was to be televised live from a specially constructed press centre that could house 1,000 journalists. The budget for the celebrations would run into billions of roubles. So much was being invested in the new Amber Room and yet no one seemed able to resolve the fate of the original masterpiece. It was now said to be worth more than 250 million dollars, a figure that made it the most valuable missing work of art in the world.

There are, we discovered, many different types of treasure hunters. Key 'Amber Room' into an Internet search engine or any online newspaper library and see over 800,000 entries pop up.

A group of salvage experts have for years been scouring the catacombs that run beneath the German city of Weimar in the belief that the Amber Room was secretly transferred to the Baltic city of Königsberg and then on to Weimar by Nazi agents acting for the Gauleiter of East Prussia.

Divers regularly explore the rusting wreck of the *Wilhelm Gustloff*, a German liner torpedoed on 31 January 1945 as it sailed from the Baltic port of Gotenhafen, north-west of Danzig. The liner was evacuating 10,582 wounded Germans away from Königsberg and the advancing Soviet front. It was also said to be carrying the Amber Room.

Mining experts regularly congregate in western Saxony and Thuringia where the countryside is honeycombed with deep ore and potash pits in the belief that as the Nazis had used mines and caves to hide important art works, the Amber Room too had been secreted in the subterranean tunnels.

These different theories and their backers, a league of treasure hunters from Europe, the United States and Russia, have spawned thousands of potential leads and a dizzying world of conspiracy. As we write this, there are more than a dozen German digs under way, each underpinned by a different theory.

However, in Russia there is an information black hole. Almost every official directly connected to the original Amber Room is dead or missing. Political and economic conditions have led to their files, diaries and memorabilia being broken up, stolen, concealed and classified. Even after glasnost and perestroika, the most important Russian archives that might contain material on the official searches for the Amber Room are arcane. The museum authorities in Moscow and St Petersburg are awkward and often inhospitable (especially to those who come without offers of international funding or research exchanges).

We had no previous experience of working in Russia or the former Eastern bloc, but had for more than a decade earned a reputation for chasing difficult stories, researching out in the field and inside archives in America, Britain, China and India, for British newspapers and broadcasters. Russia seemed like the best place to start. It was vast, obstreperous and secretive. It was also therefore likely to be the place that had retained the most secrets, even if they were difficult to extract.

In December 2001 we flew to St Petersburg and made slow progress through official channels. However, friends from the former Leningrad University, experts at living creatively, suggested another, more lateral strategy. They helped us piece together a network of subordinate characters, Red Army veterans, old comrades, serving and retired museum curators. One knew another. An introduction led to a dinner invitation. Slowly—so slowly at times that we felt as if we were going nowhere at all—we reached back in time and unearthed the stories of those directly involved in the Amber Room mystery.

In dachas and apartments, on park benches and in faceless offices, memories came alive, loosened by vodka, sweet black tea and white beer. For every official file, diary or briefing paper said by archives and libraries to be missing or inaccessible, we found draft or duplicate documents stashed away in living rooms and in hallways. For every government album that had been emptied or was lost, we discovered framed photos above mantelpieces and in bedroom drawers.

Six decades of secret and often frantic searching for the Amber Room came alive, as did the extraordinary efforts of those who struggled to suppress the truth about its fate. Our first faltering weeks in Russia grew into a two-year investigation and finally, having travelled thousands of miles from St Petersburg to Moscow, London to Washington, and from Holland, through Germany to Liechtenstein and Austria, following a paper trail that took us into the parallel worlds of the KGB and the East German Stasi, we arrived in the beat-up Russian enclave of Kaliningrad and at the heart of an extraordinary cover-up.

It was here, in a dying city on the Baltic, as the winter began to thaw, that the final pieces of the Amber Room mystery came together and we were forced to confront the truth about a story that would challenge the way we perceive the Soviet Union and its place in the Cold War.

Notes

1   Susanne Massie has researched an account of the evacuations of the Leningrad palaces. See Susanne Massie, *Pavlovsk,* Hodder and Stoughton, London, 1990.

2   See Théophile Gautier, *Voyage en Russie,* Paris, 1866.

3   The Catherine Palace had some of its rooms transformed into a museum as early as 1918.

4   Hans Hundsdörfer, who served with the 6th Panzer Division, quoted in Paul Enke, *Bernsteinzimmer Report,* Die Wirtschaft, East Berlin, 1986, pp. 15–16.

5   See footnotes in Chapter 2 [of Scott-Clark and Levy, *The Amber Room,* 2004] for a list of files to access in the National Archives, Kew, Surrey.

The Yellow Wallpaper

Charlotte Perkins Gilman

INTRODUCTION

Wallpaper often takes a latent role in the domestic interior. Charlotte Perkins Gilman, the early-twentieth-century feminist writer, recognized this and transformed wallpaper into a central figure in her short story The Yellow Wallpaper. *She began with wallpaper's familiarity as a background presence and assigned it a prominent role in addressing issues that surrounded the secondary role of women in her society.*

The characters, a young couple vacationing in a rented country house shortly after the birth of their first child, are in residence there to relieve the mother's nerves from childbirth and postpartum depression. Her husband and brother, both doctors, prescribe medical treatment. The prescription includes assigning her a children's room in the attic, away from her family, so she will not be disturbed. She is kept from her writing, which the men see as unnecessary, a hindrance in her healing. For her, writing is a means to recovery that the men have denied her. In the bedroom, the patterned yellow wallpaper becomes more and more familiar to her during the hours when she is confined to the room. What develops over the weeks is the main character's relationship to the wallpaper, which she believes becomes alive at night with the imagery of women held behind bars, symbolic of her own situation. The woman's relationship to the wallpaper intensifies, while the one with her husband wanes.

Another world is set up between the room's interior, the wallpaper, and what lies behind it. It is within this thin layer that the story develops. Anthropomorphic qualities are assigned to the wallpaper, giving it a psychological dimension not ordinarily addressed in the interior.

Writing the setting of the room allowed Gilman to build on the tangible elements of the house so that her character could reach a state of enlightenment, madness, or both. Her fictional story is now regarded as a critical

Originally appeared in *The New England Magazine* (January 1892).

contribution to the feminist discourse, yet it is rarely read in interior design curricula. Reading The Yellow Wallpaper *through the lens of interior gives wallpaper the opportunity to bring forward the importance that subtle, background imagery can play.*

———

IT IS VERY seldom that mere ordinary people like John and myself secure ancestral halls for the summer.

A colonial mansion, a hereditary estate, I would say a haunted house, and reach the height of romantic felicity—but that would be asking too much of fate!

Still I will proudly declare that there is something queer about it.

Else, why should it be let so cheaply? And why have stood so long untenanted?

John laughs at me, of course, but one expects that in marriage.

John is practical in the extreme. He has no patience with faith, an intense horror of superstition, and he scoffs openly at any talk of things not to be felt and seen and put down in figures.

John is a physician, and *perhaps*—(I would not say it to a living soul, of course, but this is dead paper and a great relief to my mind)—*perhaps* that is one reason I do not get well faster.

You see he does not believe I am sick!

And what can one do?

If a physician of high standing, and one's own husband, assures friends and relatives that there is really nothing the matter with one but temporary nervous depression—a slight hysterical tendency—what is one to do?

My brother is also a physician, and also of high standing, and he says the same thing.

So I take phosphates or phosphites—whichever it is, and tonics, and journeys, and air, and exercise, and am absolutely forbidden to "work" until I am well again.

Personally, I disagree with their ideas.

Personally, I believe that congenial work, with excitement and change, would do me good.

But what is one to do?

I did write for a while in spite of them; but it *does* exhaust me a good deal—having to be so sly about it, or else meet with heavy opposition.

I sometimes fancy that my condition if I had less opposition and more society and stimulus—but John says the very worst thing I can do is to think about my condition, and I confess it always makes me feel bad.

So I will let it alone and talk about the house.

The most beautiful place! It is quite alone, standing well back from the road, quite three miles from the village. It makes me think of English places that you read about, for there are hedges and walls and gates that lock, and lots of separate little houses for the gardeners and people.

There is a *delicious* garden! I never saw such a garden—large and shady, full of box-bordered paths, and lined with long grape-covered arbors with seats under them.

There were greenhouses, too, but they are all broken now.

There was some legal trouble, I believe, something about the heirs and coheirs; anyhow, the place has been empty for years.

That spoils my ghostliness, I am afraid, but I don't care—there is something strange about the house—I can feel it.

I even said so to John one moonlight evening, but he said what I felt was a draught, and shut the window.

I get unreasonably angry with John sometimes. I'm sure I never used to be so sensitive. I think it is due to this nervous condition.

But John says if I feel so, I shall neglect proper self-control; so I take pains to control myself—before him, at least, and that makes me very tired.

I don't like our room a bit. I wanted one downstairs that opened on the piazza and had roses all over the window, and such pretty old-fashioned chintz hangings! But John would not hear of it.

He said there was only one window and not room for two beds, and no near room for him if he took another.

He is very careful and loving, and hardly lets me stir without special direction.

I have a schedule prescription for each hour in the day; he takes all care from me, and so I feel basely ungrateful not to value it more.

He said we came here solely on my account, that I was to have perfect rest and all the air I could get. "Your exercise depends on your strength, my dear," said he, "and your food somewhat on your appetite; but air you can absorb all the time." So we took the nursery at the top of the house.

It is a big, airy room, the whole floor nearly, with windows that look all ways, and air and sunshine galore. It was nursery first and then playroom and gymnasium, I should judge; for the windows are barred for little children, and there are rings and things in the walls.

The paint and paper look as if a boys' school had used it. It is stripped off—the paper—in great patches all around the head of my bed, about as far as I can reach, and in a great place on the other side of the room low down. I never saw a worse paper in my life.

One of those sprawling flamboyant patterns committing every artistic sin.

It is dull enough to confuse the eye in following, pronounced enough to constantly irritate and provoke study, and when you follow the lame uncertain curves for a little distance they suddenly commit suicide—plunge off at outrageous angles, destroy themselves in unheard of contradictions.

The color is repellent, almost revolting; a smouldering unclean yellow, strangely faded by the slow-turning sunlight.

It is a dull yet lurid orange in some places, a sickly sulphur tint in others.

No wonder the children hated it! I should hate it myself if I had to live in this room long.

There comes John, and I must put this away—he hates to have me write a word.

We have been here two weeks, and I haven't felt like writing before, since that first day.

I am sitting by the window now, up in this atrocious nursery, and there is nothing to hinder my writing as much as I please, save lack of strength.

John is away all day, and even some nights when his cases are serious.

I am glad my case is not serious!

But these nervous troubles are dreadfully depressing.

John does not know how much I really suffer. He knows there is no reason to suffer, and that satisfies him.

Of course it is only nervousness. It does weigh on me so not to do my duty in any way!

I meant to be such a help to John, such a real rest and comfort, and here I am a comparative burden already!

Nobody would believe what an effort it is to do what little I am able—to dress and entertain, and other things.

It is fortunate Mary is so good with the baby. Such a dear baby!

And yet I *cannot* be with him, it makes me so nervous.

I suppose John never was nervous in his life. He laughs at me so about this wallpaper!

At first he meant to repaper the room, but afterwards he said that I was letting it get the better of me, and that nothing was worse for a nervous patient than to give way to such fancies.

He said that after the wallpaper was changed it would be the heavy bedstead, and then the barred windows, and then that gate at the head of the stairs, and so on.

"You know the place is doing you good," he said, "and really, dear, I don't care to renovate the house just for a three months' rental."

"Then do let us go downstairs," I said, "there are such pretty rooms there."

Then he took me in his arms and called me a blessed little goose, and said he would go down to the cellar, if I wished, and have it whitewashed into the bargain.

But he is right enough about the beds and windows and things.

It is an airy and comfortable room as any one need wish, and, of course, I would not be so silly as to make him uncomfortable just for a whim.

I'm really getting quite fond of the big room, all but that horrid paper.

Out of one window I can see the garden, those mysterious deep-shaded arbors, the riotous old-fashioned flowers, and bushes and gnarly trees.

Out of another I get a lovely view of the bay and a little private wharf belonging to the estate. There is a beautiful shaded lane that runs down there from the house. I always fancy I see people walking in these numerous paths and arbors, but John has cautioned me not to give way to fancy in the least. He says that with my imaginative power and habit of story-making, a nervous weakness like mine is sure to lead to all manner of excited fancies, and that I ought to use my will and good sense to check the tendency. So I try.

I think sometimes that if I were only well enough to write a little it would relieve the press of ideas and rest me.

But I find I get pretty tired when I try.

It is so discouraging not to have any advice and companionship about my work. When I get really well, John says we will ask Cousin Henry and Julia down for a long visit; but he says he would as soon put fireworks in my pillow-case as to let me have those stimulating people about now.

I wish I could get well faster.

But I must not think about that. This paper looks to me as if it *knew* what a vicious influence it had!

There is a recurrent spot where the pattern lolls like a broken neck and two bulbous eyes stare at you upside down.

I get positively angry with the impertinence of it and the everlasting-ness. Up and down and sideways they crawl, and those absurd, unblinking eyes are everywhere. There is one place where two breadths didn't match, and the eyes go all up and down the line, one a little higher than the other.

I never saw so much expression in an inanimate thing before, and we all know how much expression they have! I used to lie awake as a child and get more entertainment and terror out of blank walls and plain furniture than most children could find in a toy store.

I remember what a kindly wink the knobs of our big, old bureau used to have, and there was one chair that always seemed like a strong friend.

I used to feel that if any of the other things looked too fierce I could always hop into that chair and be safe.

The furniture in this room is no worse than inharmonious, however, for we had to bring it all from downstairs. I suppose when this was used as a playroom they had to take the nursery things out, and no wonder! I never saw such ravages as the children have made here.

The wallpaper, as I said before, is torn off in spots, and it sticketh closer than a brother—they must have had perseverance as well as hatred.

Then the floor is scratched and gouged and splintered, the plaster itself is dug out here and there, and this great heavy bed which is all we found in the room, looks as if it had been through the wars.

But I don't mind it a bit—only the paper.

There comes John's sister. Such a dear girl as she is, and so careful of me! I must not let her find me writing.

She is a perfect and enthusiastic housekeeper, and hopes for no better profession. I verily believe she thinks it is the writing which made me sick!

But I can write when she is out, and see her a long way off from these windows.

There is one that commands the road, a lovely shaded winding road, and one that just looks off over the country. A lovely country, too, full of great elms and velvet meadows.

This wallpaper has a kind of sub-pattern in a different shade, a particularly irritating one, for you can only see it in certain lights, and not clearly then.

But in the places where it isn't faded and where the sun is just so—I can see a strange, provoking, formless sort of figure, that seems to skulk about behind that silly and conspicuous front design.

There's sister on the stairs!

Well, the Fourth of July is over! The people are gone and I am tired out. John thought it might do me good to see a little company, so we just had mother and Nellie and the children down for a week.

Of course I didn't do a thing. Jennie sees to everything now.

But it tired me all the same.

John says if I don't pick up faster he shall send me to Weir Mitchell in the fall.

But I don't want to go there at all. I had a friend who was in his hands once, and she says he is just like John and my brother, only more so!

Besides, it is such an undertaking to go so far.

I don't feel as if it was worthwhile to turn my hand over for anything, and I'm getting dreadfully fretful and querulous.

I cry at nothing, and cry most of the time.

Of course I don't when John is here, or anybody else, but when I am alone.

And I am alone a good deal just now. John is kept in town very often by serious cases, and Jennie is good and lets me alone when I want her to.

So I walk a little in the garden or down that lovely lane, sit on the porch under the roses, and lie down up here a good deal.

I'm getting really fond of the room in spite of the wallpaper. Perhaps *because* of the wallpaper.

It dwells in my mind so!

I lie here on this great immovable bed—it is nailed down, I believe—and follow that pattern about by the hour. It is as good as gymnastics, I assure you. I start, we'll say, at the bottom, down in the corner over there where it has not been touched, and I determine for the thousandth time that I *will* follow that pointless pattern to some sort of a conclusion.

I know a little of the principle of design, and I know this thing was not arranged on any laws of radiation, or alternation, or repetition, or symmetry, or anything else that I ever heard of.

It is repeated, of course, by the breadths, but not otherwise.

Looked at in one way each breadth stands alone, the bloated curves and flourishes—a kind of "debased Romanesque" with delirium tremens—go waddling up and down in isolated columns of fatuity.

But, on the other hand, they connect diagonally, and the sprawling outlines run off in great slanting waves of optic horror, like a lot of wallowing seaweeds in full chase.

The whole thing goes horizontally, too, at least it seems so, and I exhaust myself in trying to distinguish the order of its going in that direction.

They have used a horizontal breadth for a frieze, and that adds wonderfully to the confusion.

There is one end of the room where it is almost intact, and there, when the crosslights fade and the low sun shines directly upon it, I can almost fancy radiation after all—the interminable grotesques seem to form around a common centre and rush off in headlong plunges of equal distraction.

It makes me tired to follow it. I will take a nap I guess.

I don't know why I should write this.

I don't want to.

I don't feel able.

And I know John would think it absurd. But I *must* say what I feel and think in some way—it is such a relief!

But the effort is getting to be greater than the relief.

Half the time now I am awfully lazy, and lie down ever so much. John says I mustn't lose my strength, and has me take cod liver oil and lots of tonics and things, to say nothing of ale and wine and rare meat.

Dear John! He loves me very dearly, and hates to have me sick. I tried to have a real earnest reasonable talk with him the other day, and tell him how I wish he would let me go and make a visit to Cousin Henry and Julia.

But he said I wasn't able to go, nor able to stand it after I got there; and I did not make out a very good case for myself, for I was crying before I had finished.

It is getting to be a great effort for me to think straight. Just this nervous weakness I suppose.

And dear John gathered me up in his arms, and just carried me upstairs and laid me on the bed, and sat by me and read to me till it tired my head.

He said I was his darling and his comfort and all he had, and that I must take care of myself for his sake, and keep well.

He says no one but myself can help me out of it, that I must use my will and self-control and not let any silly fancies run away with me.

There's one comfort, the baby is well and happy, and does not have to occupy this nursery with the horrid wallpaper.

If we had not used it, that blessed child would have! What a fortunate escape! Why, I wouldn't have a child of mine, an impressionable little thing, live in such a room for worlds.

I never thought of it before, but it is lucky that John kept me here after all, I can stand it so much easier than a baby, you see.

Of course I never mention it to them any more—I am too wise—but I keep watch of it all the same.

There are things in that paper that nobody knows but me, or ever will.

Behind that outside pattern the dim shapes get clearer every day.

It is always the same shape, only very numerous.

And it is like a woman stooping down and creeping about behind that pattern. I don't like it a bit. I wonder—I begin to think—I wish John would take me away from here!

It is so hard to talk with John about my case, because he is so wise, and because he loves me so.

But I tried it last night.

It was moonlight. The moon shines in all around just as the sun does.

I hate to see it sometimes, it creeps so slowly, and always comes in by one window or another.

John was asleep and I hated to waken him, so I kept still and watched the moonlight on that undulating wallpaper till I felt creepy.

The faint figure behind seemed to shake the pattern, just as if she wanted to get out.

I got up softly and went to feel and see if the paper *did* move, and when I came back John was awake.

"What is it, little girl?" he said. "Don't go walking about like that—you'll get cold."

I thought it was a good time to talk, so I told him that I really was not gaining here, and that I wished he would take me away.

"Why darling!" said he, "our lease will be up in three weeks, and I can't see how to leave before."

"The repairs are not done at home, and I cannot possibly leave town just now. Of course if you were in any danger, I could and would, but you really are better, dear, whether you can see it or not. I am a doctor, dear, and I know. You are gaining flesh and color, your appetite is better, I feel really much easier about you."

"I don't weigh a bit more," said I, "nor as much; and my appetite may be better in the evening when you are here, but it is worse in the morning when you are away!"

"Bless her little heart!" said he with a big hug, "she shall be as sick as she pleases! But now let's improve the shining hours by going to sleep, and talk about it in the morning!"

"And you won't go away?" I asked gloomily.

"Why, how can I, dear? It is only three weeks more and then we will take a nice little trip of a few days while Jennie is getting the house ready. Really dear you are better!"

"Better in body perhaps—" I began, and stopped short, for he sat up straight and looked at me with such a stern, reproachful look that I could not say another word.

"My darling," said he, "I beg of you, for my sake and for our child's sake, as well as for your own, that you will never for one instant let that idea enter your mind! There is nothing so dangerous, so fascinating, to a temperament like yours. It is a false and foolish fancy. Can you not trust me as a physician when I tell you so?"

So of course I said no more on that score, and we went to sleep before long. He thought I was asleep first, but I wasn't, and lay there for hours trying to decide whether that front pattern and the back pattern really did move together or separately.

On a pattern like this, by daylight, there is a lack of sequence, a defiance of law, that is a constant irritant to a normal mind.

The color is hideous enough, and unreliable enough, and infuriating enough, but the pattern is torturing.

You think you have mastered it, but just as you get well underway in following, it turns a back-somersault and there you are. It slaps you in the face, knocks you down, and tramples upon you. It is like a bad dream.

The outside pattern is a florid arabesque, reminding one of a fungus. If you can imagine a toadstool in joints, an interminable string of toadstools, budding and sprouting in endless convolutions—why, that is something like it.

That is, sometimes!

There is one marked peculiarity about this paper, a thing nobody seems to notice but myself, and that is that it changes as the light changes.

When the sun shoots in through the east window—I always watch for that first long, straight ray—it changes so quickly that I never can quite believe it.

That is why I watch it always.

By moonlight—the moon shines in all night when there is a moon—I wouldn't know it was the same paper.

At night in any kind of light, in twilight, candlelight, lamplight, and worst of all by moonlight, it becomes bars! The outside pattern I mean, and the woman behind it is as plain as can be.

I didn't realize for a long time what the thing was that showed behind, that dim sub-pattern, but now I am quite sure it is a woman.

By daylight she is subdued, quiet. I fancy it is the pattern that keeps her so still. It is so puzzling. It keeps me quiet by the hour.

I lie down ever so much now. John says it is good for me, and to sleep all I can.

Indeed he started the habit by making me lie down for an hour after each meal.

It is a very bad habit I am convinced, for you see I don't sleep.

And that cultivates deceit, for I don't tell them I'm awake—oh, no!

The fact is I am getting a little afraid of John.

He seems very queer sometimes, and even Jennie has an inexplicable look.

It strikes me occasionally, just as a scientific hypothesis—that perhaps it is the paper!

I have watched John when he did not know I was looking, and come into the room suddenly on the most innocent excuses, and I've caught him several times *looking at the paper*! And Jennie too. I caught Jennie with her hand on it once.

She didn't know I was in the room, and when I asked her in a quiet, a very quiet voice, with the most restrained manner possible, what she was doing with the paper—she turned around as if she had been caught stealing, and looked quite angry—asked me why I should frighten her so!

Then she said that the paper stained everything it touched, that she had found yellow smooches on all my clothes and John's, and she wished we would be more careful!

Did not that sound innocent? But I know she was studying that pattern, and I am determined that nobody shall find it out but myself!

Life is very much more exciting now than it used to be. You see I have something more to expect, to look forward to, to watch. I really do eat better, and am more quiet than I was.

John is so pleased to see me improve! He laughed a little the other day, and said I seemed to be flourishing in spite of my wallpaper.

I turned it off with a laugh. I had no intention of telling him it was *because* of the wallpaper—he would make fun of me. He might even want to take me away.

I don't want to leave now until I have found it out. There is a week more, and I think that will be enough.

I'm feeling ever so much better! I don't sleep much at night, for it is so interesting to watch developments; but I sleep a good deal in the daytime.

In the daytime it is tiresome and perplexing.

There are always new shoots on the fungus, and new shades of yellow all over it. I cannot keep count of them, though I have tried conscientiously.

It is the strangest yellow, that wallpaper! It makes me think of all the yellow things I ever saw—not beautiful ones like buttercups, but old foul, bad yellow things.

But there is something else about that paper—the smell! I noticed it the moment we came into the room, but with so much air and sun it was not bad. Now we have had a week of fog and rain, and whether the windows are open or not, the smell is here.

It creeps all over the house.

I find it hovering in the dining-room, skulking in the parlor, hiding in the hall, lying in wait for me on the stairs.

It gets into my hair.

Even when I go to ride, if I turn my head suddenly and surprise it— there is that smell!

Such a peculiar odor, too! I have spent hours in trying to analyze it, to find what it smelled like.

It is not bad—at first, and very gentle, but quite the subtlest, most enduring odor I ever met.

In this damp weather it is awful, I wake up in the night and find it hanging over me.

It used to disturb me at first. I thought seriously of burning the house— to reach the smell.

But now I am used to it. The only thing I can think of that it is like is the *color* of the paper! A yellow smell.

There is a very funny mark on this wall, low down, near the mopboard. A streak that runs round the room. It goes behind every piece of furniture, except the bed, a long, straight, even *smooch*, as if it had been rubbed over and over.

I wonder how it was done and who did it, and what they did it for. Round and round and round—round and round and round—it makes me dizzy!

I really have discovered something at last.

Through watching so much at night, when it changes so, I have finally found out.

The front pattern *does* move—and no wonder! The woman behind shakes it!

Sometimes I think there are a great many women behind, and sometimes only one, and she crawls around fast, and her crawling shakes it all over.

Then in the very bright spots she keeps still, and in the very shady spots she just takes hold of the bars and shakes them hard.

And she is all the time trying to climb through. But nobody could climb through that pattern—it strangles so; I think that is why it has so many heads.

They get through, and then the pattern strangles them off and turns them upside down, and makes their eyes white!

If those heads were covered or taken off it would not be half so bad.

I think that woman gets out in the daytime!

And I'll tell you why—privately—I've seen her!

I can see her out of every one of my windows!

It is the same woman, I know, for she is always creeping, and most women do not creep by daylight.

I see her on that long road under the trees, creeping along, and when a carriage comes she hides under the blackberry vines.

I don't blame her a bit. It must be very humiliating to be caught creeping by daylight!

I always lock the door when I creep by daylight. I can't do it at night, for I know John would suspect something at once.

And John is so queer now, that I don't want to irritate him. I wish he would take another room! Besides, I don't want anybody to get that woman out at night but myself.

I often wonder if I could see her out of all the windows at once.

But, turn as fast as I can, I can only see out of one at a time.

And though I always see her, she *may* be able to creep faster than I can turn!

I have watched her sometimes away off in the open country, creeping as fast as a cloud shadow in a high wind.

If only that top pattern could be gotten off from the under one! I mean to try it, little by little.

I have found out another funny thing, but I shan't tell it this time! It does not do to trust people too much.

There are only two more days to get this paper off, and I believe John is beginning to notice. I don't like the look in his eyes.

And I heard him ask Jennie a lot of professional questions about me. She had a very good report to give.

She said I slept a good deal in the daytime.

John knows I don't sleep very well at night, for all I'm so quiet!

He asked me all sorts of questions, too, and pretended to be very loving and kind.

As if I couldn't see through him!

Still, I don't wonder he acts so, sleeping under this paper for three months.

It only interests me, but I feel sure John and Jennie are secretly affected by it.

Hurrah! This is the last day, but it is enough. John is to stay in town over night, and won't be out until this evening.

Jennie wanted to sleep with me—the sly thing; but I told her I should undoubtedly rest better for a night all alone.

That was clever, for really I wasn't alone a bit! As soon as it was moonlight and that poor thing began to crawl and shake the pattern, I got up and ran to help her.

I pulled and she shook, I shook and she pulled, and before morning we had peeled off yards of that paper.

A strip about as high as my head and half around the room.

And then when the sun came and that awful pattern began to laugh at me, I declared I would finish it today!

We go away tomorrow, and they are moving all my furniture down again to leave things as they were before.

Jennie looked at the wall in amazement, but I told her merrily that I did it out of pure spite at the vicious thing.

She laughed and said she wouldn't mind doing it herself, but I must not get tired.

How she betrayed herself that time!

But I am here, and no person touches this paper but Me—not *alive*!

She tried to get me out of the room—it was too patent! But I said it was so quiet and empty and clean now that I believed I would lie down again and sleep all I could; and not to wake me even for dinner—I would call when I woke.

So now she is gone, and the servants are gone, and the things are gone, and there is nothing left but that great bedstead nailed down, with the canvas mattress we found on it.

We shall sleep downstairs tonight, and take the boat home tomorrow.

I quite enjoy the room, now it is bare again.

How those children did tear about here!

This bedstead is fairly gnawed!

But I must get to work.

I have locked the door and thrown the key down into the front path.

I don't want to go out, and I don't want to have anybody come in, till John comes.

I want to astonish him.

I've got a rope up here that even Jennie did not find. If that woman does get out, and tries to get away, I can tie her!

But I forgot I could not reach far without anything to stand on!

This bed will *not* move!

I tried to lift and push it until I was lame, and then I got so angry I bit off a little piece at one corner—but it hurt my teeth.

Then I peeled off all the paper I could reach standing on the floor. It sticks horribly and the pattern just enjoys it! All those strangled heads and bulbous eyes and waddling fungus growths just shriek with derision!

I am getting angry enough to do something desperate. To jump out of the window would be admirable exercise, but the bars are too strong even to try.

Besides I wouldn't do it. Of course not. I know well enough that a step like that is improper and might be misconstrued.

I don't like to *look* out of the windows even—there are so many of those creeping women, and they creep so fast.

I wonder if they all come out of that wallpaper as I did?

But I am securely fastened now by my well-hidden rope—you don't get *me* out in the road there!

I suppose I shall have to get back behind the pattern when it comes night, and that is hard!

It is so pleasant to be out in this great room and creep around as I please!

I don't want to go outside. I won't, even if Jennie asks me to.

For outside you have to creep on the ground, and everything is green instead of yellow.

But here I can creep smoothly on the floor, and my shoulder just fits in that long smooch around the wall, so I cannot lose my way.

Why there's John at the door!

It is no use, young man, you can't open it!

How he does call and pound!

Now he's crying for an axe.

It would be a shame to break down that beautiful door!

"John dear!" said I in the gentlest voice, "the key is down by the front steps, under a plantain leaf!"

That silenced him for a few moments.

Then he said—very quietly indeed, "Open the door, my darling!"

"I can't," said I. "The key is down by the front door under a plantain leaf!"

And then I said it again, several times, very gently and slowly, and said it so often that he had to go and see, and he got it of course, and came in. He stopped short by the door.

"What is the matter?" he cried. "For God's sake, what are you doing!"

I kept on creeping just the same, but I looked at him over my shoulder.

"I've got out at last," said I, "in spite of you and Jane. And I've pulled off most of the paper, so you can't put me back!"

Now why should that man have fainted? But he did, and right across my path by the wall, so that I had to creep over him every time!

The Five Senses: Boxes

Michel Serres

INTRODUCTION

The French philosopher Michel Serres unraveled the making and experience of a house through its layers, voids, apertures, and mechanisms in this essay. As a philosopher, Serres's perception of the house was not limited to the terminology of interior design, decoration, or architecture. Instead, he drew on philosophy's language and structure to adopt a reading of the house as a sensorium.

Serres's use of such terms as envelopes and layers invoke linings that wrap the body and interior. Included are skin, clothes, and bed sheets as inhabited layers often left out of the discourse of interior design and architecture because of their ephemeral associations. He described adjacent layers such as floorboards that touch carpets and bed sheets that touch skin. Specifically, bed sheets conjure up imagery of intimate spaces that the body slips into but not in the same capacity as clothing or furniture upholstery. It is a layer that resides somewhere between. The dimensions of a bed give measure to the sheets, but the poetic quality of bed sheets being the layer that supports the body and head during dreams is immeasurable. By emphasizing layers that meet the body, the domestic acts associated with the interior, such as the need for washing linens, record the passing of time. Time is registered in architecture through light and shadows, or weathered material made visible over the years, but Serres points directly to the layers that change at the scale of the inhabitant and daily routines. This descriptive approach situates the body within the terminology of architecture and interiors. Rather than dehumanize the body, he humanizes the interior.

Serres counts the number of skins made of hard and soft materials between the body and the house's exterior layer, imagining their meeting at the skin where tapestry and wall intersect. The tapestry-wall relationship recalls Gottfried Semper's principle that the first mark of architecture is the tapestry, followed by its hanging support structure. As Serres moves toward the threshold, he encounters openings and closings in the form of windows and shutters

---

From *The Five Senses: A Philosophy of Mingled Bodies*, translated by Margaret Sankey and Peter Cowley (London: Continuum, 2008), 146–48. By kind permission of Continuum International Publishing Group.

that delineate inside and outside. Through the window, the landscape appears as a tapestry composed of ground, sky, and foliage. Serres invoked the image of a tapestry with its color and pattern to compare views looking inward and outward. The tapestry he walks us through is a composition of details that together unify the interior.

———

WE MULTIPLY our skills and strategies to avoid the deadly fate of Orpheus: we will turn away, flee in horror, sweat, shiver, cover ourselves with veils, lie low; produce variations on the box, enlarging and reinforcing it.

An aid to knowledge, the box supports life. I am that box. I inhabit it.

We are soft, and construct softening boxes.

Behind a courtyard, its grills and portals closed, withdrawn, in front of the high walled garden, the house collects itself within its walls. Distant, protected, holding the world at bay. Inside, the hard stone or rough concrete is covered in gowns, envelopes, ever softer membranes, ever finer textures, smooth plaster, refined paper or liquid paint, decorated, historiated, floral wallpaper; the house multiplies layer upon layer, starting with the rough and ending with pictures. On the vertical plane, the same multi-layered progression: plumbing, girders, floorboards, carpet, rugs. Finally, embellishments and plasterwork. The house closes up its openings too: shutters, windows, double-glazing, stained glass, net curtains, drapes, decorative pelmets, and until not so along, doorways and windows with deep alcoves. Built to be closed, the box has labyrinthine openings. To open our dwellings so brutally, as we have done recently, we needed to shed our fear of the world and believe it criss-crossed by nothing more than signals. The house functions as a space of transformation where forces are calmed, like a high energy filler, or converter. Outside reigns harsh spring or unrelenting dawn, inside is the dream space of calm pictures which do not hinder conversation, inside the space of language is created. Like a skull, a brain. The box transforms the world into coloured pictures, into paintings hanging on walls, changes the landscape into tapestry, the city into abstract compositions. Its function is to replace the sun with heaters and the world with icons. The sound of the wind with gentle words. Cellars turn alcohol into aromas.

In such a house, the philosopher writes and thinks and perceives. Inside. Through the window I see an apple tree in flower, he says. He searches for the origins of knowledge and places himself at its beginnings. He discovers a garden in this Genesis, naturally, and in this garden only the apple tree interests him, tempts him: he can see its flowers. Long dissertation about the tree, the picture of it he might draw, the image he has of it or the word he finds and writes in his language—something that is absent from every orchard. He forgets the window, the alcove, the curtains, the opaque or translucent glass and, depending on whether he lives in the north or south, the sash or casement window. Forgets the house, and the opening through the house, in front of the apple tree. In strong wind, in driving rain, the tree houses squawking birds at night in the branches where they nest; one thing to prune the tree, outside, another thing to describe it, inside. Beyond the reach of water, beyond wind, cold, fog, light and dark—even beyond noise, in the past—the house protects us just as the belly of a vessel separates us from the cold of the sea. Second skin, enlarging our sensorium. Still a box, but now an eye also. Hearing and pavilion. The house observes the apple tree through the window. The house-skull quietly contemplates the tree through the porthole-eye. We might call the window a medioscope, mesoscope or iso-scope. Thus did Captain Nemo, behind the scuttle of the *Nautilus,* descend slowly into the classification of fish, into taxonomy, the dictionary of nat-ural history, more than he plunged to the depths of the sea. The scientist observes the naturalized butterfly beneath glass, or peers at Linnaeus' table from behind his spectacles, or microbes under his microscope. From behind the window-pane, the image of the apple tree is disciplined even though the window preserves its dimensions. The philosopher cares nothing for its fruits and flowers—acacia, maple? Behind the glass there is a phantom, just as we say that the soft replica of an object is formed on the retina, behind the pupil or crystalline lens. Tempest becomes moan as it crosses the shut-ter-eardrum, information as it works its way through hallway and winding staircase.

The house stares through its windows at the vineyards and tufts of thyme, ornamental oranges take shape on its walls, a tissue of lies, oranges and liemons. The philosopher forgets that the house, built around him, trans-forms a plantation of olive trees into a Max Ernst painting. The architect has forgotten this too. And is happy if the next harvest, outside, is transformed into a *Virgin with Grapes,* inside. The house transforms the given, which can assault us, softening it into icons: it is a box for generating images, a cavern or eye or *camera obscura,* a barn which sunlight only illuminates with a slim shaft piercing through the dust—an ear. Architecture produces painting, as though the fresco or canvas hanging on the wall revealed the ultimate cause of the whole structure. The aim of architecture is painting or tapestry. What we took to be mere ornament is its objective, or at the very least its end prod-uct. Walls are for paintings, windows for pictures. And padded doors for inti-mate conversations.

The philosopher holds forth about sensation, yet he inhabits it already, dwelling in a kind of sensation, a part of his house as the pupil is part of his eye. The writer forgets the window, its position and the passive work it does, and observes the painting. Or, if he contemplates a painting, thinks he is dealing with a porthole. He forgets the house, the soft box which ends at the window. Sees the picture, vaguely contemplates a few icons, now abstract, destroyed by a wave of iconoclasm, looks at his page of language where he discovers the given.

The house is a picture box, like a skull or an eye. The philosopher inhabits his own problem. In the past, the world was called God's sensorium. Let us say that the house is man's sensorium. The heavens are filled with God's glory, the house is filled with our small energies.

Within the house, the bedroom encloses a box within a box. When people got into box beds, in Ouessant, or four-poster beds, in Rambouillet or Versailles, you could add yet another box to the list, this time a slightly darker one inside the still illuminated larger one. Sheets add another pocket to the nested series, and rarely do we slide between them naked. O! frozen time of our childhood when no-one went to bed without their woollen sleeping bag. The empiricist is astonished by the number of layers, strata and partitions from rough concrete to bed linen, the number of skins until we reach our real skin. We have already counted the box of veils, of garments. No, we do not live as beings in the world the way books tell us, we cannot possibly make such a claim, there is no way we could tolerate it, but rather as a variety of mammal or soft primate which, having lost its fur, invented the house and promptly filled it with boxes within boxes. Only the external house is exposed to the world; the multi-layered apartment is merely exposed to the city. Language weaves the last protective wall in front of our delicate skin, just after images and paintings.

Radio and television would have us believe that they bring the world itself into our homes.

The house constructs an orthopædic sensorium around us; conversely, the sensorium constructs our little portable house, our fragile vessel, a soft membrane ready to burst open under the assault of the smallest thorn. The philosopher forgets the house he inhabits, but also this house of sensation, the last softening box.

Curtain as Architecture

Casa da Música, Porto, Portugal 1999–2005
Sound-, view- and light-regulating curtains

Petra Blaisse

INTRODUCTION

The traditional role of a theater curtain takes on new form and meaning in the works of Petra Blaisse and her Amsterdam-based office, Inside Outside. In her essay she guides us through her process for the design and installation of custom-made curtains in the Casa da Música in Porto, Portugal, designed by the architect Rem Koolhaas and his Office of Metropolitan Architecture (OMA). Her role as curtain designer reveals the need to respond to phenomenal and professional issues in the collaborative nature of architecture.

Contrary to conventional performance halls, OMA included large voids on the building's perimeter that required blackout curtains to mediate light and acoustics in performance spaces that were sensitive visually and audibly. For Blaisse, the challenge to design these curtains led to a design process that reinvented traditional motifs in Portuguese culture to produce a contemporary design with recognizable elements.

Blaisse started with references to culture and materials. The merging of these two began with a parallel drawn between body and building, where the large windows of the performance hall are seen as the building's eyes in need of coverage. Blaisse finds the solution by looking to Portuguese women who cover their heads with lace for church services. The lace's delicate quality was scaled up from the body to building. As a designer previously trained in apparel construction, she moves fluidly between the scale of the body and building.

Where the theater required opaque surfaces, Blaisse turned to iconography and representation. The need for blackout curtains led her to reintroduce the construction drawing of lace curtains applied as graphic imagery. She continued to reappropriate familiar materials throughout the theater, including common materials like plywood. She applied imagery of enlarged,

From *Inside Outside Petra Blaisse*, edited by Kayoko Ota (Rotterdam, The Netherlands: NAi Publishers, 2007), 364–81.

pixilated wood-grain in gold to the surface of the plywood. The application recalls Loos's laws in "The Principle of Cladding," stating specifically that: "wood may be painted any color except one—the color of wood."* As a contemporary designer, Blaisse implemented new techniques and design concepts that challenged Loos's writings, while at the same time, continuing the critical discourse that Loos had established in modern times. With a century of history between them, the design of common interior elements continued to be re-written.

————

EVERYONE COMPARES the Casa da Música to a stranded body from outer space that has landed in the middle of the old city of Porto out of nowhere. It is true that every time you see people climb the large steps up to the building, you expect the stairs to fold back and 'it' to take off.

In fact, a very low slit invites you into a cathedral: an immense volume, weightless, built entirely of white concrete; its high walls, openings, the columns that fly through space, the way sound is reflected and light filters in: it is almost a religious experience. You breathe in, you're lifted up beyond gravity. You climb the countless steps and everywhere you turn you arrive in different rooms, areas, shapes with spectacular views outward, intriguing views into some other interior space, urging you on and on, up and down, steering you in inexplicable directions until you arrive somewhere—anywhere—it doesn't really matter. You want to be there.

From Storage Clump to Concert Hall

OMA suggests that the concept for the Casa derived from a private house (a massive storage clump out of which living areas were excavated) and was enlarged to the scale of a concert hall, but I never liked that story very much, as it seems very unlike OMA to make life so simple...But whatever the true evolution of this project, from the first Casa model until the building's opening, six years later, Inside Outside worked as advisor for atmospheres, materials and landscape, and as curtain designer. Roles we have played in many projects since OMA opened its office in Rotterdam in the early eighties.

Here, our exchanges eventually led to the colours and materials of the public spaces and the soft-coloured, folded travertine plaza in which the white, rock-shaped building lies embedded. No green allowed on that plaza, only curves that hide cafes, bus stops and intimate seats; all attention focused on the beautiful circular garden of the Rotunda da Boavista in front and its monumental sculpture[1] that shows a lion conquering an eagle—representing the victory of the Portuguese Patriotists over Napoleon's army in the Peninsular War (1808–1814).

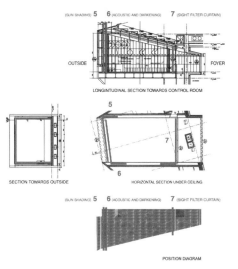

Fig. 4.1: Plans and sections of concert halls and the positions of all the curtains designed by Inside Outside.

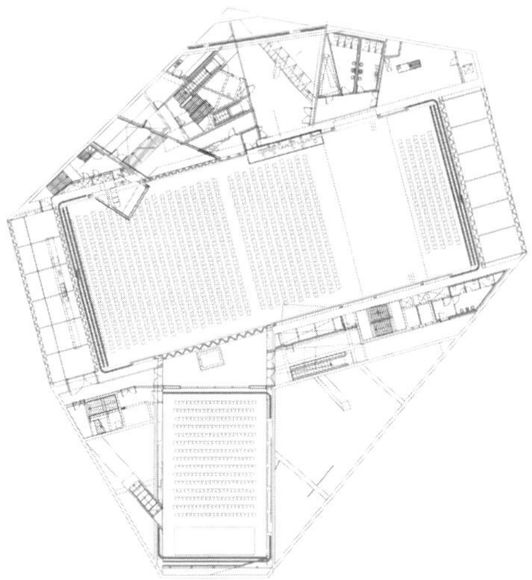

Fig. 4.2: Plan showing the two main concert halls being 'punctured' by public spaces.
Images courtesy of Inside Outside

Curtain as Facade

When the building was still a model and a stack of drawings, I could only understand its spatial implications by imagining an apple from which the skin was cut with flat strokes of a knife and then punctured by the same knife to take out the core. Piece after piece was then taken out, and those cavities became the public spaces and the small concert hall, all looking out over the city and, inside, connecting to the long tunnel that forms the large concert hall.

When do you *ever* see curtains in a concert hall? Here, because both concert halls and all public spaces were 'excavated from a massive volume' and both auditoriums are dominated by huge windows, allowing a sea of daylight in from two directions! Daylight in a concert hall, music in the sun and singers in the shade of a trombone…it is unheard of.

So curtains were part of the plan from the very beginning of the project, although the true range of their technical performance was still unclear and would only develop during the process. But one thing *was* clear: windows *that* size need something, if only to soothe the client about this revolution:…concert halls with a view. [Figs. 4.1 + 4.2]

Construction Site

During construction, the Casa da Música already felt special. It seemed somehow perfect from the first pour; down in the pit, its first idle columns stood reaching out to the sky, white and elegant as robes; countless thin,

273

swaying steel rods shooting in all directions like fireworks. At night, construction lamps cast trillions of shadows, sliding in formations from left to right with the wind. Like seaweed washing in the waves.

Close to the hole, a medieval-looking wooden shack stood squeaking in the winter cold. Inside, barely lit but warm, booted workmen with dark and light skins, heavy eyebrows and very blue eyes ate their lunch at long wooden tables. Breathing out the smell of fish and garlic and listening to melancholy music, they prepared for the next shift: moulding and pouring, filling, fencing, scraping and weaving, folding, sawing, welding, cutting, measuring, aligning; carrying enormous bundles of rods, planks, cables, pipes, packs and tools on shoulders, climbing up and down scaffoldings, balancing on planks bridging puddles and air—apparitions of men at work in the windy wet misty cold that clouds in from the sea.

The Concert Halls

From the beginning, OMA wanted to make the two concert halls into rectangular 'shoeboxes': the large concert hall (SALA 1) with its aluminium floors and stage, rows of connected chairs as one continuous plane, as if the floor folds up and down, and a wooden 'cover' forming walls and ceiling; and the small concert hall (SALA 2), with a dark floor and loose chairs that can be taken out completely leaving an empty space, and an equal wooden 'cover' forming walls and ceiling. Both 'boxes' were imagined as surfaces of rectangular wooden plates into which all additional needs would be integrated: sound, air and light; curtain storage and machinery. Everything more or less invisibly built in, solved within that one folded plane.

Structures and Veils

At first the idea of curtains was purely a visual game in the architect's models and representations: textile scraps were inserted as placeholders, very decorative elements with large birds and flowers—a counterpoint to the clean, sculptural form of the white concrete building. We soon forgot about decorations and colours and began to interpret the curtains as walls, facades, integral parts of the architecture, structures that complete a room.

As the public rooms became more and more colourful and decorated— to radiate colour into their surroundings, to implement local culture and to imply their use—we realized that all curtains should be colourless, more restrained objects. Spatial effects would only be triggered through structure and scale, with light, weight and movement.

As the requirements and expectations of the curtains changed, we did tests for each room and each function; from one material to another; from whites to blacks, thin and thick, rigid and fluid. This process was useful because, by going through these many tryouts, the entire team learnt that even the smallest shift in position, scale, material or structure has a considerable impact on the performance and potential of a room. It is always a delicate balance: solving too many issues with textile—making them too present—could work against the stark, structural character of the building.

In the end, we made six separate curtains for the large concert hall—three layers on each side—measuring between 13 and 15 m in height and 22 m in width; three curtains for the small auditorium—measuring between 12 and 7 m high by 17 m wide; and two curtains for the rehearsal studios below ground, measuring up to 8 m high by 65 m wide.

Some of these layers hardly claim any space and disappear as quietly as they come. Others, however, have a three-dimensional rhythmic structure and take up space as much as they *are* space in themselves; walls of varying degrees of transparency and mass that fold upwards into ceilings or sideways into hollow walls. Each of them adds to the acoustic and atmospheric definition of the rooms, together with sound-reflecting and absorbing surfaces, orchestra pit and public—with all planes, forms and volumes, hard and soft, porous and massive.

SALA I
Surface

Maarten van Severen († 2005) designed the chairs in strict rows of silver, like ripples in the sea. Each rigid, transparent armrest holds a little LED lamp for reading during performances.[2] First, the chairs were to be upholstered in perforated silver plastics and leathers, but as these materials didn't react well acoustically and were too vulnerable, they were replaced with light grey mohair velvet.

We thought: here is a concert hall with a scale that emanates strength and with a sobriety that radiates integrity. Its sheer uninterrupted volume and the enormous size of each plane make the space impressive. A few elements enrich the interior: the coloured glass of the balcony windows; the organs on both sides of the stage; the transparent acoustic canopy, like a modern chandelier above the orchestra; the massive pleated windows—light green—in front and behind; the large floor plane of aluminium and silver velvet; the colourless curtains that filter light and project shadows; and the views of the ochre red city, blue sky, green treetops and bronze sculpture.

Yet something was still missing, something to add scale to the wooden, monochrome walls and link everything together. Something festive, a symbol of cultural wealth, a warm glow to embellish the visitors' complexions and intensify the colours of their clothes…

Gold then, and not mathematically placed squares or rectangles but voluptuous, large-scale, rounded forms like naked angels on old paintings, like trumpets and tuba's, like the hairdos of opera singers.

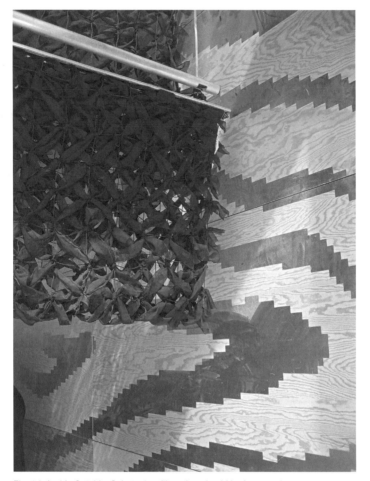

Fig. 4.3: Inside Outside, Sala 1: view filter 1b and gold leaf on wood.
Photo credit: Graham Bizley

We suggested imprinting the entire wooden shoebox with an enlarged version of the wood's own grain: a shimmering layer of organic shapes, flames of gold, that reflect the light.[3] [Fig. 4.3]

Hanging Walls and Reflective Veils
(2x) 22 x 15 or 13 m of facade

The large auditorium has three types of curtains: sun-screening, blackout/acoustic and view-filtering.

Directly aligning with the glass facades on both sides of the hall, light and transparent grey voiles with large, white, weighed-down seams screen the glare and reflect the sun. Fluorescent slits point the way to security doors. They disappear into the hollow wooden side walls.

Fig. 4.4: Inside Outside, Sala 1: blackout curtain 2a. The end of the day…time to open up. Photo credit: Leonardo Finotti

The two blackout curtains—one behind the orchestra and the other behind the audience's seats—had to be heavy and porous, so that they could also absorb sound. Positioned a few metres away from the glass facades, they fold out from the ceiling: a lid folds open, out the curtain comes, and 'hop!' the lid closes again without a sound. I had never imagined that folding and unfolding movements could be so like tai-chi: in perfect harmony and very sloooow.

These blackout curtains are made out of two connected layers. One of the two layers (looking inward) is made of thick wool to secure the right acoustic absorbance. The second layer (facing out) is made of a dense, coated cloth to block out the smallest bit of daylight from the room.

Behind the public seating area the same build-up is applied. The acoustically absorbent layers (looking inward) are made of bleached wool behind the orchestra—acting as a projection screen for light and moving images; and of matte black wool behind the audience, fulfilling the opposite role of the projection screen—absorbing light, creating a large black hole.

As both of the backsides of these blackout drapes would be visible from the city and from the foyer spaces (pressed between the two corrugated glass layers on both sides of the large concert hall), we had many discussions as to what additional role these large surfaces could have: they could provide indirect light or digital information to the foyers; they could be large paintings addressing the city—sea battle paintings of old masters, Gobelin tapestries representing nature, scientific drawings of medusas or shellfish (the sea is near!). Hard to make a convincing choice here, until someone suggested using Inside Outside's construction drawings of the actual knotted curtains inside…

We enlarged our drawings fourfold and digitally printed the blackout cloth for each side of the hall, using a different working drawing for each side in different shades of greys and whites. [Fig. 4.4]

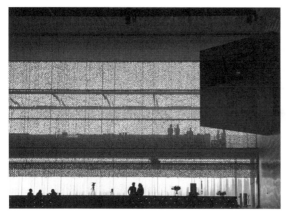 

Fig. 4.5: Sala 1: view filter 1a. The two foyer levels seen through the knotted plane.
Fig. 4.6: One of two view-filtering curtains. Images courtesy of Inside Outside

Open Structures
(2x) 22 x 15 or 13 m of facade

In addition, Rem Koolhaas wanted a 'view filter' on each side of the hall. The term 'view filter' felt totally obvious yet also very vague: a view filter to what degree, with what purpose? To filter out, to tone down, spread light, obscure, fade, blur what is visible behind it? Or to envelope the room, create an aesthetic backdrop for the orchestra, allowing the gaze to sense the outside, to see sky, trees, sculpture and city? [Fig. 4.5]

Since this curtain was meant to be used randomly, it was not allowed to have any acoustic effect on the space. To realize this 'acoustic non-existence,' we needed a weightless and open structure: a giant piece of lace. Since almost everything has an acoustic effect, we needed to do many tests and calculations in order to arrive at the right answer for a concept that was inspired by the lace voiles that Portuguese women wear over their hair in church: black for married, white for unmarried women; which we enlarged and simplified. [Fig. 4.6]

I thought of the many churches I saw when we lived in Portugal and Austria when I was a child. I remember my mother and other women covering their hair with white or black lace before entering church with those special expressions that only mass brings about: alternating between serenity, grief, concentration, boredom, dozing off until the singing brings everyone back to life. Large or small, all churches then were sober structures in themselves—except for the Stephan's Dome in Vienna—but filled with choir and organ music, littered with gold leaf or the gold thread appearing on the priest's robes, the objects on the altar, the domes and fresco's and paintings of Christ and Jesus and the apostles, sculptures of terror-struck male, female and animal figures with Mary in light blue and white robes, her veiled head surrounded by a golden halo, innocently in their midst. The stained windows spread patches of coloured light through the space, gliding over all objects in the course of mass. We were not allowed to have breakfast on Sundays and mass seemed endless, so we looked around while the Latin rhymes and flows filled our ears and soothed our minds. Communion was a welcome distraction, and the host welcome food that we glued to our palate and sucked on at length.

To achieve the lacelike effect that we wanted for the view filters, we used the technique Inside Outside had developed for the Prada store in New York: knitting bands of very thin material (zero acoustic effect) into a complex but very open structure. In our studio, we did knitting test after knitting test, trying to achieve the right recipe and scale…each test more beautiful than the other.

We used a very thin and transparent voile; in itself an insipid cloth that through manipulation acquires a totally different character. But it became clear that however ingenious the loop and knot combinations we tried were, knitting would never be stable enough at the anticipated scale. We needed a skeleton, flexible enough to move with the curtain and fold in and out of the ceiling. We found strong, large-scale fishing nets—plunging into the Dutch fishing industry, which was surprisingly interesting—and then crocheted bands of voile into them with our hands, moving from 'knit' to 'knot.'

We drew recipes and made one-to-one (1:1) samples of the knots. The cloth had to be knotted loosely yet not too much so; and the pieces of cloth that appear at each end of its width—little rectangular flags where your tear stops and you turn to start tearing in the opposite direction—had to be pulled to one side of the curtain, creating an extra three-dimensionality.

Gerriets GmbH from Germany eventually got the commission for the production of the curtains and they worked with us to refine technique and materials. They hired seventeen people in Germany and France—mostly women—to tear the white and black voile cloth into bands of 10 cm width, zigzagging their way through an entire bale and then knotting these endlessly long bands into the netting; all materials fire proof of course. Side by side, these women worked their way through six white and seven black bands of 22 x 2.5 m, knot by knot and often reknotting areas if they were too loose, too stretched or too different from the adjacent knotted areas. It took them 700 hours.

Since no two people knot the same, the whole thing had to be meticulously orchestrated. We asked Gerriets to mail us photographs of the process at regular intervals, so that we could follow the knotting from afar and react to 'impurities' if necessary. Quite a military operation!

The two view-filtering curtains—one white and one black, each appearing out of the ceiling at the outer ends of the concert hall—were composed of seven or eight knotted bands of 22 x 2.5 m. Each band was slid into an aluminium profile—two bands fit into each profile—to create one knotted plane of 22 x 15 or 13 m. Each aluminium profile, horizontally aligned, has thin steel cables attached in a vertical direction, connecting the lowest beam to each following beam and to the motor hidden inside the roof; allowing the curtain to fold up and down evenly. Eight-hundred and fifty linear metres of voile, 300 centimeters wide, was used for these two curtains: 2,550 square metres of cloth to produce 616 square metres of knotted surface. [Fig. 4.7]

Weight, Sound and Storage Effect

In each curtain project, we have regular discussions with the architects to review storage and motor spaces and to ensure that they are included in the construction drawings. The same goes for structural adjustments: we provide the engineers with the necessary information to make sure that ceilings can carry the curtain's load. A curtain can occupy from 2 to 100 m² of architectural space in storage and can weigh up to 500 or more kilos. Motors can be large, heavy and noisy; but also tiny and flexible, running along with the curtains within the tracks. Checking structural drawings and exchanging information up to the very last stage is essential.

In the end, slim doors that measure up to 15 m in height open up automatically and allow curtains to slide in and out of hollow walls effortlessly and elegantly, closing without a sound. Shifting panels in the large auditorium's ceiling allow four textile structures of 22 m width to fold down or up independently, evenly and without obstruction, leaving no trace when shut. Tracks are recessed and motors[4] are hidden and silenced behind folding or turning lids: all beautifully detailed by the architects and stage engineers.

Curtain Scrutiny

Every curtain idea we develop has to be aesthetically accepted by the architects, measured and reviewed by the acoustic engineer, then technically reviewed by the architects, users, contractors, theatre engineers and production people. The objects have to answer to acoustic, weight, volume, fire, wear and tear, financial and technical demands and have to be detailed in a way that is workable and feasible within a given schedule. Very often the review meetings unleash more questions than answers, which is always good and sometimes painful. The ultimate test follows later: the local fire brigade tests the curtains on site and either accepts them or not; and if not, well…

Tender Process

Design is a negotiation and does not come with a guarantee; not to you and not to the parties that you involve in the process. You 'massage' companies into studying technical solutions or possibilities with you, do tests

Fig. 4.7: Inside Outside, Sala 1: view filter 1a. The blackout goes down; the view filter follows.
Photo credit: Iwan Baan

and calculate budgets in a much earlier stage; lots of diplomacy required. And you have to invest all the time, as there is no way a client will invest in experiments.

You must understand that working with yarn, pigments and textiles is like working with gold and metals: prices, availability and regulations can change every single day! Who knows what will happen in India, Pakistan or China, Korea, Africa, the United States or the Arab Emirates tomorrow, what new tensions terrorism, poverty and the pressure of the market economy and religious or cultural ethics will bring? What small or large natural disasters or economic decisions will not only uproot societies but also nature—the source of everything? And if you imagine that architecture projects stretch over years and years; that an accepted design is sometimes executed five years later and has to be realized for the exact same budget that has been agreed upon years before, without inflation correction…then you understand the risk designers take at each turn, and how often we have to reposition ourselves, our ideas and solutions along the way.

Mind you, we still think it's worth it.

Notes

*   Adolf Loos, "The Principle of Cladding," in *Spoken into the Void: Collected Essays 1897–1900*, trans. Jane O. Newman and John H. Smith (Cambridge: MIT Press, 1982), 67.

1   The sculpture dates from 1909 (start)–1951 (inauguration), and was made by sculptor Alves da Sousa and architect Marques da Silva.

2   Like plankton that light up the waves on a summer night.

3   Like so many ideas that pass by between OMA and their advisors (we are one of many satellites that invest specific know-how into their projects at their invitation), this idea would have remained an idea if it would not have been taken up by Koolhaas and his team. Sure, Inside Outside made a start by sketching wood-grain patterns and suggesting scale and materialization of these forms, but it was thanks to OMA's true-to-size samples, their PhotoShop interpretations and their conviction to show it again and again in presentations to the client, and then finding the right people to realize this idea that it survived all phases and became real. In the golden wood-grain form was 'digitized' on the architect's request, meaning that its rounded forms are built up of small squares instead of fluid lines. Architectural language managed its way into this *one* organic form; the only voluptuous decoration in the building! Actually, the digitizing made me think of censored porn: sexual organs as blobs of beige, pink, white and black.

4   Two motors were installed inside the roof on both ends of the large concert hall to allow the view filters to appear and disappear separately from the acoustic/darkening curtains.

Skin: New Design Organics

Ellen Lupton

INTRODUCTION

In a survey of groundbreaking skins that build on Gottfried Semper's and Adolf Loos's precedents, Ellen Lupton surveys the evolution of forms and surface and highlights recent developments in the design and application of new skins. She reminds us of such properties as the elasticity, translucency, and plasticity of human skin that inform innovation in developing artificial skins.

Lupton's examples of clothing, furniture, and architecture have properties of being skinlike. The invention of new materials and structures has spurred the reinvention and capacity of familiar items such as textiles for clothing that have body temperature control. In a sense, temperature-regulating textiles recognize the body's limits and improve on comfort while hinting at evolutionary adaptation. At a larger scale, the integration of technologically advanced textiles on building interiors in the form of curtains offers sustainable solutions to regulating building temperatures.

Innovative skins primarily motivate and fit the scale of industrial design products such as furniture and household objects. Lupton offers examples from these related disciplines that use new materials and construction methods. The integration of these examples influences the interior realm by moving away from 2x4 wall construction. Interior architectural walls have traditionally been rigid, but through the projects highlighted by Lupton, the influence of pliable and curved surfaces generate new forms that allow interior space-making elements to move toward animation. Projects such as Erica Hanson's Objects for Walls *gravitate toward an interior wall with resemblances of human curves that peel away. In KolMac's* InversaBrane, *the wall moves further away from architecture and closer to the body as opaque surfaces disintegrate into a hybrid of skin and bone to make a screenlike appearance.*

The move toward systems that integrate skin and structure presents new options for interior designers and, with it, a new aesthetic—one that asks

From *Skin: Surface, Substance, and Design* (New York: Princeton Architectural Press, 2002), 28–41.

designers to integrate new palettes of materials and fabrication techniques. The hybridization of objects and interior surfaces invites the interior designer to actively participate in the design process and fabrication rather than the traditional model of selecting and placing objects in the interior. As these methods become more available outside product design, the interior offers a multitude of opportunities for their location.

This essay builds on and expands the introduction to the first edition of Skin *(2002). The revised essay includes new projects selected from the traveling exhibition* Second Skin, *conceived by Cooper-Hewitt, National Design Museum, Smithsonian Institution, and produced by Vitra Design Museum.*

———

THE BODY HAS been design's primary point of reference across history, not only because people like to fashion things in their own image but because functional objects come in close contact with our flesh, skin, and bones. Humans invented technologies to supplement the inadequacies of the body's natural envelope. Chairs and jackets, cups and spoons, buildings and cars, serve to extend and support the body, compensating for its failures and allowing it to survive in a world that is largely inhospitable to human life. The first shelters and the first garments, made from animal skins, protected people against harsh climates, allowing them to cultivate ever-more hostile regions of the planet.

This book explores skin as both substance and metaphor in recent design practice. Skin is a multilayered, multipurpose organ that shifts from thick to thin, tight to loose, wet to dry, across the landscape of the body. Skin responds to heat and cold, pleasure and pain. Lacking definitive boundaries, it flows continuously from the exposed surfaces of the body to its internal cavities. It is a self-repairing material whose exterior is senseless and inert while its inner layers are flush with nerves, glands, and capillaries.

Contemporary designers approach the surfaces of products and buildings as similarly complex, ambiguous forms. New tools and materials have changed the practice of design, yielding objects and buildings that resemble living creatures—modeled with complex curves and forms—while remaining distinctly artificial. This new organicism has taken shape most aggressively across the surface of things. Manufactured skins modulate the meaning, function, and dimensionality of products and buildings. New materials react to light, heat, touch, and mechanical stress. Translucency and change have replaced transparency and permanence. The outer envelope has detached from the interior volume. Flexible membranes are embedded with digital sensors and luminous substances. Thin planes of material are folded, warped, or pumped with air to become load-bearing structures.

As products become more like living things, the body is increasingly approached as a consumer product. An arsenal of cosmetic procedures are marketed to an expanding and unembarrassed public: injections of bovine fat or collagen fill shallow lines and acne scars; chemical peels remove the outermost layer of the epidermis, exposing a fresh layer of cells: toxic injections paralyze facial muscles to eliminate wrinkles. Breasts, thighs, bellies, and butts are lifted, tucked, suctioned, and prosthetically enhanced.

Natural skin is both dead and alive. The thin outer layer, the epidermis, consists of strata of cells that migrate toward the surface, where they compact into a layer of dead material. Skin's protective function relies on the inertness of this outer surface. Mark C. Taylor, whose 1997 book *Hiding* is a commentary on the culture of skin, writes, "Death, like life, is not a momentary event but is an ongoing process whose traces line the body. At the point where I make contact with the world, I am always already dead."[1] Skin, hair, and nails are products of the body, continuously sloughed off and renewed. Hair is part of the skin, its cells generated deep within the living dermis and pushed upward into shafts of protein, emerging across the body's landscape as a thicket of dead blades. Skin is connected to our bodies yet also alien, marking the exterior, the end of our selves. It is a screen on which we witness the body's amazing ability to heal itself as well as its irreversible collapse.

A technologically enhanced body emerged over the course of the last century, achieving a monstrous perfection and an alarming dependency on creature comforts. From birth, the human organism is sustained by an infrastructure that controls and delivers food, water, light, climate, and entertainment. Rarely naked, never alone, the new body requires constant attention and prophylactic shields against disaster.

In the 1940s and 1950s, organic forms and malleable materials provided designers with a humanist vocabulary that affirmed society's place within the natural world. In the 1920s and 1930s, Raymond Loewy and other pioneering industrial designers drew upon engineering principles that had been employed in naval and aeronautical design since the nineteenth century, when the curved shells of ships and zeppelins were designed to minimize drag as vessels push through air or water. Designers thus employed aerodynamic forms to impress the image of speed and modernity on the bodies of cars, trains, and planes as well as on such stationary objects as toasters, staplers, and pencil sharpeners. The teardrop became an icon of 1930s modernism.[2]

While Loewy's streamlined skins aimed to conceal, product skins today are often transparent or translucent. Industrial surfaces have become softer, more giving to the touch, enhancing the object's creaturelike presence. Mario Bellini designed an adding machine for Olivetti in 1972, covering the keyboard in flesh-toned rubber. In 2001 the design firm IDEO published

Fig. 4.8: Carla Ross Allen and Peter Allen (KnoWear), Skinthetic.
Fig. 4.9: Donna Franklin, Fibre Reactive Garment, 2004.
Fungi (pycnoporus and aureobasdium), silk, organza, acrylic case, wood base.
Encrusted with living fungi, this garment addresses the commodification of living entities.
We are accustomed to wearing the processed by-products of life, but rarely do we wear
materials that are in an active state of growth.

prototypes using ElekTex, a conductive fabric whose entire surface can sense the location and pressure of human touch: "It allows a product to have a skin that is flexible, that is itself a functioning, intelligent organ."[3]

Like skin, design performs at the frontier of life and death, body and product. Human beings, using objects to survive and conquer, rely on the world of things, merging their own identities with the objects they use. Photographer Elinor Carucci has used her camera to reveal intimate relations between skin and everyday industrial products, from lipstick and pantyhose to zippers, bras, and buttons. Carla Ross Allen and Peter Allen propose grotesque conjoinings of bodies and consumer goods in projects that predict the grafting of brand identities and digital technologies into living tissue. [Fig. 4.8] Donna Franklin creates garments encrusted with living fungi. [Fig. 4.9]

Industrial skins have assumed a life of their own. It is a life whose pedigree, however, is more alien than human. Our increasing dependence on the artificial bears with it a measure of anxiety, a phenomenon vividly expressed in science fiction. The term *cyborg* refers to a being who is part biological, part mechanical, enhanced by a host of technological devices.[4] Although the term brings to mind monstrous beings, it also describes modern creatures routinely repaired with pacemakers, hearing aids, and prosthetic limbs, and outfitted with cell phones, PDAs, and wristwatches.

The fear of invasion from within the body drives many depictions of warfare with outer space. In the *Alien* film series, the enemy is most frightening when it occupies a human host, incubating inside the body before bursting through the abdomen or chest. A dream sequence in *Aliens* (1986) shows Sigourney Weaver—prone on a hospital bed—watching with horror as a mechanical-looking object protrudes upward through her belly, threatening to erupt in a hideous birth. The clinical setting heightens the shock of the scene, with its threat of physical helplessness and humiliation.

Like cinema, design offers imaginative responses to the merging of life and technology, in turn celebrating and recoiling from it. Contemporary objects and spaces are cloaked in surfaces that have been enhanced, simulated, or engineered, surfaces that masquerade as other materials, surfaces where the physical and the virtual, the real and the imagined, collide. Hard surfaces look soft, and soft surfaces look hard. Smooth planes are rippled, bubbled, or scarred with digital imagery; luminescent fabrics, gels, and plywoods glow with preternatural life.

Jurgen Bey's Kokon series encloses traditional wooden furnishings inside a tight wrapping of PVC. The humanly scaled limbs of the found objects press through a grossly artificial skin. In Kokon Double Chair, two chairs are bound, back to back, like lovers held hostage in a dysfunctional embrace. [Fig. 4.10] Moorhead & Moorhead's Rubber Lamp No. 5 has a flexible shade of translucent rubber that peels open to direct the flow of light, evoking the alien pods from *Invasion of the Body Snatchers*, a story whose disturbing picture of the human body as host to alien life has been continually retold in science fiction movies (1956, 1978, 2006). [Fig. 4.11]

Organic design vocabularies—from the ecstasies of baroque ornament to mid-twentieth-century biomorphism—have always gestured toward the erotic, suggesting the curves and movements of the human body. In contemporary design, eroticism is present yet held at a distance, handled with rubber gloves. The fulfillment of desire and the satisfaction of touch are blunted by protective layers of material. Clothed in latex, vinyl, rubber, or resin, sensual forms are rendered clinical.

Herzog and de Meuron's Jingzi lamp resembles a spermatozoa or a giant primitive worm. Jingzi's electrical components are entirely contained inside a thin-walled silicon tube that also diffuses the bulb's light. The lamp is activated by touching the translucent membrane. Whereas electrical cords are usually inert and at best unobtrusive, the long tail of the Jingzi lamp follows the fluid gesture of a sperm cell moving toward its quarry.

TechnoGel is a soft polyurethane material developed in the 1970s for use in wheelchairs and hospital beds, where it supports the body with minimal friction. Werner Aisslinger's Gel chair is padded with slabs of TechnoGel, whose cool yet fleshy texture is said to have the consistency of human fat.[5] Hella Jongerius's Pushed washbasin is made from soft polyurethane. Whereas most bathroom fixtures are hard to the touch, her soft appliance is designed for cramped spaces where flesh is often exposed. [Fig. 4.12]

Fig. 4.10: Jurgen Bay, Kokon, Double Chair.

Fig. 4.11: Moorhead & Moorhead, Rubber Lamp.

Fig. 4.12: Pushed Washtub,
1996. Material: PU rubber, metal.
Dimensions: 57 x 34 x 18 cm.
Category: Unlimited Production.
Commission: Own initiative.
Production: Jongeriuslab.
Collection: MoMA San
Francisco, Centraal Museum
Utrecht (prototype), Droog
Design Amsterdam, FRAC Nord
Dunkerque. Photo credit: Bob
Goedewaagen

Latex is a material that combines eroticism with clinical functionality. Matthieu Manche has created latex garments that propose links among multiple wearers and the proliferation of body parts. He uses this material of self-protection to suggest the merging and elaboration of bodies. Tonita Abeyta's Sensate is a line of latex undergarments—some equipped with built-in male and female condoms—that aim to transform the tools of sexual hygiene into alluring fashion objects. Where love and fear are necessary bedfellows, the plush, dimly lit boudoir gives way to the bright, wipeable surfaces of the laboratory and lavatory.

Such works of brave new organicism reflect the convergence of nature and technology, information and biology. In the 1990s, planes and animals with altered DNA were dispersed through the global food market. The successful cloning of a sheep in Scotland in 1997 plunged a science-fiction fantasy into technological fact. In the summer of 2000, the human genome was mapped, laying bare new terrains for medical science and economic conquest. In the mid-1990s, the new field of tissue engineering emerged, charged with the manufacture of human organs. Today, while complete hearts, lungs, and kidneys cannot yet be generated from living cells, skin is a viable medical product, grown in laboratories.

One such product is Apligraf, a cellular, bi-layer living skin substitute. It is grown in a petri dish on a bed of collagen that is seeded with living human skin cells. (The cells are harvested from the circumcised foreskin of an infant boy's penis; this neonatal tissue is ideally suited for growth.) This single human harvest can generate thousands of skin grafts. The product is shipped via Fed Ex and has a shelf life of five days. Apligraf is used to repair venous leg ulcers and diabetic foot ulcers, two common ailments. Meanwhile, the search is on to create robot skins that are as intelligent or flexible as living surfaces.

A sense of horror as well as enthusiasm accompanies such developments. Environmentalists warn against an ecosystem unhinged by genetically altered species, while bioethicists fear a society dominated by a physically perfected, self-replicating elite. Scientific research is increasingly motivated by profit and loss—life-saving drugs and newly identified DNA sequences are patented and sold for financial gain, while unchecked diseases devastate local and international economics. Cosmetic surgeries are consumed by the privileged few—anxious to extend the appearance of youth into lives prolonged by medical services—even as the lack of basic health care and sanitation shortens the life spans of millions around the world.

The design of new materials has become a central activity for many architects and product designers, who see all opportunity to create surfaces and substances with subtle behaviors and new functions. Addressing the unequal distribution of technology worldwide, Sheila Kennedy has developed a textile woven with integrated photovoltaic fibers that harvest solar energy by day and emit light by night. This new material becomes a flexible, portable, and autonomous infrastructure. [Fig. 4.13]

Architects Sulan Kolatan and William Mac Donald are developing a material called INVERSAbrane with DuPont Industries. This carbon-fiber-reinforced, organo-polymeric composite is fire-resistant and anti-microbial. Formed into a complex, three-dimensional surface, INVERSAbrane has the potential to revolutionize building, as seen in Kolatan's and Mac Donald's Resirise prototype, whose undulating skin is pocked with scoops and bladders at varying scales. These deformations in the skin serve to minimize wind loads through deceleration, diffusion, and local asymmetries. They also collect and recycle air, water, and light in order to generate micro-climates within the building. [Fig. 4.14]

Contemporary designers have exchanged the transparent skins of early modernism for physically present, semi-opaque surfaces.[6] Buildings are clothed in multiple layers that trap and reflect light, from translucent marble to double thicknesses of glass, creating a sense of delay, a thickening of light and space, in place of instantaneous immediacy.

Exploring interior walls as living, multifunctional surfaces, designer Erika Hanson has developed new uses for Maplex, a remarkably strong, light-weight industrial material made from compressed, unbleached tree fibers, traditionally used for industrial applications. Hanson is creating mass-produceable wall panels that are cut, slit, or perforated, inviting touch or allowing light to emanate from behind them. [Fig. 4.15] Other new wall surfaces include Panelite, which serves as both a finished skin and a structural material. Panelite's structural honeycomb core makes it strong and stiff yet light-weight. This translucent material has been used by Rem Koolhaas and other architects for both interior and exterior walls.

Greg Lynn's concept of "animate form" stretches the skin of architecture into the dimension of time. Digital design tools plunge three-dimensional structures into a space that ripples with currents of force, as the undulating skins of Lynn's "blobs" record the object's passage through fields of pressure.[7] The Berlin-based architecture group realities:united, led by Jan and Tim Edler, transformed the curved blue envelope of the Kunsthaus Graz (designed by Peter Cook and Colin Fournier with Spacelab. UK) into a giant media screen. The BIX media facade consists of 930 ring-shaped fluorescent lights installed inside the building's translucent skin. [Fig. 4.16] A crude, low-resolution image forms as the lights dim on and off to varying degrees. The display system was conceived and built as an integral part of the architecture, allowing images to pulse from within the body of the building. In one sequence, a huge eye looks out from the building's curving, bulging envelope.

 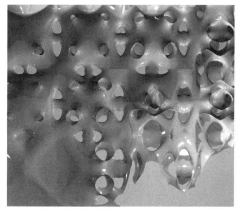

Fig. 4.13: A Huichol girl reads at night using her Portable Light Unit. Courtesy of KVA MATx

Fig. 4.14: Sulan Kolatan and William Mac Donald, INVERSAbrane (rendering), 2006.
Kol/Mac Studio, New York NY

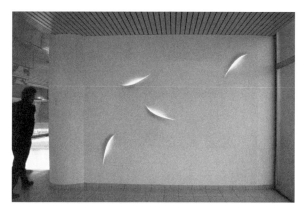

Fig. 4.15: Erika Hanson, Objects for Walls: Maplex wall system with lighting components, 2006. Manufacturer: EHV Weidman, St. Johnsbury, Vermont. Photo credit: Joe Arcidiacano

Fig. 4.16: Kunsthaus Graz, Night Alien. Photo credit: Universalmuseum Joanneum, Nicolas Lackner

291

Fig. 4.17: Adam Yarinsky and Stephen Cassell (Architecture Research Office LLC), CNC Panels: Study Models, 2005. CNC-milled medium density fiberboard.
Photo credit: Architecture Research Office, LLC

Patterns of dots of changing size or intensity are the principle behind the halftone image, which translates shades of gray into a pattern of larger and smaller spots of pigment. The deployment of this graphical device by architects and product designers reflects the interplay of two-dimensional and three-dimensional design, fields that have come to share digital tools and a communications agenda. Architecture Research Office (ARO) in New York City created a series of panels to filter light and provide changing views inside a Manhattan apartment. Perforations in each panel shift across its surface, creating a skin with fluctuating degrees of transparency. Areas of greater openness favor views from specific orientations, which relate to the design of the apartment. The panels are produced with a computer-controlled three-axis router on medium density fiberboard. The designers created numerous small-scale study models, using equipment in their own studio, to develop the final patterning. [Fig. 4.17]

Similarly, the perforations in the seat and back of Werner Aisslinger's Nic chair shift in size, creating relative degrees of transparency (as well as a varied tactile effect). Designer Jan Melis has created experimental packaging for Dutch Jenever, a distilled beverage traditionally sold in a brown ceramic jar. Using rapid prototyping manufacturing and software, Melis rendered a CAD image of a standard bottle in 3-D at low resolution, so that the tool paths used by the software to describe the shape of the bottle become perceptible to the eye and hand. Melis has thus exposed the graphical language that underlies the description of three-dimensional form in digitally-driven design and manufacturing.

Skins mediate between users and products in the digital realm. The customized buttons and controls found in computer interfaces are known as skins. Thousands of skins are exchanged via the Internet, allowing users to upload and download interfaces that are colored, coded, themed, and branded to suit individual whims. Avatars, the graphical icons used to represent players in computer games, are also known as skins—they are the digital surfaces of invented personae. In 2001, the first feature film cast entirely with digital, photoreal human characters—*Final Fantasy*—was released. Such characters, which consist of wireframe structures wrapped with digital surfaces, are feared by some actors as the death knell of the flesh-and-blood performer. The cyborg player is set free from time and imperfections—and requires no salary or profit share.

The substance of the body is under renovation. The arsenal of drugs, vaccines, and mechanical replacement parts developed during the twentieth century has been joined by the engineering of flesh itself. While living skin has become a commercially manufactured product, objects and buildings have come to resemble natural organisms. The barriers between body and product, self and other, nature and technology, are folding inward. The dense, luminous surfaces of contemporary objects—pulsing with hidden intelligence or taut with potential life—can be beautiful and disturbing, divine and grotesque. These industrial skins may be incubating something alien. They could be shielding us from invisible dangers or harboring the nascent growth of a predatory force. Everywhere, prophylactic skins slip into the space between people and things, forming seductive planes of contact as well as protective barriers, screens where image replaces tactility or where touch triggers a visual response—points of no entry or no return.

Notes

1   Mark C. Taylor, *Hiding* (Chicago: University of Chicago Press, 1997), 13.

2   Donald J. Bush, *The Streamlined Decade* (New York: Braziller, 1975) and Raymond Loewy, *Never Leave Well Enough Alone* (New York: Simon and Schuster, 1951).

3   IDEO Europe, *Fabrications* (London: IDEO and ElectroTextiles, 2001), 67.

4   Chris Hables Gray, ed., *The Cyborg Handbook* (New York: Routledge, 1995).

5   Chee Pearlman, "From Bike Seat to Chaise: Is Gel the New Black?" *New York Times,* 12 April 2001.

6   Terence Riley, *Light Construction* (New York: Museum of Modern Art, 1995).

7   Greg Lynn, *Animate Form* (New York: Princeton Architectural Press, 1999), 11. See also Joseph Rosa, *Folds, Blobs and Boxes: Architecture in the Digital Era* (Pittsburgh: Carnegie Museum of Art, 2001).

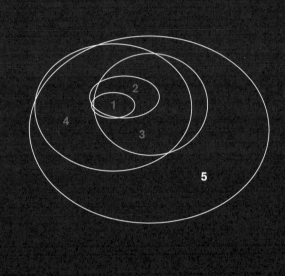

Mapping
the Interior

Introduction:
Mapping the Interior

Mapping has its place in architecture and landscape as a tool for analyzing the relationship of site and building, but the variables differ when it comes to the interior. Instead, the interior requires alternative forms of mapping specific to its topography. Chapters 1 through 4 addressed the multidimensional range of layers associated with inhabiting interiors. Clothing, furniture, and wallpaper are material items with oneiric qualities that support an argument for the importance of making observations about them. Chapter 5, Mapping the Interior, looks at the summation of these layers and how they have been mapped historically and recently. The term *mapping* is used rather than *representing* because neutral, geometric, and scientific forms of documentation that result in objective maps are inherently more reliable than subjective representations. Methodologies of mapping stem from traditional bodies of knowledge such as orthographic projection, full-scale drawing, geometry, and measuring. Using mapping as a critical practice, the interior reveals its own set of material, structural, and theoretical issues to explore, giving new perspective on how the interior is viewed and constructed.

Orthographic projection, as it appears in the following essays, is fundamental to documenting architecture and interior spaces. Principles embedded within systems of drawing conventions are extracted, tested, and reinserted. Conventional notations contribute information to drawings so they can be read objectively and guide the translation from two-dimensional drawing into three-dimensional construction. There is little room for subjectivity as preliminary and construction drawings seek to eliminate it. In the first essay, Robin Evans articulates the conventions associated with orthographic drawing, reframed from the perspective of the interior based on drawings from eighteenth-century furniture makers, who required orthographic drawings to emphasize the unity of interior finishes and furnishings. The projections' failure to represent three-dimensional relationships led to "developed surface drawings" that extracted and highlighted this information.[1] Evans observes that in the drawings, "something gained, something lost," was necessary for the furniture makers to express the importance of their craft.[2] In this case, attention to interior details revealed the loss of any exterior reference, making for a hermetic interior. Extracting information from drawings has now become commonplace, especially for digital images, whose layers can be turned on and off, but for eighteenth-century furniture makers, selective orthographic projections ushered in a new and strange way to look at the interior, and provided a tool to surpass limited earlier visualization methods.

Mapping relies on neutrality in order to register change, requiring a figure and scale that places parts in proportion. The authors in Chapter 5 discuss the scales they apply to their method of mapping, in some cases replacing abstract, proportional architectural drawings with full-scale drawing and making. The interior, it can be argued, is a place that is understood at full-scale. Humans perceive the visual and tactile qualities of materials, textiles, and light firsthand. In presentations that map furniture and objects, communication reaches outside the orthographic drawing and reflects social configurations. Architectural drawings tend to keep these actions at arm's length, lest they fall into the study of human behavior and be seen as part of an interior design discipline.

The other essays look further into the interior not only to map spatial configuration but to analyze personal possessions and investigate materials at full-scale. In "Corners and Darts," I developed a project directly inspired by Evans's essay, in which I set out to challenge the hierarchical layers of the furniture maker's drawings by emphasizing furniture as the primary artifactual layer, intentionally making architecture secondary, to analyze details in a room.

Jeanine Centuori is also concerned with objects in a room, as well as events associated with household objects, such as eating a meal. Her installation, Flattened Room, produced drawings that collapse the three-dimensional event of a meal into a two-dimensional, full-scale map of the placement and shape of objects associated with the meal.

Monica Wyatt's installation, Space-Enfolding-Breath, begins with a simple question about occupying a wall that grows increasingly complex. A full-scale map of the body begins with orthographic principles and a neutral grid altered to accommodate the body's curves. The map takes a progressive approach to dimensions, incorporating the expandable nature of human lungs, whose inhaling and exhaling cause a constant condition of change in measure.

Jeffrey Siegel also maps breathable air in his essay "Engineering the Indoor Environment." Siegel explores the contaminants that objects and architecture emit and how that affects indoor air quality. He provides a scientific map using objective data, presenting a layer of the interior that the eye cannot see.

Catherine Bédard's essay "In a Few Lines, Alan Storey" analyzes the recordings produced by artist Alan Storey's "drawing machines." Storey's machines record human movement and translate it into full-scale drawings. Because of the limitless repetition of lines, this record can only be viewed, not occupied. The machines rely on boundaries for their marks to appear. In some instances, the results are so abstracted that it is impossible to recognize what generated them. Nonetheless they represent objective data, lifted directly from an interior, defined by restrictions built into the machine and its environs. Storey's pieces uniquely contain a defined scope of information, reinforcing Robin Evans's comment on "something gained, something lost." The final drawings from Storey's *Shipping Crate Drawing Machines* share the same presentation as the eighteenth-century furniture-maker drawings, an unfolded series of interior elevations.

The last essay, "Self as Eye: The Perspective Box," by Celeste Brusati, examines painting techniques for mapping interiors. The small-scale interior appears as perspective boxes that, like Storey's crates, cannot be occupied, only peered into. Brusati focuses on paintings by Samuel Van Hoogstraten, who used complex perspectival geometry to forge lifelike scenes. His approach was scientific, relying on mapping points and understanding the viewer's perception, which provided a foundation for his painterly techniques.

Chapter 5 presents an introspective, detailed view of furniture, surfaces, clothing worn by the occupant, and the air he or she breathes. Each graphic is mapped by reliance on its own system of measure, while depending on intellectual objectivity. The drawings and essays argue that the interior needs a form of mapping that grows out of (and contains) its component parts. Interior mapping offers an adaptable methodology for going beyond architecture's inherited norms. Alternative forms specific to the interior allow interrogation, analysis, and synthesis of elements that can affect the design and construction of the interior. Sophisticated technical mapping offers the discipline a way to question itself about content and modes of representation.

Notes

1   Robin Evans, "The Developed Surface: An Enquiry into the Brief Life of an Eighteenth-Century Drawing Technique," in *Translations from Drawing to Building and Other Essays* (Cambridge, MA: MIT Press, 1997), 202.

2   Ibid., 199.

The Developed Surface:
An Enquiry into the Brief Life
of an Eighteenth-Century
Drawing Technique

Robin Evans

INTRODUCTION

Orthographic drawings allow mapping of objective information to be uniformly understood across design disciplines. Interiors commingle architecture and objects and social functions, so a drawing system that accurately encompasses the visualization and development of rooms is necessary. Architectural historian and theorist Robin Evans recognized this requirement and other nuances of drawing specific to the interior. He uncovered a deviation from the typical orthographic drawings that late-eighteenth-century furniture makers used to demonstrate their stylistic vision and highlight a continuous style. The furniture maker's vision became so central to the interior that it briefly altered how orthographic drawings were viewed. Rooms were treated like boxes that could literally unfold and reveal the interior elevations in great detail adjacent to the plan. Corners and edges were especially important in these drawings where molding acted as "the conceptual tape that bound the severed surfaces back together."*

Evans points out that to view the location of furniture in the developed surface drawing, furniture makers combined, among others, orthographic and perspective drawing techniques. The rift between these drawing types and the resultant reintegrated graphic unintentionally gives the impression of collage. In the pursuit to reorganize the conventions of the orthographic system, furniture makers integrated a new architectural logic that took the interior as its starting point. Evans reveals this trend by analyzing the drawings of Robert Adam, Thomas Lightoler, and Sir John Soane, but he also points out the moments when, later in the century, the logic failed.

The abstruse nature of the developed surface drawing allowed underlying nonarchitectural superficialities to surface. It became fashionable for designers to produce the drawings even as they strayed far from designing socially useful rooms. As abundant decoration and fashion dominated rooms,

Originally appeared in *Translations from Drawing to Building and Other Essays*, (Cambridge, MA: The MIT Press, 1997), 195–231

their effect on furniture placement resulted in awkward social interactions and ennui. The fundamental principle that inspired them—constructed unity in the interior—was abandoned in pursuit of the more energetic balancing of disparate elements.

———

THIS ARTICLE IS NOT so much the written exposition of an argument as the development of some ideas by writing them down. Much of the sense of it only emerged in the drafting and redrafting. These few prefatory words are to explain why such an enterprise should have been embarked upon, since it would not necessarily be obvious to anyone why the interiors dealt with, nor the way of drawing them, should warrant attention.

English interiors of the late eighteenth and early nineteenth century, although not within the compass of what is usually regarded as properly serious or significant in architecture, are, I believe, capable of providing what a good deal of material within that orbit has not been able to provide: evidence of strong interactions between things visual and things social, even if at what we are prone to consider (perhaps mistakenly) a lower level than the grand questions of architectural theory. This is largely due to the more explicit consciousness among the practitioners concerned that their work was socially and historically specific; that its ultimate justification lay as much within the milieu in which it flourished as in the generalized and unifying principles of a timeless art.

It is true that some of the work reviewed is of modest intrinsic interest, satisfying little more than the demands of a prevailing domestic taste. The interiors of Repton, Smith, Landi and Richardson might be seen as elements in a social history, without any great merit attaching to them except as illustrations of some wider tendency or other. This is hardly the case with Robert Adam, and yet Adam, also, has become marginal to a neo-classicism increasingly envisaged in relation to theoretical texts.

The quality of Adam's work has to be examined within a very different setting to that of Ledoux, Schinkel or Piranesi. Indeed, the admiration that Piranesi felt for Adam's talent, not entirely reciprocal, and derived from the early period of Adam's career while he was busy recording antiquities, could hardly, even then, have been based on shared motives. We might say that Piranesi's work was theoretical and Adam's not. But this seems to devalue Adam's percipience, giving the impression that his architecture was insufficiently intellectual, merely decorative and opportunistic. Likewise the comparison that would pit Piranesi's imaginary work against Adam's more practical activity, as if practical activity were necessarily an impediment to imagination. So it frequently seems, but only because we expect the imagination to have been given shape elsewhere (otherwise, amorphous and indefinite, what could get in its way?). As often as not, the imaginative in Adam's work arose from consideration of the trifling practicalities that frustrated other architects. This struck me while looking at successive plans by Chambers for Somerset House and by Adam for Harewood; where Chambers, starting with a magnificent Roman palace design, ended up with a far more subdued proposal, Adam, starting with an undistinguished plan, ended up, characteristically, with something much more vivid. I do not put this observation forward as a blanket justification of atheoretical postures among architects (far from it), but it does suggest that architecture's productive engagements are not always between explicit theory and form.

It may be better to say that Piranesi's work, in all its visibility, was enmeshed in a nexus within which his polemical writing was also prominent; while Adam's, in all its visibility, was enmeshed in a nexus within which the social activities and proclivities of his clients were prominent. These are imperfect and clumsy formulations, but at least they avoid the pre-emptive degrading of visible things not already under the protecting aegis of theory, or whose forms are not clearly conceived independent of the client relation. Adam is, after all, very susceptible to the insult thrown by the English social historian E.P. Thompson at Colen Campbell, and through him at all successful eighteenth-century British architects: obsequiousness—Thompson uses the word *toady*.

I have attempted, then, to displace the customary foci of interest, considering the interiors of the late eighteenth and early nineteenth centuries neither as objects of connoisseurship, nor as adumbrations of architectural theory, nor as moral counters for or against an ingratiating profession, but as visible entities within a particular area of human affairs. And within this area of human affairs they are meant to r*etain* their visibility, not lose it. This evasive tactic of mine, trying to write a piece that was neither this, nor that, nor the other, in an effort to conserve a property so easily lost in passage from buildings to words, would have floundered completely were it not for the substitution of an alternative focus: the drawing technique. The re-focusing that this entailed may have made it possible for me (for the first time, I think, with any success at all) to treat the formal, spatial and visible on the one hand, and the social on the other, as involved in exchanges that *do not entail the destruction or domination of the one by the other.* For is it not the case that the social is normally construed as a blinding affair which does not so much include the visual as digest it, squeezing out from its visibility the social significance that only then may be absorbed into the verbal metabolism of an existing body of knowledge concerning society?

Beneath the allegorical frontispiece to Thomas Sheraton's *Cabinet Maker and Upholsterer's Drawing Book*, published in 1793, was the following

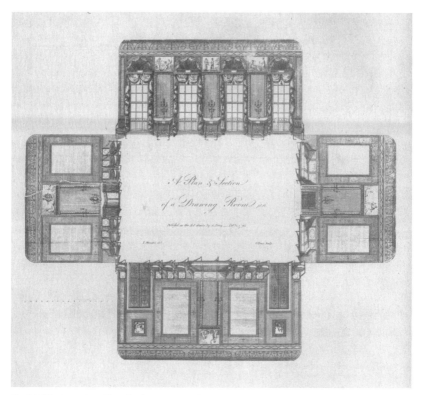

Fig. 5.1: "A plan and section of a drawing room." Reprinted from Thomas Sheraton,
The Cabinet Maker and Upholster's Drawing Book, 1793.

inscription: 'Time alters fashions and frequently obliterates the works of art and ingenuity, but that which is formed in geometry and real science will remain unalterable.' This was an extraordinary sentiment to express in a book on household furniture, a commodity subject to relatively rapid obsolescence. What Sheraton was doing was shifting emphasis from the furniture itself, subject to the vagaries of taste, to the techniques of representing it, which he thought were not. As in architecture, so in furniture design: drawing was to be regarded as fundamental. The 'geometry and real science' to which the motto referred was the geometry required for drawing: that is what Sheraton's book was about. It contained instructions for the making of perspective and orthographic projections of pieces of furniture drawn individually or grouped *in situ* within an architectural interior.

It is ironic then, to say the least, that one of the architectural drawing techniques described by Sheraton was already, at the time or his book's publication, in mortal decline. [Fig. 5.1] Moreover, it was furniture makers like Sheraton himself who were inadvertently helping to force this sort of drawing into oblivion.

In what follows it will be suggested that techniques of representation, far from being of permanent value, are subject to alterations of sense. Architectural drawing affects what might be called the architect's field of visibility. It makes it possible to see some things more clearly by suppressing other things: something gained, something lost. Its power to represent is always partial, always more or less abstract. It never gives, nor can it give, a total picture of a project, so in consequence it tends to provide a range of subject-matter that is made visible in the drawing, as opposed to all the other possible subject-matter that is left out of the drawing or is not so apparent from it.

Now it may be that some architects can see beyond this field of visibility provided by their own drawings and it may be that others cannot, or choose not to, see beyond it. But whether it is the direct sponsor of the imaginative effort, as the axonometric has been for certain contemporary designers such as Eisenman, Hejduk and Scolari, or whether it is a counterpoint to the architect's vision—a technical proof of the imagination's plausibility—as orthographic sections seem to have been for some later baroque architects,[1] we have to understand architectural drawing as something that defines the things it transmits. It is not a neutral vehicle transporting conceptions into objects, but a medium that carries and distributes information in a particular mode. It does not necessarily dominate but always interacts with what it represents.

As a formulation, though, this is far too inexact. How and where does this interaction operate? It is not a matter of simple causality. A technique of drawing does not compel designers to do this or that; there are too many ways round it. Its influence, though strong, is too local for long strings of instrumental effects to be hung on it. More likely it is a matter of things belonging in sets, of a type of drawing being conducive to a certain range of taste, lending itself to a certain kind of social practice, a certain arrangement of space, a certain pattern of planning. Such a set of related practices is described in this article, which sets out neither to increase, nor to diminish, the importance of drawing, but only to show it embedded in a nexus of other events. The subject of what follows is, therefore, as much the nexus in which the drawing technique was situated as the drawing itself.[2]

In the middle years of the eighteenth century a new way of representing interiors was to be found turning up more and more frequently in pattern books and design drawings. In technical terms, this was not a profound break from earlier methods, just a modification of existing techniques so they could be applied to a new subject-matter: the room.

At that time the customary way of showing an interior was to section a building. It was also customary to restore a sense of spatial recession into

the resulting flat projected surface by casting shadows. In this kind of drawing the interiors are shown as an accumulation of contiguous spaces, but
only one wall of any normal room is shown. A typical architectural representation of a palace, villa or house would involve plans, major elevations
and a section. Invariably the exterior would be more fully described than the
interior. From the mid-eighteenth century interiors began to be more amply
described.

Three drawings, all orthographic projections and all, as it happens,
from the late 1750s, show three different ways of extending the range of
what was represented of interiors. The most accomplished is William
Chambers's famous section of a town house for Lord Derby in Pall Mall. [Fig.
5.2] Cornforth and Fowler tell us that this was one of the first architectural
sections in England to show wall coverings, colour scheme and decor.[3] The
second is a sketch elevation by James Stuart of part of one wall of the dining
room at Kedlestone, which the same authors say is the earliest representation of mobile furniture in its architectural setting. It is not much of a sketch
but the content is novel.[4] The third is a drawing of a stair hall by Thomas
Lightoler, published in *The Modern Builder's Assistant*.[5] [Fig. 5.3] The plan is
shown in the middle of a group of four elevations which look as if they had
been folded out from their upright position and flattened into the same place
as the plan. At this stage, unlike the others, the Lightoler drawing involved
no new content but was a relatively unfamiliar sort of representation.

In descriptive geometry, folding out the adjacent surfaces of a three-
dimensional body so that all its faces can be shown on a sheet of paper is
called developing a surface, so we will call the kind of drawing done by
Lightoler the *developed surface interior*. It became a way of turning architecture inside-out, so that internal rather than external elevations were shown.
Earlier drawings of a similar kind can be found in the seventeenth century,
illustrating town squares or formal gardens with their perimeter elevations
folded out. These had most probably evolved from the common, but primitive, cartographer's practice of laying elevations of buildings, landmarks
and trees flat on a map's surface to facilitate recognition. The seventeenth-
century examples described a border-land between interior and exterior.
They illustrated things that were unequivocally outside, but which shared
one way of turning characteristic of interiors; being enclosures of one sort or
another. The novelty of the later eighteenth-century application of this technique was that it made actual individual rooms the subject of architectural
drawing, rather than the enlarged room-like areas or gardens and squares.

To go back to the Lightoler drawing: all four walls of the rectangular
stairwell are shown connected to the side of the plan they originate in. Five
discontinuous planes are therefore represented in one plane and the illustration becomes completely hermetic; nothing outside can be shown—in

Fig. 5.2: William Chambers, Section of York House, Pall Mall, 1759.
RIBA Library and Archives Collection

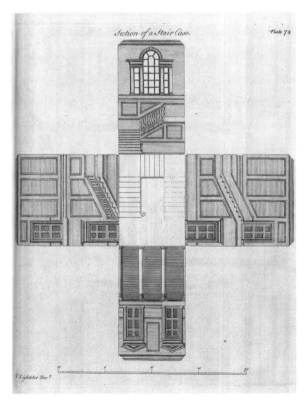

Fig. 5.3: Thomas
Lightoler, "Section
of a stair hall," from
*The Modern Builder's
Assistant*, 1757.
RIBA Library and
Archives Collection

Fig. 5.4: James Paine,
*Section of a stair hall,
Wardour Castle,
1770–76.* Drawn by George
Byfield. V&A Images, Victoria
and Albert Museum

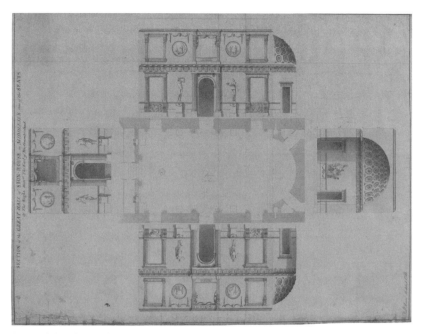

Fig. 5.5: Robert Adam, *"Section" of the Great Hall at Syon House*, 1761.
By courtesy of the Trustees of Sir John Soane's Museum

this case, not even the thickness of the walls. It is an imploded representation that discloses more of the interior and less of everything else. Like the conventional section, the developed surface interior is a three-dimensional organization reduced to two-dimensional drawing, but it is much less easy to restore apparent depth, because while the section merely compresses space, the developed surface also fractures space and destroys its continuity. Look at George Byfield's section of the stair hall at Wardour Castle and it is easy imagine the space with the room; not so the Lightoler drawing. [Fig. 5.4] The much simpler staircase is shown four different ways, but for all the multiplicity of views it seems flat and resistant to interpretation. What the Lightoler drawing does do, though, is dwell lovingly on the inside faces of the box enclosing the stair.

In the 1750s, 1760s and 1770s the developed surface interior was being used by architects with domestic commissions. In the hands of the Adam brothers, however, it became a basic mode of production and, one might also say, a basic mode of apprehension. The portfolios of Adam drawings that survive are replete with them. [Fig. 5.5] Certainly they never usurped plans and elevations, but there was a distinct move away from the shaded or tinted general section as a carrier of information about the interior, as favoured by William Chambers, toward highly worked exhaustive individual room portraits using the developed surface.[6]

A good deal of Adam's work involved additions to, or conversions of, existing buildings. In such circumstances individual description of rooms made some sense. Yet even when dealing with commissions for completely new buildings he would produce characteristic paper-thin fold-out designs for each interior. To find out why this, too, made sense, it is necessary to look at the layout of the major floor as a whole.

A comparison between the principal floors of a typical Adam house plan and a typical plan by James Gibbs indicates the considerable change that had taken place in the organization of domestic space within little more than a generation. Gibbs's plans, always much the same, thoroughly consistent, involve a sequence from a main salon, via ante-chambers, through chambers to closets. [Fig. 5.6] Four radiating routes can be plotted from the public salon in the centre to the remote terminating closets in the wings; a fundamentally hierarchical arrangement, exactly and symmetrically graded from centre to edge, from capacious grandeur to privileged seclusion, four times over.[7] Both late baroque and early Palladian plans tend to be of this sort.

In Adam's domestic plans, which are not so consistent, the rooms are also in sequence but the radial array has disappeared. Instead, in several of his major works, the rooms are joined in a circle. Look for example at the designs for Syon, Saxham, Culzean, Luton Hoo, Harewood, or Home House: access through the major accommodation is strung out into a ring.[8] [Fig. 5.7]

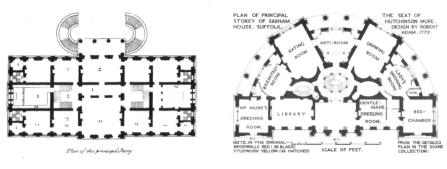

Fig. 5.6: Principal storey of house at Milton, from James Gibbs, *A Book of Architecture*, 1728.
Fig. 5.7: Robert Adam, principal storey of Saxham House, 1779. Reprinted from Arthur T. Bolton,
The Architecture of Robert and James Adams, Vol. 1, 1922.

There is little real difference between the relationship of the rooms, one to another, when they are circuited this way. The hierarchy all but disappears. Only the major points of entry can be marked out as intrinsically unlike the others. Wherever you may be in the circuit, like a mouse in a wheel, you do not change the way the rest of the ring relates to you. You are always, as in certain recent cosmologies, looking at the back of your own head, so to speak. If you walk out of a door on one side of an apartment, you will presently return through the door on the opposite side.

This essential equalization of territory within the ring, which could easily have brought with it the prospect of inescapable sameness, was in fact the basis of an orgy of variations on a theme. If, like beads on a string, all the rooms are the same in their overall relationship to one another, they are made different in every other conceivable respect. In Gibbs's work the rooms are all serially ranked in size and square or nearly square in the plan; there is little need for further description. In an Adam plan or a plan by William Thomas, James Wyatt, Thomas Playfair, John Carter or Henry Holland, they are, with scant regard to overall symmetry made deliberately into a medley of unique and distinct shapes: square, oblong, apsidal, circular, oval, quatrefoil, cruciform, hexagonal or octagonal. They are now also distinguished by use: dining rooms, breakfast rooms, parlours, tea rooms, withdrawing rooms, card rooms, music rooms and picture galleries. And by decor: green rooms, chintz rooms, rustic rooms, Etruscan rooms and so forth. The increased variegation of usage and effect is the counterpoint to a transcending homogeneity of space. A concatenation of interiors of magnified individuality dispels any sense of latent sameness; each room is its own little empire of activity, allusion and colour; each a totally encompassing enterprise. Once we recognize the strategy of pitting individuality against equality we can understand why the developed surface interior drawing was so appropriate to the houses and villas of the 1770s, 1780s and 1790s.

For that degree of difference to flourish in adjacent spaces they have to give very little of themselves away before the moment of entry. To preserve their precious identity, so easy to dilute, they are forbidden to mix. Apart from the restricted information disclosed by the enfilading of doors (an archaizing glimpse of unity), interiors are introverted and boxed in. Doors might open out onto one another but spaces rarely do. Their qualities have to be carried in memory like so many countries recollected by a traveller. In this way, too, they tend to be the same: the less they have to do with each other in terms of spatial interpenetration, the more of themselves they are able to conserve. They are therefore experienced more vividly as a temporal series than as a spatial series. We have noticed already that developed surface representation obliterates the connection between an interior and its surroundings. With its exclusiveness accentuated, an interior so drawn can flourish on its own identity and need receive none of its attributes from its relationship to anything that impinges upon it from outside, which is exactly why at that moment in history the developed surface drawing became so useful a method of describing interior space. In a circuit plan it is the equality of parts that is fundamental. The differences have to be forced into existence afterwards, one by one, room by room. The developed surface interior makes it much easier to contrive these differences by detaching the room from its situation.

The developed surface belongs with the circuit of rooms because it provides the right conditions for the countervailing production of differences within an arrangement that has quietly done away with the hierarchy of the plan, and done away also with the relational differences between rooms implanted in that hierarchy.

With the four walls arranged on a single sheet, sometimes supplemented with a carpet design, a floor pattern or an outline plan or, alternately, all six surfaces illustrated in separate drawings, the developed surface and its derivatives offered an opportunity to saturate interior surfaces with ornament. [Fig. 5.8] Insipid vignettes, grotteschi, bas-reliefs, filigree plasterwork—mostly employing a consciously etiolated iconography such as that published by George Richardson, one of Adam's assistants—were part of a subsidiary industry of Adamesque mural decoration.[9] The developed surface also offered the opportunity for an unexampled unification of the one interior. Drapes, furnishings, fittings, wall coverings, plasterwork, floor and carpet all beg to be drawn. They are not extras to be added after the essential architectural shell has been constructed, not foreign items to be imported into a readymade cavity. They are the things that the developed surface invites the draughtsman to describe. Because of its inclusion and unification of all these heretofore diverse elements, the Adam interior has justifiably been called total design, but one has to qualify that: it was total design

Fig. 5.8: Robert Adam, *The Etruscan Room with furniture as of 1782*, Osterley Park, 1775–79.

Fig. 5.9: Robert Adam, *Ceiling Plan of the Music Room, Home House, 1777.* By courtesy of the Trustees of Sir John Soane's Museum

of an *enveloping surface*, the empty space contained within was left unde-scribed and untouched. Nevertheless, anything that could be pulled toward this enveloping inner surface of the room would be absorbed into it, or flat-tened against it as if some centrifugal force had thrust it out and pressed it there. Use of the developed surface induces facile, specious, superficial architecture that sucks as much of the world as it is able into its flatness. Covering, still very heavy in English Palladian architecture, much more pon-derous in the work of Kent or even Chambers, becomes in Adam, Wyatt and their imitators a web of lightly embossed arabesques. [Fig. 5.9] Entablatures and pilasters turn into near flush gilded edges. Furniture is pushed back to the wall and dwindles into a series of modest extrusions out of the mural surface.[10] It is a painterly architecture that compares with the developed surface, intent on illusion, but it is not the illusion of *depth* that is sought, it is the illusion of *flatness*. Recesses and niches are shallow or made light, their shadows muted, as in the grand salon at Syon, appearing to be *trompe l'oeil*, never threatening to dissipate the tautness in the flat wall.

Where more considerable ruptures occur, as, for example, in the Alcove Room at Audley End or the Library at Kenwood, the illusion of flatness is maintained, even heightened, by a familiar variant of the proscenium principle. Used in the theatre to create apparent depth, the architectural frame is here used by Adam as a kind of edge stiffening which isolates the opening from the principal wall surface, then forces whatever is behind into a collapsed, exhaled space of minimum depth. Compare the Audley End Alcove Room with the model from which it derives: the French alcove recess so common all over Europe in the early eighteenth century. In the older French arrangement the head of the bed: or day-bed, would normally be placed on the back wall, facing directly outwards into the room. Not only was the recess deeper, its depth was accentuated by the orientation of the bed and, most significantly of all, by the posture of the figure occupying the bed at right angles to the wall plane. In the Alcove Room at Audley End the body of the reclining figure that occupied the day-bed, like the conventionalized empanelled bas-reliefs round about, lay in the plane of the wall, incorporated into an aesthetic unity.[11]

There were, though, distinct limitations to this technique. The developed surface interior, as has already been said, disrupts the continuity of the space it represents. Cuts have to be made between adjoining walls so as to splay them flat. To read the room as an enclosed space it is necessary to mentally fold the walls up out of the paper. It would be subversive to this thinking of the drawing into a space to fiddle with its basic, box-like geometry, and that explains why in Adam's designs the paper box is wherever possible kept intact. The Music Room at Home House, for example, has three apsidal bays inscribed in the window wall; voluptuous shapes neatly hemmed in by the rectangular wall edge. The drawing of the ceiling shows how effortless was the progression from the semicircular apsidal heads of the three projecting bays to an entire surface of circular motifs that appear to develop out of them.[12] [Fig. 5.9] But, in the event, the bays have no such relation to the ceiling, being neutralized within the frame of the window wall. The ceiling circles disappear inconclusively into a modest corner moulding which represents the real structure of the room: the inviolable rectangular frame. This moulding was the conceptual tape that bound the severed surfaces back together. Voluptuous elements were inevitably held in check within the frame, even when the illusion offered by the developed surface drawings themselves suggested otherwise. So if one difficulty was in seeing across the discontinuities opened up by the drawing technique, another was in seeing through the continuities apparent in the drawing but not transferable to the space it represented.

Circuits of rooms were being described in plans while circles of walls were being described in developed surface drawings of interiors: their coexistence in so many projects during the late eighteenth century might lead us to conclude that they are equivalent, yet they are not. Their only similarity lies in the fact that they are laid out in a ring. The circuit of rooms is a suppression of expressed centrality. Passing through the apartments of such a building, the occupant is unaware of what constitutes its centre—a feature of Adam's work noticed by Horace Walpole, who wrote of Osterley that it was 'the palace of palaces and yet a place sans crown, sans coronet.'[13] The developed surface, on the other hand, is a way of spinning architecture and its appurtenances out to the periphery of available space, consequently opening up a void in the centre of the room, toward which everything faces, non-specific and empty yet very much in evidence, the more so, in fact, because of the withdrawal of all else to the perimeter. Odd, even so, that in this apparent geometric similarity lay the real difference that would lead to the extinction of the developed surface drawing and the kind of interiors associated with it.

In planning there had been a quiet and remarkably thorough, if local, disestablishment of hierarchy. The effects of the toppled pyramid could be enjoyed only by the privileged occupants of the principal floors of large houses—hardly radical within the wider politics of the time yet significant all the same. The contraction and occasional disappearance of the central hall or salon was one aspect of it, the redefinition of sequence in terms of activity to be undertaken rather than social gradation was another. *Who* occupies a space within the confines of this precious milieu becomes less important than what is done in it, hence the proliferation of tea rooms, retiring rooms, powdering rooms and the like. The only organizing forces in the circuit plan, apart from the quest for variety as such, are weak ones; the passage from room to room corresponding to the passage from pastime to pastime through the course of the day (a strong organization would only have supplanted the tyranny of decisive social division with the tyranny of decisive temporal division), and the tendency to draw more reflective pursuits away from the more boisterous. Both were carried over from earlier practices without compromising the circuit plans, which retained their fundamental difference from the hierarchical plans that preceded them. Curiously enough, no such fundamental reorganization had occurred in the internal structure of the room. The method of description had changed, but it was the overall distribution of the house that this had helped to transform.

Furnishing gives an indication of the way rooms are used. Throughout the eighteenth century the tendency had been to do as Adam did and spread it round the edge. The developed surface drawing could hardly show anything other than peripheral furnishing, but paintings, inventories, catalogues and surviving pieces from the period confirm that it was the characteristic distribution. Around mid-century these wall-dependent items begin to whittle down to a teetering fragility, elegant and ephemeral, and, like camp furniture, to which they bore a resemblance, they become easy to move around. For some time, though, they continue to be attached to the wall. When the V&A Museum furniture and woodwork department was restoring the Etruscan Room at Osterley Park, it ascertained that the top rails on the chairs listed in the 1782 inventory stood in alignment with the surrounding dado and were painted as a continuation of it. Other correspondences were discovered between the decoration of the chairs and the wall surfaces. This seemed evidence enough, but, to underline their provisional status as free-standing elements, the rears of the chairs were painted plain white, while front and sides were meticulously painted with miniature Etruscan motifs.[14] However easily they might be moved into the open floorspace of the room, they were painted as if they did not belong there. Stranded from the parent wall, their position was indeterminate and dependent on the drift of intercourse.

The peripheral ring of chairs in particular was a long-established formation. In Daniel Marot's well-known designs for the furnishing of a palace, published in the 1690s, a ring of chairs is to be found in nearly every room.[15] With Chippendale, Hepplewhite and Adam furniture, the seventeenth-century bulk is quite gone, allowing *de facto* freedom to escape this arcane arrangement, but the magnet of convention is still strong. When the room is empty the furniture reverts to the wall.

During the last three decades of the eighteenth century, a brief equilibrium was achieved between house planning, the method of representing interiors, and the distribution of furniture. They formed a set of interrelated procedures and practices: it would be useless to speculate as to the causal priority of one over the others. They simply belonged together, each lending stability, value or intensity to the rest. The only suggestion of anything unsatisfactory was a minor equivocation over the placing of furniture, which was effectively mitigated by making it light enough to move around.

This minor equivocation, however, grew into an insuperable difficulty. It was the call for variety *within* the social landscape of the room that broke the hallowed ring of peripheral furnishing.[16] The champion of variety within the room in England—the belated champion, for this parlour revolution had been heralded in the 1750s in Paris—was Humphrey Repton. Adam stood for variety of rooms within the house; Repton stood for variety of occupations within the rooms. The circle of chairs had to be broken, redolent as it was, he said, of dull, obsequious, outmoded conversation directed at one senescent, overbearing figure, the matriarch, whose domineering presence was symbolized by a portrait in his drawing of 'the Old Cedar Parlour.' The circle of chairs was the vehicle for this old way of assembling company.[17] His intention was to destroy the remaining instrument of hierarchy. As it happens, this second disestablishment would never bring about the expected congruence between the occupation of a room and the occupation of the house as a whole so that both would work against hierarchy at once, but Repton was explicitly attempting to combine them.[18] The variety achieved in the serial organization of different rooms was to be matched by a microcosm of variety in each room. In order for this to take place, the purely *geometric* correspondence between rings of rooms and rings of walls would have to be done away with. The two kinds of similarity could not coexist. The one would inevitably cancel out the other. A geometrical figure works differently in different situations. It is not like a gene, something that always carries the same message and always produces the same results; it does not have a meaning independent of the circumstances of its employment, unless it be an entirely conventionalized meaning. In one instance (the plan), the ring was the agency for variation; in another (the room), the agency for unification. So the *geometry* of the ring was supplanted by the *logic* of variety; an idea about social intercourse took over from a configuration as the key theme.

Repton's target, the ring of chairs, was vulnerable to attack because, as noticed already: furnishing in the last half of the eighteenth century had become so light and mobile that the pattern of intercourse it politely represented in deference to past practice—the peculiar unity demanded of social events during the seventeenth century—could easily be disfigured or dispersed. What is more, the aesthetic bondage of furniture to wall surface was, by the time of Repton's animadversions in 1816, in any case loosening.

The reason why the subsequent disengagement of furniture from the wall surface was so important was that it altered the basic geography of the interior, acting as agency for a new mode of occupation. The Regency Period between 1800 and 1826 was the time or transition. A few examples: George Smith in 1808 produced a design for room furnishings that shows the customary ring of chairs, now bedded in a highly modelled wall surface. Added to the ring of chairs is a central island table surrounded by four chaiseslongues. This island is quite different to the traditional centrepiece of the dining table, or king's bed, which focused all attention inward. The Smith plan instead distributes attention around an annular ring of space between wall and centre, a centre which has been effectively taken out of service, suggesting a circle of varied activity rotating round an inactive core; in other words, a room-sized miniature of the circuit plans of the previous decades.[19]

Then there are the disquieting illustrations from Gaetano Landi's *Architectural Decorations* of 1810, showing a series of interior perspectives with different styles of decor, not one piece of furniture to be seen.[20] [Fig. 5.10] The large Grecian salon looks, for instance, as if it has been folded straight out of a developed surface drawing, while on a separate plate, a collection of furniture in the same style, Greek, stands afloat in an unbounded perspective space where the individual pieces are planted awkwardly as though meant to stand free of architecture, but still hankering for a wall. [Fig. 5.11] The clumsy division between interior and furniture suggests some conflict between them. This was not a problem of projection technique, for Landi's two plates are both perspectives. It was just that, despite its stylistic compatibility with the room, the furniture could not be effectively positioned: it was literally neither here nor there, neither in the room nor on the wall.

The publication two years later of some far more sophisticated drawings by Henry Moses, an employee of Thomas Hope, resolves these uncertainties and illuminates some salient features of the new interior landscape. The purpose of Moses' drawings, published as *Designs for Modern Costume*, was to display the Greek style of dress devised by Hope. This he did in sixteen little cameo perspectives of architectural interiors, richly furnished and decorously populated. [Fig. 5.12] The interiors are of Duchess Street, a house by Adam that Hope had redecorated. The plan is a circuit. The furniture is Hope furniture.[21] One of Moses' drawings, the 'Beau Monde,' shows a reception in the Duchess Street Picture Gallery. There are nine clusters of two, three or four persons, some using chairs and tables that edge away from the sides of the room. The Beau Monde is still the ambiguous world of Adam's interiors, where the furniture belongs to the wall, yet can be easily displaced.[22] But practically all the other scenes in *Designs for Modern Costume* are of small groups that accentuate the role of furniture laying the

Fig. 5.10: "Large Grecian salon," from *Architectural Decorations* by Gaetano Landi, 1810 (engraving) by Italian School (19th century). Private Collection/The Bridgeman Art Library.
Nationality/copyright status: Italian/out of copyright
Fig. 5.11: "Furniture in the Grecian Style," from *Architectural Decorations* by Gaetano Landi, engraved by G. D'Argenzio, 1810 (engraving) by Italian School (19th century).
Private Collection/The Bridgeman Art Library, Nationality/copyright status: Italian/out of copyright

Fig. 5.12: "Woman and child," reprinted from Henry Moses, *Designs for Modern Costume*, 1812.

groundwork for closeness and intimacy. In these touching, domestic scenes, the *furniture* occupies the room and then figures inhabit the furniture. The relation between body, dress, furniture, architecture and intercourse attains a truly comprehensive unity in these pictures, although they are unnerving, as are all such syntheses in their insistence on the homogenization of appearances. What they demonstrate is the sustenance offered to quartet, trio or couple by couches, tables and chairs, and the increasing encroachment of furniture onto the floorspace as the groups reduce in size. This littering of the floor breaks up its consistency, giving it a more complex, diverse geography which aids and abets intimacy.

The room is no longer a circus, but a miniature internal landscape. It is no longer an edge and a centre (distantly but distinctly related to those spectral archetypes, the domed space and the ideal city), always looking toward the latent authority of the centre, as was so well parodied in Repton's Cedar Parlour. It is now a topography of varied elements distributed picturesquely across the floor, without evident formality, but nevertheless with concern for the niceties of subdivided, heterogeneous association.

The emphasis had moved from the wall to the floor. We return now to the developed surface, its fate sealed with the migration of furniture out of its reach. There are, in the V&A Museum, a collection of drawings from the London company of Gillows, furniture makers. Produced between 1817 and 1832, they illustrate proposals for various interiors, for the most part drawing rooms. Gillows, then still in the forefront of the trade, understood the new mode of furnishing very well and their catalogue contained freestanding pieces that colonized open floorspace as well as a range of traditional wall-hugging items.[23] Yet their design drawings, presumably meant for clients, indicate a dislocation between the recognized technique of representing interiors and the altered geography of the floor. They needed to show the walls because some of their merchandise still belonged there. For that the developed surface was the obvious choice. They needed also to show

Fig. 5.13: Gillows and Co., *Furnishings for a small drawing room*, 1822 (engraving) by English School (19th century). Private Collection/The Bridgeman Art Library. Nationality/copyright status: English/out of copyright

each item of potential purchase, whatever its position, in sufficiently pictorial a form, and they needed to show their combined effects on the room as a whole. They ended up conflating three distinct types of drawing in a vain attempt to illustrate the topography of the floor and the flatness of the walls in one summary representation. [Fig. 5.13 + 5.14] The old technique of folding the walls outward is trundled out unflinchingly to satisfy one part of the requirement. At the same time small-scaled perspectives of the disengaged chairs, couches, footstools, card- and dining-tables float in the maelstrom of conflicting imagined spaces, each piece contributing its own idiocentric and cock-eyed cone of vision. Orientation of the drawing is utterly impossible, directly adjacent objects being frequently upside-down or sideways in relation to each other. Add to this the constant flicker between the two-dimensional representation of the wall surface and floor plan, and the splayed three-dimensionality of the autistic perspective constructions, and the confusion is complete. There is some pattern: one might guess that the individual pieces, which are viewed always from the same height, were

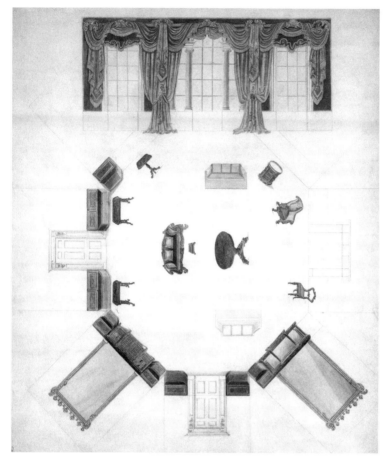

Fig. 5.14: Gillows of Lancaster, *Furnishings for an octagonal drawing room*, circa 1825. Pencil, hand-colored. V&A Images, Victoria and Albert Museum

traced from a catalogue, and their perspective vanishing-points tend to converge on the nearest wall as if not quite emancipated from it. None of this, though, is any aid to visualization.[24]

The company purveyed these masterpieces of vacillation for at least fifteen years, yet their eloquence is their failure to convey in drawing any idea of spatial consistency or relative position. Nothing could more clearly demonstrate their incapacity to show what had to be shown than this hilarious incoherence. Insufficient by itself, incapable (because of the extremity of its flatness) of incorporation with perspective, the developed surface was now a positive hindrance to comprehension.

During the nineteenth century the process of furniture accumulation continued; more of it became free-standing, and its weight increased until rooms were hardly traversable at all. Plan and perspective became the

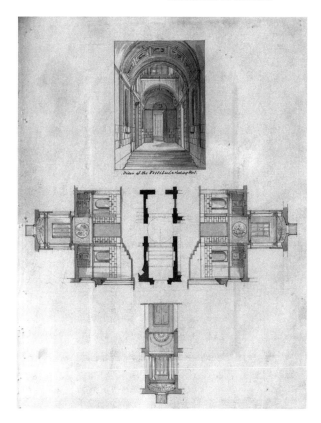

Fig. 5.15: Sir John
Soane, *Vestibule at
Pitzhanger Hall*, 1802.
By courtesy of the
Trustees of Sir John
Soane's Museum

characteristic means of representing interiors. The demise of the developed surface, complete by 1820, was the demise also of a way of making interiors. Its disappearance coincided not only with a change in the way rooms were occupied, but with a change in the prevailing conception of architectural space. John Soane's drawing of the vestibule at Pitzhanger was its swansong. [Fig. 5.15] In the published folio of drawings of Soane's suburban villa it is the only one of its kind.[25] The illustration shows a narrow defile of a room, pulled upwards into a lantern, the shaft of which opens out onto other rooms on the first floor. Sections—not elevations—of the walls are distributed around a central plan. Wall thickness and openings are therefore made visible in contravention of the Adam technique. Although the spatial outflow from the vestibule to adjacent rooms is limited in comparison with other Soane interiors, the relationships are not easy to deduce. The drawing still keeps the room relatively hermetic. Even though the thin, unfurnished hall was no doubt chosen by Soane as a good candidate for developed surface representation, the limitations of the technique are evident. The pressure to gain full-bodied three-dimensionality is so strong that the section on the fourth side thrusts back into a perspective. This is the same layout, but not really the same technique as the developed surface interior, for it has under-gone considerable redefinition.[26]

Soane's architecture, like so much to follow, broke through walls to achieve real and extended depth. Enclosures would dissolve into vir-tual presence, revealing a complex of receding, partially enclosed volumes beyond. Containment is virtual, depth real: the formula is an exact reversal of that which could be applied to Adam's work. To attempt to illustrate deep spaces expanding out from a room represented as if it were a flattened paper box was plainly futile. The Pitzhanger vestibule drawing, though a modifi-cation of developed surface projection, was not sufficient to save the species from extinction in the new surroundings.

The two mutations in the drawing of the interior, around 1760 and then around 1810, corresponded to changes in the environment in which the drawing functioned. The first mutation brought developed surface projec-tion into plans. The room was made into a ring of decorative surfaces, sim-ilar in geometry to the characteristic circuit of rooms in the house plans of which it was part. Yet while the ensemble of rooms had been to a consider-able extent freed from the old tyranny of hierarchical organization, the room itself remained much as it had before. Escape here was achieved by surrep-titiously mobilizing furniture, not by altering the formation of space. In the second mutation the room was liberated and made the scene of variety, as the house had been in the first. The developed surface belonged only with the first set of relationships, because as attention moved from the enveloping surfaces of the room to the spaces in front and behind, the interior required a different mode of investigation and therefore a different sort of drawing.

One final point: the second mutation was not an extension of the first. As the effort of liberation moved from house to room, the house plan altered yet again, suggesting that two versions of the same variegated geography, two attempts to escape from the same tyrant, could not coexist within the same shell. Repton, Nash and Soane did not employ either the ancient hier-archical plan or the circuit of rooms but something else again; varied still, but more complex, more private. A kind of hierarchy found its way into their plans nevertheless: a hierarchy based on the division between circulation and occupation rather than on sequential gradation.

But what kind of liberation was this? It was modest and, like all liber-ation, insofar as it is an experience of release, temporary. We have already noted that it was confined to a certain area of existence for a certain class of persons. It is sobering to recall that during this same period other classes of persons were being subjected to an architecture of precisely opposite ten-dency, bent on forcing consciousness as well as activity into a given mould, frequently based on just the hierarchical authority being erased from the town houses and villas of the well-to-do. Figures such as Adam, and even

Repton, were happy enough to provide either on request. Nor was this other architecture, the architecture of the prisons, workhouses, factories and model cottages, an outmoded thing soon to be got rid of. It was dreamt up and put together in the same period. And this should not be forgotten, because an architecture conceived of as altering both human consciousness and the circumstances of human intercourse, can work against liberty as well as for it. In fact, it can do the former rather more easily and effectively. So, if there was, during this period, when the great institutions of modern life were being formed, an instance of architecture being effectively deployed against authority, it must surely be of interest, even if it was restricted in scope, and only temporary.

But was it even so temporary? The answer is equivocal. An illustration from J.B. Jackson's *American Space* traces the effects of another escape.[27] Maps of a plantation before and after the Civil War show the tight authoritarian community of the slave era dispersed, sharecroppers' cabins spread out to cover the vacant peripheral territory; another rejection of personified authority, another release registered in the physical distribution of buildings—not simulated, not signified by it, but registered. There is no denying, however, that this led to a kind of sterility, the effects of which would in time develop their own species of tyranny, as those subject to the revised pattern came to realize both its power and its limits. The same could be said of the synchronized revisions that took place in the format of polite society, planning, furnishing and architectural drawing around 1760, and then again around 1810. Something of this has come down to us. Many aspects of our own domesticity emanate from these events. We no longer regard them as liberties, since they no longer represent an escape from anything. They are simply background characteristics of everyday life, occasionally irritating, but more usually taken for granted.

It is worth bearing in mind that informality, the word that was used in the eighteenth and nineteenth centuries to describe the new domestic geography, was not an abolition of formality by an alternative constitution of relations between many diverse things. For instance, in order to escape the tyranny of obsequious, unified conversation, the empty space of the room, which offered a sort of freedom of its own, was overrun by furniture which then rendered the definition of action far more specific than before.

While the results of these trivial but momentous events should therefore retain some interest for us, I would direct attention also to the pattern of interaction between the various practices involved—drawing, social intercourse, planning and furnishing. These practices form constellations. The constellations change every now and then, taking up a new shape, incorporating new elements. Is each reconstituted, constellation the result of a single idea expressing itself thus? Does a change in the informing principle account for the changes that occur in the constellation? Is the difference between the work of Adam and Repton the difference between a body of work dominated by the idea of circuits, in the one case, and informality in the other?

Not quite. In both cases the tendency to impose a distinct theme was counteracted by the recalcitrance of the medium. The theme could never express itself as a fundamental informing principle; it was closer to the surface of events than that. In both cases the theme itself was in the process of development, and its power only extended so far. Things remained out of its reach, or were seen to be unreasonably distorted by it. What we have here, then, is a tendency toward informing principles rather than fully fledged examples of the type. There is a difference between tying a group of people together with rope and saying they are related, and pointing out that they all have the same parents. Adam and Repton *et al* use rope to establish relations. Or, to make the analogy more exact, they impose a family resemblance on a diverse body of subjects, which it is all too easy for us to interpret as fundamental, when in fact it lies on the surface.

Each confronted an existing set of practices; each attempted significant alteration to the set at whatever appeared to be the critical point. Adam and his contemporaries challenged the hierarchy of the early-eighteenth-century plan; Repton and his contemporaries colonized the open floorspace of the late-eighteenth-century interior. There is no equivalent of stellar gravitation here. Each constellation was held together, not by one force, but by a multiplicity of forces. Yet in order to alter it, a stronger force had to be introduced. Reality can manage without unity, the intellect cannot. As soon as a set of practices becomes the subject of manipulation, as soon as they are altered to correspond to human intention, the unifying principle comes into play. Only in this way can any purpose or direction be given to things. And precisely because of this conscious, unifying tendency in human affairs, things do not issue from a fundamental unity but converge toward unities fitfully.[28]

Notes

*   Robin Evans, "The Developed Surface: An Enquiry into the Brief Life of an Eighteenth-Century Drawing Technique," in *Translations from Drawing to Building and Other Essays*, ed. Robin Evans (Cambridge: The MIT Press, 1997), 212.

1   I am thinking of architects such as Balthasar Neumann and Bernardo Vittone, whose surviving architectural drawings are all orthographic. They seem to have set much store by perspective sketches of the kind so well known from Juvarra, and yet the architecture they produced was decidedly scenographic. See Christian Otto, *Space into Light: The Churches of Balthasar Neumann* (Boston, 1979), pp. 37–9; also Rudolph Wittkower, 'Vittone's Domes,' in *Studies in the Italian Baroque* (London, 1975), pp. 217–8.

2   It may be useful to describe the rest in relation to the drawing, not because architectural drawing informs other ideas and practices—it has no such priority—but because it is often presumed to be a purely technical matter, related perhaps in some vague way to spatial sensibility though nothing much else. The seminal work on architectural drawing studied in its setting is Wolfgang Lotz's 'The Rendering of the Architectural Interior in Architectural Drawing of the Renaissance,' in *Studies in Italian Renaissance Architecture* (Cambridge, Mass., 1977), pp. 3–65, which provided the stimulus for this article.

3   John Cornforth and John Fowler, *English Interior Decoration in the Eighteenth Century* (London, 1974), pp. 26–8.

4   Ibid. There is at least one much earlier example of the same sort: an unattributed drawing in the V&A, showing furniture against an elevational wall surface. See Peter Ward Jackson, *English Furniture in the Eighteenth Century* (London, 1958), plate II. However, Cornforth and Fowler's attachment of importance to Stuart's drawing as first ripple of the coming tide would seem justified.

5   William Halfpenny, Robert Morris, Thomas Lightoler, *The Modern Builder's Assistant* (London, 1757), plates 71 and 72 (both stair halls) and 75 (a hall without stairs). All are shown as developed surface interiors. Other interiors in this work are shown as sections or ceiling plans. This was by no means the earliest use of the technique in England; Colen Campbell shows the great hall at Houghton thus; see *Vitrvius Britannicus,* vol. 3, plate 34. William Kent also drew interiors for the Houses of Commons and Lords this way; see RIBA, *Catalogue* of *Drawings Collection,* edited by J. Lever (London, 1973), vols. G–K, Kent W, f. 18, 21.

6   Robert Adam's own education in drawing with Clerisseau led in a completely different direction: perspective and pictorial. His acquaintance with Piranesi (whose architectural elevations, quite unlike his *vedute* and *carcere* engravings, treated the wall as a flat surface, rather like a page to be written on) may have encouraged Adam to attempt the contraction of space into surface, but even if this were the case, it is hardly to the point. I am concerned here less with where things come from, more with what is done with them. See John Fleming, *Robert Adam and his Circle* (London. 1978), pp. 65 *et seq.*

7   This arrangement is rarely as consistently portrayed in plans as in James Gibbs's *A Book of Architecture* (London, 1728), where even a variant of the Villa Rotunda is made subject to the same internal organization, but it was characteristic of much produced in the last half of the seventeenth century and the first quarter of the eighteenth. See Cornforth and Fowler, *English Interior*

Decoration in the Eighteenth Century (London, 1974), chapter 3; Peter Thornton, *Seventeenth-Century Interior Decoration in England, France & Holland* (London, 1978), pp. 55–63; and Mark Girouard, *Life in the English Country House* (London, 1978), chapter 5.

8   The 1761 proposal for Syon, with a central rotunda, puts it in a different category, although the rotunda was never built. Sometimes a complete circuit develops only on one side of a central entrance, as in Newelston, Harewood and the first Luton Hoo plan. And sometimes the clear circuit organization of early schemes degenerates into more complex, less distinct patterns, as at Luton Hoo. Indeed the most unequivocal circuit plans are pattern-book examples by John Carter, William Thomas and George Richardson. If this suggests a disinclination on the part of the clients, it also suggests a certain insistence on the architect's part. The circuit was an ideal arrangement frequently modified in practice. See Arthur Bolton, *The Architecture of Robert & James Adam* (London, 1922), vol. 1, p. 42, vol. 2, pp. 78, 81, 266, 279; William Thomas, *Original Designs in Architecture*, 1783, plate 2; John Carter, *Builders' Magazine*, 1774 and after, plates xxxix and lxxxiii.

9   Richardson, who worked with Adam for eighteen years, produced *A Book of Ceilings*, London, 1776, all Adamesque, and *Iconology*, 2 vols. (London, 1779); this latter a revision of Cesare Ripa with the figures made more Greek and agreeable, their allegorical purpose conventionalized. Giuseppe Manocchi was responsible for a great many Adam ceilings. See Walter L. Speirs, *Catalogue of Drawings of R & J Adam in the Sir John Soane Museum* (Cambridge, 1979); and Geoffrey Beard, *The Work of Robert Adam* (London, 1978), chapter 3, pp. 20–7.

10   George Smith, writing in 1826, said that Chippendale introduced the arabesque in furniture, but that the Adam brothers, following their studies of Diocletian's palace and baths, had introduced it into interior design: 'A complete revolution in the taste of design immediately followed; the heavy panelled wall, the deeply coffered ceiling, although they offered an imposing and grand effect, gave way to the introduction of a light arabesque style.' G. Smith, *Cabinet Maker and Upholsterer's Guide* (London, l826), p, v; see also Eileen Harris, *The Furniture of Robert Adam* (London, 1963).

11   The traditional posture of the body would emphasize authority by facing the figure directly out into the major space of the room, as happens, for example, in the recess of the Queen's closet, Ham House (1670s). In the Adam alcove room, a figure on the day-bed would certainly not be able to maintain frontality. She, too, would of course face out toward the room, turning sideways to do so, but to accomplish this her posture, though still classical, would become 'informal.'

12   Margaret Whinney, *Home House* (Feltham, 1969), pp. 44–6; and A. Bolton, *The Architecture of R & J Adam* (London, 1922), vol. 2, pp. 82–3.

13   Victoria & Albert Museum, *Guide to Osterley Park* (London, 1972), pp. 52–3.

14   Ibid. pp. 5, 34–5; and Maurice Tomlin, 'Back to Adam at Osterley,' *Country Life*, vol. cxlvii, 1970.

15   Daniel Marot, *Das Ornamentwerk* (Berlin, 1892), part v, plates 151–62.

16   See Mark Girouard, *Life in the English Country House*, pp. 236–9 for a discussion of breaking the circle. It is difficult to gauge how strong the circle really was during the earlier part of the eighteenth century. Hogarth's portraits of diversified groupings at Wanstead and Bowood in the 1730s, for instance, lead one to suspect that it was to some extent a property projected into the immediate past in order to clarify present intentions.

17 Humphrey Repton, *Fragments on the Theory and Practice of Landscape Gardening* (London, 1816), fragment xiii, p. 85.

18 Ibid. fragment xxv, p. 127.

19 George Smith, *Collection of Designs for Household Furniture and Interior Decoration* (London, 1808), p. 30 and plates 152, 153.

20 Gaetano Landi, *Architectural Decoration,* 1810, vol. I, plates 2 and 5.

21 David Watkin, *Thomas Hope and the Neo-Classical Idea* (London, 1812).

22 See also Thomas Hope, *Household Furniture* (London 1807), where, in the unpopulated rooms, the furniture still relates to the wall surface.

23 Department of Prints & Drawings, V&A Museum, London, Gillows Company folios 14, 14a l4b, 14c. These include also libraries, dining rooms, bedrooms and music rooms drawn in the same way.

24 The tendency to incoherent representation could already be discerned in Sheraton's developed surface (Fig. 2), about which he wrote: 'In a drawing room of this kind (i.e., with wall furniture) very little perspective is wanted....And I would not advise drawing every object on each wall to one point of sight, as those at the extremities will thereby become exceedingly distorted and unnatural. For upon supposition that the spectator moves along to different stations as he views any one side of the room, perspective will admit that the designer have as many points to draw as the spectator has stations to view from.' Thomas Sheraton, *The Cabinet Maker and the Upholsterer's Drawing Book* (London, 1793), p. 441. The suggestion of kinetic representation, directly at odds with the perspectival requirement of a fixed viewpoint, leads to a series of minor topological ruptures which in this instance glide into one another with relative ease. Even so, the mixture of perspective and orthographic drawing deprives the walls of their flatness.

25 John Soane, *Plans, Elevations and Perspective Views of Pitzhanger Manor House* (London 1802), plate vi.

26 Another example of transition can be found in the Morel and Seddon project for refurbishing Windsor. See G. de Bellaique and P. Kirkham, 'George IV and the Furnishing of Windsor,' *Furniture History,* vol. viii, 1972. The drawings for the library show the deep bay of the east wall in perspective and the flat plane of the west wall in elevation, the mode of drawing dependent on the degree of modelling in the architecture.

27 J.B. Jackson, *American Space: The Centennial Years 1865–1876* (New York, 1972), pp. 150–2, taken from *Schriber's Magazine,* April 1881.

28 Unfortunately I was unable to read Laura Jacobus's article on the drawing technique I have described until after mine was typeset (see 'On "Whether a man could see before him and behind him both at once,"' in *Architectural History,* vol. 31, 1988, pp. 148 *et seq.*) We seem independently to have arrived at similar conclusions though she gives greater emphasis to earlier examples. The most important difference is that she understands the box-like format to be a practical convenience that was restrictive of the architect's imagination, whereas I see it as expanding some horizons while restricting others.

Corners and Darts

Lois Weinthal

INTRODUCTION

Clothing, furniture, interior design, and architecture each have their own set of drawing conventions unique to the materials of their trade and methods of construction, but all design requires precision in measurement. Fashion and furniture manufacture rely on full-scale drawings for construction, whereas interior design and architecture use scaled proportions, often found at 1/4" or 1/8". In this essay, I looked at an interior where all these disciplines coexist, a catchall space that offers the opportunity to combine full and miniature scale by their common notations and conventions. Notations specific to clothing, such as the integration of the sewn line and darts, were tested in architectural construction. In these experiments, the drawing itself was treated as a two-dimensional surface that could be transformed into three dimensions. When these conventional notations are shared, new methods of construction emerge.

The starting point for this work began with a furniture maker's drawing by Gillows and Co. from 1822, originally analyzed by Robin Evans in his essay "The Developed Surface: An Enquiry into the Brief Life of an Eighteenth-Century Drawing Technique." In his essay, Evans draws the distinction between the primary orthographic plan of a room upon which furniture is secondarily placed. The plan uses walls and floor to ground stylistic elements, such as ornament, furniture, wallpaper, and curtains. These elements are secondary and by nature temporary and easily replaced. The location of furniture, the least-grounded element in the drawing, aroused my curiosity. I wanted to challenge its secondary status by reversing the drawing's hierarchy to make secondary elements primary. This reversal draws on Gottfried Semper's first task of the architect—to hang textiles and skins, giving priority to the interior. In a full-scale installation, I redistributed drawing conventions from sewing clothing to constructing a room. A chair became the central symbol of the transposition, normally rendered full-scale in furniture drawings and construction, but often miniaturized in interior and architecture drawings. The

---

Originally appeared in *Thresholds*, no. 22 (2001): 84–89.

result allowed furniture to map the interior by altering orthographic princi-
ples. At the same time, the chair emphasized elements inherent to the interior
and gave objects of personal significance priority, as a way to reflect its domi-
nant presence in the interior.

———

Scenario

The occupant sits on a chair in a room. The clothes on the occupant have
been tailored to fit the surface of the body along with pockets to carry objects.
The chair is placed upon a carpet that runs along the floor till it reaches the
surface of a wall. Upon that wall is a layer of wallpaper, tailored to fit the
openings of doorways, windows, and terminating at closets.

The tailoring of clothes, the objects in a room and the surfaces that
line the interior are made through drawings at a 1:1 scale. This project entitled Wing Chair focuses on the representation of clothing patterns, furniture
and architecture, and the ability to share notations resulting in new constructions. A drawing brought to light by Robin Evans becomes the instiga-
tor to test the reversal of these drawing conventions. The result relies upon
the borrowing of clothing pattern constructions to inform the construction
of architecture in a project for a chair that accepts rules and notations from
both disciplines.

Architecture and clothing construction have both formalized the process of representation resulting in a standard language universal in each discipline. Inherent are rules, notations and symbols that have the potential to
overlap from one discipline to another. The orthographic drawing is the convention used in the practice of architecture. It allows true measurements
and the representation of individual surfaces such as plan, elevation, section
and detail that then get keyed together through a reference system. These
flat patterns are the result of established views chosen to represent the most
important information, usually with a wall or floor as a base to the drawing. A scale is applied to the drawings at an abstract proportion. In contrast,
the role of scale in the clothing pattern is established at 1:1. Notations on the
pattern instruct the tailor of a size, centerline, notches to be cut, grain-line
direction, folding, pinning, darts and the location of additional assembly and
connection details.[1]

The clothing pattern becomes a form of documentation for the body.
The clothing pattern mimics the surface of the skin, allowing the pattern to
unfold and take precedent over a dominant organizing system, such as the
grid commonly referred to in the orthographic drawing system. In contrast,
the clothing pattern inherently locates darts by lining the irregular surface of
the body and unfolding the surface onto a plane. A pattern for a coat reveals

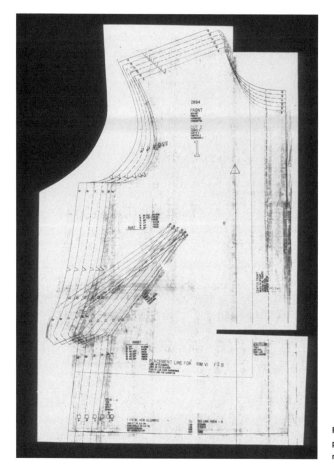

Fig. 5.16: Coat
pattern with dart
notation.

the dart notation instructing the tailor how to develop a flat surface or create a volume through the darts located by the waist. [Fig. 5.16] The clothing pattern confronts the problem of how to wrap a curved form that cannot fold or unfold with the same precision as an orthogonal form.

The question can be asked: how do the conventions of the clothing pattern enter into a dialogue with the orthographic system? One of the consequences of the orthographic system is that the people and objects that fill the interior have less presence in the drawing system, although it is these characters that we see in the immediate occupied space. Therefore, the object one would find in a room, such as a chair, becomes the focus of an investigation that references the occupant and locates itself on a floor plan. It is this situation where I form a dialogue between architecture and clothing. A chair acts as a vehicle between the body and architecture and is given precedent in the orthographic drawing as a base. This investigation requires the dart in clothing construction to become structural in architecture.

Fig. 5.17: Lois Weinthal, muslin wallpaper tailored to a door threshold with molding, 1993.

Referring back to the opening scenario of the occupant sitting on a chair in a room, we can rethink the drawing types used to represent the elements within that space. The surfaces lining the room such as wallpaper and rugs are made at a 1:1 scale and share similar characteristics to the clothing pattern. The pliable materials of interior surface linings can inherently be shaped outside of the orthographic system and take into consideration the notation of darts, allowing for a dialogue of drawing conventions between the orthographic and the clothing patterns.

Similarly, as the surface of a wall peels away, such as the layer of wallpaper, they become patterns lifted off the wall. Therefore, an association can be made between the wallpaper as a full-scale drawing, and the unfolded drawing as a pattern of a volume. The pattern allows one to manipulate the surface to form a volume, such as darts in clothing. The interior has these places, such as where the door molding projects into space, creating a volume, resulting in a pattern with darts.

To test the relationship of interior surfaces to the notation of darts in clothing patterns, an interior chamber of a home is chosen to be the testing ground where muslin—the material used for mocking up clothing patterns—acts as wallpaper, also becoming the full-scale drawing. Surfaces are lined to find how the interior might inherently have darts. As the wallpaper meets the door molding, it becomes an instance where a volume projects from the surface and the wallpaper becomes tailored to this element. [Fig. 5.17] As a result of the process, the wallpaper becomes the material for drafting upon and darts are found in architecture. A question can be asked about the wallpaper and the drawings for clothing patterns: can the wallpaper take on

329

Fig. 5.18: Gillows and Co., *Furnishings for a small drawing room*, 1822 (engraving) by English School (19th century). Private Collection/The Bridgeman Art Library. Nationality/copyright status: English/out of copyright

characteristics of these drawings and present the notations as tangible elements in the interior space? Or vice versa, and what would that mean for the clothing pattern? It is this relationship that will guide the chair project allowing the drawing system used for clothing patterns to participate in the orthographic drawing.

The Developed Surface Interior

Robin Evans writes in his essay "The Developed Surface: An Inquiry into the Brief Life of an Eighteenth-Century Drawing Technique" of a drawing example by Gillows and Company. Evans calls this drawing type the 'developed surface interior' where walls separate at their edges and unfold to be read in relation to the plan.[2] [Fig. 5.18] The orthographic system directs the surfaces as how to unfold relying upon the corner as the location where the architectural surfaces separate to show plan and elevations neatly organized. As the elevations separate from one another, a wedge shape is formed. The dart in clothing patterns offer the same scribed line and wedge shape, and is made tangible to give structure to the clothing. It is my desire to test the potential of this interior dart, the space spanning between surfaces, that I call the *wing space*. This space of latent notation in the 'developed surface interior' drawing has the potential to become the structure that pulls these walls together to form their volume. At this point, a relationship can be established where at full-scale, the corner in architecture and the dart in clothing patterns have a potential to inform one another.

Upon these surfaces, the furniture makers attempted to show how the furnishings would fit in the space. The furnishings are applied to the surfaces as if they belonged to that surface without regard to the whole. If a chair were to be placed next to a wall, the chair would gravitate toward that surface. Similarly, as objects are placed toward the center of the floor plan, their correct view becomes more difficult as the draftsman tries to locate the furniture in a view that would be most clear to understand. The furniture drawn in perspective appears to be suspended and not "exist" within the space of the orthographic drawing, leaving it up to our imagination to connect the walls at their edges and fold the room back up so it reads as a whole.[3] The drawing now consists of two different drawing types, the orthographic and the perspective.[4] This architectural drawing represents the interior elevations and floor plan as the primary architectural surfaces that act as a base for the personal objects—being secondary—to be placed upon. I question: can the personal objects that one places in the interior be the base upon which the interior architectural surfaces respond? How would the structure of a space change?

Wing Chair

A chair is chosen as a vehicle to answer these questions. The chair begins its construction under combined rules of the two drawing conventions: the 1:1 scale borrowed from clothing pattern and the unfolded view in the orthographic system as the base view. By nature, the drawing type allows singular elevations to be drawn, acting as a pattern for the chair to be made. The edges of the chair are the location for it to be unfolded and to find those spaces that offer darts, or the wing space. This act begins to address the possibility of finding those latent notations that we see in the flattened object, such as the clothing pattern, and make them tangible. The goal is to make the wing space be both a notation in the drawing and in turn, make it tangible. The wing space is located and sewn to the chair with reinforcing of steel rods as the scale of durability and materials step up. [Fig. 5.19]

The relationship of the floor to the objects that are placed on it refers back to my question of how can the objects begin to unfold the architectural surfaces giving the objects priority. The chair is given priority on the plan, and when unfolded, unfolds the floor. New edges are created in reaction to the floor as it breaks from itself to connect to the unfolded chair. [Figs. 5.20–22]

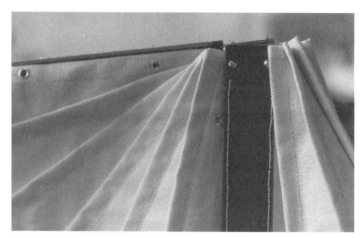

Fig. 5.19: Lois Weinthal, Wing Chair, 1993. Detail of expanded "wing" taking cues from darts in clothing construction.

Fig. 5.20: Lois Weinthal, Wing Chair, 1993. Wing Chair folded up with steel rods slipped into the "wing" darts as support for the chair.

Fig. 5.21: Lois Weinthal, Wing Chair, 1993. Detail of break line in the floor responding to the unfolded chair plan.

Fig. 5.22: Lois Weinthal, Wing Chair, 1993. Wing Chair unfolded revealing the "wings" in plan and the separation of the floor in response to the chair plan.

My previous questions: can the objects within the space take priority in the unfolding of the volume? Is there room in the drawing system for latent notations to become tangible? And can two drawing systems, the one used for architecture, the other for clothing patterns, provide compatible information with the possibility of furthering one another? These questions are addressed through the relationship of parts in the Wing Chair.

Conclusion

The dart is a notation that informs the tailor how to make a flat surface become developed. Is it possible for architecture to reconsider the corner by taking a cue from the dart in clothing construction? The established orthographic drawing shows plan, section and elevation where the drawing is usually cut off when it turns a plane at a corner, it is at these locations that we can see a way for the convention to accept a counterpart in the tailoring of clothing. The conventional architectural drawing is represented on a standard sheet size with no alteration to the physical character of that paper. The drawing must supply all the information regarding how a building comes together with the graphic language of architecture. This process of construction is represented as two-dimensional, with the key word being representation. In contrast, the approach of clothing construction allows notations to be visible at full-scale, where the element of representation is simultaneously part of the construction and the finished product. Is it possible to even consider in the profession, if the standard architectural drawing sheet could change? And vice versa, how would the standards of the architectural drawing ever change the clothing pattern?

I would like to conclude with a question as a result of this investigation. If we take cues from related disciplines such as clothing patterns and see them in the light of architecture, would we discover new pockets of space that offer something new to architecture? I think so.

Notes

1   Reader's Digest. *Complete Guide to Sewing*. (New York: The Reader's Digest Association, 1989), 54–7.
2   Robin Evans, "The Developed Surface: An Enquiry into the Brief Life of an Eighteenth-Century Drawing Technique," in *Translations from Drawing to Building and Other Essays* (Cambridge: The MIT Press, 1997), 202.
3   Evans, 211.
4   Evans, 221.

Flattened Room

Jeanine Centuori

INTRODUCTION

Jeanine Centuori's project, Flattened Room, is built on the language of ortho-graphic drawing, but extends away from walls, floors, and ceilings toward objects that fill the interior, like tables, chairs, and silverware. Her project recalls Robin Evans's essay "The Developed Surface: An Enquiry into the Brief Life of an Eighteenth-Century Drawing Technique" as a precedent for map-ping the interior, where furniture makers' drawings centered attention on the walls and floor, leaving furniture to float on the drawings.

Centuori steps into the virtual acts of drawing, borrowing, and reinter-preting conventions from orthographic projection in order to map floating objects in her own arrangement. Her meal setting, for instance, included typ-ical objects: a table, chair, dish, wine bottle, and soup spoon. The complexity of these forms, with their curved surfaces, rendered the traditional method of pencil and paper inadequate. Instead, the map was constructed out of latex. After encasing all of the objects and letting the liquid latex dry, Centuori began mapping by deciding where and how she would make the first cuts to estab-lish her system for unfolding the objects from the room. She used geometri-cal shapes to produce flattened maps whose recognizable shape carries hints about the details recorded in the latex.

Centuori's maps feel familiar for several reasons. First, latex looks like skin, which we understand is a container for the body—its curved surfaces wrap around bone, tendons, muscle, and fluid. Although not explicit, Centuori's process has an underlying association with the body. Her flattened maps recall the anatomical drawings of Henry Gray's Anatomy of the Human Body. The latex maps also have patterns that reveal the function of the cast items, such as the seat of a chair or the profile of a boot. Once we visually reattach the edges, we recognize objects by piecing together views to form complete wholes. In Flattened Room, Centuori reveals the elegance and simplicity of the two- and three-dimensional relationship and her ability to "think around objects" of the everyday in the interior.

Originally appeared in *Architecture Studio: Cranbrook Academy of Art 1986–1993*, edited by Dan Hoffman (New York: Rizzoli International Publications, Inc., 1994), 186–93..

———

Text by Dan Hoffman

The Architecture Studio persists in believing that the processes used to manipulate material can both inspire and manifest an architectural pursuit. Though material processes are necessary to construct buildings, much of our work is devoted to ways in which these processes can carry and intensify architectural ideas.

Jeanine Centuori investigates the potential of latex rubber to record topological or multidimensional surfaces of objects. This material can be applied in a liquid state to complex surfaces, becoming, as it dries, an elastic skin. This can then be peeled off and flattened to reveal the continuous, developed surface. As a liquid, latex can cover surfaces that would be impossible to describe with conventional, orthographic drawing, enabling us to think *around* objects rather than through the two-dimensional cuts of a section or the flat projection of an elevation.

The site for this project was a table setting for a meal in a room within the architecture studio. Each item in the room was covered with latex and then unwrapped onto six four-by-eight-foot panels in the order that they were covered. The unwrapping was done in a manner particular to each object: radial patterns for circles, orthogonal patterns for rectangular forms, and so on. The resulting picture is unpredictable yet curiously familiar. It is as if the flattened skins were waiting for a breath of volume to peel themselves off the panel and be reconfigured, their surfaces carrying the memory of the original volumes. We sense their potential to occupy volumetric space and unconsciously fill them. They recall John Hejduk's masque objects, whose distinctive profiles flatten dimensions like shadows on the ground, volumes that carry the ghost of their drawings around with them; however, in Centuori's project the volumes themselves are the ghosts.

Though the flattened skins could be described as representations of the original objects, their material presence offers something more in the evidence, or trace, of the material and processes involved. Unanticipated details are picked up in places which offer a texture of readings in addition to the geometry involved in re-forming the objects. For example, the difficulty of a particular detail or pattern an object leaves upon the surface gives a temporal and material dimension to the work.

A running description of the objects in the room, written by Centuori, accompanies the flattened objects, thereby providing an additional reading of the piece. The combination of image and text offers a structure similar to that of a musical score, enabling us to reinhabit the room within the space of multiple interpretations.

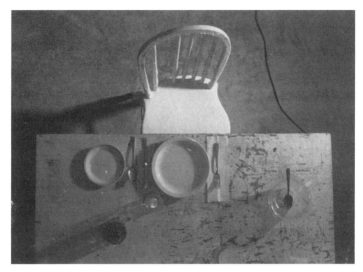

Fig. 5.23: Jeanine Centuori, Flattened Room, 1991.

Text and Work by Jeanine Centuori

In the center of the room, there is a table. The table is made of a wooden top which is white, or at least the very top layer is white. It's a thin layer of paint which is very worn. There are a lot of scratches and marks on it. It appears to have been worked on quite a bit, mostly with a sharp object. On the table there are several objects which are mostly dishes. On the table, furthest to the right of the chair, is a small white porcelain dish with an insignia on it that says *Ford* in gray script letters. Just in front of the dish, a little bit to the left, there is a green wine bottle. Just to the left of the small Ford dish there is a silver spoon, a soup spoon. To the top or front of that is a glass which is empty, and it appears as though it could hold about eight ounces of liquid. At the very left of the knife, there is a large dinner plate; it's an off-white porcelain dish. To the left of the plate there is a napkin, which is really a paper towel. Sitting on the paper towel is a fork whose design seems to almost match the knife and spoon. To the top, or toward the front, of the fork and napkin there is a jar, a glass jar with a white lid which is tightly closed down around the jar. To the left, almost near the edge of the table, is a glass bowl with a spoon in it. The underside of the table is bare wood which is quite splintery, and it has a lot of knots in it which are depressions in the surface. The supports of the table are metal, and seem to have been put there by hand. The table contacts the floor at four points, and there is a black rubber stopper at each of the points. Along the long side of the table, and near the dinner plate, there is a wooden chair, which is slightly tilted out from the

337

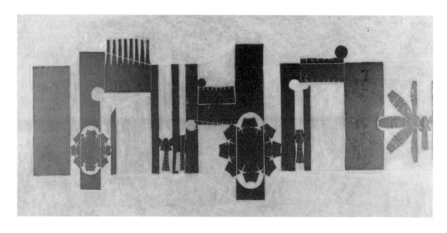

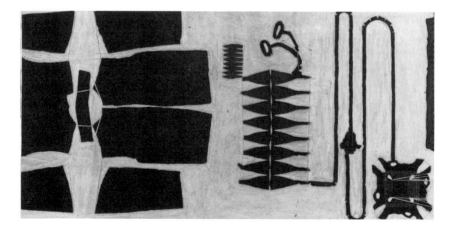

Figs. 5.24–5.29: Jeanine Centuori, Flattened Room, 1991.

table as though someone had just left. There are four legs which are seemingly identical, except for their angle. Behind the chair to its left, if you were sitting in it, is a chest of drawers. It sits in the corner of the room, touching three of its surfaces. The frontmost object on the chest of drawers is a book, a small red book, with the title *Waste*. On the very right side of the chest of drawers, almost near the right edge, there is a porcelain cup which is white with a blue image on it. The picture is a bucolic scene with a windmill, a body of water, a boat, a tree, and a house. Around the edge of the image there is a scrolling line that frames it. In the mug are some objects, mostly pencils, a scissor, erasers, and some odd implements. To the left of the mug, there is a plain wooden rectangular box with a white-and-blue ceramic inlay in its top. Behind this box there is another wooden box. Its top is obscured by a third box. This last box is a blondish wood with a metal clasp at the front. On top of it is a very ornate wooden box which appears to open on a hinge. To the left of the two boxes there is a pink alarm clock with the image of the globe on its face. On the left of the alarm clock there is a small green porcelain cup. The side of the dresser is a brown wood, also painted, and appears to be the same color as the top, although the side is not as worn as the top. At the very base of the chest of drawers, next to its side, there is an outlet, or extension cord, which has a brown plug in it. The extension cord disappears behind the chest of drawers. There is another white extension cord coming out of the first cord, and going up and away from it. To the very left of the chest of drawers, on the floor, is a pair of black rubber boots. Above the boots, hanging on the wall at about eye level, there is a jacket. It's plaid and very colorful. The purple and the red are very distinct large lines, and the areas filled in-between are green and brown. Just to the left of the jacket, attached to a pipe running on the wall, is a lamp which has a clamp connector with rubber ends that holds itself on the pipe with pressure. The cord attached to this lamp is connected to the extension cord on the floor, which continues to connect another lamp located on the other side of the table. It's a tall, thin floor lamp, which is made of metal and marbled glass pieces. At the opposite corner, next to the clamp lamp, there is a door which is connected to the walls of the room. [Figs. 5.23–5.29]

* Jeanine Centuori, "Flattened Room," in *Architecture Studio: Cranbrook Academy of Art 1986–1993*, ed. Dan Hoffman (New York: Rizzoli International Publications, Inc., 1994), 187.

Space-Enfolding-Breath

Monica Wyatt

INTRODUCTION

Monica Wyatt asks what it means to occupy architecture, not just ordinary interior spaces but also those that are inaccessible, such as a wall and its poché. Acting as a physical limit, a wall is a boundary that cannot be traversed without an opening, but the reality of a wall's thickness and the peculiar desire to be in a wall inform Wyatt's curiosity about occupying this space. When educating architects and interior designers, the question is often resolved by expanding the wall's thickness to contain programmed space, or left behind as a space deemed unoccupied. Wyatt does not give in to either direction. Rather, she looks to the wall, entering it to find answers to these questions.

Wyatt's experiment began with a series of full-scale studies. First she compared the wall itself to skin, then the poché became breath. She analyzed wrapping to compare poché and breath, wrapping a building material— a brick—in paper, which acted as the skin. Once the brick was removed and the paper folded back up, it left a void that became a metaphor for the containment of breath. Her study of the skin presented a two-dimensional surface problem, which she resolved by folding it over and over, turning the surface inside out. The map's creases contributed to a two-dimensional surface that recorded the exchange between interior and exterior.

Wyatt weaves these studies together to form a map of the body using a flexible textile that registers the expansion and contraction of breathing. Although the difference in dimension is minimal, it becomes the dress pattern for occupying the skin of a wall. The result is a map and a body wrapped with wallpaper, where body and wall share the same material. Wyatt finds an entry point into the wall, through a map of the body that also reinserts the body back into the wall.

Wyatt uses poetric interpretations of poché and interior space to produce these unconventional mappings. While this project and Jeffrey Siegel's essay "Engineering the Indoor Environment" undertake different approaches to measuring air, notice that they both offer alternative forms that return back to the body and breath.

Originally appeared in *Architecture Studio: Cranbrook Academy of Art 1986–1993*, edited by Dan Hoffman (New York: Rizzoli International Publications, Inc., 1994), 194–201.

_____

Text by Dan Hoffman

Monica Wyatt began her work with a list of questions, noted in her thesis, in search of a definition of a wall:

> To define a wall: What is a wall?
>
> Is a wall defined by its thickness, height, and resistance to penetration?
>
> Is a wall measurable, finite, with two sides, this side and the other?
>
> Is a wall defined by what occurs on the other side?
>
> Is a wall an object such as myself with space separating us?
>
> Can I be (in) a wall, fixed and watching bodies move with space
> separating us?
>
> Can a wall be merely the surface with which one comes in contact, with
> the substance behind/beyond the surface as something else?
>
> Can I define a wall considering only the frontal relationships, just one of
> the surfaces?
>
> Is a wall the surface with which I am immediately confronted?
>
> (Can the wall be that which always separates me from the other object?
> Is space the medium that always separates, or does it merely fill the
> gap that is impassable?)

The questions are phenomenological and psychological, attempting to account not only for the physical presence of the wall itself but for how it is there for *her*. Like Wyatt's own body, walls have fronts and backs, interiors and exteriors. They can separate and bind, and they also possess the point of view of an other from which one is viewed. For Wyatt the wall is ambiguous: even though it presents itself as a physical limit to her body, it provokes the desire to move beyond its bounds. Her confessed desire is to "get into the wall," to escape from the physical limits of the surroundings so that she may see herself from the other side. Wyatt desires to be simultaneously in both places, impossible if one accepts the materialist proposition that two bodies cannot occupy the same space at the same time. She desires, however, to make this possible, to conceive of a situation in which space and material become intertwined, as if consciousness and body were intertwined with in the space of a fold.

This project documents Wyatt's search, starting with simple folding operations performed with thin sheets of lead and ending with the surface of the wall being transformed into the skin of the body. In the end Wyatt entered the wall through a logic that allows for multiple faces of consciousness. It is possible to occupy a wall only if we accept that we are present for others as well as for ourselves. By projecting ourselves into another's point of view, we construct a space within which being is defined and constituted.

Pressed-Brick Wrappings

The effort to enter the wall began with the idea that a wall must have space within it to be entered. Monica Wyatt constructed this "space" symbolically by wrapping a brick in lead sheet and extracting the brick. She then flattened the brick wrapping by running it through a printing press. Though flat, the print of the collapsed brick bears the traces of its former volume, and though the interior is not physically accessible, one feels that its space has come to the surface. Here the flattened lead wrapping is impressed on soft, white paper. [Fig. 5.30]

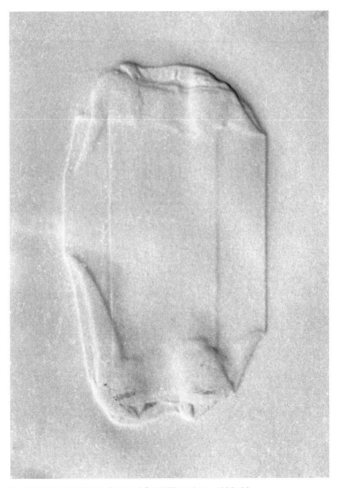

Fig. 5.30: Monica Wyatt, Pressed-Brick Wrappings, 1992–93.

Cruciform Folding

These prints are from a series of foldings performed on a cruciform-shaped lead sheet. One image shows the interior side of the lead pressing through to the visible surface. Wyatt states: "In my prints the surface alludes to spaces seemingly hidden inside—inside made by folding, originally on the outside, pressed to the inside, with a new surface created. The skin is malleable; the surface can be unfolded exposing the 'inside' but with a permanent alteration in shape. This is the persistence of past actions, transformations."

The fold is the key. For within this action the exterior is brought to the interior. With the second action of enfolding there exists the possibility of having the interior reappear on the exterior. [Figs. 5.31–5.34]

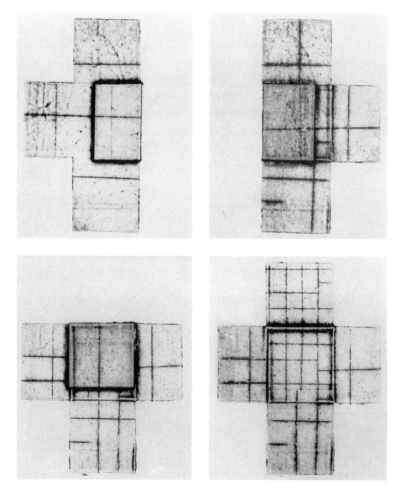

Figs. 5.31–5.34: Monica Wyatt, Cruciform Folding, 1992–93.

Lead Box Plans

The problem here was to produce a box from a single piece of lead. The process of folding was not to be planned in advance; the plan was to result from the construction process. Wyatt established the following operating rules:

> The plan is constructed on a single piece of material.
>
> No raw edges may show.
>
> Excess is good; it can represent density, create structure, allow for expansion.
>
> Each material requires a different plan; though the difference may be small, the rules of construction follow the properties of the material and its possible everyday use.
>
> Everything must follow a logic, whether fictional or not.
>
> [Figs. 5.35 + 5.36]

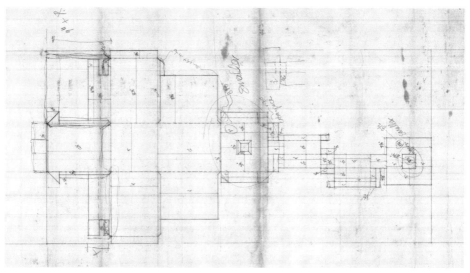

Fig. 5.35: Monica Wyatt, Lead Box Plans, 1992–93.

Fig. 5.36: Monica Wyatt, Lead Box Plans, 1992–93.

345

Planning the Body

Through the operation of the fold a flat continuous surface can be developed into a body. The task again is to develop a plan.

The body itself presents certain difficulties. Its surfaces are continuous and pliable and constantly change with movement. Planning such a surface requires a material that can come in direct contact with the skin itself. Liquid latex rubber conforms precisely to the surface that it touches. As it dries, it must accommodate bodily movements such as the expansion of the rib cage during breathing. Here the plan pattern was cut and filled with enough cotton gauze to accommodate this expansion. This extra space allowed the body to slip out of the skin. [Fig. 5.37]

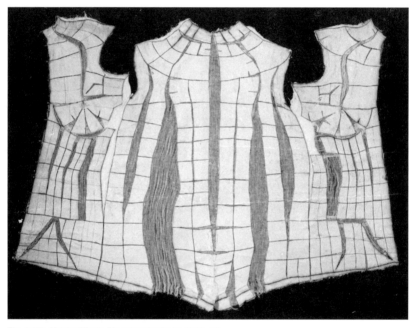

Fig. 5.37: , Monica Wyatt, Planning the Body, 1992–93.

Inhabiting the Wall

Once the plan was produced, it was used to cut out a pattern on a wall covered with wallpaper. The resulting shape was peeled off the wall and made into the form of the body from which it was drawn, its pleats gathered and held with snaps. By putting on the body-dress, Wyatt was able to gather the interior surface of the wall around her, fulfilling her desire to "be in the wall." [Figs. 5.38–5.40]

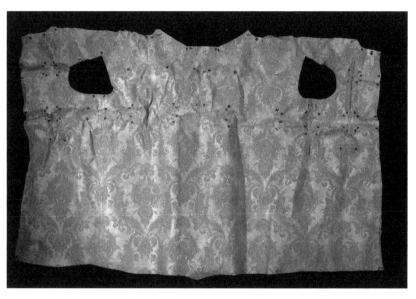

Figs. 5.38–5.40: Monica Wyatt, Inhabiting the Wall, 1992–93.

Engineering the Indoor Environment

Jeffrey Siegel

INTRODUCTION

The interior realm is layered with familiar materials: textiles, wallpaper, and floor covering, along with materials in functional objects like furniture and appliances. Living with these tangible, visible layers is second nature to the occupants, but many of these materials emit unseen pollutants that occupy the same space. Indoor air quality is not easy to grasp for interior designers because it is an engineering issue. Jeffrey Siegel provides a mechanical engineer's perspective of the indoor environment, studying the invisible pollutants that people breathe. He considers domestic interiors to be repositories for indoor air pollutants and opportunities to trace their paths from a material as they potentially form biochemical combinations while they circulate through mechanical systems. Siegel looks to everyday activities (cooking, smoking, burning candles) and ordinary objects and their material compositions to uncover how indoor air pollutants are formed. He translates measured data into a language that should translate with designers.

The scientific measuring scale registers elements not visible to the eye in parts per billion (ppb). Because this measurement registers such a small scale, Siegel offers insight through comparisons that help situate the presence of indoor air pollutants. In one example, the measurement of harmful pollutants is compared with those found in drinking water. The analogy is easy to grasp because of water's visibility and tactile quality.

Interior design as a discipline is learning to answer the demands of sustainability by specifying environmentally friendly materials. Students and professional designers find sustainable materials through course work and manufacturers, but the knowledge of how materials interact in the interior environment is crucial to developing a body of knowledge about building materials and their impact on human health. Siegel's measurement of the effects of materials and their ability to generate pollutants is laying the foundation for sustainable interior design practice at a time when the professional practice is concerned with ever-more-complex definitions of health.

Courtesy of the Department of Civil, Architectural and Environmental Engineering, The University of Texas at Austin, 2010.

OUR INTERIOR environments define us. The average American spends 18 hours indoors for every hour spent outside.[1] This temporal reality, as well as the fact that many common pollutants exist at much higher concentrations indoors[2], largely governs our exposure to airborne pollutants. To put this in the context of our health, the known risks that we face from indoor air pollution vastly exceed those from any other environmental media (outdoor air, soil, water).[3] The hazards associated with indoor air pollution are not limited to industrialized nations: the second-leading global cause of sickness and death are respiratory issues related to the combustion of low-grade fuels for cooking and heating.[4] Despite its importance, there is very little attention paid to indoor air contaminants and the purposes of this essay are to explore the interior from an engineering perspective and provide a context for understanding and improve the indoor environment.

Documentation of Health Risks

Before discussing an explicit mapping of contaminants in indoor environments, it is critical to understand the magnitude of the risks that we face in a typical interior. There are many well-known sources of indoor air pollution, including radon from soil, formaldehyde from pressed wood products, allergies to dust mites and pet dander, and odors from paints and solvents. However, there are many more sources that are poorly understood and considerably less well-known. Many have an understanding that carpet can harbor or emit hazardous compounds, but fewer understand that other flooring materials may also be of concern. As an example, a large study of Swedish children found that those that lived in homes with PVC flooring had an elevated risk of asthma and allergy[5], particularly if there were increased indoor concentrations of certain phthalates, plasticizers that are common in many indoor materials.

A clear example of how we perceive the health risks associated with indoor air involves a comparison to water quality. Consider that global consumption of bottled water exceeds 150 billion liters, presumably because of real or perceived health benefits. However, the average person breathes, by mass, approximately ten times more indoor air than they consume water (in both food and drink). Thus, from a very approximate perspective because of differences between inhalation and ingestion, any contaminant in indoor air will have a ten times larger health effect than the same concentration of that contaminant in water. Said differently, if we care about the quality of our drinking water, then we should certainly care about the quality of indoor air. As a specific example, consider benzene, a volatile organic compound (VOC) that is a known carcinogen. In 1990, Perrier recalled its entire inventory of bottled water in the United States because of the presence of benzene at a concentration of 12.3–19.9 parts per billion (ppb) in a small sample of bottled water.[6] Drinking water standards at the time limited benzene to 5 ppb, which was the level that was determined to cause a very small risk of approximately one in a million excess risk of cancer over a lifetime of consumption. The finding of elevated benzene led to a flurry of testing, media attention, and general concern about benzene. Meanwhile, two decades later, benzene is a common airborne pollutant in indoor environments. It comes from cigarette smoke, burning candles, motor vehicles and gas-powered devices in attached garages, and a variety of other sources. Typical concentrations in American homes lead to lifetime cancer risks in excess of ten in a million[7], much larger than that associated with consumption of a small amount of bottled water. But, because there are no real standards for private indoor environments, this much larger health risk receives almost no attention.

Benzene is just one example, but there are thousands of other compounds in indoor environments with known or suspected health risks. Table 1 describes some of the major categories of indoor pollutants, known health effects, and likely sources. [Fig. 5.41] Table 1 also belies the complexity of the indoor environment. As an example, there are thousands of VOCs in a typical indoor environment. Most are benign or have no known health effects at typical indoor concentrations. Others are carcinogenic or have other serious health consequences, some at concentrations that are so low that it is very difficult to measure. Adding to this complexity is the fact that the easiest measurement to make of VOC concentrations is a broad measurement of the total VOC concentration in air without any assessment of the contribution of different specific compounds. Furthermore, measuring the concentrations of specific VOCs require different and expensive techniques that depend on the chemical properties of the compound in question and so it is generally not practical to document specific VOC concentrations in indoor environments. Other pollutant categories in the table have similar complexity.

Given the wide range of health hazards in typical indoor environments, there is an obvious question about why more attention is not paid to indoor air quality. The primary reason is that it is extremely difficult to pass laws that regulate private indoor environments. The interior environment is considered a sanctuary where regulation is unwelcome. In the United States, the environmental protection agency consistently ranks indoor air pollution as one of our greatest environmental risks[8], much greater than those from outdoor air or water quality, and yet it does not promulgate or support any indoor air regulations. This lack of regulation, as well as a reluctance to demonstrate that our homes are hazardous and not the sanctuaries that we envision, have dramatically limited research funding to explore indoor environmental hazards. Furthermore, it is difficult to envision viable regulation

Compound Category	EXAMPLE		
	Compounds	Sources	Health Effects
Particulate matter	allergens, combustion byproducts, fibers, microbiological aerosols	cooking, vacuuming, indoor ozone chemistry	respiratory disease, cardiovascular disease, asthma, cancer, irritation
Volatile Organic Compounds (VOCs)	benzene, toluene, formaldehyde	consumer products, building materials, combustion, office equipment	irritation, cancer, headaches,
Semi-Volatile Organic Compounds (SVOCs)	plasticizers, pesticides, flame retardants	Building materials, pest control, textiles, electronics	Asthma, allergies, male reproductive issues, obesity
Inorganic compounds	Nitrogen dioxide, carbon monoxide	Cooking, unvented/ malfunctioning water heaters, furnaces, and fireplaces	Irritation (NO2), decreased lung function, flu-like symptoms, death (CO, at very high concentrations)
Oxidants	Ozone	Outdoor air, ion generating air cleaners, photocopiers and laser printers	Respiratory irritant, asthma trigger, diminished lung function

Fig. 5.41: Table 1: Indoor Air Pollutants

for many indoor air quality problems because apartment dwellers in adjoining units influence each others air quality, some indoor pollutants originate from outdoors, and many of our own activities, even those as seemingly benign as cleaning[9] or cooking[10], emit contaminants of concern. Further complicating this issue is the fact that most known indoor air hazards, particularly at the typical indoor concentrations, cause health effects that do not manifest until late in life, long after exposure may have occurred, such as cancer, cardiovascular disease, and respiratory disease.

There are also technical and scientific realities that complicate regulation of the indoor environment. In addition to direct emissions of compounds, there is substantial evidence about chemical reactions that occur indoors. An example of this occurs when ozone, an important outdoor pollutant that is ubiquitous in urban areas, particularly in the summer months, reacts with a group of compounds called terpenes. Terpenes are important constituents of many consumer products (usually added as scenting agents) and are naturally emitted by trees and other plants. Scents associated with different terpenes include lemon and pine odors. By themselves there is no evidence that terpenes are hazardous, even at very high concentrations. When they react with ozone that comes from outdoors or is emitted by certain air cleaners and some office equipment, terpenes can produce ultrafine particles, formaldehyde, carboxylic acids, and a variety of other compounds that are irritating or hazardous.[11] These reactions are common outdoors, but become particularly important indoors where ventilation rates are low, which encourages reactions and prevents byproducts from dispersing. It is challenging to develop regulation to address this situation as there are many products that contribute to indoor terpenes (cleaning agents, air fresheners, wood products, etc.), all of whose manufacturers can (correctly) argue that their products are not hazardous. It is only in the presence of ozone completely unrelated to these products that a potential health hazard occurs. Recent research suggests that we are an important part of this problem as ozone reactions with skin oils[12] and personal care products[13] produce a variety of compounds of concern.

Another example of complexities in improving the indoor environment is the emissions from architectural coatings. One of the first forms of environmentally friendly paints were low-odor paints that utilized VOCs that had little or no smell. However, odor is generally completely disconnected from health hazard and thus these paints were not necessarily any safer than conventional paints. A later innovation was low-VOC paints that emitted a much lower mass of VOCs than ordinary paints. But again, given the diversity of VOCs that are used in paints, the total amount of emission is much less important than the specific chemical make-up of the emissions. There is even some evidence that some low-VOC paints are more hazardous than their conventional counterparts because the VOCs that they emit are more toxic even though their total emissions are much lower.[14] No-VOC paints are currently widely touted as being environmentally superior and often contain linseed oil and similar compounds. Linseed oil is unsaturated which makes it very reactive with ozone, similar to terpenes discussed above, and thus surfaces painted with "eco-paints" can produce a wide variety of hazardous or irritating compounds.[15, 16]

A final comment on indoor air hazards is that the impact on human health is not the only reason to be concerned with the quality of indoor air. Art objects, electronics, and indoor surfaces are all affected by poor indoor air quality. There are numerous examples of historically important indoor environments being damaged by indoor pollutants.[17, 18] More recently, there has been alarming evidence of the indoor environment affecting the outdoor environment. Flame retardants from textiles and electronics, and other persistent organic compounds, have been found in polar bear tissue in the arctic.[19] The bidirectional influence of the indoor and outdoor environment on each other increase the urgency and complexity of the problem.

Mass Balances

Given the importance of the interior environment, we need tools to understand and track indoor air pollutants. Scientists and engineers who study the interior environment have created a physical framework to map the interior. The concept, called a mass balance, is based on reactor models and other tools used widely in chemical and environmental engineering. The idea is to consider an indoor space as a well-mixed contiguous volume. If we consider all of the flows of a pollutant into and out of the space, as well as internal generation from emissions and human activities, we can know the concentration of the pollutant at any given time in the space. For engineering purposes, a mass balance takes the form of a differential equation that is a representation of the following equation:

Change in pollutant in concentration over time
= Rate of generation from sources
− Loss rate

Typical sources of indoor pollution include human activities (cooking, smoking, vacuuming, cleaning), chemical reactions, and transport from outdoors. Typical losses include ventilation, air cleaning (i.e., a filter in a heating/cooling system), chemical reactions, and interactions with interior surfaces. Although seemingly simple, the mass balance allows for the exploration of the impact of different sources and strategies for control, as well as provides an estimate of human exposure that occurs in a building.

From the perspective of the study of the indoor environment, the application of mass balances allows for the quantitative comparison of different strategies for maintaining a healthy indoor environment. Practically, there are three main control strategies for improving the indoor environment. Two focus on getting rid of the pollutant once generated (the loss rate in the equation above), ventilation and air cleaning. Ventilation refers to diluting indoor pollutants with generally cleaner indoor air and air cleaning generally refers to the use of portable or central filters or other technologies to remove pollutants. The final strategy, source control, is the elimination of a source of indoor pollution (the rate of generation in the equation above). Each of these strategies is discussed in more detail below:

1) Ventilation to dilute indoor contaminants is responsible for approximately 25 percent of all energy used in buildings[20] and thus should be used judiciously. For example, when outdoor air quality is poor, for example in some urban and industrial areas, ventilation can serve to make indoor pollution worse. Tying ventilation to indoor sources: for example, flushing out new or renovated buildings before occupancy, avoiding over-ventilation when there is a conditioning energy penalty, basing ventilation on occupancy, and using local ventilation fans near sources (i.e., a kitchen rangehood fan), all increase the efficacy of ventilation.

2) It is tempting to believe that all pollutants can be filtered from indoor environments. Air cleaning, such as filtration for particles, can be enormously useful but like ventilation it has to be carefully matched to sources. Most filters used in central heating and cooling systems in homes are completely ineffective against VOCs and other gaseous pollutants. They are surprisingly ineffective at removing particles as well because of the challenges and expense of designing a system that can remove all particle sizes of concern. For example, a filter that is very effective at removing many allergens may also be completely ineffective at removing the much smaller particles from combustion, such as from a burning candle. Even if a filter is matched to a source, it has to be installed and maintained correctly for acceptable performance.[21] There is widespread use of portable air cleaning devices: although they can be effective, many have insufficient air flowing through them to be effective at reducing pollutant levels.[22] Most importantly, current technologies and systems are in their infancy for controlling many pollutants of concern.

3) Given the limitations of air cleaning and ventilation, most improvement to the indoor environment comes from eliminating sources. Human activities are responsible for a large part of indoor air pollution. Many of our ordinary indoor activities are potentially harmful, including combustion (smoking, cooking, burning candles), cleaning (cleaners, dusting, vacuuming), scenting (personal care products, air fresheners), and even simply walking across a room can kick up previously deposited particles and dust.[23] This provides a vast opportunity for improving the indoor environment with better education. For example, simply encouraging the use of effective kitchen rangehood fans can dramatically reduce human exposure to harmful particles, VOCs, and other compounds.[24] Making sure that sensitive individuals are not present during cleaning events is another reasonably innocuous lifestyle change that improves the indoor environment. Encouraging alternatives for problematic sources is another important component of source control. An example of this is *para*-dichlorobenzene, a compound used in only two widely-used consumer products, moth crystals and toilet bowl deodorizers, and not present in outdoor air. Despite these limited uses, *para*-dichlorobenzene is a significant contributor to cancer risk for the U.S. population, particularly for some population subgroups.[25] A harder source to eliminate is formaldehyde, one of the largest cancer risks in indoor air, from pressed-wood products widely used in furniture and building materials. Eliminating formaldehyde is challenging and raises the price of these materials.

The real value of mass balances from an engineering perspective is to allow these three options to be compared. How many portable filters are needed to achieve the same benefit as a rangehood fan? How much energy will be required to ventilate a given pollutant source? How much flooring material needs to be replaced to avoid phthalate exposure? In my own research, the application of mass balances has also provided useful information on indoor air quality and interiors, including the importance of ozone chemical reactions on different indoor materials[26], the role of different flooring materials in particle resuspension[27], and the possibility of using novel indoor materials to remove ozone and other pollutants.[28]

Summary

It is important to put the hazards of indoor air pollution in context. We live in a sea of risk and generally do a poor job of assessing these risks. Many ordinary activities are considerably more dangerous than we perceive them to be. In terms of risk from environmental pollution, the data clearly support the perspective that if we (rightfully) care about the quality of our outdoor air and drinking water, then we should also care about the quality of our indoor air. The challenges in addressing this risk are the wide range of indoor pollutants and sources (including many that are not yet known), the interplay between the products and actions that we have control over and those that we don't, and the complexity and lack of comprehensive information for many indoor pollutants. These challenges also offer the opportunity for novel approaches and technologies to improve our health and diminish the health risks associated with interior environments.

Notes

1 Klepeis, N. E., W. C. Nelson, W. R. Ott, J. P. Robinson, A. M. Tsang, P. Switzer, J. V. Behar, S. C. Hern, and W. H. Engelmann. "The National Human Activity Pattern Survey (NHAPS): a resource for assessing exposure to environmental pollutants." *Journal of Exposure Analysis and Environmental Epidemiology* 11, no. 3 (June 2001): 231–252.

2 Ott, W. R., and J. W. Roberts. "Everyday exposure to toxic pollutants." *Scientific American* 278, no. 2 (February 1998): 86–91.

3 Corsi, R. L. "Indoor Air Quality: A Time for Recognition," *Environmental Manager*, September, 2000, 10–15.

4 World Health Organization, 1997. Health and Environment in Sustainable Development, WHO/EHSG/97.8. WHO, Geneva.

5 Bornehag, C. G., J. Sundell, C. J. Weschler, T. Sigsgaard, B. Lundgren, M. Hasselgren, and L. Hagerhed-Engman. "The association between asthma and allergic symptoms in children and phthalates in house dust: A nested case-control study." *Environmental Health Perspectives* 112, no. 14 (October 2004): 1393–1397.

6 James, George. "Perrier Recalls Its Water in U.S. After Benzene Is Found in Bottles," *New York Times*, February 10, 1990.

7 Hun, D. E., J. A. Siegel, M. T. Morandi, T. H. Stock, and R. L. Corsi. "Cancer Risk Disparities between Hispanic and Non-Hispanic White Populations: The Role of Exposure to Indoor Air Pollution." *Environmental Health Perspectives* 117, no. 12 (December 2009): 1925–1931.

8 Corsi, R. L. "Indoor Air Quality: A Time for Recognition," *Environmental Manager*, September, 2000, 10–15.

9 Wolkoff, P., T. Schneider, J. Kildeso, R. Degerth, M. Jaroszewski, and H. Schunk. "Risk in cleaning: chemical and physical exposure." *Science of the Total Environment* 215, no. 1–2 (April 23, 1998): 135–156.

10 Wallace, L., F. Wang, C. Howard-Reed, and A. Persily. "Contribution of Gas and Electric Stoves to Residential Ultrafine Particle Concentrations between 2 and 64 nm: Size Distributions and Emission and Coagulation Rates." *Environmental Science & Technology* 42, no. 23 (December 1, 2008): 8641–8647.

11 Weschler, C. J. "Ozone's impact on public health: Contributions from indoor exposures to ozone and products of ozone-initiated chemistry." *Environmental Health Perspectives* 114, no. 10 (October 2006): 1489–1496.

12 Wisthaler, A., and C. J. Weschler. "Reactions of ozone with human skin lipids: Sources of carbonyls, dicarbonyls, and hydroxycarbonyls in indoor air." *Proceedings of the National Academy of Sciences of the United States* 107, no. 15 (April 13, 2010): 6568–6575.

13 Corsi, R. L., J. Siegel, A. Karamalegos, H. Simon, and G. C. Morrison. "Personal reactive clouds: Introducing the concept of near-head chemistry." *Atmospheric Environment* 41, no. 15 (May 2007): 3161–3165.

14 James, J. P., and X. D. Yang. "Emissions of volatile organic compounds from several green and non-green building materials: A comparison." *Indoor and Built Environment* 14, no. 1 (February 2005): 69–74.

15 Toftum, J., S. Feund, T. Salthammer, and C. J. Weschler. "Secondary organic aerosols from ozone-initiated reactions with emissions from wood-based materials and a "green" paint." *Atmospheric Environment* 42, no. 33 (October 2008): 7632–7640.

16 Knudsen, H. N., P. A. Clausen, C. K. Wilkins, and P. Wolkoff. "Sensory and chemical evaluation of odorous emissions from building products with and without linseed oil." *Building and Environment* 42, no. 12 (December 2007): 4059–4067.

17 Nazaroff, W. W., and G. R. Cass. "Protecting Museum Collections From Soiling Due to the Deposition of Airborne Particles." *Atmospheric Environment Part A—General Topics* 25, no. 5–6 (1991): 841–852.

18 Cass, G. R., W. W. Nazaroff, C Tiller, and P. M. Whitmore. "Protection of Works of Art from Damage Due to Atmospheric Ozone." *Atmospheric Environment Part A—General Topics* 25, no. 2 (1991): 441–451.

19 Muir, D. C. G., S. Backus, A. E. Derocher, R. Dietz, T. J. Evans, G. W. Gabrielsen, J. Nagy, et al. "Brominated flame retardants in polar bears (*Ursus maritimus*) from Alaska, the Canadian Arctic, East Greenland, and Svalbard." *Environmental Science & Technology* 40, no. 2 (January 15, 2006): 449–455.

20 Liddament, M. W., and M. Orme. "Energy and Ventilation." *Applied Thermal Engineering* 18, no. 11 (November 1998): 1101–1109.

21 VerShaw, J., J. A. Siegel, D. B. Chojnowski, and P. J. Nigro. "Implications of Filter Bypass." *ASHRAE Transactions* 2009, vol. 115, pt. 1 (2009): 191–198.

22 Offermann, F. J., R. G. Sextro, W. J. Fisk, D. T. Grimsrud, W. W. Nazaroff, A. V. Nero, K. L. Revzan, and J. Yater. "Control of Respirable Particles in Indoor Air with Portable Air Cleaners." *Atmospheric Environment* 19, no. 11 (1985): 1761–1771.

23 Zhang, X. Y., G. Ahmadi, J. Qian, and A. Ferro. "Particle detachment, resuspension and transport due to human walking in indoor environments." *Journal of Adhesion Science and Technology* 22, no. 5–6 (2008): 591–621.

24 Li, C. S., W. H. Lin, and F. T. Jenq. "Removal Efficiency of Particulate Matter by a Range Exhaust Fan." *Environment International* 19, no. 4 (1993): 371–380.

25 Hun, D. E., J. A. Siegel, M. T. Morandi, T. H. Stock, and R. L. Corsi. "Cancer Risk Disparities between Hispanic and Non-Hispanic White Populations: The Role of Exposure to Indoor Air Pollution." *Environmental Health Perspectives* 117, no. 12 (December 2009): 1925–1931.

26 Waring, M. S. "Indoor Secondary Organic Aerosol Formation: Influence of Particle Controls, Mixtures, and Surfaces." PhD Diss., University of Texas at Austin, 2009.

27 Mukai, C., J. A. Siegel, and A. Novoselac. "Impact of Airflow Characteristics on Particle Resuspension from Indoor Surfaces." *Aerosol Science and Technology* 43, no. 10 (2009): 1022–1032.

28 Kunkel, D. A., E. T. Gall, J. A. Siegel, A. Novoselac, G. C. Morrison, and R. L. Corsi. "Passive reduction of human exposure to indoor ozone." *Building and Environment* 45, no. 2 (February 2010): 445–452.

In a Few Lines, Alan Storey

Catherine Bédard

INTRODUCTION

For Catherine Bédard, Alan Storey's drawing machines are examples of alternative forms of drawing and mapping. Moving back and forth between room-sized installations and small crates, each machine registers movement within an interior. The machines develop a relationship with their installation, as if they were inhabitants becoming familiar with the interior through scribing and drawing. In this essay Bédard focuses on two pieces, his Draw (Machine for Drawing on Walls) *and* Shipping Crates Drawing Machines. *Both produce drawings at full-scale with minimal requirements except that the limits of the interior must make the boundaries.*

Draw (Machine for Drawing on Walls) *is an analog mechanism with a rotating arm affixed with a thin ink-fed wheel that rolls along surrounding walls to produce a drawing. Because of the rotating arm's limitations, corners become voids marked by their absence. In contrast to the wall drawings, which originate from a static point, the* Shipping Crates Drawing Machines *rely on random movement that occurs while the boxes are in transport to kinetically produce the drawings. The crates are sent on a transatlantic journey. Labels are applied that instruct freight handlers to rotate them, which are followed unpredictably. When the crate reaches its destination, it is splayed open to display the resulting travel lines—the machine's markings reveal an interior that has no preference for orientation.*

The mechanical constructions of these two machines are mechanically similar yet different structurally—one draws at the scale of the body, the other at the scale of a hand. In both cases, the machines are tailored to their respective interior space. They demonstrate how to draw using atypical conventions that emphasize time and movement. As landscape measurement has its own set of tools for surveying, Storey's machines propose a new set of tools to survey the interior. These machines will never produce the same line, unlike conventional orthographic projections. Instead they produce a new form of precision interior drawings that seeks to make latent lines visible.

Excerpted from Drawing Machines, Alan Storey (Paris: Services culturels de l'Ambassade du Canada, 1999), 8–24, 29–30, 55, 63.

OF ALL THE INVENTIONS of Alan Storey, his drawing machines are the ones which constitute the central cortex of a multiform production where each project has the look of a laboratory experiment. And the laboratory, for this artist, is the place where the work becomes visible: the exhibition hall, the public space, in opposition to the studio which is reserved for conceiving and fine tuning instruments. It is outside of the studio, during the time of the exhibition, that the work creates itself, and this stepping out in to the world brings a measure of the unexpected and the accidental to the work, inscribed as a network of fine traces within a frame work rigorously defined by the artist.

The main theme in the art of Alan Storey is decidedly the line. But a line attached to a device that makes it expand indefinitely over a surface untouched, then progressively blacker. This progressively opaque darkening makes it imperative to end the strange artistic process by which the apparition of the drawing, under the accumulation of lines, signifies its slow and irreversible disappearance. Apparently driven to turn in circle in the sense that it makes an interminable circle around a closed space by marking a rotating cylinder or criss-crossing its own convolutions the line does not needlessly furrow the surface upon which it unfurls in curves and charts.

Our objective with this exhibition at the Canadian Cultural Centre was to show several "samples" of the experiments undertaken by Alan Storey over a fifteen-year period. More than allowing a European audience to understand the mechanisms of this young and yet already monumental work, our desire was to show to what degree the machines, when compared to each other, are entirely determined by the place they are made to function and exist in. Whether they are imposing constructions (such as the pivoting arm in *Machine for Drawing on Walls*), a chain of complex devices (as in *Thirteen*), or extremely sensitive crates or cages, which reduce the movements and transports of the exterior world to the scale of a microscopic trace (which the two works realized for the CCC, *Bird in a Cage, Writing Its Own History* and *Shipping Crates Drawing Machines*, are, each in their own way), all of these instruments do the same and simplest thing possible: they draw lines on a white surface.

By articulating the circular (the pulley, the wheel, the paper drum, etc....) and the linear (the thread connecting the surrounding movements to those of the pen, the pen's indefinite flow of ink, producing an uninterrupted line, etc....), Alan Storey manages to make each drawing a picture of the world perceived through the movements which animate it: from the smallest movement—when it deals with showing the physical limits of the exhibition hall—to the largest—when it deals with representing a map of the world and the web woven by the Internet, for example. Drawings in their own right (neither expressionist nor abstract, anything but figurative, the line ignoring everything but the eventual contour of the space), in other words made to be contemplated, once finished, as real works of art, they are distinguishable by the fact that they are neither completed nor finished, rather, let us say, simply "stopped."

More than a substitute for the artist's hand, the machine is a medium (motorized or not, and from a technological viewpoint, knowledgeably tinkered more than refined) that evokes the obvious and the banal in an unexpected manner: the graphic network is revelatory of a reality which escapes our sight (that is, one lying so close under our noses that we can't even see it), but which is perceptible on a daily basis through its effects. An example would be the configurations impressed on the minds of a farming community where the dominant image could well be the network of lines drawn by tractor harrows (*Machine for Drawing on Prairies*), or for other communities the networks of urban highways or global communications (*Machine for Drawing All Over the World*). The surface on which the machine draws is not just any old support; its form, like its dimension, adheres to the surrounding space, when it isn't the miniaturized echo of the architecture which contains it (*Bird in a Cage, Writing Its Own History*).

Among this collection of seven projects which are all built on the principle of the drawing machine (divided into models, photographs, objects and original works), one can distinguish three groups:

1) Direct recording instruments (as in *Machine for Drawing* on *Walls, Climatic Drawing Machine, Thirteen, Bird in a Cage…*), for wind, precipitation, itineraries, comings and goings, etc., which have in common the principal of acting on a vertical surface. These drawings are the transposition of environmental phenomena which art is typically called upon to make us forget by transporting us into a separate, sheltered world. Note that the phenomenon of rotation which lies at the center of this drawing mechanism does not entail circular lines.

2) Representation instruments with their measure of arbitrary movements (*Machine for Drawing on Prairies, Machine for Drawing all over the World*) which have the principle characteristic of acting on horizontal surfaces. One observes that the phenomenon of traction which makes the pen move bring about the circular lines.

3) A direct recording instrument which combines rotation (a vehicle on a round base, to which a pen is attached, turns around on the surface) and the absence of traction (this non-motorized vehicle is turned upside down by the exterior movements imposed on it, i.e., by the displacement of the crate containing it), and which has the principle characteristic of acting on the temporarily horizontal side of a cube that is moved around and rotated. The six sides become marked according to how the cube is moved. When such transportation has ended, this cubic crate, which contains nothing but the drawing machine, allows us to identify by deduction which surfaces were the most often horizontal and which were held vertically. What results is the graphic history of the voyage of a work created "underway."

"Draw" is one of those words with multiple meanings. Among the most important is "to pull" (and all the connotations this word implies) and "to sketch," which leads us to think that drawings are intrinsically linked to the act of "drawing a line." But there is also the idea of "a draw," which could spell the real motive behind all these games where neither the artist nor the machine is the winner. The surprise these drawings evoke is what matters most; it permits us to go beyond the calculation according to which mechanical gestures should rival those of artists, or the idea that the machine has freed art from the cultural weight associated with the pictorial mark of the male artist.

With extreme delicacy, which also marks a break with the rough handling to which one imagines the crates were subject during their transport, the drawings produced by the *Shipping Crates Drawing Machines* allow a startling geometry to appear: a square where each of the four corners is prolonged into a perfect circle. This geometry is the result of rotation movements or linear displacements of the small non-motorized vehicle placed in the empty crate before its pan-Canadian and trans-Atlantic voyages. But this skittish geometry has registered the multiple shocks of a contraption brilliantly conceived to respect the limits of a predefined playground: out of the rather chaotic network of lines arises the main lines corresponding to the zones marked by the repeated displacements of the instrument which carried the pen along the sides of the square and from one corner of the surface. Still, one admires the immaculate sides which seem to have miraculously escaped the scratches of the registering pen, as if one could find there the trace of a certain attention paid to the displacement of a work meant to voyage under conditions of relative immobility.

Text by Alan Storey

Draw (Machine for Drawing on Walls)

This machine, a lumbering, heavy, massive timber construction, had the appearance of danger and menace compressed into the small gallery space. Yet when "alive" as a drawing device, it had a very delicate and sensitive touch. It gingerly traced its way across the walls and glass windows of the gallery leaving a fine imprint of its life/existence/history. [Fig. 5.42]

Figs. 5.42 + 5.43: Alan Storey, *Draw (Machine for Drawing on Walls)*, 1984. Mechanical parts, wood, lead, ink, four gallery walls, 3.6 m x 6.6 m x 2.4 m. Installation views at the Or Gallery, Vancouver, 1984.

This machine was built to the exact dimensions of the space that it was contained in. The central post was on a bearing. A motor, powered by battery, turned the spoked wheel. A combination of weights and springs maintained a constant pressure of the wheel against all sections of the wall, thus driving itself around the room. A small brush kept the wheel wet with black ink. It took about 20 to 30 minutes to complete a revolution. Through the duration of the exhibition the machine recorded a history of its travels. [Fig. 5.43]

Shipping Crate Drawing Machines

The drawings shown here were created during the transport of the crates from Vancouver to Paris. The two crates in the back of the gallery were transported by truck between Vancouver and Montreal, then shipped by plane to Paris. The two crates near the entrance of the gallery (including the one containing the drawing) were shipped by plane from Vancouver to London, then transported by truck from London to Paris. The various, and often contradictory, instructions to the transporters ("other side up" or "this side up") indicate how each box should be handled. [Figs. 5.44–5.47]

Figs. 5.44–5.47: Alan Storey, *Shipping Crates Drawing Machines*, 1999. Exterior of crate (top left); Drawings out of their crates, complete view (top right); Dimensions of each crate: 80 cm x 80 cm x 80 cm. (middle). Dimensions of the drawings: 2.25 m x 3 m. Wood, metal paper, pen, 1999; Installation views at the Canadian Cultural Centre, Paris, 1999 (bottom).

Self as Eye: The Perspective Box

Celeste Brusati

INTRODUCTION

The Italian Renaissance saw the development of mathematical construction in perspective drawing. A century after its first application, Dutch painter Samuel Dirksz van Hoogstraten had taken it one step further, exploring the variables of constructed perspectives. By the sixteenth century, the underlying framework of perspective drawing was altered to produce drawings with embedded imagery that reconfigured the relationship of parts in the perspective drawing while staying true to geometry. The most notable of these is Hans Holbein's The Ambassadors *(1533), with an anamorphic image integrated into the bottom of the painting. These embedded images were revealed only to those viewers who had learned how to look for them, reflecting an elite status. Van Hoogstraten reinterpreted the constructed perspective to create illusions in what would be called "perspective boxes." Celeste Brusati analyzes these boxes in her essay, with particular attention to those by van Hoogstraten, who received criticism at the time for his paintings' perceived deception and counterfeit experience.*

The perspective box was large enough to contain a painting yet small enough to walk around, like a piece of furniture. The eyehole was located at the height of a typical keyhole, mimicking the effect of a peeping tom spying into a room. The decision to locate the opening at that height transitioned the viewer from the threshold of the full-scale world to the interior miniature world. Van Hoogstraten often featured a traditional Dutch domestic scene that might include details of his own belongings, signifying his personal identity and investment in the paintings. Various views displayed rooms typical of the time and reflected the materials, proportions, and layout of Dutch homes. In her essay, Brusati highlights an additional layer of livable qualities seen in objects, light, shadow, reflection, depth, and paintings within the painting. These qualities, coupled with a view of occupants, allowed events and narratives to unfold within the painting. Van Hoogstraten joined these elements, creating an illusion of people and objects that appeared life-sized, demonstrating an

---

: From Artifice and Illusion: The Art and Writing of Samuel van Hoogstraten, 169–82. The University of Chicago Press. © 1995 by The University of Chicago.

ability to alter the geometry of perspective and replicate imagery at a minia-
ture scale. Perspective box techniques represented the interior in ways that led
to an "experience of wonder" and provoked curiosity about the interior.

————

TODAY THERE ARE only six surviving examples of the uniquely Dutch art
form known as the perspective box or *perspectyfkas*.[1] Various contrivances
commonly referred to as perspective boxes had been made in fifteenth-
century Italy in connection with the development of linear perspective
methods. But these devices, along with the so-called "peep shows" made
in Germany during the sixteenth century and the stagelike boxes used by
Poussin and other seventeenth-century artists, differed both in purpose and
construction from the Dutch perspective box.[2] Whereas the others were
furnished with wax models of figures or other objects or were intended as
apparatus for viewing stage set-like images placed inside them, the Dutch
perspective box contained nothing at all—except for a single, multifaceted
image projected and painted over the discontinuous surfaces of the box's
interior.

One of the few extant Dutch perspective boxes, now in the National
Museum in Copenhagen, depicts a view down the nave of a Dutch Reformed
Church.[3] The church's interior is represented on two surfaces which join to
form one corner of a triangular box. Opposite this corner, the third face of
the box is equipped with a viewing hole, with a windowlike opening above
it through which light is admitted. When viewed from the eyehole, the distorted and disintegrated image of the nave is made to appear continuous, and
the figures, columns, and furnishings represented in miniature on the interior faces of the box appear not only to be life-size but to stand free within
the fictive space of the church. [Figs. 5.48–5.50]

Van Hoogstraten expressed particular delight in the marvelous illusions of scale created by these devices when he noted with nearly audible
pleasure in his painting treatise that the perspective box, when properly executed, could make "a finger-length figure appear to be life-sized."[4] Indeed,
the striking illusion produced by the perspective box was more than a
source of delight for Van Hoogstraten; it exemplified the qualities which
he ascribed to the perfect painting. Such a picture, to recall his paraphrase
of Philostratus, "makes things that do not exist appear to exist and thus
deceives in a permissible, pleasurable, and praiseworthy manner."[5]

The perspective boxes which Van Hoogstraten commended and constructed not only offered compelling counterfeits of what he called the visible world; they also provided a graphic demonstration of the deceptive
artifice which he understood to be common to the painter's art and the

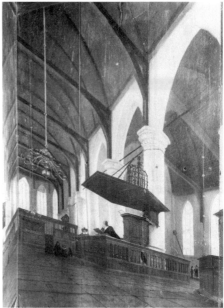

Figs. 5.48–5.50: Hendrick van Vliet, *Perspective Box of a Protestant Church Interior.*
Interior, oil on panel. Copenhagen, National Museum, museum photo

operations of the eye itself. For all of these devices were contrived not only to create delightful deceptions but also to reveal the principles by which they produced the experience of wonder which was, as we have seen, a central aim of the experimental arts.[6] Later generations came to regard these pictorial experiments simply as children's amusements and "mere curiosities" designed to please a naive public, and this is doubtless one reason why so few have survived. Although perspective boxes were indeed regarded as curiosities in Van Hoogstraten's time, they were not then thought of as toys but rather as works of experimental art. The fascination of Van Hoogstraten's contemporaries with such devices testifies to a larger interest in experimental demonstration as a mode of investigating nature and representing what was often referred to as "natural knowledge." The crafting of appropriate apparatus was fundamental to this empirical mode of scientific inquiry. By way of such devices, the experimenter sought to counterfeit nature's own workings and thereby to offer concrete explanations of the natural phenomena which he replicated. By calling attention to their own artifice, curiosities like the perspective box sought to stimulate the intellectual curiosity of the beholder and to incite discovery of the secrets of nature revealed in their making. The ingenuity of these contrivances was further intended to induce in the beholder feelings of wonder not only for nature but also for the artifices and the ingenious men who devised them. It is with an appreciation of such experimental artistry that Van Hoogstraten encourages his readers in the *Inleyding* to try their hands at devising automata and similar artifices. "For such artful deceptions," he writes, "are marveled at by the whole world and insure that the maker is held in high esteem."[7] In the following discussion we shall be considering the London perspective box in both of these contexts, as a consummate display of ingenuity and as a complex pictorial demonstration of how the eye is deceived by nature and by the painter's art.

Exhibiting his usual drive not to be outdone in the "race for artistic laurels," Van Hoogstraten executed what is by far the most complex and accomplished of the six extant works in this genre, the *Perspective Box with Views of a Dutch Interior*, now in London.[8] It consists of a rectangular wooden cabinet, about two feet high, three feet wide, and two feet deep. [Fig. 5.51] Light is admitted through the open front face, which was originally covered with some kind of translucent paper and is now fitted with a clear plastic panel. The box is further equipped with two small openings placed opposite each other on the cabinet's short sides. Thanks to the modern pedestal on which the cabinet rests these viewing holes are situated suggestively at keyhole level. Through either of these apertures the beholder peers into a domestic interior intricately described on the five interior faces of the box. Open doors and windows offer multiple views into the house's nine separate rooms and spaces, plus framed glimpses of an outside world beyond. [Figs. 5.52–5.56]

All images pp. 368–69:
Samuel van Hoogstraeten,
(1627–1678), *A Peepshow
with Views of the Interior
of a Dutch House*, about
1655–60. Oil and egg on
wood, 58 x 88 x 60.5 cm.
Presented by Sir Robert
and Lady Witt through
The Art Fund, 1924.
Location: National Gallery,
London, Great Britain.
© National Gallery, London /
Art Resource, NY

Fig. 5.51: Box on pedestal
seen from front.

Fig. 5.52: Left interior face.

Fig. 5.53: Right interior face.

Fig. 5.54: Rear interior face.

Fig. 5.55: Bottom interior face.

Fig. 5.56: Detail of a woman in bed rendered in strong foreshortening.

Fig. 5.57: Circle of Pieter Janssens Elinga, *Perspective Box with View of a Dutch Interior.* Interior, oil on panel. Museum Bredius in The Hague, Holland

The intricacy of the London perspective box is striking in comparison with other extant boxes. The simplest and apparently the most common type of Dutch perspective box was triangular in shape. John Evelyn recorded seeing one of these boxes in London in 1656:

> Was shew'd me a prety Perspective & well represented in an triangular Box, the greate Church at Harlem in Holland, to be seene thro a small hole at one of the corners, & contrived into an hansone Cabinet. It was so rarely done that all the Artists & Painters in Towne, came flocking to see & admire it.[9]

Three of the six surviving boxes, namely the two church interiors in Copenhagen and the domestic interior in the Bredius Museum, are of this simple triangular type.[10] [Fig. 5.57] Van Hoogstraten's works in this genre are notably more ambitious both in design and subject matter. Both his London box and the unusual pentagonal box in Detroit depict composite views far more complex than those shown in either the Copenhagen or the Bredius boxes. There are, moreover, no extant parallels either for the double peepholes in the London box or for the pentagonal format of the Detroit box.

In addition to being the most ambitious of the surviving perspective boxes the London box is also the only one which so clearly functions as a self-representation of its maker. Among the various inscriptions that mark the box's diminutive world as both made and possessed by Van Hoogstraten are a self-addressed letter lying on the floor under the chair at the left front end of the box, a portrait bearing the Van Hoogstraten family crest (visible to the left of the bedroom door), and a stained glass window showing his wife's family arms (just above the table in the room beyond the bedroom). Like the *Feigned Bookshelf,* and the *Feigned Painting of a Letter Rack,* the London perspective box presents Van Hoogstraten's skill at fooling the eye as a possession which offers access to honor, wealth, status, and ultimately dominion over the entire visible world. But the perspective box goes beyond the illusionistic virtuosity of his trompe l'oeil self-images. Besides its compelling illusions of scale and three-dimensionality, the device graphically demonstrates Van Hoogstraten's understanding of how the eye is deceived both by the painter's art and by the act of seeing itself. As such it offers an invaluable presentation of the assumptions about the nature of vision and picture making that inform Van Hoogstraten's art and writing. Before considering how those assumptions are built into this apparatus let us look at how he describes the art of painting within the miniature world of the perspective box.

Looking into the London box, we find a veritable encyclopedia of images and "imagings" within a domestic interior which the artist presents as his own home. It is furnished with painted landscapes (above the bedroom doors) and history paintings, along with a printed map (at the far right under the broom), a portrait print, and little paintings on glass that adorn the windows. These products of human artistry are displayed along with various pictures made by nature through the action of light: a shadow cast by the broom, the reflected image of the window and its frame imprinted on the wall (behind the chair to the left of the dog), the fragmented image of the tiled floor and threshold caught on the shining surface of the mirror hanging to the right of the bedroom. And finally, there are the pictures produced by the viewer's eye in the act of looking through the framing gridwork of doorways and windows, forming a seemingly infinite number of views which are perforated in turn by yet other views.

In its aggregate of pictures and picturing the perspective box sets up a parallel between vision and painting as image-making processes. Van Hoogstraten's representational strategy here is similar in many ways to the pictorial descriptions of the art of painting which we find in the

Fig. 5.58: Willam van Haecht (1593–1637), *The Studio of Apelles*. Oil on canvas. The Hague, Mauritshuis, The Netherlands. Scala: Art Resource, NY

kunstkamer paintings, sometimes known as "Pictura allegories," which began to appear in the southern Netherlands in the early decades of the seventeenth century.[11] In their painstaking counterfeits of the objects and images commonly found in encyclopedic collections, these works assert the all-encompassing power of pictorial representation. In many of these paintings, for which Willem van Haecht's *Studio of Apelles* may serve as an example, Pictura herself is shown within the collection which constitutes her realm. [Fig. 5.58] Painting, presented as a universal science of representation, is celebrated as the key to the encyclopedia. Particular subjects, such as the "Contest of Apollo and Pan," "The Victory of Minerva over Ignorance," and "Christ Healing the Blind," appeared frequently among the images depicted in the *kunstkamer* and served to underscore the thematic importance given to pictures as a means of comprehending and communicating our knowledge of the world. With their richly elaborated representations of the pictorial arts the *kunstkamer* paintings offer a pictorial version of the defenses of painting's epistemological importance found in the writings of Carel van Mander and his Netherlandish followers.[12]

Van Hoogstraten alludes to this pictorial tradition in the perspective box by including within it a painting of "Minerva Conquering Ignorance" (to the left of the doorway behind the dog) and a picture showing "The Contest of Apollo and Pan" (in the room in front of the woman reading). [Figs. 5.52 + 53] He thus associates his own fictive house with Pictura's realm. Indeed, one might say that Van Hoogstraten domesticates the painted *kunstkamer* tradition, turning the pictorial description of the visible world his art encompasses into a miniature representation of his home and his possessions.

Van Hoogstraten's identification of the realm of painting with his own house also provides a curious version of another tradition of artists' self-representations, namely the painted decoration of their homes. Among the best-known examples of this practice are the houses of Vasari and Rubens, which were ornamented with elaborate allegories of painting.[13] Both of these artists chose to celebrate their art and allude to the dignity of their profession by commemorating the achievements of their ancient predecessors. In their studies of the decoration of Rubens's house in Antwerp, both Elizabeth McGrath and Jeffrey Muller have shown that Rubens gave a special place in his decorative program to his own pictorial recreations of the achievements of the ancients, which he based on classical texts and ekphrases of their lost paintings.[14]

One of the scenes which Rubens included in his program, "The Contest of Apollo and Pan," was, McGrath noted, unusual in that it was not known to be the subject of any ancient painting. The picture is of particular interest for us since it figures in both Rubens's house and Van Hoogstraten's perspective box. Though the subject had scarcely any mythographical tradition in antiquity, it was popular in later Flemish art and appeared frequently in the painted *kunstkamers*. The story involves Midas's unenlightened preference for Pan over Apollo and his consequent receipt of ass's ears, an emblem of ignorance and ill-informed aesthetic judgement. Rubens and Van Hoogstraten show Midas, his ignorance thus marked, behind the subjugated Pan, while Apollo, or true art, reigns triumphant. Rubens and Van Hoogstraten repeat a theme frequently found in the *kunstkamer* paintings in associating the protection of Painting by her patrons with the symbolic demise of Midas. Rubens makes the connection by placing his "Apollo and Pan" opposite a depiction of "The Calumny of Apelles," a scene in which Ignorance is mitigated by the restraining hand of Minerva. Van Hoogstraten makes a similar pairing by showing the painting of "Minerva Conquering Ignorance" opposite a painting of "The Contest of Apollo and Pan" in the perspective box.

While the artists allegorically celebrate the victory of art over ignorance in similar ways, the art that triumphs is nonetheless different for each. For Rubens, this art was epitomized in the humanist ideal of painting that culminated in the *istoria*. And it was in this, the most exalted of genres, that

Rubens displayed his superb command of his art, decorating his house with spirited inventions and recreations of famous history paintings. Even in his tour de force of imitative skill—a fresco of "Perseus and Andromeda" illusionistically painted as a feigned canvas hanging in the courtyard of his house—Rubens reinforced his commitment to the humanist hierarchy of subject matter and media.[15] Rubens's feigned canvas, in addition to being a counterfeit history painting, was also executed in fresco, the technique privileged by the Italians as the measure of artistic skill because of its extreme difficulty. For Van Hoogstraten, on the other hand, it was not history painting per se but pictorial representation in the largest sense which triumphed over ignorance. In the perspective box he demonstrates the power of painting in the terms set forth within the painted *kunstkamers,* linking the knowledge and possession offered by painting both to its universal compass and its capacity to reproduce what the eye sees.

Van Hoogstraten's perspective box, however, goes even further than the painted *kunstkamers* in its emphasis on the power of pictures to duplicate the artifice of vision itself and thereby to fool the eye. Insofar as it constitutes the ultimate pictorial deception, the perspective box is for Van Hoogstraten also the ultimate aesthetic conquest. Let us look for a moment at the ways he thematizes this aesthetic conquest within the imagery and the apparatus of the box itself.

As an apparatus, the perspective box constructs a specific physical relationship between the viewer and the world depicted inside of it. The artifice of the peephole isolates the viewer's eye in much the same way as lenses and other optical devices do, and thus sets up the expectation of privileged ocular access to a normally invisible world. At the same time, however, as a condition of having its reach enhanced, the viewer's eye is quite literally held captive at the juncture of its own world and that of the artist's crafting.

Van Hoogstraten thematizes this aesthetic conquest in the explicitly gendered imagery he uses inside the box. There he figures his art's power to seduce and gratify the desirous eye, offering a quiet domestic space and its female inhabitants to the curious gaze of a male voyeur. Van Hoogstraten calls special attention to the beholder's simultaneous corporeal exclusion from and optical absorption into the painted world in a number of ways. The viewer looking into the box from the left sees a version of his or her own covert viewing represented by a man with his eye pressed to the window secretly watching a woman absorbed in her reading. This Peeping Tom figure duplicates the activity of the beholder, who in turn spies not only on him, but also on the woman reading and on a second unsuspecting woman asleep in the adjacent bedroom. With his characteristic delight in accessories that covertly explain something, Van Hoogstraten alludes pictorially to the specular relationship of the painted peeper and the viewer by placing a mirror on the wall between the two *doorkijkjes,* or little "views into" the house, which each peeper enjoys. On the empty chair below the mirror lies a string of pearls and a comb, emblems of Venus and, one might say, of the feminine charms which ensnare the eye of the beholder. Through the inclusion of his own and his wife's coats of arms (on the portrait to the left of the bedroom and in the window of the room visible through a doorway beyond the bedroom), Van Hoogstraten inscribes both the seductive charms of the sleeping woman and, by implication, the captivating power of painting as his own possessions.

If the viewer is captivated by the sights visible through the peephole at the left, the view through the right aperture seduces again, but this time by a different strategy, which places the beholder imaginatively at the center of the box as the invisible object of the dog's gaze. From this vantage point, instead of looking in unseen at female figures framed by sealed-off passages and closed windows, the viewer looks out into the world beyond the house. The beholder is thus flattered, put into the position of the artist or the man of the house. His aristocratic trappings—coats, hat, sword, and sash—hang before him on the wall. But how does this imaginary owner see himself reflected in these possessions: as the seducer, returning to the world after his optical and/or sexual conquest of the women on the other side? Or as disarmed and disrobed by being represented as part of the world he views and paints? These narratives of beholding, fraught with anxious pleasure, convey something of the delightful yet strangely disturbing viewing experience that Van Hoogstraten contrives in the perspective box. On the one hand, the box's detailed mise-en-scène and relentless clarity of execution stimulate the viewer's visual curiosity and taste for aggressive peering and probing. On the other hand, its imagery and construction confront the beholder repeatedly with reminders of the furtive and vaguely illicit character of its seductive visual pleasures. The fantasy of ocular ubiquity offered by the perspective box not only gratifies but also disarms and disembodies the viewer, for the box's seductions and possessions are not available to an embodied beholder but only to the eye placed at the peephole. This curious identification of the eye and the viewing subject, so graphically demonstrated through the artifice of the perspective box, is worth considering in some detail. Far from being peculiar to this device, it is a characteristic feature both of Van Hoogstraten's art and the pictorial tradition to which it belongs.

Notes

1   For a catalog of these see Susan Koslow, "De Wonderlijke Perspectyfkas: An Aspect of Seventeenth Century Dutch Painting," *Oud Holland* 82, nos. 1–2 (1967): 35–56, esp. 48–56.

2   See, for example, Wolfgang Born, "Early Peep-Shows and the Renaissance Stage," *Connoisseur* 107 (1941): 67–71, 161–64; Anthony Blunt, *Nicolas Poussin,* 2 vols. (New York and London, 1967), 1:242 ff; Oskar Bkschmann, *Dialektik der Malerei von Nicolas Poussin* (Munich, 1982), 36–38; and Martin Kemp, "Science and Non-Science: The Interpretation of Brunelleschi's Perspective," *Art History,* 1, no. 2 (June 1978): 134–62.

3   On this box see Koslow, "De Wonderlijke Perspectyfkas," 48, cat. no. 1; and Walter Liedtke, "The *View in Delft* by Carel Fabritius," *Burlington Magazine* 118, no. 875 (February 1976): 63.

4   "Through the knowledge of this science one can also make the wonderful perspective cabinet which, when painted correctly and with skill, makes a finger-length figure appear to be life-sized." ("Door de kennisse van deeze weetenschap maektmen ook de wonderlijke perspectyfkas, die, alsze regt en met kennisse geschildert is, een figuur van een vinger lang als leevensgroot vertoont.") *Inleyding,* 274–75.

5   "Want een volmaekte Schilderey is als een spiegel van de natuer, die de dingen, die niet en zijn, doet schijnen te zijn, en op een geoorlofde vermakelijke en prijslijke wijze bedriegt." *Inleyding,* 25.

6   See above, chap. 3, "Pictorial Illusion and Experimental Artifice at Court" and "Gentleman, Artificer, and Student of Nature: England, 1662–1667" [in Brusati, *Artifice and Illusion,* 1995].

7   "Want dusdanige konstige bedriegeryen stellen al de werelt in verwondering, en maken dat men een groot gevoelen van den vinder heeft." *Inleyding,* 21 1. On the culture of curiosity and the value placed upon this type of wondrous effect, see Krzysztof Pomian, *Collectors and Curiosities: Paris and Venice,* 1500–1800, trans. Elizabeth Wiles-Porter (Cambridge: Polity Press, 1990), and the essays in Joy Kenseth et al., *The Age of the Marvellous* (Dartmouth College, Hood Museum of Art, 1992). On the cultural and art theoretical significance of optical deceptions in particular, see the interesting article by Muylle, "'Fascinatio.' De betovering van en door het oog."

8   See Brown and MacLaren, National Gallery Catalogues, *The Dutch School,* 203–6; Clothilde Briére-Misme, "Deux 'bôites-à-perspective' hollandaise du XVIIe siècle," *Gazette des Beaux-arts,* ser. 5, 11 (1925): 156–66; Uwe Schneede, "De Wonderlyke Perspectiefkas: Hoogstraten's perfekte Täuschungen," *Artis* 18 (1966–67): 25–26; S. Koslow, "De Wonderlijke Perspectyfkas," 38–53; Brown et al., "Samuel van Hoogstraten: Perspective and Painting," 60–84; and Martin Kemp, *The Science of Art: Optical Themes in Western Art from Brunelleschi to Seurat* (New Haven, 1990), 204–6.

9   *The Diary of John Evelyn,* ed. E. S. de Beer (Oxford, 1965), 3:165. Evelyn's entry is the first mention of one of these devices.

10   See Koslow, "De Wonderlijke Perfectyfkas," cat. nos. 1, 2, 6.

11   See Matthias Winner, *Die Quellen der "Pictura-Allegorien" in gemalten Bildergalerien des 17. Jahrhunderts,* Dissertation (Cologne, 1967); S. Speth-Holterhoff, *Les peintres flamands de cabinets d'amateurs au XVIIe siècle* (Brussels, 1957); and Zirka Filipczak, *Picturing Art in Antwerp,* 1550–1 700 (Princeton, 1987).

12 See above, chapter 1, n. 15, and below, chapter 6 [in Brusati, *Artifice and Illusion*, 1995].

13 Other well-known artists who decorated their homes with allegories of art include Andrea Mantegna, Federigo Zuccaro, and Giulio Romano in Italy and Cornelis Ketel and Frans Floris in the north. On this phenomenon, see *Künstlerhauser von der Renaissance bis zur Gegenwart,* ed. Eduard Huttinger (Zurich, 1985). On the decoration of the Vasari's houses in Florence and Arezzo, see Winner, *Pictura-Allegorien,* 20ff.; Alessandro Cecchi, "La Casa del Vasari in Arezzo," in the exhibition catalog *Giorgio Vasari: Principi, Litterati e artisti nelle carte di Giorgio Vasari,* ed. Laura Corti et al. (Florence: Edam, 1981); Fredrika Jacobs, "Vasari's Vision of the History of Painting: Frescoes in the Casa Vasari, Florence," *Art Bulletin* 64 (1984): 399–417. On Floris, see Carl van de Velde, "The Painted Decoration of Floris' House," in *Netherlandish Mannerism: Papers given at a symposium in the National Museum of Stockholm,* 127–34 (Stockholm, 1985), and Catherine King, "Artes Liberales and the Mural Decoration on the House of Frans Floris, Antwerp, c. 1565," *Zeitschrift für Kunstgeschichte* 52, no. 2 (1989):239–56.

14 Elizabeth McGrath, "The Painted Decoration of Rubens's House," *Journal of the Warburg and Courtauld Institutes* 41 (1978): 245–77; and Jeffrey Muller, "The *Perseus and Andromeda* on Rubens's House."

15 For the pictorial *topos* to which Rubens's painted deception refers, see Muller, "The *Perseus and Andromeda* on Rubens's House," 139.

Private Chambers

Introduction:
Private Chambers

The domestic realm is the container of private rooms. Upon closer examination, personality nuances can be revealed that suggest a character-based narrative. Intimate spaces draw attention to gender but also reference modeled interiors, such as a dollhouse—the interior as theater. Together, these spaces create a view of private chambers where the role of intimacy in interior design can be discussed candidly, for once.

Children, for example, make their first attempts at configuring privacy in play. Dollhouses symbolically and figuratively present children with rooms where they can imagine varying degrees of interaction from social to private. Dollhouses share characteristics, like scale and materials, with architectural models, but also include details like kitchenware, bedroom linens, upholstered furniture, and wallpaper. The dollhouse is a highly focused interior, unlike the abstract interior of architectural models used to convey spatial configuration.

A dollhouse is not limited to furniture arrangement, because it invites play. Play reveals how daily events in the home are observed and reenacted in the miniature. It is no wonder that dollhouses are associated with interior design and decoration rather than architecture, with their inward-looking view and theatrical setting. A dollhouse is conducive to make-believe; its small inhabitants are truly anthropomorphic compared to the anonymous scale figures in architectural models. An outfitted dollhouse reinforces the interior as the site where intimacy is not inhibited. Like a stage set, it is where narrative, furniture, and objects are combined to create a setting in which real or imagined characters act on the space and the space acts on them.

Small-scale models and mention of the dollhouse appear in Witold Rybczynski's essay "Domesticity" where he looks at the origins of domesticity and its association with the seventeenth-century Dutch home. Pride of home and its care was commemorated by commissioned custom-made architectural models detailed as dollhouses. Another essay on the scale of the miniature, by Mark Wigley, reveals how the contemporary photographer James Casebere constructs and photographs modeled interiors to produce images that blur the line between dollhouse and architectural model.

Ed Lilley and Henry Urbach both write about the private chambers of the eighteenth and nineteenth centuries, the closets, boudoirs, libraries, and cabinets historically associated with intimate rooms that provided privacy within the larger domestic setting. They were often found at the end of a sequence of rooms, giving them distance from public spaces. Each room invoked an identity, whether it held collections of books or antiquities, or was associated with sexual liaison because of its appearance in romance novels. As a result, the rooms were an extension of self: personal identity in physical form. The intimate relationship crafted between room and person afforded its occupant the power to admit or deny visitors. Access to personalized rooms is akin to revealing details about self.

Other essays propose that gender and marginalized spaces are intertwining themes. Lilley and Urbach both allow for a comparison of demure rooms, in some cases so diminutive that the body is denied access to them. Urbach's focus on the closet is one example of how the self is reflected not only in a mirror but in the contents stored within. Lilley examines the boudoir and the evolution of room types where smaller and smaller rooms appear in floor plans as a way to further seclude rooms. Gender inherently enters into these rooms. The boudoir is associated with femininity, and the closet is gender neutral. Urbach develops the double architectural and social meaning of the closet with its euphemistic metaphor as a site for hiding gay and lesbian identity.

These two essays provide examples of marginalized spaces: the more private a room, the more its location is pushed to the edges of the house. But some peripheral spaces come to the foreground, for example, the attic used by Anne Frank's family to hide in during World War II in Amsterdam. It has been studied extensively as part of the war's history, but is an understudied space in the archives of interior design. With summaries of Anne's diary by Hans Westra, the Anne Frank House curator, the attic as a hiding place opens up new interpretations of marginalized interior spaces.

Orchestrated views are the subject of Diana Fuss and Joel Sanders's essay "Berggasse 19: Inside Freud's Office" about Sigmund Freud's Vienna office and study, and Beatriz Colomina's essay "Interior" about the residential interiors of Adolf Loos. Analytic diagrams and photographs in both essays reveal uses of direct light from windows and the placement of mirrors, furniture, and objects to establish theatrical interiors that located both actor and audience. The documentation of these interiors through drawings and photographs reveals views that are highly controlled depending on who the viewer is and the degree of privacy. Fuss, Sanders, and Colomina all invoke the organization of a theater and the relationship of parts to guide the analysis of interiors.

By focusing on private rooms at the periphery of architecture, subtle themes come into focus that are often left out of interior design literature, but present new criteria for viewing and writing about the interior. Through these wide-ranging essays on photography, history, gender, and politics, a borrowed richness characterized by intimacy is invited into the contemporary discourse.

Inside the Inside

Mark Wigley

INTRODUCTION

Model making is inherent to the practice of architecture and interior design. Mark Wigley analyzes the role of interior models through the photographs of James Casebere, who challenges the conventions of the architectural model mainly by rendering atmosphere on the interior. Casebere's models draw on archetypal structures common to such public institutions as schools, prisons, hallways, places of worship, sewer systems, and subway tunnels, all the while focusing on the interior. Before constructing these models, Casebere visits archetypal variations of these places and reconstructs them as models to the point of fluctuating between real and not real, dollhouse and architectural model. His documentation of these sites involves performing tasks of an architect that include measuring, surveying, controlling light, and crafting details. In the end, the models retain a sense of collective familiarity owing to Casebere's editing of form and detail to arrive at a typology. The result of these operations and discoveries: large-scale photographs that document and visually allow us to enter their virtual space. For Casebere, the photograph is the final work, yet the model is necessary to get there.

It is easy to draw associations between the dollhouse and interior design because of their shared emphasis on objects, textiles, and furniture. This comparison further emphasizes the role of interior design as being secondary to architecture. But Casebere's work challenges the secondary nature of the dollhouse through his attention to details, whether they are ornament or dust, taking his models one step further toward object and emotion than both the dollhouse and the architectural model.

Casebere crafts dirt, worn surfaces, interior finishes, and light picking up dust in the air—all things associated with the interior but not necessarily the dollhouse. His use of these elements to create a sense that someone just occupied the space offers a reinterpretation of the interior model. When Wigley describes Casebere's models as being in a "state of suspension," it is a result

Originally appeared in *The Architectural Unconscious: James Casebere + Glen Seator*, edited by Joseph N. Newland (2000), 16–23. Courtesy of the Addison Gallery of American Art, Phillips Academy, Andover, Massachusetts.

*of crafting atmospheres that imply well–worn, familiar spaces—unlike the newness of architectural models made of glue and foam core, or the kitsch of dollhouses.**

———

EMPTY. THE ROOM IS EMPTY. All we see is room. We are completely surrounded by a monotonous, unyielding, massive, yet ultimately vague material. Blank surfaces everywhere. Floors, walls, and ceiling all made of the same whitish stuff. Only soft lines between them. Everything merging to form a monolithic interior. As if a space has been carved out of an endless heaviness at some unknown time. A man-made cave with no way out. Our prison.

James Casebere traps us in haunting images by constructing architectural models and photographing them. The sense of realism is palpable. The camera seems to be peering into an actual building. It is as if the photographer is simply taking us to some curious structure that he has found. Yet what is curious is the strange sense that its reality is somehow unreal. Rather than a cardboard and plaster model cannily reproducing the effect of a building, a full-scale building seems to have the quality of a model. The spaces we are shown have neither been found in the outside world nor constructed in the artist's studio. They are suspended between the two. Casebere's craft is to precisely engineer a state of suspension. Every image forces a confusion between real and unreal that gives space an elusive quality. Something mysterious slides back and forth between model and building. Something is found in the model that resides in buildings yet usually remains hidden. It lurks there. Almost there.

This sense of the uncanny is symptomatically absent when Casebere photographs existing buildings. Faced with architecture, whether abandoned or newly built, he remains strictly within the conventions of black and white documentary realism. And yet particular buildings are used as the starting point for most of his models. In the case of the remarkable prison images, for example, institutional spaces are reconstructed. Though never exactly. From the beginning, the geometry is slightly different. Walls are never quite square or straight. Proportions are rearranged. Windows and doors move, grow, shrink, or disappear. And everything keeps changing. The specific source is made unspecific in a long process of rebuilding and reshooting, a patient search for a generic quality. In an obsessive, almost philosophical, kind of research, the artist constructs a model of the historical idea of prison rather than a particular prison. Anonymous spaces are used to force a meditation on the meaning of incarceration. In addition, we are asked to confront the impossibility of separating incarceration from everyday life.

The unique atmosphere of these images is produced by the removal of detail. If each model begins as a realistic approximation of a building, details are progressively taken away until the critical sense of haunting suspension is approached. If the sensitive point is passed and the model looks too much like a model, something must be added. This point of suspension is so elusive and fragile that every part of the image has to be continuously reworked in interaction with ever-shifting camera angles, lighting, focus, exposure, etc. Months go by before countless outtakes give way to a final image, an image in which there are no traces of the artist's work other than the effect of space, an image in which a space seems to have simply been discovered in all its strangeness.

This requires an expertise in surface, form, proportion, space, and light—the traditional palette of the architect. And architects do routinely make models and photograph them in a way that disguises the fact that they are models to give an impression what a space would be like. Clients and colleagues are invited to bring their eyes closer and closer until the model is the only thing in view and the imagined space is no longer subordinate to that of the room it is displayed in. People and cameras are pointed into miniature interiors. Models are carefully photographed in the outdoors to give a sense of a real landscape and sky fully integrated with the designed spaces. Model photographs are seamlessly grafted into photographs of the site. Images of the outside landscape are cut into the window frames of interiors. And so on. Every architect is adept at the tricks. Architectural design typically culminates in the most sophisticated of models. The realistic effect of such a model is more often than not the endpoint of the project. Only a very small proportion of designs get beyond the model. Architects photograph it to act as if it has already been built or in the hope that it will be. Today, the magic is increasingly done with computer modeling. Architectural fantasies are walked in or flown through. With virtual technologies, the spaces can be felt and heard. The model is occupied by the body rather than observed.

While architects try to suppress the surrealism of these procedures, Casebere heightens it. Where they add detail, he removes it. The presence of detail in an architect's model is a sign of its believability as a proposal. As the camera moves in, it discovers the rhythm and texture of each surface, the precise play of light off the fittings. Like the sophisticated models used by filmmakers, the more detail there is, the more the space can be taken for granted and the action can begin. Casebere's spaces can never be taken for granted, and there is no action. The resources of the architect are deployed to subtly disturb architecture. Or, rather, to reveal something already disturbing about it.

Casebere slides under the skin of the architect. Indeed, the minimalism of stripping away detail without abandoning realism aligns him with a particular architectural tradition, that of the historical avant-garde in the 1920s. The removal of detail was the mantra for the modern architects, as exemplified by their trademark white walls—smooth uninterrupted surfaces that wrap and define spaces with a minimum of fuss. This paradoxically facilitated detailed models. If what the model had to convey was the loss of superfluous detail, each of the few remaining details could be precisely registered. Models could all the more easily capture the qualities of a built space. The camera became a key design tool. One of the reasons that figures like Le Corbusier and Mies van der Rohe were leaders of the architectural avant-garde was that they knew how to photograph models. The conventional association of the camera with realism allowed experimental fantasies to be given a sense of reality. Photography literally realized designs.

Modern architecture is inseparable from the logic of the photographed model. Small models took on the effect of large buildings and buildings took on the effects of models. Model gives way to building which gives way to model in an endless ecological cycle that blurs the distinction between them. All modern buildings were meant to assume the polemical force of models. They were full-scale models of a new way of life. To live in a modern house was to occupy an idealized world. Photographs of the completed building are uncannily like those of models. It is as if the attempt to strip away excess detail gave the structures a permanent model-like quality. This effect was so marked that by the end of the twenties, Frank Lloyd Wright was repeatedly criticizing modern architecture for looking "as though cut from cardboard with scissors" and calling for a recovery of "realism," solid forms embedded in the ground rather than thin planes floating lightly above it, surfaces highly detailed rather than blank, and so on. But within a few decades the world had been filled with cardboard boxes. To construct a modern building was first and foremost to construct an image. Buildings anticipated being photographed. The first modern designs had many colored surfaces in addition to the trademark white walls, but these surfaces appeared white in photographs. The images returned the building to the effect of a monochrome model. Within a few years, the colored surfaces started to be bleached out from the designs as if in readiness for the black and white film. Buildings appeared on the site like a monochrome model in the studio. In the world but not quite of it. An idealized structure.

Casebere's models likewise anticipate the camera. Their relentless whiteness is even accentuated by the use of color film. When the viewer realizes any other color would have been registered, monochrome becomes even more polemical. The black and white effect becomes visible as an effect. Modern architects argued that the blank white surface had an archaic quality. It was timeless and therefore could register the flow of time. Casebere uses it to give particular historical forms a sense of archetypal permanence.

Yet his surfaces are not simply blank in the end. They are subtly marked. So subtly, in fact, that the sense of blankness is ultimately more intense than the naked walls dreamed of by the architects. The endless rebuilding and refinishing of the model in the quest for the right image produces surfaces with a unique sense of depth. Like the bumps in a wall where wallpaper or paint has been added and taken away over the years, there is a sense of history on each surface we see, without any of the details being given away. Each freshly modeled space seems to have been used for a long time. Much seems to have happened there. The short life of the model in the studio conjures up a long history just as its small size conjures up a large space. Time slows to a stop. Like an abandoned building, there is an eerie calm, haunted by unknown events and occupants. Only the furniture in some of the images gives the sense of a body that has or will inhabit the space. And even then the beds, tables, and toilets are made of the same white material as the room. Part of the space rather than in it. Nothing tangible occupies the space. Only a pervasive emptiness.

The images are archeological, full of missing details that force us to complete the picture by telling some story about the space. No help is offered. The titles give very little away. They simply describe the most obvious features of the image. For Casebere's first exhibition of the prison interiors, in 1995, he wrote a press release explaining the work, but never again. Likewise, his images used to be surrounded by standard wooden frames, but now they stand alone. In every sense, the framing of the work has been stripped down. Detail has been removed from the frame in the same way as it has been taken away from the image. The minimalism is relentless.

The images ultimately refuse to answer the questions they so insistently raise. Instead of being told what to think about prison, the viewer is simply thrown into it. As part of taking detail out of the frame, the edges of the image are usually out of focus and dark, encouraging the eye to jump into the center of the photograph, to jump, that is, into the room. Once there, the viewer is trapped. No way out. No escape. An inmate of the image. Like a visitor startled when the cell door closes, a sudden impression of what it is to be imprisoned. Not knowing if we will leave before anything happens. Confined between events, wondering who has been there before and who will arrive next. Not even able to leave our marks on the walls. Just pacing up and down in the image.

The spaces are occupied by the viewer rather than looked into. To visit an exhibition or read a publication of Casebere's photos is to be successively trapped in a number of spaces. In the gallery, the prints are very large, facilitating an easy entry to the architecture. And what kind of world do we enter? Each space goes all around us and way over us. We seem to be low down, dwarfed by high walls and distant ceilings. The space exceeds us.

Windows cannot be looked out of. Sometimes they are out of view—behind us, above us, or around a corner, or above our view, their presence only indicated by the pools of light they send into the dark interior. Sometimes they are cut into the ceiling or are unreachably high up in the walls. Rarely do they appear at eye level and even then they are just bright geometric flashes of intense white. Rather than offering an opening to the outside, they continue the surface of the interior, completing the sense of closure rather than breaching it. In the end, there is only the interior.

This intense sense of interiority is even preserved in images of the exterior. At first, the scheme seems reversed. The windows become pitch-black punctures in the bright white facade of the prison building. But almost immediately we realize that we are still in the dark looking at surfaces that have been lit by a light that comes from an outside we cannot access. We stand in the shadow of the outer prison wall that is cast across the facade, the softened image of the barbed wire putting us back in our place. Inmates still. Exercising, not escaping. The exteriors are actually interiors. The prison series is an extended meditation on the interior. All the spaces are structured by absence—of people, details, and exterior—forcing the eye to restlessly explore the terrain by scrutinizing every surface.

The same construction of a sense of interior can be seen in all of Casebere's images. Not just the literal interiors (suburban house, courtroom, library, arcade, church, asylum, shooting gallery, cave, storefront) but also the exteriors (house, tenement, mill, ghetto, street, subdivision), the in-between spaces (driveway, porch, and collections of objects like boats, wagons, or toys), and even the landscapes. Every image is of an internalized space, lit from an invisible outside. What would normally be openings—like windows, doors, sky, or gaps—are either pitch black or blinding white. The extreme tonal limits of the image act as the limits of the enclosure, with a monolithic surface stretched between them to hold us inside.

This effect is partly coming from the fact that these are literally images of interiors, miniature closed spaces constructed in an artist's studio. But this could have been easily dissimulated. Casebere chooses to intensify the effect, projecting, as it were, a sense of interiority onto the outside world. In so doing, he exposes as much about photography as he does about each model. The camera, with its relentless frame, always creates an interior, a division between the selected space within the frame and an unseen outside. It is a mechanism for producing a sense of interior. It is itself an interior, of course, a camera, a room, a closed box. The model, in turn, resembles a camera. In the studio it is even covered with a black cloth like an old plate camera. A small opening in the cloth lets light enter and activate the inner surface. When Casebere photographs a model, two small rooms are placed together with the shutter connecting them for a fraction of a second. The model is thrown away after the image is constructed. It only lives for the photograph. In a sense, it is just an attachment of the camera. Even when the same basic model is photographed from different angles, it never appears to be the same architecture. The structure and the shot are always adjusted. Different lighting, surface treatment, shooting angle, fog, composition, size of print, and furniture remove the sense that the camera is reexamining a ready-made space. The illusion that the camera can be detached from the scene it observes is systematically dissolved. The camera no longer has a position in space, a point of view. Looking at space and constructing it become the same thing. Unable to take the traditional safe position of the discrete camera, that of the voyeuristic mobile eye that is free to leave any scene, the viewer is thrown into the inside of the inside, confined within a frame whose limits are no longer clear.

Yet, precisely what is haunting about these images is that we are at home in them. It is not by chance that Casebere's survey of interiority began with five years of models of the inside of a suburban house. After all, the models are themselves constructed on a tabletop in a domestic apartment. The intimate exchange between architecture and camera occurs in a living room. The sense of interior exemplified in the prison series is thoroughly domestic, as became clear in the 1993 lithograph *Home and Prison,* where the facade of a suburban bungalow is juxtaposed with the facade of a prison. The big house aligned with the little one. Casebere presents everyday life as a set of interiors, institutionalized spaces from which escape is not possible, or even desired. The prison cell is no longer a space cut off from the everyday. Radical enclosure is the very mechanism of the everyday, of our dreams of freedom even. In the end, the way these images hover between real and unreal is more familiar than strange. The only menace they pose is the realization that we always live in models.

But what is it to occupy a model? How do we inhabit space? Casebere's most recent work forces us to admit that we are not sure. The viewer is thrown into transitional spaces, ones that are designed to be moved through and are difficult to stand still in. Yet the sense of confinement increases. This starts in 1998 with images of tunnels. The edges of the frame are again blurry, launching us into the middle of the space and down the line of movement. But the end of the path is always hidden. The tunnel immediately turns or goes completely dark. Sometimes there is more than one possible path. The tunnel forks and smaller openings are cut into the sides or above. Each potential opening is closed by being too bright or too dark. There is no wall behind us or in front of us, yet there is no way out. In theory we are able to move, perhaps very fast and very far, but we remain trapped. The tunnel offers no escape. Instead of passing through, we are caught, suspended, staring at the texture of the heavy surface that envelops us. Occupying a space

left
Fig. 6.1: James Casebere, *Four Flooded Arches from Right*, 1999. Dye destruction print, 60 x 48 inches.
Copyright James Casebere

below
Fig. 6.2: James Casebere, *Flooded Hallway from Right*, 1999. Dye destruction print, 24 x 30 inches & 48 x 60 inches.
Copyright James Casebere. Images are courtesy James Casebere and Sean Kelly Gallery, New York

built for something else, wondering what else might come toward us or from behind at any moment. The more roughly surfaced tubular tunnels seem to be spaces made by a burrowing animal or for the flowing of liquids, while the smoothly arched tunnels are clearly man-made for the liquid that is subtly suggested on the floor. We are intruders who cannot leave. The liquid starts to take over with the images of *Flooded Arches*. [Fig. 6.1] An intense, even claustrophobic, sense of interior is produced without showing any walls, ceiling, or floor. Just a series of arches passing into the distance. Water occupies the space, not people. At first, there seems to be a clear distinction between the water and the arches. The arches likely continue beneath the surface, but it is unclear how deep they go or what kind of bottom lies below, if any. Liquid flow and solid form collaborate to create an enclosure. Light bounces around between them from unseen openings and starts to blur the limits. Rippling movements appear high up on the smooth surface of the arches and the clear geometric form of the arches is reflected down on the wavy surface of the water. The mirrored image of the arches produces the sense of a complete tube. Positioned low over the water, we are thrown into this semi-solid or semi-liquid tube, confined there at the interface as the water pulls in one direction and the solid pulls in another. The confusion of liquid and solid becomes even more extreme when the tunnel images give way to those of hallways, another transitional space of movement. Despite titles like *Flooded Hallway*, the spaces have not simply been flooded. [Fig. 6.2] Rather it seems that the solid floor has uncannily started to become liquid. More precisely, it is hovering between the two. Once again there is the odd sense of being forced into a space that cannot simply be entered or exited. One cannot stand, sit, lean, lie, or walk here. One can only float. Not on the surface of the liquid but in the blurring of liquid and solid. A very familiar, simple, and spare geometry quietly turns surreal. The dancing play of light bouncing off the horizontal surface swaps places with the vertical surfaces that now swim below. The line between vertical and horizontal remains but is challenged. To look at such an image is to think about what it is to occupy even the simplest of spaces. The walls and floor around us can no longer be trusted. With the latest image series commissioned for the Addison Gallery exhibition, the construction of space becomes indistinguishable from dissolving it. In *Pink Hallway #2* there is a clear sense that an interior has been flooded, with the pattern of the floor tiles showing through the swirling yet strangely dense liquid. But in *Pink Hallway #3* there is no sense of a solid layer below the ripples. [Fig. 6.3] The floor itself has become liquid and the line at the center of our view between the building and its reflection is disappearing. At a certain undefined point, the walls and doors just start rippling. One can just as easily read the building as a straightening out of the ripple as read the reflection as an optical distortion of the building. This doubt is even greater in *Blue*

Fig. 6.3: James Casebere, *Pink Hallway #3*, 2000. Digital chromogenic print, 30 x 24 inches, 60 x 48 inches & 96 x 77 inches. Copyright James Casebere

Fig. 6.4: James Casebere, *Converging Hallways from Left*, 1997. Dye destruction print, 24 x 38.5 inches, 48 x 67 inches & 86 x 120 inches. Copyright James Casebere

Fig. 6.5: James Casebere, *Monticello #3*, 2001. Digital chromogenic print, 24 x 30 inches & 48 x 60 inches. Copyright James Casebere. Images are courtesy James Casebere and Sean Kelly Gallery, New York

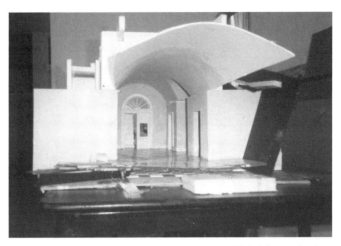

Fig. 6.6: James Casebere, View of model in progress for *Pink Hallway* series in artist's studio, 2000. Copyright James Casebere. Image courtesy James Casebere and Sean Kelly Gallery, New York

Hallway. The level of the subtly wavy surface has risen much higher, but the effect is neither that of a very deep flood nor of strangely stunted doors. It is as if the whole interior has simply become molten, fragile, indeterminate. And it is this blur that encloses us. In the end, architecture appears to be intimately engaged with, and dependent upon, the very forces that at first seem to erode it. These last images bring Casebere's extended exploration of the interior full circle. The building being modeled actually stands across the road from the gallery where the images were first displayed. The photographs have returned from the domestic tabletop to the seemingly external world that they so cannily challenge. For the first time, building and image face off. They expose each other. Every tiny shift is evident as the proportions, details, and colors of the hallway have been changed, then change again between images. But the remarkable effect is not that a space has been represented in different ways or transformed with liquid. The effect is that the building itself is just another model, just another enigmatic assemblage of fragile elements whose limits are never clear. It seems that we are forever living within such interiors, forever inside the inside, but it is a strange thing. There is no such thing as a simple room. [Fig. 6.4–6]

Notes

* Mark Wigley, "Inside the Inside," in *The Architectural Unconscious: James Casebere + Glen Seator*, ed. Joseph N. Newland (Andover: Addison Gallery of American Art, Phillips Academy, 2000), 16.

Domesticity

Witold Rybczynski

INTRODUCTION

Witold Rybczynski identifies the Dutch seventeenth-century interior as the point of origin of a gestalt describing the occupation and care of the bourgeois household in small urban, live-work structures. He references Johannes Vermeer's domestic scene paintings as reasonable resources for reconstructing the reality of life in the architectural interiors—and within a burgeoning domestic culture different from other European enclaves. In Vermeer's paintings, he depicts elements of the everyday that include clothing, domestic objects, light, and people interacting and undertaking domestic chores as layers surrounding the body, from clothing to walls. Rybczynski provides an analysis of these layers through a historical reading of paintings. Together they complete a picture of a family's identity.

By taking a closer look at Dutch interiors versus those found in contemporary bourgeois France, Rybczynski draws a connection between family income and identity. Separate from family structure and home economics, he identifies a distinct functionality placed on objects in the Dutch home. Rybczynski sees the care and attachment of the Dutch to their homes as a unique and identifying characteristic of the initiation of a culture of house interiors. Dutch middle-class householders commissioned three-dimensional models that, like dollhouses, documented their homes in miniature. As portraits they went beyond exterior architecture and replicated the home in detail and viewpoint with such interior artifacts as textiles, objects, and furniture. The interior focus of the dollhouselike models was inherent in form because the dollhouses de-emphasized exterior walls owing to the construction method of parti-walls for adjacent homes.

The use of the dollhouse to replicate personal living space is obsolete. From today's vantage point, dollhouses reveal a layer of detail that gives a unique sense of interiority that pushes architecture aside. Rybczynski emphasizes that the details in them can be described with such words as "homeness," "household," and "snug," to show how the interior was used and perceived. They also express the duality of occupying two spaces: a full-scale version and a miniaturized, idealized version. The dollhouse performed the role of being a portrait of the house's full-scale reality, forever and simultaneously capturing its idealized state.

———

Domesticity, privacy, comfort, the concept of the home and of the family: these are, literally, principal achievements of the Bourgeois Age.
—John Lukacs, *The Bourgeois Interior*

THE APPEARANCE OF intimacy and privacy in homes in Paris and London, and soon after even in such out-of-the-way places as Oslo, was an unwitting, almost unconscious, reaction to the changing conditions of urban life, and it appeared to be more a question of popular attitudes than of anything else. It is difficult to trace the evolution of something so amorphous, and it would be dangerous to claim that there was a single place where the modern idea of the family home first entered the human consciousness. There was, after all, no identifiable moment of discovery, no individual inventor who can be credited with the intuition, no theory or treatise on the subject. There was one place, however, where the seventeenth-century domestic interior evolved in a way that was arguably unique, and that can be described as having been, at the very least, exemplary.

The United Provinces of the Netherlands was a brand-new state, formed in 1609 after thirty years of rebellion against Spain. It was among the smallest countries in Europe, with a population one-quarter that of Spain, one-eighth that of France, and with a landmass smaller than Switzerland's. It had few natural resources—no mines, no forests—and what little land there was needed constant protection from the sea. But this "low" country surprisingly quickly established itself as a major power. In a short time it became the most advanced shipbuilding nation in the world and developed large naval, fishing, and merchant fleets. Its explorers founded colonies in Africa and Asia, as well as in America. The Netherlands introduced many financial innovations that made it a major economic force—and Amsterdam became the world center for international finance. Its manufacturing towns grew so quickly that by the middle of the century the Netherlands had supplanted France as the leading industrial nation of the world.[1] Its universities were among the best in Europe; its tolerant political and religious climate offered a home for émigré thinkers such as Spinoza, Descartes, and John Locke. This fecund country produced not just venture capitalists and the speculative tulip trade, but also Rembrandt and Vermeer; it devised not only the first recorded war game, but also the first microscope; it invested not only in heavily armed East Indiamen but also in beautiful towns. All this occurred during a brief historical moment—barely a human lifetime—which lasted from 1609 until roughly the 1660s, and which the Dutch call their "golden age."

These unlikely achievements were the result of several different factors, such as the Netherlands' advantageous location in European maritime trade, as well as the defensibility of its national borders, but it was in great measure a result of the peculiar character of the Dutch social fabric, which was different from that of the rest of Europe. The Dutch were primarily merchants and landowners. Unlike England, the Netherlands lacked a landless peasantry (most Dutch farmers owned their land); unlike France, it had no powerful aristocracy (the nobility, decimated by the wars for independence, was small and no longer wealthy); unlike Spain, it had no king (the head of state, or *stadhouder,* was a national symbol, but with limited real power). This republic—the first in Europe—was a loose confederation ruled by a States General, which consisted of representatives of the seven sovereign provinces, chosen from the patrician upper middle class.

The pattern of human settlements was also markedly different than elsewhere. Already in 1500, the Low Countries (which then included Brabant, or Belgium) had numbered more than 200 fortified towns and 150 large villages.[2] By the seventeenth century, most of the population in its three most powerful provinces—Holland, Zeeland, and Utrecht—lived in towns. Amsterdam became a major city of Europe, Rotterdam was a growing port, and Leiden was an important manufacturing and university town. However, it was not its major cities but its many smaller towns that distinguished the Netherlands; there were more medium-sized towns than in much larger countries, such as France, England, or Germany.[3] The eighteen largest towns had one vote each in the assembly of the provincial states, which indicated their importance and their independence. In short, at a time when the other states of Europe remained primarily rural (even in urbanized Italy, most of the people were still peasants), the Netherlands was rapidly becoming a nation of townspeople. Burghers by historical tradition, the Dutch were bourgeois by inclination.[4]

The bourgeois nature of Dutch society in the seventeenth century needs some explanation. To say that it was "bourgeois" does not mean that it consisted exclusively of a middle class. There were farmers (*boers*), seamen, and, in manufacturing towns such as Leiden, factory workers. The last-named, especially, did not share in the prosperity of that time, and their living conditions were as miserable as in other countries. There was also, as in all European cities, an urban rabble (*grauw*), composed of paupers and criminals, the unemployed and the unemployable, itinerant beggars and tramps. However, the middle class predominated, and was broad enough to encompass the international financier as well as the shopkeeper. The former did not, of course, identify, or even associate with the latter, even if, as was often the case, his economic ascent was recent, for Dutch society was not static, and social position was defined largely by income. Bourgeois also was the patrician elite—a ruling class—which provided the magistrates and burgomasters who governed the towns, and through them the country. By European standards, this was a greatly expanded democracy, and this "social dictatorship of the merchant class," as one historian called it, created the first bourgeois state.

Everyday life in the Netherlands in the seventeenth century reflected the traditional bourgeois virtues—an unruffled moderation, an admiration for hard work, and a financial prudence bordering on parsimony. Thrift evolved naturally in a society of merchants and traders who, moreover, lived in a country which required a constant communal investment in canals, dikes, sluices, and windmills to keep the North Sea at bay. They were also a simple people, less passionate than the Latins of southern Europe, less sentimental than their German neighbors, less intellectual than the French. The Dutch historian Huizinga claimed that the flat, restful landscape of polders and canals, which lacked dramatic features such as mountains or valleys, encouraged the simplicity of the Dutch character.[5] Equally important was religion. Although only about a third of the Dutch were Calvinists, this became the state religion and exercised a major influence on everyday life, contributing a sense of sobriety and restraint to Dutch society.

All these circumstances produced a people who admired saving, frowned on conspicuous spending, and naturally evolved conservative manners. The simplicity of the Dutch bourgeois expressed itself in many ways. The dress of a Dutch male, for instance, was plain. The doublet and trousers were the seventeenth-century equivalent of the modern businessman's three-piece suit, and like it they were unaffected by fashion; the quality of the cloth might vary but the style remained unchanged for generations. The favorite colors were dark: black, violet, or brown. The officials of the clothmakers' guild, in Rembrandt's famous group portrait, were prosperous (as their lace collars and amply cut cassocks indicate) but somber to the point of drabness. Their wives dressed with similar moderation, and neither exhibited the nervous flamboyance and constantly changing chic that was so characteristic of the French bourgeoisie. So circumspect were the Dutch that in paintings of the period it is not always easy to distinguish between an official and his clerk, between a mistress and her servant.

The same simplicity and thrift were apparent in Dutch houses, which lacked the architectural pretension of townhouses in London or Paris, and which were built of brick and wood instead of stone. These materials were used for their light weight, since the boggy soil of the Low Countries frequently required pile foundations, the cost of which could be reduced if the foundations carried less weight. Brick does not lend itself to elaborate decoration—unlike stone, it cannot be carved, and unlike cement plaster, it cannot be formed into moldings and reliefs. Consequently, Dutch buildings were plain, only occasionally relieved by stonework at the corners and around the doors and windows. The material was appreciated mainly for its pleasant texture; undoubtedly its economy also appealed to the practical-minded Dutch, who used it even for their public buildings.

The expense of building canals and pilings dictated that street frontages be reduced as much as possible; as a result, the building plots in Dutch towns were extremely narrow, sometimes only one room wide. The houses were built adjacent to each other in a row, usually sharing common walls. The roofs were covered in red clay tiles. Their gable ends, which were often stepped, faced the street and produced the characteristic silhouettes for which Dutch towns became famous. At the top of the gable was a wooden bracket and hook, used for hauling furniture and other goods to the upper floors. The interior of the medieval Dutch house consisted of a "front room" (where commercial activities took place) and a "back room" (where the household cooked, ate, and slept). In front of the house, and slightly raised above the level of the street, was a wide verandah-like *stoep*, or stoop, with benches, sometimes protected with a wooden canopy. Here the family sat in the evenings and socialized with passersby. Below the house was a shallow cellar, its floor never lower than the water level of the adjacent canal. As families became more prosperous, these low houses were extended in the only direction possible—up. Two, and sometimes three, floors were added.

The original ground floors of Dutch houses were often high, so that the first additional space consisted of a gallery or loft, which was reached by a ladderlike stair. As the house grew, this pattern was continued, so that often no two rooms were on the same level, and all were connected by steep, narrow staircases. Initially, these rooms, with the exception of the kitchen, did not have special functions. By midcentury, however, the subdivision of the house into day and night uses, and into formal and informal areas, had begun. The upper floors of the house began to be treated as formal rooms, reserved for special occasions. The second-floor room facing the street was turned into a parlor, the old front room became a kind of living room, and other rooms began to be used exclusively for sleeping. As in the rest of Europe there were no bathrooms, and privies were a rarity. (One reason that privies were rare was that most Dutch towns were built on marshy land, and privy pits and cesspools filled with water and ceased to function. The usual alternative was the chamber pot, which was emptied into the canal. Unlike Venice, however, Dutch towns had no sea tide to remove these wastes, with the unfortunate consequence that these pretty towns probably had an unbearable odor. There were occasional efforts to remedy the situation. Canals were periodically dredged, and in some towns night soil was collected from the houses in wooden containers and barged out to the countryside for the benefit of the farmers, a practice that was medieval in origin but continued in some towns until the 1950s.)[6] The Dutch were a seafaring people, and there was something shipshape about these compact interiors, with the tarred brick walls (to protect them against the humidity) and painted woodwork, the steep, narrow stairs, and the rooms as small as ships' cabins. The atmosphere could best be described as snug—a word which is coincidentally both of nautical and of Dutch origin.

Building on pilings on reclaimed land had its drawbacks, but it also produced an unexpected benefit for the occupants. Since the shared side walls of these houses carried all the weight of the roof and the floors, the external cross-walls served no structural function, and, given the high cost of foundations, there was an advantage to making them as light as possible. To accomplish this, the builders of Dutch houses pierced the facades with many and large windows, whose function may have been to save weight, but which also allowed light to penetrate far into the deep, narrow interiors. In the days before gaslight, this was important. Paintings of Dutch houses in daytime show bright, sunlit rooms whose cheerfulness was in contrast to the dark interiors that were typical in other countries. Before the seventeenth century, the upper parts of Dutch windows had fixed glass, and only the lower portions, which were solid wood, were openable; later these too were glazed. The light coming through these windows was controlled by shutters, and by a new device—window curtains—which also provided privacy from the street. As these openings became larger, they became more awkward to open the windows in the conventional way, and the Dutch invented a new type of window, the sash or double-hung window, which could be conveniently opened without sticking into the room. Like the two-part Dutch door, the sash window was soon copied in England and France.

New inventions such as the sash window were not typical; Dutch houses in the seventeenth century were hardly bristling with innovation, and in fact retained many medieval features. This mixing of the old and new was a characteristic feature of Dutch society. At the same time as it pioneered new political forms of organization, it combined these with traditional institutions such as guilds and self-governing towns; these social revolutionaries (although they would have hardly considered themselves that) dressed like their grandfathers, and in many ways lived like them as well. Their houses continued to be built out of wood and brick. In the traditional way, signs indicated the owner's profession—scissors for the tailor, an oven for the baker. The gabled facades of private houses were topped off with a figurative sculpture with literary or biblical connotations. The Dutch loved allegories, and in some houses stone tablets, inscribed with a suitable epigraph, were set into the wall. The small houses with their colorful signs had a medieval, toylike charm. Indeed, they, and their owners, were often described as "old-fashioned."

Unfortunately, the thermal charms of these houses were also medieval. (I once spent a week in January in a seventeenth-century house in Leiden. In this historically protected neighborhood the old house was without insulation, double glazing, or central heating; it was a chillingly authentic experience.) The Dutch climate is not a particularly severe one, but the situation of the country makes for damp winters. In the absence of firewood (Holland has few forests) the main heating fuel in the seventeenth century was peat, which can be burned effectively but requires special stoves. These were unknown at that time and instead, to promote combustion, the peat was piled in tall, open stacks on the fire grate inside the fireplace, or was burned in so-called fire pots; this got rid of the foul-smelling smoke, but unfortunately produced little heat.[7] The only way to achieve some comfort under such circumstances was to wear many clothes, which, as amused visitors noted, is exactly what the Dutch did. Men wore half a dozen waistcoats, several pairs of trousers, and heavy cloaks; their wives wore as many as six petticoats under their skirts. The effect was hardly flattering to the figure and at least partially explains the apparently dumpy physiques of the burghers and their wives in contemporary paintings.

These houses were "small houses," literally as well as figuratively. They did not need to be large, because they contained few people; the average number of people per house in most Dutch towns was not more than four or five, compared to as many as twenty-five in a city such as Paris. Why was this? For one thing, there were no tenants, for the Dutch preferred, and were prosperous enough, to afford the luxury of owning their own homes, however small. The house had ceased to be a place of work, and as many artisans became well-to-do merchants or *rentiers*, they built separate establishments for their businesses, and employees and apprentices had to provide their own lodgings. Nor were there as many servants as in other countries, for Dutch society discouraged the hiring of servants and imposed special taxes on those who employed domestic help.[8] Individual independence was more highly prized than elsewhere, and, equally importantly, it could be afforded. As a result, most homes in the Netherlands housed a single couple and their children. This brought about another change. The publicness that had characterized the "big house" was replaced by a more sedate—and more private—home life.

The emergence of the family home reflected the growing importance of the family in Dutch society. The glue that cemented this unit was the presence of children. The mother raised her own children—there were no nurses. Young children attended infant school at the age of three, and then primary school for four years. The Netherlands had, it is generally agreed, the highest level of literacy in Europe, and even secondary education was not uncommon. Most children lived at home until they were married, and the relations between Dutch parents and their children were characterized by affection, rather than by discipline. Foreign visitors considered this permissiveness to be a dangerous habit. Given the excessive indulgence with which parents treated their children, one observed, "it is surprising that there is not more disorder than there is."[9] For the Frenchman who wrote this, children were small and unruly, but nevertheless adults; the idea of childhood did not yet exist for him. The historian Philippe Ariès has described how the substitution of school for apprenticeship throughout Europe reflected a rapprochement between parents and family, and between the concept of family and the concept of childhood.[10] This is precisely what happened in the Netherlands, where the family centered itself on the child and family life centered itself on the home, only in the Dutch home it occurred about a hundred years earlier than elsewhere.[11]

It was the opinion of more than one contemporary visitor that the Dutch prized three things above all else: first their children, second their homes, and third their gardens.[12] In these narrow houses, built directly on the street and sharing their side walls with their neighbors, the garden was an important space, all the more so because in the mild climate it was used most of the year. Within the restricted area available, there evolved a particularly formal type of landscaping, as artificial, in its own way, as the small urban gardens of the Japanese. The precisely clipped hedges, geometrically shaped box trees, and colored gravel walks echoed the orderliness of the interiors. The Dutch garden was a further indication of the transition from the communal big house to the individual family home. The typical European townhouse of this period, whether in Paris or in Oslo, was built around a courtyard which was essentially public in nature. The secluded back garden of the Dutch house was different—it was private.

While Dutch houses and gardens may have been private, they nevertheless contributed to the overall appearance of the towns. Because of the canals, which were built with tree-lined roadways on both sides, the spaces between the houses were the width of boulevards (this was two hundred years before Baron Haussmann built the Champs-Elysées). Because of the wide use of brick and a building style that was imitative rather than inventive, Dutch towns had a pleasant uniformity. This prompted the Danish historian Steen Eiler Rasmussen to write that whereas the French and the Italians created impressive palaces, the Dutch created incomparable towns.[13]

The rapid, and, as it seemed to many, improbable prosperity of the Netherlands—as that of Japan today—aroused much interest in other countries. Sir William Temple, who was the English ambassador at The Hague from 1668 to 1670 and knew the country well, wrote a widely read book attempting to explain this curious phenomenon to his countrymen. The fourth chapter, entitled "Of Their People and Dispositions," concluded: "Holland is a Countrey where the Earth is better than the Air, and Profit more in request than Honour; Where there is more Sense than Wit; More good Nature than good Humor; And more Wealth than Pleasure; Where a man would chuse rather to travel, than to live…" Harsh words, although intended, perhaps, for a jingoistic audience, since later in life their author gave up the chance to be Secretary of State in favor of returning to his old job in The Hague. Despite what he perceived as penny-pinching cheerlessness in the Dutch character, Temple did point out that in one area, at least, the Dutch did not hold back in their expenditures: they were inclined to invest all their surplus income in "the Fabrick, Adornment, or Furniture of their Houses."[14]

The Dutch loved their homes. They shared this old Anglo-Saxon word—*ham, hejm* in Dutch—with the other peoples of northern Europe. (This wonderful word, "home," which connotes a physical "place" but also has the more abstract sense of a "state of being," has no equivalent in the Latin or Slavic European languages. German, Danish, Swedish, Icelandic, Dutch, and English all have similar sounding words for "home," all derived from the Old Norse "heima.") "Home" brought together the meanings of house and of household, of dwelling and of refuge, of ownership and of affection. "Home" meant the house, but also everything that was in it and around it, as well as the people, and the sense of satisfaction and contentment that all these conveyed. You could walk out of the house, but you always returned home. The Dutch affection for their homes was expressed in a singular practice: they had elaborate scale models built of their houses. These replicas are sometimes—inaccurately—referred to as dollhouses. Their function was more like that of ship models, not playthings but miniature memorials, records of dearly beloved objects. They were built like cupboards which did not represent the exterior appearance of the house. But when the doors were opened the entire interior was magically revealed, not only the rooms—complete with wall coverings and furnishings—but even paintings, utensils, and china figurines.

The furniture and adornment of a seventeenth-century Dutch home were meant, although in a typically restrained way, to convey the wealth of its owner. There were still benches and stools, especially in the homes of the less prosperous, but, as in England and France, the chair had become the most common sitting device. It was almost always without arms, padded, and upholstered in velvet and other rich materials, usually attached to the frame with copper nails. Tables, like chairs, were of oak or walnut and had elegantly turned legs. Curtained four-poster beds were similarly constructed, but less common than in England or France; instead, the Dutch slept in beds that were built into the wall. Such beds, of medieval origin, were set into an alcove, completely enclosed on three sides, and the opening was screened with a curtain or solid shutters. The most important piece of bourgeois furniture was the cupboard, which the Dutch borrowed from Germany, and which replaced the horizontal chest as the means of storage. There were usually two such cupboards, often ornamented with inlays of precious wood, one for the linens and another for tableware. For storing and displaying the latter there were also glass-fronted credenzas, descendants of the medieval plate cupboards, which held silver and crystal, Delft porcelain and oriental china. (Chinese porcelain was evidence of the Netherlands' international trade and its growing colonial empire. It is also a reminder that the Dutch frequently played the role of middlemen of culture, as well as of trade.[15] They were the first Europeans to use Turkish carpets, for instance, occasionally on the floor, but more frequently as a table covering. It was the Dutch, also, through their East India Company, who introduced Europe to japanned and lacquered finishing from the Orient, to the arts of inlaying and veneering furniture from Asia, and, not the least, to tea-drinking.)

The type of furniture in a Dutch house was similar to that found in a Parisian bourgeois home; the difference was in the effect. The French interior was crowded and frenetic, the many pieces of furniture jostling each other in rooms whose papered walls were illustrated with scenic landscapes and where all surfaces were embroidered, gilded, or decorated. Dutch decor, by comparison, was sparse. Furniture was to be admired, but it was also meant to be used, and it was never so crowded as to detract from the sense of space that was produced by the room and by the light within it. The walls were rarely papered or covered, although they were adorned with paintings, mirrors, and maps—the last-named a uniquely Dutch practice. The effect was far from severe, and was not intended to be. These rooms, with one or two chairs under a window, or a bench beside the door, were intensely human, and were directed to private use, rather than to entertaining and socializing. They exhibited an intimacy that is inadequately described by words such as "serene" or "peaceful."

As every homemaker knows, the less furniture there is, the easier it is to keep a room clean, and this too may have had something to do with the relative sparseness of the Dutch interior, for these houses were spotlessly, immaculately, unbelievably clean. The well-scrubbed Dutch stoop is famous and has come to serve as an example of public exhibition and bourgeois pretentiousness. Public it certainly was—not only the stoop but the entire road pavement in front of the house was washed and sanded by the householder—but it was no pretense; the interiors of Dutch houses were equally scrubbed and scoured. Sand was scattered on the floor, recalling the medieval practice of covering floors in rushes. Pots were shined, woodwork varnished, brickwork tarred. This was all taken seriously by the Dutch, and produced some curious customs which never failed to elicit comment from foreigners. A German visitor to Delft in 1665 wrote that "in many houses, as in the holy places of the heathens, it is not permissible to ascend the stairs or set foot in a room without first removing one's shoes."[16] Jean-Nicolas de Parival, a French traveler, observed the same thing, adding that frequently straw slippers were put on over one's shoes.[17]

This gives the impression that the streets of Dutch towns were unkempt; instead the opposite was true. Save for those in the oldest neighborhoods, where the poor lived, the streets were paved in brick, and included sidewalks for pedestrians. Whereas in London and Paris the public street was unbearable—a combination of open sewer and garbage dump—in Dutch towns this waste material was disposed of in the canals, leaving the street relatively clean. Moreover, since it was the custom for each household to wash the street in front of its house, these streets were generally as well scrubbed as the stoops. If the streets were so clean, certainly cleaner than elsewhere in Europe, how to explain this collective obsession with cleanliness inside the home? Was it the product of Calvinism (stoops in Calvinist Scotland were equally scoured), or merely of bourgeois decorum? Or was this homely virtue the result of the simplicity of the Dutch spirit, a delight in the neat and the orderly? (The Dutch word for clean, *schoon,* also expresses beauty and purity.) Huizinga suggested the latter, adding that it was made possible by the easy availability of water, the dustless marine atmosphere of the Netherlands, and the tradition of cheese making, an activity requiring special attention to cleanliness.[18] This sounds too deterministic, and in any case, cheese-making was hardly confined to the Netherlands. Another explanation is that the care lavished on their homes by the Dutch was a kind of preventive maintenance. That, at least, was Temple's suggestion: "The same moisture of Air makes all Metals apt to rust, and Wood to mould; which forces them by continual pains of rubbing and scouring, to seek a prevention or cure: This makes the brightness and cleanness that seems affected in their Houses, and is call'd natural to them, by people who think no further."[19]

The importance that the Dutch attached to domestic cleanliness is all the more striking since we know that in their personal habits the Dutch were not especially clean; there is plenty of evidence that they were considered, even by the insalubrious standards of the seventeenth century, to be dirty.[20] "They keep their houses cleaner than their bodies," wrote an English visitor.[21] The Dutch house did not contain a room for bathing, for instance, and public baths were almost unknown. Bathing was further discouraged by the multiple layers of clothing that both men and women wore in the damp winters.

Temple remarked on the unhealthy climate and situation of the Netherlands. Although the Dutch originated modern medicine, they were unable to control the many infectious diseases that struck almost every Dutch town during the seventeenth century. The generally low level of public health was indicated by the series of annual epidemics that ravaged Amsterdam for six years during the 1620s, reducing the population by thirty-five thousand. Leiden lost more than a third of its forty thousand citizens in six months of 1635.

It is precisely because Holland's scrubbed floors and polished brass-work did not reflect a profound understanding of health or hygiene that they are significant. The cleanliness of the Dutch interior was not simply a part of the national character, nor a response determined by external causes, but evidence of something much more important. When visitors were required to take off their shoes or put on slippers, it was not immediately on entering the house—the lower floor was still considered to be a part of the public street—but on going upstairs. That was where the public realm stopped and the home began. This boundary was a new idea, and the order and tidiness of the household were evidence neither of fastidiousness nor of a particular cleanliness, but instead of a desire to define the home as a separate, special place.

That we are able to know so much about the appearance of Dutch homes is thanks to two happy accidents: the predominance of painting in seventeenth-century Holland, and the popularity of domestic scenes as a subject of these paintings. The Dutch loved paintings. The richest and the most humble person bought them and hung them in their homes. This was partly as an investment, but also for their own pleasure. Paintings could be found not only in parlors and front rooms but also in taverns, offices, and workplaces and behind shop counters. The bourgeois public supported many painters who, like furniture makers or other craftsmen, were organized in guilds. These Dutch painters diligently worked their way up in their profession, beginning at the age, of fourteen as apprentices, then as journeymen assistants, until after six years they could apply for membership in the guild and become independent "masters," at which point they were permitted to sell paintings under their own names.

Although the market for paintings was large, the supply was as well, and few Dutch painters became wealthy. Portraits were painted on commission, but much painting was done on speculation and sold through dealers. The public desired paintings of suitable subjects, whose artistry they could admire and understand. The technically skilled painters, with a direct, uncomplicated approach to painting, and without the self-consciousness of later artists, were happy to oblige. As a result, seventeenth-century Dutch paintings serve not only as art, but also as an unusually accurate representation of the time.

Given the affection of the Dutch for their neat, well-kept houses, it was not surprising that in addition to biblical subjects and family portraits, there developed a genre of painting that dealt with the home itself. To recall the work of an American illustrator such as Norman Rockwell conveys a little of their artistry, but it does give a sense of a type of painting that appealed to a home-loving public. Pieter de Hooch painted wonderful scenes of domestic life, as also did Jan Steen and Gabriel Metsu. Less than forty paintings remain by the great Jan Vermeer, and almost all of them are set within the home. But it was Emanuel de Witte, who specialized in views of church interiors, another popular genre, who painted a domestic scene that has come to epitomize the seventeenth-century Dutch interior. [Fig. 6.7] This little masterpiece, painted around 1660, shows a series of rooms opening off each other, bathed in sunlight that falls through the large leaded windows. (Genre paintings, since they were to be hung in the home, were usually small; de Witte's was only thirty by forty inches. Many were less than half that size.) Judging from the way that the light passes into all three rooms and the hint of trees visible through the windows, this house is probably on the outskirts of the town. The central figure in the painting, and the one from which it gets its name, is a young woman playing the virginals, a precursor to the spinet, that was popular in Holland at that time.

Like many Dutch painters, de Witte intended his picture to tell a story. On the surface this is an idyllic, peaceful scene. It is early in the day—that is implied by the low angle of the sun, and by the maidservant busy with the morning chores, visible in a distant doorway. The mistress of the house—who else could it be?—sits at the musical instrument. The room in which she is playing, typically, serves many functions. It contains, in addition to the virginals, a table, three chairs, and a curtained bed.

But all is not what it appears to be. Closer inspection of the painting reveals that the woman is not playing for herself alone; on the bed, behind the curtains, someone is listening to the music. It is unquestionably a man—the figure wears a mustache—and, although he is hidden, his clothing is fully visible on the chair in the foreground. The hilt of a sword that is barely within the picture and the casual fashion in which the clothes have been thrown on the chair—instead of being hung neatly on the hooks behind the door—hint, in a delicate way, that this man may not be the woman's husband. Marital infidelity was frowned upon in Calvinist Holland and de Witte fulfilled his social obligations by making it the subject of an allegory, although

Fig. 6.7: Emanuel de Witte, *Interior with a Woman Playing a Virginal*, circa 1660.
Oil on canvas. The Montreal Museum of Fine Arts, Purchase, John W. Tempest Fund.
Photo credit: The Montreal Museum of Fine Arts, Denis Farley

that tale is hidden in a series of riddles, symbols, and secondary meanings. The jug and towel on the table, the water pump, and the woman sweeping the floor suggest something along the lines of "Cleanliness is next to godliness." But part of the delight of this genre is the painter's ambiguity toward his subject. Is the woman properly penitent? If so, why is she playing and not weeping? She has her back turned, as if in shame, but in the mirror hanging on the wall over the virginals, her face is tantalizingly not quite reflected. Maybe she is smiling; we will never know.

One does not need to unravel the turgid story that lies hidden in the shadows and details of de Witte's painting. He was interested not only in narrative but also, like most Dutch painters, in portraying the material world as he saw it. This love of the real world—"realism" is too weak a word—was evident in many details. We can enjoy the way that the shadow of the windows falls on the partly open door, the red taffeta curtains that color the light in the room, the shiny brass of the chandelier, the rich gilt of the mirror frame and the matte texture of the pewter jug. There is a little dog curled up beside the bed; sheet music lies open on top of the virginals. Nothing is too small to escape the painter's attention.

It should be said immediately that it is unlikely that de Witte's was a depiction of an actual house; photographic as his paintings appear, they are imagined, not real. De Witte's churches, for example, were not portraits of existing buildings; although they were based on sketches of identifiable interiors, the finished paintings combine elements from different churches. What we cannot ignore, however, is that while the house may have been imagined, the effect is real, and it is above all one of extreme intimacy.

The furniture is not complicated; the padded chairs look comfortable but lack the fringes and embroidered material that were then popular in France. The rooms are *enfilade,* but the effect is not intimidating. The walls are plain, although they are typically adorned with a mirror, as well as with a map visible through the doorway. The stone floor is a simple pattern of black and white squares of marble. This is a well-to-do household—the musical instrument, the oriental carpet and the gilded mirror attest to that—but the atmosphere is not one of luxury. Objects are not on display; instead, we have the impression of a simple practicality from the way that the furnishings are arranged. The bed is located in a corner, behind the door; the rug is thoughtfully placed beside the bed, to take the morning chill off the cold stone floor. The mirror hangs over the virginals. The table and chairs sit next to the window, near the light. And what light! The rooms are illuminated to emphasize their depth and distance, as well as their physical, material reality. It is above all this sense of interior space, and hence of insideness, that distinguishes this painting. Instead of being a picture of a room, it is a picture of a home.

De Witte's true subject was the domestic atmosphere itself, which is the reason that this genre of painting was for so long dismissed as a minor one, and which is precisely why it is of interest here. De Witte was not, of course, the only practitioner of the domestic genre. Pieter de Hooch, a Delft neighbor, produced an entire oeuvre documenting the everyday life of the ordinary bourgeois. He showed them in their homes, usually at work, engrossed in some commonplace task, and he carefully depicted their houses and gardens with architectural accuracy. Unlike de Witte, he was less concerned with narrative and more interested in portraying an idealized domesticity. Although he subordinated the human figure to its background, his scenes always included one or two persons, usually women with children. During the Renaissance, when women had been solitary figures in a painting, it was as Madonnas, saints or biblical personages, the Dutch painters were the first to choose ordinary women as their subject. It was natural for women to be the focus of de Witte's paintings, because the domestic world that he was depicting had become *their* realm. The world of male work, and male social life, had moved elsewhere. The house had become the place for another kind of work—specialized domestic work—women's work. This work itself was nothing new, but its isolation was. Medieval paintings had always shown women at work, but they were rarely alone, and inevitably their work occurred amid the activities of men—people talking, eating, conducting business, or lounging about. De Hooch's women work alone, quietly.

Jan Vermeer, another Delft painter, was predominantly interested in the female human figure and less in the domestic interior, but since almost all his masterly paintings are set in the home, they also convey something of its character. His subjects act with a concentration that is mirrored in the still atmosphere of the room and its furnishings. Through Vermeer's paintings we can see how the house has changed: it has become a setting for private acts and personal moments. *The Love Letter* shows the mistress of the house being interrupted by her maid bringing her a letter. We can see the corner of an ornate fireplace, as well as a gilt leather wall panel and a seascape hanging on the wall (the last two items actually belonged to Vermeer). Ignoring the narrative clues—the letter, the mandolin, the seascape—what is most striking is the relationship between the two women sharing a private moment, and the way that Vermeer has placed us in another room, emphasizing the intimacy of the event and also achieving a sense of domestic space in a highly original way. The various objects in the home—a laundry basket, a broom, clothing, a pair of shoes—establish the predominance of the women in this space. The man, from whom the letter presumably comes, is far away; even if he were not he would have to tread warily on the freshly cleaned black-and-white-tiled marble floor. When a male is included in a Vermeer, one has the sense that he is a visitor—an intruder—for these women do not simply inhabit these rooms, they occupy them completely. Whether they are sewing, playing the spinet, or reading a letter, the Dutch women are solidly, emphatically, contentedly at home.

The feminization of the home in seventeenth-century Holland was one of the most important events in the evolution of the domestic interior. It had several causes, chief among them the limited use made of servants. Even the wealthiest household rarely employed more than three servants, while a typical prosperous bourgeois family included, at most, a single maidservant. Compare this to the Bruns, who had, in addition to their three employees, two servants, or to the typical British bourgeois family of that time which would have had at least half a dozen domestics. Dutch law was explicit on contractual arrangements and on the civil rights of servants, so that the relationship between employer and employee was less exploitive and closer than elsewhere in Europe; servants ate with their masters at the same table, for instance, and housework was shared instead of delegated. All this produced, for the seventeenth century, a remarkable situation: Dutch married women, irrespective of their wealth or social position, did most of their own household chores. It has been recorded that when the wife of Admiral de Ruyter was visited on the day after her husband's death by an envoy of the *stadhouder,* the Prince of Orange, she could not receive him, since she had recently sprained her ankle—while hanging out the laundry![22] When de Witte was commissioned to paint a wealthy burgher's wife, Adriana van Heusden, he depicted her shopping with her little daughter in an Amsterdam fish market. It would be impossible to imagine a wealthy French or English lady performing the same duty, or wishing to be immortalized in such prosaic surroundings.

Dutch married women had "the whole care and absolute management of all their Domestique," according to Temple.[23] This included taking charge of the cooking. Contemporary accounts by foreign visitors were clear on this point, although, particularly in the case of Frenchmen, characteristically disparaging remarks were made about the unsophisticated cuisine of the Dutch. However that might be, this small change had far-reaching consequences. When servants were doing the cooking, the room containing the kitchen was hardly differentiated from the other rooms, and was in any case accorded a secondary position. In Parisian bourgeois houses, for example, the kitchen occupied a room off the courtyard but without direct access to the main rooms. In English terrace houses the kitchen, adjacent to the servant quarters, continued to be located in the basement until the nineteenth century. In most *appartements* the "kitchen" was no more than a pot hanging in the fireplace.

In the Dutch home the kitchen was the most important room; according to one historian, "the kitchen was promoted to a position of fantastic dignity and became something between a temple and a museum."[24] Here were located the cupboards that held the prized table linens, china, and silver. Copper and brass utensils, brightly polished, hung on the walls. The chimney piece was enormous and elaborately decorated—overly so to modern tastes— and contained not only the hearth with the traditional hanging pot, but also a simple kind of stove. The sink was copper, sometimes marble. Some kitchens had interior hand pumps (one is visible in de Witte's painting) and even reservoirs with a continuous supply of hot water. The presence of such amenities signified the growing importance of domestic work and the premium that was beginning to be placed on convenience. This was natural. For the first time, the person who was in intimate contact with housework was also in a position to influence the arrangement and disposition of the home. Servants had to put up with inconvenient and ill-thought-out arrangements because they had no say in the matter. The mistress of the house, particularly when she was as independent-minded as the Dutch woman, did not.

The importance accorded the kitchen reflected the central position of the woman in the Dutch household. The husband may have been the head of the family and led the mealtime prayers, but in household matters he was no longer "master in his own house." It was the wife, not her husband, who insisted on cleanliness and tidiness, not the least because it was she who had to do the cleaning. This simple self-interest is a much more convincing explanation of the clean Dutch house than either climate or national character.

There are many examples of domestic order in Holland maintained by women. Smoking tobacco was popular among Dutch men, and their wives went to great lengths to keep the odor out of their homes. Some women even had "no smoking" clauses inserted into their marriage contracts; if all else failed they set aside a "smoking room" for their nicotic spouses. In any case, once a year the entire house was emptied for a major cleaning (this was in addition to the regular weekly washings). Men, forbidden access and deprived of hot meals, referred to this period as "hell." Formal parlors were also cleaned regularly, although they were used rarely. One burgher confessed to Temple that there were two rooms in his own house that he was not permitted to enter, and had never done so.[25] Although Dutch men continued to wear their hats at the table (except when saying grace) and rarely washed their hands before eating, the evolution of bourgeois—as opposed to courtly—manners had begun.

The imposition of a special code of behavior within the home was considered odd by foreign visitors, although that opinion may have been biased, since those visitors whose records have survived were exclusively male. Stories of the strictness, if not tyranny, of the Dutch mistress abounded; undoubtedly many were apocryphal. But they all pointed to a change in domestic arrangements. Not only was the house becoming more intimate, it was also, in the process, acquiring a special atmosphere. It was becoming a feminine place, or at least a place under feminine control. This control was tangible and real. It resulted in cleanliness, and in enforced rules, but it also introduced something to the house which had not existed before: domesticity.

To speak of domesticity is to describe a set of felt emotions, not a single attribute. Domesticity has to do with family, intimacy, and a devotion to the home, as well as with a sense of the house as embodying—not only harboring—these sentiments. It was the atmosphere of domesticity that permeated de Witte's and Vermeer's paintings. Not only was the interior a setting for domestic activity—as it had always been—but the rooms, and the objects that they contained, now acquired a life of their own. This life was not, of course, autonomous, but existed in the imagination of their owners, and so, paradoxically, homely domesticity depended on the development of a rich interior awareness, an awareness that was the result of the woman's role in the home. If domesticity was, as John Lukacs suggested, one of the principal achievements of the Bourgeois Age, it was, above all, a feminine achievement.[26]

Notes

1   G. N. Clark, *The Seventeenth Century* (Oxford: Clarendon Press, 1929), p. 14.

2   Steen Eiler Rasmussen, *Towns and Buildings: Described in Drawings and Words,* trans. Eve Wendt (Liverpool: University Press of Liverpool, 1951), p. 80.

3   Charles Wilson, *The Dutch Republic and the Civilization of the Seventeenth Century* (New York: McGraw-Hill, 1968), p. 30.

4   "Our national culture is bourgeois in every sense you can legitimately attach to that word." J. H. Huizinga, "The Spirit of the Netherlands," in *Dutch Civilization in the Seventeenth Century and Other Essays,* trans. Arnold J. Pomerans (London: Collins, 1968), p. 112.

5   J. H. Huizinga, "Dutch Civilization in the Seventeenth Century," in ibid., pp. 61–63.

6   N. J. Habraken, *Transformations of the Site* (Cambridge, Mass.: Awater Press, 1983), p. 220.

7   Paul Zumthor, *Daily Life in Rembrandt's Holland,* trans. Simon Watson Taylor (New York: Macmillan, 1963), pp. 45–46.

8   Ibid., p. 135.

9   Ibid., p. 100.

10   Philippe Ariès, *Centuries of Childhood: A Social History of the Family,* trans. Robert Baldick (New York: Knopf, 1962), p. 369..

11   Bertha Mook, *The Dutch Family in the 17th and 18th Centuries: An Explorative-Descriptive Study* (Ottawa: University of Ottawa Press, 1977), p. 32.

12   Petrus Johannes Blok, *History of the People of the Netherlands* Part IV, trans. Oscar A. Bierstadt (New York: AMS Press, 1970), p. 254.

13   Rasmussen, *Towns,* p. 80.

14   William Temple, *Observations upon the United Provinces of the Netherlands* (Oxford: Clarendon Press, 1972), p. 97.

15   Wilson, *Dutch Republic,* p. 244.

16   Quoted in Madlyn Millner Kahr, *Dutch Painting in the Seventeenth Century* (New York: Harper & Row, 1982), p. 259.

17   Quoted in Zumthor, *Daily Life,* p. 137.

18   Huizinga, *Dutch Civilization,* p. 63.

19   Temple, *Observations,* p. 80.

20   Blok, *History,* p. 256.

21   Quoted in Zumthor, *Daily Life,* pp. 53–54.

22   Ibid., pp. 139–40.

23   Temple, *Observations,* p. 89.

24   Zumthor, *Daily Life,* p. 41.

25   Ibid., p. 138

26   John Lukacs, "The Bourgeois Interior," *American Scholar*, Vol. 39, No. 4 (Autumn 1970), p. 624.

The Name of the Boudoir

Ed Lilley

INTRODUCTION

The emergence of the boudoir in the eighteenth century raised issues of gender, hierarchy, and space. In the following essay, Ed Lilley looks for reasons why the boudoir became a private space for women. Lilley walks us through the development and location of the boudoir to establish its seclusion from public areas, indicating that the boudoir was pushed to the periphery. At the same time, his analysis offers an alternative reading for the emergence and disappearance of the boudoir.

Lilley describes the use of the boudoir for changing clothes, practicing religion, and attending to one's "toilet." Because the boudoir emerged alongside romantic novels, Lilley proposes that it was also used as a place for women to read, that is, to gain knowledge. This space signified the need for female privacy that took on multiple interpretations depending on which gender was defining it. From a male perspective, Lilley raises an important question: "Why did women in the eighteenth century develop the need of a room in which to sulk? (Or maybe, why did men think that women needed such a space?)." The boudoir was seen as the "subspecies" of the male library or cabinet, not an equivalent. As the boudoir was placed at the end of a hierarchy of spaces, so too was its perception by men. Rather than make visible the notion that women were reading, and being seen as equals, it was easier to accept that women's activities only took place in private.*

These activities were located in contiguous rooms within the bedroom's sphere. Lilley conveys through floor plans the point at which these elongated thresholds—or rooms growing out of rooms—were no longer useful, and ultimately led to their disappearance.

The role of education for women in the eighteenth century helps explain the emergence of the boudoir as a female space and enters into the dialogue of programming room types. Lilley reminds us that our actions have an effect on the way we occupy rooms, even if they are not necessarily labeled as such; that room types can emerge from less-prescriptive agendas.

Originally appeared in *Journal of the Society of Architectural Historians* 53, no. 2 (June 1994): 193–98. © 1994 by the Society of Architectural Historians. Republished by permission from the University of California Press.

———

THIS ARTICLE ATTEMPTS to discover possible reasons for the emergence of the boudoir in eighteenth-century France. It acknowledges that there was a general increase in the desire for privacy, but seeks to determine why a space designed specifically for primarily female occupation should have appeared. Drawing particularly on the work of feminist historians, it seeks to situate the development of the boudoir in specific attitudes toward women at the time. While noting that the boudoir later became associated with illicit sexual liaisons, it suggests that the original reasons behind its development were more complex than might have been imagined to date. It charts the appearance of the term *boudoir* and the boudoir's apparently later arrival as a physical entity and raises questions as to why this particular name was used and what activities might originally have been envisaged for the room. The general aim is to situate the discussion of a concrete architectural entity in the context of a wider sphere to suggest that the boudoir emerged not simply as a result of changing style or architectural innovation, but as an intervention in a wider historical process.

> "Third dialogue [Madame de Saint-Ange, Eugénie, Dolmancé]
> The scene takes place in a delightful boudoir
>
> EUGÉNIE (Very surprised to see in this cabinet a man whom she was not expecting) 'Oh, God! My dear friend, this is a betrayal!'"[1]

In *La Philosophie dans le boudoir,* the Marquis de Sade reminds us, in his excessive way, that the boudoir was the *locus classicus* of sexual intrigue, although it is significant that in the title he further associates the room with something more cerebral, *philosophie* (in the sense of that term intended by the eighteenth-century *philosophes*). In this short extract, he also tells us rather more about the form and function of this quintessentially eighteenth-century space. He defines the boudoir as "delightful," and there is no shortage of texts and images to convince us that this room, ideally, was elegant and rather frivolous. The architect Le Camus de Mezières insisted that "the boudoir is regarded as the abode of sensual delight, where plans may be meditated and natural inclinations followed. It is essential for everything to be treated in a style in which luxury, softness and good taste predominate."[2] Sade defines the code that regulated who had access to this female-controlled venue. The occupant would certainly admit her "dear friend," and men were also allowed entrance, but only if they had been specifically invited. Dolmancé's penetration of the boudoir, which will lead to much worse horrors, is nothing less than a betrayal, perhaps even a treason.

The tone of libertinage survives, albeit transformed, in a much more sober analysis by a twentieth-century commentator. "It is fanciful to see the *philosophes* dissolutely chasing from 'boudoir' to 'boudoir,' or to think that all they wished for was the right to snigger at obscene pictures or to produce pornographic novels. The *philosophes* sought to break with the conventional—that is to say, Christian and bourgeois—morality because in their opinion it constrained and even degraded man's nature."[3] The juxtaposition of boudoir to sexuality remains, but Peter Gay insists in retaining the triad derived from the work of Sade: boudoir/sexuality/philosophy. Gay also sets the tone for the society in which the boudoir emerged; it was a challenging world in which radically revised concepts of desirable behavior were emerging. It seems that the boudoir was much more than a room: it generated discourse about sexual power relationships and was at the center of discussions about morality. The boudoir has become associated with light-hearted fictions of upper-class amorous dalliance, but it can, and arguably should, be treated rather more seriously. One should note the dates of both Sade's (1795) and Le Camus's (1780) works. By then the boudoir was firmly associated with luxury and sexual intrigue, but its genesis suggests other influences at work.

There is general agreement that rooms became increasingly function-specific during the eighteenth century. The process began earlier, but during the period of the Enlightenment, with its increasing insistence on the autonomy of the individual and a consequently augmented demand for privacy, new room-types developed, and new distribution meant that access to one room did not necessitate (as in the past) passage through several others. Recent research has shown that changes toward specificity and privacy spread a good way down the social scale, but my examination of the boudoir is limited to the most privileged residences, as only the homes of the economic and social elite contained such rooms.[4] For those lower down the socioeconomic scale, there remained the *ruelle* or alcove, a space next to the bed, if possible away from the door.[5] This intimate area had developed in the sixteenth century, but while it remained a valuable resource for those who lacked a private room, it is difficult to see it as the precursor to the boudoir since its function would have been multivarious. In this particular instance, as in a more general sense, "it was the interior of the aristocratic *hotel* which saw the most significant architectural innovations."[6]

There is no clear evidence as to when exactly the boudoir developed as a distinct location within the house, although the use of the term in texts predates, to my knowledge, its appearance on architectural plans. The word was certainly in existence by 1730, and some sources date its emergence to the Regency (1715–23), which may be the case, but this may also derive from a desire to have as contemporaneous a period noted for sexual license and a room associated with like practices.[7] I have not found it on plans before the 1760s, and it seems significant that it has no place in the relevant volume of d'Alembert and Diderot's *Encyclopédie* (1751), with its insistence on the up-to-date. This source includes a good deal of information on particular rooms, the most interesting of which, for my purposes, describes the *cabinet*: "Under this name one understands rooms dedicated to study or in which one conducts private business, or which contain the finest examples of one's collections of paintings, sculptures, books, curios, etc. One also calls *cabinets* those rooms in which ladies get dressed, attend to their devotions or take an afternoon nap, or those which they reserve for other occupations which demand solitude and privacy."[8] This is a revealing text, making it evident that, on one level, the boudoir emerged as a subspecies of the *cabinet*. The latter, in different forms, is designated for activities that demand privacy, itself an increasingly perceived need in the eighteenth century, but there is also a clear indication here that men and women have different needs for their private rooms. While a man might study, deal with his private business, or admire his collections, a woman might adorn herself, perform her religious duties, or rest. All of the activities so far mentioned might be performed most expeditiously when alone but they do not, of themselves, absolutely demand seclusion. It was, one might remember, quite normal at the time for women to receive visitors while attending to their *toilette*. All the male activities are spelled out clearly, but just what were the unspecified female occupations that demanded being alone? The insistence on solitude and contemplation suggests, in all probability, entirely respectable diversions, reading, for example, but the lack of detail might just allow a little space for the more questionable activities that later took place in boudoirs.

Turning from the text of the *Encyclopédie* to the evidence of architectural plans, the picture remains somewhat ambiguous. The classic arrangement of a woman's apartment might be suggested as that in Claude-Nicolas Ledoux's Pavilion Hocquart (1765), where the sequence of rooms is bedroom–dressing room–boudoir–wardrobe. Variations do exist, as in the same architect's palatial Hôtel Thélusson (late 1770s), where a suite runs wardrobe–bedroom–cabinet–boudoir, suggesting perhaps a differentiation between the polite activities of the study and the intrigues of the boudoir. Ledoux again shows his variety in the plan of the Hôtel d'Attily (late 1780s), where one can see bedroom–dressing room–boudoir or *cabinet*. The indecision over the last room would suggest uncertainty as to whether the rooms were to be occupied by a man or a woman. In an extremely expansive residence, a woman might enjoy both boudoir and *cabinet,* but there seems to be no evidence that men possessed boudoirs.

The etymology of the term boudoir should, at the outset, warn us against thinking of the room as primarily the location for illicit sexual

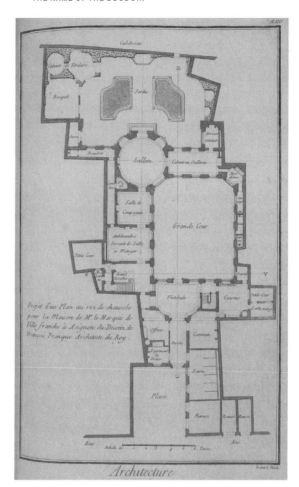

Fig. 6.8: François Franque, house for the marquis de Villefranche, Avignon. Plan of the ground floor from the *Recueil de planches* of the *Encyclopédie*, 1762, plate 25. The boudoir is left of the circular *sallon* top left, with windows giving on to the garden. The *méridienne* is to the right, separated from the *sallon* by the *cabinet en galerie*.
© The British Library Board.
65.g.6-66.g.4

liaisons. The edition of the *Dictionnaire de Trévoux,* published in 1752, has the following: "Small closet, very confined cabinet, adjacent to the room one normally occupies, apparently thus named because of the habit of retiring there, to sulk unseen, when one is in a bad mood."[9] There is not even the suggestion here that the boudoir is for female occupation, although the literary source used to situate the word chronologically does make this clear with its insistence on the feminine gender: "Becoming gloomy and dreamy, as if in your boudoir, / You deepened your dark mood until it turned to black."[10]

At this stage the boudoir is anything but the sumptuously decorated love nest of later literature and popular imagination. It is a strait space, useful for hiding one's black moods. Although the *Encydopédie* fails to record a term (and an entity) noted by a virtually contemporary dictionary, the boudoir does in fact occur in the former source, although admittedly in the plate volume, only published in 1762. [Fig. 6.8] Here, significantly, in the plan by

417

François Franque, it is not a commodious place of enchantment, but a narrow construction that only communicates directly with a corridor, the latter
being, of course, a prime enabler of privacy. Importantly, there is easy access
by stairs from the *cabinet* above, but the boudoir on this plan seems only susceptible to the activity described in the dictionary. A peculiarity of this early
boudoir design is the presence of a division within the room. In the smaller
of the two spaces thus created, there is a circle on the plan adjacent to the
exterior wall. This might indicate a latrine, but without written confirmation
it is impossible to be sure. In other buildings—for example, Ledoux's Hôtel
d'Attily—the boudoir does give directly on to a toilet, but here the two rooms
are obviously discrete spaces. The unusual layout in Franque's design further suggests a lack of precision about the use of the room. Intriguingly, the
plan separates out another function previously associated with the *cabinet,*
since almost opposite the boudoir is a small space designated a *méridienne.*
This space, interestingly, never became fashionable, perhaps because a further private room was seen as excessive. One authority has dated this plan to
as early as circa 1740, but I have found no evidence to confirm this date and
would hesitate to assign it to a time much earlier than that of publication.[11]
What seems to have happened, then, is that the perception of a need for a
boudoir predated its physical construction. Presumably some small space
was designated a boudoir and only later did such rooms feature *ab initio* on
architects' plans. Franque is following early thinking in showing a confined
space rather than the larger and often exotically shaped rooms that appeared
later. This evidence might argue for an early date for his plan, but it is not
conclusive.

One crucial problem now remains: why did women in the eighteenth
century develop the need of a room in which to sulk? (Or maybe, why did
men think that women needed such a space?) Franque's plan is helpful in
insisting on the need for a discrete space, but it was obviously not for taking a nap, as the *méridienne* served this purpose, and one cannot accurately
judge if it usurped some, or all, of the functions of the *cabinet.* The narrow
room looks about as suitable for amorous adventures as a telephone booth
(admittedly, however, there are specialized tastes), and we need to look elsewhere for further information. Some provisional answers may be suggested
by assessing the differing attitudes of and toward upper-class women in
mid-eighteenth-century France. It has been suggested that "the only indis-
putable marks of progress for women—aside from a growing freedom from
death in childbirth and, for poor women, from death from starvation—
appear to have been literacy and education."[12] Indeed, it was at precisely the
time of the development of the boudoir, around mid-century, that the watershed occurred in the educational process of women. Upper-class women
were increasingly abandoning their roles as courtiers and *salonnières* and

were taking more seriously their position as wives and mothers. As a result, one authority has suggested that "by the last half of the eighteenth century, noblewomen began to expect more out of marriage than a chance to be left alone."[13] This stress on sociability rather than solitude might seem to argue against the need for a private space such as a boudoir, but the implication must be that whereas noblewomen were previously casually neglected by their husbands, they increasingly became partners (if not equal partners) in a situation where they were accorded (or perhaps demanded) some room specifically for themselves. Why then call this space a boudoir?

The specified private female activities outlined in the *Encydopédie* were dressing, dozing, and devotions, but the other, unnamed, occupations that required solitude and meditation could certainly have included the increased number of educationally oriented pastimes such as reading. The very act of reading, certainly the development of silent, solitary reading, was in and of itself an indication of an increased concern for privacy. Reading quietly by oneself developed particularly quickly during the seventeenth century, but with the eighteenth-century emergence of the novel, for which there was initially a strong female readership, one may posit a connection between reading and the development of a private female space.[14] It now seems evident that education for aristocratic women became at least tolerated if it was confined to the private world of the home, although such opportunity for learning brought with it a perceived threat to the emerging world of professional male writers.[15] Elizabeth Fox-Genovese has another point about the new definition of wife and mother. "Conjugal domesticity and motherhood were gradually seen to offer the perfect molds within which to confine female sexuality and female authority. They also had the advantages of offering [upper-class] women a new and flattering image of themselves, control of their own sphere—however marginalized—and a model with which women of different social and economic backgrounds could identity."[16] These new opportunities and attitudes led to a complicated situation. On the one hand, women were becoming educated and they needed somewhere to pursue their learning; on the other hand, men felt threatened by women's new role and sought to limit its development and certainly to restrict it to the home. From this, it seems reasonable to proceed to the formulation that women could be allowed a space of their own, but those with the power (that is, men) would not dignify it with a title such as *cabinet d'étude de Madame* (*chamber à coucher de Madame* was common enough), but would call it a room to sulk in.

I have not been able to ascertain why, specifically, the term *boudoir* emerged rather than another neologism, although the tone smacks of male condescension. Leaving aside questions of education, the designation, even on an emotional level, is low-key. The lady has not retired to contain unbridled rage or passionate despair, but simply because she is a little moody.

The name could have originated with men seeking a derogatory term which would confine and disempower ideas of women's education, but the emotional resonance might suggest that it was connected with what some would now call premenstrual tension. The *Encyclopédie* sets out the symptoms clearly and notes that upper-class women, with their relative lack of physical exertion, suffered more from menstrual problems than those lower down the social scale.[17] Sulking and the need for retirement can, of course, have many causes, and may affect men as well as women, but if this room, designed for female privacy, was named by men, then the nomenclature may even have resulted from their received ideas of what occasioned female moodiness.

Women could, and presumably did, use their boudoirs for a variety of occupations, but the term quickly became associated specifically with sexual pleasure. It was surely the licentious association that made a nineteenth-century manual of etiquette decree: "The *chambre ornée* became the *cabinet,* and this name is still used by people of good taste, although decorators, chambermaids, and the *nouveaux riches,* as well as guides to the royal palaces, never fail to call this room a boudoir."[18] No purpose would be served in this context by detailing the numerous adventurous couplings that took place in boudoirs in eighteenth-century fiction, but one minor text, Jean-François de Bastide's *La petite maison,* is worthy of mention.[19] In this short story, the marquis de Trémicour wagers Mélite that she will no longer be able to resist him once she has visited his "little house" ("little" proves to be a relative term). Mélite is given a guided tour, much in the manner of a nineteenth-century or present-day tour through a royal palace, but here the aim is seduction, not edification or diversion. The young woman is particularly taken with the boudoir, which Bastide describes in some detail. "All the walls were hung with mirrors, and the joints of the latter were covered with artificial trees carved with great skill into leafy patterns. These trees were arranged in such a manner that they seemed to form a quincunx. They were strewn with flowers and hung with chandeliers, the candles of which provided a graduated light because of the cunning disposition, at the end of the room, of gauze hangings, either tightly stretched or hanging loose over the mirrors. This artifice was so successful that one could imagine oneself in a natural wood, illuminated by the forces of art. The niche which contained the ottoman, a sort of day bed, had a parquet floor of rosewood and was decorated with green and gold fringes and strewn with different-sized cushions. The wall and ceiling of the niche were also covered with mirrors. Finally, all the woodwork and plaster was painted in the colors appropriate to what it represented, this color having been applied by Dandrillon, so that it gave off the scent of violets, jasmine, and roses."[20] This description is so close to that provided by Le Camus de Mezières in his *Le Génie de l'architecture* that it seems evident that he drew from the textual source rather than from an architectural one.[21] Written and visual descriptions alike, however, tend to stress the elaboration and sumptuousness of the boudoir. It is difficult to see such places as suitable for business or study, as Mélite was to discover. "Mélite was in an ecstatic trance. She examined the boudoir for more than a quarter of an hour, but if she was silent, her heart did not stop talking; it warned against those men who engage the talents of others to express a sentiment that they themselves are incapable of putting across."[22] The house is the active seducer, not the marquis, but Mélite resists the erotic insistence of the boudoir, despite being totally overcome. Thereafter the couple eat in a marvellous dining room and then comes the *coup de grâce*. Mélite moves into the *pièce de résistance* (or nonresistance)—a second boudoir. "The threat was dreadful and the situation even worse...Mélite trembled, became confused, sighed, and lost the wager."[23]

The association of the boudoir with seduction is commonplace, but Mélite does not pause to consider what might be the boudoirs' purpose in the marquis's house. These boudoirs must surely imply some pre-existing female occupation which, had she stopped to think, might have given her pause. That she nevertheless succumbs gives further weight to the idea of the house, rather than Trémicour, as the active principle, but it remains a bizarre reversal. In this instance, at least, the boudoir signifies sexual activity so strongly that the woman does not stop to consider whose space it is. This is an invasion as transgressive as that of Dolmancé in Sade.

Those great advocates of a feminine eighteenth century, the Goncourt brothers, have surprisingly little to say about the boudoir. One might have imagined that they would have recounted tales of "boudoir diplomacy" or "boudoir politics," to stress the behind-the-scenes power that they count women as having had. In fact, and this is perhaps more consistent with their general stance, they describe a more powerful situation: "And some women had, to accommodate their pleasure, little houses just the same as the little houses of the *roués,* little houses for which they themselves arranged the purchase and engaged the gate-keeper, in order that everyone would be obliged to them and so that nothing could discommode them, even if they chose to cheat on their lover."[24] Such "little houses" were evidently very different from Bastide's and show that some women, at least, did not have to rely on the controlled atmosphere of the boudoir for their pleasure.

Discourse on the boudoir has until now comprehended material from architectural history, social history, and literature (to name the main components), but the latter has provided the dominant tone. It is very difficult to think of a boudoir without imagining something like the scene depicted in Nicolas Lavreince's *L'heureux moment*. [Fig. 6.9] Beneath a painting of Cupid, an elegantly dressed woman in a revealing gown sits on a sofa while an equally elegant man, down on one knee before her, makes ready to embrace

Fig. 6.9: Nicolas
Lavreince, *L'heureux
moment*. Engraved by
Nicolas De Launay,
circa 1778. Bibliothèque
nationale de France

her. This is the boudoir as signifier of an eighteenth century in which hand-some gentlemen dally with gorgeous ladies in sumptuous interiors, all the while hoping that their spouses do not come in and ruin everything. Assuredly this image is not just a fiction, although it is equally sure that there was in the eighteenth century, as in others, more sex in art than in life; still, to take this as the boudoir's defining image seems shortsighted. The boudoir was not the only gender-specific room in the eighteenth-century home.[25] But this factor, together with its association with privacy and its place in the erotic imagination, make it uniquely determined and worth more investigation than is provided by this introduction, which attempts to sketch the pre-liminaries of a possible new approach to the study of the boudoir.

Notes

*   Ed Lilley, "The Name of the Boudoir," *Journal of the Society of Architectural Historians* v.53 n.2 (June 1994): 195.

1   Donatien Alphonse François, marquis de Sade, *Oeuvres complètes*, ed. Gilbert Lely, 16 vols. (Paris, 1966–67), 3:381. "Troisieme dialogue [Madame de Saint-Ange, Eugénie, Dolmancé] La scène est dans un boudoir délicieux EUGÉNIE (très

surprise de voir dans ce cabinet un homme qu'elle n'attendait pas) 'Oh! Dieu, ma chère amie, c'est une trahison!'" *La philosophie dans le boudoir* is not normally classed with Sade's theatrical works, but it is set out in the manner of a play, with lists of characters and stage directions, as above. All translations are by the author, unless otherwise stated.

2 Nicolas Le Camus de Mezières, *Le Génie de l'architecture* (Paris, 1780). Quoted in Jean Starobinski, *The Invention of Liberty,* trans. Bernard C. Swift (Geneva, 1964), 56.

3 Peter Gay, *The Party of Humanity* (London, 1964), 137.

4 Annik Pardailhé-Galabrun, The *Birth of Intimacy, Privacy and Domestic Life in Early Modern Paris,* trans. Jocelyn Phelps (Cambridge, 1991).

5 Orest Ranum, "The Refuges of Intimacy," in *A History of Private Life,* ed. Philippe Ariès and Georges Duby, 5 vols. (Cambridge, Mass., 1987–90), 3:207–63.

6 Monique Eleb-Vidal and Anne Debarre-Blanchard, *Architectures de la vie privée* (Brussels, 1989), 50. "C'est l'intérieur de l'hôtel aristocratique qui est alors le champ privilégié des innovations architecturales."

7 The *Dictionnaire universel françois et latin* (Paris, 1752), commonly known as the *Dictionnaire de Trévoux,* notes its appearance in the work of Jean-Antoine du Cerceau, who died in 1730. The *Grand Dictionnaire Encyclopédique Larousse* (Paris, 1982), suggests that the term dates from the Regency.

8 Denis Diderot and Jean Le Rond d'Alembert, *Encyclopédie,* 33 vols. plus supplements (Paris, 1751–77), 2:488. "Sous ce nom on peut entendre les pièces destinées à l'étude ou dans lesquelles l'on traite d'affaires particulières, ou qui contiennent ce que l'on a de plus précieux en tableaux, en bronzes, livres, curiosités, etc. On appelle aussi cabinet, les pièces où les dames font leur toilette, leur oratoire, leur méridienne, ouautres qu'elles destinent à des occupations qui demandent du recueillement et de la solitude."

9 *Dictionnaire universel,* "Petit réduit, cabinet fort étroit, auprès de la chambre qu'on habite, ainsi nommé apparemment, parce qu'on a coutume de s'y retirer, pour bouder sans témoin, lorsqu'on est de mauvaise hurneur."

10 "Tantôt sombre et rêveuse, et comme en ton boudoir, Tu renfonçois ton gris, et me montrois ton noir." Jean-Antoine du Cerceau (1670–1730) was a Jesuit who passed the principal part of his career at the collège Louis-le-Grand in Paris. He was employed as a tutor to young noblemen and wrote plays and poems. I have not been able to trace the source of the couplet in which he refers to the boudoir.

11 Wend Graf Kalnein and Michael Levey, *Art and Architecture of the Eighteenth Century in France* (Harmondsworth, 1972), 268. Born in 1710, Franque would have been of an age to have made the plan in 1740, but Kalnein's suggestion lacks acceptable proof Blondel was an admirer of Franque, but the fact that there is no mention of a boudoir in Blondel's monumental *Architecture françoise,* 4 vols. (Paris, 1752–56) makes one doubt that it was in regular use in the architectural world at this date.

12 Elizabeth Fox-Genovese, "Introduction," in *French Women and the Age of Enlightenment,* ed. Samia I. Spencer (Bloomington, Ind., 1984), 1–29, esp. 19.

13 Cissie Fairchild, "Women and Family," 97–110, esp. 98, in Spencer, ed., *French Women.*

14 Roger Chartier, "The Practical Impact of Writing," in Ariès and Duby, eds., *A History of Private Life* (see n. 5), 3:111–59.

15 Fox-Genovese, "Introduction" (see n. 12), 13.

16 Ibid., 16.

17 Diderot and d'Alembert, *Encyclopédie* (see n. 8), 14:26.

18 Comtesse de Brady, *Du savoir-vivre en France au XIXe siècle* (1844). Quoted in Eleb-Vidal and Debarre-Blanchard, *Architectures* (see n. 6), 236–38. "La chambre ornée prit le nom de cabinet, et ce nom lui est encore conservé par les gens de bon goût tandis que les tapissiers, les femmes de chambre et les nouveaux initiés à la magnificence ainsi que les hommes de livrée qui montrent les maisons royales ne manquent jamais de désigner cette pièce sous le nom de boudoir."

19 Jean-François de Bastide, *La petite maison* (Paris, 1879). According to the preface of this nineteenth-century edition, Bastide's story was first published in the *Journal oeconomique* in 1753 or 1754 and was reprinted in the *Nouveau spectateur,* vol. 2 (1758–59) before appearing in Bastide's collected *Contes* (Paris, 1763).

20 Bastide, *La petite maison,* 14–15. "Toutes les murailles en sont revêtues de glaces, et les joints de celles-ci masqués par des troncs d'arbres artificiels, mais sculptés, massés et feuillés avec un art admirable. Ces arbres sont disposés de manière qu'ils semblent former un quinconce; ils sont jonchés de fleurs et chargés de girandoles dont les bougies procurent une lumière graduée dans les glaces, par le soin qu'on a pris, dans le fond de la pièce, d'étendre des gazes plus ou moins serrées sur ces corps transparens, magie qui accorde si bien avec l'effet de l'optique que l'on croit être dans un bosquet naturel éclairé par le secours de l'art. La niche où est placée l'ottomane, espèce de lit de repos qui pose sur un parquet de bois de rose à compartimens, est enrichie de crépines d'or mêlées de verd et garnie de coussins de différens calibres. Tout le pourtour et le plafond de cette niche sont aussi revêtus de glaces; enfin la menuiserie et la sculpture en sont peintes d'une couleur assortie aux différens objets qu'elles représentent, et cette couleur a encore été appliquée par Dandrillon, de manière qu'elle exhale la violette, le jasmin et la rose."

21 See Starobinski, *Liberty* (see n. 2), 56–57.

22 Bastide, *La petite maison,* 16–17. "Mélite étoit ravie en extase. Depuis plus d'un quart d'heure qu'elle parcouroit ce boudoir, sa langue étoit muette, mais son coeur ne se taisoit pas: il murmuroit en secret contre les hommes qui mettent à contribution tous les talens pour exprimer un sentiment dont ils sont si peu capables."

23 Bastide, *La petite maison,* 46. "La ménace étoit terrible, et la situation encore plus. Mélite frémit, se troubla, soupira, et perdit la gageure."

24 Edmond and Jules de Goncourt, *La Femme au dix-huitième siecle,* ed. E. Badinter (Paris, 1982), 159–60. This book was originally published in 1862. "Et les femmes auront, pour loger leur plaisir, des petites maisons pareilles aux petites maisons des *roués,* des petites maisons dont elles feront elles-mêmes le marché d'achat, dont elles choisiront le portier, afin que tout y soit à leur dévotion et que rien ne les gêne si elles veulent y aller tromper leur amant même."

25 Eleb-Vidal and Debarre-Blanchard, *Architectures* (see n. 6), 58, notes that the *chambre de parade* was where, specifically, the woman of the house received guests on grand ceremonial occasions.

Closets, Clothes, disClosure

Henry Urbach

INTRODUCTION

Henry Urbach uncovers the dual meaning of the closet as an architectural container and metaphoric location to conceal sexual identity. A parallel is drawn between these two meanings, the closet as a place of demarcation where one side of the threshold conceals and the other reveals. Urbach views the closet as a container for putting away what is not needed or wanted for display in order to make a clean room. Similarly, society stuffs homosexual identity in the closet, hence the phrase "coming out of the closet."

Urbach outlines an overview of the closet's evolution in the nineteenth century, from its origin as freestanding armoires and chests for storage to being separated from a room and absorbed into walls. Where the wall was once a solid line represented as poché on architectural plans, it then became a wall compartment, unprogrammed space, a cavity with personal items associated with identity. With the loss of highly particularized spaces such as the boudoir and cabinet, the closet became the substitute interior space for possessions. The boudoir and cabinet, typically associated with female and male, respectively, were large enough to be occupied intimately and concealed enough to be the originating source site of intrigue and scandal. The modern closet is reduced in scale and character.

To expand the closet's theoretical space, Urbach finds a solution in the space of the door swing, or "ante-closet," "an interstitial space that appears, disappears, and reappears again and again."* Urbach grounds the door swing in the language of architecture by noting its representation as an arc, but also identifies it as "a space of changing" and "a moment of graphic folding."† By aligning space and action, Urbach locates an appropriate—though formerly almost invisible—psychoanalytic context for defining the meaning of the fold in interiors.

In the conceptual drawing practice of interiors, the fold is the place of architectural motion, such as the door swing versus the static lines of walls, floors, and ceilings. If interiors can be defined as a space of change, owing to

Originally appeared in *Assemblage*, no. 30 (1996): 62–73. The MIT Press. © 1996 by the Massachusetts Institute of Technology.

ease of retrofitting, whether through refashioning or a change in occupants, the fold itself situates this space of social and relational alteration. Urbach offers this parallel reading of the closet and the potential that overlooked perimeter rooms contain.

———

THE WORD *CLOSET* holds two distinct but related meanings. On the one hand, a closet is a space where things are stored. In this regard, we might say, "Your clothes are in the closet." But when we observe that "Joe has been in the closet for years," we are concerned less with his efforts to match trousers and tie than with how he reveals his identity to others. In this sense, the closet refers to the way that identity, particularly gay identity, is concealed and disclosed. Concealed *and* disclosed because gay identity is not quite hidden by the closet, but not quite displayed either. Rather, it is represented through coded gestures that sustain the appearance of uncertainty.

These two closets are not as different as they might appear. Taken together, they present a related way of defining and ascribing meaning to space. They both describe sites of storage that are separated from, and connected to, spaces of display. Each space excludes but also needs the other. The non-room, the closet, houses things that threaten to soil the room. Likewise, in a social order that ascribes normalcy to heterosexuality, the closet helps heterosexuality to present itself with authority. The stability of these arrangements—a clean bedroom free of junk and a normative heterosexuality free of homosexuality—depends on the architectural relation between closet and room.

The two closets resonate against one another within a linguistic and material network of representations that organize the relation between storage and display, secrecy and disclosure. The sexual closet refers, through an operation of metaphor, to the familiar architectural referent. The built-in closet, in turn, petrifies and disseminates, as architectural convention, the kind of subjectivity described by the homosexual closet. The built-in closet concretizes the closet of identity, while the closet of identity literalizes its architectural counterpart.

Despite their overlapping meanings in the present, the two closets bear histories that remain distinct and irreducible. We will take each of these in turn, beginning with the built-in closet and focusing in particular on the clothes closet, even though closets have also been used for storing linens, cleaning supplies, and other provisions. The closet we know today was invented as a new spatial type in America around 1840. For centuries, Europeans and North Americans had stored clothing in furniture; sometimes it hung from wall pegs or hooks. Now, for the first time, a wall cavity was produced for household storage. Briskly disseminated among all social classes, the closet effectively outmoded wardrobe, armoire, and chest. These freestanding, mobile cabinets (which still exist, but without the same primacy) had encased clothing within the precinct of the room. Now, the place of storage was at, or more precisely beyond, the room's edge.

Armoires, chests, and the like are volumetric objects with unambiguous spatial presence. They display locks or key holes to indicate their hollow interior along the outside surface. Moreover, these cabinets are ornamental objects, often lavished with paint, carving, and inlay. Freestanding, upright, and decorated, they evoke the clothed human body. By contrast, the closet displays itself more surreptitiously. It relies on the spatial effects of the hollow wall to present itself as not quite there.

From the moment of its first appearance, the closet not only concealed its contents, but also (almost) hid itself. Numerous mid-nineteenth-century American "pattern books" treat the closet as an obvious but irrelevant fact of domestic planning. In *Cottage Residences,* first published in 1842, Andrew Jackson Downing describes the closet as follows:

> The universally acknowledged utility of closets renders it unnecessary for us to say anything to direct attention to them under this head. In the principal story, a pantry or closets are a necessary accompaniment to the dining room or living room, but are scarcely required in connection with any of the other apartments. Bedrooms always require at least one closet to each, and more will be found convenient.[1]

As spaces that merely *accompany* fully described rooms, closets are outlined in plan drawings but not otherwise elaborated. [Fig. 6.10] This is also the case with Samuel Sloan's *The Model Architect* of 1852. Although Sloan lavishes attention on myriad aspects of house planning and construction, he mentions closets only in passing to say that they must be "fitted up and fully shelved."[2] Their height, ventilation, light, surface treatment, and other spatial qualities are not discussed at all. In these mid-nineteenth-century texts (not to mention constructed domestic space and subsequent architectural historiography), the closet was barely visible.

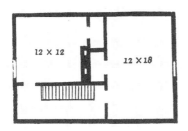

Fig. 6.10: Second-floor plan for a laborer's cottage, 1850.
Reprinted from Andrew Jackson Downing, *The Architecture of Country Houses.*
New York: DaCapo Press, 1968, page 75.

Concealing the storage of clothes and other possessions, the closet may have served to address a widespread ambivalence about material acquisition and the accumulation of excess wealth. This ambivalence appears clearly in an 1882 lecture by Harriet Beecher:

> The good sense of the great majority of business men—and women— is in favor of enterprise, and of that frugality and economy which shall result in amassing property....And yet there exists at the same time in the community...a vague sense of the unspirituality of the treasures of this life, and of the dangers that inhere in them, together with some sort of conscience—they know not what—or fear.[3]

For Americans of the period, encountering an expanding industrial economy alongside the resurgence of Christian morality, wealth had come to represent both virtue and decadence. It could be amassed but not comfortably shown. In this context, it seems, Americans looked to the closet to moderate display without diminishing actual possession.

The closet worked, along with other architectural strategies, to advance an extensive reform movement that aimed to invest the American home with signs of moral propriety. Increasingly strict codes of behavior were given architectural form as, for instance, the stairway to second-floor bedrooms moved out of the entrance hall to a less prominent position. Likewise, programs and spaces once joined were separated into discrete rooms with distinct degrees of privacy. At a wide range of architectural scales, efforts mounted to moderate the visibility of spaces now deemed private. Downing proposed that "the ideal" of domestic planning was to keep "each department of the house...complete in itself, and intruding itself but little on the attention of the family or guests when not required to be visible."[4] Consistent with other transformations of the American house, in a relatively small but powerful way, the closet helped people to put things away without getting rid of them.

Holding clothes in abeyance, the closet not only hid "excess" in general terms, but, more specifically, the sartorial multiplicity of the wardrobe. If a person's various garments offer a kind of repertory for self-representation, the closet served to ensure, instead, that only those garments worn at any particular moment would be visible. In this way, one's outfit could gain singular legitimacy, unchallenged by the other clothes tucked away in the wall. The closet contained the overflow of garments and their meanings to heed Downing's maxim, a statement that neatly captures the spatial thrust of the era: "The great secret of safe and comfortable living lies in keeping yourself and everything about you in the right place."[5]

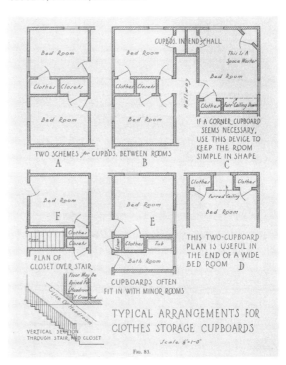

Fig. 6.11: Plans of clothes storage cupboards, ca. 1940. Reprinted from Wooster Bard Field, *House Planning*. New York: McGraw-Hill, 1940.

In the course of the last century and a half, the architecture of the closet has sustained a particularly strict relation between closet and room. Regardless of adjacent conditions, the closet usually opens to a single room—a room it is said to be "in"—even though it is actually *next to* this room or between one room and another. In general, closets receive neither anterior nor lateral expression. Windows or doors rarely appear at the rear or side of the closet, even though they might serve to admit light and air as well as passage.[6] A relationship of faithful codependence thus emerges between closet and room. The room relies exclusively on its closet and the closet communicates uniquely with its room.

The threshold between closet and room mediates their relation, simultaneously connecting and dissociating the two spaces. Although the closet door may take many forms (among them, sliding, pocket, and hinged single or double doors), the door always shuts to conceal the interior of the closet and opens to allow access. Moreover, the door is usually articulated to minimize its own visibility, often set flush or painted to match the surrounding wall. As much as possible, the closet presents itself as an absence, a part of the (not so) solid wall at the room's edge. According to a domestic planning manual from the 1940s: "Closets should not interfere with main areas of activity in a house. They should be accessible but inconspicuous."[7]
[Fig. 6.11]

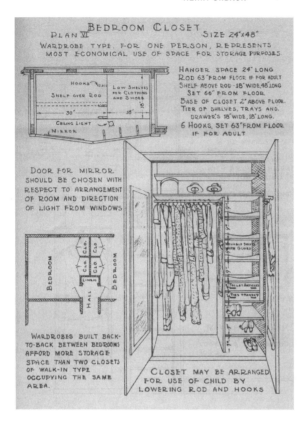

Fig. 6.12: Bedroom closet for one person, ca. 1934. Reprinted from Maud M. Wilson, *Closets and Other Storage Arrangements for the Farm Home.* Washington, D.C.: U.S. Department of Agriculture, Bureau of Home Economics, 1934.

The tension between visual concealment and physical access has driven the architectural elaboration of the closet/room pair. But, despite its formidable architectural strength, it fails to contain the tension exerted by contrary imperatives: storage versus display, keeping things hidden versus keeping things handy. The closet, in the end, can only be so inconspicuous. The door cannot help but hint at the space beyond its planar surface. There is always some seam, gap, hinge, knob, or pull that reveals the door as a mobile element and the wall as a permeable boundary. Furthermore, the door displays the presence of the closet beyond by setting parameters for decorating and furnishing the room. One does not, for example, place furniture in front of a closet door as though it were part of the wall. [Fig. 6.12]

Holding things at the edge of the room, at once concealing and revealing its interior, the closet becomes a carrier of abjection, a site of *interior* exclusion for that which has been deemed dirty. Julia Kristeva's psychoanalytic and sociocultural analysis of abjection examines how things that are considered dirty and therefore subject to exclusion are never fully eliminated. Rather, they are deposited just beyond the space they simultaneously soil and cleanse. This partial elimination, this spatial juxtaposition, keeps present that which has been deemed dirty so it can constitute, by contrast, the cleanliness of the clean.[8]

It is with this in mind that we can understand the peculiar architecture of the closet/room pair, along with its urgency for mid-nineteenth-century Americans and its continuing presence. Closet and room work together to keep the room clean and the closet messy, to keep the contents of the room proper and those of the closet abject. They do not eliminate dirt, but hide it in plain sight across a boundary that is also a threshold, a doorway that undermines their separation while stabilizing their difference.

The closet of sexual secrecy, named after the built-in closet, existed long before it was first called "the closet." For at least a century, as Eve Sedgwick, D. A. Miller, and others have demonstrated, the closet was a social and literary convention that narrated homosexuality as a spectacle of veiled disclosure.[9] The closet was the late-nineteenth-century device by which "the love that dare not speak its name" could be spoken and vilified. It served a larger social project committed, as Michel Foucault has shown, to establishing homo- and heterosexuality as distinct and unequal categories of identity. Instead of polymorphic sexual practices, there was now a taxonomy of new sexual types. In Foucault's account, "the sodomite had been a temporary aberration; the homosexual was now a species."[10]

The closet organized homosexual identity as an open secret, a telling silence. Like the wall seams and door pulls that betray the closet, the absence of wedding bands and other positive assertions of heterosexuality would effectively raise the specter of gay identity even without forthright disclosure. One could neither be fully legible nor fully invisible as homosexual; instead, secrecy would reveal a condition not otherwise stated.

"Heterosexuality" cast its abject other into the (yet-unnamed) closet, at once nearby and far-off, hidden and accessible. Positioned in this way, the category of homosexuality accrued all the fantasmatic impropriety required by heterosexuality to secure its own proper domain, the idealized sanctity of its own, tidy bedroom.[11] Excluded, but always just over there, homosexuality was identified with promiscuity and degeneracy. By contrast, heterosexuality was identified with procreation, fidelity, and true love.

Despite its presence throughout the early part of this century, the homosexual closet was not named as such before the 1960s. The term "closet," in this sense, arose in America during the period of political foment that produced, among other events, the Stonewall riots of June 1969. The nascent gay rights movements identified the closet as a tool of homophobic violence and advanced a new battle cry: "Out of the closets! Into the streets!"

From then on, "coming out" has been understood as the origin of gay identity, the sine qua non of physical security, legal protection, and social dignity. "Coming out" is imagined, rather naïvely, as a way of rejecting the closet and its hold on gay self-representation. And, indeed, within the regime of (almost) compulsory heterosexuality, the personal and political value of coming out must not be underestimated. But its effects on the architecture of the closet should not be overstated. Where heterosexuality is presumed, coming out can never be accomplished once and for all. As Sedgwick has argued, the sustenance of gay identity (where straight identity is presumed) depends on continuous acts of declaration.[12] To reveal gay identity in one situation does not obviate the need to reveal it again in the next. Every new acquaintance, every new situation demands a repetition of, or retreat from, disclosure.

For the past century, then, imagining an opposition of "in" and "out," gay identity has found itself in a double bind. Wherever one is, relative to the closet, one risks *both* exposure and erasure. But the binary logic of the closet/room pair, the rigid opposition of in and out, does not account for the dynamic entanglement of these spaces, the ways in which they constantly separate and reattach, the ways in which one is always *both* in and out, *neither* in nor out. This binary obsession has radically constricted the ways that gay people feel they can "disclose," rather than perform, identity.[13]

To come out and declare "I am gay"—whether to another person or to oneself—is to submit to a host of ideological imperatives: self-unity ("I"); immutability over time ("am"); and the given characterization ("gay"). These are crude and brittle words, unable to capture the diachronicity and multivalence of identity and sexuality as played out in social space. Performer k. d. lang seemed aware of this when, shortly after coming out in the national media, she appeared on the Radio City Music Hall stage, took the mike, and gingerly teased her audience: "I…AM…(by now, soap bubbles had begun to fill the stage)…A…LLL…L…L…LL…LLLL…LLL…LLLLLLL… Lawrence Welk fan."

Gay people have learned to work with and against the closet, since its invention more than a century ago. Toying with the architecture of the closet and its codes of disclosure, k. d. points toward the possibility of manipulating language—verbal and sartorial codes alike—to elaborate "identity" as a lively, ongoing process of signification. This is something Mikhail Bakhtin theorized in his model of language as a site of social contest. The word, for Bakhtin, becomes "one's own" only when the speaker populates it with his or her own accent and adapts it to his or her own semantic intention.[14] Consider, then, the reinvention of the once derogatory "queer," "fag," and "dyke" as affirmative terms. Or the practice, widespread among gay men during the 1970s, of displaying a colored handkerchief in the rear jeans pocket. Appropriated from the uniform of laborers, the handkerchief served not only to display sexual orientation but also to indicate, with considerable nuance, particular sexual interests. Extending from the inside of the pocket to the outside of the trousers, the handkerchief also recapitulated, at the scale of the body, the larger spatial relation governing the storage and display of gay identity.

In recent years, gay people have learned to rearticulate other, more overtly homophobic codes of dress: (macho) tattoos, (Nazi) pink triangle, (gym teacher) hooded sweatshirt, (military) crew cut, (femme fatale) lipstick, and (skinhead) Doc Marten boots. These gestures of *détournement*— when done well, and before they ossify into new norms—underscore the relation of homo- and heterosexualities without necessarily adopting the violence and inequity of their opposition. They are simultaneously effects of the closet and moments of its loosening.

The impressive architectural stability of the closet notwithstanding, it did not always, and need not, describe a spatiality so rigid. A wide range of spatial practices, including architectural scholarship and design, offer opportunities to redress, provoke, and reconfigure the relation of closet and room. Working with and against the closure of the closet, it is possible to produce an expanded space between closet and room. Here, in this realm marked by the interpenetration of dirty and clean, of storage and display, new architectures of "identity" may emerge.

Long before the built-in closet was invented, there was another kind of closet, a very different kind of space. From the late fourteenth through the nineteenth centuries, the closet referred, in terms both architectural and social, to an inhabitable room. In England and much of continental Europe, the "closet" (or its analogue, such as the French *grand cabinet*) described a place for retreat, prayer, study, or speculation.[15] It served not only as a private sanctuary, but also as a special repository for both storage and display of books, paintings, and other treasured objects.

During the fifteenth century in England, a closet particular to royal residences emerged. Closely associated with the private apartments of the sovereign or other nobility, this closet referred to a chamber used for retreat, writing, contemplation, small receptions, and religious activities.[16] At Hampton Court, "holy-day closets" were added in 1536 to provide the king, queen, and their invited guests with semiprivate spaces of worship apart from the court.[17] Eventually, "closet" came to refer to the pew occupied by a lord and his family in the chapel of a castle. Through its various incarnations, the royal closet provided privacy, but also allowed for gathering and interaction with others.

An intimate retreat, a space for gathering, a wall cavity used for storage, a condition of gay secrecy: in what ways can the "closet" continue to unfold, opening itself to other spatial forms, uses, and meanings? Consider this: extending from the inside of the closet door frame to some distance in front of the closet, there is an interstitial space that appears, disappears, and reappears again and again. Where the door slides or folds, the space is not so deep but, in the case of the ordinary hinged door, it is a space of considerable dimension. This is a space I call the *ante-closet,* the space before the closet. The ante-closet is where one selects clothes. It is the space of changing.

I recall my discovery of the ante-closet when I was a young boy. There, standing before a built-in closet, I learned something about my own representational range. To be frank, this did not happen in front of my own closet, not the closet filled with the clothes little boys wore in New Jersey in the late 1960s. Instead, it was in my parents' room, in-between the hinged doors to my mother's closet, that I first found and learned to occupy this important little space.

On the inside surface of both doors was a tall mirror lit by delicate, vertically mounted fluorescent tubes. I remember pushing the switch as the lights flickered and hummed, then positioning the doors so the mirrors reflected space, and me, to infinity. Before removing my own clothing, I carefully selected an outfit from my mother's wardrobe—dress, shoes, necklace, handbag. The transformation was brief and private, as I never chose to display my new look to others. But it was a privacy that was profoundly limitless, a moment where self and other became completely entangled. The paired mirrors redoubled every gesture to infinity as I saw myself, in a moment of utter plenitude, transformed: grown-up, autonomous, and lovely.

Nowadays, despite my more gender-consonant wardrobe, I continue to extend my representational range in the ante-closet. Between the closet and the room, in this ephemeral space, I explore the effects of sartorial gestures and imagine their significance to others. Respectable merino cardigan? Raw leather tunic? Mao jacket? Velour cigarette pants? Where the ante-closet contains a mirror, I am able to consider these modes of identification visually, as others might see them. Where there is no mirror, I rely instead on memory and imagination. Private and social realms interpenetrate as the line between what I hide and what I show breaks down and I start to see myself as someone else.

The ante-closet can be further elaborated with reference to Gilles Deleuze's notion of the *pli* or fold. The *pli* is a space that emerges, both within and against social relations, to constitute a space of self-representation at once connected to and free from social norms. In the *pli,* Deleuze writes, "the relation to oneself assumes an independent status. It is as if the relations of the outside, folded back to create a doubling, allow a relation to oneself to emerge, and constitute an inside which is hollowed out and develops its own unique dimension."[18] The *pli* is not a secure idyll, but it is, provisionally, an enclave. Social codes, inequities, and violence penetrate the *pli* through and through, and yet it remains possible, in this space, to work with them. In the *pli*, the representational range of clothing, the multivalence of sexualities and identities, does not threaten and therefore does not need to be foreclosed.

The ante-closet has a curious status in architectural drawings, conventionally rendered as a kind of graphic interruption. The notation for "door swing" is an arc that traces the passage of the unhinged edge from open to shut. Whether drawn as a light solid line or a series of dashed segments, this arc does not indicate, as other lines do, "cut" material. Instead, it records the possibility of architectural movement, of changing spatial relations. At once conventional and incredibly bizarre, a moment of graphic folding, the notation for "door swing" registers the making and unmaking of architectural space.

We can imagine many ways of elaborating the ante-closet: Apertures that open the closet to other spaces; closet fixtures that leap into rooms; doors that evoke the closet interior at its surface: these are among the many possibilities open to further architectural research. In thinking about my childhood encounter, I have observed that one way the ante-closet enriches the relation of storage and display is by invoking a play of scales—from the bodily to the infinite—and by inviting acts of architectural manipulation: sliding, pressing, adjusting, grabbing.

Like tattoos and hooded sweatshirts, like the terms "queer," "fag," and "dyke," the ante-closet is an effect of reappropriations and resignifications without end. It resists the violence of fixed identities by allowing spaces to fold, unfold, and fold again. The ante-closet does not obliterate closet or room, but brings them into a more fluid and generous adjacency. It waits between these spaces, ready to burst when relations of affiliation and abjection need to be refigured. Working with and against closet and room, the ante-closet dismantles their tired architecture to sustain the possibility of other arrangements.

Many people have helped this essay to unfold. I particularly want to thank Stephen Hartman, Catherine Ingraham, Mary McLeod, Joan Ockman, John Ricco, Brian Walker, and Mark Wigley. Thanks as well to the organizers and audiences of the following conferences: the Sixth National Gay and Lesbian Studies Conference, the Gender/Architecture/Modernity symposia at Columbia University, Graduate School of Architecture and Planning, and Desiring Practices, sponsored by the Kingston and Bartlett Schools of Architecture.

Notes

*   Henry Urbach, "Closets, Clothes, disClosure," *Assemblage* 30 (1996): 70.

†   Ibid., 72.

1   Andrew Jackson Downing, *Cottage Residences* (New York: Wiley and Putnam, 1842), 7.

2   Samuel Sloan, *The Model Architect* (Philadelphia: E. S. Jones, 1852), 14.

3   Harriet W. Beecher, "The Moral Uses of Luxury and Beauty," *Outlook* 25 (16 March 1882): 257.

4   Downing, *Cottage Residences*, 3.

5   Quoted in E. C. Gardner, *The House That Jill Built, after Jack's Had Proved a Failure* (New York: W. F. Adams, 1896), 166.

6   An American house planning guide from 1940 notes: "*Ventilation* of the clothes closet generally waits for the opening of the door into the bedroom.... Daylight, particularly sunlight, is valuable as a sterilizer, but we seldom manage to admit it to the closet" (Wooster Bard Field, *House Planning* [New York: McGraw-Hill, 1940], 149).

7   Maud M. Wilson, *Closets and Storage Spaces*, Farmers' Bulletin no. 1865 (Washington D.C.: United States Department of Agriculture, 1940), 1.

8   Julia Kristeva, *Powers of Horror: An Essay on Abjection*, trans. Leon S. Roudiez (New York: Columbia University Press, 1982).

9   See D. A. Miller, *The Novel and the Police* (Berkeley and Los Angeles: University of California Press, 1988), esp. chap. 6, "Secret Subjects, Open Secrets." Also see Eve Kosofsky Sedgwick, *Epistemology of the Closet* (Berkeley and Los Angeles: University of California Press, 1992).

10   Michel Foucault, *The History of Sexuality*, vol. 1, trans. Robert Hurley (New York: Random House, 1978), 43. He further writes: "This new persecution of the peripheral sexualities entailed an *incorporation of perversions* and a new *specification of individuals*. As defined by the ancient civil or canonical codes, sodomy was a category of forbidden acts; their perpetrator was nothing more than the juridical subject for them. The nineteenth-century homosexual became a personage, a past, a case history, and a childhood, in addition to being a type of life, a life form, and a morphology, with an indiscreet anatomy and possibly a mysterious physiology. Nothing that went into his total composition was unaffected by his sexuality" (42–43).

11   "Homosexuality, in a word, becomes the excluded; it stands in for, paradoxically, that which stands without. But the binary structure of sexual orientation, fundamentally a structure of exclusion and exteriorization, nonetheless constructs that exclusion by prominently including the contaminated other in its oppositional logic. The homo in relation to the hetero, much like the feminine in relation to the masculine, operates as an indispensable interior exclusion—an outside which is inside interiority making the articulation of the latter possible, a transgression of the border which is necessary to constitute the border as such" (Diana Fuss, "Inside/Out," in *inside/out*, ed. Diana Fuss [New York: Routledge, 1991], 3).

12   "Furthermore, the deadly elasticity of heterosexist presumption means that, like Wendy in *Peter Pan*, people find new walls springing up around them even as they drowse: every encounter with a new classful of students, to say nothing of a new boss, social worker, loan officer, landlord, doctor, erects new closets whose fraught and characteristic laws of optics and physics exact from at least gay

people new surveys, new calculations, new draughts and requisitions of secrecy or disclosure" (Sedgwick, *Epistemology of the Closet,* 68).

13 Judith Butler asks: "Is the 'subject' who is 'out' free of its subjection and finally in the clear? Or could it be that the subjection that subjectivates the gay or lesbian subject in some ways continues to oppress, or oppresses most insidiously, once 'outness' is claimed? What or who is it that is 'out,' made manifest and fully disclosed, when and if I reveal myself as lesbian? What is the very linguistic act that offers up the promise of a transparent revelation of sexuality? Can sexuality even remain sexuality once it submits to a criterion of transparency and disclosure, or does it perhaps cease to be sexuality precisely when the semblance of full explicitness is achieved?" ("Imitation and Gender Subordination," in Fuss, *inside/out,* 15).

14 Michael Holquist, ed., *The Dialogic Imagination: Four Essays by M. M. Bakhtin,* trans. Caryl Emerson and Michael Holquist (Austin: University of Texas Press, 1981). Bakhtin writes: "As a living, socio-ideological concrete thing, as heteroglot opinion, language, for the individual consciousness, lies on the borderline between oneself and the other. The word in language is half someone else's. It becomes 'one's own' only when the speaker populates it with his own accent, when he appropriates the word, adapting it to his own semantic intention. Prior to this moment of appropriation…it exists in other people's mouths, in other people's contexts, serving other people's intentions: it is from there that one must take the word, and make it one's own" (293–94).

15 *Oxford English Dictionary,* 2d ed., s.v. "closet." A text from 1374 notes: "In a closet for to avyse her bettre, She went alone." A novel of 1566 states: "We doe call the most secret place in the house appropriate unto our owne private studies…a Closet."

16 Ibid. According to a text from 1625: "If the Queens Closet where they now say masse were not large enough, let them have it in the Great Chamber."

17 John Bickereth and Robert W. Dunning, eds., *Clerks of the Closet in the Royal Household: 500 Years of Service to the Crown* (Phoenix Mill: Alan Sutton, 1991), 5–6.

18 Gilles Deleuze, *Foucault,* trans. and ed. Sean Hand (Minneapolis: University of Minnesota Press, 1988), 100.

Inside Anne Frank's House: An Illustrated Journey through Anne's World

Hans Westra

INTRODUCTION

The Anne Frank House falls outside the typical realm of examples of interiors, yet the attic where the Franks hid was an extremely charged interior. Anne Frank's family of four, along with four others, went into hiding in 1942 as Amsterdam was anticipating German occupation during World War II. It was a rarity for families to hide together, and compared to many others, the people in the Secret Annex enjoyed a relatively large amount of space. The house, located in central Amsterdam, is now a museum that has collected possessions of the families so that it can be understood in its original context. Hans Westra, the museum's former director, along with staff members of the Anne Frank House, reconstructed daily life in the attic based on Anne Frank's diary and photographs showing the rooms occupied before and after the house's renovation into a museum. The photographs included in this essay represent a special reconstruction of daily living not typical of the museums everyday exhibition. Combined with Frank's diary, the photographs vividly describe the rooms, how people used them and interacted in them, and where details about living took place. Small moments that could have been unnoticed were highlighted in Frank's memoirs. The museum descriptions include such basics as the type of beds slept on to the limited number of possessions the family and the others were able to carry without drawing attention to themselves the morning they left to make their way to the attic. Although there were limits, the teenaged Anne was able to establish an identity in her room decoration by taping images and photographs to the wall.

The removed space of the attic reflects the marginalized position of those in hiding, in this case because they were Jewish. The reason for hiding directly reflects the link between politics and interiors. The attic had to be altered to prevent detection of its inhabitants from the outside. Hidden passageways and alterations to interior facades, especially the windows, were created to provide security. One such example, a movable bookcase, concealed the entryway into the attic. Common elements such as a map on the wall had been placed

Excerpted from *Inside Anne Frank's House: An Illustrated Journey Through Anne's World*, translated by Epicycles/Amsterdam (Woodstock, NY: Overlook Duckworth, 2004), 40–41, 52, 57, 67, 98–99, 102, 106–07, 112–13, 116, 130, 164, 148–49, 161, 164–65, 176.

near the movable bookcase to give the illusion that the surrounding arrangement was ordinary. In addition to appearances, the attic's occupants remained aware of every noise they made, because the house's lower levels were in use as a warehouse, with those workers unaware. Subtle noises, such as a cough or water in the plumbing could have revealed the hidden rooms. In the Anne Frank House, what is typical in our everyday took on grave consequences during the war.

––––

On Monday July 6th, Anne Frank was awakened at five-thirty in the morning by her mother. It was less warm than Sunday and it rained throughout the day. In order to bring as much as possible the family dressed in thick layers of clothing. Anne put on two undershirts and three pairs of underpants, over that a skirt, a jacket, a raincoat, two pairs of stockings, heavy shoes, a cap, a scarf, and more. Miep Gies came along on a bicycle, taking Margot Frank, Anne's sister, to the hiding place.

At seven-thirty, the rest of the family left the house on Merwedeplein and traveled on foot to the Secret Annex located behind Otto Frank's company on the Prinsengracht. The house was left in such a state that it appeared as if they had all fled in haste. One week later the Van Pels family—Hermann, Auguste, and their son Peter—also came to hide in the Annex. On November 16, 1942, yet an eighth person, Fritz Pfeffer, joined. These eight people were cared for by Otto Frank's most trusted employees.

When the Frank family arrived at the location of the hiding place, all the rooms were filled with furniture, boxes, and food supplies.

From the moment they went into hiding, Otto and Edith kept track of how much their daughters grew. In those two years, Anne grew more than five inches and Margot around two.

The seven original residents would spend more than two years hiding in the Annex; Fritz Pfeffer spent just under two years.

Simply looking at the exterior of a canal house reveals little about its interior floor plan—each one differs. At Otto Frank's warehouse, the two doors to the left of the warehouse entrance open directly onto staircases. The left-hand door is the entry to a long, steep "leg-breaking" stairway that continues up to the third floor. The right-hand door opens onto a short staircase that leads to the office on the second floor. The office staff used this staircase. People

Fig. 6.13: The Warehouse front door of the Anne Frank House, Amsterdam, the Netherlands. Photo credit: © AFS, Amsterdam

could enter the warehouse through the larger doors on the right. Therefore the office and the warehouse have completely separate entrances. [Fig. 6.13]

The people in hiding could not move around too much during office hours. This time was usually reserved for studying and reading. They walked around in socks.

Danger of discovery presented itself not only from the street side, but also from the gardens in the back. During the day, the workers in the warehouse must not hear the people in hiding. The windows of the Annex were concealed from the view of the warehousemen by an extension built onto the rear of their work space. The neighbors must also not notice anything suspicious, so making noise at night was just as dangerous. The longer the war lasted, the more times the building was burglarized. These break-ins were a continual threat to those in hiding.

Essentially, the Annex was well concealed from the outside world. In the evenings, blackout panels were placed in front of the windows. During the day, the windows were covered with curtains.

Once the Frank family and the Van Pels family had been in hiding for more than a month, a decision was made to camouflage the entry door to the Annex. To do this, the stoop leading up to the Annex's gray door needed to be removed so the door itself could be lowered. The warehouse manager, Voskuijl, built the movable bookcase. [Fig. 6.14–16] The short staircase opens onto the landing, in front of the bookcase, and leads down to the office

Fig. 6.14: View of a moveable bookcase on display inside the Anne Frank House, Amsterdam, the Netherlands, 1999. Photo credit: © AFS/Allard Bovenberg

Fig. 6.15: View of a room with a swinging bookcase inside the Anne Frank House museum, Amsterdam, The Netherlands, 1999. Photo credit: © AFS/Allard Bovenberg

Fig. 6.16: The helpers' staircase to the Secret Annex.
Photo credit: © AFS/Allard Bovenberg

spaces on the second floor. The helpers used this stairway when they visited the Annex. [Fig. 6.16] In the evenings and on weekends, when the people in hiding came out of the Annex, they descended this staircase to reach the offices below.

During the war years, a dense, semitransparent paper (glassine) was affixed to the windows on the landing so policeman could not see into the Annex. Yet the people in hiding were still very worried.

Today the stairwell is sealed off with a piece of glass. During the hiding period, policemen unexpectedly came up these stairs. On April 8, 1944, the company building had been broken into once again. The outside door was damaged and a couple passing by warned the police. The people in hiding huddled together on the uppermost floor, afraid to move at all.

By pulling on a cord hanging next to the bookcase the helpers were able to unlatch the hook and swing open the bookcase. The people in hiding could pull the door closed from the inside and latch it once again. The same piece of cloth filled with wood-wool that Peter van Pels once nailed above the door continues to hang there today.

A panel was used to board-up the opening at the top of the doorway. A map-was hung in front of that panel. This panel covered the opening created when the door was lowered, and is still visible today.

On November 16, 1942, Margot started sleeping in the same room as her parents on a folding bed that was previously kept upstairs in the attic. [Fig. 6.17] In the early months of hiding it was used for sunbathing.

Anne began to glue prints from her collection to the two blank walls of her small room. These images give us an impression of her broad range of interests, for example: film stars, nature, history, and royalty: Leonardo da Vinci and Rembrandt alongside Greta Garbo and Ginger Rogers. [Fig. 6.18]

Tensions were unavoidable between eight people living so closely together for such a long time. Besides temperamental clashes between various persons, clear differences of opinion sometimes emerged between "upstairs" (van Pels family) and "downstairs" (Frank family). For example, about how to raise children, what they may or may not read, eat, or know.

Eight people having access to only one toilet and sink also meant that those in hiding often have to wait their turn. [Fig. 6.19] An additional problem was

Fig. 6.17: Interior
of Otto, Edith and
Margot Frank's room
inside Anne Frank
House, Amsterdam,
the Netherlands.
Photo credit: ©AFS/Allard
Bovenberg

Fig. 6.18: Interior of
Anne Frank and Fritz
Pfeffer's bedroom in
the Anne Frank House
Museum, Amsterdam,
the Netherlands,
1999. Photo credit:
©AFS/Allard Bovenberg

Fig. 6.19: The
bathroom in the Anne
Frank House set
up to look as it did
when German Jewish
holocaust victim Anne
Frank (1929–1945)
and her family hid in
the house from July
1942–September
1944, Amsterdam,
the Netherlands,
1999. Photo credit:
©AFS/Allard Bovenberg

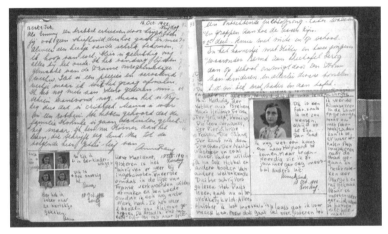

Fig. 6.20: Anne Frank's Diary. Photo credit: ©AFF, Basel/AFS, Amsterdam

above

Fig. 6.21: The common living room, dining room, and room of the Van Pels family in the Anne Frank House set up to look as it did when German Jewish holocaust victim Anne Frank (1929–1945) and her family hid in the house from July 1942–September 1944, Amsterdam, Netherlands, 1999.
Photo credit: ©AFS/Allard Bovenberg

left

Fig. 6.22: The Westerkerk or Western Church in Amsterdam, seen from the window of the Anne Frank House, circa 1970. Photo credit: ©AFF, Basel/AFS, Amsterdam

that the facilities could not be used too often, because the sound of streaming water could give them away. The toilet, for instance, might be flushed in the daytime during office hours, but not too frequently. It can definitely be heard in the warehouse, but the workers there do not suspect that anyone other than the office employees could be responsible for the sound. The toilet was also a place for the people in hiding to retreat to, to find some privacy in the crowded Annex. If there was imminent danger, this room is the furthest away from the entrance and therefore the safest. If there was someone in the house who was unaware of the situation, such as the cleaning lady, the carpenter, or burglars, the people in hiding gathered nervously together in this room and remain as quiet as possible. Once the door was closed, few sounds penetrate.

Anne wrote regularly about the tensions in the Annex and the despondent moods of its inhabitants. [Fig. 6.20] Constantly feeling unsafe is just one of the reasons for this. Anne could not believe, for instance, that the warehouse employees never noticed a thing.

As a result of the burglaries, the people in hiding agreed to new security measures. Everybody had to be back in the Annex by 9:30 p.m., when the movable bookcase was shut.

In the evenings and on the weekends the people in hiding sometimes went to get warm water from the kitchen. There were curtains hanging so they could not be seen from the garden side. [Fig. 6.21]

The stove was in the corner next to the sink. The heater not only provided warmth, but was also used to burn the trash. Those in hiding could not put any garbage in the trash cans because the warehousemen would notice. Therefore everything had to be burned, even when outdoor temperatures were extremely high, which risked raising the suspicions of neighbors, especially on weekends. To avoid this, the heater was stoked very early on Sunday mornings, when the neighbors were still asleep.

During the working week, Anne came upstairs to the attic at lunchtime for three-quarters of an hour to get a breath of fresh air. [Fig. 6.22].

Berggasse 19: Inside Freud's Office

Diana Fuss and Joel Sanders

INTRODUCTION

Diana Fuss and Joel Sanders analyze Sigmund Freud's London office based on a series of photographs commissioned and executed by Edmund Engelman before Freud was expelled from Vienna at the onset of World War II. The photographs were initially used to reconstruct the office and catalog the numerous antiquities Freud collected. Most importantly, the placement of objects and furniture with regard to the doctor-patient relationship were documented. Through a series of diagrams, Fuss and Sanders make visible underlying structures embedded in the office and consultation room. The complex weaving of invisible relationships between Freud and patient are identified by inscribing sight lines to connect objects, views, and occupants' locations seen in the photographs and through them map out hidden agendas of Freud's analytic technique. These diagrams have a visual collage effect. Drawing connections between the relationship of the room's items to one another and the location of occupants in orthographic projection, these images are connected back to Engelman's photographs. The mapped connections are in the form of solid or dotted trajectory lines, depending on which type of image they traverse. Even though the diagrams represent things in different scales and views, they map the subtle plays among all scales found in the office.

The essay addresses the emphasis placed on the iconic mirror hanging in front of Freud's office window. Because it is an object symbolizing psychoanalytic transference, there is a subtle play of elements that creates a stage set for the drama acted out in the office space. The narrative involves the timing of entry, what the analysand sees when seated, and the interplay of objects and psyche. Once Freud and the patient enter the office, the space is charged with their choreographed appearance, and the objects themselves are put in motion, and in the service of the analysis.

Freud's office was not only the home of his antiquities collection but was also densely packed with furniture, textiles, books, and photographs. His

Originally appeared in *Stud: Architectures of Masculinity*, edited by Joel Sanders (New York: Princeton Architectural Press, 1996), 112–38.

possessions created a second interior skin. Gottfried Semper's writings in The Four Elements of Architecture *and creating "a room within a room" come to mind especially in light of the Persian rugs that draped interior walls and of course the prototypical couch.* Beautiful objects, color, patterns, and a sense of interiority seduced patients into an atmosphere that supported the incredible intimacy required to reveal their innermost thoughts. Freud's rooms in Berggasse 19 were akin to the boudoirs of the seventeenth century.*

———

IN MAY OF 1938, on the eve of Sigmund Freud's expulsion from Vienna and flight to London, Freud's colleague August Aichhorn met with the photojournalist Edmund Engelman at the Café Museum on the Karlsplatz in Vienna to make a proposal. Would it be possible, Aichhorn wondered, to take photographs of Freud's office and apartment without drawing the attention of the Gestapo who, since Hitler's annexation of Austria two months earlier, had been keeping the home of one of Vienna's most famous Jewish intellectuals under constant surveillance? The purpose of this photographic documentary was to provide an inventory of Berggasse 19 so exact that, as Aichhorn envisioned it, the home of psychoanalysis might be painstakingly recreated as a museum after the impending war.[1] Engelman, a mechanical and electrical engineer who ran a local photography shop on the Karntnerstrasse, agreed to try to provide a pictorial record of Berggasse 19. In the course of four days and using two cameras (a Rolleiflex and a Leica), two lenses (a 50mm lens and a 28mm wide-angle lens), and a light meter, and working without the aid of either flashes or floodlights, Engelman took approximately one hundred shots of Berggasse 19, focusing on the consulting room, study, and family living quarters.[2] These photographs, together with a short film segment of Freud's office taken by Marie Bonaparte in December 1937, provide the only extant visual record of the place where, for forty-seven years, Freud treated his patients, met regularly with his colleagues, and wrote his scientific papers and case histories.

Freud's biographers have written eloquently of his traumatic expulsion from his home in Vienna; cultural historians have studied in fascinating detail the peculiarities of Freud's domestic arrangements and the routine of his office schedule; psychoanalysts have analyzed at length the procedures of Freud's clinical practice; and art historians have recently begun to examine the meaning of Freud's extensive collection of antiquities and the links between psychoanalysis and archaeology. But we have yet to consider the significance of the site that housed these practices and objects. We have yet to fully enter, in other words, Berggasse 19. How might the spatial configuration of Freud's office, and the arrangement of furniture and objects with in it, frame our understanding of psychoanalytic theory and practice? What might an architectural study of Berggasse 19 tell us about the play of vision, power, gender, and transference that structures the analytic scene?

Taking as its point of departure Engelman's black-and-white photographs, as well as our own architectural drawings gathered from site visits to Freud's offices in London and Vienna, this project traverses the porous boundary between the two-dimensional space of photography and the three-dimensional space of architecture. The convergence of these two languages of space reflects the tensions that inform not only this essay but what it seeks to read, highlighting the confusion of surface and depth, inside and outside, subjects and objects, that characterize psychoanalysis's own primal scene. Until recently, questions of spectatorship have been theorized largely in terms of a subject's perception of a two-dimensional image (photography, film, television).[3] This essay explores the role of vision in three-dimensional space, examining how architecture organizes the physical and visual interaction of bodies as they move through the interior of Freud's professional office. Architecture and psychoanalysis come together here in a reading of the interior, for both are cultural discourses of the seen and the unseen, the visible and the invisible—of public and private space.

This collaborative project is impelled by a powerful fantasy, the same fantasy that drives Engelman's photographs—namely, the illusion that one can relive the experience of early psychoanalysis by retracing the footsteps of Freud's patients. But the space of Freud's office is a fundamentally irrecuperable one. The photographs of Berggasse 19, originally taken for the postwar construction of a Freud museum, have themselves become the museum—miniature sites of preservation and display. Today visitors to the consulting room and study in Berggasse 19 will find a space emptied of Freud's possessions (currently housed in the Freud Museum in London) but encompassed with enlargements of Engelman's photographs displayed on the walls. This highly unusual mode of museum exhibition insists on the mediating function of the photographs, while preserving the empty rooms of the office as a space of exile and absence: the place Freud was finally forced to flee at the end of his life "to die in freedom."[4] To the extent that our own research project is an attempt at recovery, at reconstituting from the fragments of history what has been buried and lost, our reading of Berggasse 19 is inevitably a work of mourning, framed by the same logic of memorialization that, we will argue in what follows, so pervasively organized the space of Freud's office.

I.

Engelman's photodocumentary opens with three exterior shots of Berggasse 19, motivated, as he was later to write, by a presentiment that the building itself would be destroyed in the war.[5] The façade of this typical late nineteenth-century Viennese apartment house comes into focus through a progressive sequence of long, medium, and closeup shots of the entry door. Exerting a kind of centrifugal force, the swastika placed over the door of Berggasse 19 by the building's Aryan owner pulls the camera in, gradually focussing and delimiting the social boundaries of the photodocumentary's visual field. What kind of space is the urban street space? For the European, the street is the place of chance encounters and accidental dramas. It is also, historically, the site of political uprising and counterrevolution—the birthplace of the modern revolutionary subject. But, as Susan Suleiman notes of the modern wayfare, "after 1933, any attempt to think politically about the street had to grapple with its profound ambiguity."[6] The street, formerly a place of collective resistance to state intervention, becomes, with the rise of fascism in Europe, a public venue for Nazi torchlight parades and other forms of national socialist ideology.

Engelman's three views of the street, taken with a wide-angle lens, capture a near-deserted Berggasse. Far from removing us from the sphere of political action, however, these daytime shots of a scarcely populated urban street illuminate, in visually arresting fashion, the realities of political occupation for the predominantly Jewish residents of Vienna's Ninth District. Most of the Ninth District's Jewish population was located on eleven streets, including the Berggasse, which ran from the fashionable upper-middle class neighborhood of the University of Vienna at one end, to the junk shops of the Tandelmarkt owned by poor Jewish shopkeepers at the other.[7] Though located just outside the Ringstrasse, the Berggasse was very much at the center of the German occupation. By the time Engelman embarked on his pictorial record of Freud's residence in May 1938, the image of a scarcely populated urban street operated as a potent indexical sign of political danger and social displacement. For Vienna's Jewish residents, occupation meant incarceration; to be "occupied" was to be exiled, driven out of the public space of the street and into the home.

Operating without the use of a flash ordinarily employed for interior shots, and continuing to use a wide-angle lens designed for exterior shots, Engelman transports the codes and conventions of street photography inside Berggasse 19. The building becomes an interior street as the camera's peripatetic gaze traffics through domestic space. Engelman begins his pictorial walking tour by bringing us across the entry threshold and into the lobby, a wide linear space which, with its cobblestone floor and coffered ceiling, resembles a covered arcade. At the end of the entry corridor, a pair of glazed doors—their glass panes etched with antique female figures—provides a view of an aedicule located, on axis, in the rear service courtyard beyond. These symmetrical semi-transparent doors establish a recurring visual motif that is progressively disrupted and finally displaced as we approach and move through the suite of rooms comprising Freud's office. Interestingly, Berggasse 19 wears its façade on the inside; those architectural elements normally found on the exterior of a building can be seen on the interior of Freud's apartment house. At the top of the switch-back stair, for example, we encounter a translucent window—an interior window that looks not onto an exterior courtyard but directly into the Freud family's private apartment. Illuminated from within, but draped with an inside curtain, Freud's interior window troubles the traditional distinction between privacy and publicity by rendering completely ambiguous whether we might be on the outside looking in or the inside looking out.

The architectural transposition of public and private space chronicled by Engelman's camera captures Freud's own relation to his work place, for although located at the back of the apartment and insulated from the street, Freud's office nonetheless operated as a busy thoroughfare. [Fig. 6.23] Patients, colleagues, friends, family, and even pets moved in and out at regular intervals. When he needed privacy, Freud would seek refuge on the Ringstrasse where he would retreat for his daily constitutional, occasionally with a family member or friend to accompany him. For Freud, the interior space of the office and the exterior space of the street were seamless extensions of one another; both were places of movement and conversation, of chance words and surprise meetings, of accident and incident.[8] The commerce of everyday encounters constituted the primary source materials of interior reflection his patients brought to their private sessions with Freud. The transactions of the street quickly became the transferences of the therapeutic scene.

Inside Freud's consulting room and adjoining study, we are confronted with a confusing assortment of furniture and objects: couch, chair, books, bookcases, cabinets, paintings, photographs, lights, rugs, and Freud's extensive collection of antiquities. Freud displayed in the close space of his office the entirety of his collection, acquired mainly from local antique dealers with earnings set aside from his daily hour of open consultations.[9] The experience of viewing Engelman's photographs of Freud's office is like nothing so much as window shopping, as we are permitted to view, but not touch, the objects before us, many arranged in glass showcases. Ultimately, what Engelman seeks to document in these photographs is not just the objects but their particular sites of display. It is the very specific spatial arrangement of objects within the interior that constitutes the photodocumentary's visual field and that offers a blueprint for the future reconstruction of the office-museum.

The gaze of Engelman's camera is systematic, not random: it documents and surveys, inventories and catalogs. It moves from one corner of the room to the next, from wall to wall, window to window, memorizing the details of the office interior. This archival gaze is also a slightly manic one, obsessively traversing the same spaces, partitioning the office into a series of

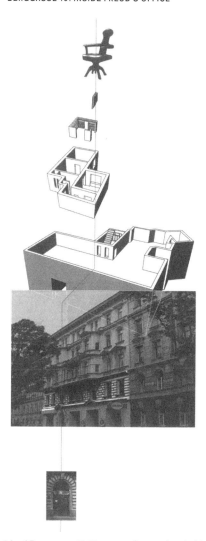

Fig. 6.23: Exploded Axonometric of Berggasse 19. The zone of rooms located immediately behind the protective surface of Berggasse 19's front facade buffers Freud's office (isolated in the back of the apartment) from the street. The office walls, outfitted with double sets of casement windows and lined with bookshelves and antiquities, heighten the impression of Freud's office as a sequestered, private, interior space. Diana Fuss and Joel Sanders

overlapping but discrete perceptual fields, at once contiguous and enclosed. The prosthetic eye of the camera attempts to take everything in, but finds its efforts frustrated by the very objects it seeks visually to preserve. The visual space becomes a carceral one as Engelman's camera repeatedly tries, and fails, to negotiate the crowded terrain of Freud's office, so cluttered with objects that many of the two thousand antiquities can be seen in these photographs spilling onto the study floor.[10]

Two months after his father's death in October 1896, Freud began assembling the antiquities that would transform his office into a veritable tomb. The debilitating illness and lingering death of Jakob Freud is generally recognized as the emotional crisis that galvanized Freud's compensatory interest in collecting. A father's demise is "the most important event, the most poignant loss, of a man's life" (4: p. xxvi), Freud famously opines in *The Interpretation of Dreams*, a book that has itself been read as an extended work of mourning, Freud's gradual coming to terms with the loss of his father. But it is not just his father whom Freud mourns through his accumulation of reliquary objects; it is also, in some profound sense, himself. Freud's self-described "death deliria"[11] played a central role in shaping the psychical and physical space of his office. Long before his father died, Freud was preoccupied with foretelling the exact time of his own future death. In a letter to Wilhelm Fliess dated June 22, 1894, Freud insists that although he has no scientific basis for his predictions, he "shall go on suffering from various complaints for another four to five to eight years, with good and bad periods, and then between forty and fifty perish very abruptly from a rupture of the heart."[12] As Freud moved into the period forecast for his "rupture of the heart," it was not his own death that occurred but that of his father, who fell fatally ill and died of heart failure shortly after Freud's fortieth birthday. "All of it happened in my critical period," Freud writes to Fliess a day after his father's funeral, "and I am really quite down because of it."[13] Freud apparently felt that his father died in his place, prompting a labor of self-entombment that exhausted itself only with Freud's own painful and prolonged death almost half a century later.

Like Osiris buried alive in his coffin,[14] Freud began surrounding himself with disinterred objects: Egyptian scarabs, Roman death masks, Etruscan funeral vases, bronze coffins, and mummy portraits.[15] The attempt to chronicle the space of Freud's office for the purposes of erecting a future museum upon its ruins was, by 1938, a touchingly belated act, for Freud's office was a museum long before Engelman arrived to document it. Like all museums, this particular memorial site doubled as a mausoleum, showcasing the self-enshrinement of a collector buried among his funerary objects. "Museum and mausoleum are connected by more than phonetic association," Adorno once commented; "museums are the family sepulchers of works of art."[16] Engelman's photographs dramatically capture what half a century of Freud commentary has overlooked: the location of the analytic scene within the walls of a crypt. When patients arrived at Freud's office, they entered an overdetermined space of loss and absence, grief and memory, elegy and mourning. In short, they entered the exteriorized theater of Freud's own emotional history, where every object newly found memorialized a love-object lost.

We might recall at this juncture that Berggasse 19 was not Freud's first professional office. Freud initially set up his medical practice in a new residential building erected on the ashes of one of Vienna's most famous edifices, the Ring Theater, which burned to the ground in 1881 in a spectacular fire, killing over six hundred people inside. Austria's Franz Josef commissioned the Viennese architect F. Y. Schmidt to construct on the ruins an apartment house for the *haute bourgeoisie,* a portion of whose rent would be allocated to assist the hundreds of children orphaned by the fire. It was here, in an architectural monument to the dead of Vienna's Ring Theater, that psychoanalysis first took up residence. Not even the birth of the Freuds' first child, which brought the newly married couple an official letter from the Emperor congratulating them on bringing new life to the site of such tragic loss, could completely erase for Freud the symbolic connotations of treating patients' nervous disorders in a place that came to be known as the *Sühnhaus* (House of Atonement).[17] Freud's psychoanalytic practice, from the very beginning, was closely associated with loss and recovery, the work of mourning.

II.

The patient's entry into Freud's office initiates a series of complicated and subtle transactions of power, orchestrated largely by the very precise spatial arrangement of objects and furniture. Freud held initial consultations, between three and four every afternoon, in the study section of his office. [Fig. 6.24] Preferring a face-to-face encounter with prospective patients, Freud seated them approximately four feet away from himself, across the divide of a table adjacent to the writing desk. Located in the center of a square room, at the intersection of two axial lines, the patient would appear to occupy the spatial locus of power. As if to confirm the illusion of his centrality, the patient is immediately presented, when seated, with a reflection of his own

Fig. 6.24: Freud's Study.
Photographer: Edward Engelman

453

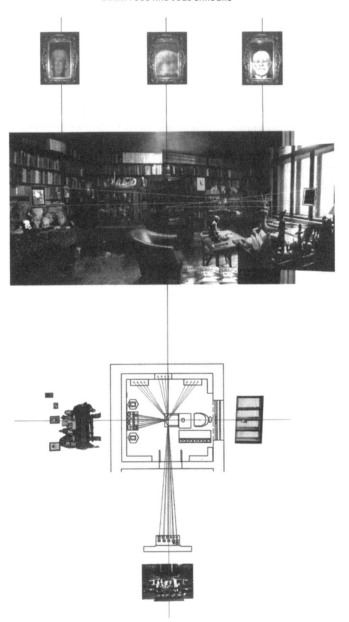

Fig. 6.25: Study Diagram. During the initial consultation with Freud, the patient, seated at the center of the square shaped study, sees his reflection framed within the portrait-sized mirror on the central mullion of the window behind Freud's desk. Myriad gazes, issuing from Freud's collection of stone heads and antique figurines, survey the patient from the tables and vitrines that terminate the room's other three axes. When Freud sits in his desk chair, his head blocks and replaces the patient's image in the mirror, initiating the transferential dynamics governing future therapeutic encounters. Diana Fuss and Joel Sanders

image, in a small portrait-sized mirror, framed in gold filigree and hanging, at eye-level, on a facing window. As soon as Freud sits down at his desk, however, interposing himself between patient and mirror, the patient's reflection is blocked by Freud's head. [Fig. 6.25] Head substitutes for mirror in a metaphorical staging of the clinical role Freud seeks to assume. "The doctor," Freud pronounces in *Papers on Technique,* "should be opaque to his patients and, like a mirror, should show them nothing but what is shown to him" (12: p. 118).

Freud's clinical assumption of the function of the mirror, and the substitution of other for self that it enacts, sets into motion the transferential dynamics that will structure all further doctor-patient encounters. In preparation for the laborious work of overcoming their unconscious resistances, patients are required to divest themselves of authority while seated in the very center of power. In a reverse panopticon, the most central location in Freud's study (the point from which the gaze normally issues) turns out to be the most vulnerable, as the patient suddenly finds himself exposed on all sides to a multitude of gazes. Viewed from both left and right by a phalanx of ancient figurines (all displayed at eye-level and arranged to face the patient), as well as from behind by a collection of detached antique heads and from in front by Freud's imposing visage, the patient is surveyed from every direction. Power in this transferential scene is exercised from the margins. From the protected vantage point of his desk chair, Freud studies his patient's face, fully illuminated by the afternoon light, while his own face remains barely visible, almost entirely eclipsed by backlighting from the window behind him.

"The process of psychoanalysis," Freud goes on to remark in *Papers on Technique,* "is retarded by the dread felt by the average observer of seeing himself in his own mirror" (12: p. 210). The analogy of the mirror, used to describe the process of psychoanalytic self-reflection, makes its first appearance in Freud's work in his reading of the memoirs of Daniel Paul Schreber. Mirrors figure prominently in Schreber's transvestic identification: "anyone who should happen to see me before the mirror with the upper portion of my torso bared—especially if the illusion is assisted by my wearing a little feminine finery—would receive an unmistakable impression of a *female bust*" (12: p. 33). And what did Freud see when, alone in his office amongst his classical heads and ancient figurines, he turned to face his own image in the mirror? Freud, too, saw the unmistakable impression of a bust—head and shoulders severed from the body, torso-less and floating, like the Roman head overlooking his consulting room chair or the death mask displayed in his study. His head decapitated by the frame of the mirror, Freud is visually identified with one of his own classical sculptures, transformed into a statuary fragment.

Looking in the other direction Freud also saw only heads. A wooden statue of a Chinese sage sitting on the table between Freud and his patient severs the patient's head in the same way Freud's head is decapitated by the frame of the mirror. From the vantage point of the desk chair, the patient's disembodied head assumes the status of one of Freud's antiquities, homologous not only to the stone heads filling the table directly behind the patient (the only table in the office displaying almost exclusively heads) but also to the framed photographic portraits above them, hanging at the exact same level as the mirror.

For Freud, every self-reflection reveals a death mask, every mirror image a spectral double. In his meditation on the theme of doubling, Freud remarks in "The 'Uncanny'" that while the double first emerges in our psychical lives as a "preservation against extinction," this double (in typically duplicitous fashion) soon reverses itself: "from having been an assurance of immortality, it becomes the uncanny harbinger of death" (17: p. 235). By captivating our image, immobilizing and framing it, the mirror reveals a picture of our own unthinkable mortality.

Yet, as Freud notes elsewhere, it is finally impossible to visualize our own deaths, for "whenever we attempt to do so we can perceive that we are in fact still present as spectators" (14: p. 289). The mirror that memorializes also reincarnates, reconstituting us as phantom spectators, witnesses to our own irreplaceability. The mirror thus functions simultaneously like a window, assisting us in passing through the unrepresentable space of our violent eradication, and helping us, in effect, to survive our own deaths. This was indeed the function of Etruscan mirrors (so prominent in Freud's own private collection) on whose polished bronze surfaces mythological scenes were engraved. By differentiating between pictorial space and real space, the frame of the Etruscan mirror offers the illusion of a view onto another world. These mirrors, originally buried in tombs, assisted their owners in passing through their deaths: the Etruscan mirror opened a window onto immortality.

Lacan saw as much in his early reflections on the mirror stage. Radically dislocating the traditional opposition of transparency and reflectivity (window and mirror), Lacan instructs us to "think of the mirror as a pane of glass. You'll see yourself in the glass and you'll see objects beyond it."[18] In Freud's office, the placement of a mirror on a window frame further complicates this conflation of transparency and reflectivity by frustrating the possibility of opening up the space of looking that both crystalline surfaces appear to offer. Normally, when mirrors are placed against opaque walls, they have the capacity to act as windows; they dematerialize and dissolve architectural edges, creating the illusion of extension and expanding the spatial boundaries of the interior. But in this highly peculiar instance of

Fig. 6.26: Sections through Entry Vestibule and Study Window. The window in Freud's study possesses certain compositional similarities with the building's rear entry doors. Seen frontally, both sites present us with a rectangular figure (aedicule and mirror) framed by a bifurcated glazed ground (door and window). But Freud's placement of the mirror before the study window inverts the traditional relationship of figure to ground. Disrupting the reassuring trajectory of a sovereign look (embodied by the transparency of the back entry doors), the mirror redirects the patient's gaze inwards, relaying the gaze back upon itself. Diana Fuss and Joel Sanders

a mirror superimposed on a window, visual access is obstructed rather than facilitated. Unlike the glass panes on Berggasse 19's rear entry doors, which allow the viewer's gaze to pass easily along a central axis from inside to outside, the composition of Freud's study window, with the mirror occupying the central vanishing point, redirects the gaze inward. [Fig. 6.26] By forcing the subject of reflection to confront an externalized gaze relayed back upon itself, the mirror on Freud's window interrupts the reassuring classical symmetries of self and other, inside and outside, and seeing and being seen that constitute the traditional humanist subject.[19]

The architectonics of the Freudian subject depends fundamentally upon a spatial dislocation, upon seeing the self exteriorized. It is not only that when we look in the mirror we see how others see us, but also that we see ourselves occupying a space where we are not. The statue that confronts us in the mirror permits us to look not only at but through ourselves to the "object who knows himself to be seen."[20] The domain delimited by Lacan's *imago,* "the statue in which man projects himself,"[21] is thus a strangely lifeless one. As Mikkel Borch-Jacobsen pictures it in "The Statue Man," this mirror world is "a sort of immense museum peopled with immobile 'statues,'

Fig. 6.27: Freud's
Consulting Room.
Photographer: Edward
Engelman

'images' of stone, and hieratic 'forms.'" It is "the most inhuman of possible worlds, the most *unheimlich*."[22]

What Freud sees in his mirror is a subject who is, first and foremost, an object, a statue, a bust. The "dread" of self-reflection that Freud describes in *Papers on Technique* appears to issue from a fear of castration, of dramatic bodily disfigurement. If, as Freud insists in "Medusa's Head," the terror of castration is always linked to the sight of something, then it is the sight of *seeing oneself seeing* that possesses lethal consequences for the figure in the mirror. Like Medusa, who is slain by the fatal powers of her own gaze reflected back to her by Perseus's shield, Freud's narcissistic gaze makes him "stiff with terror, turns him to stone" (18: p. 273). Self-reflection petrifies. Perhaps this is the knowledge that so frightened, and so fascinated, Freud: the realization that the subject's "optical erection" could only be achieved at the price of its castration, its instantaneous, fatal transformation into a broken relic.

III.

As the clinical treatment moves from the initial consultation in Freud's study to the sessions on the consulting room couch, the distribution of objects in the room produces a new kind of body, and a reconfigured doctor-patient relation. [Fig. 6.27] In the study, the patient, sitting isolated and exposed at the center of the room, occupied the point of maximum exposure; in the consulting room, the patient finds herself securely situated outside a circuit of visual surveillance. The arrangement of couch and chair, with their occupants

458

Fig. 6.28: Consulting Room Diagram. The position of Freud's treatment chair behind the head of the couch effectively prohibits any direct visual exchange between patient and doctor. While Freud's corner chair offers a view of the entire consulting room, as well as the study desk in the adjoining room, the couch directs the reclining patient's gaze to the bare corner above the Viennese stove, the only surface in the office uncluttered by artifacts. Diana Fuss and Joel Sanders

facing outward at perpendicular angles, ensures that, once the analysis formally begins, there will never be an unobstructed line of vision between patient and doctor. The most intimate space in the room is thus also the most highly mediated, as if such close physical proximity between patient and doctor can only be sustained by the structural elimination of any direct visual transaction. [Fig. 6.28] The placement of articles on and around the consulting room couch—the heavy Persian rug hung vertically from the wall and anchored to the couch by a matching rug, the chenille cushions supporting the patient's head, neck, and upper back, and the blanket and porcelain stove warming the patient's feet—all create the impression of a protected enclave, a room within a room, a private interior space.

The profusion of sensuous Oriental rugs and throw pillows, and the horsehair sofa in the consulting room in Berggasse 19 suggests the subtle encroachment of "female" domestic space into the public sphere of the office. Freud's professional office as a scene of domestic comfort is precisely how the Wolf Man remembers it thirty-eight years after the completion of his formal analysis:

> I can remember, as though I saw them today, his two adjoining studies, with the door open between them and with their windows opening on a little courtyard. There was always a feeling of sacred peace and quiet here. The rooms themselves must have been a surprise to any patient, for they in no way reminded one of a doctor's office....A few potted plants added life to the rooms, and the warm carpet and curtains gave them a homelike note. Everything here contributed to one's feeling of leaving the haste of modern life behind, of being sheltered from one's daily cares.[23]

In her autobiographical work, *Tribute to Freud,* the American poet H.D. recalls Freud's office in similar terms, emphasizing the feelings of safety and security generated by the space encompassing the consulting room couch: "Today, lying on the famous psychoanalytical couch,...[w]herever my fantasies may take me now, I have a center, security, aim. I am centralized or reoriented here in this mysterious lion's den or Aladdin's cave of treasures."[24]

H.D. goes on to describe the "smoke of burnt incense" (TF, p. 23) and the "fumes of the aromatic cigar" (TF, p. 132) that waft above the couch, emanating from the invisible corner behind her. Freud considered his passion for collecting "an addiction second in intensity only to his nicotine addiction."[25] The air in Freud's treatment room, densely humidified by ceramic water tubes attached to the Viennese stove, hung heavy with the smell of Freud's favorite cigars, which he often smoked during analytic sessions. Reading the visual record of Freud's office alongside these verbal accounts, a carefully staged orientalist scene insistently begins to take shape. Reclining on an ottoman couch, cushioned by Eastern carpets, and wreathed in pungent smoke, patients find themselves at home in a late Victorian fantasy of the opium den.

In Europe's *fin-de-siècle* fascination with the East, oriental interiors— especially the smoking room—were closely associated with leisure and relaxation. The bright dyes, luxurious textures, and bold designs of increasingly popular Persian carpets were instrumental in importing into the bourgeois Victorian home a stereotypical aura of Eastern exoticism. In fact, the last decades of the nineteenth century found Europe in the grip of what one German design historian has called "Oriental carpet fever."[26] The first major European exhibition of Oriental carpets took place at the Imperial Austrian Trade Museum in Vienna in 1891, the very year Freud moved his home and office to Berggasse 19. For Freud, these Persian carpets and Oriental fabrics may well have reminded him of his father, by profession a wool merchant who traded in Eastern textiles. For Freud's patients, the enchantment and mystery of these Oriental rugs further sequestered them in the interiorized, reclusive space of the consulting room couch—a place of private fantasy and quixotic danger: "[a] mysterious lion's den or Aladdin's cave of treasures."

As if in compensation for the risks that must be taken there, Freud envelops the patient on the couch in all the comforts of a private boudoir, ordinarily the most interior and secluded room of the Viennese home. Freud's office, in fact, is located in the back wing of what was originally designed to be part of a domestic residence, in that area of the apartment house typically used as sleeping quarters.[27] It is the sexual overtones of the famous couch—the sofa as bed—that most discomforted Freud's critics and, if Freud himself is to be believed, no small number of his patients.[28] In one of the few essays to take note of the spatial organization of the scene of analysis, Luce Irigaray has pointed out that the sexual connotations of lying supine can vary dramatically, depending on the sex of the patient. A woman reclining on her back with a man seated erect behind her finds her relation to the doctor inevitably eroticized.[29] The same could be said for Freud's male patients, whose daily sessions of private sex talk with their male doctor tacitly homoeroticized the clinical encounter. "Some men," Freud once commented, "scatter small change out of their trouser pockets while they are lying down during treatment and in that way pay whatever fee they think appropriate for the session" (6: p. 214). The association of lying down with scattered change—in short, of sex with money—invokes the specter of (male) prostitution, a connection that Freud appears to intuit here but not fully register.

What is being staged, or restaged, around the privileged, centralized, over-invested figure of the consulting room couch? "I cannot put up with being stared at by other people for eight hours a day (or more)," Freud acknowledges, defending his mandate that all patients, without exception, assume a reclining position on the couch. But why a couch? The couch turns out to be yet another museum relic—a "remnant," Freud calls it, "of the hypnotic method out of which psycho-analysis was evolved" (12: p. 133). While Freud abandoned his early hypnotic practice of placing patients into a somnambulistic sleep, he retained the couch as a serviceable memorial to psychoanalysis in its infancy. The couch, given to Freud as a gift by his former patient Madame Benveniste around 1890, operated as a nostalgic reminder of his professional past.

But there is more to this couch than its store of personal memories for the doctor; the analytic couch served a mnemonic function for the patient as well. The following anecdote, recounted by Freud in *The Psychopathology of Everyday Life,* provocatively suggests a different way of thinking about the prominence of the consulting room couch:

A young lady suddenly flung open the door of the consulting room though the woman who preceded her had not yet left it. In apologizing she blamed her 'thoughtlessness'; it soon turned out that she had been demonstrating the curiosity that in the past had caused her to make her way into her parents' bedroom. (16: p. 214)

What is being subtly replayed here, across the threshold of two rooms, is none other than the spectacle of the primal scene. The patient in the waiting room, hearing sounds through the consulting room door, bursts into Freud's office, propelled by the same "curiosity" that drew her, as a child, to cross the threshold of her parent's private bedchamber. Freud's intruding female hysteric sees all too clearly the highly eroticized choreography made possible by the very particular configuration of consulting room couch and chair, so closely juxtaposed that if one were to remove the arm of the couch and the arm of the chair behind it, the patient's head (formerly propped at a thirty-five degree angle) would fall nearly into Freud's lap. Shortly after this incident of analysis *interruptus*, Freud soundproofed his consulting room by adding a second set of doors lined with red baize. The sound barrier between treatment room and waiting room now insulated the analytic couple, whose muffled voices previously risked transporting the patient in the next room back to the trauma of the primal scene, to that interior place of fantasy where "uncanny sounds" are registered but only belatedly understood.

Freud's own placement in this scene is by no means a simple one; the question of the analyst's identificatory position is far more complicated than Irigaray's "orthogonal"[30] pairing of prone patient/erect doctor might suggest. Significantly, Freud chooses to assume a passive position in his exchange with the patient. Advising against the taking of notes during treatment sessions, a practice that prohibits the doctor from maintaining a posture of "evenly suspended attention" (12: p. 111), Freud recommends that the analyst "should simply listen, and not bother about whether he is keeping anything in mind." This passive listening technique represents the exact correlative to the fundamental rule of analysis for patients, the injunction to say anything that enters one's head "without selection or censorship" (12: p. 112).[31] The analyst must never engage in the work of scientific research while involved in the clinical act of listening. He must instead make himself vulnerable and receptive; he must "lay…[himself] open to another person" (12: p. 116); he must allow himself "to be taken by surprise" (12: p. 114).

> To put it in a formula: he must turn his own unconscious like a receptive organ toward the transmitting unconscious of the patient. He must adjust himself to the patient as a telephone receiver is adjusted to the transmitting microphone. Just as the receiver converts back into sound

waves the electric oscillations in the telephone line which were set up by sound waves, so the doctor's unconscious is able, from the derivatives of the unconscious which are communicated to him, to reconstruct that unconscious, which has determined the patient's free associations. (12: pp. 115–116)

Opening himself to the risk of feminization, Freud assumes the role of an orifice, a listening ear, while the patient becomes a mouth, an oral transmitter. Freud, as office receptionist, opens a direct line to the patient, adjusting the patient's unconscious to the frequencies of his own psychical interior. This interconnection between patient and doctor, transmitter and receiver, mouth and ear, sets up a technology of oral transmission: transference operates telephonically.

The gratification Freud derived from the "electric oscillations" of the transferential line suggests that at the center of psychoanalysis's primal scene is a performance of what Neil Hertz has dubbed "oral intercourse in that other sense of the term." Freud's choice of a telephone to describe the intimate exchanges between doctor and patient highlights the "epistemological promiscuity" that characterizes psychoanalysis's therapeutic practice.[32] The very arrangement of couch and chair facilitates an erotics of voice, privileging sound over sight, speech over spectatorship. In the consulting room, telephone replaces mirror as the governing topos of the doctor-patient relation.

However, like the mirror on the window, Freud's imaginary telephone immediately connects us to the place of mourning. This indeed is the lesson of Avital Ronell's *The Telephone Book*, which reminds us that the telephone has always been involved in a hermeneutics of mourning, in a call to an absent other: "like transference, the telephone is given to us as effigy."[33] Invented originally as a device for the hearing and speech impaired, the telephone works as a prosthesis to compensate for radical loss. Freud, partially deaf in his right ear, detected in the electric speech of the telephone the soft reverberations of distant connections, the sound of the unconscious. A powerful transmitter of disembodied presence, Freud's telephone was capable of summoning the very spirits of the dead-modulated voices from beyond the grave.[34]

IV.

In one respect, the arrangement of bodies in the consulting room bears a certain disquieting resemblance to a wake, with Freud holding vigil over the body of his patient lying immobilized on the couch, most likely enshrouded (mummy-like) in the blanket provided, and surrounded by hundreds of funerary objects. *Eros* and *thonotos* turn out to be comfortable bedfellows as Freud's analytic couch doubles as not just a bed but a bier. Occupying the space of an off-screen presence, the analyst's listening ear and ventriloquized speech offer the patient the promise of reestablishing a tenuous connection to the Other who has been lost. By assuming the position of telephone receiver, the one who accepts the call to the Other, Freud thus finds himself addressing the patient from the borderline between presence and absence—the threshold between life and death.

In the minds of his patients, Freud was not only healer, prophet, and shaman but gatekeeper to the underworld, "patron of gate-ways and portals" (TF, p. 106). Like the stone Janus head on his office desk, Freud "faced two ways, as doors and gates opened and shut" (TF, p. 100).[35] A modern-day Hermes or Thoth, Freud keeps vigilant watch over the dangerous passage across the invisible borders of past and present, memory and forgetting. "In analysis," Freud once explained to H.D., "the person is dead after the analysis is over," to which H.D. responded, "which person?" (TF, p. 141) With characteristic acuity, H.D. troubles the notion of physician as mourner, alluding to the possibility that it is Freud himself who is mourned, Freud who may already find himself on the other side of the portal. In the journey through death staged by the work of analysis, the question of who is the traveler and who the guide remains, at the very least, open.

In one of Freud's most interesting metaphorizations of the scene of treatment, he imagines doctor and patient as fellow passengers on a railway journey. Tutoring the patient on the technique of free association, Freud recommends: "Act as though…you were a traveler sitting next to the window of a railway carriage and describing to someone inside the carriage the changing views which you see outside" (12: p. 135). The train, associated throughout Freud's work with death and departure, carries doctor and patient along the same track, advancing the familiar genre of the travelogue as a model for the talking cure. The picture of easy companionship and leisurely conversation that Freud paints for his patient clearly seeks to domesticate what threatens to be a terrifying venture. Yet what is particularly striking about Freud's scenario of the fellow train travelers is his own severely circumscribed role within it, for Freud is the passenger whose vision is impaired, who can only imagine the view outside the window that his companion is invited to describe. While doctor and patient are located on the same side of the window, the patient alone is visually empowered while Freud is functionally blinded. Freud can listen but he cannot see; hearing must compensate for a radical loss of vision. Once again, then, Freud imagines himself as a passive, responsive organ: "two open ears and one temporal lobe lubricated for reception."[36]

In depriving himself of visual authority, Freud assumes the role of the blind seer, the one who "sacrifices sight…with an eye to seeing at last."[37]

Through his figurative self-blinding, Freud inserts himself into a long line of blind healers and sightless soothsayers: Oedipus, the guilty son, who achieves wisdom by putting out his own eyes; Tiresias, the prophet of two sexes, who suffers blindness at the hands of the goddess Hera after testifying to women's greater sexual pleasure; and Tobit, the man of last respects, who never stops asking his sons to close his eyes as the time approaches for his own burial. It is impossible to forget the dream Freud had on the night after his own father's funeral—a dream about closing the eyes. Freud dreamt that he was in a place (in one account, a railway station) where a sign was posted that read: "you are requested to close the eyes." Late for his own father's funeral, Freud reads this dream as an expression of guilt for his failure to give his father a proper burial. Freud explains that "the sentence on the sign has a double meaning: one should do one's duty to the dead (an apology as though I had not done it and were in need of leniency), and the actual duty itself. The dream thus stems from the inclination to self-reproach that regularly sets in among survivors."[38]

"You are requested to close the eyes" refers to the literal act of performing a burial rite and to the symbolic necessity of taking one's leave of the dead. As Didier Anzieu perceptively notes, however, the request to "close the eyes" is also one of the instructions Freud habitually gave to his patients when beginning an analytic session.[39] The clinical rehearsal of this particular ritual provides what is perhaps the clearest illustration of the extent to which Freud envisioned the work of psychoanalysis as an elaborate funeral rite. Freud eventually discontinued the practice of enjoining his patients to close their eyes,[40] but vision and blindness continued to define for Freud the core dynamic of the therapeutic relation. Eyes now open, the patient on Freud's consulting room couch encounters the penetrating look of Gradiva, a plaster cast bas-relief hanging on the wall at the foot of the ottoman, carefully positioned to stare directly down at the patient. It is Wilhelm Jensen's Gradiva—for Freud the very incarnation of immortality—who offers patient and doctor (eye and ear) a new set of instructions: "look, but not with bodily eyes, and listen, but not with physical ears. And then…the dead wakened" (9: p. 16).

In Freud's theater of inversions, where a healing ritual can lull the living into a nether world of dreams and a funeral rite can waken the dead, subjects and objects are also transposed. When H.D. first enters the office in Berggasse 19, it is the objects, not their owner, that seize her attention: "The statues stare and stare and seem to say, what has happened to you?" (TF, p. 110) There are more sculptures in Freud's vast collection of antiquities than any other kind of art object, figures with a more immediate and anthropomorphic presence than either painting or photography.[41] Apparently these statues are endowed with the vision that Freud himself is denied; the figurines, their faces and their sight animated, stand in obverse relation to Freud, his face composed and his eyes veiled. In one of H.D.'s only physical descriptions of Freud, she describes him as though she were appreciating a piece of statuary, sculpted by an expert craftsman:

> His beautiful mouth seemed always slightly smiling, though his eyes, set deep and slightly asymmetrical under the domed forehead (with those furrows cut by a master chisel) were unrevealing. His eyes did not speak to me. (TF, p. 73)

The portals of Freud's eyes are closed to his patients, as if he himself were an inanimate statue. By prohibiting the patient from looking at him during analysis, Freud, ostensibly seeking to ward off the possibility of idolatry, actually lays its foundations. Positioning himself in the place of "the one who must not be looked at," Freud immediately assumes the status of an otherworldly presence, concealed behind the inscrutable exterior of a powerful and mysterious graven image.

Is this why the view from Freud's consulting room chair resists all attempts to reproduce it technologically? And why Engelman's camera, when it attempts to see the space of the office through Freud's eyes, is effectively rendered blind? "I wanted to see things the way Freud saw them, with his own eyes, during the long hours of his treatment sessions and as he sat writing," Engelman concedes in his memoir, "[but] I couldn't…fit my bulky tripod into the tight space between Freud's chair at the head of the couch and the little table covered with an oriental rug on which [were] set a half-dozen fragile looking Egyptian statuettes."[42] Unable to simulate the view from the analyst's chair, Engelman finds that he must redirect his gaze back to the perspective of the patient. The consulting room chair stands as a fundamentally uninhabitable space, a tribute to the imposing figure of the analyst who remains, even to the searching eye of the camera, totally and enigmatically other.

V.

"Tucked" away in his "three-sided niche" (TF, p. 22), Freud once again can be seen to occupy a spatially marginalized position. But while Freud's physical mobility in the consulting room may be more severely restricted than that of his patient, his field of vision is actually far greater. From his treatment chair, Freud can see not only the cabinet of antiquities below the now famous reproduction of Pierre Albert-Brouillet's engraving, *La Leçon clinique du Dr. Charcot,* but also the room's two main apertures (window and door) that frame it on either side. While from this position he is capable of monitoring any movements in or out of the consulting room, Freud's view of the entry door is partially obscured by a set of fully intact antiquities displayed on the table in front of him, a double row of figurines that, like the patient on the couch, are carefully arranged on a Persian rug. Are we to see these unbroken antiquities as visual surrogates for Freud's patients ("there are priceless broken fragments that are meaningless until we find the other broken bits to match them," H.D. writes [TF, p. 35]; "I was here because I must not be broken" [TF, p. 16])?[43] Or are we to see Freud's patients as simply another part of his collection, a conjecture reinforced by the photographs of Marie Bonaparte and Lou-Andreas Salomé, two of Freud's former patients, placed on the study bookcases alongside Freud's other antiquities?

It seems likely that the relation between Freud's antiquities and his patients is more complex than either of these two possibilities allows. Notably, the Egyptian statues in front of the consulting room chair are visible to Freud from the side, like the figures in profile found on the Egyptian papyrus hanging on the wall closest to Freud's immediate line of vision. This particular mummy covering, which depicts a scene of embalming,[44] holds a privileged place amongst Freud's antiquities, its location next to the treatment chair permitting hours of careful study. For Freud, interpreting a patient's dream is like deciphering an Egyptian hieroglyph. Pictographic script emblematizes the work of dream interpretation, offering a visual analog to the template of the dream text, the "picture-language" (13: p. 177) of the unconscious.

From his consulting room chair, Freud also has an unobstructed view of the desk in the adjoining study, where he will adjourn late in the day to take notes on his sessions and to write up his research. "One of the claims of psycho-analysis to distinction is, no doubt, that in its execution research and treatment coincide" (12: p. 114), Freud remarks, immediately qualifying that it is, in fact, unwise to begin scientific research on a case while treatment is still in progress. The architectural design of the office accordingly splits the interior in two, artificially divorcing the space of listening from the space of reflection. But the strict methodological barrier Freud erects between study and consulting room is nonetheless breached by the two doors that remain, like listening ears, perpetually open between them. [Fig. 6.28] A single axial line links desk chair to treatment chair, reflection to reception. While Freud listens to the patient from his consulting room chair, he has a clear view of the desk that awaits him, and a vision of the work of analysis toward which the clinical session aspires. Similarly, while Freud composes his scientific notes and theoretical papers at the study desk, consulting room couch and chair stand before him like an empty stage set, a visual reminder of the drama that has recently unfolded there in which Freud himself played a prominent role. The centers of knowledge in these adjoining rooms are thus visually continuous: treatment anticipates research; research rehearses treatment.

The immediate view from Freud's desk chair is no less phantasmatically staged, with many of Freud's favorite figurines lined up in a row on his desktop like so many members of a "silent audience."[45] Freud's desk, the most interior place in the office and the most difficult to access, is also the site of greatest structural fortification. Surrounded on three sides by three wooden tables, Freud's work area marks out yet another protected enclave, more confining yet more secure than the interior room created for the patient on the couch. It is at his desk that Freud makes the perilous transition from listening to writing; it is at his desk that he enters into dialogue with his professional demons; it is at his desk that he struggles to put his own manuscripts to rest. Visible in Engelman's photographs of the study desk are the spectral outlines of Freud's *Moses and Monotheism*—Freud's last completed work that, he confesses, "tormented me like an unlaid ghost" (23: p. 103).

In what sense might Freud's office, and the clinical encounter that takes place there, be read not just as an elegiac space but as a haunted one? Freud, it appears, was forever exorcising ghosts. A year after moving his office into a wing of his living quarters, Freud writes to Carl Jung of what he calls his "poltergeist"—a cracking noise issuing from the two Egyptian steles resting on top of the oak bookcases. Believing at first that these ancient grave-markers are possessed by spirits whenever Jung is in the room, Freud only reluctantly relinquishes his fanciful superstition when the steles continue to groan in his friend's absence: "I confront the despiritualized furniture," Freud laments, "as the poet confronted undeified Nature after the gods of Greece had passed away."[46]

But the Greek gods are not the only apparitions haunting the furniture and antiquities in Freud's office; for Freud's patients, these possessions operate as spectral doubles for the analyst himself. At least once in every analysis, Freud explains, the patient claims that his free associations have stopped; however, if pressed, he will admit that he is thinking of the objects around him—the wallpaper, the gas-lamp, the sofa: "Then one knows at once that he has gone off into the transference and that he is engaged upon what are still unconscious thoughts relating to the physician" (18: p. 126).[47] A transferential force emanates from Freud's possessions; these overinvested forms operate, for the patient, as shadowy substitutes for the analyst who must not be seen. Whether or not Freud's patients actually related to their physician's objects in this way is perhaps less interesting than the revelation of Freud's own deeply cathected relation to his things, which his theory of animation implicitly betrays. For this quasi-mystical account of the patient's transference onto the doctor through the medium of surrogate-objects is based on Freud's ready presumption that these inanimate possessions *could* somehow function as versions of himself.

Fig. 6.29: Freud at Study Desk. Photographer: Edward Engelman

The possibility that Freud may identify with these objects, may actually see himself as a part of the vast collection amassed around him, finds ironic visual confirmation in the last of Engelman's office photographs. In the only office photograph that includes a human figure, Freud's upper torso and head appear behind the study desk like yet another classical sculpture. [Fig. 6.29] Captured in a moment of statuary repose, Freud's imperturbable facial features appear to imitate the bust of him sculpted seven years before by the Yugoslavian artist Oscar Némon. This final image of Freud amidst his collection provides eloquent testimony to Jean Baudrillard's claim that, while "a given collection is made up of a succession of terms,...the final term must always be the person of the collector," for in the end "it is invariably *oneself* that one collects."[48]

The very medium of the photograph participates in the process of memorialization that so deeply permeates the space of Freud's office. Theorists of photography inevitably return to the camera's technological capacity to objectify the subject, to turn the image of the living into a memorial to the dead. "The home of the photographed is in fact the cemetery," Eduardo Cadava writes; "a small funerary monument, the photograph is a grave for the living dead."[49] Engelman's camera captures that moment, identified by Roland Barthes, when the one who is photographed is neither subject nor object but a subject becoming an object, a subject who is truly becoming a specter.[50] The photograph of Freud amongst his relics mortifies its living subject—it embalms Freud in a tomb he spent over forty years preparing. It is a suitable memorial to the man who seemed to glimpse, more assuredly than anyone, the many elusive ways in which our deaths anticipate us and our lives encrypt us.

Photography might be said to haunt psychoanalysis in another way, for a principle of photographic likenesses, of double exposures and exposed doubles, animates and reanimates the transferential scene. Insofar as the mechanism of transference works precisely by means of a double exposure—a superimposition of one figure onto another—the process of psychoanalysis can be seen to operate as a form of photographic development. Like photography, the technology of transference performs a kind of spirit work in which the phantoms of missing or lost others come back to life in the person of the analyst. In "Introjection and Transference," Sandor Ferenczi refers to the physician as a "revenant" in whom the patient finds again "the vanished figures of childhood."[51] Freud, as object of his patients' transferences, was just such a revenant, the living image of an absent person. Psychoanalysis, in this respect, was never very far from the schools of nineteenth-century spiritualism it so vigorously sought to bury. The ghost of the spirit medium speaks through the psychoanalyst every time the patient, through the agency of transference, communes with the dead.

A year and four months after Engelman took his clandestine photographs of Freud's Vienna office, Freud died of cancer in his new home at 20 Maresfield Gardens in London. He died in his office, a room that had been renovated by his architect son Ernst and arranged by his maid Paula Fichtl to reproduce, as closely as possible, the office at Berggasse 19. In this, the most painful period of his sixteen year battle with oral cancer, Freud's office became his sickroom. It was here that Freud slipped into a coma after Max Schur, at Freud's request, administered the fatal doses of morphine that would end Freud's life on 23 September 1939. Cremated three days later, Freud's ashes were placed, according to the family's wishes, in a Greek urn—a red-figured Bell Krater presented to Freud as a gift by Marie Bonaparte. One might say that Freud at last found a resting place amongst his beloved antiquities.

This essay is part of a longer book-length project on the space of Freud's office. We would like to thank the many curators who made this research possible: Lydia Marinelli of the Freud Haus in Vienna; Erica Davies and J. Keith Davies of the Freud Museum in London; and Christian Witt-Doring of the MAK (Österreichisches Museum für angewandte Kunst) in Vienna. We also thank Kim Yao, who assisted in the production of the architectural drawings. Most of all, we extend our gratitude to Edmund Engelman, who graciously agreed to be interviewed for this essay.

Notes

*   Diana Fuss and Joel Sanders "Berggasse 19: Inside Freud's Office," In *Stud: Architectures of Masculinity*, ed. Joel Sanders (New York: Princeton Architectural Press, 1996), 124.

1   See Edmund Engelman, "A Memoir," which follows the published English-language version of the photographs, *Berggasse 19: Sigmund Freud's Home and Offices, Vienna* 1938 (New york: Basic Books, 1976), p. 134. Rita Ransohoff's photographic captions visually orient the reader, while Peter Gay's preface to the volume, "Freud: For the Marble Tablet," provides an eloquent historical and biographical introduction. Readers might also wish to consult the more recent

German edition of Engelman's photographs, *Sigmund Freud: Wien IX. Berggasse 19* (Vienna: Verlag Christian Brandstätter, 1993), which includes an introduction by Inge Scholz-Strasser, General Secretary of the Freud Haus.

2 Edmund Engelman, interview by the authors, 14 September 1995. Of these 100 photographs, 56 have been published in the English-language version of *Berggasse 19*, regrettably now out of print.

3 An exception is Beatriz Colamina's analysis of spectatorship in the architectural interiors of Adolf Loos and Le Corbusier in her important book, *Privacy and Publicity: Modern Architecture of Mass Media* (Cambridge: MIT Press, 1994).

4 Freud, Letter to his son Ernst, 12 May 1938. In *Sigmund Freud, Briefe 1873–1939*, ed. Ernst L. Freud (Frankfurt am Main: S. Fischer, 1960), p. 435.

5 Engelman, "A Memoir," p. 136.

6 Susan Suleiman, "Bataille in the Street: The Search for Virility in the 1930s," *Critical Inquiry* 21 (Autumn 1994), p. 62.

7 Hannah S. Decker, *Freud, Dora, and Vienna, 1900* (New York: The Free Press, 1991), p. 24. Bruno Bettelheim has speculated that Freud's choice to settle on this respectable but undistinguished street was motivated by a deep cultural ambivalence, as Freud sought to reconcile loyalty to his Jewish beginnings with competing desires for assimilationist respectability. See Bettelheim's *Freud's Vienna & Other Essays* (New York: Vintage, 1991), p. 20. Bettelheim argues in this review of Engelman's photographs that "studying the psychoanalytic couch in detail does not necessarily give any inkling of what psychoanalysis is all about, nor does viewing the settings in which it all happened explain the man, or his work" (19). Our own reading of Berggasse 19 suggests that just the opposite is the case: Engelman's photographs and the space of the office provide important clues not only to Freud's role as clinician but also to the historical development of psychoanalysis, a practice that evolved in response to the changing social, political, and cultural spaces it inhabited.

8 On the street as a site of "accident and incident," see Peter Jukes, A *Shout in the Street: An Excursion into the Modern City* (Berkeley and Los Angeles: University of California Press, 1990).

9 We might note in this regard Edmund Engelman's personal recollection of the ambiance of Freud's office, which he compares to the feeling of being "inside the storage room of an antique dealer." Interview, 14 September 1995.

10 As early as 1901, only five years after beginning his collection, Freud writes of the shortage of space in his office study, already filled with pottery and other antiquities, and of his visitors' anxieties that he might eventually break something. See Freud's *Psychopathology of Everyday Life,* in *The Standard Edition of the Complete Psychological Works of Sigmund Freud,* trans. and ed. James Strachey, 24 vols. (London: The Hogarth Press, 1953–1974), 6: p. 167. All citations from the *Standard Edition* hereafter cited in the text by volume and page number.

11 Letter to Fliess, 19 April 1894, in *The Complete Letters of Sigmund Freud to Wilhelm Fliess: 1887–1904,* trans. and ed. Jeffrey Moussaieff Masson (Cambridge: Harvard University Press, 1985).

12 Letter to Fliess, 22 June 1894.

13 Letter to Fliess, 26 October 1896.

14 Freud possessed many representations of Osiris, king of the underworld and god of resurrection. Osiris, in some accounts the first Egyptian mummy, was locked into a coffin by his brother and set adrift on the Nile. Three different bronze statues of Osiris (two complete figures and a large head fragment) adorn Freud's desk, testifying to the importance Freud accorded this particular Egyptian deity.

15 For a more complete discussion of Freud's antiquities, see the essays and selected catalogue in *Sigmund Freud and Art: His Personal Collection of Antiquities,* eds. Lynn Gamwell and Richard Wells (London: Thames and Hudson, 1989). John Forrester provides an especially fascinating reading of Freud's antiquities in his essay "'Mille e tre': Freud and Collecting," in *The Cultures of Collecting,* eds. John Elsner and Roger Cardinal (Cambridge: Harvard University Press, 1994), pp. 224–251.

16 Theodor Adorno, "Valéry Proust Museum," in *Prisms,* trans. Samuel and Shierry Weber (Cambridge: MIT Press, 1981), p. 175. Freud's office bears striking similarities to the house-museum of Sir John Soane in London. For a discussion of the museum as a place of entombment, see John Elsner's "A Collector's Model of Desire: The House and Museum of Sir John Soane," in *The Cultures of Collecting,* pp. 155–176. See also Douglas Crimp, *On the Museum's Ruins* (Cambridge: MIT Press, 1993).

17 For fuller accounts of the *Kaiserliches Stiftungshaus,* Freud's first home and office, see Ernest Jones, *The Life and Work of Sigmund Freud,* 2 vols. (New York: Basic Books, 1953), I: p. 149, and Bettelheim, *Freud's Vienna,* pp. 11–12.

18 Jacques Lacan, *Seminar I: Freud's Papers on Technique,* ed. Jacques-Alain Miller, trans. John Forrester (New York: Norton, 1988), p. 141.

19 For an excellent discussion of challenges to the traditional humanism of the architectural window, see Thomas Keenan, "Windows: of vulnerability," in *The Phantom Public Sphere,* ed. Bruce Robbins (Minneapolis: University of Minnesota Press, 1994), pp. 121–141. See also Colomina, *Privacy and Publicity,* esp. pp. 80–82, 234–238, and 283 ff. An earlier discussion of windows and mirrors can be found in Diana Agrest, "Architecture of Mirror/Mirror of Architecture," in *Architecture from Without: Theoretical Framings for a Critical Practice* (Cambridge: MIT Press, 1991), pp. 139–155.

20 Lacan, *Seminar I,* p. 215; see also p. 78.

21 Jacques Lacan, "The Mirror Stage as Formative of the Function of the I as Revealed in Psychoanalytic Experience," in *Écrits,* trans. Alan Sheridan (New York: Norton, 1977), p. 2.

22 Mikkel Borch-Jacobsen, *Lacan: The Absolute Master,* trans, Douglas Brick (Stanford: Stanford University Press, 1991), p. 59.

23 *The Wolf-Man, by the Wolf-Man,* ed. Muriel Gardiner (New York: Noonday, 1991), p. 139. Sergei Pankeiev also takes note, as all Freud's patients did, of the many objects in the room: "Here were all kinds of statuettes and other unusual objects, which even the layman recognized as archeological finds from ancient Egypt. Here and there on the walls were stone plaques representing various scenes of long-vanished epochs.…Freud himself explained his love for archeology in that the psychoanalyst, like the archeologist in his excavations, must uncover layer after layer of the patient's psyche, before coming to the deepest, most valuable treasures" (139). For more on the dominance of the archeologicalmetaphor in Freud's work, see Donald Kuspit, "A Mighty Metaphor: The Analogy of Archaeology and Psychoanalysis," in *Sigmund Freud and Art,* pp. 133–151.

24 H.D., *Tribute to Freud* (New York: McGraw-Hill, 1975), p. 132. Hereafter, abbreviated "TF" and cited in the text. H.D.'s autobiographical account of her psychoanalytic sessions with Freud provides us with the most complete recollection we have, from the point of view of a patient, of Freud's consulting room. Her memoir offers a narrative counterpart to Engelman's photographs, describing, in surprisingly rich detail, the view from the couch and the sounds, smells, and objects around her.

25 Max Schur, *Freud: Living and Dying* (New York: International Universities Press, Inc., 1972), p. 246.

26 Friedrich Spuhler, *Oriental Carpets in the Museum of Islamic Art, Berlin,* trans. Robert Pinner (London: Faber and Faber, 1988), p. 10. See also David Sylvester, "On Western Attitudes to Eastern Carpets," in *Islamic Carpets from the Joseph V. McMullan Collection* (London: Arts Council of Great Britain, 1972); Kurt Erdmann, *Seven Hundred years of Oriental Carpets,* ed. Hanna Erdmann, trans. May H. Beattie and Hildegard Herzog (London: Faber and Faber, 1970); and John Mills, "The Coming of the Carpet to the West" in *The Eastern Carpet in the Western World, from the 15th to the 17th Century,* ed. Donald King and David Sylvester (London: Arts Council of Great Britain, 1983). For a more detailed treatment of Orientalism in the context of Western architecture and interior design, see John M. MacKenzie's *Orientalism: History, Theory and the Arts* (Manchester: Manchester University Press, 1995). While many of the older carpets on display in the Vienna exhibition came from mosques, Freud's newer carpets were woven in Northwest Persia, most likely in court workshops.

27 Freud's first office in Berggasse 19 was located on the building's ground floor, beneath the family apartment, in three rooms formerly occupied by Victor Adler. Freud conducted his practice here from 1891 to 1907, when he moved his offices in to the back rooms of the apartment immediately adjacent to the family residence.

28 Freud admits toward the end of *Papers on Technique* that "a particularly large number of patients object to being asked to lie down, while the doctor sits out of sight behind them" (12: p. 139).

29 Luce Irigaray, "The Gesture in Psychoanalysis," in *Between Feminism and Psychoanalysis*, ed. Teresa Brennan (New York and London: Routledge, 1989), p. 129.

30 Ibid., p. 128.

31 Freud's own practice was to take notes from memory after all his sessions that day had been completed. For particularly important dream texts, the patient was asked to repeat the dream until Freud had committed its details to memory (12: pp. 113–114).

32 Neil Hertz, "Dora's Secrets, Freud's Techniques," in *In Dora's Case: Freud, Hysteria, Feminism,* eds. Charles Bernheimer and Claire Kahane (New York: Columbia University Press, 1985), pp. 229 and 234.

33 Avital Ronell, *The Telephone Book: Technology, Schizophrenia, Electric Speech* (Lincoln: University of Nebraska Press, 1989), p. 84.

34 Ibid., esp. pp. 88–96. Freud lost much of the hearing in his right ear after his surgery for oral cancer in 1923. Peter Gay writes that Freud actually moved the couch from one wall to another so he could listen better with his left ear. See Gay, *Freud: A Life for Our Time* (New York: Anchor Books, 1988), p. 427.

35 Psychoanalysis generally reads the space of the doorway as a symbol of change and transition, but in at least one instance the doorway became for Freud a powerful image of arrested movement. In a letter to Minna Bernays dated 20 May 1938, written as he anxiously awaited permission to emigrate, Freud compares the experience of impending exile to "standing in the doorway like someone who wants to leave a room but finds that his coat is jammed." Cited in *The Diary of Sigmund Freud, 1929–1939*, trans. Michael Molnar (New York: Charles Scribner's Sons, 1992), p. 236.

36 Letter to Fliess, 30 June 1896.

37 Jacques Derrida, *Memoirs of the Blind: The Self-Portrait and Other Ruins,* trans. Pascale-Anne Brault and Michael Naas (Chicago and London: University of Chicago Press, 1993), p. 30. In this elegant book Derrida traces a tradition of prints and drawings depicting figures of blindness, including three of the visionary blind men alludded to here: Oedipus, Tiresias, and Tobit.

38 Freud recounts this dream both in the letter to Fliess cited here, dated 2 November 1896, and later, in slightly altered form, in *The Interpretation of Dreams* (4: pp. 317–318). See also Freud's analysis of another death-bed dream, "Father on his death-bed like Garibaldi" (5: pp. 427–429).

39 Didier Anzieu, *Freud's Self-Analysis,* trans. Peter Graham (Madison, CT: International Universities Press, 1986), p. 172.

40 According to Anzieu, Freud discontinued this practice in 1904; ibid., p. 64.

41 Lynn Gamwell has noted that "almost every object Freud acquired is a figure whose gaze creates a conscious presence." See her "The Origins of Freud's Antiquities Collection," in *Sigmund Freud and Art,* p. 27.

42 Engelman, "A Memoir," p. 137.

43 H.D. saw immediately the significance of Freud's reliquary objects, their mirror relation to the patients who came to Freud every day to be "skillfully pieced together like the exquisite Greek tear-jars and iridescent glass bowls and vases that gleamed in the dusk from the cabinet" (TF, p. 14.).

44 C. Nicholas Reeves identifies this particular piece of ancient cartonnage as a frontal leg covering from the mummy of a woman. The two lower panels once again depict Osiris, king of the underworld. For a fuller description of this Egyptian mummy covering and its hieroglyphics, see *Sigmund Freud and Art,* p. 75.

45 Gamwell in *Sigmund Freud and Art,* p. 28.

46 Letter to Jung, 16 April 1909, in *The Freud/Jung Letters,* ed. William McGuire, trans. Ralph Manheim and R.F.C. Hull (Cambridge: Harvard University Press, 1988), p. 218. This story of the haunted steles appears in the same letter in which Freud analyzes another episode of his death deliria (the superstition that he will die between the ages of 61 and 62) and where he makes reference to what he identifies as "the specifically Jewish nature of my mysticism" (220).

47 On the subject of a patient's transference onto the doctor through the medium of objects, see also Freud's *Papers on Technique:* "[the patient] had been occupied with the picture of the room in which he was, or he could not help thinking of the objects in the consulting room and of the fact that he was lying here on a sofa.... [E]verything connected with the present situation represents a transference to the doctor, which proves suitable to serve as a first resistance" (12: p.138).

48 Jean Baudrillard, "The System of Collecting," in *The Culture of Collecting,* p. 12.

49 Eduardo Cadava, "Words of Light: Theses on the Photography of History," in *Fugitive Images: From Photography to Video,* ed. Patrice Petro (Bloomington and Indianapolis: Indiana University Press, 1995), pp. 223 and 224.

50 Roland Barthes, *Camero Lucida: Reflections on Photography,* trans. Richard Howard (New York: Farrar Straus & Giroux, 1981), p. 14.

51 Sandor Ferenczi, "Introjection and Transference," in *Sex in Psychoanalysis* (New York: Basic Books, 1950), p. 41.

Interior

Beatriz Colomina

INTRODUCTION

Beatriz Colomina frames Adolf Loos's residences in the context of theatrics, and thus provides a script for the domestic realm as a stage set awaiting its occupants. A saying by Walter Benjamin, "To live means to leave traces," adds to the drama analogy and draws attention to cues on the interior that reveal traces of occupation.* Colomina materializes these traces by referencing photographs of Loos's interiors in which domestic objects played a temporal role, often anchored to a specific place in the image. More ephemeral still, a photograph of Loos's Moller House depicts a cup and saucer on the floor, which we see left in the middle of the room, informing the making of a narrative and a layer of intimacy uniquely inherent to the interior, unlike the static realm of architecture. As narrative informs theatrics, so does lighting, views, and props, all of which played leading roles in Loos's interiors.

Loos carved spaces using his conceptual invention of the Raumplan. *Not only did the spaces result in hierarchical ordering of occupation, they also incorporate attributes of theaters—often in the form of a perch or alcove-like space comparable to a theater box. Colomina narrates the processional sequence by highlighting the roles of actor and audience in the interior spaces that most elaborate on strategies of theatrical device. In her description, light through windows act as a spotlight on a room entry, and built-in furniture in front of the window provided seating for the viewer whose gaze is directed to the interior. Colomina emphasizes architectural elements of the interiors-as-theater that include window, furniture, floor, and entry as a way to assemble the stage set in anticipation of actors. In some instances, these theatrical platforms were gender specific, such as the perchlike room meant for the woman of the house in the Villa Müller. Loos placed the woman's sitting room in the center of the house and provided screenlike openings at an intimate scale to imply that when the woman was in the room, she also had watch over spaces around her. The interior was conceived as a container of delicate moments.*

Originally appeared in *Privacy and Publicity: Modern Architecture as Mass Media*, 9,190 word excerpt from pages 233–82, 369–74. © 1994 Massachusetts Institute of Technology, by permission of The MIT Press.

Loos used the houses to reinforce his agenda that the interior was the site where luxurious use of material could be applied as long as it met his rules from "The Principle of Cladding." The exterior, on the other hand, remained unembellished, like that of a man's dinner jacket, providing anonymity and inconspicuousness, because to do so was to be modern. Loos's expression of material application for interior and exterior skins is made analogous to cloth-ing: "All the architecture of Loos can be explained as the envelope of a body."[+]

———

"TO LIVE IS TO LEAVE TRACES," writes Walter Benjamin, discussing the birth of the interior. "In the interior these are emphasized. An abundance of covers and protectors, liners and cases is devised, on which the traces of objects of everyday use are imprinted. The traces of the occupant also leave their impression on the interior. The detective story that follows these traces comes into being....The criminals of the first detective novels are neither gentlemen nor apaches, but private members of the bourgeoisie."[1]

There is an interior in the detective novel. But can there be a detective story of the interior itself, of the hidden mechanisms by which space is constructed as interior? Which may be to say, a detective story of detection itself, of the controlling look, the look of control, the controlled look. But where would the traces of the look be imprinted? What do we have to go on? What clues?

There is an unknown passage of a well-known book, Le Corbusier's *Urbanisme* (1925), that reads: "Loos told me one day: 'A cultivated man does not look out of the window; his window is a ground glass; it is there only to let the light in, not to let the gaze pass through.'"[2] It points to a conspicu-ous yet conspicuously ignored feature of Loos's houses: not only are the win-dows either opaque or covered with sheer curtains, but the organization of the spaces and the disposition of the built-in furniture (the *immeuble*) seem to hinder access to them. A sofa is often placed at the foot of a window so as to position the occupants with their back to it, facing the room, as in the bedroom of the Hans Brummel apartment (Pilsen, 1929). [Fig. 6.30] This even happens with the windows that look into other interior spaces—as in the sit-ting area of the ladies' lounge of the Muller house (Prague, 1930). Or, more dramatically, in the houses for the Vienna Werkbundsiedlung (Vienna, 1930–1932), a late project where Loos has finally brought himself to make a thor-oughly modern, double-height window; not only is this opening still veiled with a curtain, but a couch in the sitting nook of the upper-level gallery places the occupants with their back to the window, hovering dangerously over the space. [Fig. 6.31] (Symptomatically, and we must return to this point, when the sitting nook in an identical house is used as a man's study, the seat

Fig. 6.30: Adolf
Loos, flat for Hans
Brummel, Pilsen,
1929. Bedroom
with a sofa set
against the window.
Albertina, Vienna

Fig. 6.31: Adolf
Loos, house
for the Vienna
Werkbundsiedlung,
Vienna, 1930–
1932. Living room
on two levels with
a sofa "against"
the window and
suspended in the
space. Albertina,
Vienna

faces the window.) Moreover, upon entering a Loos interior one's body is continually turned around to face the space one has just moved through, rather than the upcoming space or the space outside. With each turn, each return look, the body is arrested. Looking at the photographs, it is easy to imagine oneself in these precise, static positions, usually indicated by the unoccupied furniture. The photographs suggest that it is intended that these spaces be comprehended by occupation, by using this furniture, by "entering" the photograph, by inhabiting it.[3]

In the Moller house (Vienna, 1928) there is a raised sitting area off the living room with a sofa set against the window. Although one cannot see out the window, its presence is strongly felt. The bookshelves surrounding the sofa and the light coming from behind it suggest a comfortable nook for reading. But comfort in this space is more than just sensual, for there is also a psychological dimension. A sense of security is produced by the position of the couch, the placement of its occupants against the light. Anyone who, ascending the stairs from the entrance (itself a rather dark passage), enters the living room, would take a few moments to recognize a person sitting on the couch. Conversely, any intrusion would soon be detected by a person occupying this area, just as an actor entering the stage is immediately seen by a spectator in a theater box.

Loos refers to this idea in noting that "the smallness of a theater box would be unbearable if one could not look out into the large space beyond."[4] While Kulka, and later Münz, read this comment in terms of the economy of space provided by the *Raumplan,* they overlook its psychological dimension. For Loos, the theater box exists at the intersection between claustrophobia and agoraphobia.[5] This spatial-psychological device could also be read in terms of power, regimes of control inside the house. The raised sitting area of the Moller house provides the occupant with a vantage point overlooking the interior. [Fig. 6.32] Comfort in this space is related to both intimacy and control.

This area is the most intimate of the sequence of living spaces, yet, paradoxically, rather than being at the heart of the house, it is placed at the periphery, pushing a volume out of the street facade, just above the front entrance. Moreover, it corresponds with the largest window on this elevation (almost a horizontal window). [Fig. 6.33] The occupant of this space can both detect anyone crossing-trespassing the threshold of the house (while screened by the curtain) and monitor any movement in the interior (while "screened" by the backlighting).

In this space, the window is only a source of light, not a frame for a view. The eye is turned toward the interior. The only exterior view that would be possible from this position requires that the gaze travel the whole depth of the house, from the alcove to the living room to the music room,

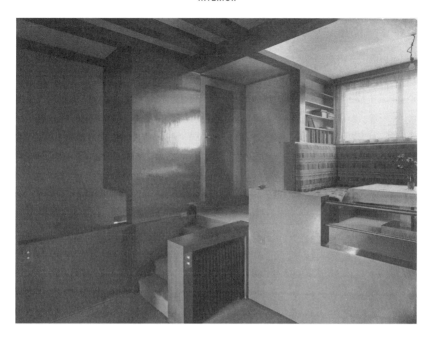

above
Fig. 6.32: Adolf
Loos, Moller
House, Vienna,
1928. The raised
sitting area off
the living room.
Albertina, Vienna

right
Fig. 6.33: Moller
House. View
from the street.
Albertina, Vienna

Fig. 6.34: Moller House. Plan and section tracing the journey of the gaze from the raised sitting area to the back garden. Drawing by Johan van de Beek. Reprinted from Max Risselada, ed., *Raumplan versus Plan Libre*. Rotterdam: 010 Publishers, 2008.

which opens onto the back garden. [Fig. 6.34] Thus, the exterior view depends upon a view of the interior.

The look folded inward upon itself can be traced in other Loos interiors. In the Müller house, for instance, the sequence of spaces, articulated around the staircase, follows an increasing sense of privacy from the drawing room to the dining room and study to the "lady's room" (*Zimmer der Dame*) with its raised sitting area, which occupies the center or "heart" of the house.[6] [Fig. 6.35] But the window of this space looks onto the living space. Here, too, the most intimate room is like a theater box, placed just over the entrance to the social spaces in this house, so that any intruder could easily be seen. Likewise, the view of the exterior, toward the city, from this "theater box" is contained within a view of the interior. Suspended in the middle of the house, this space assumes the character both of a "sacred" space and of a point of control. Comfort is produced by two seemingly opposing conditions, intimacy and control.

This is hardly the idea of comfort that is associated with the nineteenth-century interior as described by Walter Benjamin in "Louis-Phillippe, or the Interior."[7] In Loos's interiors the sense of security is not achieved by simply turning one's back on the exterior and immersing oneself in a private universe—"a box in the world theater," to use Benjamin's metaphor. It is no longer the house that is a theater box; there is a theater box inside the house, overlooking the internal social spaces. The inhabitants of Loos's houses are both actors in and spectators of the family scene—involved in, yet detached from, their own space.[8] The classical distinction between inside and outside, private and public, object and subject, becomes convoluted.

Traditionally, the theater box provided for the privileged a private space within the dangerous public realm, by reestablishing the boundaries between inside and outside. It is significant that when Loos designed a theater in 1898 (an unrealized project), he omitted the boxes, arguing they "didn't suit a modern auditorium."[9] Thus he removes the box from the public theater, only to insert it into the "private theater" of the house. The public has entered the private house by way of the social spaces,[10] but there is a last site of resistance to this intrusion in the domestic "theater box."

above
Fig. 6.35: Müller House.
The raised sitting area in
the Zimmer der Dame
with the window looking
onto the living room.
Albertina, Vienna

right
Fig. 6.36: Müller House.
The library.
Albertina, Vienna

The theater boxes in the Moller and Müller houses are spaces marked as "female," the domestic character of the furniture contrasting with that of the adjacent "male" space, the library. [Fig. 6.36] In these, the leather sofas, the desks, the chimney, the mirrors represent a "public space" within the house—the office and the club invading the interior. But it is an invasion that is confined to an enclosed room—a space that belongs to the sequence of social spaces within the house, yet does not engage with them. As Münz notes, the library is a "reservoir of quietness," "set apart from the household traffic." The raised alcove of the Moller house and the *Zimmer der Dame* of the Müller house, on the other hand, not only overlook the social spaces but are exactly positioned at the end of the sequence, on the threshold of the private, the secret, the upper rooms where sexuality is hidden away. At the intersection of the visible and the invisible, women are placed as the guardians of the unspeakable.[11]

But the theater box is a device that both provides protection and draws attention to itself. Thus, when Münz describes the entrance to the social spaces of the Moller house, he writes: "Within, entering from one side, one's gaze travels in the opposite direction till it rests in the light, pleasant alcove, raised above the living room floor. *Now we are really inside the house.*"[12] So, where were we before? we may ask, when we crossed the threshold of the house and occupied the entrance hall and the cloakroom in the ground floor or while we ascended the stairs to the reception rooms on the second or elevated ground floor. The intruder is "inside," has penetrated the house, only when his/her gaze strikes this most intimate space, turning the occupant into a silhouette against the light. The "voyeur" in the "theater box" has become the object of another's gaze; she is caught in the act of seeing, entrapped in the very moment of control. In framing a view, the theater box also frames the viewer. It is impossible to abandon the space, let alone leave the house, without being seen by those over whom control is being exerted. Object and subject exchange places. Whether there is actually a person behind either gaze is irrelevant:

> I can feel myself under the gaze of someone whose eyes I do not even see, not even discern. All that is necessary is for something to signify to me that there may be others there. The window if it gets a bit dark and if I have reasons for thinking that there is someone behind it, is straightway a gaze. From the moment this gaze exists, I am already something other, in that I feel myself becoming an object for the gaze of others. But in this position, which is a reciprocal one, others also know that I am an object who knows himself to be seen.[13]

Architecture is not simply a platform that accommodates the viewing subject. It is a viewing mechanism that produces the subject. It precedes and frames its occupant.

The theatricality of Loos's interiors is constructed by many forms of representation (of which built space is not necessarily the most important). Many of the photographs, for instance, tend to give the impression that someone is just about to enter the room, that a piece of domestic drama is about to be enacted. The characters absent from the stage, from the scenery and from its props—the conspicuously placed pieces of furniture—are conjured up.[14] The only published photograph of a Loos domestic interior that includes a human figure is a view of the entrance to the drawing room of the Rufer house (Vienna, 1922). A male figure, barely visible, is about to cross the threshold through a peculiar opening in the wall.[15] But it is precisely at this threshold, slightly off stage, that the actor/intruder is most vulnerable, for a small window in the reading room looks down onto the back of his or her neck. This house, traditionally considered to be the prototype of the *Raumplan*, also contains the prototype of the theater box.

In his writings on the question of the house, Loos describes a number of domestic melodramas. In *Das Andere*, for example, he writes:

> Try to describe how birth and death, the screams of pain for an aborted son, the death rattle of a dying mother, the last thoughts of a young woman who wishes to die…unfold and unravel in a room by Olbrich! Just an image: the young woman who has put herself to death. She is lying on the wooden floor. One of her hands still holds the smoking revolver. On the table a letter, the farewell letter. Is the room in which this is happening of good taste? Who will ask that? It is just a room![16]

One could as well ask why it is only the women who die and cry and commit suicide. But leaving aside this question for the moment, Loos is saying that the house must not be conceived of as a work of art, that there is a difference between a house and a "series of decorated rooms." The house is the stage for the theater of the family, a place where people are born and live and die. Whereas a work of art, a painting, presents itself to a detached viewer as an object, the house is received as an environment, as a stage, in which the viewer is involved.

To set the scene, Loos breaks down the condition of the house as an object by radically convoluting the relation between inside and outside. One of the strategies he uses is mirrors that, as Kenneth Frampton has pointed out, appear to be openings, and openings that can be mistaken for mirrors.[17] Even more enigmatic is the placement, in the dining room of the Steiner house (Vienna, 1910), of a mirror just beneath an opaque window.[18] Here again the window is only a source of light. The mirror, placed at eye level, returns the gaze to the interior, to the lamp above the dining table and the objects on the sideboard, recalling Freud's studio in Berggasse 19, where a small framed mirror hanging against the window reflects the lamp on his work table. [Fig. 6.37] In Freudian theory the mirror represents the psyche. The reflection in the mirror is also a self-portrait projected onto the outside world. The placement of Freud's mirror on the boundary between interior and exterior undermines the status of the boundary as a fixed limit. Inside and outside cannot simply be separated. Similarly, Loos's mirrors promote the interplay between reality and illusion, between the actual and virtual, undermining the status of the boundary between inside and outside.

This ambiguity between inside and outside is intensified by the separation of sight from the other senses. Physical and visual connections between the spaces in Loos's houses are often separated. In the Rufer house, a wide opening establishes a visual connection between the raised dining room and the music room that does not correspond to the physical connection. Similarly, in the Moller house there appears to be no way of entering the dining room from the music room, which is 70 centimeters below; the only means of access is by unfolding steps that are hidden in the timber base of the dining room.[19] [Fig. 6.38] This strategy of physical separation and visual connection, of "framing," is repeated in many other Loos interiors. Openings are often screened by curtains, enhancing the stagelike effect. It should also be noted that it is usually the dining room that acts as the stage, and the music room as the space for the spectators. What is being framed is the traditional scene of everyday domestic life. [Fig. 6.39]

But the breakdown between inside and outside, and the split between sight and touch, is not located exclusively in the domestic scene. It also occurs in Loos's project for a house for Josephine Baker (Paris, 1928)— a house that excludes family life. However, in this instance the "split" acquires a different meaning. The house was designed to contain a large top-lit, double-height swimming pool, with entry at the second-floor level. Kurt Ungers, a close collaborator of Loos in this project, wrote:

> The reception rooms on the first floor arranged round the pool—a large salon with an extensive top-lit vestibule, a small lounge and the circular cafe-indicate that this was intended not for private use but as a *miniature entertainment centre*. On the first floor, low passages surround the pool. They are lit by the wide windows visible on the outside, and from them, thick, transparent windows are let into the side of the pool, so that it was possible to watch swimming and diving in its crystal-clear water, flooded with light from above: an *underwater revue*, so to speak.[20]

Fig. 6.37: Adolf Loos, Steiner House, Vienna, 1910. View of the dining room showing the mirror beneath the window.
Albertina, Vienna

Fig. 6.38: Moller house. View from the music room into the dining room. In the center of the threshold are steps that can be let down.
Albertina, Vienna

Fig. 6.39: Moller House. View from the dining room into the music room.
Albertina, Vienna

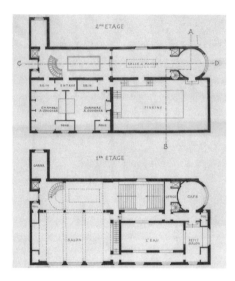

Fig. 6.40: Josephine Baker
House. Plans of first and
second floors.
Albertina, Vienna

As in Loos's earlier houses, the eye directed toward the interior, which turns its back on the outside world; but the subject and object of the gaze have been reversed. The inhabitant, Josephine Baker, is now the primary object, and the visitor, the guest, is the looking subject. The most intimate space—the swimming pool, paradigm of a sensual space—occupies the center of the house, and is also the focus of the visitor's gaze. [Fig. 6.40] As Ungers writes, entertainment in this house consists in looking. But between this gaze and its object—the body—is a screen of glass and water, which renders the body inaccessible. The swimming pool is lit from above, by a skylight, so that inside it the windows would appear as reflective surfaces, impeding the swimmer's view of the visitors standing in the passages. This view is the opposite of the panoptic view of a theater box, corresponding, instead, to that of a peephole, where subject and object cannot simply exchange places.

The *mise-en-scène* in the Josephine Baker house recalls Christian Metz's description of the mechanism of voyeurism in cinema:

> It is even essential…that the actor should behave as though he were not seen (and therefore as though he did not see his voyeur), that he should go about his ordinary business and pursue his existence as foreseen by the fiction of the film, that he should carry on with his antics in a closed room, taking the utmost care not to notice that a glass rectangle has been set into one of the walls, and that he lives in a kind of aquarium.[21]

But the architecture of this house is more complicated. The swimmer might also see the reflection, framed by the window, of her own slippery body superimposed on the disembodied eyes of the shadowy figure of the spectator, whose lower body is cut out by the frame. Thus she sees herself being looked at by another: a narcissistic gaze superimposed on a voyeuristic gaze. This erotic complex of looks in which she is suspended is inscribed in each of the four windows opening onto the swimming pool. Each, even if there is no one looking through it, constitutes, from both sides, a gaze.

The split between sight and the other physical senses that is found in Loos interiors is explicit in his definition of architecture. In "The Principle of Cladding," Loos's most Semperian text, he writes: "The artist, the architect, first senses the *effect* that he intends to realize and [then] sees the rooms he wants to create in his mind's eye. He senses the effect that he wishes to exert upon the *spectator*…homeyness if a residence."[22] For Loos, the interior is pre-Oedipal space, space before the analytical distancing that language entails, space as we feel it, as clothing; that is, as clothing before the existence of readymade clothes, when one had first to choose the fabric (and this act required, or I seem to remember as much, a distinct gesture of looking away from the cloth while feeling its texture, as if the sight of it would be an obstacle to the sensation).

Loos seems to have reversed the Cartesian schism between the perceptual and conceptual. Whereas Descartes, as Franco Rella has written, deprived the body of its status as "the seat of valid and transmissible knowledge" ("In sensation, in the experience that derives from it, harbors error"),[23] Loos privileges the bodily experience of space over its mental construction: the architect first senses the space, then he visualizes it.

For Loos, architecture is a form of covering. But it is not simply the walls that are covered. Structure plays a secondary role, and its primary function is to hold the covering in place. Following Semper almost literally, Loos writes:

> The architect's general task is to provide a warm and livable space. Carpets are warm and livable. He decides for this reason to spread one carpet on the floor and to hang up four to form the four walls. But you cannot build a house out of carpets. Both the carpet on the floor and the tapestry on the wall require a structural frame to hold them in the correct place. To invent this frame is the architect's second task.[24]

The spaces of Loos's interiors cover the occupants as clothes cover the body (each occasion has its appropriate "fit"). José Quetglas has written: "Would the same pressure on the body be acceptable in a raincoat as in a gown, in jodhpurs or in pyjama pants?…All the architecture of Loos can be explained as the envelope of a body." From Lina Loos's bedroom (this "bag of fur and cloth") to Josephine Baker's swimming pool ("this transparent bowl of water"), the interiors always contain a "warm bag in which to wrap

Fig. 6.41: Adolf Loos's flat. Lina Loos's bedroom. Albertina, Vienna

oneself." [Fig. 6.41] It is an "architecture of pleasure," an "architecture of the womb."[25]

But space in Loos's architecture is not just felt. It is significant, in the quotation above, that Loos refers to the inhabitant as a "spectator," for his definition of architecture is really a definition of theatrical architecture. The "clothes" have become so removed from the body that they require structural support independent of it. They become a "stage set." The inhabitant is both "covered" by the space and "detached" from it. The tension between sensation of comfort and comfort as control disrupts the role of the house as a traditional form of representation.

It also disrupts any representation of the house. The status of the architectural drawing, for example, is radically transformed. In "Architecture" Loos writes: "The mark of a building which is truly established is that it remains *ineffective* in two dimensions."[26] By "ineffective" he means that the drawing cannot convey the "sensation" of space, as this involves not only sight but also the other physical senses.[27] Loos devised the *Raumplan* as a means of conceptualizing space as it is felt, but, revealingly, he left no theoretical definition of it. As Kulka has noted, he "will make many changes during construction. He will walk through the space and say: 'I do not like the height of this ceiling, change it!' The idea of the *Raumplan* made it difficult to finish a scheme before construction allowed the visualization of the space as it was." Or as Neutra recalls, Loos "prided himself on being an architect without a pencil":

In the year 1900, Adolf Loos started a revolt against the practice of indicating dimensions in figures or measured drawings. He felt, as he often told me, that such a procedure dehumanizes design. "If I want a wood paneling or wainscot to be of a certain height, I stand there, hold my hand at that certain height, and the carpenter makes his pencil mark. Then I step back and look at it from one point and from another, visualizing the finished result with all my powers. This is the only human way to decide on the height of a wainscot, or on the width of a window." Loos was inclined to use a minimum of paper plans; he carried in his head all the details of even his most complex designs.[28]

But Loos was not simply opposing sensual experience to abstraction. Rather, he was dealing with the intranslatability of languages. Because a drawing cannot convey the tension between the other senses and sight it cannot adequately translate a building. For Loos, the architect's drawing was a consequence of the division of labor, it could never be more than a mere technical statement, "the attempt [by the architect] to make himself understood by the craftsman carrying out the work."[29]

Loos's critique of the photography of architecture and its dissemination through architectural journals was based on the same principle, that it is impossible to represent a spatial effect or a sensation. When he writes: "It is my greatest pride that the interiors which I have created are totally *ineffective* in photographs. I am proud of the fact that the inhabitants of my spaces do not recognise their own apartments in the photographs, just as the owner of a Monet painting would not recognise it at Kastan's,"[30] his point is that photographs and drawings could not adequately reproduce his interiors because these possess tactile as well as optical qualities.

But also, inhabitants fail to recognize their own houses in the photographs because of the transformation that occurs in the process of reproduction. The inhabited house is perceived as an environment, not as an object, and therefore its reception occurs in a state of distraction. The photographs of a house in an architectural journal require a different kind of attention, an attention that presupposes distance. This distance is closer to that required of a spectator in the contemplation of a work of art in a museum: Loos's Monet example. Loos interiors are experienced as a frame for action rather than as an object in a frame.

However, there is something systematic about the photographs of Loos's interiors that seems to suggest his involvement in their production. The repeated presence of certain objects, such as the Egyptian stool, in nearly every interior view has been noted by Kenneth Frampton. Loos also seems to have adjusted the photographs to better represent his own idea of the house. The archives containing the photographs used to illustrate Kulka's book reveal a few of these tricks: the view through the "horizontal window" in the photograph of the Khuner villa (near Payerbach, 1930) is a photomontage,[31] as is the cello in the cabinet of the music room of the Moller house. A story was added to the photograph of the street facade of the Tristan Tzara house (Paris, 1926–1927) so as to make it more like the original project, and numerous "distracting" domestic objects (lamps, rugs, plants) were erased throughout. These interventions suggest that images were carefully controlled, that the photographs of Loos's buildings cannot simply be considered as a form of representation subordinate to the building itself.

For example, Loos often frames a spatial volume, as in the bedroom of the Khuner villa or the fireplace nook of his own apartment. This has the effect of flattening the space seen through the frame, making it seem more like a photograph. As with the device of obscuring the differences between openings and mirrors, this optical effect is enhanced, if not produced, by the photographs themselves, which are taken only from the precise point where the effect occurs.[32] Loos's critique of the photographic representation of architecture should not be mistaken for a nostalgia for the "real" object. What he achieves in this play with reflective surfaces and framing devices is a critique of photography as a transparent medium, and by extension a critique of classical representation. Such framing devices undermine the referential status of the photographic image and its claim to represent reality "as it is." The photographs draw the viewer's attention to the artifice involved in the photographic process. Like drawings, they are not representations in the traditional sense; they do not simply refer to a preexisting object, they produce the object; they literally construct their object.

Loos's critique of traditional notions of architectural representation is bound up with the phenomenon of an emergent metropolitan culture. He recognized social institutions as systems of representation, and his attacks on the family, Viennese society, professional organizations, and the state, launched in *Das Andere*, were implicit in his buildings. Architecture in all its possible manifestations—drawing, photograph, text, or building—is, after all, only a practice of representation. The subject of Loos's architecture is the citizen of the metropolis, immersed in its abstract relationships and striving to assert the independence and individuality of its existence in the face of the leveling power of society. This battle, according to George Simmel, is the modern equivalent of primitive man's struggle with nature; clothing is one of the battlefields, and fashion is one of its strategies.[33] He writes: "The commonplace is good form in society.…It is bad taste to make oneself conspicuous through some individual, singular expression.…Obedience to the standards of the general public in all externals [is] the conscious and desired means of reserving their personal feelings and their taste."[34] In other words, fashion is a mask that protects the intimacy of the metropolitan being.

Loos writes about fashion in precisely such terms: "We have become more refined, more subtle. Primitive men had to differentiate themselves by various colors, modern man needs his clothes as a mask. His individuality is so strong that it can no longer be expressed in terms of items of clothing.…

His own inventions are concentrated on other things."[35] Fashion and etiquette, in Western culture, constitute the language of behavior, a language that does not convey feelings but acts as a form of protection—a mask. As Loos writes, "How should one dress? Modern. One is modernly dressed when one stands out the least."

Significantly, Loos writes about the exterior of the house in the same terms as he writes about fashion:

> When I was finally given the task of building a house, I said to myself: in its external appearance, a house can only have changed as much as a dinner jacket. Not a lot therefore.…I had to become significantly simpler. I had to substitute the golden buttons with black ones. The house has to look inconspicuous.[36]

> The house does not have to tell anything to the exterior; instead, all its richness must be manifest in the interior.[37]

Loos seems to establish a radical difference between interior and exterior, which reflects the split between the intimate and the social life of the metropolitan being: "outside," the realm of exchange, money, and masks; "inside," the realm of the inalienable, the nonexchangeable, and the unspeakable. Moreover, this split between inside and outside, between the other senses and sight, is gender-loaded. The exterior of the house, Loos writes, should resemble a dinner jacket, a male mask, as the unified self, protected by a seamless facade, is masculine. The interior is the scene of sexuality and of reproduction, all the things that would divide the subject in the outside world. However, this dogmatic division in Loos's writings between inside and outside is undermined by his architecture.

The suggestion that the exterior is merely a mask that clads some preexisting interior is misleading, for the interior and exterior are constructed simultaneously. When he was designing the Rufer house, for example, Loos used a dismountable model that would allow the internal and external distributions to be worked out simultaneously. The interior is not simply the space that is enclosed by the facades. A multiplicity of boundaries is established, and the tension between inside and outside resides in the walls that divide them, its status disturbed by Loos's displacement of traditional forms of representation. To address the interior of Loos is to address the splitting of the wall.

Take, for instance, the shift of drawing conventions in Loos's four pencil drawings of the elevation of the Rufer house. Each one shows not only the outlines of the facade but also, in dotted lines, the horizontal and vertical divisions of the interior, the position of the rooms, and the thickness

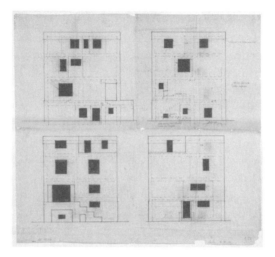

Fig. 6.42: Rufer House. Elevations. Albertina, Vienna

of the floors and the walls, while the windows are represented as black squares, with no frame. [Fig. 6.42] These are drawings of neither the inside nor the outside but the membrane between them: between the representation of habitation and the mask is the wall. Loos's subject inhabits this wall. This inhabitation creates a tension on that limit, tampers with it.

This is not simply a metaphor. In every Loos house there is a point of maximum tension, and it always coincides with a threshold or boundary. In the Moller house it is the raised alcove protruding from the street facade, where the occupant is ensconced in the security of the interior yet detached from it. The subject of Loos's houses is a stranger, an intruder in its own space. In Josephine Baker's house, the wall of the swimming pool is punctured by windows. It has been pulled apart, leaving a narrow passage surrounding the pool, and splitting each of the windows into an internal window and an external window. The visitor literally inhabits this wall, which enables him to look both inside, at the pool, and outside, at the city, but he is neither inside nor outside the house. In the dining room of the Steiner house, the gaze directed toward the window is folded back by the mirror beneath it, transforming the interior into an exterior view, a scene. The subject has been dislocated: unable to occupy the inside of the house securely, it can only occupy the insecure margin between window and mirror.

This tampering with the limits is intensified in Loos's Goldman & Salatsch men's wear store in Vienna of 1898. The space of this shop is halfway between the private universe of the interior and the outside world. It occupies the intersection between body and language, between the space of domesticity and that of social exchange, of economy. Goldman & Salatsch provided its clients with underwear and external accessories such as ties,

Fig. 6.43: Adolf Loos, showroom, Goldman & Salatsch men's wear shop, Vienna, 1898. Reprinted from *Das Interieur*, 1901.

hats, and walking sticks—that is, with the most intimate garments, the clothes most closely held to the body, as well as the objects that support (literally and symbolically) the body as a figure (the body's props, its prostheses). In this store, the "invisible," the most intimate garments, are exhibited and sold: they have abandoned the sphere of domesticity for the sphere of exchange. Conversely, the "visible," the objects that most obviously represent the site of exchange, the mask that safeguards the coherence of the human figure in the public realm, have entered the interior.

A photograph published in *Das Interieur* in 1901 shows a space clad with tall rectangular mirrors set in dark frames. Some of the mirrors are fixed, others are cabinet doors, yet others coincide with openings into other spaces. [Fig. 6.43] There are two male figures, one presumably a client emerging from the intimate atmosphere of the fitting room, the other an accountant who has entered from the exterior world of finance. They are both occupying the same wall, but the nature of that occupation is unclear. One of them seems to be standing at the threshold of an opening, his image reflected on the mirror-door, perhaps again in the cupboard door to the right. Even more enigmatic is the other figure, for only the upper part of the body is visible, behind bars, as if confined within a cage. Even with the recently reconstructed plan of the shop (which no longer exists), the actual position of the figures within the space cannot be established. One of them seems to be standing beside the image of his back—or is it the other way around? The depth of his body, its material presence, has been erased. Other reflections appear throughout the space, without any body to ground them.

In the midst of the intricate space of this photograph, only the figure of a woman is "complete" and clearly there, *in* the space. As if to indicate, once more, that in modernity it is the male subject, or rather the construct of masculinity itself, that no longer knows where to stand. The threat of modernity, how to master the uncontrollability of the metropolis, is that of castration. In this sense, perhaps one should pay closer attention to the repeated association of the metropolis and its undefined boundaries with femininity.

Furthermore, the subject that is split and its fragments multiplied in the photograph of Goldman & Salatsch is not the only "inhabitant" of the space. The dissolution of the figures into the wall surfaces questions not only their position but also that of the person viewing the photograph. The spectator of the photograph, attempting to master the image, no longer knows where he or she stands in relationship to the picture.

Even Loos, supposedly the very figure of mastery as the architect of the space, is also a troubled spectator of his own work. The illusion of Loos as an authority, a man in control, in charge of his own work, an undivided subject, is suspect. In fact, he is constructed, controlled, and fractured by the work. The idea of the *Raumplan,* for example: Loos constructs a space (without having completed the working drawings), then allows himself to be manipulated by this construction. Like the occupants of his houses, he is both inside and outside the object. The object has as much authority over him as he over it. He is not simply an author.[38]

The critic is no exception to this phenomenon. Incapable of detachment from the object, the critic simultaneously produces a new object and is produced by it. Criticism that presents itself as a new interpretation of an existing object is in fact constructing a completely new object. The Loos of the 1960s, the austere pioneer of the modern movement, was replaced in the 1970s by another Loos, all sensuality, and in the 1980s by Loos the classicist. On the other hand, readings that claim to be noninterpretive, purely objective inventories, the standard monographs on Loos—Münz and Kunstler in the 1960s and Gravagnuolo in the 1980s—are thrown off balance by the very object of their control. Nowhere is this alienation more evident than in their interpretations of the house for Josephine Baker.

Münz, otherwise a wholly circumspect writer, begins his appraisal of this house with the exclamation: "Africa: that is the image conjured up more or less firmly by a contemplation of the model," but he then confesses not to know why he invoked this image.[39] He attempts to analyze the formal characteristics of the project, but all he can conclude is that "they look strange and exotic." What is most striking in this passage is the momentary uncertainty as to whether Münz is referring to the model of the house or to Josephine Baker herself. He seems unable either to detach himself from this project or to enter into it.

Like Münz, Gravagnuolo finds himself writing things without knowing why, reprimands himself, then tries to regain control:

> First there is the charm of this gay architecture. It is not just the dichromatism of the facades but—as we shall see—the spectacular nature of the internal articulation that determines its relined and seductive character. Rather than abandon oneself to the pleasure of suggestions, it is necessary to take this "toy" to pieces with *analytical detachment* if one wishes to understand the mechanism of composition.[40]

He then institutes a regime of analytical categories ("the architectural introversion," "the revival of dichromatism," "the plastic arrangement") that he uses nowhere else in the book. And he concludes:

> The water flooded with light, the refreshing swim, the voyeuristic pleasure of underwater exploration—these are the carefully balanced ingredients of this gay architecture. But what matters more is that the invitation to the spectacular suggested by the theme of the house for a cabaret star is handled by Loos with discretion and *intellectual detachment,* more as a poetic game, involving the mnemonic pursuit of quotations and allusions to the Roman spirit, than as a vulgar surrender to the taste of Hollywood.[41]

Gravagnuolo ends up crediting Loos with the "detachment" (from Hollywood, vulgar taste, feminized culture) in "handling" the project that the critic himself was attempting to regain in its analysis. The insistence on detachment, on reestablishing the distance between critic and object of criticism, architect and building, subject and object, is of course indicative of the obvious fact that Münz and Gravagnuolo have failed to separate themselves from the object. The image of Josephine Baker offers pleasure but also represents the threat of castration posed by the "other": the image of woman in water—liquid, elusive, unable to be controlled, pinned down. One way of dealing with this threat is fetishization.

The Josephine Baker house represents a shift in the status of the body. This shift involves determinations not only of gender but also of race and class. The theater box of the domestic interiors places the occupant against the light. The body appears as a silhouette, mysterious and desirable, but the backlighting also draws attention to it as a physical volume, a bodily presence within the house with its own interior. The occupant controls the interior, yet it is trapped within it. In the Baker house, the body is produced as spectacle, the object of an erotic gaze, an erotic system of looks. The exterior of the house cannot be read as a silent mask designed to conceal its interior; it is a tattooed surface that does not refer to the interior, it neither conceals nor reveals it. This fetishization of the surface is repeated in the "interior." In the passages, the visitors consume Baker's body as a surface adhering to the windows. Like the body, the house is all surface; it does not simply have an interior.

Notes

* Walter Benjamin, "Paris, Capital of the Nineteenth Century," in *Reflections,* trans. Edmund Jephcott (New York: Schocken Books, 1986), pp. 155–156.

† Beatriz Colomina, "Interior," *Privacy and Publicity: Modern Architecture As Mass Media,* Beatriz Colomina (Cambridge: The MIT Press, 1994), 265

1 Benjamin, "Paris, Capital of the Nineteenth Century," pp. 155–156.

2 "Loos m'affirmait un jour: 'Un homme cultivé ne regarde pas par la fenêtre; sa fenêtre est en verre dépoli; elle n'est là que pour donner de la lumiére, non pour laisser passer le regard.'" Le Corbusier, *Urbanisme* (Paris, 1925), p. 174. When this book was published in English under the title *The City of To-morrow and Its Planning,* translated by Frederick Etchells (New York, 1929), the sentence read: "A friend once said to me: 'No intelligent man ever looks out of his window; his window is made of ground glass; its only function is to let in light, not to look out of'" (pp. 185–186). In this translation, Loos's name has been replaced by "a friend." Was Loos "nobody" for Etchells, or is this just another example of the kind of misunderstanding that led to the mistranslation of the title of the book? Perhaps it was Le Corbusier himself who decided to erase Loos's name. Of a different order, but no less symptomatic, is the mistranslation of "laisser passer le regard" (to let the gaze pass through) as "to look out of," as if to resist the idea that the gaze might take on, as it were, a life of its own, independent of the beholder.

3 The perception of space is produced by its representations; in this sense, built space has no more authority than do drawings, photographs, or descriptions.

4 Ludwig Münz and Gustav Künstler, *Der Architekt Adolf Loos* (Vienna and Munich, 1964), pp. 130–131. English translation: *Adolf Loos, Pioneer of Modern Architecture* (London, 1966), p. 148: "We may call to mind an observation by Adolf Loos, handed down to us by Heinrich Kulka, that the smallness of a theatre box would be unbearable if one could not look out into the large space beyond; hence it was possible to save space, even in the design of small houses, by linking a high main room with a low annexe."

5 Georges Teyssot has noted that "the Bergsonian ideas of the room as a refuge from the world are meant to be conceived as the 'juxtaposition' between claustrophobia and agoraphobia. This dialectic is already found in Rilke." G. Teyssot, "The Disease of the Domicile," *Assemblage* 6 (1988), p. 95.

6   There is also a more direct and more private route to the sitting area, a staircase rising from the entrance of the drawing room.

7   "Under Louis-Philippe the private citizen enters the stage of history.... For the private person, living space becomes, for the first time, antithetical to the place of work. The former is constituted by the interior; the office is its complement. The private person who squares his account with reality in his office demands that the interior be maintained in his illusions. This need is all the more pressing since he has no intention of extending his commercial considerations into social ones. In shaping his private environment he represses both. From this spring the phantasmagorias of the interior. For the private individual the private environment represents the universe. In it he gathers remote places and the past. His drawing room is a *box in the world theater*." Walter Benjamin, "Paris, Capital of the Nineteenth Century," in *Reflections*, p. 154. Emphasis added.

8   This calls to mind Freud's paper "A Child Is Being Beaten" (1919), where, as Victor Burgin has written, "the subject is positioned both in the audience *and* on stage—where it is both aggressor *and* aggressed." Victor Burgin, "Geometry and Abjection," *AA Files*, no. 15 (Summer 1987), p. 38. The *mise-en-scène* of Loos's interiors appears to coincide with that of Freud's unconscious. Sigmund Freud, "A Child Is Being Beaten: A Contribution to the Study of the Origin of Sexual Perversions," in *Standard Edition of the Complete Psychological Works of Sigmund Freud* (London: Hogarth Press, 1953–1974), vol. 17, pp. 175–204. In relation to Freud's paper, see also Jacqueline Rose, *Sexuality in the Field of Vision* (London, 1986), pp. 209–210.

9   Münz and Künstler, *Adolf Loos*, p. 36.

10   See note 7 above. There are no social spaces in the Benjaminian interior. He writes: "In shaping his private environment he [the private person] represses both [commercial and social considerations]." Benjamin's interior is established in opposition to the office. But as Laura Mulvey has noted, "The workplace is no threat to the home. The two maintain each other in a safe, mutually dependent polarisation. The threat comes from elsewhere:...the city." Laura Mulvey, "Melodrama Inside and Outside the Home" (1986), in *Visual and Other Pleasures* (London: Macmillan, 1989), p. 70.

11   In a criticism of Benjamin's account of the bourgeois interior, Laura Mulvey writes: "Benjamin does not mention the fact that the private sphere, the domestic, is an essential adjunct to the bourgeois marriage and is thus associated with woman, not simply as female, but as wife and mother. It is the mother who guarantees the privacy of the home by maintaining its respectability, as essential a defence against incursion or curiosity as the encompassing walls of the home itself." Laura Mulvey, "Melodrama Inside and Outside the Home."

12   Münz and Künstler, *Adolf Loos*, p. 149.

13   Jacques Lacan, *The Seminar of Jacques Lacon: Book I, Freud's Papers on Technique 1953–1954*, ed. Jacques-Alain Miller, trans. John Forrester (New York and London: Norton, 1988), p. 215. In this passage Lacan is referring to Jean-Paul Sartre's *Being and Nothingness*.

14   There is an instance of such personification of furniture in one of Loos's most autobiographical texts, "Interiors in the Rotunda" (1898), where he writes: "Every piece of furniture, every thing, every object had a story to tell, a family history." *Spoken into the Void: Collected Essays 1897–1900*, trans. Jane O. Newman and John H. Smith (Cambridge: MIT Press, 1982), p. 24.

15 This photograph has only recently been published. Kulka's monograph (a work in which Loos was involved) presents exactly the same view, the same photograph, but without a human figure. The strange opening in the wall pulls the viewer toward the void, toward the missing actor (a tension that the photographer no doubt felt the need to cover by literally inserting a figure). This tension constructs the subject, as it does in the built-in couch of the raised area of the Moller house, or the window of the *Zimmer der Dame* overlooking the drawing room of the Müller house.

16 Adolf Loos, *Das Andere*, no. 1 (1903), p. 9.

17 Kenneth Frampton, from a lecture at Columbia University, Fall 1986.

18 It should also be noted that this window is an exterior window, as opposed to the other window, which opens into a threshold space.

19 The reflective surface in the rear of the dining room of the Moller house (halfway between an opaque window and a mirror) and the window in the rear of the music room "mirror" each other, not only in their locations and their proportions but even in the way the plants are disposed in two tiers. All of this produces the illusion, in the photograph, that the threshold between these two spaces is virtual—impassable, impenetrable.

20 Letter from Kurt Ungers to Ludwig Münz, quoted in Münz and Künstler, *Adolf Loos*, p. 195. Emphasis added.

21 Christian Metz, "A Note on Two Kinds of Voyeurism," in *The Imaginary Signifier* (Bloomington: Indiana University Press, 1977), p. 96.

22 Adolf Loos, "The Principle of Cladding" (1898), in *Spoken into the Void*, p. 66 (emphasis added). Loos is explicitly referring here to Semper's concept of space as cladding, borrowing even the term "principle of cladding" from Semper. Aside from this instance, the influence of Semper on Loos can be found throughout Loos's theories and could perhaps be traced back to his studies in the Technische Hochschule in Dresden where he was an auditor in 1889–1890. Gottfried Semper taught at this school from 1834 to 1848 and left an influential theoretical legacy.

23 Franco Rella, *Miti e figure del moderno* (Parma: Pratiche Editrice, 1981), p. 13 and note 1. Rene Descartes, *Correspondance avec Arnauld et Morus*, ed. G. Lewis (Paris, 1933): letter to Hyperaspistes, August 1641.

24 Adolf Loos, "The Principle of Cladding" (1898), in *Spoken into the Void*, p. 66. Compare Semper's statement: "Hanging carpets remained the true walls, the visible boundaries of space. The often solid walls behind them were necessary for reasons that had nothing to do with the creation of space; they were needed for security, for supporting a load, for their permanence, and so on. Wherever the need for these secondary functions did not arise, the carpets remained the original means of separating space. Even where building solid walls became necessary, the latter were only the inner, invisible structure hidden behind the true and legitimate representatives of the wall, the colorful woven carpets." Gottfried Semper, "The Four Elements of Architecture: A Contribution to the Comparative Study of Architecture" (1851), in *Gottfried Semper: The Four Elements of Architecture and Other Writings*, trans. Harry Francis Mallgrave and Wolfgang Herrmann (Cambridge: Cambridge University Press, 1989), p. 104.

25 José Quetglas, "Lo Placentero," *Carrer de la Ciutat*, nos. 9–10, special issue on Loos (January 1980), p. 2.

26 Adolf Loos, "Architecture" (1910), trans. Wilfried Wang, in *The Architecture of Adolf Loos* (London: Arts Council of Great Britain, 1985), p. 106.

27 See in this respect Loos's use of the word "effect" (*Wirkung*) in other passages. For example in the fragment of "The Principle of Cladding" quoted above, the "effect" is the "sensation" that the space produces in the spectator, the feeling of "homeyness" in a house.

28 Richard Neutra, *Survival through Design* (New York: Oxford University Press, 1954), p. 300.

29 Adolf Loos, "Ornament und Erziehung" (1924), in *Sämtliche Schriften,* vol. 1, p. 392.

30 Adolf Loos, "Architecture," p. 106. Emphasis added.

31 This window, the only "picture" window to appear in Loos's work, points to the difference in his work between architecture in the context of the city and in that of the countryside (the Khuner villa is a country house). This difference is significant not only in terms of architectural language, as often discussed (Gravagnuolo, for example, talks of the differences between the "whitewashed masterpieces"—the Moller and Müller houses—and the Khuner villa, "so vernacular, so anachronistically alpine, so rustic"; see Benedetto Gravagnuolo, *Adolf Loos* [New York: Rizzoli, 1982]), but in terms of the way the house sets itself in relation to the exterior world, the construction of its inside and outside.

32 In the photograph of the dining room of the Moller house, the illusion that the scene is virtual, that the actual view of the dining room is a mirror image of the space from which the view is taken (the music room), thus collapsing both spaces into each other, is produced not only by the way the space is framed by the opening but also by the frame of the photograph itself, where the threshold is made to coincide exactly with the sides of the back wall, making the dining room into a picture inside a picture.

33 "The deepest conflict of modern man is not any longer in the ancient battle with nature, but in the one that the individual must fight to affirm the independence and peculiarity of his existence against the immense power of society, in his resistence to being levelled, swallowed up in the social-technological mechanism." Georg Simmel, "Die Grosstadt und das Geistesleben" (1903), English translation "The Metropolis and Mental Life," in *Georg Simmel: On Individuality and Social Forms,* ed. Donald Levine (Chicago, 1971), p. 324.

34 George Simmel, "Fashion" (1904), in ibid, pp. 313ff.

35 Adolf Loos, "Ornament and Crime" (1908), trans. Wilfried Wang, in *The Architecture of Adolf Loos,* p. 103.

36 Adolf Loos, "Architecture," p. 107.

37 Adolf Loos, "Heimat Kunst" (1914), in *Sämtliche Schriften,* vol. 1, p. 339.

38 One of the ways in which the myth of Loos as an author is sustained is by privileging his writings over other forms of representation. Critics legitimize observations on buildings, drawings, and photographs by the use of written statements by the architect. This practice is problematic at many levels. Critics use words. By privileging words they privilege themselves. They maintain themselves as authors (authorities). This convention is dependent on the classical system of representation, which I am here putting in question.

39 Münz and Künstler, *Adolf Loos,* p. 195.

40 Gravagnuolo, *Adolf Loos,* p. 191. Italics added.

41 Ibid. Italics added.

Public
Performance

Introduction:
Public Performance

Public interiors, regardless of their specific program, share a theaterlike quality where viewer and performer act interchangeably in unscripted narration, see, and are seen. Interior space, spatial views, and architectural objects create the setting where internal and cultural dramas are played out. A classic example is Charles Garnier's Opéra de Paris, which marked a significant shift toward understanding that a performance hall functions as more than a stage: the public areas offstage invite unorchestrated performances. This is especially apparent in the grand staircase where the public goes to see and be seen.

Public Performance, as a categorical aspect of the study of interiors, stems from the observation that the theatrics of viewer and spectacle in public space has many manifestations in museums, film, and exhibitions. Spaces are designed to enhance the sensory experience of observers and their presence in a space simultaneously occupied by others. By viewing these diverse platforms as public performance in interiors, themes of nostalgia, narration, and registration of time can be seen along with the architectural devices that produce them and are themselves metaphors.

Opera houses and museums establish a relationship between viewer and object and between viewer and viewer. Subtle dances take place as museumgoers vie for optimal viewing positions. Once the desired viewpoint is achieved, the relationship of viewer to object is often mediated by a regulated distance from the work of art or by a protective vitrine. The location and sequencing of objects in a museum guides the viewer through a narrative, often with a beginning and an end. Curators interpret works of art for the public, and exhibition designers physically frame them. Strategies of visual analysis are employed to design the sequence to draw attention to objects and allow the eye to rest between objects. The use of vitrines suggests the precious nature of sequestered objects, but they also entice the viewer to inspect the work closely.

The first two essays in this chapter amplify points of view about museums that are eccentric, internal, and microcosmic. The Sir John Soane Museum, the Museum of Jurassic Technology, and the Salon de Fleurus, although established in different centuries, evoke longing for the past and the recovery of time, reflecting their creators' desires to communicate with timelessness in the present and with what has lasting value. The Sir John Soane Museum and Salon de Fleurus make reference to the past with both interior design and collections. The Museum of Jurassic Technology is a contemporary cabinet of curiosity, or *Wunderkammer*, with exhibit design that, instead of commingling antiquities and objects of later technologies and developments, marries science and a sense of curiosity and wonder.

Set design for film, where attention to detail is necessary for a convincing performance, parallels interior design. Set design mimics reality, taking into account details that register the traces of living.

When the work of the architect and interior designer is eventually complete they exit; occupants move in and pattern their actions in response to living within the space. The set designer must virtually inhabit interior space to understand how a character in a play would move and use objects—so that they can be rematerialized in a detailed set, as if they were real. Filmmakers like the Quay Brothers, who work with small-scale models in stop-motion animation, and Alfred Hitchcock, have fabricated sets that include not only interiors but also entire city blocks. In the work discussed here, both engaged similar qualities even though their outcomes were different. The Quay Brothers's animation takes place in models that articulate the effects of gravity, light, and shadow. They utilize these conditions as if they are characters in their narrative.

Hitchcock's *Rear Window*, on the other hand, required a larger, more complex set that included buildings, interiors, streets, and sky. Apart from the set design and actors' performances, the film's theme connects one interior space to another through a public courtyard. The film relies on this courtyard to bind multiple private interiors—as a way to reflect on the narrative's development. Both filmmakers integrated details as small as a purse, camera, screws, and dust to materially induce their film atmospheres.

The criteria for displaying objects in museums require their own articulation. Architects Elizabeth Diller and Ricardo Scofidio use display as a strategy to reveal the social constructs and cues encountered in public space. They focus on experimental and critical forms of culturally conditioned display, with emphasis on the body, interiors, and objects. In Aaron Betsky's essay "Display Engineers," he describes their concern with how "display functions to present a consumable reality."[1] Their design strategy analyzes everyday rituals to arrive at narratives that are then fabricated in geometries where performance, display, architecture, and interior meet.

Interaction among people in public places animates interiors that, when otherwise empty, are said to be stage sets anticipating actors. The inclusion of furniture and equipment that are typically within the purview of interior designers, like props in a theater production, are the means at hand of envisioning and constructing features that bind the body and movement to architecture and to life in public places. Making theater out of people moving through life and public space, understanding the dramatic qualities of objects as aspects of place-making, and sensing the materials that are placed in public space are all disciplines critical to interiors practice.

1   Aaron Betsky, "Display Engineers," in *Scanning: The Aberrant Architecture of Diller + Scofidio*, Aaron Betsky, K. Michael Hays, and Laurie Anderson (New York: Whitney Museum of American Art, 2003), 24.

The Specular Spectacle of the House of the Collector

Helene Furján

INTRODUCTION

Visiting nineteenth-century English architect Sir John Soane's Museum at Lincoln's Inn Fields in London, one notices that the view is continuously redirected into and through the house by architectural apertures and mirrors strategically located throughout the interior. The house is primarily known for Soane's collection of antique artifacts and architectural prints, including a portfolio of Giovanni Piranesi's original proofs. The collection was organized in anticipation of transforming Soane's private, professional collection into a public museum. Helene Furján highlights this lesser-known collection and the disposition of mirrors throughout the house that reflect, fragment, and multiply views of the antiquities.

Furján speculates on the significance of the mirrors in reference to the emergent technology's symbolic and philosophical meaning to the representation of knowledge, nature, religion, and painting. Soane's ongoing integration of mirrors, according to Furján, increased illumination by directing light into windowless areas of the house. As a result, the mirrors inadvertently emphasized shade and a perception of depth on the surface of the antiquities. Dramatic spatial illusions were constructed with mirrors that reflected spaces and rooms, and gave the overall appearance of a larger, deeper house. She observes that this light guides the viewer's gaze toward the details of antique fragments throughout the house. The placement of antiquities and the mirrors were orchestrated to produce such effects as doubling their quantity and space.

Mirrors were fashionable machined objects at the time, such that Furján characterizes the Soane house as combining "antiquity and modernity." The mirrors and antiquities visually merged in the same way as did the programs of house and museum, or private and public. The house was configured to display the collection of antiquities for his practice. The result recalled Renaissance cabinets of curiosity that rescaled the full-scale interior into portraits of a miniaturized world when viewed in convex mirrors. Furján concludes that*

Originally appeared in *Assemblage*, no. 34 (1997): 57–69.

Soane installed mirrors as a constructed look on antiquities. His latent identi-fication with classical architects and his ambition to preserve his longevity in their company, along with his cultural affiliations, conditioned him to prepare the collection for posterity in the form of a public museum.

———

Much will the Mirrour teach, or evening gray,
When o'er some ample space her twilight ray
Obscurely gleams; hence Art shall best perceive
On distant parts what fainter lines to give.
—William Mason, *The English Garden*

IN 1792 JOHN SOANE, by then a well-established architect, began building at Lincoln's Inn Fields in London. This was to mark the start of an occupa-tion that would extend over three adjoining sites, charting a history of con-tinuous construction and reconstruction. His first house, at no. 12, was made possible in large part by a legacy left by his wife's uncle, George Wyatt, who had died in 1790. The inheritance also allowed Soane to begin to amass a col-lection, although his collecting activities here remained modest—a library and a set of plaster casts of architectural detail that inhabited a corridor connecting the house to his office at the rear. The first significant museum space at no. 12 was a room he added behind no. 13 after its purchase in 1808, a space that was filled with the by then sizable collections moved from his country house, Pitzhanger Manor, on its sale in 1810.[1] By this date, the house had already undergone many permutations. Soane built his final residence at Lincoln's Inn Fields, no. 13, between 1812 and 1813 once the existing house on the site was demolished; it continued to be altered, in a history that con-structs a narrative as convoluted and labyrinthine as the spaces of the house themselves came to be.[2] By the 1820s, the house in its present form was largely in place, although the collections still expanded and small adjust-ments were made until Soane's death in 1837. [Fig. 7.1]

In a surprisingly small space, Soane managed to elaborate multiple narratives of display and collecting, exhibiting his interests as an antiquar-ian, an architect, and a man of taste in collecting and storing inscriptions of culture and history. The objects that bore such inscriptions encompassed not only the fragments and collectibles of high culture and antiquity, but also the very domestic environment in which they were located. As a house-museum, in which the collections cannot be distinguished from the domestic objects, the furniture and furnishings, of the house itself, Lincoln's Inn Fields not only incorporated the collection into the house, but significantly, incorpo-rated the house into the collection.

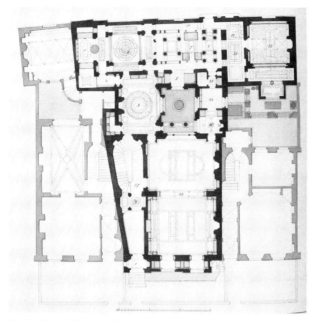

Fig. 7.1: Plan of the ground floor of nos. 12, 13, and 14 Lincoln's Inn Fields.
By courtesy of the Trustees of Sir John Soane's Museum

The mirror—the convex mirror in particular—figuratively duplicates the collections housed here, and it is perhaps significant that by the time Soane died the house and its museum contained over a hundred mirrors, most of them convex and most of them concentrated in the Breakfast Room.[3] [Fig. 7.2] Re-collecting the interior within their compass, the mirrors present a collection of images that capture the carefully preserved and minutely constructed professional environment of a late-eighteenth-century architect, the collections of a late-eighteenth-century antiquarian and connoisseur, and the domestic interior of a late-eighteenth-century gentleman. These mirrors proffer up a miniaturized (and thus *collectible*) image of the world of the viewing subject for the very *reflection* of that subject.

Ironically, it is through its very capacity to distort that the convex mirror most reflects the collecting act, gathering and concentrating, in comparison with the plane mirror, which merely "reproduces what lies within its field."[4] The convex mirror helps to select and organize the interior, as crucial a part of its arrangement as the furniture it tends to fix in its images: "Its curved surface reduced the world to an idyll, to a small cleanliness."[5] Gathering in the interior, and even what lies outside its windows, the convex image provides a "coordinated world" reduced to the scale of comprehension. A domestic object that reflects, and thereby holds and collects, the collections, the mirror is also, in its proliferation in this house, a collection

Fig. 7.2. Convex
mirror in the
Breakfast Room.
Helene Furján

in itself. It is one, moreover, that in its sheer repetition threatens to exceed its capacity to organize, confounding and confusing, or better, dissolving, the spaces of the house into images.

But the mirror also operates as a figure for history itself. As Siegfried Giedion was to note a century later: "History is a magical mirror. Who peers into it sees his own image in the shape of events and developments."—an observation that neatly points to the personal investment to be located in Soane's "desire for history."[6] The mirror could represent, for him, a scrying apparatus that magically conjured up the image of the past that he himself wished to inhabit. This was not simply a desire to be immersed in the past. It was a desire to see his collections of that past in a context of architectural history that included himself, his work, his role as preserver of the past, and, most significantly, the very container of that past, the house itself. In other words, the house-museum could function as a mediation, or even continuity, between the past and the present, or rather, the antique and the modern; or indeed, between his own past and a future safely predetermined by the frozen collections of art, antiquity, and domesticity that form the house as museum.

That in addition to a "union" of the arts, Soane was interested in a union between antiquity and modernity can be seen in this house that, with its mass of antiquities, is equally filled with works contemporary with Soane and is, furthermore, built using the latest developments in technology and the latest fashions of design and interior decoration.[7] And the mirror that populates this interior is itself a result of the industrial advances and mass production of the time: cast plate glass having been produced in England since 1773 at the British Cast Plate Manufacturers' casting hall in Ravenhead, then the largest industrial building in the country.[8] Cast glass was quickly adopted by the Adam school, which also popularized the overmantel mirror and the ovalframed mirror and returned the convex mirror to fashion.[9] By the time that Soane was building in Lincoln's Inn Fields, then, the mirror was very much in vogue, an indispensable item of interior decoration employed in all manner of ways: pier glasses, overmantel mirrors, looking glasses and cheval glasses, pilaster insets, door facings, display-case backings, convex mirrors, vista mirrors, catoptric devices, and so on. As such, the mirrors of Soane's house are a compendium of their fashionable usages at both the end of the eighteenth century and the beginning of the nineteenth.

By 1825, for instance, when C. J. Richardson produced a series of watercolors surveying the house,[10] there were no less than five pier glasses in the North Drawing Room to compensate for its northern aspect. The South Drawing Room accommodated an overmantel mirror, a pier glass between the two front windows, and three convex mirrors. [Fig. 7.3] The Dining Room held four large convex mirrors (with ornamental circles on the top that were removed by 1830) set up in the corners of the east and west walls, adjacent to mirror-backed niches on the north and south that contained classical busts.[11] [Fig. 7.4] Strips of mirror appeared on the window frames and on the fronts of the two projecting piers that separated this room from the Library, where, in turn, a pier glass hung between the front windows over a mirror-paneled chest. The Breakfast Room had strips of mirror set into pilasters and around the glazing of the bookcases. The museum area housed two mirrors: one in the Corridor and another in the Colonnade, set in the window recess under an odd and very small oculus cut in the ceiling. In the Monk's Parlor, a large paneled mirror lined the north wall to reflect the colored glass of the window opposite, and in Soane's bathroom, a large overmantel mirror was divided into three and canted forward so that he could see himself better.[12] There would, of course, be many more: the myriad convex mirrors of the Breakfast Room and its mirror-backed niche and overmantel mirror were yet to come, as were the convex mirrors and the catoptric niche in the stair hall. The Library windows facing onto the street were to acquire mirrored shutters, while opposite, those in the Dining Room facing onto a courtyard were to acquire angled mirrored panels on either side. Mirror strips would be added to a pilaster and a relief panel in an anteroom between the Breakfast Room and museum area when it was rearranged around 1826, and in 1836, a large convex mirror would be placed in a north-wall recess of the Egyptian Crypt. And a canted mirror device was to be set into a window in the Crypt anteroom, with a pane of glass placed at a ninety-degree angle over one of mirrored glass, designed to reflect light from above into the depths of the interior.

Fig. 7.3: View of the South Drawing Room, showing one of the convex mirrors.
Helene Furján

Fig. 7.4: Convex mirror and bust of Dione in a mirror-backed niche in the
Dining Room. Helene Furján

What is remarkable, though, is not so much the mirrors' various employments, but their accumulation; their association both with and as a collection. Here are to be found all the possible concerns—from the archaeological to the fashionable, from the mirroring of the self to the interiorized landscape of vista and perspective—that the mirror could invoke. Their primary function at Lincoln's Inn Fields remained, of course, to multiply the level of illumination from the inadequate sources of natural daylight and candlelight, introducing light into the farthest reaches of these complex interiors through reflections and refractions.[13] But they nonetheless provided, or amplified, poetic and picturesque effects of light and shade, expanded the spaces of the house, sometimes even providing the illusion of additional rooms, and contributed, figuratively and literally, to the collecting impulses of the interior.

The Mirror of History

During the Middle Ages and beyond, the mirror received a theoretical usage that exceeded its power merely to reflect. There was the mirror of God; the mirror of wisdom and the mind, which pointed both to religious truth and to the world as a place of transient semblance; the mirror of the soul, a reflection of ideal virtue; mirrors of creation; and mirrors of human nature, which set out guidelines for proper conduct. These figurative (always convex) mirrors suggested that the image contained allegorical or symbolical significations capable of revealing truth and knowledge beyond the visual surface. In other words, the mirror contained the possibility of distilling meaning, if only its signs could be interpreted; or its surface besmirched, like the crystal ball or gazing sphere, and its hidden depths suddenly rise to that surface.

In the medieval mind, such knowledge was usually connected with divine agency, and the scryers who made its recovery their trade were thus theological readers.[14] But "mirrors" were also texts, whether exhaustive books of instruction or histories, that sought to fix aspects of the world or of the past within their covers as did the surface of the mirror: they posited a belief, which would culminate in the encyclopedic projects, that the world could be captured in a text as faithfully as in the visual arts, reflecting it back in an objective and unmediated fashion. In the 1590s, for instance, John Norden embarked on a never-to-be-completed project to provide a comprehensive "chorography" of Britain, his *Speculum Britanniae*. Chorographies, the specular texts perhaps closest to Soane's own interests, were a "type of topographical-historical-antiquarian literature," an attempt to unite an antiquarian interest in inscriptions and relics to history and to a visual and often pictorial interest in landscape. These written descriptions accompanied by maps undertook to survey minutely both the past and present of regions in order to recover and record their identities.[15]

Visual representation, of course, had a strong affinity with the mirror. Art had long been tied to the mirror through theories of mimesis, from Plato through Alberti and into the eighteenth century.[16] In painting, mirrors served most commonly as signs of vanity, but they also appeared as portents. An example of the latter, painted by Petrus Christus in 1449, is *Saint Elijah and the Betrothed*, in which the convex mirror that rests on the jeweler's table at the lower right edge of the frame depicts the future married life of the betrothed couple collecting their wedding ring. Mirrors could also operate as representational aids, revealing what was otherwise unavailable to

Fig 7.5: Convex mirror
in the Corridor, no. 13
Lincoln's Inn Fields.
Helene Furján

the eye. The convex mirror in Quentin Metsys's early sixteenth-century painting *The Banker and His Wife*, for instance, shows a beggar in front of the window forming the frame for the interior view presented. In Jan van Eyck's *Amolfini Marriage*, representation was self-consciously foregrounded, the mirror's image not only providing the view of the room in front of the picture plane, and hence of the artist himself, but also reinforcing the effect of his signature placed above it, the medieval eye of God giving way to the self-referential authorial gesture.

For Soane, the figurative mirror perhaps most at home among his collections is the mirror of history. And in the section of the museum proper where fragments of antique ruins abound we find such a mirror. In the Corridor a large convex mirror hangs amid these fragments, reflecting those hanging on the walls opposite it. [Fig. 7.5] Moreover, it forms the focal point of a vista receding from the Colonnade and the Dome area as a visible image of the fragments that are themselves concealed from this view by the architecture. [Fig. 7.6] This catoptric trick recalls the earliest precursor of Soane's museum, the cabinets of curiosity whose intention was to place the world in a room, forming a miniaturized, representative universe. These assemblages of radical heterogeneity collected together wonders and rarities that offered not only a mirror of nature but also, through their very marvelousness, the reflection of divine agency. And, in fact, the mirror and the marvel are closely connected, the word *mirror* deriving from "*mir,* the root of *mirabilis* (marvelous, wonderful) and *mirari* (to wonder at)."[17] In this regard, such cabinets

Fig 7.6: View through the Colonnade revealing the convex mirror in the Corridor.
Helene Furján

were close to another display device popular around the same time, catoptric boxes that were either lined with mirrors or contained two plain mirrors set at various angles to each other so that objects or scenes were multiplied, providing optical illusions.[18]

The catoptric box and the cabinet of curiosities come together in Soane's house as a means of creating a fully internalized world, from the wondrous universe in microcosm of the cabinet to the Leibnizian monadic world of the catoptric device. Indeed, the catoptric device could be seen as a cabinet of wonder in its own right, and Soane's house, with its Chinese-box effect of cabinets within cabinets and its mirrors lining every available surface, is, in effect, itself a catoptric device. Individual catoptric devices actually exist in the museum; in particular, the mirror-backed display niches composed, in one instance, in the hall, of two angled mirrors. But perhaps most significantly, the mirrored shutters of the Library windows that face onto Lincoln's Inn Fields were not lined with mirrors, as was common at the time, on the outside, so that when open they would bring, along with the daylight, the image of the park and street into the house. On the contrary, the mirrors line the inner surfaces, radically excluding the outside world when shut and reflecting in its place the candlelit interior back to itself.

Is this, then, Soane's attempt to turn his back on the world outside and recreate his own internal world? If so, this is not yet quite the space of contemplation that would characterize the mid-nineteenth century (figured by Kierkegaard's internal reveries), but rather, a compensatory space, replacing the marauding urban world outside that threatened to annihilate or, perhaps worse, overlook him. Soane substituted for urban civil society, the arena of the long and bitter fights in which he was embroiled, including the extended battles with his son George, a world of things. And these things had a special, genealogical, significance. They were not only signs of culture and history, they were also signs of Soane's rise to a gentlemanly status, markers of taste, connoisseurship, and antiquarian erudition. Together they formed Soane's own history: the legacy he wished to leave, the material remainders of his collecting activities, and a history of architecture.

But the most powerful message evident in the fragments themselves, especially those of the Corridor area, may be the crumbling and decaying state of these traces of history. Bathed in a musty yellow light, these pieces of ruins speak of antiquity, in the manner that Winckelmann himself proposed, as a past age irrevocably lost. The mustard hue of the Corridor depicts the sun set on the classical age, and the image inscribed on the surface of the mirror suggests the faint vestiges that are all that remain. In this sense, the fragments tell of the mortality of artifacts, destined to "die" as their human makers do. Soane knew this, and often had his own work depicted, projected into a future moment, as ruins. But he was also clearly interested in artifacts as markers of a human mortality, to which his collection of funerary objects attests. And as the decaying fragments served to remind, as a memento mori of the ephemerality of all things.[19]

Yet, lest this space conjure too well the molding and musty scene suggested—the sublime infinitude of fragmentation and ruin and the attendant losses of meaning—we should remember the *reconstructive* element of the antiquarian trade. The yellow light, just as readily evocative of the first light of early morning, heralds the promise of ruins to be salvaged. And it is no doubt significant that the Corridor of this museum is, in fact, a threshold space, leading to the stairs of the mezzanine studio above. This architectural studio can be seen from below, illuminated by the bright, clear light of invention and imagination, a romantic reflection of genius, framed by the decayed and ruined fragments of antiquity barely visible in the yellowed gloom. In a sense, then, Soane is playfully combining Gothic gloom with fantasies of restitution, mortality, and redemption. Though irrevocably of the past, and perhaps importantly so, they nevertheless form the material of Soane's antiquarian and architectural projects: fragments of classical architecture that operate as signs of history, didactic architectural examples, and generative details.[20]

Most of the "antique fragments" are, in truth, plaster casts and can therefore be seen as souvenirs, or simulacra, of ruins. Moreover, the yellow light is caught up in the ruse, "for it is that soft primrose hue so peculiarly adapted for the exhibition of the marbles, imparting the tint of time to those who have not yet attained it."[21] Although Soane did not collect most of his fragments directly from their source, they were indeed often made precisely as souvenirs, the casts taken off ruins and ancient buildings visited on Grand Tours. Not all the fragments are of ancient origin, but all were seen as material for the study of architecture and as an aid to production in the studio. Thus the fragments would offer several possibilities for Soane. In antiquarian terms, they would be valued for their "pastness," that is, their ability to represent historicity, if not history itself. In connoisseurial terms, they served to impress colleagues and (gentlemanly) clients with his taste and knowledge. And in architectural terms, they would provide a catalogue from which the architect could draw for the invention of new designs, assembling and recombining the fragments in new ways. As Peter Thornton points out, "Soane's was the collection of a working architect and was used as an anthology of antique architecture and decoration as well as a teaching collection."[22] But what he does not make clear is that this *was* Soane's design method, inherited from such architects as Piranesi and George Dance the Younger: the collecting together and framing of selected fragments; or, as Christopher Hussey writes, speaking of Piranesi's reconstructions, the "pouring together, as from a combined treasury, armoury, and museum the hoarded relics of an epoch."[23]

In other words, the museum collects itself both as the fantasy and fiction of reconstruction, one ordered through the narrative coherence of history. It is in this sense that the mirrors of Soane's house-museum are important: as poetic figurations of these imagistic operations. They reflect, that is, double, the operation of the museum itself, providing a vehicle through which the past becomes accessible to representation. The convex mirror, in particular that in the Corridor, though part of the collection itself, collects history in a catoptric fashion, a visual trick attempting to pull the discrete fragments together in a cohesive image that would form such a narrative, a mirroring of the antiquarian trade.[24] For the antiquarian, history so poeticized in this "delightful" image remains as evocative as the unreadable inscription on the ruined monuments of which his fragments form the traces. Like the sublime image of the ruined monument that this scene evokes,[25] the mirrors transform fragments into something that, though not a totalizable whole, is nevertheless expressive of a gathered heterogeneity: history, in other words.

Notes

*   Helene Furján, "The Specular Spectacle of the House of the Collector," *Assemblage* 34 (1997): 60.

1   Sir John Soane (1753–1837) built an extension to no. 12 behind the existing house at no. 13 between 1808 and 1809, containing the central tribune area that still exists and Soane's professional offices, the Colonnade of the present museum. Pitzhanger Manor in Ealing, purchased in 1800 and occupied as a country residence from 1804 to 1810, was largely demolished and rebuilt, with the notable exception of parts of the house worked on by Soane's revered first master, George Dance the Younger. It was to a great extent here that Soane began seriously not only to collect, but to construct the spaces of his house around, and even as, the collection.

2   Soane was able to purchase no. 13 by moving its (obliging) resident into a new house built at no. 14. The new house at no. 13 occupied parts of no. 12 and in 1823 was extended into the rear of no. 14.

3   The only existing record of the purchase of convex mirrors for Lincoln's Inn Fields is a bill dated 1794 for two from the opticians P. and J. Dolland. Although this paper will concentrate on no. 13, and especially in its later manifestations, this suggests that not only were there mirrors in no. 12, but that some of them were convex, placing Soane at the forefront of their return to fashion around 1800. These mirrors may well have been reused in no. 13.

4   Wolfgang M. Zucker, "Reflections on Reflections," *The Journal of Aesthetics and Art Criticism* (Spring 1962): 243.

5   Ibid., 245.

6   Siegfried Giedion, *Mechanization Takes Command: A Contribution to Anonymous History* (New York: Norton, 1969), 2. Giedion seems to refer to the divining properties of the scrying mirror (see n. 14), although, ruling out an attempt to foresee the future, he uses it to peer backward. The phrase a "desire for history" is from Stephen Bann, who links it to the renewal of "curiosity" in the late eighteenth and early nineteenth centuries, resulting in the spread of interest in history from connoisseurs, professional historians, and antiquarians to a mass public, particularly through such representational mediums as the historical novel, history painting, and such spectacles as the history museum. See Stephen Bann, *Romanticism and the Rise of History* (New York: Twayne Publishers, 1995), esp. 3–30.

7   Soane was one of the first in Britain to patronize contemporary, especially British, artists. See John Britton, "The Union of Architecture, Sculpture and Painting," in Sir John Soane, *Description of the House and Museum on the North Side of Lincoln's-Inn-Fields, Etc.* (London: James Moyes, 1830).

8 Until the introduction of this industrial process, glass had been produced under a monopoly by the older and less efficient blown method that restricted the size of glass sheets. This method would not become competitive again until modernized in 1832 by Robert Lucas Chance, who developed the "broad" sheet glass that, despite the development of patent plate in 1839, would be used for the Crystal Palace in 1851. Modern "silvering" techniques, where silver foil replaced the tin-mercury backing, were not developed until 1840.

9 Historically the predominant type until eclipsed by casting processes, the convex mirror returned briefly to popularity roughly between 1800 and 1820, a fashion captured enthusiastically in Soane's museum. For further details on the history of the mirror in England, see Raymond McGrath and A. C. Frost, *Glass in Architecture and Decoration* (1937; London: The Architectural Press, 1961), 314–15.

10 These watercolors were bound together in a volume entitled "Sketches and Drawings of the House and Museum J. Soane Esq., R.A., 1825," vol. 82, Sir John Soane's Museum Archive.

11 In the Dining Room, the mirror panels that now surround three sides of both Sir Thomas Lawrence's portrait of Soane over the chimneypiece and Sir Joshua Reynolds's *Love and Beauty* were not added until very late, sometime in 1836. To my knowledge, they do not appear in any of the views that contain these paintings after their hanging around 1829, and they are certainly missing from the illustrations for the revised edition of *Description of the House and Museum on the North Side of Lincoln's-Inn Fields,* 2d ed. (London: Levey, Robson, and Franklyn, 1835–36). This is also true of the mirrors added to the back of the niches above the Library bookcases.

12 Some of these mirrors were to disappear as the house evolved.

13 The most evident examples are the angled mirrored panels to either side of the windows in the Dining Room; the pier glass set between the two tall windows of Library, which largely reflects light from the dining windows opposite; the lantern in the Dressing Room, which has mirrors around its base, angled to diffuse light over the whole room; and the canted mirror device in the Crypt anteroom, which not only reflects light into the basement room, but also provides reflections of the opposite wall of the Dressing Room and study and of the parapet as well as, on the underside, of the pebbled pavement of the courtyard.

14 *Specularii,* or scryers, as they were known in England, were professional readers of distant events (in time and space) prevalent in the Middle Ages. They "read" spherical and semispherical reflective surfaces, especially convex mirrors and crystal spheres, interpreting the reflections through a theological medium.

15 See Stan A. E. Mendyk, '*Speculum Britanniae*': *Regional Study, Antiquarianism and Science in Britain to 1700* (Toronto: University of Toronto Press, 1989), esp., 38–81.

16 As M. H. Abrams notes in his book on romanticism, *The Mirror and the Lamp: Romantic Theory and the Critical Tradition* (London and New York: Oxford University Press, 1953): "The recourse to a mirror in order to illuminate the nature of one or another art continued to be a favorite with aesthetic theorists long after Plato. In Renaissance speculation the reference to a looking-glass is frequent and explicit. 'What should painting be called,' asked Alberti, 'except the holding of a mirror up to the original as in art?' Leonardo repeatedly appeals to a mirror to illustrate the relation to nature both of a painting and the mind of the painter....As late as the middle of the eighteenth century important critics continued to illustrate the concept of imitation by the nature of a looking-glass. Dr. Johnson was fond of this parallel, and found it the highest excellence of Shakespeare that he 'holds up to his readers a faithful mirrour of manners and life'" (32).

17 Alan Shelton, "Renaissance Collections and the New World," in *The Cultures of Collecting*, ed. John Elsner and Richard Cardinal (London: Reakton Press, 1994), 179.

18 Catoptric devices were even found within the cabinets of curiosity: for instance, Ole Worm's museum in Copenhagen, one of the more famous cabinets of the mid-seventeenth century, had such a device in its collection. See Jurgis Baltrusaitis, *Le Miroir: Révélations, science-fiction et fallacies* (Paris: Elmayan/Le Seuil, 1978).

19 Compare *The Artist Contemplating Ancient Fragments* by Henry Fuseli (Johann Heinrich Füssli).

20 Soane himself described the fragments as "sermons in stones" that were to appeal to the antiquary, "who loves to explore and retrace them through ages past"; the student, "who, in cultivating a classic taste, becomes enamoured of their forms"; and the imaginative man, "whose excursive fancy gives to each 'a local habitation and a name' in association with the most interesting events and the most noble personages the pages of history has transmitted for our contemplation" *(Description of the House and Museum* [1835–36], 13).

21 Barbara Hofland, in ibid., 12. One hundred fifty copies of the 1835–36 edition were printed, the text interspersed with poetry and descriptive remarks by Barbara Hofland.

22 Thornton also points out that Soane's collection of fragments was not uncommon, although its display may have been; Robert Adam and Henry Holland also had them, some of which ended up in Soane's own collection. See Peter Thornton and Helen Dorey, *Sir John Soane: The Architect as Collector, 1753–1837* (New York: Harry N. Abrams, 1992), xi.

23 Christopher Hussey, *The Picturesque: Studies in a Point of View* (London: Frank Cass & Co., 1927), 200. John Summerson strongly suggests this approach to Soane's design methodology; that is, the selecting and recombining of figures and motifs from a repertoire of stylistic devices. He even goes so far as to claim that by 1806 this stock of motifs was closed: "They may be distorted and rearranged, but they were the old themes, and the old themes alone" ("Soane: The Man and the Style," in *John Soane* [London: Academy Editions; New York: St. Martin's Press, 1983], 14).

24 Soane was clearly interested in historical narrative subjects in his choice of art works, an interest that could be seen as a romanticism such as found in Fuseli, whom he collected: "Fuseli, the most eccentric of all romantic artists, valued poetical (that is, historical or narrative) painting above realistic art (portraits, for example)" (Helen Dorey, "Soane as a Collector," in Peter Thornton and Helen Dorey, A *Miscellany of Objects from Sir John Soane's Museum* [London: L. King, 1992], 126).

25 Soane "shared the feeling for 'the terrible sublime' evoked in the works of Fuseli, James Barry, John Martin and John Mortimer, all of whose work is represented in his collection though, in the case of the last three, only in the form of prints or drawings" (ibid.).

Polyvalent Spaces:
The Postmodern Wunderkammer
and the Return of Ambiguity

Pablo Helguera

INTRODUCTION

The Museum of Jurassic Technology in Los Angeles and the Salon de Fleurus in New York City can be categorized as museums, yet both institutions reconstruct the museum experience and reinterpret familiar standards and conventions for conveying interpretive communications. Pablo Helguera emphasizes how the two institutions challenge these standard conventions and propose alternative methods of viewing art and natural history for the visitors.

Helguera explores how these two museums use displacement. The familiarity of museums is presented in slightly altered interpretations within the museum space. Upon entering each of these exotic museums, the visitor registers a departure from the expectations of a conventional museum. Crossing into the atypical fields of these quasi-public realms puts visitors on alert that they do not know how to interact with the exhibits in a traditional manner. Both museums objectify the exhibit design to connect the familiar and unfamiliar.

Helguera points out that the Museum of Jurassic Technology references science as a form of objectifying artifacts. This sense of familiarity—used widely in natural history and science museums—provides a seductive sense of security as the admitted viewer becomes an active part of the dialogue. The Salon de Fleurus rewrites the authorship of familiar by replicating an early-twentieth-century Paris salon. Paintings only slightly different from those that would have populated Gertrude Stein's collection hang on the walls, and their labels are all titled anonymous, a direct critique of the conventions of large, well-funded, public museums. At both institutions, the exhibit designs do not appear contemporary. Rather, the curators display odd objects that, in turn, inform how other odd objects should be displayed. The design solutions provide inventive ways to interpret and participate in the dialogue between display, viewing, and viewed.

The exhibit design contributes to the atmosphere of the two museums, but interior design and decoration are what really provide the spatial character of these oddities. Entering modern-day Wunderkammern *("cabinets of*

Courtesy of the Department of Education, Museum of Modern Art, New York, 2010.

curiosities") transports the viewer into a fictional world that turns the interiors into objects of display, in ways similar to (but unlike) the display of objects and collections elsewhere. Familiar objectivity is overrun by the eccentricity of the interiors and the quirky, mercurial ambiguity of the museum gestalt.

––––

> When the real is no longer what it used to be, nostalgia assumes its full meaning.
> There is a proliferation of myths of origin and signs of reality; of second-hand
> truth, objectivity and authenticity. There is an escalation of the true, of the
> lived experience; a resurrection of the figurative where the object and substance
> have disappeared. And there is a panic-stricken production of the real and the
> referential, above and parallel to the panic of material production. This is how
> simulation appears in the phase that concerns us: a strategy of the real,
> neo-real and hyperreal, whose universal double is a strategy of deterrence.
> —Jean Baudrillard, *Simulations*

SOMETIME IN 1987, on a modest block of Venice Boulevard in downtown Culver City, of West Los Angeles, the Museum of Jurassic Technology quietly opened its doors to the public. The project was the creation of an unassuming man named David Wilson, offering viewers an immersive, exquisitely installed Victorian-era museum environment full of dimly-lit dioramas and exhibitions. The theatrical displays offer a wide variety of natural and historical oddities that narrate what Wilson defines as "the Lower Jurassic," ranging from horned ants and Flemish moths to microscopic sculptures made out of human hair and representations of old-time remedies. The MJT recurs to obscure chapters of human knowledge to offer a Borgesian universe of poetic and cosmic connections, guiding us, as the museum itself claims, "as a chain of flowers into the mysteries of life." The museum's perplexing exhibits, with their elaborate narratives, beautiful presentation, and, to many, suspicious veracity, have generated an enthusiastic cult-like following amongst contemporary artists, taking a unique spot as an "artist's Wunderkammer."

A second example of a contemporary Wunderkammern, although this one on the East Coast and taking art history as its subject, is located on a rear building near the corner of Spring and Mulberry Streets in New York's SoHo. Opened to the public in 1992 and still in operation, The Salon de Fleurus doesn't have a web page nor does it advertise itself through any means. Instead, it has existed mainly by word of mouth for two decades in Manhattan, and its hidden feel is vital to its own anachronistic condition (as it references a historical period far before the digital age). The Salon is open only in the evening hours (I was told this was done in order to give a certain quality to the experience). I will not describe the interior in detail, so as to not disrupt a potential visiting experience of the reader, but suffice to say that the name relates to Gertrude Stein's apartment at 27, Rue de Fleurus, where she held what was likely the very first collection of modern art. The evocative environment, presented against the background of an Édith Piaf album, oscillates between the domestic and the public space, or between an antiques bazaar and a museum. Several paintings hang on the dim lit walls are described as the work of "anonymous authors" but appear to be replicas of works by Cezanne, Braque, and Picasso. Together, they conjure up a defining yet fragile moment in history when these pieces were hanging for the first time in history. Visitors to the Salon (the Salon only admits a very small group of people at a time) are welcomed at the door by the curator, who describes himself only as the "caretaker" of the collection. He conducts the group to the rear end of the building and, once entering the Salon and letting the visitors take it all in, starts with a narration that further enhances the space as a perfect hybrid of a historical house and a mythical place—namely, the birthplace of modernism.

I

Because neither the curators of the MJT or the Salon de Fleurus claim their spaces as art project nor describe themselves as artists, this doesn't seem to be an accurate label to give to either of them; yet the pedagogic license taken over the interpretation of the objects, the opaque mission statement of their enterprises and the unusual conditions of the exhibitions also would prevent one to place them in the roster of Los Angeles or New York cultural institutions. Wilson's decidedly ambiguous positioning of his museum has made it, for the most part, impossible to extract from its original environment and inserted into a traditional art historical narrative. A case in point would be a casual conversation I had on the subject in 1999 with MoMA's curator Kynaston McShine, who had just opened his exhibition *The Museum As Muse*—MoMA's attempt to document and chronicle both the institutional critique generation and the Postmodern impulse by artists to use museums as their subject. When I inquired about the conspicuous absence of the MJT in MoMA's exhibition, McShine shrugged: "I just didn't know how to fit the Jurassic into the show." A similar problem arose when curator Larry Rinder selected the Salon de Fleurus to be part of the 2002 Whitney Biennial. While some objects of the Salon were placed in the galleries, they felt out of place inside an art museum. The effect of being inside the Salon was impossible to recreate and the true experience was left for only a few scheduled visitors to the actual location during the biennial.

McShine and Rinder are not the only ones who have had trouble pinning down these Postmodern Wunderkammern—like the MJT's conceptually elusive Flemish moths—into art history. The constant conundrum of how to place these projects in a curatorial context—what is true or not about the exhibits, on whether this should be regarded as an art work or not, on whether the institution should be treated like any other museum, and so forth—is also the main reason of their success, and may simply just point to the fact that they may actually be all these things at once. It was the late Marcia Tucker who first gave the most accurate assessment of the MJT: "It's like a museum, a critique of museums and a celebration of museums,—all rolled into one."[1]

Much has been written about the MJT in terms of its history, its exhibitions, and its connection to the traditional cabinet of curiosities—most notably by Lawrence Weschler in his 1995 book *Mr. Wilson's Cabinet of Wonder*—so I will not repeat Weschler's insightful description and analysis. What I will focus on in this short text is in offering some thoughts on where these contemporary Wunderkammers like the MJT and the Salon de Fleurus could be placed in the larger historical context of contemporary art practice, tracing a brief typology of these projects and their spatial and narrative strategies, and argue how its manipulation of spatial, cognitive and narrative conventions proposes models that in fact are now helping redefine the notion of the alternative space employing, in an unorthodox way, community building notions that are comparable to Ray Oldenburg's theory of the "third place." I will argue that their slipperiness, achieved through a delicate choreography of physical and conceptual space, has become one of the most important contributions to rethinking today's artist enterprises, merging earnestness with irony, certainty with self-doubt.

II

One of the great gifts that Postmodernism brought in the visual arts was, via Minimalism, the appropriation of historical models through the filters of irony and self-awareness. This attribute is common of artists' insertions into institutional frameworks roughly ranging from the 1970s to the early 90s (such as Michael Asher, Fred Wilson, Hans Haacke, Barbara Bloom, Andrea Fraser, and many others) that became associated with institutional critique. These groups of artists used the theatrical and pedagogical conventions of museums as a medium to build a phenomenology of the viewer and increase awareness, self-reflexivity, and critical thought on issues such as the authoritative voice of the museum, the subjective narratives of art history, and the alignment of cultural institutions with economic and political power. The more ancillary practice by artists to concoct museums as critical and autonomous mechanisms could be traced back to the inauguration in 1968 of Marcel Broodthaers' *Musée d'Art Moderne, Départment des Aigles*. By creating conceptual and nomadic museum without a permanent collection, Broodthaers' project displayed the self-consciousness, irony, confrontation, and mutability that became the basis of institutional critique. Broodthaers' fictional museum model, as well as the later works by artists who took on the institutional disguise, were more than an atavistic simulation: it was a reappropriation of the experiential ritual of art, a criticism of the purported knowledge onto which modernism laid its foundation, and an attempt to blur the boundaries of art and life and historical and fictional narratives.

These type of hybrid "museums" adopt a museological narrative model that from the onset counters the rational linearity of Modernism and a rebellion to the tenets of its pristine ideals of neutral space. In terms of space, it is natural that, because the canonical modernist narrative in the visual arts had been staged using the white cube, that its counterpoint should be constructed using an opposite device. In the case of the Salon, there is an attempt to re-enact the pre-modern environment that led to the construction of the white cube: the domestic space where artists socialized, exchanged ideas, and lived their lives. Similarly, the MJT appropriates elements of the entire history of museums, ranging from the XVIIth century cabinets of curiosities to the XIXth century natural history museum, as if searching for a new historical referent that would altogether bypass the avant-garde.

In terms of narrative linearity, the MJT's exhibits don't deal with art necessarily, but rather with curiosities of science and history, returning, as it were, art to an encyclopedic mission, a primal habitat where it once shared space with scientific and religious items, as well as with objects of superstition and of wonder, liberating it from the modernist demand of speaking about itself. The Salon de Fleurus, by presenting replicas of famous paintings that are claimed as anonymous, proposes a questioning of authorship that is not only pre-modern, but pre–art historical, returning to the time when art in churches had no authors.

III

Different and unique as they both are, both the Museum of Jurassic Technology and the Salon de Fleurus employ a strategy of contextual displacement and immersion, where the viewer has to ask oneself where he or she is. This slight confusion is key to introduce the viewer into a situation where objects and the place itself, although are being assigned specific names (*this* is a museum, *that* is an exhibit, *this* is an artwork, *you* are a museum visitor, etc.) they soon start looking like something else and shedding their officially assigned meaning (in the same way in which the MJT's scientific exhibitions don't appear to be objective, the Salon doesn't feel like an anonymous location, but rather a very accurate historical reconstruction of a very concrete place and the events around it). What is regained by this strategy of displacement, interestingly, is a more heightened awareness of the visual information being presented to us.

Connected to the feeling of displacement is the playful tension that both spaces employ with the notions of authenticity and truth as conveyed by an institution. While using formal devices and authoritative interpretive tools such as the ones used by museums, but also presenting statements that are at best dubious or arguable, one is left to *wonder*, perennially left with more questions about the answers that are being given. The more one scratches for the "truth" of these places, the more one sinks into ambiguity.

Another, equally important component of these two spaces is their intimacy. Both the MJT and the Salon are relatively small locations, so the social dynamics that take place in there are closer to the one that would take place in a small or medium size shop than in a public art museum. Size allows also for a more personal relationship with the art, and perhaps for an unexpected kind of isolation where we are not surrounded by others to influence our thoughts on what we are experiencing—instead we are there to reflect on our own and to have one-to-one dialogues. Additionally, spaces like these become conversation pieces amongst the initiated, offering a mystery that can be discussed and debated. Amongst those close to the spaces, the humor of deceit also becomes important.

It goes without saying that all the above-described conditions are very difficult, if not impossible, to recreate in public art museums today. A museum's public mission and duties toward access, interpretation, and their sheer mandate to accommodate large groups of people to every exhibition greatly reduce the possibility to preserve the one-to-one experience of art. In reality, this is the great irony about museums, which in theory should offer viewing situations where the art works come to life in the mind of the viewer. Yet, because the public demands access and information in all sorts of formats, much of the art experience needs to be mediated through a series of frames, labels, and explanations that can quickly turn each artwork into a dead specimen. Contemporary Wunderkammern, by contrast, can afford to dispense with any demands of public service and create a world where a seemingly opaque and surreal logic erases every sort of frame, or rather, the frames that it presents appear to fuse into the work itself (the mission statement of the MJT, for instance, instead of explaining anything, only becomes an extension of the opacity of the interior space).

Jean Baudrillard's quote at the beginning of this essay refers to how the inevitable effect of a perfect simulation is the nostalgia of the real. There is indeed a pervasive sense of longing on these places, a romantic impulse to restore a kind of knowledge that had been lost (or, quoting one of the exhibition titles of the MJT, "no one will ever have the same knowledge again"). In the postmodern context, this nostalgic sensibility should not be interpreted just as a Pre-Raphaelite-like movement toward recapturing some kind of lost innocence or building an artistic Arcadia, but instead as another kind of impulse as described before: the restoration of the viewing experience, and the attainment of secret knowledge, as in an alchemical process that bestows the visitor with a prized possession through mysterious means.

IV

Both the MJT and Salon de Fleurus emerged during a period where the global expansion of the art world in post-wall Europe led to a oversize biennial landscape, where major museums focused on blockbuster exhibitions that would attract the larger public, and where incremental rise of the art market, and the decline of public funding for the arts in the United States led to the closing of many alternative spaces and displaced many artists communities in search for spaces to present their work. At the same time, in the late 80s and early 90s, urban changes in American cities led sociologists to propose new models for neighborhood design and about local solutions to community building. In 1989, sociologist Ray Oldenburg famously proposed the notion of the "third place," that location between work and home where individuals find an environment that is structured just so that they can feel at ease but also stimulated enough so that they can engage in activities that reinforce their sense of selves and their sense of belonging (the notion was taken, and successfully implemented, by the corporate chain Starbucks which expanded exponentially in the 90s selling the idea of a location that was just between work and home).

The Oldenburgian third place is grounded on the notion of a participatory public, where the primacy is personal interaction, and where participants can feel most at ease. In perhaps a counter-intuitive way, spaces like the MJT and the Salon de Fleurus proposed a version of the third place for the art community: a place for the initiated, where experience of the work takes primacy, but simultaneously serves as a social glue. By making it difficult to access, the membership becomes more enthusiastic. Furthermore, I would posit that these third spaces in the visual arts go beyond the normal duality of work and home: they propose a space between truth and fiction; between the museum and the artist studio, and between public and private, and between knowing and unknowing. While theoretically grounded in postmodernism, they point to a step beyond traditional oppositionalities where we by necessity need to adopt simultaneous roles as architects and inhabitants, or as curators/narrators and actors. The viewer, in this case, becomes a complicit participant in furthering the dialogue of fiction (that is, by playing along as a regular museum visitor).

Looking at the new generation of artists and artist spaces in Los Angeles, one could argue that at least in the case of the MJT, its example has been followed by a number of new experiments, if not on museum-building, certainly on the ambiguous spaces. The Center for Land Use Interpretation, founded in 1994, describes itself as an "education and research organization" but it participates directly in the art world through site-specific projects and activities. Machine Project, a space run by artist Mark Allen, while it doesn't operate like a museum, has adopted a hybrid model of community center, Kunsthalle, and school. Artist Fritz Haeg turned his house in Los Angeles into a school organizing a variety of activities that ranged from basic learning experiences to performance. Many more spaces emerge on a nearly daily basis. New York has also seen a remarkable proliferation of such hybrid spaces (although due perhaps to the much more higher rents in the city, they tend to live much briefer lives).

What is clear from the experiment of the Postmodern Wunderkammern is that, drawing from the tools of Institutional Critique, they emerged as autonomous spaces that refused definition as a key part of their identity, small in scale in order to retain individual relationships and experiences, and reached out to a type of knowledge that may be obscure, universal, erudite, or simply strange, to produce moments of wonder and communal experience, always by participating in a simulated representation. Their nostalgic aura is yet another of their disguises: they are as much about the present as they are about the past. They point to a need to abandon permanent structures and move, as we already do in so many phases of our contemporary life, into movable platforms of experience.

Notes

1   Quoted by Lawrence Weschler, in "Mr. Wilson's Cabinet of Wonder," 40.

A Metaphysics of Space:
The Quay Brothers' Atmospheric Cosmogonies

Suzanne H. Buchan

INTRODUCTION

The Quay Brothers's set decor in their stop-motion animation films resemble artifacts within architectural models. Integrating movement and animation of their puppets contributes to an overall sense of atmosphere in the mis-en-scène of their film architectures. Suzanne H. Buchan guides us through the Quays's sets and their use of details, music, and atmospheric conditions, whose overall multisensory aesthetic is steeped in the nostalgia their work promotes.

The Quay Brothers look mainly to Eastern European literature for both their narrative content and design aesthetic. This holistic embrace of literature also provides identities for their sets, which are seen as non-narrative, material constructions that create the atmosphere of an abstracted narrative. Buchan introduces several of the Quays's films to describe and analyze the aesthetics of the interiors that the puppets inhabit. In doing so, she establishes associative precedent and lineage in their work.

In contrast to the absence of occupants in typical architectural models used in practice, the Quay Brothers populate their architectonic spaces with puppets made from vintage and well-worn found objects. Their interiors are often laden with nostalgia, either in the form of historical styles or familiar objects. They also incorporate discarded objects ranging from antique porcelain doll heads, scissors, and feathers to screws. Through Buchan, we learn that the Quay Brothers "ask of our machines and objects to act as much if not more than the puppets."* This intensifies the emotional charge within the aesthetic field of the set decor and produces a nonhierarchical sense of ordering the mood.

In the dreamlike atmosphere crafted by the Quay Brothers, puppets and interiors are not limited to the rules of our world. In their films we enter a world that reveals the hidden life of objects when we are not looking. Interior spaces accommodate their dancelike movement, altered to help animate details often left unnoticed. In the background, surfaces are malleable elements

*reconstructed for the puppets to engage. Interior surfaces retain a sense of
wear and tear revealed in graphics, ornament, and text. Buchan reveals the
synthesis of these elements that are accompanied by musical scores, reminding
us of the role sound plays in our interiors that further animates our everyday.*

––––

THE QUAY BROTHERS are among the most accomplished filmmak-
ers to emerge out from the 'Renaissance' of British animation in the 1980s.[1]
Whether puppet animation short or feature films, watching any of their
works means entering into a complicity of furtive glances, choreographed
shadows and a mélange of artistic, musical and literary tropes. Their opus
bears an instantly recognizable style, a shifting composite of chiaroscuro,
and assemblage of obscure and fragmented non-narrative structures. Their
works are closer to music than to dialog, closer to poetry than literature,
closer to interior monologue than to fictional narrative. Their imagery obeys
the enigmatic laws particular to their idiosyncratic cinematic universe. A
creative palimpsest of music, literature, dance and architecture, graphic
design, the sacred and the occult, pathology and metaphysics is compacted
into the graphic stylization, spatiotemporal play and material textures of
their films. Their works function at a tension between concrete phenomenal
'stuff'—the matter the sets and puppets are built of—and poetic, philosophical and perceptual concepts, often from literature. This essay aims to reveal
some of the many formal and aesthetic elements of their cinematic works'
interiors. It also invites reconsideration of how we perceive and understand
the built interior environment, specifically when this environment is occupied by, and in some instances actively created by, *objects* filmed in single
frame animation.

Like many artists working with the static graphic image or sculptural
object, the Quay Brothers' first encounters with film and the kinetic possibilities of frame-by-frame animation began during a course at the Philadelphia
College of Art, where they made live-action shorts and two cut-out animation films. After graduation in illustration in 1969, their interest in European
graphics brought them to London where they enrolled in the Royal College
of Art, continuing their illustration training and filmmaking. They eventually settled in London and in 1979 made the prize-winning animation film
Nocturna Artificialia. This brought them closer to the literary and musical regions of Europe, a self-imposed exile to a mid-point between modern
America and tradition-rich Eastern European culture. The Quay Brothers'
preferred authors and artists tend to be found in the direction of forgotten,
enduring or rediscovered works: Archimboldo, Lewis Carroll, Franz Kafka,
Max Ernst, Michel de Ghelderode, Bruno Schulz, Robert Walser, Robert

Roussell, Adolfo Bioy Casares, Stanislaw Lem. They themselves are contemporary cinematic conspirators in this continuum, and their work has
developed into homages to exiles, foregrounding these authors particular
preoccupation with metaphysics and singular cosmogonies that are psycho-
grammes of existence. Whether their first documentary or literary-inspired
puppet animations or the 2010 *Maska* short, the ambiguousness of the
anachronistic world of their puppets has introduced a new quality of spatial
poetry to animated cinema.

Authentic Trappers in Metaphysical Playrooms

The Quay Brothers' research and studio process is more often than not rooted
in an utterly tactile sensibility and in their notion of 'the liberation of the
mistake.' An example of this emerged from an interest in anonymous architectures and a strong fascination for Hans Poelzig and the entire realm of
the Baroque—in particular the German Asam brothers and the Zimmermann
brothers. Holding a postcard of the St. Johann-Nepomuk church, also
known as the Asamkirche (Asam Church) built in the mid eighteenth century by Rococo architect and sculptor Egid Quirin Asam and his brother
Cosmas Damian in Munich, they turned it upside down. What was an ornate,
skyward-reaching ceiling vault transformed into a deep, concave space, walls
lined with architectural oddities, paintings, plaster decoration and other
religious artifacts, the floor now a ceiling. This ornate grotto inspired the
interior space and ethereal, liquid mood of Lisa Benjamenta's refuge, the
subterranean realm in the live-action feature *Institute Benjamenta* (1995).
[Fig. 7.7] The kind of research the Quay Brothers undertake respects existing
creative origins and identifying features while reinventing them in sets and
visual compositions that result in their unmistakable cinematic style.

The Quay Brothers regard themselves as 'authentic trappers.'[2] In countries they have travelled to around the world, the archive, the faded grandeur of buildings, the used book seller, the antique shop, the museum, the
library, each with their own idiosyncratic ordering and disordering, are the
secreted and astonishing sources of ideas, materials, sounds, music and figures that find their way into over 30 films to date.[3] Distinct from the 'mythic'
origins of their preferred authors' descriptions of matter, the objects, architecture, décors and other elements in their set designs for theatre and opera
and their films' mise-en-scène have physical, tangible origins; they are constructed out of a variety of materials, including mirrors, posters, fabrics,
glass, wood and metal. [Fig. 7.8] The materials retain historical references;
objets trouveés, faded fabrics showing the effects of age and wear, Duchamp-
esque 'readymades' and bachelor machines—all are suggestive of the eras in
which their literary sources set their tales. Watching any of their animation
films means entering a dream world of visual poetry; part of their poetics lies

Fig 7.7: Still of an interior created using puppet animation and special effects from *Institute Benjamenta*, 1995. Courtesy of and © the Quay Brothers

Fig. 7.8: Model décor for "Le Bourgeois Gentilhomme" of Molière for the National Theatre London. Courtesy of and © the Quay Brothers

in the subtly choreographed interplay between lighting, exquisite set fragments and unusual puppets and objects. In their own words: "Puppet films by their very nature are extremely artificial constructions, even more so depending at what level of 'enchantment' one would wish for them in relation to the subject, and, above all, [depending on] the conceptual mise-en-scène applied."[4] Their striking decors and unique puppets, their attention to the 'liberation of the mistake' and their casual and lingering macro close-ups combine to create an ingenious alchemy of animated cinema.

Fig. 7.9: Décor from *Stille Nacht 1: Dramolet* as it was displayed in the 'Dormitorium' exhibition. Image © and courtesy of Mark Bartlett

The Quay Brothers' sets and puppets are often exhibited at festivals, and in 2007 they curated 'Dormitorium,' a collection of *Wunderkammer*, of their meticulously designed and crafted sets and stage designs.[5] What fascinates is not simply the detail and the miniature scale—the *performance* of these sets in the cases also pulls the viewer in. Bending over to look into the non-perspectival depth of a set from Th*e Piano Tuner of Earthquakes* or peering through one of the convex glass windows, the distorted vision of a set fragment becomes cinematic, similar to the macro lenses and focus pulls the Quay Brothers use in their films. The sets' materials are the stars here: fabrics and cultivated dust (*Street of Crocodiles*, 1986), nurtured patinas on metal and wood (*The Piano Tuner of Earthquakes*, 2005*)*, mottled and textured surfaces (*Rehearsals for Extinct Anatomies*, 1988), starry, magnetized iron filing 'fur' (*Stille Nacht 1: Dramolet*, 1988). [Fig. 7.9] The opportunity to linger over these interiors' exquisite detailing that can go undiscovered in a film's crepuscular lighting and time-based projection is one of the exhibition's attractions.

Although they provide audiences the opportunity to see the relation between the screen world and the mechanical and technical investment required for puppet animation, for the Quay Brothers, these displays are not representative of the films:

They are in no way meant to be seen as finished objects when seen in isolation out of the natural context of the very films themselves. They lack entirely the further additional multiple potentials of sound, music, lighting, the choreography of rhythm and movement of puppets or objects through framing; and lastly, the interpretative mise-en-scène applied to all these. Retroactively, they are a reminder of the static imitation of the film's otherwise natural evanescent flux.[6]

The sets are the environment for the films' 'actors'—the natural evanescent flux of their cosmogony of puppets, automata and 'metaphysical machines.'

Cinematic Set Design in *Street of Crocodiles*

One of the Quay Brothers' best-known short films is the 21-minute colour film *Street of Crocodiles* (1986) based on the short story "The Street of Crocodiles" by Polish author Bruno Schulz. *Street of Crocodiles* gathers and reassembles fragments of materials from his writings, transporting Schulz's literary descriptions into the locations that are the sets of the film. The main figure is a male puppet, perhaps Schulz himself, and the film records his aimless wanderings through a maze of alleys, mirrors and dimly lit shop windows. The hapless hero is a fragile construction of the Quay Brothers' preferred materials. An oversize head roughly crafted of ravaged plaster, with eyes so liquid that their gaze is set in a permanent state of disorientation and longing, a tailcoat hung over his haggard frame, and thin, delicate hands which are so expressive that each gesture they make is poignantly helpless. We follow his erring and cautious steps into the 'Antechamber' and through miniature dust-filled street corners until he pauses, caught by a flickering portal window in the distance. [Fig. 7.10] Sometimes the camera assumes his point-of-view: one sequence, when he looks through the flickering window, now an eyehole, reveals a space that contains animated automata: one of the film's 'Metaphysical Museums.'[7] The space he sees (and we see) through the portal is undefined, in part due to extreme play with focal planes. Then the camera is turned on his watching eye as he gazes through it, one of the mysterious drawers, openings and shadowy holes which dot the architecture of many a Quay film, windows and passages to subconscious desire.

Mapping the architecture, spaces and objects of the Quay Brothers' films, and of *Street of Crocodiles* in particular here, means investigating how the architectural constructions and materials create the spatialities particular to the film's 'world.' Characteristic is a preference for patina, rough edges, folds and visually rich tactile surfaces—for *Street of Crocodiles* all in keeping with the inspiration from Schulz's descriptions of the alleys, shop windows, moods and textures in his story. The Quay Brothers often use materials that have had a past use in the physical world (a strip sample of thread colours

Fig. 7.10: A glowing window of desire beckons from beyond the *Crocodile* portal frieze. Courtesy of Suzanne Buchan and © the Quay Brothers

that adorns the Tailor's shop cabinets, bent screws, antique doll fragments, tapestry fabric), and they re-appropriate this past use in the design and composition of the puppet or set constructions. An example of this is Schulz's combing of history that is mirrored by the filmmakers' excursions to Poland to the locations of these mythologies to gather the stuff, the forgotten materials from attics, shops and markets, in immersions in the emotional capacity of music, or in the 8mm films they shot on their travels, and in the photographs, postcards and old prints that once were contemporary to Schulz.

Critics have described *Street of Crocodiles* as labyrinthine. I interpret this threefold here: firstly, because it takes cues from Schulz's metaphysical descriptions of space and time for its cinematic images; second, as a collaged, convoluted and disconnected space created through montage it incites spatial uncertainty. And finally, littered with puppets and objects, discrepancies of scale and miniatures contribute to the credibility of the realm.[8] Before addressing these, I will briefly explain some formal concepts of cinematic set design and how they are relevant (or not) for animation set design.

Film architecture (or what is generally understood as set design) represents a fictional space not completely bound to physical laws, such as gravity or weight bearing limitations. This puts it in a privileged position in relation to the 'lived-in' spaces of built architecture. Juan Antonio Ramirez assigns the properties of cinematic set design to the following categories: it is illusory, fragmentary, flexible and moveable, it is non-orthogonal, demonstrates distorted size and proportions; is quickly built and usually quickly dismantled or destroyed.[9] The same conditions apply to the Quay Brothers' puppet sets: the actions and movement of the puppets take place within an existing space that presents spatial dimensions and perspectival depth.[10] Set design in puppet animation has a lesser degree of controllability than other techniques of animation because although a film is shot frame-by-frame using stop-motion, the images are produced in front of the camera using a mise-en-scène similar to live-action studio productions.

In *Street of Crocodiles*, the main formal parameters are texture (materials), spatial constructions (zones) and scale (miniatures). Yet puppet animation can subvert and expand upon Ramirez' definitions of live-action set design, since the artificiality inherent in film architecture is exaggerated in puppet animation and it does not have to exhibit an architectural logic. Analogous in some respects to live action, puppet set design can be tailored to create illogical architecture and highly artificial spaces. Keeping scale, camera angles and lenses in mind, like live-action filmmakers, the Quay Brothers can 'cheat' on architectural requirements, distort perspective and, since they are building miniature sets, they can use materials that would otherwise not be feasible in a 1:1 scale. Using time-based animation, animators can create an experience of architectural construction that does not need to fulfil Vitruvius' architectural principles of *utilitas* or *firmitas*.[11] The architectural imagination of animation is *venustas*, the artistic design.

Spatial Collage

The Quay Brothers develop and build their sets in an intimate tabletop working space where mostly just the two of them are engaged in developing ideas and trying them out: "The first thing you do is build the sets—you're really building your mise-en-scène when you've built the sets. It's important when you say 'are there going to be two windows; is there going to be one window and two doors?'"[12] [Fig. 7.11] They have been assisted with many of the technical challenges of their sets, puppets and automata by master craftsman and technical adept Ian Nicholas. The *Street of Crocodiles* sets were built in fragments that were then interrelated and diegetically connected in the film editing process. The convoluted and disconnected littering of space developed from a concept of set design based on a collage principle, in part because it allowed the Quay Brothers the possibility to randomly join architectural images with varying perspectives:

> [A]rchitecturally that was the first time that we'd really attempted something on that scale and tried to use space in a way to deliberately confuse....We realised in making [*Street of*] *Crocodiles* that we would need a whole collage technique of putting building fronting onto backs, backs onto fronts and to sides. It was the easiest way to actually execute that kind of confusion.[13]

Fig. 7.11: Miniature scale and proportions of the set: the Quay Brothers shooting the "Tailor's shop" sequence, for *Street of Crocodiles*, ca. 1985.
Courtesy of and © the Quay Brothers

A recurring awareness during watching *Street of Crocodiles* (and perhaps any puppet animation film) that can momentarily break engagement with the film's fictional world is the knowledge that the set is small scale and positioned in the artists' studio. This is the kind of knowledge that we tend to suppress; otherwise, we are recurrently preoccupied with what its spatial relations are to the rest of the room: where are the filmmakers standing? How is the set positioned? If more than one set is used in the film, where is it placed in relation to the one we see on screen? The complexity of the Quay Brothers' elliptic collage construction of interiors and of time creates ambiguous space where the viewer cannot reconstruct 'where' she 'is' in the film. We are not given enough visual clues to imagine a rational extension of the real space off-screen outside the shooting setup; our expectations of the spatial relations of 'beside, through, in and beyond' are disrupted in the film.

Street of Crocodiles' interiors, as in most of their puppet animation films, seem to be air-tight. It is hard to imagine a gust of wind ever disturbed the accrued, sedimentary dust that glows softly in the bright light that infiltrates these spaces. These are akin to Gaston Bachelard's drawers, chests and wardrobes, like a "lovingly fashioned casket [that] has interior perspectives that change constantly as the result of daydream. We open it and discover that it is a dwelling-place, that a house is hidden in it."[14] Bachelard's unparalleled phenomenological exploration of spaces evoked in literature and poetry resonates with Schulz's creative imagination of mnemonics, metaphysics and place. The collaged set fragments, partially organised around puppets' point-of-view structures, interconnect to become the 'world' of the film. Besides the ten set fragments that create the cinematic 'world,' 'interiors the Quay Brothers' particular cosmogony includes both puppets and non-anthropomorphic mechanical apparati. Along with the ones in the 'Metaphysical Museum,' they conjure the undercurrent 'life of the realm.'

Bruno Schulz's *'generatio aequivoca'*

The Quay Brothers possess a predilection for rootless, abandoned materials. Their studio is a tactile atmosphere saturated with Richard von Krafft-Ebing, Kafka and Archimboldo, and populated by various objects suspended by strings or collecting their own unique dust on shelves. Salvaged from various *marchés aux puces* they seem to lie waiting for their opportunity to slip into one of the films. Their continuance of the *trompe-l'oeil* tradition of Max Ernst's metamorphoses, their use of organic and inorganic matter and automata mocking human form, and their animated autonomy of material from human behaviour and laws of the physical world, all seem intertwined in the challenge to animate and sensualise deadness. This emphasis on matter rather than anthropomorphic puppets is clear in a statement from the Quay Brothers: "We ask of our machines and objects to act as much if not more than the puppets."[15]

They circumscribe the limitations of traditional puppet animation by exposing the fragile, crumbling materiality of their constructions that invokes Antonin Artaud's aesthetic engagement with the sick mind and the sick body, or his concept of a Theatre of Cruelty. Armatures are visible, like tortured and crushed bones tweaking out of the crumbling fabrics that encase them, or are reduced to a single body part, a head, an eye. In a critique of German Romantic Ludwig Tieck's "The Cup of Gold," Artaud suggests: "Perhaps we do live in the mind, but what a larval, skeletal, foetal life it remains, where all the simplest intellectual steps, sifted by our rotten minds, turn into some ominous dust, some grotesque posturing or other."[16] Some of the Quays' interpretations of literature recall not the romantic notions of innocence, but rather the images of the mind that Artaud describes—and the concept of the automaton is a central trope throughout their work. The life of the mind translates visually into the grotesque architecture and puppets in the films; even the dust has a disturbing life of its own. In an uncanny reversal of disconcerting density, we understand what it is to be trapped in a sawdust and cloth form, and become privy to its sinister and sensual potential. Macro close-ups, calibrated pans and lingering shots enable the viewer intimate experiences of the private moments of this slumbering matter. In *Street of Crocodiles* an animated drop of spit sets the metaphysical machineries off in motion, This is the inanimate made animate, the *secret life of materials on screen.*

The world of the inanimate made animate is also the world of the fairy tale. Walter Benjamin brilliantly draws analogies between children's fascination with waste objects and how they use these to create their own 'worlds':

> Children [...] are irresistibly drawn by the detritus generated by building, gardening, housework, tailoring or carpentry. In waste products they recognize the face that the world of things turns directly and solely to them. In using these things they do not so much imitate the works of adults as bring together, in the artifact produced in play, materials of widely differing kinds in a new intuitive [volatile] relationship. Children thus produce their own small world of things within the greater one.[17]

The Quays grew up in Philadelphia that had a large immigrant population, which might explain an early infiltration of immigrant European culture in their imaginations. One could easily imagine two little boys rummaging in back alleys of the little shops where dislocated watchmakers, butchers or dressmakers enclosed their private ghosts of distant Europe. The way the Quay Brothers visualise fairy tale elements in their films is a collecting of material, their salvaged material—the 'detritus' Benjamin speaks of—and rearranging it in a way that transforms it into a 'world' in which these materials' animistic properties prevail. An example is *Street of Crocodiles* tailor's assistants, combinations of puppet fragments, armatures and a wooden cabinet for a 'skirt' are examples of portmanteau constructions.[18] [Fig. 7.12] In their

Fig. 7.12: Tailor's shop with puppets and full-scale sewing notions from the set of *Street of Crocodiles* as it was displayed in the 'Dormitorium' exhibition. Photograph by Lois Weinthal and © the Quay Brothers

Fig. 7.13: Screws
embedding
themselves in front
of a cymbal-playing
"metaphysical
machine."
Courtesy of Suzanne
Buchan and
© the Quay Brothers

work with 'anonymous objects,' the filmmakers suggest "You accept their very physicalities palpably as objectified dream or as music, and it's at this point that you can convey compound zones, darker ranges, deeper possibilities as well as perpetuate other narratives, other secret liberties."[19] Animated matter and collaged mise-en-scène relaxes expectations of a cinematic equivalent of human life form, allowing metaphor and analogy to enter into the performative 'otherness' of the objects. This is a cinematic expression of Bruno Schulz's *generatio aequivoca*, "a species of beings only half organic, a kind of psuedofauna the result of a fantastic fermentation of matter."[20] The materials, objects and puppets in the Quays' studio are the *generatio aequivoca* in an undead slumber, objects that retain their cultural and historical referents when animated in the films' interiors.

Most of the metaphysical machines—pulleys with wires propelled into the distance, a bowl of metal parts, a rubber band machine, the trio of screws—were filmed in brief sequences in interiors that appear either independent of the rest of the film's spaces or are intercut with them to suggest the life of matter and automata in the film. And screws move like nomads, or a mischievous gang, through many of the interiors, often embedding themselves in surfaces. [Fig. 7.13] These hiatus-like cameos are scattered throughout the film—there is no reason for these to appear in the film, no narrative motivation. We see them simply as a spectacle of the miniature, a performance that has the sole point of celebrating itself. Laura Marks proffers that haptic visuality—which is what these cameos generate—requires the viewer to work to constitute the image, "to bring it forth from latency…in this mutually constitutive exchange [she] finds the germ of an intersubjective eroticism."[21] This can explain in part the fascination the Quay Brothers' film's hold for many viewers, as the filmmakers experiment with a visual erotics Marks defines as: "one that offers its object to the viewer but only on the condition that its unknowability remain intact."[22] The need to describe action of the animated inanimate is thus replaced by a sensual lingering, a haptic eroticism, that remains spectacular. Susan Sontag has suggested that there is a beautification of the grotesque, the common and the ugly by virtue of being photographed.[23] The conscious eschewal of continuous space and a shifting of focus is further complicated by the Quay Brothers' use of extreme close-up and macro lenses, which provide virtually no depth of field; gestures and metaphysical machines become gargantuan and some of the dusty, shabby and pockmarked machines are indeed grotesque: The Quay Brothers' lingering shots extend this photographic beauty into a mythopoetic one: dandelion clocks are gossamer rainfall, pulleys become spectacular titans; dust, a living layer.

Miniature 'Worlds'

The Quay Brothers' interpretation of Schulz's labyrinthine spaces takes place in a world that is in miniature scale, and part of the enchantment of *Street of Crocodiles* has to do with animation of inanimate 'things' and particularly with the miniature aspect of them. During screening, these miniatures usually appear in proportional relation to the space and architectures that presents a world that is miniature no longer—rather, it is the world of the film, and puppets occupy interiors constructed to accommodate their relative sizes. But there are sequences in *Street of Crocodiles* and other films that subvert proportional rules, where we may become aware of the actual size of such an object used in an unconventional way. In the 'Metaphysical Museum' ice cubes or dandelion clocks that fill the frame call attention to the size of the human hand that places them there. Elsewhere, we see these objects in the same frame as one of the puppets, undermining the illusion that the scale is equivalent to human proportions. The Quay Brothers also occasionally include elements and tools of their own handwork; screwdrivers and hand scissors (like those we would find in a workshop drawer at home), the tips of a scissors that looms over 'Bruno' or a tiny scissors held by the Tailor. [Fig. 7.12]

The miniature is perceptually close to our experience of the fantastic. Neither the miniature nor the fantastic 'exist' in the natural world—they are cocreated by the reader/observer. The Quay Brothers seem to understand the fantastic as Tzvetan Todorov defines it: there is a moment of hesitation between a phenomenal and supersensible explanation distinct from both the uncanny and the marvellous that have natural explanations. The fantastic, however, is when the reader (or viewer) cannot decry whether a narrative phenomenon belongs to the genres of the marvellous or the uncanny, as the fantastic exists between these two categories.[24] Todorov's category of the fantastic is "that hesitation experienced by a person who knows only the laws of nature, confronting an apparently supernatural event."[25] This is the origin of a pleasurable apprehension their films can evoke. The Quay Brothers are cautious in their use of the fantastic:

> If you are thrown too much into the fantastic, so that you lose all hand-hold, then it defeats you. In a sense you create a fantastic world, like in the Gilgamesh film [*The Songs of the Chief Officer of Hunar Louse, or, This Unnameable Little Broom*, 1985], it is important to establish that [the puppet] has certain functions in that world, so that when further elements of the marvellous happen, you can move up to that plane, then back off, and then come back down.[26]

The fantastic is not decorative here; it is an aesthetic means to express a visual correlation for the permeable borders between reality and vitality, between natural physical laws and the increasingly seamless inclusion of fantasy in fictional realism. Watching the scenes described above, we oscillate between understanding that this space exists outside the cinematic experience—in constructed miniatures—and giving ourselves completely to the haptic experience of aestheticised, defamiliarised objects. A still or single-frame image can still be contextualised as a moment isolated from a continuum of living and moving through the world, whether cinematic or 'real.' This is, of course, part of the reason why the Quay Brothers can construct narrative that uses miniatures, but, in their framing and convergences of scale within the frame, with some exceptions mentioned above they appear believably proportional, are haptically experienced and we engage with them physically. The animation reveals its 'secret life.'

Calligraphing Space

The Quay Brothers' prowess in illustration seeps into many formal elements through their works, often as graphic embellishment in the set decoration, Calligraphy defines many of the Quays' interiors. They vary from film to film, from the thick black Expressionist lines in *Nocturna Artificialia*, the inked, faded Polish words on walls, tables and cupboards in *Street of Crocodiles*, or the stark black and white posters and signs and decorative ornaments like woodcut etchings on the cupboard drawers, floors and walls of the 'Wunderkammer' in *The Cabinet of Jan Svankmajer* (1984). [Fig. 7.14] These 'wallpapers' and paper 'appliqués' create trompe-l'oeil, develop mood and atmosphere and add cultural referents from illustration, signage and histories of graphic arts. And even the film titles, intertitles and credits appear in a variety of handwritten styles that stylistically match each film, ranging from Expressionistic, angled fonts in earlier films to the ornate curves and curls in *In Absentia* (2000).

Fig. 7.14: Exploring the drawers of the "metaphysical playroom" in *The Cabinet of Jan Svankmajer*.
Courtesy of and © the Quay Brothers

Discussing the 'home-dweller' in *The System of Objects* Jean Baudrillard suggests that

> our environment is…a *directly experienced* mode of existence… [and the object] a humble and receptive supporting actor…beyond their practical function, therefore, objects—and specifically objects of furniture—have a primordial function as vessels, a function that belongs to the register of the imaginary.[27]

This can be conceived analogous to the centrality of the role of mise-en-scène and decors in The Quay Brothers works as articulated in an early 'manifesto': "We demand that the decors act as poetic vessels and be foregrounded as much as the puppets themselves."[28] Yet distinct from Baudrillard's directly experienced mode of 'supporting actors,' we experience these objects as non-human subjects in the animated 'world' of the film. An example of this is the inventive cinematic graphic stylization (with the added dimension of time which cinema permits) in *Rehearsals for Extinct Anatomies*. Visually, it is a collection of austere spaces and idiosyncratic objects—metaphysical machines—loosely knit together more by technical and spatial aspects of the camera's point-of-view than by any narrative source, a combination of the prosaic and the poetic. The film is a composition of camera pans back and forth between three striking interiors. One is a darkened room lined with striped fabric literally flowing from the walls that is populated by two mostly

541

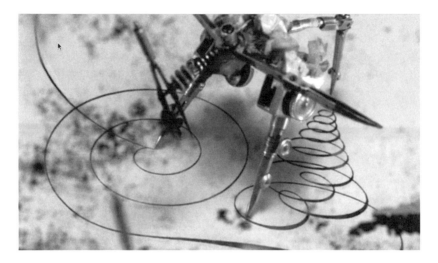

above
Fig. 7.15: An animated "metaphysical machine" creating the decorations in *Rehearsals for Extinct Anatomies*. Courtesy of Suzanne Buchan and © the Quay Brothers

left
Fig. 7.16: Décor for *The Calligrapher*, three station idents commission for the BFI, but never screened. Courtesy of and © the Quay Brothers

immobile puppets, one reclining and one sitting. The two human-like puppets, strangely familiar in stature and gesture from earlier films, wait for—what? Perhaps for an illness to run its course, perhaps not. The oppressive atmosphere is momentarily relieved with an existential Beckettian humouresque: the sitting puppet scratches his head in the same gesture as a one-eyed wire homunculus in another space. It is precisely in this existential sense of nothingness that the 'action' of the Quay Brothers' elliptic narratives takes place.

The white Classicism of the two other spaces that flank the dark room are playgrounds for bizarre puppets, balls and metal forms. These brilliant white spaces are invaded by animated, stark calligraphic lines. Transmogrifying in form between ink, coarse wooly thread and curved wire springs, they climb walls and traverse floors. Lines of a barcode tremble in accord to the sounds of a plucked guitar, then 'drain' down the wall and disappear. A caliper and compass-based metal figure cavorts and pirou-ettes throughout the room, leaving a trail of ink behind that develops spirals, curves and varying thickness of calligraphic line. [Fig. 7.15] In the dark room, thick white lines creep up furniture, climb dark walls and even embrace del-icate folds of cloth. These graphic ornaments escape the fixity of paper and course throughout the decors that they also actively develop and define. In one of the airy paper and ink sculpture idents *The Calligrapher* (1991), seven hands with feathered nibs collaboratively create an ink-drawn bird wing that lifts itself from a sheet of paper. [Fig. 7.16] In *Rehearsals*, as well as providing such decorative embellishment the lines have an additional important func-tion, temporally developing decorative interiors as self-reflective 'poetic vessels,' drawing attention to the potential of animation to free the line and the geometric object from their static destinies to actively invade and alter the films' interiors. The 'long shots' of the full sets are crisp, in medium and close-up shots, and extreme focus pulls are made in almost every scene of *Rehearsals*. This transforms the interiors, creating the effect of landscapes revealed when travelling through fog, sometimes to the extent that forms become grey and pale, blurred abstract forms without outline. Underlying the entire film is a music track from Leszek Jankowski, also mysterious and hermetic, embellished by whispered monologues that hint at seduction or the disparate and unconnected, elliptical experience of solitude.[29] Michael Atkinson captures the film's mood:

> But nowhere is the tension between psychological translation of any stripe and the Quays' ferocious hermeticism more tangible than in *Rehearsals For Extinct Anatomies*, their starkest and most oblique film, free as it is of any (discernible) relationship with outside source material.[30]

The Quays' experiments with new stylistic elements in this film—high-key lighting, blurred animated balls swinging at dizzying frequency, Expressionistic decors and meandering musical scores that occasionally lapse into silence—also enhance the set design.

Conclusion

The Quay Brothers engagement with spatial themes of inside/outside and imagined/experienced may mirror our own continual negotiation between the physical, phenomenal and a metaphysical world. Throughout their opus a continuity can be observed in their artistic devotion to the mar-ginal, and to matter, quietly elevated into the sublime; this is why most of the Quay Brothers short films resist anthropocentric narrative interpre-tations. They transform the objects and materials they work with into imagery that expresses both real and imagined experiences of space and interiors devoid of human life, yet redolent with the intimated past human cultures of the materials they use. Atkinson has suggestively described the Quay Brothers' narratives as "parabolic."[31] Whether labyrinths, zones or maps, what predominates is a poetic preoccupation with dream and disorientation. Emotionally charged with music and sound effects, (and almost a total lack of spoken language), their animated films let matter and architecture 'speak' of an undercurrent metaphysical 'life' that is the Quay Brothers' unique animated cinematic cosmogony. The juxtaposition of imperious logic and alchemy is a fertile terrain for their visual and lyrical imaginations. On screen, these terrains are transmuted into the animated textures and collaged spaces that their camera effortlessly traverses, intimating the secret relationships of spastic machinery, occluded mirrors and fetishised dust.

Notes

* Suzanne Buchan, "A Metaphysics of Space: The Quay Brothers' Atmospheric Cosmogonies," Animation Research Centre at the University for Creative Arts, England, 2010, see page 536.

1 This essay contains elements from my 'The Quay Brothers: Choreographed Chiaroscuro, Enigmatic and Sublime.' published in *Film Quarterly*, Vol. 51, Number 3, Spring 1998.

2 McLatchy, J. D. "Movie Magic. The Quay brothers: the toast of eight film festivals." *Connoisseur Magazine* (1989): 93.

3 In addition to the puppet films, the Quay Brothers' work encompasses various animated shorts, artist documentaries, pop promos, advertising commissions and television station breaks, set design for theater, ballet and opera productions on international stages.

4 Quay Brothers, "In Deciphering the Pharmacist's Prescription 'On Lip-Reading Puppets.'" London: unpublished manuscript, 1986: 1.

5 The exhibition has been displayed at venues around the world, most recently in New York's Parsons The New School for Design, July–October 2009.

6 Quay Brothers Interview, 1996.

7 This set construction appears to be inspired by the peephole window of Marchel Duchamp's assemblage installation *Given: 1. The Waterfall, 2. The Illuminating Gas* that was gifted to the Philadelphia Museum of Art in 1969 (the year the Quay Brothers left Philadelphia).

8 I have also explored a related notion of an animated architectural uncanny in "Uncanny Space, Narrative Place: The Architectural Imagination of Animation." In *What is Architecture?/ Text Anthology (Co To Jest Architektura? / Antologia tekstow)*. (Adam Budak, Ed.): pp 354–391. Krakow: Bunkier Sztuki Contemporary Art Gallery, RAM, Goethe Institut, 2002.

9 Ramirez, Juan Antonio, cited in: Affron, Charles and M. J. Affron. *Sets in Motion. Art Direction and Film Narrative*. New Brunswick and New Jersey: Rutgers University Press, 1995: 31.

10 For an extended discussion of the spectators' experience of the Quays' films,

see Buchan, "The Animated Spectator: Watching the Quay Brothers' 'Worlds.'" In *Animated 'Worlds,'* Suzanne Buchan (Ed.), pp 15–38. Eastleigh: John Libbey Publishing, 2006.

11   Kruft, Hanno-Walter. *History of Architectural Theory: From Vitruvius to the Present.* [Trans Ronald Taylor, Elsie Callander and Antony Wood] Princeton: Princeton Architectural Press, 1994: 14.

12   Quay Brothers Interview, 1992.

13   Quay Brothers Interview, 1996.

14   Bachelard, *The Poetics of Space.* Trans. Maria Jolas. Boston: Beacon Press, 1994: 86.

15   Quays, "In Deciphering the Pharmacist's Prescription,": 2.

16   Artaud, Antonin. *Collected Works Vol 2.* Originally published as *Antonin Artaud: Oeuvres Completes, Tome II.* Paris: Editions Gallimard, 1961. Trans. Victor Corti. London: Calder & Boyars, 1971: 197.

17   Benjamin, Walter. 'Old Forgotten Children's Books.' In *Selected Writings* [translation of 'Alte vergessene Kinderbücher' (1924)]. Translated by Rodney Livingstone. © 1996, pp. 406–413. Cambridge, Mass., and London: Harvard University Press, 2004: 408.

18   For an extended discussion of portmanteau construction and its analogies with the literary technique coined by Lewis Carroll used by James Joyce, see Buchan, Suzanne, *The Quay Brothers: Into a Metaphysical Playroom,* University of Minnesota Press 2010.

19   Quay Brothers Interview, 1992.

20   Schulz, Bruno. *The Street of Crocodiles.* 1963. Translated by Celina Wieniewska, Introduction translated by Michael Kandel. New York: Penguin, 1977: 66.

21   Marks, Laura. *Touch. Sensuous Theory and Multisensory Media.* Minneapolis and London: University of Minnesota Press, 2002: 13.

22   Marks, Laura. *The Skin of the Film. Intercultural Cinema, Embodiment, and the Senses.* Durham and London: Duke University Press, 2000: 193.

23   Sontag, Susan. *On Photography* (1977). London: Penguin Books, 1979: 15.

24   Todorov, Tzvetan. *The Fantastic: A Structural Approach to a Literary Genre.* [Trans. Richard Howard] Ithaca: Cornell University Press, 1973: 31–33.

25   Ibid.

26   Quay Brothers interview, 1992.

27   Baudrillard, Jean. *The System of Objects.* [1968] London: Verso, 2006: 26.

28   Quay Brothers, 1986: 2.

29   Janskowski has collaborated on most of the Quay Brothers' films. Music and the sound track are central in their montage methods and poetics as I describe in *The Quay Brothers. Into a Metaphysical Playroom.*

30   Atkinson, Michael. "The night countries of the BROTHERS QUAY." *Film Comment,* September/October (1994): 39.

31   Ibid.

Architecture of the Gaze:
Jeffries Apartment and Courtyard

Steven Jacobs

INTRODUCTION

In the set design for the 1954 film Rear Window, *Alfred Hitchcock used neighboring interiors to fabricate a voyeuristic ambiance. In the following essay, Steven Jacobs analyzes the film's spatial relationships and famous visual tension while reporting on the extensive set design work he uncovered in his search to understand Hitchcock's construction of a fictitious Greenwich Village block in New York City. Using it as the site for his film, Hitchcock sought to intensify the close proximity of interior spaces in city life. The film's action is symbolic, showing and referencing its themes through window frames and camera lenses. Hitchcock bridges interior and exterior through framed views where the characters, the dynamics of urban dwelling, and the social rules of conduct guiding the characters are witnessed through a camera's eye. Jacobs guides us into the details of Hitchcock's interior space and highlights moments in the film that help establish the identity and symbolism of characters. This is accomplished primarily by isolating the main character, L. B. Jeffries, a photographer whose apartment is replete with visually oriented objects such as cameras and binoculars.*

Jacobs's analysis of the set design includes not only the details of Jeffries's apartment but also Hitchcock's strategy of emphasizing color in each apartment that Jeffries (and the camera) will see, as a way to associate occupant with interior. This color code even extends to clothing as a link to individual apartment interiors. This strategy, coupled with the camera's introductory pan across apartments at the start of the film, helps establish an important elevational map of the characters' apartments. Hitchcock pans the camera across the courtyard facades to help familiarize the audience with the location of apartments and their occupants. Both Jeffries and the audience are transformed from innocent bystanders to peeping toms.

A level of intimacy with the film viewer is established from the window-picture plane of Jeffries's centrally located apartment. Hitchcock

Originally appeared in *The Wrong House: The Architecture of Alfred Hitchcock* (Rotterdam, The Netherlands: 010 Publishers, 2007), 278–95.

subtly reinforces the relationship between film and window by assigning the same proportional dimensions of a film screen to the windows in the film set. Doing so draws the audience further into the film and setting.

———

Rear Window
West 10th Street
Greenwich Village, New York
Color
Paramount, 1954

Art Direction:
Hal Pereira
Joseph MacMillan Johnson

Set Decoration:
Sam Comer
Ray Moyer

This apartment is a smallish studio with the kitchen hidden from view by a bookshelf. The only interior door, apart from the entrance, is the one of the bathroom, of which the inside is never seen in detail. It is not clear whether there is a separate bedroom. The big window looks out unto a courtyard, enclosed by the rear walls of a three-story apartment building in a vernacular 'Federal Brick' style. Only one narrow alleyway leads to a parallel street. The apartment itself is situated on 10th Street, just east of Hudson Street, Manhattan. As Donald Spoto and Juhani Pallasmaa among other commentators have argued, its location can be deduced from the address mentioned of the apartment on the other side of the courtyard: 125 West 9th Street.[1] Because American law required that a film crime was not situated at an existing place, the address is fictitious: in reality, 9th Street changes into Christopher Street west from 6th Avenue. However, at 125 Christopher Street, the building was situated that inspired Hitchcock, who, according to a Paramount Advance Campaign document, "dispatched four photographers to that colorful section of New York with instructions to shoot the Village from all angles, in all weather and under all lighting conditions, from dawn to midnight."[2]

The 10th Street apartment is the residence of L.B. Jeffries (James Stewart), who is confined to his wheelchair due to a leg fracture. Killing time by watching his neighbors through a rear window, his attention is drawn in particular by Lars Thorwald (Raymond Burr), who murdered his wife—at least, this is Jeffries' interpretation of a series of incidents he witnessed: the disappearance of Thorwald's bedridden and nagging wife; Thorwald inspecting her personal belongings such as a purse and wedding ring that are still in the apartment; Thorwald cleaning a butcher knife and bathroom tiles; Thorwald leaving the apartment with a big suitcase in the middle of the night; et cetera.

The protagonist of *Rear Window*, a film dealing with voyeurism, is even a professional voyeur: a photojournalist accustomed to nosing into other people's affairs and owning an arsenal of professional viewing devices (binoculars, telephoto lens), he eagerly deploys to spy on his neighbors. Precisely because of its voyeuristic theme, its tension between watching and being watched, and its outspoken attention to optic instruments, *Rear Window* has been repeatedly seen as an allegory of the gaze and the cinematic apparatus.[3] Hitchcock himself described the film's plot as "the purest expression of a cinematic idea" and as a meditation on the famous Kuleshov effect.[4] The film's protagonist is almost a hybrid creature: half man half camera, he even comes with his own tracking apparatus[5]—a few years later, cameraman Raoul Coutard would famously use a wheelchair for the tracking shots in Jean-Luc Godard's *A bout de souffle* (1959).

Revealing himself in earlier films as a master of point-of-view editing, Hitchcock presented *Rear Window* as a film in which the subjective point of view dominates (though not to an absolute degree). This resulted in a very specific topography. Since distance is important to the plot, we seldom get close to the characters on the other side of the courtyard. Furthermore, the predominantly fixed viewpoint implies an important spatial restriction: the film takes place in a single, but gigantic and diversified set that represents a Greenwich Village block comprising 31 apartments. [Figs. 7.17 + 7.18] Based on the hundreds of photographs and sound recordings obtained by the party exploring the neighborhood, the $100,000 set was designed by Paramount unit art director Joseph MacMillan Johnson under the supervision of Hal Pereira, head of Paramount's art department. For months, Hitchcock, Pereira, and MacMillan Johnson did nothing but plan the design of what was to become the largest indoor set ever built at Paramount. Hitchcock himself superintended the huge and complex construction that took six weeks to set up. [Fig. 7.19] The entire set was fit with a sophisticated drainage system for the rain scene and with an ingenious wiring mechanism for the highly complex lighting of day and night scenes in both the exterior of the courtyard and the interiors of the apartments. The earlier mentioned Paramount Advance Campaign document proudly displayed an impressive collection of statistical data: The set "consumed 25,000 man-hours. It used 175,000 board-feet of lumber, 200 sacks of plaster, 750 gallons of paint, and 12 tons of structural steel for flooring and for eye-beams from which to hang balconies.

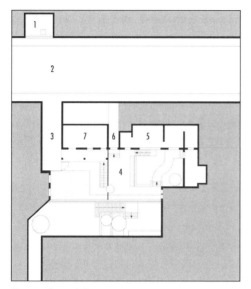

Fig. 7.17: Ground Floor. Drawing by David Claus

1. Restaurant
2. Street
3. Alley
4. Courtyard
5. Apartment Miss Lonelyheart
6. Corridor
7. Apartment Sculptress

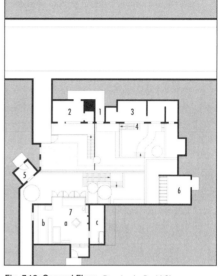

Fig. 7.18: Second Floor. Drawing by David Claus

1. Corridor
2. Apartment Miss Torso
3. Thorwald Apartment
4. Balcony with Fire Escape
5. Apartment Newlyweds
6. Apartment Composer
7. Jeffries' Apartment
a. Living Room
b. Kitchen
c. Bathroom

Fig. 7.19: Courtyard. Set Photograph, Royal Film Archive, Brussels

Steel was also used for roof vents, down-spouts, chimneys and fire-escapes, all of which were 'practical,' which is the film term for usable, as opposed to plainly ornamental. More than 20,000 square feet of imitation brick was cast-staff, in a new method introduced solely for this film."

However, the set was not only a huge piece of machinery, it also contained numerous well-considered details. Since about a dozen of the apartments play a role in the story line and because the camera peeked into the interiors by means of giant booms, they were upholstered or furnished extensively by Sam Comer and Ray Moyer to match the character of their occupants. A publicity handout announced that New York designer Grace Sprague (uncredited) had been hired to work out "visualizations" of the apartments as well as sketching "the kind of costumes needed for the actors working in them."[6] An unsigned Paramount memo further states that "Hitchcock feels due to the fact that he will be jumping around in the various apartments so much that the color of the background walls within the apartments, as well as color of wardrobe, will help orient the audience quicker than anything."[7] Such a meticulous attention to details gave the set its realist but also its uncanny look: a feeling of threat and danger gradually penetrates into an everyday and familiar environment. "This movie could never have been accomplished on location with the same dramatic impact," Pereira assured.

The careful attention to details already characterizes the impressive camera movement that opens the film and immediately evokes the claustrophobic atmosphere of the courtyard. In the first place, this crane shot serves as a classical establishing shot that gives the spectator an understanding of the architectural organization of the situation and of the spatial relations between the different places important to the narrative. [Fig. 7.20] During the long take, the camera rises and descends, slows down and accelerates slightly: from the very beginning, specific areas of the set are emphasized. However, after plunging through the window into the courtyard, the camera returns to the interior of Jeffries' apartment and explores his belongings. It is a perfect illustration of Hitchcock's visual way of storytelling: gliding past a broken camera, a snapshot of a racecar accident, war pictures, all kinds of photographic equipment, and stacks of illustrated journals successively, the shot gives us a lot of information on the inhabitant without any dialogue or voice-over. In a general study on art direction, the opening scene of *Rear Window* is described as "a good example of production design which, with the help of art works and props, presents a story (narration)—not only supporting it, furthering and interpreting it but actually telling it."[8]

The theme of voyeurism combined with the spatial confinements of a single set turns the architectural construction of *Rear Window* into a magisterial

Fig. 7.20: Hitchcock and cameraman Robert Burks in Jeffries' apartment.
Set Photograph, Royal Film Archive, Brussels

viewing device. The architecture becomes an instrument of the gaze, a kind of *camera obscura* on an urban scale. First and foremost, Hitchcock presents the architecture as a tool of the scopic drive by emphasizing the window, which, as the film's title suggests, is also the veritable subject of the film. Unmistakably, he presents the window as a metaphor for the film screen. In *Rear Window*, the window has become a cinematic equivalent of the old pictorial metaphor that dates back to the Renaissance, when the Italian architect and art theoretician Leone Battista Alberti defined painting, in his *De Pictura* (1435), as a window onto the world. Instead of a flat surface that is being looked *at*, the painting is a frame that is looked *through*. This concept, which is often visualized in the countless illustrations of so-called perspective machines of the fifteenth and sixteenth centuries, demonstrates that the visual understanding and the optical domination of the world is dependent on the construction of a frame situated between the world and its beholder.

Not coincidentally, the image of the window, which serves as the opening credits of *Rear Window,* is an important architectural motif in Hitchcock's entire œuvre. *The Lady Vanishes*, *Shadow of a Doubt*, *Rope*, *I Confess*, and *Psycho*, as well, start with the image of a window that marks the transition from an urban exterior to the seclusion of an interior. In contrast with these films, the trajectory in *Rear Window* is made from inside to outside: by means of an impressive dolly shot, we plunge through the window, then slide, from right to left, along the facades of the courtyard and, eventually, end up inside Jeffries' apartment back again.

Fig. 7.21: Miss Torso's apartment (Digital Frame). Courtesy of Universal Studios Licensing LLLP

Not only the window of Jeffries' flat functions as a film screen, each window on the other side of the courtyard does as well—the proportions of these windows even match perfectly the aspect ratio (1.66:1) of the film. Viewed across the courtyard, the characters seem just real enough, something half-remembered, like the images on a cinema screen.[9] The facade on the other side is like a movie library. Each window, each film, answers to specific generic conventions: a comedy of newly-weds during their turbulent honeymoon, a musical comedy with the eligible dancer Miss Torso, a melodrama of a woman nicknamed Miss Lonelyhearts, a biopic of a young composer of popular songs, and, of course, the Hitchcockian murder mystery in Thorwald's flat. [Figs. 7.21 + 7.22] In addition, the film offers a view of some other residents of the building, such as the couple with the little dog that sleeps on the escape ladder and the woman who makes abstract sculptures. This last character alludes, together with the composer, dancer, and photographer, to the different senses but also to the fact that the story is situated in a neighborhood that is a perfect biotope for the fine arts.

Given this perspective, *Rear Window* contains a series of films into one single film. Each window offers a view to a singular picture and the entire courtyard is a kind of urban equivalent of a cable television mosaic with Jeffries (as well as the spectator) zapping between channels. Strikingly, each film deals with love or marriage: the lonely woman waiting for prince to come, the newly-weds making love all the time, the dancer desired by many men, the childless couple that adore their little dog, the couple that quarrels until the wife gets murdered, and, last but not least, Jeffries, who is unwilling

Fig. 7.22: Composer's apartment (Digital Frame). Courtesy of Universal Studios Licensing LLLP

to marry his ravishing fiancée Lisa Freemont (Grace Kelly). As critics such as Robin Wood have noted, all windows, in short, represent alternative scenarios for Jeffries' own life.[10] The windows on the other side of the courtyard are also cinematic screens of desire and the events become the gratification of the voyeuristic longings of both Jeffries and the spectator.

Since the windows on the other side of the courtyard function primarily as screens, the rooms behind them are squashed. The reconstruction drawing of the floor plan indicates that the flats across the courtyard are narrower than Jeffries' apartment. Thorwald's apartment and the one underneath (occupied by 'Miss Lonelyhearts') and above (by the couple with the dog) only connect to the hallway. They seem to be so-called 'railroad apartments' which are quite common in New York brownstone apartment buildings. Similar in design to a railway car, such an apartments comprise a series of rooms, connecting to each other in a line. Often, there is no adjacent hallway, such that in order to move from the first to the third room, one must cross the second. Of course, such one-sided apartments with flattened spaces posited linearly next to one another are perfectly suited to the plot. In so doing, the rooms are arranged parallel to the range of vision of both Jeffries and the spectator.

Because the architecture is subjected to the gaze, the entire building shows several similarities with building types that serve as perspectival machines such as the theater and the panopticon. The space of *Rear Window* can be considered a theatrical or scenographic device because the story depends on the repression of the fourth side of the city block. Although, as Michel Chion has noted, this fourth side is briefly exposed, the dominant point of view makes us forget that there may be on Jeffries' side of the block other apartments from which one can see just as well and perhaps even better what goes on in Thorwald's place.[11] Furthermore, the image Jeffries is watching from his theater seat resembles the archetypical stage set: Jeffries' rear window offers a view of the city, which was also the stage image of the earliest examples of modern theater architecture in the sixteenth century. The modern Renaissance theater building does not only incorporate all kinds of urban architectural fragments (windows, balconies, balustrades, stairs, et cetera) in its decorative scheme, the stage itself represented invariably an urban street in shortened perspective. With their perspectival vistas of the city, both Vincenzo Scamozzi's design for the permanent stage of Andrea Palladio's *Teatro Olympico* in Vicenza (1584) and Sebastiano Serlio's famous drawings of a tragic and comic scene illustrate that the origins of the modern theater coincides with those of modern urban planning—both are disciplines subjecting space to the gaze and to the new logic of geometric perspective.

Since Hitchcock, as opposed to most other Hollywood directors, had a sound grasp of the optical aspects of filmmaking, he undoubtedly exploited skillfully the perspectival distortions of the camera. Already at the start of his career, Hitchcock knew perfectly how a set would look like in the film. It was a lesson that he learned in the early 1920s from German masters such as Murnau: "What you see on the set does not matter. All that matters is what you see on the screen."[12] In *Rear Window*, the viewpoint determines the space even more than usual since Jeffries watches the spectacle from a distance and from a fixed position. As a result, his apartment serves as a box in the theater. This tallies with Hitchcock's frequent use of the theatrical metaphor. Crucial scenes in several films (*The Pleasure Garden, Downhill, Murder, The 39 Steps, Stage Fright, I Confess, The Man Who Knew Too Much, Torn Curtain*) occur in theater and concert halls. In addition, Hitchcock frequently employs architectural or decorative elements referring to the theater. *Rear Window*, as *Stage Fright*, opens with the rise of a curtain. At the end of the film, the curtains in Jeffries' box are lowered. Midway through the story, Lisa endorses the theatrical metaphor by literally closing the curtains while stating that "the show's over for tonight." Several authors have interpreted the presence of theatrical places and conventions in Hitchcock's *œuvre* as a Brechtian estrangement effect—a striking feature in the work of a director who presents cinema as almost the opposite of theater by means of fluent camera movements, dynamic editing, and the extensive use of point-of-view shots.[13] According to John Belton, *Rear Window* plays self-consciously "with the differences between theatrical and cinematic film space, relying on set design and certain kinds of camera movements to establish a concrete, unified theatrical space and on editing, framing, and camera movement to construct a more abstract, psychological, cinematic film space."[14] In the Paramount Advance Campaign document, production designer Pereira pointed out that the impressive single set reversed the usual rules. "It's ambition of every New York producer to acquire a property using a single set. The great properties of motion pictures have often resulted from the purchase of stage plays and then the movies have amplified these to create added scope and interest." Yet, the same document emphasizes, *"Rear Window* uses only a single set which never could have been duplicated on the stage. Hitchcock has reversed the time-worn rules by creating a one set movie which could only be done as a movie."

The subjection of the environment to the logic of the look gives the space of *Rear Window* not only qualities of the theater but also of the panopticon.[15] In the late eighteenth century, Jeremy Bentham presented this circular building with central surveillance unit as a building type perfectly fit for all institutions dealing with control. Whereas the theater directs the gaze of many onlookers to the single focal point of the stage, the panopticon inverts this logic by subjecting the space to a single point of view. The space of *Rear Window* adopts the imaginary form of a cone, whose apex is constituted by Jeffries' living room (or his head) and then extends out toward its base in the courtyard. Just as the panopticon combines spectacle with surveillance, Hitchcock subjects the space to an all-encompassing gaze that transforms the environment into spectacle. The spectator/voyeur himself is invisible. As Bentham's guard, who bases his absolute and demonic power on his own invisibility in the dark core of the building, *Rear Window's* voyeurs hide themselves in the dark: Jeffries pulls back in the shade or extinguishes the light when Thorwald can notice him. Thorwald himself hides in the only non-lighted flat when the little dog of one of the neighbors has been found dead.

Nonetheless, the panoptic power is limited. As in every classical Hollywood film, *Rear Window* comprises many spatial ellipses and there are doors of which it is unclear where they are leading to. In *Rear Window*, however, these features have an added value because of the unusual cinematic space of the single set. In addition, not everything is exposed to the gaze of the protagonist. On the one hand, he is not able to perceive everything (because he sleeps, for instance). On the other, some areas, which can only be imagined by the viewer, are invisible because of the fixed viewpoint. Still other spaces are rendered invisible by characters such as the newlyweds closing the curtains. Moreover, Hitchcock rewardingly uses the border between visible and invisible spaces. The bare walls between the windows, for instance, play an important part in the scene of the quarrel between

Thorwald and his wife or in the one in which Lisa intrudes the Thorwald apartment. Hitchcock, as it were, introduces, on screen, an off-screen space. Because of this, he rouses the spectator's curiosity and imagination and he maximizes suspense. Furthermore, in contrast with the logic of the panopticon, the gaze is mirrored at a climactic moment in the film: Thorwald looks back at Jeffries and, through him, at the camera, the director, and the spectator.

Michel Foucault, who presented Bentham's panopticon as an allegory of the processes of normalization and discipline of modernity, noted that in Bentham's building, "every cage is a small theater in which the actor is alone, perfectly individualized and permanently visible."[16] As in Bentham's panopticon, there seems to be no communication among the individual residential units. Foucault noted that, consequently, the visual logic of the spectacle is turned upside down. Instead of exposing some individual bodies to a community (as the architecture of the temple, theater, and circus in antiquity did), the panoptic courtyard of *Rear Window* provides the lonely surveyor with an overview of many separated individuals. As the panopticon, the urban courtyard belongs to a modern society without a ritual mediation between particular individuals and the abstract concepts of the state or the law. The voyeur sees a collection of anonymous metropolitans that are part of a *Gesellschaft* of autonomous individuals. The inhabitants rather live isolated from than *with* each other. Even the courtyard is not that of a single apartment block but consists of a number of individual back yards attached to distinct, architecturally different buildings on a single city block.

Given this perspective, *Rear Window* is an interesting meditation on modern urban society. The film, as it were, offers a cross-section of an urban segment in a manner that resembles the popular nineteenth-century prints showing Paris apartment buildings. These prints, which show an unseen density and social diversity within a single architectural construction, illustrate the development of a new, modern, and urban way of life in a metropolis radically transformed by Baron Haussmann. Hitchcock's evocation of Greenwich Village shows a colorful urban universe in which inhabitants live as strangers next to each other. Nonetheless, *Rear Window*'s characters are no monads existing only on themselves. Their dwellings have windows and they open up to the world. The characters exist as representations and as images. The dialectic between seeing and being seen touches not only on the essence of Hitchcock's *œuvre* but also, as authors such as Erving Goffman and Lyn Lofland have demonstrated, on that of the urban way of life. In light of this, *Rear Window* is a wonderful evocation of the way in which the spatial organization of the city determines the lives of its residents.[17] The behavior of some inhabitants is unmistakably connected to the fact that the story takes place in this kind of semi-public courtyard in the midst of a metropolis.

Hitchcock, whose films comprise many hidden or impenetrable spaces, maximizes the voyeuristic pleasure by showing a space, which is usually invisible for most of us. The story develops not before a window but, tellingly, in front of a rear window. The set consists of an informal backside containing a capricious combination of terraces and little gardens and which undoubtedly sharply contrasts with the invisible front side. *Rear Window* clearly deals with the contrast between formal and representative facade and informal backside, which is one of the essential characteristics of urban architecture since early modernity—the set, moreover, contains little pieces of such representative front sides in the form of a protruding brownstone facade with a cornice and window mouldings on the other side of the street. Hitchcock realizes that some inhabitants would hesitate to perform the same acts behind a window on the front side or street side of the building. On the informal backside facing the courtyard, by contrast, nobody takes pain to hide or to close the windows with curtains or shutters. The urbanites perform their daily rituals without screening off their rooms. Jeffries too sits in front of the window in his pajamas and shaves. Instead of an absolute privacy behind doors and walls, the courtyard is characterized by a conditional or mediated form of privacy, which is based on the knowledge that others can watch but usually do not. It is a delicate social balance based on the collective use of spaces and on implicit rules of conduct between neighbors. Precisely the relative isolation and the lack of interference in the everyday life of others are the attractive elements of big city life. The story of *Rear Window* is unthinkable in a small town or in suburbia since the balance between individualism and collectivity is completely different in such places.

Dealing with social representation and its dialectic between coded forms of voyeurism and exhibitionism, the film is much more than simply "a commentary on the alienation of urban life."[18] The film discusses the relation between urban alienation and visual power—something that has become much more important in an era when cameras and other systems of surveillance are ubiquitous in both public and private spaces.[19] *Rear Window* announces a postmodern urban space, the boundaries of which are no longer defined by architectural structures but by the screen and the lens.

Notes

1   Spoto, *The Art of Alfred Hitchcock,* 217; Pallasmaa, *The Architecture of the Image,* 145.

2   "Rear Window: Paramount Advance Campaign," document in the Royal Film Archive Brussels. See also the correspondence and documents in the Paramount Files 14 and 17 on *Rear Window,* Margeret Merrick Library, Los Angeles. See also Curtis, "The Making of *Rear Window,*" 29.

3   Douchet, "Hitch et son public"; Stam & Pearson, "Hitchcock's *Rear Window*"; Harris, *"Rear Window* and *Blow-Up"*; and Shariff, *The Art of Looking in Hitchcock's Rear Window.*

4   François Truffaut, *Hitchcock* (New York: Simon & Schuster, 1984), 214–16.

5   David Kehr, "Hitch's Riddle," *Film Comment* (May–June 1984), 12.

6   Bill Krohn, *Hitchcock at Work* (London: Phaidon, 2000), 141.

7   Ibid. See also Gavin, "Rear Window"; and Atkinson, "Hitchcock's Techniques Tell *Rear Window* Story."

8   Heidi Lüdi & Toni Lüdi, *Movie Worlds: Production Design in Film* (Stuttgart: Edition Axel Menges, 2000), 20.

9   Brougher, "Hitch-Hiking in Dreamscapes," 8.

10   Wood, *Hitchcock's Films Revisited,* 100–107.

11   Chion, "Alfred Hitchcock's *Rear Window,*" 110–17.

12   McGilligan, *Alfred Hitchcock,* 63. See also Leff, *Hitchcock and Selznick,* 30–31.

13   The tension between cinema and theater and references to theater as an estrangement effect are recurrent themes in Hitchcock criticism. Authors such as William Rothman, Donald Spoto, Tania Modleski, Raymond Bellour, Jean Douchet, Alenka Zupancic, and many others have focused on this topic.

14   Belton, "The Space of *Rear Window,*" 80.

15   The similarities between *Rear Window*'s spatial setup and the panopticon have been noted before by commentators such as Robert Stam and Juhani Pallasmaa. See Stam, Burgoyne, and Flitterman-Lewis, *New Vocabularies in Film Semiotics,* 212–13; and Pallasmaa, *The Architecture of Image,* 164.

16   Michel Foucault, *Surveiller et punir: Naissance de la prison* (Paris: Gallimard, 1975).

17   James Sanders, *Celluloid Skyline: New York and the Movies* (New York: Alfred A. Knopf, 2001), 228–41.

18   John Fawell, *Hitchcock's Rear Window* (Carbondale: Southern Illinois University Press, 2000), 112.

19   See AlSayyad, *Cinematic Urbanism,* 147.

References

Belton, John, "The Space of *Rear Window,*" in Walter Raubicheck & Walter Srebnick (eds.), *Hitchcock's Rereleased Films* (Detroit: Wayne State University Press, 1991), 76–94.

Chion, Michel, "Alfred Hitchcock's *Rear Window*: The Fourth Side," in John Belton (ed.), *Alfred Hitchcock's Rear Window* (Cambridge: Cambridge University Press, 2000), 110–17.

Leff, Leonard J., *Hitchcock and Selznick: The Rich and Strange Collaboration of Alfred Hitchcock and David O. Selznick in Hollywood* (Berkeley: University of California Press, 1987).

McGilligan, Patrick, *Alfred Hitchcock: A Life in Darkness and Light* (New York: Regan Books, 2003).

Pallasmaa, Juahani, *The Architecture of the Image: Existential Space in Cinema* (Helsinki: Rakenustieto Oy, 2001).

Stam, Robert, Robert Burgoyne, and Sandy Flitterman-Lewis, *New Vocabularies in Film Semiotics* (London: Routledge, 1992)

Display Engineers

Aaron Betsky

INTRODUCTION

In "Display Engineers," Aaron Betsky highlights the role of ritual and familiar spaces in the work of Diller + Scofidio (now Diller Scofidio + Renfro). Betsky reveals how these themes reveal and augment narrative structures that are often invisible. Diller + Scofidio's practice uses familiar objects from the domestic sphere, such as furniture and clothing, to build structures that reveal the temporary nature of rituals.

Betsky provides examples from works by Diller + Scofidio where their early work sets a foundation for their later. Both stages are performative, including exhibitions and installations. Their early performances mimics or fits the body, while the later work materializes structures at a larger scale, where interiors and architecture take on performance while referring back to the body. Diller + Scofidio attain dual capacities for performance applied to the body and building. Through familiar conventions of architectural language, such as orthographic projection and model-making techniques, the conventions embedded within architectural language are translated into clothing, by using ironing to develop new lines in a shirt for Bad Press, for example, or in Slow House, transposing the drawing section onto a model that influences a house design.

Aligned with the performative aspect of Diller + Scofidio's oeuvre are themes of fetish and display. These themes originate within the interior, and are projected outward to expose the undisclosed matters of the private realm. Their theoretical projects recall the visibility found in retail display windows. Together, fetish and display imply a private interior to which we are privy but not allowed to enter. The nature of interiors and their ability to retain privacy is the site for their performative assemblages. By revealing the conceptual constructs through custom-machined details and graphics, Diller + Scofidio reveal invisible structures such as social constructs and the temporary nature of how

---

Originally appeared in *Scanning: The Aberrant Architecture of Diller + Scofidio*, Aaron Betsky, K. Michael Hays, and Laurie Anderson (New York: Whitney Museum of American Art, 2003), 23–36.

we occupy rooms. The emphasis on custom-machined details especially shows how the concepts and objects were linked. The resulting fetishizing of objects, as seen in Vanity Chair, for example, incorporates the role of vintage vanity tables minimized into the essential idea of an underlying quest for beauty. Diller + Scofidio tease out the unspoken desires of occupants and fabricate frameworks that bridge the conceptual and physical.

———

THE WORK OF Diller + Scofidio is a form of display that removes from architecture the idea that it is always and only about shelter, comfort, and functionality. The principals in this collaboration, Elizabeth Diller and Ricardo Scofidio, are hybrid architects/artists who make visible the technologies of desire and reveal the surveillance of objects of desire. They reconstruct the rituals of buying and selling, of control and negotiation that make up a world that may be our daily reality, but that goes unnoticed. They articulate the invisible into the all-too-apparent. In doing so, Diller + Scofidio construct an alternative to our culture of display, in which the continual presentation of consumable goods—including human beings—appears to be the central task of the social and economic system. In short, these artists display display.

In order for ourselves, our goods, and our information to work, they cannot merely have a presence; they must be designed to catch our attention, to seduce, to make sense in an ever more confusing environment.[1] Diller + Scofidio want to make us aware of this fact by heightening, questioning, or frustrating the act of display, and by doing this within display itself. They make art out of and in shopping, security, sexual role-playing, and a panoply of the other display-oriented activities we engage in every day.

Display is central to our culture. We display our goods in packaging, advertising, and retail environments, we display ourselves in our clothes and through our body language, and we display our information in signs and icons.[2] More than in an "empire of signs," we live today in the realm of display.[3] Without making judgments about whether there is a true nature of things outside of appearances, or if our culture is becoming more superficial, it is easy to observe the increased importance not of how things appear to us, but how they are displayed. There is an economic reason for this. Shopping, buying, and all the rituals that go with them have displaced production as the pivot of economic and cultural life. The regulation of those rituals—through a web of security that extends through the visible and invisible surveillance cameras mounted from factory floor to store, but also through the clerical acts that make goods available at the right time and place—provides an invisible structure beneath our slippery reality of surfaces.[4]

In the vast retail industry, where up to $50 million can be spent on the construction of one store (Rem Koolhaas's Prada Soho), both art and architecture have taken on the function of framing, stating, and representing the objects to be desired.[5] Thus the central task of the architect is no longer the construction of the central institutions of the state, as it had been from the moment the term was codified by the French Academy in the eighteenth century. Rather, it is the making of places for display: the display of power, of goods, of the art that validates, through its very unavailability, the culture of consumption.[6]

This culture of display allows the architect to maintain her or his role as the designer of the central parts of our urban environments, since our stores, restaurants, bars, theaters, and other places where display takes place are the institutions around which our lives now revolve. We come to cities more to have an experience—to see, to be seen, to buy, to acquire well-packaged information—than we do to work or live.[7] To remain relevant, then, the architect must concern her- or himself with the spaces where this occurs. The other functions the architect has, such as organizing space, figuring out how to construct buildings, and orchestrating complex material choices, can now be done more efficiently by engineers of various sorts. What these specialists, each of them concerned above all else with reducing costs, cannot do, however, is what "wasteful" architects, trained to care about appearances and staging, are still good at: manipulating space, light, proportion, and material so that we, our goods, and our data can be displayed. So it is the architect who sets the scene for the rituals of buying and selling, defines the sequence of events, controls the flow of people and goods, and contains acts of desire in coherent frameworks. The architect has become an engineer of display.[8]

Diller + Scofidio concern themselves with the ways display functions to present a consumable reality. Their work also asks the question of where and how the architect must define her- or himself in this task. They answer this by turning display back into ritual art, and by making art out of our daily rituals. In so doing, they find a new way to attach value to the objects of architecture (or art) itself. In primitive cultures, the derived value of things, the value not inherent in an object itself, was stored in icons of religious devotion or in objects representing the wealth of those in power. The surplus of meaning and wealth these objects contained was preserved through acts of power and devotion—staged in temples, palaces, and other tombs—meant to make real the invisible value of things, including that of human life.[9] In our culture, this surplus is so dispersed and so pervasive that we no longer notice it. Value now exists everywhere we turn—in the excess of consumer goods through which we define ourselves, in the artificial heroes and heroines whose images we desire, in the miniature palaces we want our homes to be, and in the temples of consumption where we shop.[10]

Diller + Scofidio thus operate differently than traditional organizers of space and materials. They refuse to accept the myth that art and architecture are simply the production of functional elements. They do not start from the premise that the aim of architecture should be the production of an object that houses a defined function and that behaves in a responsible fashion. They are not concerned, at least not primarily, in modulating environmental inputs to produce an efficient and sensible place to live, work, or play. And they do not make the way in which the building continues or contributes to the context in which it appears the focal point of their design activities.[11] These architects/artists also do not offer escape or direct criticism—they do not make art that shows us the image of a world more perfect than our own, nor do they present direct commentary on our reality. Their work is not consumable bits of cultural commentary that lives on white walls or on museum pedestals. Rather, it has the character of art as a concentrated form of value, the form of architecture, and the function of providing a self-conscious form of display.

This confusion of modes of making is central to Diller + Scofidio's œuvre. Their work is also no longer "unique," in the sense of stating itself as either of one time or place or as an object of desire. In other words, they do not make "critical" objects that in their strange appearance or novelty are meant to offer alternatives to our current reality. They also do not try to perfect prevalent styles, as do some architects working in "neoclassical" or "neo-modern" modes. Instead, they map and mirror the rituals of display, from going shopping to eating in a restaurant to attending a state fair, then frustrate those mechanisms of seduction and packaging. Diller + Scofidio's work seeks to surf on our culture of display, and then to frustrate its smooth workings.[12]

Still, Liz Diller and Ric Scofidio are both architects, and thus have inherited the anxiety about the role of the architect. When they started their joint practice in 1979, however, they were part of a New York milieu in which questions of display were central. Because of their affiliation with the Cooper Union School of Architecture and with the New York art scene, and because they began to work together during a period when making buildings was difficult for purely economic reasons, they were completely wrapped up in three basic issues: taste, technology, and organization.

During this era, Diller + Scofidio started to use the techniques they found in performance, site-specific art, and Pop art to make an architecture that was exactly about those issues.[13] They made work that played on the accepted norms of good taste. They used technological innovation, but at a scale and in a way that denied its inherent logic. Rather than smoothly functional buildings, they made performances, installations, and exhibition displays that worked within existing buildings and their conventions, changing how they appeared through the display of an alternative set of images, bodies, and signs.

While these were the basic questions Diller + Scofidio were addressing, they were also exploring a series of themes, including domesticity, rituals of daily life, security and surveillance, gender roles, and prosthetics. Today, after some twenty years of working, their themes and many of their techniques have begun to merge in work that has, above all else, the quality of blur, or of limbo. Diller + Scofidio make mechanisms of display in which sharpness and clarity disappear (blur), and which leave us uncertain how to interpret what should be seductively displayed phenomena (limbo). These qualities represent a final criticism of productive society and a statement of the singularity of what it is the architect/artist does. The resulting work is almost like an anti-building.

To start with the techniques: Diller + Scofidio have exquisite taste.[14] They pose themselves very carefully within an aesthetic that is fashionable yet recognizable, as it is built on historical and popular images. To work, this tastefulness has to be new-seeming, elegant, and still slightly disturbing. This may sound like a negative thing to those trained to think that the balancing act between the new and the familiar is the sign of somebody who is not a "true" artist. But if we are willing to admit that a person who makes images, objects, and spaces that we think of as art or architecture does so in a way that is part of a wider culture, we have two choices: We either have to believe that the artist or architect is doing so unconsciously, or that they are doing so in a self-conscious and even ironic manner.

Whether unconsciously or ironically, Diller + Scofidio evidence great taste. The objects they make have a seemingly effortless grace and appropriateness that we do not have a proper critical language to assess. We (or at least this author) experience the work as beautiful, and are therefore willing to accept what it does. The sources for this beauty seem to lie in a combination of standard architectural representational techniques, such as section drawings, perspectives, and finely wrought models.

It also extends into the craft of making both buildings and objects, where Diller + Scofidio employ the kinds of details architects are fond of using to accentuate the salient elements of their buildings. Generating this sensibility are, at least in part, the color, compositional, and other formal techniques taught at art and architecture schools.[15]

One might think of the result of all this as the aesthetics of display itself.[16] Diller + Scofidio engage in a kind of meta-display, integrating the methods by which things are presented with the presentation objects themselves. Their exquisite line drawings, the giant lips on a video screen (in *Soft Sell*), the carefully constructed scaffolding for monitors (in almost all of their works), and the glasses seen in the case (*Vice/Virtue Glasses*), are all part of the same construction. It is almost impossible to separate out what is the fetish and what is the ritualistic element that surrounds that object of desire. They give such objects a highly controlled and integrated framework that itself becomes an object of desire.

Diller + Scofidio have also become masters of innovative technology, scavenging hardware and electronics stores to find the latest devices to activate their work. This is a very American attitude toward technology; they work in a culture that includes not only Frank Lloyd Wright, Buckminster Fuller, and "dead tech" designers such as Eric Moss and Morphosis, but also the tinkering mechanics that produced the automotive and movie industries, to name just a few examples.[17] The basic components of Diller + Scofidio's work are thus not found in architects' standard catalogues. Rather than follow traditional modes of construction, they turn to a manner of assembly that might be common in a workshop or on a movie set. This gives their work a sense of temporary rightness. All the pieces have been assembled for a highly specific purpose; they function for precisely the length of time needed. Like a scene's set or a store, they are temporary mechanisms of display. But it is display itself that is on show.

This care taken with the display of various technological gadgets makes Diller + Scofidio's work appear at first glance as if it consists of highly individual pieces that have no all-encompassing form. Elements often float in space, as either objects or as images, without an immediately clear ordering principle. The presence of so many switches, screens, and miscellaneous pieces of hardware often threatens to usurp the overall design. Their work has also included, almost from the beginning, electronic components that produce images and sounds as if by magic. As a result, their œuvre has a quality Americans are familiar with from *The Wizard of Oz*: the hidden technology that transforms or controls the world is revealed, and at the same time reveled in.[18] There is also a sense of mystery about their work that recedes as the viewer lifts more and more of the veil that surrounds its inner workings. It is not surprising, then, that Diller + Scofidio's first major public art work, *Delay in Glass* (aka *The Rotary Notary and His Hot Plate*; 1987), was a restating of Marcel Duchamp's *Large Glass* (aka *The Bride Stripped Bare by Her Bachelors, Even*), in which the technology stripping the bride became visible, then reversed itself.

The third technique Diller + Scofidio use is the efficient organization of their production processes. In their work, they act as organizers of resources into coherent objects, places, and images. While this is the quality that makes their work successful, it is also the most difficult one to grasp. Architects have long claimed that they were orchestrators, coordinators, or conductors, wrangling into coherence the disparate elements that make up a building. Today, however, this self-image is usually reserved for those who lead larger architectural offices. The avant-garde architect instead often revels in the "artist" image, struggling in a studio with limited resources, making things that always come too late and don't always perform as advertised. Diller + Scofidio have some of these qualities, as they worked in a small loft in New York, were always running late on deadlines, and projected an image of being artists who could not be bothered with the bureaucratic structures of commissioning.

Yet Scofidio had run a large architecture office before starting Diller + Scofidio, and both he and Diller are highly adept at organizing their projects and highly controlling of the final results.[19] Unlike some of their avant-garde contemporaries, they have produced work that can actually be seen, inhabited, and experienced. That might sound like faint praise, but it is of signal importance; one easy definition of Diller + Scofidio is that they are artists who get things built. What is built, however, often has the exact quality of an orchestration, rather than of a building, as in the choreography of their dance works, the assembly of pieces in their *American Lawn: Surface* of *Everyday Life* and *Tourisms: suitCase Studies* installations, and the timing of the images on the lenticular screens of *Travelogues,* an installation at John F. Kennedy International Airport.

The dance of thoughtfully assembled bits and pieces of technology in an elegant manner serves as a good, if reductive, definition of Diller + Scofidio's work. But the work is also resolutely about something, and that is display itself. The problem with this as a subject is that it—or its derivatives and counterpoints, such as desire and security—is so inherent in any objects made as either art or architecture that it becomes difficult to discern. So display as a subject is something Diller + Scofidio have worked out in or through a number of different themes.

The first of these themes is the nature of domesticity, which initially emerged in their 1987 installation *The withDrawing Room,* at the Capp Street Project in San Francisco. This theme uses as its basic elements the props of everyday life: beds (sawn in half and rotating), chairs (with mirrors inserted in their middle), tables (hanging right below the ceiling), and what the French call *meubles,* or movables, such as towels (for Him and Her, in one installation). Each of these objects is recognizable, but no longer usable in the way it was originally designed to be.

There are several things that make this theme of domesticity important. First, it is also an aesthetic technique—the assembly of elements taken from everyday life, placed within a frame, and made no longer legible or usable. It is, in effect, assemblage or collage. In this way the theme asks the question of how we can use or understand the most basic elements of the modern world.[20] Second, instead of theoretical questions about the nature of humanity in a modern age, Diller + Scofidio have concerned themselves with

Figs. 7.23 + 7.24:
Vanity Chair, 1988.
Images courtesy of
Diller Scofidio + Renfro

the basic things that we use every day. They address the much more essential issue of what it means to have a human body, and how that body behaves
in social relations when the implements it uses are inherited or mass-
produced. They often pose these questions through objects that we can—
or exactly can't—sit on (the unusable chairs in *Para-site),* or gather around
(a table we can't reach, in *The withDrawing Room*), or see (a mirror that
stands where we want to sit, in *Vanity Chair*). [Figs. 7.23 + 7.24] Such unus-
ability gives their work an immediacy; it also makes it part of the world
around us in a way many Pop artists aspired to, but which they often found
difficult to achieve because of their work's status as "high art."[21]

Diller + Scofidio's focus on domesticity has expanded to include the
design of living environments. (One of these, a 105-unit apartment building in Gifu, Japan, has actually been constructed.) The architects/artists
are always most interested in what one sees and uses in the house or apartment, however, instead of in the enclosure of (or for) moments of domesticity. The apartment block in Gifu is a curving assembly of small cells that
are assembled in a stepped plan; there is no stable floor plan, and no simple
facade. The individual apartments appear as indistinguishable elements that
never cohere into a whole. This is true of apartment buildings in general, but
here the contradiction between mass production and the need for individual
homes people can identify as their own is made evident.

The *Slow House*, an unrealized project for a vacation home on Long
Island, is a machine for viewing. [Figs. 7.25 + 7.26] This would seem an appropriate function for a beach-side second home, but Diller + Scofidio again
push the issue to the extent that the view takes over completely, defining
the building's shape and producing a window that is completely out of scale
with the house's other attributes. Moreover, the view is duplicated on a monitor, which plays a recorded version of the scene, so even the authenticity of

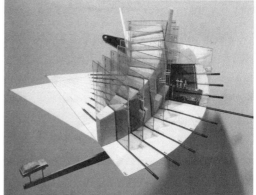

Fig. 7.25: *Slow House*, 1991. Photo-Drawing, 1989
Fig. 7.26: *Slow House*, Woodblock Model with X-rays, 1989
Images courtesy of Diller Scofidio + Renfro

that to which all the house's functions genuflect is questionable. Nowhere does the *Slow House* become a home in the traditional sense of the word.

The notion of ritual is not just implicit in Diller + Scofidio's mechanisms of display, it has also become a theme. It has been expressed mainly in their theater work, but it is also present in the way elements are arranged and used in their installations, permanent and otherwise. The ritual of swinging the bed in *The withDrawing Room,* for example, becomes the abstracted dance of measuring sticks in *Moving Target*. The ironing of *Bad Press* is as much the point of the piece as the deformed clothes that result from these actions. [Fig. 7.27] The murder mystery in *Indigestion* is just an excuse to work through the intricacies of negotiated financial and sexual relations. The rituals in Diller + Scofidio's work often mimic mass production, as in the robots endlessly rotating in the installation *Master/Slave*. Here the architects/artists are indicating that a large part of our daily actions are not our own, but are dictated either by the norms of our society or by the need to be productive. Their art consists of making us aware of such rituals by perverting them, structuring them so they have a logic that is believable, productive, and yet profoundly disturbing.

Much of Diller + Scofidio's recent work exists as performance or as documentation in time-based media. Their collaboration with several gifted choreographers, for example, has led to a number of elaborate performance pieces. They have also organized a loose troupe of performers who are able

Fig. 7.27: *Bad Press*: Dissident Housework Series, 1993–98. This series of "mis-ironed" men's white dress shirts examines ironing as one among many household tasks conventionally guided by principles of motion economy. With their abnormal creases and origami-like folds, the *Bad Press* shirts are the various results of ironing having been freed from the aesthetics of efficiency.
Image courtesy of Diller Scofidio + Renfro

Fig. 7.28: *Blur Building*, 2002. Night view. Image courtesy of Diller Scofidio + Renfro

to bring their work quite literally to life, as in the video piece that accompanies the *Blur Building* in Yverdon-les-Bains, Switzerland. [Fig. 7.28] Rather than acting as conductors or choreographers through architecture, they have taken on that task directly. They have become engineers of display.

To experience these works, however, one has to either be present or give one's self over to the ritual that is so central to our culture, watching television. By abstracting this activity—such as in *Soft Sell,* where a pair of lips asks if you want to buy various goods, both tangible and intangible, like a parody of a television commercial—and perverting its purpose, Diller + Scofidio have, like other video artists, turned the tables on the mass media. Unlike most of the work in this emerging field, however, their time-based work is made as objects (installations) that have their own presence. The craft of assembling the various components of these installations ties the work to everyday reality, while the architects/artists' refusal to make an enduring, all-encompassing object echoes their theme of domesticity by stating the importance of effect.

Two other themes in Diller + Scofidio's work, gender and prosthetics, give it a dramatic engine. The way in which our society stereotypes women has been a central concern to Diller + Scofidio since at least their 1987 *Delay in Glass* performance. To a certain extent this theme is autobiographical, as it traces Diller's emergence as a partner in the firm and her struggle to define herself as an architect in a profession that has usually assigned women to interior design or craft. It has also been a way for Scofidio to move away from the traditional role of the master architect in which he was trained and had worked. The pair uses the methods that have been reserved for women, such as the organization of domestic elements, in combination with the technological tricks for which male architects are famous, to make perverse reversals of gender roles.[22]

Diller + Scofidio did not stop, as other artists and critics have, at stating the artificiality of gender role assignments. Rather, their work has made it clear that there is a more general problem in defining both what the body is and what our reality as bodies is. The architects/artists do not just reveal (and toy with) the idea that we have erected a fantastically elaborate system of acting out particular functions based on the properties of the body. They also make clear that we manipulate the body itself. We don't just play roles as men and women, but also as workers, viewers, critics, rulers, etc. The way we extend our body in order to do this becomes a harness or straitjacket that eventually imprisons us.

Diller + Scofidio have used many elements one might call prosthetic, especially in their early work. It is in these pieces that display and control come together; through prosthetics we both internalize the world around us and extend our bodies and the technologies they have assimilated out into the world. Prosthetic elements stand in for our arms, our legs, and our eyes. They bring perverse actions beyond what our bodies are capable of into the realm of possibility. The cameras, chairs, and other metal ganglia of *Para-site*, their 1989 MoMA Projects Room installation, summed up many of these ideas, bringing the body of the museum and that of the visitor together into a kind of spatial robot that stood in for both. The robots that circulated around the Fondation Cartier a decade later in the *Master/Slave* installation echoed these concerns. Encapsulating memory into concrete *aides memoire* such as the *suitCases* is another way the architects/artists have extended the body's ability to control space and time. Again, Diller + Scofidio do not talk about the alienation of labor, but merely show us to be puppets manipulated by strings, reveal our limbs to be levers meant for work, and make visible the invisible ways in which we subject the world to our gaze in order to evaluate and use it.

This last concern, of the gaze, has taken on more significance in Diller + Scofidio's recent work, to the extent that surveillance is now what critics most identify as their signature subject or style. Surveillance was the central theme in *Para-site,* the installation that first brought them to wider public attention, and it is an element that runs through almost all of their current designs. We are always being watched while we desire what is displayed; our ability to think and act freely is always running up against the controlling actions of an authority of surveillance.[23] All that remains of the controlling and organizing functions architecture used to have are little cameras and sensors and the responses they generate—sometimes with force, sometimes, say, with more air forced into a building as more occupants enter. Diller + Scofidio lavish their greatest care and attention on this last redoubt of control.

They have also developed a defense mechanism against surveillance in recent years: the effect of blur. Starting with their use of the "snow" of an untuned television in the installation *Non-Place*, and with the limbo spaces of airplane travel they later explored in *Jet Lag*, Diller + Scofidio have concentrated on the undefined. It is almost as if they are reacting against their own desire to control and produce recognizable images, places, and objects by creating works in which one is never quite certain what one is seeing.[24]

By making objects that have no presence other than as mutable, ephemeral, or indistinct images, but then become spatial and environmental effects, Diller + Scofidio seem to be moving beyond a practice that has tried to rethink architecture's concerns in terms of the techniques of art to produce instead a form of critical display. Domesticity, gender roles, rituals, and prosthetics are less important in their recent work than the delight in the confusion of edges, spaces, and messages that occurs when technology is used against itself. Stories are broken off or impossible to understand, as in *Travelogues* at JFK; lips speak no longer with insistent messages but in an unintelligible language in the entrance to the *Blur Building*. Display is being directly denied.

Ironically, in shifting their mode of working Diller + Scofidio began making things that look more like buildings. Indeed, they have long wanted to prove that they are architects, albeit on their own terms, and that means making buildings. If the structures they produce are a little strange-seeming, at least to those who don't think of clouds as a proper place of habitation, or who like their buildings with beginnings and ends, that does not make them any less buildings. The danger in these new works, however, is that Diller + Scofidio will reduce themselves to the production of more fashion-ably innovative buildings. In time they may become monuments to the firm's achievements, and thus the artfully decorated tombs of their architectural ambitions.

I, for one, am not overly worried about this. In fact, Diller + Scofidio have already moved on to their next set of concerns, which seem to be coalescing around the nature of display as subject matter. Their ambition is to use the techniques of blur to make constructions in which one is never quite sure what one is experiencing, where one is, or how one should behave. The codes of behavior that tell us what to want and what to buy no longer work, as we don't know what we are meant to do. But other codes are hard at work, crunching away inside Diller + Scofidio's computers, creating always different effects. Beautiful uncertainty, hovering at the moment of desire, when one doesn't know whether to buy or admire, to be disgusted or delighted, to think of architecture or give one's self over to art, will result. It is at this moment that the freedom both of the maker and of the viewer, who keeps her- or himself alive by always deferring the fulfillment of the aim of display and desire, becomes completely and sublimely apparent.

Notes

1   Explanations of the centrality of display in our culture have generally come from the worlds of sociology and anthropology. The roots of display have been effectively sketched by Claude Levi-Strauss (see *Myth and Meaning* [New York: Schocken Books, 1995] and *The Savage Mind* [Chicago: University of Chicago Press, 1966]) and Clifford Geertz (see *The Interpretation* of *Cultures* [New York: Basic Books, 2000]). For a good survey of current thinking on the importance of display in our culture, see Lynne Cooke and Peter Wollen, eds., *Visual Display: Culture Beyond Appearances* (New York: The New Press, 1999). Display's effects in architecture have ranged from resistance to acceptance. For variations on these responses, see Ada Louise Huxtable, *The Unreal America: Architecture and Illusion* (New York: The New Press, 1997), and Ole Bouman and Roemer van Toarn, eds., *The Invisible in Architecture* (London: Academy Editions, 1994).

2   For a recent survey of the role of shopping in our culture, see Ann Satterthwaite, *Going Shopping: Consumer Choices and Community Consequences* (New Haven: Yale University Press, 2001).

3   The phrase is Roland Barthes's, who saw our culture as dominated by "empty signifiers." The book that carries the phrase as its title (*The Empire* of *Signs*, trans. Richard Howard [New York: Noonday Press, 1963]), however, addresses Japanese culture. For a more relevant collection of essays, see his *The Fashion System*, trans. Richard Howard (Berkeley: University of California Press, 1990).

4   See Thomas Hine, I *Want That: How We All Became Shoppers* (New York: HarperCollins, 2002).

5   Rem Koolhaas designed this store as part of an effort to formulate and codify a "scientific" approach to shopping. See his *Projects for Prada* (Milan: Fondazione Prada, 2001) and *The Harvard Guide to Shopping* (Cologne: Taschen, 2001).

6   I discussed the interdependency of art and retail through the reductive power of the brand or icon in *Icons: Magnets of Meaning* (San Francisco: San Francisco Museum of Modern Art, 1997). Two evocative discussions of this phenomenon are Mario Perniola, *Enigmas: The Egyptian Moment in Society and Art*, trans. Christopher Woodall (London: Verso, 1995), and Julian Stallabrass, *Gargantua: Manufactured Mass Culture* (London: Verso, 1996).

7   The phrase "experience economy" was coined at Harvard Business School in the mid-1990s and has made economists and politicians aware of something observers of architecture had noted long before: that "themed" environments and city centers have merged as attractors that give meaning to both consumer goods and the lives of consumers—for better or worse. See B. Joseph Pine, B. Joseph Pine II, and James H. Gilmore, *The Experience Economy* (Boston: Harvard Business School Press, 1999). For a critique of this phenomenon, see Michael Sorkin, *Variations on a Theme Park: The New American City and the End of Public Space* (New York: Hill & Wang, 1992).

8   For the rules that such engineers must follow, see Paco Underhill, *Why We Buy: The Science of Shopping* (New York: Simon & Schuster, 1999).

9   For the importance and functioning of ritual, see Levi-Strauss and Geertz, op. cit., as well as Levi-Strauss's *The Origin of Table Manners*, trans. John and Doreen Weightman (Chicago: University of Chicago Press, 1990). For ritual's social meaning in developing and developed cultures, see Pierre Bourdieu, *The Field of Cultural Production*, trans. Randal Johnson (New York: Columbia University Press, 1993).

10   Many critics would argue that such constructions are in fact impossible, and that we must instead make a strict distinction between what has grown historically and organically, and the meaningless and valueless places produced by capitalism (see Marc Auge, *Non-Places: Introduction to an Anthropology of Supermodernity*, trans. John Howe [London: Verso, 1995]). I think that this is a simplistic distinction and that the architect can and must find ways of deriving value from a place, however bare it may seem.

11   These are commonly accepted ways of judging architecture, starting from the simple observation that the discipline revolves around the making of buildings that are meant to house their occupants in a safe and comfortable manner. Such is the implicit message of the profession's educational, licensing, and code standards.

12 I would thus argue that Diller + Scofidio provide a way out of the choice between a resistance to modernity, capitalism, and the grinding aspects of commercial life, and a resistant, time- and place-bound architecture that would remove itself from the realities of modern life.

13 See Rose Lee Goldberg's essay, "Dancing about Architecture," in [Betsky, Hays, and Anderson, *Scanning*, 2003.]

14 Such taste is defined by the social class to which both the architects and this author belong. See Pierre Bourdieu, *Distinction: A Social Critique of the Judgement of Taste* (Cambridge: Harvard University Press, 1984), and Herbert Gans, *Popular Culture and High Culture: An Analysis and Evaluation of Taste* (New York: Basic Books, 1999).

15 See Hyungmin Pai, *The Portfolio and the Diagram: Architecture, Discourse, and Modernity in America* (Cambridge: MIT Press, 2002). The critic Mark Wigley has also been researching the modes of taste and presentation in the culture of architecture and has expressed his ideas in lectures that this author has found very persuasive, but have not yet been published.

16 For a survey of the ways artists have looked at and used techniques of display, see Max Hollein and Christoph Grunenberg, eds., *Shopping: A Century of Art and Consumer Culture* (Frankfurt: Hatje Cantz, 2002).

17 I have described this movement as "dead tech" and "Home Depot modern." Its roots go all the way back to the work of architects such as Thomas Jefferson, who adopted and adapted English aesthetics and technologies to local conditions.

18 See David E. Nye, *American Technological Sublime* (Cambridge: MIT Press, 1996).

19 The firm, Berman, Roberts, and Scofidio, existed from 1967 to 1970.

20 For a definition of and discussion of the importance of collage, see John Elderfield, ed., *Essays on Assemblage* (New York: The Museum of Modern Art/Harry N. Abrams, 1992); Christine Poggi, *In Defiance of Painting: Cubism, Futurism, and the Invention of Collage* (New Haven: Yale University Press, 1993); and Thomas Brockelman, *The Frame and the Mirror: On Collage and the Postmodern* (Evanston, Illinois: Northwestern University Press, 2001).

21 Their approach to the art of the everyday is much more active than the one that has been popularized by such architects as Deborah Berke, which relies on mimicking existing structures and forms. See Steven Harris and Deborah Berke, eds., *Architecture of the Everyday* (New York: Princeton Architectural Press, 1997).

22 Diller + Scofidio have been working in this field longer than any other practitioners. See my *Building Sex: Men, Women, Architecture, and the Construction of Sexuality* (New York: William Morrow, 1995).

23 See Nan Ellin, ed., *Architecture of Fear* (New York: Princeton Architectural Press, 1997). Visuality and the importance of the gaze has been a standard part of the architectural discourse in recent years. A signal contribution connecting this theoretical discussion to technology is Graham MacPhee, *The Architecture of the Visible: Technology and Urban Visual Culture* (London: Continuum Books, 2002).

24 The notion of blur as an aesthetic quality, and as something that can be used to organize information, was researched at the MIT Visual Language Laboratory in 1992 and 1993, where it led to several advances in computer interface design. Diller + Scofidio say they have not been aware of this work.

Bridging the
Exterior
and Interior

Introduction:
Bridging the Interior and Exterior

In an architectural plan or sectional drawing, the poché blurs the distinction between interior and exterior. They gradually transition from one to the other, but overall they share the same wall or line thickness: the poché. Their indistinguishableness prompts the existential question: where does the interior end and the exterior begin? Is it at the plan's threshold from inside to outside, or is it in the thickness of walls where structure is embedded? The word *poché* has two meanings. In architecture, it is a technical term that defines wall, floor, and ceiling drawn as a thick line. It also means "pocket" in French. Pockets in clothing and pockets in walls share an ambiguous conceptual space between clothing and body in the former, architecture and interior in the latter.

Pockets allow items to be stored on the body. Imagine a full coat pocket—a section drawing made through its poché would reveal an irregular profile, since underlying forms affect the drape of textiles. The muffled shape of objects only hints at their identity. Pockets are akin to shelves in the interior. Acting as a container, poché opens an undefined zone between interior and exterior, a porous boundary that is both room and poché. At the scale of the interior, a wall's thickness can be tailored to accommodate built-in cupboards, bookshelves, and seats. The similarity between a coat and a wall raises questions. Does occupying a wall differ from a hand occupying a pocket? Which is more intimate? And which is more interior?

The essays in this chapter, Bridging the Interior and Exterior, address these mysteries and challenge conventional beliefs that determine where interior and exterior begin and end. Through works of art, architecture, photography, and literature, definitions of interior and exterior are explored. Three themes emerge that engage the nature of boundaries. The first begins with the voyeuristic eye that looks past poché, taking visual access from spaces that is typically denied. The second theme explores the idea of inside out, both as a physical investigation and in its consequent results. The third looks at boundary elements that bridge public and private spaces.

Voyeurism enters private spaces through windows, apertures, and cameras. The camera lens gives photographers the ability to frame compositions. The human eye is replaced by the camera's mechanical eye that extends and impersonally facilitates voyeuristic opportunism. The precursor of the mechanical eye, the camera obscura, is introduced by Frances Terpak in her essay about the history and knowledge of the camera obscura. Diana Gaston also writes about the Renaissance device, looking at contemporary collagelike imagery in the photography of Cuban-American photographer Abelardo Morell. Because the camera obscura allows the exterior to be projected onto the interior in one collapsed view, Morell captures single images in photographs that read as double exposures. Both Terpak and Gaston emphasize the role of the interior with the camera obscura without having to ground the essays in the field of interior design. Their essays offer designers alternative ways to think about the subtle and invisible dialogues established between window and room.

Foundational design studios in art and architecture schools employ terms such as *inside out* as a way to teach about three-dimensionality. This can be seen, for example, in a project where students cast objects in plaster, bringing the outside of an object to the inside, or vice versa, in a section cut. It is a simple term, easy to understand and almost impossible to physically construct at an architectural scale. Buildings do not turn inside out (but clothing does). In the works of Gordon Matta-Clark and Rachel Whiteread, the static nature of architecture is liberated by their methods of cutting and casting buildings. They literally turn architecture inside out. Whiteread's *House* redraws the definition of poché, the term normally reserved for denoting the thickness of a wall. The *House* project removed the perimeter walls that separated interior from exterior. As a result, the private nature of the interior realm, as well as the innards of the house construction, are exposed to the public eye in solid form. Matta-Clark turns architecture inside out by making the building's section-cut tangible. Interior views are revealed through his photographic representations from a hybrid section-cut and one-point perspective. Matta-Clark redraws the interior with his camera lens under the rules of architectural drawing conventions. Where the camera obscura merges interior and exterior through reversed, projected two-dimensional imagery, Matta-Clark and Whiteread turn that relationship three-dimensional.

Interior design typically begins as an additive process, furniture plus textiles plus objects. The results are tangible elements that constitute an interior but also contribute to a sense of atmosphere established by the identity of occupants. Likewise, the visible wear and tear on personal possessions contributes to an accumulated sense of inhabitation over time. In "Rodinsky's Room," Rachel Lichtenstein and Iain Sinclair search for details about the disappearance of David Rodinsky, whose single-room apartment was discovered—untouched—after more than a decade later. His possessions, including handwritten notes, newspapers, books, and daily objects, provided a lens into his life that led the authors to different countries in their attempt to weave decades of history together like detectives in search of a single disappeared occupant. Their essay symbolically constructs a multivalent bridge between interior and exterior, bridging the life in one room to the city and beyond in a search for answers.

The concluding essay of this chapter (and the book), Wolfgang Meisenheimer's "Of the Hollow Spaces in the Skin of the Architectural Body," dwells on the thickness of poché. Where this book began with the body and ends with the threshold between interior and exterior, Meisenheimer weaves these two scales together. He compares the thick-skinned building—one that has poché—to the modern skinless building to understand the different experiences of occupying and crossing the threshold of a wall. His examples address fundamental questions about distinguishing between interior and exterior and what it means to occupy a wall. These are the richest and simplest questions to ask of a wall that ultimately contains the experience of the interior. One by one, each essay in this chapter addresses a scale larger than the previous, bridging interior to exterior.

Thèâtre de l'univers

Frances Terpak

INTRODUCTION

Unlike film or digital cameras, the camera obscura does not rely on mechanisms. It separates optics from the camera's physical body so that the two are discrete. By dissecting the inner workings of early camera obscuras, Frances Terpak situates them as tools used in natural science (to view solar eclipses), at the scale of a room, and in art. Terpak describes the simplicity of the camera's assembly as a pinhole aperture that projects an exterior image onto an interior surface. Whether at the scale of a small box or a large room, the only random variable is the scale of the pinhole to the scale of the space, and the need for all other light sources to be diminished. Movement on the exterior brings a filmic image that can be simultaneously viewed albeit inverted because of the optically manipulated light on the interior.

Terpak cites various camera obscuras, from pinhole cameras disguised within books to portable rooms set up in the landscape. These variations allowed the camera obscura to be used "for the study of human proportion, architecture, stage design, and cartography," a characterization that allows it to be seen as a tool to translate information across disciplines, such as in Terpak's examples from projected optical illusion to drawing.* The camera obscura relied on an interior space to project images at different scales. In one direction, the exterior was miniaturized on the interior of a small camera obscura. In another, the projection could occupy large spaces as if it were a theater. Like a planetarium, a sixteenth-century camera obscura was used to project solar eclipses into a small interior. Terpak also introduces the psychologically dark side of the device, describing a seventeenth-century camera obscura set up on Paris's Pont Neuf by thieves as a sideshow theater that doubled as a trap; naive audience members unwittingly surrendered their purses in the dark interior while they were distracted by the spectacle.

Sixteenth-century camera obscura constructions surveyed in "Thèâtre de l'universe" transformed their interior components into receivers of images.

Originally appeared in *Devices of Wonder: From the World in a Box to Images on a Screen*, edited by Barbara Maria Stafford and Frances Terpak (Los Angeles: Getty Research Institute, 2001), 307–14.

*Implanting a light-opening lens or a pinhole in a wall or fabric separating
inside and outside dissolved the virtual poché between interior and exterior by
penetrating it with a device (even one as simple as a hole) that captured natural phenomena as if by magic.*

———

"ALL THE WORLD'S A STAGE / And all the men and women merely
players," philosophized the melancholic Jaques in William Shakespeare's
As You Like It (2.7.139–40). Over a century later his metaphor was charm-
ingly reframed and made concrete by a portable camera obscura built into
a folio binding stamped *Thèâtre de l'univers* on the spine. [Fig. 8.1] When this
"book" is opened on a sunny day and the concealed optical device properly
set up, miniature reflections of the proximate world and its inhabitants move
silently across the stage of the book's inside back cover. Within the curtained
space of the camera obscura, figures enter and exit, playing for the observer
the fleeting scenes handed out by chance.

Noted in Alexandre Savérien's *Dictionnaire universel* (1753) as a new
type, book camera obscuras are rare today. Of the handful of extant examples, most have *Camera Obscura* stamped on the spine, and two are very
nearly identical. The slightly smaller one was presented by the English portrait painter Joshua Reynolds to Lady Yates (mid-1700s; London, Science
Museum); the other was supplied to Harvard University by the London
instrument maker Benjamin Martin for £3.13.6 (ca. 1765; Cambridge,
Massachusetts, Harvard University, Collection of Historical Scientific

Fig. 8.1: Book-form camera obscura from the Nekes Collection, ca. 1750.
The Getty Research Institute, Los Angeles, 93.R.118

Instruments). Nonetheless, book camera obscuras turn up regularly in the advertisements of eighteenth-century instrument makers. One was listed along with other optical, philosophical, and mathematical devices in one of the broadsheet advertisements issued between 1768 and 1782 by Henry Pyefinch of Cornhill, London. At £4.4.0, it cost the same as Pyefinch's compound microscope with three pillars. Some years later, the London instrument maker George Adams II, in his *Lectures on Natural and Experimental Philosophy* (1794), described a book camera obscura improved with interchangeable convex lenses of various focal lengths set in an adjustable head. The book camera obscura offered for £8.18.6 in the price list published by the London firm of William and Samuel Jones in 1797 may well have incorporated such refinements.

Although the book camera obscura was a mid-eighteenth-century innovation, other types of camera obscuras had been in use for hundreds of years. In the fourth century B.C., Aristotle had identified the principle of image formation through an aperture: in the darkened space behind an aperture, rays of light will form an inverted image of the scene passing in front of that tiny hole (*Problemata* 15.11 [912.b.11–26]). The earliest recorded practical application of this principle in Europe was in the thirteenth century, when the English scientist Roger Bacon and his contemporaries began using room-size camera obscuras in studying solar eclipses. These optical devices allowed scholars to make observations without endangering their eyesight by looking directly at the sun.

From the early Renaissance until the sixteenth century, the camera obscura was used chiefly for astronomical studies. It would finally accrue its modern functions of drawing aid and optical toy primarily through the publication of several popular treatises in which portable and room versions were illustrated. The most influential of these was by Giambattista della Porta. His *Magiae Naturalis* (1558) went through at least six printings before 1589—when the much expanded second edition was issued—and was translated from Latin into Italian, French, Dutch, and English. At about this time, two considerable improvements to the camera obscura were made: a convex lens was inserted in the aperture to sharpen the image, and a concave mirror placed an angle of forty-five degrees was added to right the image. Daniel Barbaro's treatise *La pratica della perspettiva* (1569), in which the author documented his use of the camera obscura for the study of human proportions, architecture, stage designs, and cartography, presents a clear description of how one version of the enhanced camera obscura could be made and employed:

> you should drill a hole of the size of an eyeglass in a shutter of a window of a room from where you want to see. Take an eyeglass for elderly

people, quite thick in the middle and not concave, not like those eye-glasses for short-sighted young people. Fit this eyeglass into that hole, close all windows and doors of that room so that there is no light in the room except from the eyeglass; take a sheet of paper and place it against the hole at a distance such that you can see in detail on the sheet every-thing that is outside; at a specific distance you can see in the most distinc-tive way. You will find the proper distance by moving the sheet in relation to the eyeglass until you find the right place. Here you will see the shapes on the sheet, as well as the proportions, the colors, the shadows, the movements, the clouds, the flickering of the water, the flying of the birds and everything else that one can see. For this experiment the sun must be clear and shining, because the light of the sun has great power in high-lighting what is visible. When you want to do this experiment, you should choose the eyeglasses that are most effective; and if you cover the eye-glass leaving only a small opening in the middle, bright and uncovered, you will have an even better quality image. Viewing on the sheet of paper the outlines of the objects, you can mark with a brush their perspective as it appears, shading, and coloring according to what nature shows you, holding the sheet tight, till you have completed the drawing.

During the rise of experimental science in the eighteenth century, room-size camera obscuras were adapted for staging scientific demonstra-tions. For instance, the abbé Nollet, tutor to the dauphin and the foremost public lecturer of his time, noted in his *Leçons de physique expérimentale* (1764) that the effect of particular optical experiments, such as the creation of a rainbow by a beam of light striking a globe of water, was heightened when presented inside a camera obscura. The room-size camera obscura was ideal for such occasions, but it was limited in the number of subjects it could capture to those in front of its aperture. To address this problem, a variety of portable camera obscuras were developed during the seventeenth and eighteenth centuries. The most direct translation of the room-size device was the tent camera obscura. In 1620, Sir Henry Wotton, traveler and diplomat, described the one that the astronomer Johann Kepler employed when he drew landscapes as "a little black tent…which he can suddenly set up where he will in a field." Wotton commented about the resulting images, "surely no painter can do them so precisely."

Other portable camera obscuras included an enclosed sedan chair, a compact room version, and an elegantly styled desk version that could be set in front of a window in a salon or taken to the garden, where it and the user would be draped with a cloth to achieve the effect of a darkened inte-rior. [Fig. 8.2] There were as well many variations of the portable box cam-era obscura, which could be placed on a table when sketching or held at

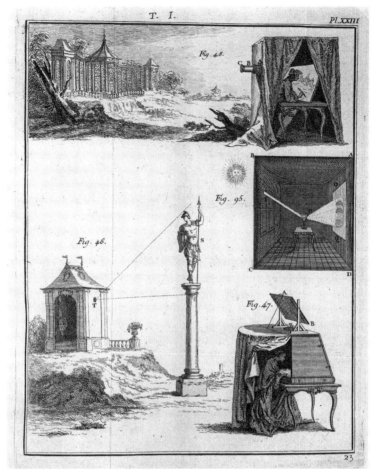

Fig. 8.2: *Tent, room, and book camera obscuras*, 1753 engraving. Alexandre Savérein, *Dictionnaire universel de mathématique et de physique…*, 1753, vol. 1, pl. 23.

This item is reproduced by permission of The Huntington Library, San Marino, California

waist height for rapid viewing. These ranged from inexpensive pocket versions no more than a few inches on a side to fairly expensive book versions two feet in height when closed. Such devices allowed the user great freedom, although portability sometimes rested in the mind of the owner. When collapsed, the camera obscura that went to North Africa with the English gentleman and adventurer James Bruce, after he was appointed British consul to Algiers in 1763, looked like a "huge folio book, about four feet long and ten inches thick." Made to Bruce's specifications by Edward Nairne and Thomas Blunt of London, this device accompanied him on his archaeological travels, as he ranged across the Barbary coast, Egypt, Palmyra in Syria, and Baalbek in Lebanon. Several of Bruce's drawings of ancient ruins, which he sketched with the aid of his camera obscura and presented to King George III, are now at the Royal Library, Windsor.

That the hand-held box-style camera obscura was a forerunner of the photographic camera is widely recognized. Basically, the fathers of photography—including Nicéphore Niépce, Louis Daguerre, and William Fox Talbot—were simply trying to fix the image visible inside a camera obscura on a light-sensitive surface. As John H. Hammond explains, "The coated material was placed on the image plane of a camera obscura where it was exposed to the image and then processed (developed). At this stage each inventor employed different techniques, with the result that Daguerre produced a single finished picture, Niépce made a printing plate (the forerunner of photogravure printing), and Fox Talbot produced a negative from which many prints could be made."

Less well understood is the part played by the camera obscura in laying the foundations for the dominance of the visual in contemporary culture. When standing in a room camera obscura or with the device in hand, individuals possessed their own moving images, long before the modern film and video industry would make that a commonplace. In addition, along with the microscope and the telescope, this device encouraged individuals to look at physical phenomena through an aperture and to think of optical technology as accessible, affordable, useful, and even entertaining. Moreover, because the camera obscura framed landscapes and urban scenes for sketching, it was uniquely suited to influencing the perception of the world visible to the naked eye. An observation made by Arthur Young, one of England's landed gentry, in a letter dated 13 July 1767 captures its effect: "The next opening in the hedge (I should tell you, by the by, that these breaks and openings are all *natural*, none *stifly artificial*) gives you at one small view, all the picturesque beauties of a natural *camera obscura*." It was also uniquely suited to nefarious uses, as Jean François Nicéron registered in *La perspective curieuse* (1652). On the Pont Neuf in Paris, according to the good monk, charlatans operating a large room-size camera obscura equipped with a very well cut and polished lens duped an audience into believing that people who were actually passing by outside had entered the darkened camera obscura, stolen their purses, and counted out their money—an early instance of the undue influence exerted on the visually naive by lifelike illusions. The camera obscura's "theater of the universe" was, it seems, one of the devices that introduced us to the delights and dangers of watching images of events as they unfold.

Bibliography

Adams, George, II. 1799. *Lectures on Natural and Experimental Philosophy, Considered in Its Present State of Improvement…* Ed. William Jones. 2d ed. London: J. Dillon. Vol. 2: 253–55.

Barbaro, Daniel. 1569. *La pratica della perspettiva…* Venice: Camillo & Rutilio Borgominieri fratelli. Pp. 192–93.

Della Porta, Giambattista. 1658. *Natural Magick by John Babtista Porta, a Neapolitane: In Twenty Books… Wherein Are Set Forth All the Riches and Delights of the Natural Sciences.* London: Thomas Young & Samuel Speed. Pp. 364–65.

Gernsheim, Helmut, and Alison Gernsheim. 1969. *The History of Photography from the Camera Obscura to the Beginning of the Modern Era.* Rev. ed. London: Thames & Hudson. Pp. 23–29.

Hammond, John H. 1981. *The Camera Obscura: A Chronicle.* Bristol: Adam Hilger.

Hammond, Mary Sayer. 1986. *The Camera Obscura: A Chapter in the Pre-History of Photography.* Ph.D. diss., Ohio State University.

Kemp, Martin. 1990. *The Science of Art: Optical Themes in Western Art from Brunelleschi to Seurat.* New Haven: Yale Univ. Press. Pp. 188–200.

Mannoni, Laurent, Donata Pesenti Campagnoni, and David Robinson. 1995. *Light and Movement: Incunabula of the Motion Picture, 1420–1896.* Gemona, Italy: Le Giornate del Cinema Muto [etc.]. Pp. 198–99.

Martinet, Marie-Madeleine. 1980. *Art et nature en Grande-Bretagne: De l'harmonie classique au pittoresque du premier romantisme XVIIᵉ-XVIIIᵉ siècles.* Paris: Aubier-Montaigne. Pp. 22–25.

Nicéron, Jean François. 1663. *La perspective curieuse…* [New ed.] Paris: La veufue François L'Anglois dit Chartres, 1652; reissue, Paris: Jean Du Puis. P. 22.

Nollet, Abbé [Jean-Antoine]. 1764. *Leçons de physique expérimentale.* 3d ed. Paris: Hippolyte-Louis Guerin & Louis-François Delatour. Vol. 5:529–35.

Playfair, R. Lambert. 1877. *Travels in the Footsteps of Bruce in Algeria and Tunis: Illustrated by Facsimiles of His Original Drawings.* London: C. Kegan Paul. Pp. 4–9.

Saverien, Alexandre. 1753. *Dictionnaire universel de mathématique et de physique…* Paris: Jacques Rollin [&] Charles-Antoine Jombert. Vol. 1:145–46, pl. 23.

Smith, Logan Pearsall. 1907. *The Life and Letters of Sir Henry Wotton.* Oxford: Clarendon. Vol. 2:205–6.

Wheatland, David P. 1968. *The Apparatus of Science at Harvard, 1765–1800.* Cambridge, Mass.: Harvard University. Pp. 126–27.

Wheelock, Arthur K., Jr. 1977. "Constantin Huygens and Early Attitudes towards the Camera Obscura." *History of Photography* 1:93–103.

[Young, Arthur]. 1768. *A Six Weeks Tour, through the Southern Counties of England and Wales.…* London: printed for W. Nicoll. P. 138.

Notes

* Frances Terpak, "Théâtre de l'univers," in *Devices of Wonder: From the World in a Box to Images on a Screen*, ed. Barbara Maria Stafford and Frances Terpak (Los Angeles: Getty Research Institute, 2001), 308.

The Secrets of Rooms

Diana Gaston

INTRODUCTION

Abelardo Morell merges interior and exterior in his photographs by trans-
forming everyday interiors into full-scale camera obscura. The experiments
result in photographs that merge images of real interiors with camera pro-
jections from the outside. Presenting a dilemma of public and private divide,
the pictures reveal the transformed room so that the viewer has to discern a
photograph that looks like a double exposure. Diane Gaston uncovers the way
Morell created these images, revealing how to appreciate the photographs that
emerge from a patient optical process.

Morell finds the familiar in everyday interiors. A bedroom, conference
room, or hotel room merges with the inverted context of its neighboring exte-
rior. The furniture and domestic detail in the room give it a consistent scale
and tone of intimate occupation. In contrast to this dominant interior, the
exterior aspect varies greatly because of borderlessness brought on by two
converging scales—a room and a city or landscape—synthesized into one that
is relative and indiscernible.

Gaston positions Morell's photographs between science and poetry, the
former necessary to produce the latter. Morell undertakes his relationship with
the camera obscura as a process of trial and error, letting individual light fac-
tors determine the opportune time exposure to produce his images, which are
exposed over hours on film in a camera on a tripod. Gaston establishes Morell
as a bystander to the photographic process once he sets up his camera in the
blackened room—except for establishing the position of the light through the
pinhole. Because the exposure can take anywhere between eight hours and two
days, Gaston recognizes the absence of people and the dialogue between sci-
ence and art at play in Morell's work, as movement and atmosphere embed-
ded in the photograph. Her analysis of Camera Obscura Image of Times
Square *in particular notes how familiar objects from a hotel room exist in the*
photograph without revealing the passage of time, such as the obscured glow

---

Originally appeared in *Abelardo Morell and the Camera Eye*, edited by Arthur Ollman, Abelardo
Morell, and Diana Gaston, 9–12. © 1998 Museum of Photographic Arts,
San Diego, California.

of an alarm clock and countless numbers of people passing through Times Square who are missing from the image projected on the hotel room's interior. The fleeting and temporal go missing in Morell's photographs, yet the walls secretly retain what is not always evident to the eye. Through Morell's photographs, Gaston reveals the photographic, virtual, and real overlap of interior and exterior.

———

INSPIRED IN EQUAL PARTS by the magical properties of scientific phenomena, the potential of poetry to transform the mundane, and the camera as an agent of vision and light, Abelardo Morell's photographs explore the workings of the everyday world. He approaches the medium as a philosopher might, constantly questioning and probing its inherent properties, seeking a more complete understanding of the camera's logic and mystery. Through the most fundamental principles of photography he explores optical phenomena that have long been understood by artists and scientists but never fully visualized as images. His subjects are decidedly familiar—domestic objects and interiors, water running from a faucet or spilled on a tabletop, illustrated books and maps, his children at play—as if to demonstrate the extraordinary visual possibilities at work on the surface of the commonplace.

Morell's exploration of the domestic environment began with the birth of his son, Brady, in 1986. He had, up until that time, worked as a black-and-white street photographer in the tradition of Henri Cartier-Bresson, Robert Frank, and Garry Winogrand. He describes his early pictures as being somewhat removed from their subjects, the result of reacting quickly, snatching frames intuitively from a distance. This approach is indicative of the strong tradition of street photography taught at Yale University when he received his MFA in photography in 1981, but also reflects the cultural distance he experienced as an immigrant living in the United States.

Born in Havana, Cuba, in 1948, Morell immigrated with his family to the United States when he was fourteen. They settled in New York City, where his father worked as a building superintendent and they lived in one of the basement apartments. Morell describes this period of his life as something of a subterranean existence, living below ground, helping his father in the evening hours with the building maintenance, watching the world outside through a single, street level window. He gradually adjusted to the cold grey light of the region and a new language. In school he was given Ernest Hemingway novels to help him learn English, and the teenager Abelardo was immediately struck by the potential of such simple, concise sentences to carry complex human dramas. After high school he received a full scholarship to attend Bowdoin College in Maine where, after a brief attempt to study engineering, he settled into a course of study in Comparative Religion. It was during his undergraduate program that he discovered photography in classes with John McKee, who also introduced him to the writings of Minor White and John Cage. For a young student, their work signaled the potential of the everyday world to yield evidence of the spiritual, and he remembers carrying their writings around like a bible.

For Morell, who grew up Catholic but did not maintain any strong belief in the teachings of the Church, the mystical qualities of Minor White's photographs and writings were particularly meaningful. In much the same way that White found art to be "a minor mysticism," Morell was drawn to the powerful transformative qualities of photography in its purest form.[1] The photographic image, much like a poem, invites the viewer to experience the spiritual, the fantastic, and the sublime in the flesh of the everyday world. And over the past decade, beginning with the birth of his first child, he has searched out a kind of beauty in ordinary things.

The Secrets of Rooms

Revealing the closed space of the camera and the optics of the camera eye are at the core of Morell's most ambitious series to date. His ongoing work with the remarkable effects of the *camera obscura* (which literally translates as dark room or chamber) began with a demonstration for his students at the Massachusetts College of Art in Boston, where he teaches. Every semester he transforms a classroom into a *camera obscura*, demonstrating the principles of photography through the first and most rudimentary of photographic devices. "When my students see projections of people on Huntington Avenue walking upside down on the classroom walls, their reaction is always total amazement that something this low tech could be so magical,"[2] he explains.

The principles of the *camera obscura* have been recognized for at least four hundred years, long before the actual development of the modem photographic camera.[3] [Fig. 8.3] Just as the *camera obscura* was frequently employed to demonstrate human vision, Morell now uses the device to demonstrate the workings of the camera eye. As Morell's simple cardboard box in *Light Bulb*, 1991, so clearly reveals, when a beam of light passes through the opening of a lens into an enclosed, darkened room or chamber, an inverted outside world is projected onto the opposite wall. As the illuminated light bulb shows us, the image appears inside the box upside down and reversed. Morell immediately recognized the potential picture in the cardboard box camera, its homely materials only underscoring the photographer's pursuit of extraordinary occurrences within the world of everyday things. It also prompted him to explore the construction of a darkened chamber on a much larger scale.

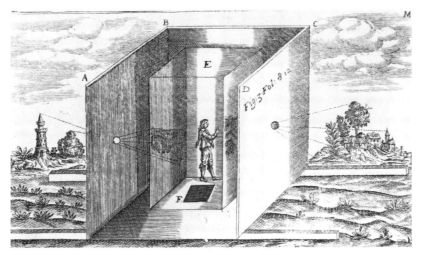

Fig. 8.3: Athanasius Kircher, *Large Portable Camera Obscura*, 1646, engraving.
Courtesy of George Eastman House, International Museum of Photography and Film

As new technology radically alters the means by which we visualize and record the world, it is somewhat remarkable that Morell would retreat to the poetic space of the *camera obscura*. His extensive experimentation with the device reveals his general interest in optics, but his actual use of the device—turning entire rooms into cameras—seems to be inspired by an almost childlike fascination with its transformative effects. "I want my photographs to reflect a time when science, art, philosophy and religion were closer brothers and sisters, as they were during [William Henry] Fox Talbot's time," he explains. He makes frequent reference to scientific inquiry, as in his photographs of the optical effects of the *camera obscura*, or the shadowy imprint of a solar eclipse reflected through the leaves of a tree onto the street below (a picture first imagined by Aristotle).[4] Not intended as scientific records of such optical phenomena, even so, they effectively draw us in to the magical properties of the physical world. These images convey the photographer's simple, hopeful message, that his imagery might restore in the viewer a sense of wonder.

Given this moment in our technological history, inspiring a state of visual innocence is no mean feat. As we become more and more entrenched in information systems, and photographic imagery increasingly mediates and distances us from firsthand sensory experience, the *camera obscura* stands in stark relief, almost otherworldly in its purity of translation. With the exception of selecting the view, or positioning the aperture, the artist who makes use of a *camera obscura* has no real control over its operation. A box which relies on optics rather than the subjective eye of the photographer, the *camera obscura* produces images purely through the vehicle of light traveling in straight lines through a narrow opening. Like the first observers who viewed the effects of the *camera obscura,* the contemporary viewer stands similarly transfixed by the clarity and detail with which the darkened chamber frames the world in real time.

In the close, a space of Morell's room-size *camera obscura* he collapses the history of optical devices, turning his own view camera back upon the imagery of its precursor. The ongoing *camera obscura* series began fairly simply in 1991, with the photographer first converting his living room, then his bedroom and finally his son's room into light-tight chambers. Doors and windows are covered with dark plastic and a small circular opening, approximately 3/8" in diameter, is made, which serves as the camera's aperture. He does not use a lens to focus the view, preferring instead the purity and immediacy of the uncorrected image that is emitted through the handmade opening. Once the outside view is positioned within the room's interior, the photographer sets up his camera on a tripod, opens the shutter and leaves the room, allowing the image to register on film over the course of several hours. A fair amount of trial and error determined that most views require an eight-hour exposure. Eight hours of real time collected on a single frame. During his early experimentation with the room-size *camera obscura* the family watched, as if from their own private theater, as the scene from across the street emerged, suspended and upside down, on the opposite wall.

Following his work within his own house, photographing familiar rooms occupied by evidence of real life, he gradually began to find opportunities to photograph interiors with views of well-known landmarks. [Fig. 8.4] Through careful alignment of two cameras he merged the intimate space of the domestic or human realm with the public space of the outside world. A clean white attic encloses a view off the coast of Marblehead, Massachusetts; a simple bedroom is visited by the elegant form of the Empire State Building; a sparsely furnished Manhattan penthouse holds the expanse of the city skyline hovering upside down on its ceiling; an empty hotel room is crammed full of Times Square. [Fig. 8.5-8.7] These were among his *camera obscura* subjects between 1991–1997. Following such highly trafficked urban sites he began to seek out landscapes to expand his series of well-known public views. A trip west to Wyoming with his son secured the image *Camera Obscura Image of the Grand Tetons in Resort Room,* 1997. [Fig. 8.8] Here, the human element of the picture is suggested by two Adirondack chairs visible just outside the window, clearly positioned to share the camera's spectacular view of the mountains.

Morell describes his *camera obscura* images as recording "what a room sees."[5] And not unlike a painting by Edward Hopper, an artist who has been particularly influential for the photographer, his rooms are pronounced in their quiet loneliness. By the sheer duration of the exposure, it is not

Fig. 8.4: Abelardo Morell, *Boston's Old Customs House in Hotel Room I*, 1999.
Image courtesy of Bonni Benrubi Gallery

surprising that Morell's rooms would be unpopulated; and yet there is the unmistakable presence of people inhabiting these spaces. It is as though they have momentarily left their room, their physical presence still hanging in the air. Here he inverts the ordinary relationship of a person inhabiting a room, presenting instead a room that holds the lingering presence of its keeper. It is the memory of the room that we see in these images.

The *camera obscura* series might also be seen as a poetic interpretation of the Latin term *in camera*, generally used in reference to a private conversation taking place in the secure space of a judge's chamber.[6] Here too, Morell invites the viewer to linger "in camera," in the private space of his pictures. By the very necessity of creating an enclosed, light-tight area for their production, these photographs are unusually intimate, even secretive. Too slow to be treated as surveillance records, they still possess the irresistible quality of a picture made unannounced. Here the patience and careful planning of their maker is balanced against the whims of natural lighting conditions and an extraordinary element of chance. Given the duality of these pictures—containing degrees of stasis and change, of technology

Fig. 8.5: Abelardo Morell, *The Sea in Attic*, 1994.

Fig. 8.6: Abelardo Morell, *The Empire State Building in Bedroom*, 1994.
Images courtesy of Bonni Benrubi Gallery

Fig. 8.7: Abelardo Morell, *Manhattan View Looking South in Large Room*, 1996.

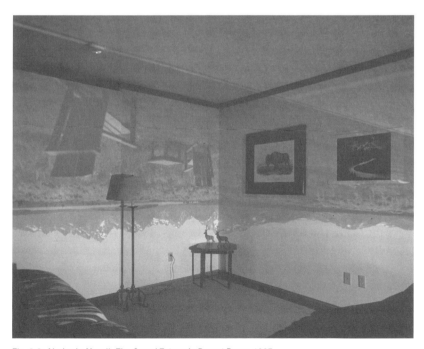

Fig. 8.8: Abelardo Morell, *The Grand Tetons in Resort Room*, 1997.
Images courtesy of Bonni Benrubi Gallery

Fig. 8.9: Abelardo Morell, *Times Square in Hotel Room*, 1997.
Image courtesy of Bonni Benrubi Gallery

and magic, of description and illusion—they are remarkably intense in their psychological capacity. The viewer is drawn in to survey the intricacies of a dark room and a strange looming representation of the outside world. In the case of *Camera Obscura Image of Times Square*, 1997, for instance, commissioned by the *New York Times*, Morell worked from a carefully selected hotel room, bringing the visual chaos of Broadway inside through a small aperture. [Fig. 8.9] Because direct sunlight is blocked by skyscrapers during a portion of the day, this photograph required an unusually long exposure of two days. With its unblinking eye open for the duration, the camera slowly registered the passage of time on film. The light of the alarm clock on the bedside table glows, but the time does not register. The hands of the wall clock spin into oblivion. The light under the door fights to enter. Over the course of two days thousands of people pass through Times Square, and yet not a single person registers on film. The long exposure lends an eerie presence to the empty streets below, not unlike the ghostly representations of many nineteenth-century photographs.

Notes

1   Quoted in Minor White, *Mirrors, Messages, Manifestations* (New York: Aperture, 1982), unpaginated.

2   Quoted in *A Camera in a Room: Photographs by Abelardo Morell* (Washington and London: Smithsonian Institution Press, 1995), p. 7.

3   The phenomenon which the *camera obscura* demonstrates was first described in tenth-century optical treatises by Arabian scholars. Its optical effects were later detailed in Leonardo da Vinci's manuscripts. The invention of the *camera obscura* is often credited to Giovanni Battista della Porta, who fully described it in his *Magia Naturalis* of 1558. The *camera obscura* became widely used by artists during the seventeenth and eighteenth centuries. For a detailed account of the *camera obscura* see Jonathan Crary, "The Camera Obscura and Its Subject," in *Techniques of the Observer: On Vision and Modernity in the Nineteenth Century* (Cambridge and London: MIT Press, 1992), 25–66.

4   The optical phenomenon of the solar eclipse casting crescent-shaped images through the leaves of a tree and onto the ground below was first described by Aristotle during the fourth century B.C. What came to be known as "Aristotle's Problem" was not solved until the sixteenth century with the development of the *camera obscura*. See John J. Hammond, *The Camera Obscura: A Chronicle* (Bristol: Adam Hilger Ltd., 1981) and Richard Torchia, *Live Projections by Richard Torchia* (exhibition brochure), (Tucson: Center for Creative Photography, The University of Arizona, 1997).

5   Quoted in "Assignment: Times Square," *The New York Times Magazine*, May 18, 1997, section 6, p. 50.

6   Eugenia Parry introduced this idea of interior spaces paralleling the psychological state of the photographer in her exhibition and accompanying essay *In Camera*, presented at the Museum of Fine Arts, Museum of New Mexico, Santa Fe in 1993. Abelardo Morell's *Camera Obscura Image of Houses Across the Street in Our Bedroom,* 1991, was included in this exhibition.

Gordon Matta-Clark

Dan Graham

INTRODUCTION

Gordon Matta-Clark straddles art and architecture to produce work on the threshold of interior and exterior. His full-scale architectural cuttings provide an interior perspective that is seldom seen in the discourse of interiors. Dan Graham contextualizes the work in the urban environment, framing his essay with two points. The first: site matters, especially with programs that rely on interiors as gathering spaces, like galleries. The second point: how Matta-Clark challenged gallery conventions by making site-specific work that existed primarily outside the site. These two points provide access to Matta-Clark's work and its effect on the interior.

Matta-Clark relied on his background as an architect to translate the metaphoric act of cutting sections and plans into full-scale building cuts. His results reveal both interior spaces and the economic classes found within. Once the buildings are demolished, the cut fragments move to the gallery accompanied by photographs and drawings that ask the viewer to piece together the fragments. As familiar architecture in a new format, this collection of work asks the viewer to consider both deconstruction and reconstruction centered on the interior.

Two works that convey Matta-Clark's ideas are Splitting *and* Conical Intersect. *Both reveal the social structure of the interior through drawing, projecting, and cutting.* Splitting *looks to a suburban single-family home and the iconic form of a house, which Matta-Clark exposes through a section cut.* Conical Intersect *also reveals the private interior but in an urban realm, with a cut through an apartment building to open up new views, as if a scope had been inserted. Although the intent is to reveal the relationship of the interior and exterior of private and public, the views reveal historical usage of the interior surfaces through orthographic cuts. Hints of wallpaper and familiar spaces help create immediacy for onlookers to place themselves within these spaces. For Matta-Clark, orthographic cut lines are not limited to lines on a page. Instead, he treats the built world as his paper.*

From *Gordon Matta-Clark*, edited by Juan Manuel Bonet (Valencia: Instituto Valenciano de Arte Moderno, 1999), 378–80.

Orthographic cuts lend themselves to an objective reading of architecture. At the same time, Matta-Clark captures the house as artifact and opens up subjective readings of the interior. Even with the house dismantled and the occupants long gone, narrative surfaces from the intimate scale of rooms and remnants of decorative surfaces left behind by the last occupant.

———

In the seventies, artists attempted to leave the politically coercive bounds of the art gallery. They deserted the city to make neoprimitive earth works, relocations, or simply maps of their walks in the landscape. But in the display (documentation) of this work to the public, ironically, the art gallery came back as a support.

> Landscape (is) co-extensive with the gallery. I don't think we're dealing with matter in terms of a back to nature movement…(or, said inversely) the world is a museum.[1] (Robert Smithson)

Smithson wanted to deny any reading of his work in terms of the currently "fashionable" ecology movement or any "political" reading; rather, it was to be read as formalist or as an ambiguously "romantic" stance.

Not only couldn't the earth artists escape the need for the gallery to document their work, but they were in danger of taking part of nature and exhibiting it as a "found object." This was a great dilemma for Gordon Matta-Clark, a young artist and friend of Smithson's. He describes his first work:

> I made a series of visits to…ghetto areas…moving into spaces with a handsaw and cutting away rectangular sections of the floor or walls to create a view from one space into another. The sections were…removed from their original positions (and taken) to an art gallery.[2]

Matta-Clark came to the position that work must function directly in the actual urban environment. "Nature" was an escape; political and cultural contradictions were not to be denied. By making his removals something like the spectacle of a demolition for casual pedestrians, the work could function as a kind of urban "agit-prop," something like the acts of the Paris Situationalists, in 1968, who had seen their acts as public intrusions or "cuts" in the seamless urban fabric. The idea was to have their gestures interrupt the induced habits of the urban masses, which might then unrepress certain concealed realities. Matta-Clark saw his "cuts" as probes, liberating "areas …from being hidden," opening up socially hidden information beneath the surface and:

...breaking through the surface (to create) repercussions in terms of what else is imposed upon a cut...it was kind of the thin edge of what was being seen that interested me as much, if not more than, the views that were being created...the layering, the strata, the different things that are being served. Revealing how a uniform surface is established. The simplest was to create complexity without having to make or build anything.[3]

Matta-Clark used houses and building structures which were about to be demolished and created de-constructed "ruins" which reveal hidden layers of socially concealed architectural and anthropological family meaning. In the early eighteenth century deliberately ruined pavilions which served as "Temples of Contemplation," "Hermitages" (for homeless monks) and elegiac evocations of ruined classical structures were built in parks. Today ruins are created each moment as buildings are demolished and replaced as part of the cycle of endless architectural consumption. Matta-Clark's work attached itself to the notion of the instant ruin of today: the demolition. Half-remembered, the existence of a Matta-Clark work now takes the form of a photograph or film or drawing in conjunction with the viewer's own memory and knowledge of the city. In Marie-Paule MacDonald's and my "Museum for Matta-Clark" we used the outward media image of *Splitting* as "ruin" to memorialize the late artist's work. However, the intent of the "Museum" is to relate Matta-Clark's cutting methodology to urban planning.

If his "dematerialized" methodology is conceptual art, this "Museum for Matta-Clark," a form of conceptual art, wishes to re-materialize his work. It also wishes to equate urban planning and conceptual art. Matta-Clark's work starts by setting up a dialogue between art and architecture or architecture's own territory. It doesn't generalize the art gallery as the site of a repressive architecture, identified with the Establishment, but now links itself to the urban environment on an experienced political architectural historical basis which includes its relation to itself as a memory of archetypal architectural form. These ideas about architecture and the city have been espoused by the architectural critic Manfredo Tafuri, who has criticized modern architecture for its destruction of the city as context.[4]

Tafuri starts with the assumption that the idea of every new building as a self-sufficient utopian vision began with the French Revolutionary architects, Boullée and Ledoux; individual works of architecture were, in each particular architectural proposal, a unique symbol for a social vision projected to be contained, solely, however, within the work's formal properties. During the nineteenth century, as the Industrial Age produced both novel materials for construction and a taste for historical eclecticism, the city became full of proliferating new buildings as innovative formal utopias.

Old buildings were seen as "reactionary" failures and torn down to make way for the new, more progressive forms. In fact, this process was connected to the capitalist organization of architectural practice which structured architecture in terms of competing buildings which would each be judged for having superseded all previous buildings. The economic effect was to keep the consumption/production cycle progressively stimulated as new buildings constantly replaced old ones. All of this was at the expense of the cohesiveness of the city structure and tended to constantly displace urban districts which were redeveloped to generate money for an expanding economy.

This position is "Marxist" in its commitment to a revolution of the oppressed, the underclasses, but in opposition to Karl Marx's ideological rejection of an appeal to the memory of past events. Marx wanted to break the ideological blinders of the past which he thought obscured the implications of the future in technological progress:

> The social revolution of the nineteenth century cannot draw...from the past, but only from the future. It cannot begin with itself before it has stripped off all superstition in regard to the past. Earlier revolutions required recollections of past world history in order to drug themselves concerning their own content. In order to arrive at its own content, the revolution of the nineteenth century must let the dead bury their dead.[5]

Walter Benjamin observed, in this century, that, on the contrary, bourgeois ideology is "maintained" by the notion of progress and that that view is supported by an empirical, "scientific" ideology of "objective" historical progress. In opposition to the twentieth-century ideology of "progress," Benjamin proposed a recuperation of historical memory. Without the concept of historical memory and the redemption of "past" oppression, Marxism would, itself, only fall into the trap of reducing itself to the dominant terms of rationalism as capitalist society:

> The past carries with it a temporal index by which it is referred to as redemption. There is a secret agreement between past generations and the present one...like every generation which has preceded us, we have been endowed with a "weak" Messianic power, a power to which the past has a claim....Nothing that has ever happened should be regarded as lost for history....[The oppressed have a] retroactive force and their struggle calls into question every victory, past and present, of the rulers....The true image of the past can be seized only as an image which flashes up at the instant when it can be recognized and is never seen again....To articulate the past historically does not mean to recognize

it "the way it really was" (Ranke). It means to seize hold of a memory as it flashes up at a moment of danger....Only that historian will have the gift of fanning the spark of hope in the past who is firmly convinced that "even the dead" will not be safe from the enemy if he wins.[6]

All of us "are living in a city...[whose] whole fabric is architectural...[where] property is so all-pervasive," noted Gordon Matta-Clark. He wanted his work to expose this "containerization of usable space" in the interests of capitalism.[7] To achieve this, instead of building, restoring or adding new elements to existing architecture to call attention to the "innovative" or "progressive" elements of each new "idea" manifested in a new work of architecture. Matta-Clark proposes to attack the cycle of production and consumption at the expense of the remembered history of the city. Such ideas have also been espoused by Tafuri, and also Aldo Rossi and Leon Krier. But Matta-Clark's approach differs from, say, Krier's by a refusal to construct; Matta-Clark's practice, instead, is to subtract from architectural structures already in existence. No new buildings are added to the world; what is gained is a newly available historical time/popular memory of the city. Matta-Clark usually focuses on one, singular, vernacular syntax at a time (row houses, seventeenth-century twin mansions, etc.) and through his deconstruction opens up his selected building's (and by implication other nearby or similar style buildings') external relation to property lines and codes of public and private. "By undoing a building...[I] open a state of enclosure which had been preconditioned not only by physical necessity but by the industry that proliferates suburban and urban boxes as a pretext for ensuring a passive, isolated consumer..."[8]

These deconstructions can, paradoxically, "still" be a form of architecture; for the effect of stripping or cutting into buildings functions to enhance or preserve the site. Matta-Clark notes that in *Splitting*: "...what the cutting's done is to make the space more articulated, but the identity of the building as a place, as an object, is strongly preserved, enhanced."[9] [Figs. 8.10–8.12]

Fig. 8.10: Gordon Matta-Clark, *Splitting*, 1974. Four gelatin silver prints, cut and collaged, 24 x 36 inches, 61 x 91.4 cm. Courtesy The Estate of Gordon Matta-Clark and David Zwirner, New York

Fig. 8.11: Gordon Matta-Clark, *Splitting*, 1974. Silver dye bleach print (Cibachrome), 26 1/2 x 39 inches, 68 x 99 cm.

Fig. 8.12: Gordon Matta-Clark, *Splitting*, 1974. Five gelatin silver prints, cut and collaged, 32 x 22 3/4 inches, 81.3 x 57.8 cm. Courtesy The Estate of Gordon Matta-Clark and David Zwirner, New York

In *Splitting*, Matta-Clark operated on a standard suburban dwelling type in a working-class neighborhood. He divided the building into two halves with a vertical cut, removed the four corners at the roof intersection, and removed material from the foundation so that one half of the house lifted forward. In *Splitting*, the cut, the operative element, opens the compartmentalized disposition of the rooms in the house in the sequence of suburban lots. The model places the representation of the house at 332 Humphrey Street in an abstracted context, suggesting the spatial condition which existed around the house and indicating its relationship to a system of division and terrain in a larger scale.

The cutting practice of Gordon Matta-Clark responded precisely to the imposed suburban order of the New Jersey site.... Matta-Clark's negative architectural activity operated on an existing architectural logic; the interaction between the two produced an analytical transgression of a series of architectural and urbanistic constraints. The cut is able to emphasize the organizational capability of the architectural logic, as the observer realizes how the space is composed, how it "should have been" before the cut, which has disclosed the order using a process of selection.[10]

To strip, eviscerate, deconstruct a building is a statement against conventional professional architectural practice. To destroy and not to construct (or reconstruct) a building also amounts to an inversion of functionalist architectural doctrine. While Mies van der Rohe, for instance, constructed with materials such as glass and steel to reveal both the material structure and the previously revealed interior, Matta-Clark looks for already existing "gaps, void places that were not developed." These only exist as negation in modern architecture. In fact, the sheer glass and steel openwork often are measures taken by modern architecture, like the modern bureaucratic thinking it reflects, to cover over these contradictions (often in definitions of public property against definitions of private property). A Matta-Clark "deconstruction," unlike "minimal," "pop" or "conceptual" art, allows an historical time to enter.

There is a kind of complexity which comes from taking an otherwise completely normal, conventional, albeit anonymous situation and redefining it, retranslating it into overlapping and multiple readings of conditions past and present.[11]

Matta-Clark grew up in both Paris and New York: his work must be located at both in terms of twentieth-century French art and in terms of contemporary American Art, especially "minimal" art like reductivism and "process-art."

Many of Matta-Clark's American works deal with vernacular apartment or two-family house structures. The cuts reveal private integration of compartmentalized living space, revealing how each individual family copes with the imposed social structure of its container. The constructural imposition becomes revealed, along with the private family and/or person's adaptation to the architecture's socially conformist concealed order, to the outside public in the form of "sculpture."

Describing the logic of a Genoa office block he dissected, Matta Clark notes:

> Normally they divided the other half into a quarter which became the office, and divided the remaining quarter in half again for the coatroom and bathroom. And then divided that again to make a shower or something. Everything was progressively divided so that the remaining last piece was 1/32 of the whole. I used the idea of division around the center. Therefore, I removed a square section out of the roof apex, then projected that cut from the roof down into the building and spread it out laterally through the walls and doors.[12]

Matta-Clark fragments or splinters architecture, turning it into a kind of reverse Cubism or "anti-monument," but one whose task is to reconstitute memory, not conventional memory as in the traditional monument, but that subversive memory which has been hidden by social and architectural façades and their false sense of "wholeness."

> (There) is a type of space we all…have stored in memory: spaces that are detailed and precise, fragments generally, at all levels of reminiscence. And, of course, once you get into reminiscence, an infinite number of associations emerge. Memory seems to create a unique kind of space setting up an about-to-be-disintegrated level.[13]

It is only the specialized professional architects in society who can penetrate the facade and read general schematic structures to building units. This professional world is itself institutionalized and containerized in its own place of work: the engineer's or architect's office suite.

> The *Datum* Cuts…took place in an engineer's rooms and offices. I couldn't deal with the outside because there wasn't enough exterior enclosure to really penetrate anything. What fascinated me was the interior central plan. The engineers took a small, square, primitive hut shape and divided it in half to make one big drafting room.

Fig. 8.13: Gordon Matta-Clark, Documentation of *Conical Intersect*, 1975. Paris.
Courtesy The Estate of Gordon Matta-Clark and David Zwirner, New York

Unlike the conventional monument designed to smoothly link past to present to implied future, Matta-Clark's "monument" is profoundly pessimistic. It will be quickly demolished; as a work it is something of a useless gesture as opposed to a permanent symbolic form. It accepts its fate—to be remembered only as a photo/text representation, as "conceptual art," *and* to disappear into the anonymous rubble. It is close to an instant ruin—a photo of what was once a spark of hope and is now erased by more dominant forms. These negative "monuments" or remembrances of works desire to "open up" history and historical memory, which could lead to a critical view of present oppression.

In effect, Matta-Clark's work, although negative as to architectural practice, still hopefully opts, from the view of historical materialism, for a communication value; which is the ideal, of "conceptual art": "The determining factor is the degree to which my intervention can transform the structure" into an act of communication."[14]

He identifies his deconstructions in terms of linguistic acts: "It's like juggling with syntax, or disintegrating some kind of established sequence of parts…the piece is a way of imposing a presence, an idea, it's a way to disorientation by using a clear and given system…"[15]

His most (propagandistically) effective work was *Conical Intersect*, in the Les Halles district of Paris, then under demolition for the erection of the Centre Pompidou and luxury housing. Matta-Clark was aware of the specifically Parisian connotations of this area's symbolic meaning and of the

Fig. 8.14: Gordon Matta-Clark, Documentation of *Conical Intersect*, 1975. Paris.
Courtesy The Estate of Gordon Matta-Clark and David Zwirner, New York

relation of the new Centre to its visual alignment with the Tour Eiffel: one, a monument of contemporary French national ideology, the other, a monument of nineteenth-century French progress.

Matta-Clark used two seventeenth-century "twin" townhouses from which he cut out a massive conical base of four meters on the diameter. [Figs. 8.13–8.15]

> The central axis made an approximately 45° angle with the street below. As the cone diminished in circumference, it twisted up through the walls, floors, and out of the attic roof of the adjoining house…[becoming] a new standard in sun and air for lodgers.[16]

The conical removals penetrated through the buildings, the holes optically functioning like periscopes in their directing the attention of the people on the street to, specifically, the alignment of the building to both the Tour Eiffel and the new Centre Pompidou as well as to these two landmarks' relation to each other. With the aid of this "periscope" they could look not only into the interior of the Matta-Clark sculpture/building, but "through" the conical borings to these other buildings that form past and present eras of Paris. The Centre Pompidou's modernist infrastructure, with its throwback to a 1960s "Archigram"—science-fiction look—has service ducts exposed to look like a circuitry diagram. Both interior and exterior pipes are color-coded and exposed to those passers-by who wish to read the information concerning

Fig. 8.15: Gordon Matta-Clark, Documentation of *Conical Intersect*, 1975. Paris.
Courtesy The Estate of Gordon Matta-Clark and David Zwirner, New York

the technical functioning of the building. Its technological popular optimism seems in contrast to the rubble of the rest, of the older section of Paris. The new Centre, then, is a talisman, linking contemporary French technology/ culture to the Paris of the Tour Eiffel. Matta-Clark's "monument" alludes to the destruction of any historical continuity between old and new Paris, evidencing a profoundly negative view of progress. Its negative form mimics both the Centre Pompidou and the Tour Eiffel. Matta-Clark's view of the Tour Eiffel echoes Barthes' description of this monument: "...an object when we look at it, it becomes a look-out in its turn when we visit it, and now constitutes as an object, simultaneously extended and collected beneath it, that Paris which just now was looking at it."[17]

Appositely, Matta-Clark's "antimonument" alludes both to the destruction of the old historical *quartier* and the shattering of any real historical continuity between old and new Paris for those who live there. Its formal openness mimics both the symbolic Tour Eiffel and the new Centre Pompidou. It takes a gamble: that by deconstructing an existing architectural object, designed to be destroyed anyway (a kind of double negation being involved here), the work has "more" (not less) articulation or symbolic meaning than the two other competing monuments. In art terms, Matta-Clark's work in Paris evokes a succession of Parisian forms: it suggests synthetic and analytic Cubism—but a reversed Cubism, for where Cubist collage consists of fragments of the real world brought into (gallery) art, Matta-Clark's work cut away from (into) things to subtract from the real world, in order to make a "sculpture." The conical borings, in their sinuous form, suggest Art Nouveau, for example, Hector Guimard's Paris "Métro" entrances. The effect of stripping or cutting away in Matta-Clark's work is to reveal the usually hidden constructional and historical layering; this is inverse to such display of compositional or functional inner workings as in the Centre Pompidou's constructed, only "apparently" open, display to the public which promulgates an ideological notion of "progress." Matta-Clark's aim can be viewed as a form of urban "ecology"; his approach is not to build with expensive materials, but to make architectural statements by removing in order to reveal existing, historical aspects of vernacular, ordinary buildings. Thus, the capitalist exhaustion of marketable material in the name of progress is reversed.

Of course, Matta-Clark himself was influenced by theories and existing examples of architecture. His restoration of the archetypalness of a typical house might be compared to Michael Graves' 1969-70 Benerraf House in New Jersey. Graves' "add-ons" leave the form of the old house intact, but build a Corbusier- or Léger-like schematic front extension which places the house in dialectical juxtaposition with its "Heroic Modernist Revival," architect-built extension. Both, in a sense, are archetypalized. What holds the composition together is that the addition is actually derived from the elevation diagram (hidden behind the facade of the house…only known to Graves, the architect). Or compare Matta-Clark's deconstruction of a house to a new house by Robert Venturi. One of Venturi's most radical compositional ideas is that architectural façades must be composed through inflection towards (mimicking) other publicly visible buildings in the surrounding, immediate environment. This is a way of looking at, or reflecting, the world as it actually is, and eliminating the authoritarian imposition of the architect's self-contained utopian building.

What Matta-Clark's projects attempted, but which is avoided by the many compositional stratagems of modern architecture, is to expose to the outside public the property lines and general containerization of the space to which the urban environment is subjected. This question is usually hidden within the composition of the modern building by the architect's composition.

Notes

1 Robert Smithson, quoted in a symposium at Cornell University, Ithaca, in connection with the exhibition *Earth*, 1970.

2 Interview with Gordon Matta-Clark, in *Matta-Clark,* (exhib. cat.), Internationaal Cultureel Centrum, Antwerp 1977, p. 8.

3 "Gordon Matta-Clark: *Splitting*, The Humphrey Street Building," an interview by Liza Bear, in *Avalanche*, Dec. 1974, p. 34.

4 Manfredo Tafuri, *Theories and History of Architecture*, Grenada, New York 1980. See especially first chapter.

5 Karl Marx, *The Eighteenth Brumaire of Louis Bonaparte*. International Publishers Co., New York, 1963, p. 18.

6 Walter Benjamin, *Illuminations*, ed. Hannah Arendt, trans. Harry Zohn, Schocken Books, New York 1969, pp. 254–255.

7 "Gordon Matta-Clark: *Splitting…*," *op. cit.*, p. 34.

8 Interview with Gordon Matta-Clark in *Matta-Clark, op. cit.*, p. 9.

9 "Gordon Matta-Clark: *Splitting…*," *op. cit.*, p. 37.

10 Marie-Paule MacDonald, "Project for 'Gordon Matta-Clark Museum' for Paris," in *Flyktpunkter/Vanishing Points*, (exhib. cat.), Moderna Museet, Stockholm 1984).

11 Interview with Gordon Matta-Clark in *Matta-Clark, op. cit.*, p. 10.

12 Donald Wall, "Gordon Matta-Clark's Building Dissections," in *Arts Magazine*, March 1976, pp. 74–79; reproduced in *Matta-Clark, op. cit.*, p. 40.

13 *Ibid.* p. 41.

14 *Ibid.* p. 39.

15 "Gordon Matta-Clark: *Splitting…*," *op. cit.*, p. 36.

16 Interview with Gordon Matta-Clark in *Matta-Clark, op. cit.*, p. 12.

17 Roland Barthes, *The Eiffel Tower and Other Mythologies*, trans. Richard Howard, Hill and Wang, New York 1979, p. 4.

House 1993

Charlotte Mullins

INTRODUCTION

Rachel Whiteread's House *addressed simple principles of solid and void. Activating these principles on the scale of a house, she presented complex issues like domesticity and memory. Here, Charlotte Mullins reviews the project, which began as a rowhouse in East London slated for demolition and evolved into a full-scale concrete cast of the building. Empty rooms became solid concrete forms, creating an iconic representation of a house. The marks of wallpaper and paint left on the concrete surface of fireplaces, staircases, sinks and window frames revealed the house's temporary and permanent nature. At times, these architectural forms and interior fixtures are defined by their absence, as the solidity of formerly negative space absorbs them. Whiteread's project captured an after-the-fact condition, documenting what was previously there as if it were a ghost.*

House *brought the interior to the exterior at its periphery. Where an exterior brick surface defines a house's boundary, Whiteread's cast interior treated the brick as formwork that could be peeled away, revealing a face. Traces of color and pattern remain. Windows, porous boundaries between interior and exterior, were abruptly halted when cast in concrete. As the house was turned inside out, Mullins compares the monolithic modernist object to a blank-slate projection screen for onlookers to interpret. The sculpture resists reconstructing the lives of the house's occupants, yet it holds the memory of their occupancy. The idea of occupation lingers on the exterior, as Mullins emphasizes the social spaces that contain the trace of dialogues from former occupants.*

While interior design occurs at the beginning of a house's life, House *recorded its end, making the layers of history embedded within visible. The sculpture offers interior design a unique view of everyday details such as light switches and window frames abstracted into archeological fragments. The concrete cast captures domestic details that go unnoticed because we have*

From *Rachel Whiteread* (London: Tate Publishing, 2004), 50–57.

grown accustomed to them. But seeing them in a new form—negative and homogeneous—offers the opportunity for interior design to re-envision these latent details.

———

ON 25 OCTOBER 1993, a small group of people gathered on a piece of featureless parkland in East London to celebrate the completion of *House* Whiteread's largest and most ambitious work to date. [Fig. 8.16] It was her first public sculpture, and over the course of the next three months it was responsible for transforming her from a relatively unknown promising young artist to a household name.

The idea for *House* had first arisen three years earlier, a few weeks after she had completed *Ghost*.

> *House* was a continuation of my early work from the late 1980s, like *Yellow Leaf* 1989 and *Closet* 1988, where elements of the originals became an integral part of the work. When making *House* we cast a concrete skin throughout the whole building—casting around the wooden stairs and floors.

Initially Whiteread obsessed over how to cast a whole house without destroying it, as she had previously managed to do with the room in *Ghost*. But when she teamed up with art facilitators Artangel, the idea of using a house due for demolition was presented to her. A giant cast of the inside could be made, with no requirement to preserve the building. The problem then became one of finding a suitable condemned house to use as a mould. For more than two years Whiteread scoured London for suitable properties. She came close to using a building on the proposed site for the controversial new M11. A fake blue heritage plaque, which had been attached to the property, read: 'This house was once a home.' But she finally settled on 193 Grove Road, a Victorian terraced house in Bow, where the tenant—Mr. Gale—had refused to move out when the rest of the street was cleared to make way for a park. Eventually he was persuaded to vacate the property, and Bow council granted Whiteread access to the house to enable her to create a temporary sculpture from it.

> This was a semi-derelict house in East London and I was very clear that it had to be in an area I was absolutely familiar with, and a building that was going to be knocked down. Grove Road was on a green corridor with a view to Canary Wharf, one of Thatcher's troubled economic babies, originally envisaged as an urban utopia.

Fig. 8.16: Rachel Whiteread, *House*, 1993. Courtesy of the artist, Luhring Augustine, New York, and Gagosian Gallery

On 2 August 1993, with a team of engineers, construction people, assistants and student volunteers, Whiteread set to work preparing the inside of the property for casting.

The previous tenants were obviously DIY fanatics. The house was full of fitted cupboards, cocktail bars and a tremendous variety of wallpapers and floor finishes. I was fascinated by their personal environment, and documented it all before I destroyed it. It was like exploring the inside of a body, removing its vital organs. I'd made floor pieces before in the studio, and had always seen them as being like the intestines of a house, the hidden spaces that are generally inaccessible. We spent about six weeks working on the interior of the house, filling cracks and getting it ready for casting. It was as if we were embalming a body.

To build a building within a building, we had to make new foundations. We worked meticulously on the interior, stripping it to its carcass. Then we applied a release agent, sprayed one centimetre of top-coat concrete [Lockrete, used to 'retouch' the white cliffs of Dover] over it, put the metal armature in place, and heavy-filled it with the rest of the concrete. It was a very strange place inside, like a cave or grotto. We used that process throughout the whole building; essentially the building became a mould. Then we stripped the whole thing by hand—every brick, every fireplace, and every door. When we'd finished casting, we got out through a four-foot square in the roof. The construction people said that it could just be patched over with wood, but I insisted that it had to be cast so that it would be a completely sealed space.

It took over a month for the interior of the whole house to be cast, and a further ten days for the concrete to cure and set. Then scaffolding was erected around the outside, and Whiteread and her team began removing the exterior of the building.

As we stripped away the building, it was amazing to me how much detail the casting had picked up, like *Ghost* but much more substantial, not just because of its size, but because of the material and the brutality with which it had been made.

The interior volumes of the family house had been solidified, and as the bricks were pulled away, sheer concrete walls imprinted with the idiosyncrasies of 100 years of domestic use were revealed. Soot clung to the bulges that protruded where fireplaces had once been; lemon paint from a top-floor bedroom clung to one wall, recalling a damaged fresco. Flexes that had once supplied electricity to switches had left their mark as tiny recessed

Fig. 8.17: Rachel Whiteread, *House*, 1993. Commissioned and produced by Artangel. Photo by John Davies

spaces embedded in the concrete skin; the light switches themselves had been reversed and rendered unusable. The social spaces that had once been privy to secrets and arguments and love and despair had been petrified, making amateur archaeologists of the onlookers, who could only reconstruct the past uses of each room and stairwell from the tiny fossilised fragments that were left, captured in the concrete like prehistoric mosquitoes in resin.

House was in fact the inverse of a house. All that had been air was now solid; few things that were solid had remained (only the staircases and the wooden floors were left in place, because Whiteread couldn't find a way to cast the house without them). [Fig. 8.17] It was an uncanny sculpture, having the proportions of a house, replicating the window frames, the doors, even the lean-to extension at the back, but in fact presenting everything in negative; fireplaces were now protrusions, window-frames like shallow crosses etched into the surface. [Fig. 8.18] *House* offered no way in, and—significantly—no protective roof over your head, since Whiteread had chosen not to cast the attic space. Instead it had a flat top cast from the upper-floor ceiling, and *House* appeared as a white-walled modernist pile, created from a Victorian terrace that was riddled with the woodworm of history.

During the two-and-a-half months that *House* stood silently on Grove Road, it generated an unrelenting storm of media noise. Over 250 newspaper and magazine articles were written about it, and it was debated everywhere from the House of Commons to the back of black cabs. Tabloids and

Fig. 8.18: Rachel Whiteread, *House*, 1993. Courtesy of the artist, Luhring Augustine, New York, and Gagosian Gallery

broadsheets across Britain carried pictures of it on their front pages; the local paper the *East End Advertiser* ran stories every week, from the vox pop 'If this is art then I'm Leonardo da Vinci', to a piece that ran on 13 January 1994, two days after *House* was torn down by bulldozers, headlined 'Bringing the House down'. The Bow Councillor Eric Flounders pilloried the sculpture in a series of vitriolic letters to the *Independent* and elsewhere (which was rather ironic, since he was responsible for securing the licence for *House* in the first place). This provoked a counter attack by campaigners, who presented petitions and proposals to save the sculpture.

On 23 November, the same day that Bow Council made the decision not to grant *House* a stay of execution, Whiteread won the Turner Prize. She used her acceptance speech to condemn the Council's edict. She was also awarded a £40,000 prize for 'worst' artist of the year, an event staged outside the Tate on the night of the Turner announcement by an attention-seeking group calling itself the K Foundation (comprising former members of the pop group KLF). Whiteread divided the £40,000 between a fund for young artists and Shelter, a charity for London's homeless.

In the end, the relentless campaigning on Whiteread's behalf paid off, and a month later Bow Council capitulated and granted an extension to the lease on the site occupied by *House* until 12 January 1994. A number of people—from museum directors to collectors to sponsors—had by this point

Fig. 8.19: Rachel Whiteread, *House*, 1993.
Commissioned and produced by Artangel. Photo by Stephen White

offered to buy *House*, but Whiteread was adamant that it shouldn't be moved. While she had wanted the sculpture to remain in place long enough for it to become part of the fabric of the neighbourhood, she had always intended *House* to be a temporary structure.

By the time the bulldozers were ordered in on 11 January 1994, *House* had been seen by thousands of people from around the world, and discussed by thousands more. From the outset, Whiteread couldn't even stand in front of the sculpture for fear of being mobbed, and had to resign herself to looking at it from afar, sitting in her car at the end of the street and peering round a newspaper. *House* was a mute memorial for the area and its history, and a tomb that visualised the darker side of domestic life. But it also came to be a pawn in the political discourse, and was called variously a 'bunker', an 'eyesore', a 'mausoleum', and an 'exceptional work of art'. It was clever yet simple, a monument to thoughts and dreams and sensations, a human-sized foil to the faceless scale of Canary Wharf. And suddenly it was gone. [Fig. 8.19]

> By the day of the demolition, it was covered in graffiti and beginning to look pretty sad; birds were living on it. It took three and a half years to develop, four months to make, and thirty minutes to demolish.

Now Grove Road is flanked by an unbroken stretch of flat green grass, and *House* exists only in photographs, drawings and the fragments that Whiteread collected from the ruins. But it also exists in the memories of all who saw or read about it—perhaps the most appropriate site for this silent monument to lost conversations and past lives.

Rodinsky's Room

Rachel Lichtenstein and Iain Sinclair

INTRODUCTION

The personal possessions found in an interior can help construct an image of its occupant. The aesthetic is not always about style—sometimes it reveals a pathological obsession with collecting and hoarding. The sufferer's idea of home is formed by literally surrounding him- or herself in everything from scraps of paper to furniture and clothes. The case of the reclusive Collyer brothers in New York City, who compulsively collected everyday objects beyond reasonable use only to perish under the weight of their collection in 1947, is an extreme example of this exaggerated possession-identity phenomenon. Identifying this type of behavior is not part of interior design curricula, but their story reminds us that interiors can be dangerously overburdened with objects acquired in psychologically obsessive states, often hidden from view.

Rachel Lichtenstein and Iain Sinclair uncover the true story of one such hidden room, found in a London synagogue. Sealed for over a decade, the room was discovered filled with personal effects. The artifacts revealed clues to the life of its previous resident, David Rodinsky. The discovery led Lichtenstein on an extended journey from London to North America, Eastern Europe, and the Middle East in search of a private life memorialized in possessions and scraps of paper.

After Lichtenstein and Sinclair heard of his disappearance, they began to investigate Rodinsky. Traces left in his room provided a complete picture of his home, as if he had just stepped out. The authors describe a room that resembled a Dutch still life painting, with photographs, papers, and books strewn alongside glass bottles and newspapers piled on a table. A closer look revealed a possible obsession that went beyond ordinary collecting. Lichtenstein discovered pencil marks on piano keys and handwriting on peeling wallpaper. The two authors used measurements determined from his clothing to estimate his height and compare it to the low-ceilinged room he occupied. Over time, his possessions were turned inside-out to discover what happened to Rodinsky and why his room was left intact.

Excerpted from *Rodinsky's Room* (London: Granta Books, 1999), 3–5, 22–23, 26–35, 256–57.

Looking for the origins of Rodinsky's possessions brings to light the cir-cuitous path taken by those archeologists of his interior—to link interior and exterior through time and place. The story of Rodinsky's room can be extended in a logical trajectory that suggests that inhabitation as well as its absence is established through transitory routes from one place to another.

———

Rachel Lichtenstein in Place, Iain Sinclair

"Did you see the black coat? A zaddik.
They can make themselves invisible I've heard."
—David Hartnett, *Black Milk*

A young Englishwoman, heavily pregnant, is admitted to the office suite of a New York literary agent. She endures all the usual status games with an amused sense of being in an over-rehearsed play: the long wait in the outer chamber, the low chair that leaves her staring across a shimmering meadow of carpet at the big desk, the gilded blitz of family photographs. 'So, you got twenty minutes. A *frummer* in the attic, he disappears. Who should care? Where's the story?' She laughs, delivers her pitch. She's told it before, often, but it always has the same effect. Rachel becomes the thing she is talk-ing about. He listens. (In the film version you could freeze-frame the cigar smoke.) It's a performance and it's true. Rachel Lichtenstein *is* the story, a mad quest to discover all that is to be known about a synagogue caretaker, a Talmudic scholar, a holy fool; a man who invented himself through his disap-pearance. A simpleton who achieved competence in half a dozen languages, alive and dead. A sink-school dropout who made translations from the cune-iform texts of the Fertile Delta. A penniless haunter of cafés. A city wanderer who assembled a library that filled more than fifty cases. Rodinsky was a shape whose only definition was its shapelessness, the lack of a firm outline. The more documentation Rachel could file, the more artefacts she could photograph and label, the more elusive this fiction, David Rodinsky, became. She improvised with all the required roles: private detective, archaeologist, curator, ghost-writer, ventriloquial deliverer of Rodinsky's voice and art. She realized, with a proper sense of dread, that the business of her life, this stretch of it, was to complete whatever it was that Rodinsky had begun: to pass beyond ego, and all the dusty particulars of place and time, into a paral-lel state. Disincarnate. Unbodied. Eternally present.

There was something mesmeric, possessed, in the way Rachel told her tale. Agents, editors, patrons were instantly persuaded by the pas-sion in that calm, reasonable, Esturine voice. They were dazzled by the wide-set, almond-shaped eyes. Fixed, burning. The young woman with the careful *maquillage* had arrived for this meeting, unflustered, at the very last moment. What she is describing is happening *now,* on the instant. The past is adapted, absorbed. She seems to have witnessed events that occurred long before her birth. Like the best detective stories, her narrative is broken into not-quite-resolved episodes. Hooks, cliff-hangers. Telephone calls from the officially dead. Recently found evidence that contradicts all that has gone before. There are no comfortable assumptions to be made. They *had* to know how it turned out, this tale that began with a sealed room in a deactivated Spitalfields synagogue, and moved out to the eastern borders of Poland and the Ukraine, to New York, Israel, Toronto. The factual and the fabulous met in riotous conjunction. Shallow-breathed whispers from ancient relatives. Internet connections. Death certificates. Numerous fragments that composed an unreliable biography. The man became intimately associated with the place, the dissolution of the Jewish ghetto. There was even, if you wanted to find it, a conspiracy of sorts. Vested interests who preferred to keep the wretched caretaker buried in the files. Files that had long since been lost or destroyed. Rodinsky's life was pressed into legend. It belonged at the end of an era, before memories became memorial plaques. An abandoned room contained all that was left of a man's life and Rachel Lichtenstein understood that it was her task, nobody else could do it, to live that life again, and to complete it. Find some resolution or lose herself forever in the attempt. That was her joy. That was her burden. That was what terrified and excited the men to whom she made her pitch.

The Princelet Street Synagogue, Rachel Lichtenstein

The moment I entered 19 Princelet Street I knew I was meant to be there. When I spoke with my father about the building later that night, he told me my grandparents had their first marital home and ran a watchmaking shop at 32 Princelet Street. He supposed they had been married in the synagogue. These revelations only fuelled my desire to spend time in the building. After numerous telephone calls I managed to track down Donald Chesworth, the chairman of the project. We met, a week after my first visit; by then I had an over-ambitious proposal to become artist-in-residence at Princelet Street. This would involve running guided tours of the area and the building; conducting educational events with just about every section of the community imaginable; archiving and cataloguing the entire museum collection; organizing and curating historical and artistic exhibitions; and, in my spare time, producing my own art work. Mr. Chesworth was very supportive of my plan and presented the proposal to the Heritage Centre committee. It was accepted. I was to become the unpaid artist-in-residence. On completing my degree that summer I moved to London and found a flat in Brady

Street, Whitechapel. I took up my new post, beginning with an exhibition of my own work [....]

I soon abandoned my desire to make sculpture in the synagogue as the building left me in a state of artistic paralysis. Its aesthetic richness and history were overwhelming, there was little I could do to compete with it. I sat alone in silent admiration on the empty wooden benches, visually saturated by the scene before me: twisted brass chandeliers against a backdrop of golden hand-painted Hebrew names, sepia-stained plaster walls framed by dusty velvet drapes, lit with a soft pink hue from the stained-glass roof.

Once a month or so the building would be hired out to film crews eager to take advantage of the unique setting. A major part of my time in residence was spent arguing with these crews. I would skulk around in the shadows of the women's balcony, watching their every move below, shouting out furiously as I spotted a set designer about to paint the ark a different colour so he could get the right shot, wincing inside as I heard the shattering of the glass lamps on the *bimah* as a cameraman carelessly backed into them. I took over what I thought of as Rodinsky's role, becoming the unpaid caretaker of the Princelet Street synagogue, fiercely defending its fragile construction.

Unable to produce my own work I became increasingly drawn to Rodinsky's room. It no longer existed in its original state, as an abandoned tomb. The room had been dismantled, the contents boxed up by the Museum of London, then taken to storage rooms to dry out in stable conditions before being returned to the synagogue. When I first saw the room, Rodinsky's belongings were neatly piled away in archival boxes lining the walls in large stacks. At first, outside the boxes, the room seemed to contain little evidence of Rodinsky's long time in residence. But gradually I began to uncover the clues. I found his old gramophone records lying under the bed, and a large collection of dust-covered empty beer bottles in a cupboard in the corner. Stiffened pyjamas and fossilized blankets still remained in his wardrobe. While fondling his piano one day, I lifted the lid to discover faint traces of pencil on the ivory keys: strange indecipherable symbols, written in his own hand. In the centre of the wooden ceiling was a rusty gas lamp, surrounded by a charcoal halo from constant use. The peeling wallpaper behind the door had also been marked, with faint traces of handwriting hidden beneath the sodden edges. The floorboards were bent and cracked next to the enamel sink where I presumed he had washed every day [Fig. 8.20]

His table stood in the centre of the room, covered in a green baize cloth, and it was here that I would perform my daily ritual of excavating his remains. Wearing protective cotton gloves. I would slowly remove his belongings from their archival boxes, gently unveiling them from their

Fig. 8.20: Rodinsky's Room. Photo credit: John Freeman and courtesy of the John Freeman and 19 Princelet Street Charity

acid-free wrappings, before photographing each one and attempting to define and catalogue it.

At first this seemingly arbitrary archaeology revealed little, the objects appearing mute with the loss of their originator's voice to explain them. I spent countless hours in his room. Heaps of inaccessible, rotting material piled up around me. Most of the languages in which he wrote I could not read. A large amount of Rodinsky's clothes, saucepans, shoes and other personal items were thrown away. I arrived one day to find them bagged up on the street, and sneaked them back upstairs.

More often than not the cold, or the overwhelming sensation of being watched, would drive me out of the room, with the hairs on the back of my neck prickling. But every day I would be back at the table, fascination overcoming fear. Gradually, over time, through careful examination of his vast collection, a faint image of a man began to emerge: a scholar harbouring secrets, a meticulous annotator of texts, a comedian, an enigma.

I discovered handwritten notebooks revealing his knowledge of languages—Sumerian, Arabic, Japanese, Hebrew, Yiddish, Greek and Russian—and of Egyptian hieroglyphics. I found an old rent book that dated back to 1936. There were foreign travel books, though I doubted somehow that Rodinsky ever visited these places. I found one notebook full of Irish drinking songs written in thick red capital letters, and I discovered a crumpled cabbalistic diagram stashed behind his wardrobe.

There were other scraps of evidence suggesting he had been orthodox in his beliefs: the kosher food packets, the religious books, the battery-operated razor, the shopping list for Shabbat: 'two challahs, candles, meat, six eggs, *kiddush* wine'. I unwrapped hundreds of artefacts, thousands of small scraps of paper covered in coded messages, in different languages, by his own hand. On the backs of chocolate wrappers, inserted inside his diaries and books, were hand-drawn maps, indications of journeys around London, from Hainault to Chigwell, Clapton to Hendon, with no clues as to who he was seeing or what the visits were about. At first I was convinced he lived alone, but bits of evidence kept cropping up suggesting he had shared the room with other family members. I found an envelope addressed to a Mrs. C. Rodinsky, his mother maybe, postmarked 'Essex January 1961'. And another, sad letter from St. Clement's Hospital social services department concerning the death of his sister, Bessie Rodinsky. It required him to come and collect her possessions, 'one pair of gold earrings'. He had scrawled over the type in red ink the words 'diabolical concentration camp'.

I decided to take Bill Fishman's advice to visit the local history department of the Bishopsgate library. I wanted to know what the room had looked like when it was first opened up. Bill had told me to ask for David Webb, the chief librarian, which I did on my arrival. A small, greasy-haired bespectacled man appeared behind the tall mahogany desk. I asked if he had any information on the Princelet Street synagogue. He told me he often had people coming to the library with that request, furious that they were unable to gain access to the building. He knew of a number of demonic attempts over the years to enter the abandoned room, with people banging on the door for hours and journalists throwing bricks through the window. A few years ago, he thought, the whole story had reached a level of hysteria, when there were claims that the first person into the room tripped over a mummified cat. He thought that in another fifty years the story would become as misrepresented an urban myth as Dirty Dick. 'It'll be on the stop of every tour guide, with tales of ever-increasing exaggeration.' He scurried off into the back, returning with a large blue folder full of newspaper clippings. I settled myself into a secluded corner of the room and devoured the information before me.

There were a number of articles concerning Rodinsky's room. The *East London Advertiser* described one visit under the headline:

SECRET OF THE LOST ROOM:
Workmen refurbishing one of Spitalfields' historic buildings have revealed a twenty-year-old secret. They have uncovered a lost room in the weaver's attic on Princelet Street. The room was the home of a reclusive Polish Jew called Michael Rodinsky. He was a self-taught language fanatic who spent lonely days studying ancient dialects. His huge collection of dictionaries has been found in his room. So have his spectacles

and a weighing machine ticket that he used as a bookmark. But suddenly in 1969 he disappeared. Rodinsky's room has remained untouched ever since, changed only by a thick covering of dust. To this day no one knows what became of him.

I found various other articles, all more or less telling the same story: a David or Michael Rodinsky, of Polish or Russian origin, mysteriously disappeared from his attic room in 19 Princelet Street some time in the late Sixties [....]

And then I found what I had been longing to set eyes on: photographs of Rodinsky's room when it was first opened. They were fantastically seductive, beautifully lit and composed, fulfilling every element of my romantic fantasy of what the room must have looked like. There was an image by Danny Gralton, in a newspaper article, that particularly excited me. It showed Rodinsky's table in exactly the same situation as it still stood, covered in the same green baize cloth I had been working on only hours before. The table was piled high with books and papers, giving the room the appearance of the scholar's garret that I imagined it to have been. Behind his table I could see his wardrobe, full of clothes, and I spotted an enamel wash bowl resting on the sideboard. It looked like the same bowl I had managed to rescue from the street when someone had tried to throw some of Rodinsky's belongings into the skip. There was another beautiful photograph in the book *The Saving of Spitalfields*. The caption read: 'Rodinsky's room as revealed when the Trust opened the door for the first time since his mysterious disappearance twenty years earlier, photograph by Danny Gralton.' The image was serene, carefully composed like a Vermeer painting, with a tactile quality that made the viewer want to reach out and touch the wallpaper so seductively dripping off the walls, that made the viewer gaze in wonder at the headline on a newspaper on the table, ISRAEL REBORN, perfectly positioned in the foreground. The light from the weaver's windows falling on the book-laden table added to the feeling that one was looking at an old Dutch masterpiece. It was easy to see why the story, backed up with these perfect pictures, had attracted so much curiosity back in the early Eighties. I was drawn further into the Rodinsky web.

The last article I came across revealed a more sceptical point of view. It was a piece in the *Guardian*, by Iain Sinclair, entitled 'The Man Who Became a Room.'

Patrick Wright alerted me to a fable that is acquiring great potency in the amoebic principality of Spitalfields—the myth of the disappearance of David Rodinsky. Rodinsky, a Polish Jew from Piotsk or Lublin or wherever, was the caretaker and resident poltergeist of the Princelet

Street synagogue: an indistinguishable *chevra* without the funds to keep a scholar-in-residence. He perched under the eaves, a crow, unremarked and unremarkable—until that day in the early Sixties when he achieved the great work and became invisible. It is uncertain how many weeks or years passed before anyone noticed his absence. He had evaporated, and would remain as dust, his name unspoken, to be resurrected only as a feature, a necessary selling point, to put alongside Nicholas Hawksmoor in the occult fabulation of the zone that the Eighties demanded to justify a vertiginous inflation in property values.

The legend had escaped and the street doors were padlocked behind it; the windows were sealed in plasterboard, painted versions of themselves. Rodinsky's room was left as he abandoned it: books on the table, rug flung from the bed, cheap calendar with the reproduction of Millet's *Angelus* fixed forever at January 1963.

The newcomers, salivating over an excavated *fricassée* of chicken, followed by smoked collops and green flummery, had discovered a quaint little myth of their own, without blood and entrails, a Vanishing Jew. They fell upon it, like a wood-panelled stairwell or a weaver's bobbin. The synagogue, complete with dark secret, passed rapidly into the hands of the Spitalfields Heritage Centre—where it is now possible, with the aid of a good torch, to climb the damaged staircase and by confronting the room, discover the man.

On August 2 1957, Rodinsky weighed 12 stone 12 pounds: he preserved the weighing machine ticket as a bookmark. His height, to judge from the jackets hanging in the wardrobe, would be about 5 foot 9 inches—which put the ceiling less than a foot above his head. He wore spectacles: the empty cases are inscribed with his name. And though his clothing was drab he favoured exuberant Kenneth More–style paisley cravats or even a glittering gold-painted tie: soberly putting on the Ritz. Perhaps not too soberly—the chest of drawers is decorated with enough empty Wincarnis bottles to support an all-night session of Harold Wilson's kitchen cabinet. The inner man found solace at the piano or the gramophone, with a collection of 78s that ranged from D'une Prison to Ol' Man River. Newspapers were trusted friends, never to be turned out: DUKE'S GUARDED THE HONEYMOON, 1923; 72 YEAR OLD WOMAN TIED TO A CHAIR, 1932. The headlines never change. All stars are swallowed by the Sun.

But if Rodinsky did not simply walk out, fade into another social identity, or fall victim to some arbitrary cancellation by violence, then the search for his secret would begin with the books and diaries. The obsession with language as code: dictionaries and primers in Hebrew, Russian, French, Ancient Middle Eastern texts. As the room itself had been converted from a refuge to a shrine so Rodinsky translated a Letts Schoolgirl's diary to his own system of universal time and language—moving through Julian, Georgian and Armenian versions, breaking from Indian to Latin to Sumerian markings. The work ceases only with his disappearance. 'KI-BI-MA...SPEAK!' 'by he she/aren't so not take' is the final entry.

The irrelevant details pile up and the man begins to fade. He does not go away, that was unnecessary. There is still so much of him here that he no longer needs to be present in any other form. The room, as he left it, has gone and will never return: Rodinsky is what remains, a museum of ephemera and dust-breath. A trap. He converted himself into these shards, tempting to carry them off, so that his work is continued. The ruin is immortal.

Visitors, Iain Sinclair

Rodinsky's room was the module through which an important narrative of immigrant life, hardship and scholarship, would be recovered. I wasn't qualified to hunt down the human story, that would be the task of someone even crazier than I was, someone capable of handling bureaucratic obfuscation, working the files, spending days chasing dead ends on a hot telephone; travelling like a spy, winning the sympathy of fragile family connections. Someone who belonged here by birthright. Someone who could read the history of the room as an analogue of their own undisclosed heritage.

It was the room, the set, that obsessed me. Millet's *Angelus* calendar like a secondary Surrealist window, a window on the inside of the inside. A window that opened, in cartoon form, on to a landscape of peasant piety. What possible significance could this image have for David Rodinsky? Salvador Dali, in *Le Mythe tragique de L'Angélus de Millet,* was happy to comb the dim painting for transgressive fetishes and talismans: the pitchfork that becomes a crutch. But Rodinsky's Millet, found in large and small versions, was one item from a catalogue of astonishingly disparate objects. The notebooks and papers of the secret scholar, the old 78s, the cigarette packets, the bottles, the chunky tweed jackets, so hairy that they appeared to be still growing. It was difficult to believe all this belonged to one person. The man himself, as far as I was concerned, had to be taken on trust. He was as remote as a character from Leo Perutz's Prague stories *By Night under the Stone Bridge*, or from Gustav Meyrink's *The Golem*. My attitude towards the room at the top of this forgotten building was unforgivably predatory. Cheesy romanticism was only the latest outrage in a long chain of exploitation. I wanted to bring outsiders here, writers and painters whose work I admired, or simply those with an interest in the hidden attics and subterranea of the city. I would construct a picture from bounced light. By seeing how the room affected other people, I would perhaps discover what it meant to me.

Of the Hollow Spaces in the Skin of the Architectural Body

Wolfgang Meisenheimer

INTRODUCTION

Poché occupies a threshold between interior and exterior. Its dimensional thickness and material convey different experiences trackable over time as wall sections, influenced by technology and culture, evolve. In the following essay, architect and author Wolfgang Meisenheimer considers poché and material composition in cultural forms of occupation. At a time when technology results in thinner and thinner wall sections, Meisenheimer reminds us that there is both history and poetry embedded in a thick wall. He identifies where poché has all but disappeared through thin materials dissolving mass into transparency. He returns to thickness to remind us of the curiosity of poché merging with program, whether as niches, built-in bookcases, or chambers. He describes these interstitial spaces as "conversational zones," where both sides of a wall meet in dialogue.* Neglecting these common walls results in forgetting how a wall and its threshold can be occupied.

Meisenheimer also reveals how thin wall sections offer transparency and reconstructed views that bond interior to landscape. But despite the transparency, it becomes evident that mechanical systems are needed to resolve issues like regulating air temperature for bodily comfort. He offers additional examples of thick walls from historical sources and a range of cultures to remind us of how walls mediate the zone between exterior and the interior, helping negotiate the relationship of mass to void.

Given multiple layers of organized material that serve the life within, Meisenheimer's proposal comparing architecture and body invariably draws on the analogy of clothing as a secondary wrapper for both body and building. This comparison and the image of the poché as possessing two skins— interior and exterior, separated by elements embedded in the thickness between them—recalls the meaning of the original French. Just as clothing acts as a secondary layer of protection on the body, the architectural poché interprets the wall as a place of cushioning inhabitation that protects the core

Originally appeared in *Daidalos*, no. 13 (1984): 103–11.

interior of architecture. The crossing of a threshold, where entry and invitation are offered and interior and exterior are felt, reveals the continuity and discontinuity of a spatial wrapper.

———

THE SURROUNDING SPACE outside the building-covering, the interior, which it surrounds, and thirdly the body of the building itself with its interior and exterior relief, its hollow spaces, niches, and projections—these three zones have three different spatial qualities for us to experience. The surrounding space, which is perceived from the interior of the building as the "space outside," is experienced outside as a continuous spatial area rather, into which the buildings themselves appear to have been set. We imagine it as being "occupied" only at particular places, but nevertheless it is these places which give it its structure as artificial, formed space. For the rest it is identified with Nature's all-embracing, pre-given space, against which it stands out only in the vicinity of the building. Thus we see the building penetrated and filled with the topographical structures of the earth as well as with the atmospheric effects of air and light. Natural things as well as artefacts, mountains, trees, and rivers as well as houses, vehicles, and streets appear to be placed in the continuous flow of the atmosphere. This space is conceived of as being unending, even though it seems limited to various degrees all around us, while from above offering an open, limitless expanse.

By contrast the interior is experienced as another kind of spatial quality. It is closed in all around, it ends with the surface of the material, which more or less surrounds it on all sides. Interiors are experienced as the real containers of the immediately adjacent living space. It is above all for the sake of the interiors that architecture has been made now for thousands of years. Their peculiar characteristic is precisely the fact that they close us in. Yet their reality, which is so very suggestive of a wholeness around our body, exists only in our imagination, for we see and hear only varying fragments of them and they are not in the least palpable as "interiors."

Finally the body of the building structure, its material mass, gives form to both of these so very different spatial qualities by virtue of the surface-relief both within and without. The space-bestriding, space-moulding expression of the building-mass is completely and utterly tied to the formed material, which not only extends in three dimensions like geometrical volumes, but challenges all our senses, physically, standing in a relationship to our body. Thus the spatial quality of the "work body" (Rudolf Schwarz) is neither that of an imaginary, infinite structure nor that of a negative, freely enterable body. The building, a material workpiece concretely manufactured with all its interfoldings and projections, crevices and openings, is comprehended as the reproduction of the most concrete of all realities: that of our body and this even prior to all "under-standing" of the architectonic language. To experience the body of the building is like experiencing the physical body as a spatial entity—what is so fascinating is that we can draw close to the work body even from within.

Thus the body of the building has a crust, a zone where inside and outside meet, a zone of contradiction. This is where qualities of experience tip over into each other or out of each other, it especially is a fixed point for our experiences of space. This zone might be called the "conversational zone" of the architectonic language, in which the demands of the environment are accepted or rejected, in which decisions are made as regards entering or not entering, in which one behaves in an exacting manner or with reserve, hurriedly or with due thought and reflection. Here the hesitation before the appearance assumes meaning. Last but not least, the openness of the decisions to be taken makes this border-area into the most eloquent backdrop of the architectonic stage.

In early modern architecture quite specific qualities of this protective zone were neglected, above all those which have to do with physical-spatial plasticity. Stimulated by the technological euphoria of early Functionalism, an ever-increasing number of such load-bearing members gained acceptance as could dispense with all but a minimum of material. The thick covering of the body of the building was well-nigh systematically reduced, skeleton con-struction was preferred to massive construction. Something approaching an "ideology of thin skin" made the disappearance of the threshold between inside and outside seem meaningful, desirable, even imperative—a most curi-ous reversal. The broad expanse of natural landscape was to penetrate into the interior of the cities and also of the houses, the limits of the building were to dissolve away. The predominant spatial conceptions of the young Le Corbusier, for example, establish topological structures which are rather determined by field-effects than by the effects of closed space. Places of particular signifi-cance occupy an "unending" space, imagined as being continuous; the associ-ated urban area runs through the zone of the *pilotis* into the ground floor of the houses; the floor-surface, together with fixtures and partition-walls, gives the appearance of homogeneity. It goes without saying that the strict minimalis-ing of the material expenditure also had an economic aspect: building with ele-ments under industrial conditions signifies thin walls. The "work body" lost its flesh. The protective zone of the building-body was thinned out to the extent that it became a membrane between air-conditioned and non-air-conditioned space. But that had negative consequences as well as positive ones, and not only in technical respects.

Just the design-maxim that it must be possible to tell the shape of the interior from without (a strictly functionalistic, ascetically technical atti-tude) has led to an unbelievable loss of formal qualities. As late as 1960 Max Taut could write: "The unity of the exterior with the interior is the highest goal that we can possibly reach. At that point we also no longer need to talk about beauty any more, for that has become a matter of course." The "superfluous" recesses and projections, the cavities of the skin, the coat-pockets of the building-body, were lost in this ideology. Fanatics of the thin skin were all too quick in renouncing the charm of deep jambs, of staggered thresholds, of anterooms and "sluices," of niches in the wall and seats by the window…

I would like to term these cavities in the outer frame of the building interiors of the second order. Though they are subordinated to the main figures of the ground-plan, it is precisely they that bring nuance to the transitions from outside to inside, these fertile "zones of doubt." Now that a primarily engineering viewpoint has been superseded by a lively interest in a nuance-laden designing of closed spaces, this is a chance to go beyond classical modern architecture.

One need only look at the astonishing results of research into the culturally determined aspects of human behaviour in rooms and spaces! For example the sensitivity of the German and the Dutchman in stepping over a threshold: the person entering is obliged to give an account of himself, is initially perceived as an intruder. But in the cultural area of middle-class North Americans that person is still not accepted even when he is inside the house. Whereas in Central Europe it is absolutely essential for a door to be closed and kept under surveillance, in the USA it can stand open, the area associated with it does not yet belong to the interior of the room. For us in Germany to articulate the spatial sense of well-being we need clear, differentiated entrances, for which the visitor must come suitably prepared. That gives a special importance to the house doors, anterooms, and hallways, to porches and "cluices." The visitor does not "fall" into the house with the door; rather he wishes to loiter in the adjoining area. It is here that the curiosity-game of expectation and disappointment is enacted; the other person comes to meet (or accompanies) the visitor as far as this point, or does not, as the case may be. Good architecture utilises the door-area to offer a scene for the contradictory meeting, to provide room for cultivated doubt. Thus it might be said that it is above all on the periphery of the building-body that architectural statements as to our cultural identity are expected. It would seem that in Europe the covering around the interior, closed and capable of being opened only by means of careful ceremonial, is understood as an image of an intact psychic gestalt, perhaps even of the integrity of the self. A typology of spatial behaviour would reveal how very much the game of attention in Central and Northern Europe requires subtly differentiated transitions. Before the actual entry into the interior of a space we need to linger for a moment. When we step out into the open we wish still to feel the protection of the house for an instant. Even before they have learnt to walk, babies play games for month on end that probe into the curiosity-zone around the threshold, half protected, half exposed. Similarly the elderly used to love their seat at the window's jamb (as long as it existed), from which point the outer world can be seen and observed, but which belongs to the territory of the interior. For many of these situations between inside and out we need such interiors of the second order, our "coat-pockets."

Let us enquire into the syntax of this spatial type. Thick outer walls are no longer necessary for constructive reasons, but for psychological ones as can be seen. Thus, we will be interested in simulating thick outer walls, the plastic styling of a distinctly noticeable spatial coat. Heavy materials will be welcome, massive construction in this connection. The deep recessing of the inner faces, the hollowing out of the outer wall as body, and the placing of the façades behind each other are welcome means. A glance into the "history of the bodily aspect" of building structures reveals the abundance of possibilities for utilizing the openings and hollow chambers of the skin, for stylising them and fitting them into the architectonic language.

Let us first cast a glance over the ruins of the Baths of Caracalla. Even today it is possible for us to follow the twofold execution of the architecture. While the huge spaces in the middle form figures which are held together by impassioned gestures, figures which once served the basic function of these baths—the meeting of acceptable society on a semi-public stage—, the interior of the masonry provides an abundance of chambers, passageways, corridors, and niches for secondary purposes. From here people were served, observed, watched over, and shadowed. This was where people left their clothes behind, their food and gear, this was where people retired to eat, to sleep, to make love, and to read. Likewise, when we scrutinise the centres of mediaeval fortresses and castles, we discover hidden chambers, niches and narrow exits, secret stairs and anterooms, channels and storerooms for things, for provisions, for the stuff of everyday. Even the rooms for the preparation and clearing away of food are there, sideboards, sinks, and sanitary closets, cells for personal hygiene with bathtubs, basins, and tanks; also secondary staircases and lift-niches, connecting corridors, weather-, noise-, and air-locks. In addition there are concealed seats by doors and windows, the galleries which formed part of the fortifications, the vaults for the animals and their feed. The load-bearing member is usually massive and thick in the extreme: from the engineering viewpoint out of all proportion. The hollow spaces are there, embedded in so much mystery, unfathomable, uncontrollable.

Another role is played by the niches, the gaps and pockets of space in the "speaking walls" of Islamic mosques, such as in the Friday Mosque in Tinmal. The ranks of Mohammed's warriors in prayer have a strict geometric order, turned to the wall with the "Mihrab" niche. In the mecca-coordinate it announces the World of God and determines the direction in which the shoulders of all the Faithful are set. Very often, as in the case of the Sultan Hassan Mosque in Cairo, the main entrances are set in "holy caves" or grottos with hanging honeycomb-like vaults (mukarnas), to recall this most important of all niches. The Ivane, huge mussel-shaped inlets in the building-mass that open onto the central inner courtyard (Sahn), can be understood as monumental forms of such "Paradise-niches." Thus the deep and shallow hollows of the protective zone become signs in architecture's symbolic language-area: they tell of the passage of worlds, of this world and the Beyond.

In Balthasar Neumann's court-church at Würzburg the plastic volume of the building body is determined by two different geometric schemes simultaneously. Seen from the outside it appears as a sharply-cut block, covered over with prismatic roof-styles; on the inside it reveals itself as a vibrant hollow-form, as a system of ovals in the ground plan, over which mutually penetrating baldachins tower. The interior of the work body, the volume between external and internal skin, contains a cavity above the vaults; this cavity holds the wooden constructions of the roof and makes them invisible. The lateral volume-sections are massive bodies of masonry of various thickness, interspersed with physically accessible "pockets of space," which create vantage-points for the viewer. They allow an unbroken view of the interior, but lie outside the baldachins. From there the spatial shells seem like freestanding tabernacles which appear to detach themselves from the covering of the outer walls. The enormous innerface recesses of the windows admit of a specially directed play of light which makes the beholder's every movement into a theatrical event. In an intensive alternation lateral light and shadows give rhythm to the spatial depth. The windows themselves are scarcely seen. That amidst such classic forms of Baroque the body of the edifice both without and within is organised according to *varying* geometric structures—precisely this is so breathtaking for the visitor entering the building. The surprise is successful: cavities appear in the crystal, in the midst of predictability spatial illusions appear; in daily life pictures of the Beyong become manifest.

With the beginning of the Functionalism of early modern architecture the heavy coat of the building-body comes to appear as an encumbrance. The opposite—extremely thin separations of interior from exterior, curtaining façades, light skin—veils the "enclosed area" over thousands of square metres—at least since the post-war reconstruction era and its passion for things big. Nonetheless in the search for observers in that artificial cavity, "the interior," some of the doyens recalled time and again the secrets of the double outer wall—to the surprise and sometimes to the mortification of representatives of minimalistic architecture. In his church in Ronchamps, for example, the later Le Corbusier begins an illusionistic theatrical play with light and our feeling for heaviness: he discovers a coating-body of monumental proportions, one such as gives form to space both inwards and outwards, although it is hardly palpable as a load-bearing body: a hollow body draped around a skeleton structure. Beneath the Indian sun Louis Kahn staggers non-identical facades in a row like pieces of scenery, light-filters with histrionic gestures. His profoundly enigmatic design for the Hurva Synagogue in Jerusalem (1968) is much more far-reaching in its consequences. A ring of outer candle-niches envelops a group of galleries, concrete baldachins, including "chambers of contemplation," which are, for their part, placed in an umbrella-formation around the Holy of Holies: space-shells around space-shells, as "event filters," a most subtle preparation for a precious interior.

But I see how this instrument of planning performs its proper function. In my own work I have endeavoured to frame main rooms with side rooms in the thick coat of the building-body; living spaces with lockable bookcases, work rooms with bed- and cupboard-niches, kitchen and play-area with storerooms for things. The result is rooms of differing atmosphere and usefulness. Even in experimental designs from the orbit of Post-modernist invention it can happen that "interiors of the second order" can once more play an important role: when processes of collage involve spatial groups, axes, and grids being tilted at angles to each other and telescoped, so that fragments of space, packing, surface-remnants remain left behind between the main figures of the ground plan and can thus be used by the attendant services.

All these examples—Baths of Caracalla, Friday Mosque, Würzburg court church, Hurva-Synagogue—even a number of fragmented works of the most recent trends of modern architecture—draw their life from the subtly diversified language of their twofold, threefold hidden coverings. While the primary interior spaces fulfill central functions of representation, the hollow spaces and gaps, the slits and holes of the skin provide accompanying services. They prepare us and put us in the right state of mind, they endow the main text with special significance and emphases by the very act of their framing it.

Be that as it may, the implied differentiation of the interior assumes an appropriate significance only when dominant and subordinate patterns of action (functions) as well as dominant and attendant spatial forms are related to each other analogously. Otherwise there would be Babel. (Perhaps in the history of architecture such counter-examples are already at hand in the context of mannerism: the subordinate spaces of the coat-zone would have the main functions assigned them. In the vocabulary of a new "speaking" architecture the intended dualism of the interiors of the first and second order could play a clarifying role, as a restful and enhancing influence on the feeling for space.

Notes

* Wolfgang Meisenheimer, "Of the Hollow Spaces in the Skin of the Architectural Body," *Daidalos* 13 (1984): 103.

Biographies

Kobo Abé was born in Tokyo in 1924 and grew up in Mukden, Manchuria. As a young man, Abé was interested in the works of Poe, Dostoevsky, Nietzsche, Heidegger, Jaspers, and Kafka. He is the author of several books, including *The Crime of Mr. S. Karuma* (1951), for which he received the most important Japanese literary prize, the Akutagawa. His book *The Woman in the Dunes* (1962) won the Yomiuri Prize for Literature. It was made into a film by Hiroshi Teshigahara in 1963 and won the Jury Prize at the Cannes Film Festival.

David Batchelor is Senior Lecturer in Critical Theory at the Royal College of Art, London. He has written and edited a number of books, including *Chromophobia* (2000) and *Minimalism* (1997), and is editor of *Colour* (2008). He has contributed to a number of journals, including *Artscribe*, *Frieze*, and *Artforum*. He has exhibited widely in the UK, Europe, the United States, and Latin America. He was a member of the Tate Britain Council from 2002–2005, an advisory body on development and programming at Tate Britain. Two of his works are held in the collection of the Tate.

Catherine Bédard is an art historian, curator, and specialist of contemporary Canadian art. As Deputy Director of the Canadian Cultural Centre in Paris, she has been running its exhibition program since 1993. She created The Esplanade Collection, a series of books that highlight the works of contemporary Canadian artists. She is the author of approximately fifty exhibition catalogs and has contributed many articles to collective publications. Since 2010, she has taught at the Université Paris III-Sorbonne Nouvelle.

Aaron Betsky is Director of the Cincinnati Art Museum. He is a former professor with the School of Architecture and Interior Design (now DAAP) at the University of Cincinnati, and he continues teaching and lecturing in the United States and abroad. Most recently he has taught architecture at the University of Michigan and the University of Kentucky in Lexington. Betsky's leadership of major institutions in the world of art and architecture includes serving as the Director of the Netherlands Architecture Institute in Rotterdam, the Curator of Architecture and Design of the San Francisco Museum of Modern Art, and the Artistic Director of the 11th International Architecture Biennale Venice, Italy, in 2008.

Petra Blaisse started her career at the Stedelijk Museum in Amsterdam, in the Department of Applied Arts. From 1987, she worked as a freelance designer and won distinction for her installations of architectural work. Gradually her focus shifted to the use of textiles, light, and finishes in interior space and to the design of gardens and land-scapes. In 1991, she founded Inside Outside. The studio works in a multitude of creative areas and across disciplines, including textile, landscape, and exhibition design.

Andrew Blauvelt is a designer, writer, and educa-tor. He has organized exhibitions and publications on a range of topics, from the use of commonplace materials and quotidian rituals in contemporary design to the changing nature of the American suburban landscape, for the Walker Art Center in Minneapolis, where he is Curator of Architecture and Design. He writes about design from a wider cultural perspective for a variety of publications and is a contributing writer to DesignObserver.com. A graduate of Cranbrook Academy of Art, Blauvelt is a practicing communications designer whose work has won numerous awards and has been exhibited and published worldwide.

Celeste Brusati is Professor of History of Art and Art & Design at the University of Michigan. She is the author of *Artifice and Illusion: The Art and Writing of Samuel van Hoogstraten* (1995), *Johannes Vermeer* (1993), and articles on still life, self-imagery, perspective, illusionism, and relations between visual and literary discourses on art in the Netherlands. She is co-editor, with Walter Melion and Karl Enenkel, of *The Authority of the Word: Reflecting on Image and Text in Northern Europe, 1400–1800* (2011). Current projects include a book on fictions of seeing in Dutch art, and editing an English translation of Samuel van Hoogstraten's *Inleyding tot de hooge schoole der schilderkonst* for the Getty Research Center.

Suzanne Buchan, PhD, is Professor of Animation Aesthetics and Director of the Animation Research Centre at the University for the Creative Arts, England. Her research focuses on interdisciplinary approaches to animated media, curatorship, and spatial politics. She is founding Editor of *Animation: An Interdisciplinary Journal* and has published widely, including *The Quay Brothers: Into a Metaphysical Playroom* (2011) and "Oscillating at the 'high/low' Art Divide: Curating and Exhibiting Animation" in J. Rugg (ed.), *Issues in Curating, Contemporary Art and Performance* (2008). Other projects include a curatorial advisory role for the London Barbican's 2011 *Watch Me Move* animation exhibition and *Pervasive Animation*, an AFI anthology.

Jeanine Centuori is Director of the Center for Community Research and Design at Woodbury University in Los Angeles, whose mission is to connect students with architecture projects of a social and/or political nature. Primary issues include the examination of overlooked and marginalized public spaces in urban areas, and creative interpretations of the Americans with Disabilities Act. Projects have received grant funding, including the National Endowment for the Arts, and have received national level awards, including a PA award, and a Best of Category for Environments from *ID Magazine.* Centuori is also a principal of UrbanRock Design, a practice that explores architecture, public art, and policy.

Beatriz Colomina is Professor of Architecture and Founding Director of the Program in Media and Modernity at Princeton University. She is the author of *Domesticity at War* (2007), *Privacy and Publicity: Modern Architecture as Mass Media* (1994), and *Sexuality and Space* (1992), which was awarded the 1993 International Book Award by the American Institute of Architects. She co-edited the catalog of the exhibition, *Clip/Stamp/Fold: The Radical Architecture of Little Magazines 196X–197X* (2010), with Craig Buckley. Her current research project is "X-Ray Architecture: Illness as Metaphor."

Caroline Evans is Professor of Fashion History and Theory at Central Saint Martins College of Art and Design where she teaches and writes on twentieth-century and contemporary fashion. She is the author of *Fashion at the Edge: Spectacle, Modernity and Deathliness* (2003, 2007), and co-author of *The London Look: Fashion from Street to Catwalk* (2004), *Fashion & Modernity* (2005), *Hussein Chalayan* (2005), and *The House of Viktor & Rolf* (2008). She has been a consultant on exhibitions held at the Museum of London, MoMu,

Antwerp, Victoria & Albert Museum, London, the Musée Galliera de la Mode de la Ville de Paris, and Museu Tèxtil i d'Indumentària, Barcelona.

Robin Evans (1944–1993) was an architect, teacher, historian, and theoretician. He was a Visiting Professor at Harvard University, Lecturer at the University of Westminster, and Visiting Lecturer at the Architectural Association. His essays and reviews were published in journals including *Lotus*, *Casa Bella*, *Architectural Review,* and *AA Files*. Before his death he completed *The Projective Cast: Architecture and its Three Geometries* (1995). Evans looked at architectural history through representation from the Renaissance to post-modernity as a way to explore how space, perception, and imagination were conveyed. His writings provided first-hand experience, arriving at his insights from direct observation often through his own analytical drawings.

Helene Furján is an Assistant Professor in the Department of Architecture at the University of Pennsylvania, where she is Director and a founding editor of *viaBooks*, and Director of the *Conversations Series* of interdisciplinary debates. She recently published *'Glorious Visions': John Soane's Spectacular Theater* (2011), and has had essays and reviews published in journals including *Gray Room*, *AAFiles*, *Assemblage*, *Casabella*, *Journal of Architecture, JAE, Art Forum*, and *Interstices*. She published *Crib Sheets: Notes on the Contemporary Architectural Conversation* with Sylvia Lavin (2005), and has chapters in *Intimate Metropolis* (2008), *306090: Models* (2008), *Softspace* (2006), *Gen(H)ome* (2006), and *Performalism: Form and Function in Digital Architecture* (2008).

Diana Fuss is a Professor in the Department of English at Princeton University. She is the author of *Essentially Speaking* (1989), *Identification Papers* (1995), and *The Sense of an Interior: Four Writers and the Rooms that Shaped Them* (2004), which won the MLA James Russell Lowell Prize for outstanding scholarly book of the year in 2005. Over the years she has published on a variety of topics, from fashion photography to literary corpses. Fuss is a past recipient of NEH and ACLS Fellowship Awards, as well as a Guggenheim Fellowship. She received her PhD from Brown University in English and Semiotics.

Diana Gaston served as the Curator at the Museum of Photographic Arts in San Diego from 1993–1999, during which time she curated the traveling exhibition *Abelardo Morell and the Camera Eye*. She served as associate director of San Francisco Camerawork. She currently lives in Boston, where she is a curator for a corporate art collection.

Dan Graham is a conceptual artist working in New York. He is an influential figure in contemporary art, both as a practitioner of conceptual art and an art critic and theorist. Graham focuses on the relationship between his artwork and the viewer through his use of film, video, performance, photography, architectural models, and glass and mirror structures. His work is represented in the collections of numerous major institutions including Moderna Museet, Stockholm; Centre Pompidou, Paris; and Tate Gallery, London. He has had exhibitions at the Museum of Contemporary Art, Los Angeles; Whitney Museum of American Art, New York; The Museum of Modern Art, New York; and the Walker Art Center, Minneapolis.

Pablo Helguera is Director of Adult and Academic Programs of the Museum of Modern Art in New York. Originally from Mexico City, he is a visual and performance artist who has exhibited widely internationally. His works, which are usually performative in nature, have included making phonograph recordings, composing orchestral pieces, inventing fictional artists and museums, founding educational and research institutions, and writing scripted symposia with actors. He has performed or exhibited at the Museum of Modern Art, New York, the Royal College of Art, London, and the Havana Biennial. He is the author of five books and is a Guggenheim Fellow.

Anne Hollander is an independent art historian, critic, and historian of dress. A Fellow of the New York Institute for the Humanities and former President of PEN American Center, she is the author of *Fabric of Vision* (2002), *Feeding the Eye* (1999), *Sex and Suits* (1994), *Moving Pictures* (1989), and *Seeing through Clothes* (1978, 1993).

Steven Jacobs is an art historian specializing in the visualization of architecture, cities, and landscapes in film and photography. He has taught at several universities and art schools in Belgium and the Netherlands. His publications include *The Wrong House: The Architecture of Alfred Hitchcock* (2007), and *Framing Pictures: Film and the Visual Arts* (2011). As a member of the Ghent Urban Studies Team (GUST), he co-edited and co-authored *The Urban Condition: Space, Community, and Self in the Contemporary Metropolis* (1999) and *Post Ex Sub Dis: Urban Fragmentations and Constructions* (2002).

Jeffrey Kipnis is Professor of architectural design and theory at the Knowlton School of Architecture of The Ohio State University. His writings on art and architecture have appeared in *Harvard Design Magazine*, *2G*, *El Croquis*, *Art Forum*, and *Assemblage*. His books include *Choral Works: The Eisenman-Derrida Collaboration* (1997), *Perfect Acts of Architecture* (2002), *The Glass House* (1993) and his study of Stephen Holl's Bloch Addition to the Nelson Atkins Museum appears in his book, *Stone and Feather* (2007). As architecture and design curator for the Wexner Center for the Arts, he has organized a number of exhibitions on architecture, furniture, and graphics.

Kerstin Kraft is the first graduate "textile scientist" in Germany. She studied textile sciences at the Institut für Kulturanthropologie des Textilen at Dortmund University and history and art history at the Ruhr-Universität Bochum. Her curatorial work at museums includes topics in the culture and history of dress. She is a research fellow at the Institute of European Ethnology/cultural sciences at the Philipps-University Marburg. Kraft's research includes material culture, sources and methodology of dress studies, and basic textile phenomena like patterns, folding, and cutting.

Le Corbusier, born Charles-Édouard Jeanneret (1887–1965), was a Swiss architect, designer, and urbanist and was one of the pioneers of Modern architecture or the International style. Le Corbusier advocated the use of modern industrial techniques to transform society into a more efficient environment with a higher standard of living on all socioeconomic levels. His book *Vers une architecture* (1923) (*Towards a New Architecture*) was written in response to industrial changes and their application into architecture and design. These values can be found in his early works, such as the Villa Sovoye and furniture designs.

Rachel Lichtenstein is an artist, writer, oral historian, and curator. She is the author of *Rodinsky's*

Whitechapel (1999), *Keeping Pace* (2003), *A Little Dust Whispered* (2004), and co-author with Iain Sinclair of the highly praised *Rodinsky's Room* (1999) and *On Brick Lane* (2008), which was shortlisted for the Ondaatje Prize. Lichtenstein has exhibited her work internationally, including in venues such as The Whitechapel Gallery, The Tate Modern, The Barbican Art Gallery, The Victoria and Albert Museum, and The Jerusalem Theatre. In 2003 Lichtenstein became The British Library's first Creative Research Fellow. She is currently the Writer in Residence for Westminster University.

Ed Lilley retired from the History of Art Department at the University of Bristol in 2010. His chief research interest has been French art and art criticism of the eighteenth and nineteenth centuries, engendering studies of the Salon criticism of Stendhal, and of the late work of Jacques-Louis David. A more recent focus has been on the work of Edouard Manet and its reception, leading to an engagement with the history of fashion. A current project involves the meaning of Daumier's caricatures of Salon exhibits.

Adolf Loos (1870–1933) was an Austrio-Hungarian architect who contributed to the shaping of Modernist architecture and ideals in Europe through his built work and writings. He sought to educate people on Modern design through a series of essays that were later published as a collection in *Spoken into the Void* (1982). In his essays, Loos renounced the ornamental style of the Vienna Secession and expressed his opinion about the use of materials in his best-known essays, "The Principle of Cladding" and "Ornament and Crime." He implemented these ideals in built works that include Villa Müller in Prague, and in Vienna, the Steiner House, Rufer House, and Villa Moller.

Ellen Lupton is a writer, curator, and graphic designer. She is director of the Graphic Design MFA program at Maryland Institute College of Art (MICA) in Baltimore, where she also serves as director of the Center for Design Thinking. As curator of contemporary design at Cooper-Hewitt, National Design Museum since 1992, she has produced numerous exhibitions and books, including *Mechanical Brides: Women and Machines from Home to Office* (1993), *Mixing Messages: Graphic Design and Contemporary Culture* (1996), *Letters from the Avant-Garde* (1996), and *Skin: Surface, Substance + Design* (2002). Her book *Thinking with Type* (2004) is used by students, designers, and educators worldwide.

Robert McAnulty is a writer, architect, and educator. He has taught at Columbia University, Parsons The New School for Design, and more recently at the University of Illinois at Chicago and the School of the Art Institute of Chicago. Publications include essays in *Explorations: The Architecture of John Ronan* (2010), *Strategies in Architectural Thinking* (1992), and *Praxis: Journal of Writing + Building*. McAnulty served on the advisory/editorial board of *Assemblage*. He is a partner with Donna Robertson in *macro*, a design firm working in architecture, urban design, and research.

Wolfgang Meisenheimer, PhD, received his diploma from the Technische Hochschule Aachen and wrote his dissertation on "The space of architecture, structures, figures, and definitions." From 1978 until 1998 he was a professor at the University of Applied Sciences in Dusseldorf and Chair of Principles of Design in addition to serving as Dean of the Faculty of Architecture. During this time, he was a founder of *Ad-books*, a documentation of annual architectural theory seminars published by the University of Applied Sciences Dusseldorf and a co-editor of the journal *DAIDALOS* (Berlin). He is an independent architect in Düren.

Charlotte Mullins has written widely on contemporary art, architecture, design, and art history. Her books include *Painting People* (2008) and the monograph *Rachel Whiteread* (2004). She has served as a judge for the BP Portrait Award at the National Portrait Gallery and has been a selector for many exhibitions, including the Jerwood Sculpture Prize and the Hunting Art Prize. Mullins studied at the Courtauld Institute of Art and Sotheby's Institute in London and is currently completing her PhD at the University of Sussex and National Maritime Museum, London. She was previously the arts editor of the *Independent* and editor of *Art Review* and the *V&A Magazine*.

Juhani Pallasmaa, Architect SAFA, Hon. FAIA, Int FRIBA, has practiced architecture since the early 1960s and established Pallasmaa Architects in 1983. In addition to architectural design, he has been active in urban planning, exhibition, and product and graphic design. He has held positions as Professor and Dean at the Helsinki University of Technology, Director of the Museum of Finnish Architecture, and Rector of the Institute of Industrial Arts, Helsinki. Pallasmaa's books include: *The Embodied Image: Imagination and Imagery in Architecture* (2011), *The Thinking Hand: Embodied and Existential Wisdom in Architecture* (2009), *Encounters: Architectural Essays* (2005), and *The Eyes of the Skin: Architecture and the Senses* (1996, 2005).

Charlotte Perkins Gilman (1860–1935) was a prominent American writer of novels, short stories, poetry, nonfiction and a lecturer for social reform. She was a utopian feminist during a time when her accomplishments were exceptional for women, and she served as a role model for future generations of feminists because of her unorthodox concepts and lifestyle. She wrote "The Yellow Wallpaper," a semi-autobiographical short story after a severe bout of postpartum psychosis. In 1909 she founded and edited her own magazine, *The Forerunner*, which gave her a platform to express her views on feminism.

Witold Rybczynski, of Polish parentage, was born in Edinburgh, raised in London, and attended Jesuit schools in England and Canada. He has written fifteen books on subjects as varied as the evolution of comfort, a history of the weekend, American urbanism, the development of a new community, and a search for the origins of the screwdriver. *Home* (1987) has been translated into ten languages, and was nominated for a Governor General's Literary Prize, while *A Clearing in the Distance* (1999), a biography of Frederick Law Olmsted, received the J. Anthony Lukas Prize. His current book is *Makeshift Metropolis: Ideas about Cities* (2010).

Joel Sanders is an Associate Professor of Architecture at Yale University in addition to being the Principal of Joel Sanders Architect. He is dedicated to the creation of innovative environments in response to today's rapidly changing culture by combining teaching with practice, and speculative projects with built commissions. As the editor of *Stud: Architectures of Masculinity* (1996), he frequently writes about art and design. A monograph of his work, *Joel Sanders: Writings and Projects,* was published in 2005, and he will release *Groundwork: Between Landscape and Architecture*, with Diana Balmori, in 2011. Sanders received Bachelor of Architecture and Master of Architecture degrees from Columbia University.

Louise Schouwenberg studied psychology at the Radboud University Nijmegen, sculpture at the Gerrit Rietveld Academy in Amsterdam, and philosophy at the University of Amsterdam and the Erasmus University Rotterdam. After establishing her career as a visual artist, from 2000 onwards her primary focus has been on design theory. She has contributed to a range of publications, one of the latest being the monograph *Hella Jongerius–Misfit* (2010). Currently she leads the Masters research programme Contextual Design of Design Academy Eindhoven (DAE). In 2010 she was appointed Lector (Professor) Design Theory at DAE.

Catherine Scott-Clark and **Adrian Levy** are authors and journalists, occasional broadcasters, and filmmakers. They currently write for *The Guardian* and worked for many years as foreign correspondents in Asia for *The Sunday Times*. Their documentary work has been screened by the BBC and Channel 4, and they regularly contribute to the BBC World Service. Their book, *Stone of Heaven* (2001), was named book of the year by the **New York Times**, and *Deception* (2007), was a *Washington Post* Pick of the Year. Levy and Scott-Clark won the One World Media award in 2005, and were nominated as feature writers of the year at the British Press Awards in 2008. They won Journalist of the Year at the One World Media awards 2009.

Michel Serres is a French philosopher who explores the parallel developments of scientific, philosophical, and literary trends. He attended the naval college and subsequently the Ecole Normale Supérieure. In 1968, Serres gained a doctorate for a thesis on Leibniz's philosophy under the supervision of Gaston Bachelard. During the 1960s he taught with Michel Foucault at the Universities of Clermont-Ferrand and Vincennes and was later appointed to a chair in the history of science at the Sorbonne, where he still teaches. Serres has also been a professor at Stanford University since 1984. In 1990, he was elected to the French Academy.

Jeffrey A. Siegel, PhD, is an Associate Professor and the J. Neils Thompson Centennial Teaching Fellow in Civil Engineering in the Department of Civil, Architectural, and Environmental Engineering at The University of Texas at Austin. Dr. Siegel and his research team have ongoing research on indoor air quality, energy use, and sustainable buildings. He is the co-principal investigator of the National

Science Foundation funded Integrative Graduate Education and Research Traineeship (IGERT) graduate program in Indoor Environmental Science and Engineering.

Iain Sinclair has lived in and written about Hackney, East London, since 1969. His novels include *Downriver* (2004), which won the James Tait Black Prize and the Encore Prize for the Year's Best Second Novel, *Radon Daughters* (2001), *Landor's Tower* (2002), and most recently, *Dining on Stones* (2005), which was shortlisted for the Ondaatje Prize. Non-fiction books exploring the myth and matter of London include *Lights Out for the Territory* (2003), *London Orbital* (2003), and *Edge of the Orison* (2005). He edited *London, City of Disappearances* (2006) and his most recent book is *Hackney, That Rose-Red Empire* (2009).

Manon Slome is President and chief curator of No Longer Empty where she has curated exhibitions and related educational programming since its formation in 2009. Slome was Chief Curator of the Chelsea Art Museum from 2003–2008 and curated exhibitions at the Guggenheim Museum between 1995–2003. Slome has curated exhibitions in Israel, Italy, Germany, and Hong Kong and has published and lectured widely on contemporary art. She is also a curatorial consultant to the Annenburg Foundation. Slome is a recipient of the Helena Rubinstein Curatorial Fellowship at the Whitney Independent Study program.

Trevor Smith is Curator of Contemporary Art at the Peabody Essex Museum. From 2003–2006 he was Curator at the New Museum of Contemporary Art in New York where, among other projects he co-curated the widely acclaimed exhibition *Andrea Zittel: Critical Space*. Smith was born in Canada and studied Art History at the University of British Columbia. From 1992–2003 he was based in Australia where he worked first at the Biennale of Sydney, then as Director of the Canberra Contemporary Art Space, and from 1997–2003 as Curator of Contemporary Art at the Art Gallery of Western Australia. He has published widely in exhibition catalogues and journals in North America, Europe, Australia, and Asia.

Frances Terpak is curator of photographs at the Getty Research Institute, where she has built the photographic and optical devices collections. She curated the exhibition *Devices of Wonder: From the World in a Box to Images on a Screen* with Barbara Maria Stafford at the J. Paul Getty Museum in 2002 and is co-author of the book with Stafford that accompanied the exhibition. In 1999, she curated the exhibition *Framing the Asian Shore: Nineteenth-Century Photographs of the Ottoman Empire* held at the Getty Research Institute. She has published and lectured on French Romanesque sculpture and related topics.

Henry Urbach is the Curator of Architecture and Design at the San Francisco Museum of Modern Art. Urbach previously owned and directed the Henry Urbach Architecture gallery in New York, a gallery of contemporary art and architecture that he founded in 1997. Urbach has vast experience as a curator, teacher, lecturer, and published writer. He has served on curatorial and advisory panels for the Storefront for Art and Architecture, the Architectural League of New York, and the Whitney Museum of American Art. Urbach has been published in many journals and books devoted to architectural history, theory, and criticism.

Milena Veenis teaches in the Anthropology Department of the University of Amsterdam. Her PhD focused on East German fantasies about the western consumer world. She continued her postdoctoral studies at Eindhoven University of Technology (the Netherlands) in an international historical research project on the American influence on the development of consumer societies in Europe, where she investigated (amongst other things) the history of cola in the former German Democratic Republic.

Doris von Drathen is a German art historian who lives in both Paris and New York. She has taught at Cornell University, Ecole des Beaux-Arts in Paris, Kunsthochschule in Berlin, Architectural Association, the University of North Carolina at Chapel Hill, and Columbia University. Through her teaching and writing, she has developed a method for understanding art, which she termed "ethical iconology." This approach grew from her studio visits while working on monographs for contemporary artists such as Marina Abramovic, Louise Bourgeois, Rebecca Horn, Agnes Martin, and Gerhard Richter. Her approach is conveyed in *Vortex of Silence: Proposition for an Art Criticism Beyond Aesthetic Categories* (2004).

Lois Weinthal is Associate Professor and Graduate Advisor for the Master of Interior Design Program at The University of Texas at Austin. Previously she was Director of the Interior Design Program at Parsons The New School for Design. She is co-editor of *After Taste: Expanded Practice in Interior Design* (2011). Her practice focuses on the relationships between architecture, interiors, clothing, and objects, resulting in works that take on an experimental nature. She has received grants from the Graham Foundation, a Fulbright Award, and the DAAD Award for residency in Berlin. She received her Master of Architecture from Cranbrook Academy of Art and Bachelor of Architecture from the Rhode Island School of Design.

Wim Wenders is a director and writer and oversees his production company Neue Road Movies. Films include *Wings of Desire* (1987), which won the award for Best Director at Cannes, as well as the European Film Award and the German Film Prize, *Paris, Texas* (1984), which won the Golden Palm at Cannes and the Best Director award of the British Academy of Film and Television Arts, and the *Buena Vista Social Club* (1999), which received an Oscar nomination. He has served as the chairman and president of the European Film Academy. Wenders is a Professor at the College of Fine Arts in Hamburg.

Hans Westra studied pedagogy at the University of Amsterdam and began work at the Anne Frank House in Amsterdam in 1974. He was the Executive Director from 1983–2011, at which time he retired. His "farewell gift" to the Anne Frank House is *The Amsterdam of Anne Frank*, which will take the form of a virtual tour of Amsterdam focusing on traces of Anne Frank and the Jewish community.

Mark Wigley is a Professor of Architecture and Dean of the Faculty of Architecture, Planning and Preservation at Columbia University in New York. Residencies and awards include a resident fellowship at the Chicago Institute for Architecture and Urbanism, the Triennial Award for Architectural Criticism, and the Graham Foundation. Wigley co-edited with Philip Johnson the exhibition and publication *Deconstructivist Architecture* (1988) at the Museum of Modern Art in New York. This may be seen to be the first of his many influential, international pieces of work, to which also belongs a series of books, including *White Walls, Designer Dresses: The Fashioning of Modern Architecture* (2001).

Monica Wyatt: "I played in my brother's bedroom as a small child because that is where the Lincoln Logs lived. The living room coffee table bore Lego houses from which I drove my matchbox car to work. My dolls had an endless variety of homes in the corners made by furniture, while they sat idle. The many houses of my life are etched in my brain, the colors, the textures, the details, the plans. Spaces are worn like a favorite cloak. Architects are not made, they are born. I have constructed, dreamed, imagined, designed the built environment and its layers. I always will."

Bibliography

Abé, Kobo. *The Box Man*. Translated by E. Dale Saunders. New York: Alfred A. Knopf, 1974.

Batchelor, David. "Chromophobia." In *Chromophobia*, 21–24, 27–31, 36–37, 39–49. London: Reaktion Books, 2000.

Bédard, Catherine. "In a Few Lines, Alan Storey." In *Drawing Machines*, by Alan Storey, 8–24, 29–30, 55, 63. Paris: Services culturels de l'Ambassade du Canada, 1999.

Benjamin, Walter. "Paris, Capital of the Nineteenth Century." In *Reflections*. Translated by Edmund Jephcott, 155–56. New York: Schocken Books, 1986.

Betsky, Aaron. "Furnishing the Primitive Hut: Allan Wexler's Experiments Beyond Buildings." In *Custom Built: A Twenty-Year Survey of Work by Allan Wexler*. Edited by Christopher Scoates and Debra Wilbur, 11–31. Atlanta, GA: Atlanta College of Art Gallery, 1999.

Betsky, Aaron. "Display Engineers." In *Scanning: The Aberrant Architecture of Diller + Scofidio*, by Aaron Betsky, K. Michael Hays, and Laurie Anderson, 23–36. New York: Whitney Museum of American Art, 2003.

Blaisse, Petra. "Curtain as Architecture." In *Inside Outside Petra Blaisse*. Edited by Kayoko Ota, 364–81. Rotterdam, The Netherlands: NAi Publishers, 2007.

Blauvelt, Andrew. "Strangely Familiar: Design and Everyday Life." In *Strangely Familiar: Design and Everyday Life*. Edited by Andrew Blauvelt, 14–24. Minneapolis, MN: Walker Art Center, 2003.

Brusati, Celeste. "Self as Eye: The Perspective Box." In *Artifice and Illusion: The Art and Writing of Samuel van Hoogstraten*, 169–82. Chicago: The University of Chicago Press, 1995.

Buchan, Suzanne. "A Metaphysics of Space: The Quay Brothers' Atmospheric Cosmogonies." Animation Research Centre at the University for Creative Arts, England, 2010.

Centuori, Jeanine. "Flattened Room." In *Architecture Studio: Cranbrook Academy of Art 1986–1993*. Edited by Dan Hoffman, 186–93. New York: Rizzoli International Publications, Inc., 1994.

Colomina, Beatriz. "Interior." In *Privacy and Publicity: Modern Architecture as Mass Media*, 233–82. Cambridge, MA: The MIT Press, 1994.

Evans, Caroline. "No Man's Land." In *Hussein Chalayan*. Edited by Caroline Evans, Suzy Menkes, Ted Polhemus, and Bradley Quinn, 8–15. Rotterdam, The Netherlands: NAi Publishers, 2005.

Evans, Robin. "The Developed Surface: An Enquiry into the Brief Life of an Eighteenth-Century Drawing Technique." In *Translations from Drawing to Building and Other Essays*. Edited by Robin Evans, 195–231. Cambridge, MA: The MIT Press, 1997.

Furján, Helene. "The Specular Spectacle of the House of the Collector." *Assemblage*, no. 34 (1997): 57–69, 86–87.

Fuss, Diana, and Joel Sanders. "Berggasse 19: Inside Freud's Office." In *Stud: Architectures of Masculinity*. Edited by Joel Sanders, 112–38. New York: Princeton Architectural Press, 1996.

Gaston, Diana. "The Secrets of Rooms." In *Abelardo Morell and the Camera Eye*. Edited by Arthur Ollman, Abelardo Morell, and Diana Gaston, 9–12. San Diego, CA: Museum of Photographic Arts, 1998.

Gilman, Charlotte Perkins. "The Yellow Wallpaper." In *The New England Magazine* (January 1892).

Graham, Dan. "Gordon Matta-Clark." In *Gordon Matta-Clark*. Edited by Juan Manuel Bonet, 378–80. Valencia: Instituto Valenciano de Arte Moderno, 1999.

Helguera, Pablo. "Polyvalent Spaces: The Postmodern Wunderkammer and the Return of Ambiguity." Department of Education, Museum of Modern Art, New York, 2010.

Hollander, Anne. "Drapery." In *Seeing Through Clothes*, 26–36. New York: Viking Press, 1978.

Jacobs, Steven. "Architecture of the Gaze: Jeffries Apartment & Courtyard." In *The Wrong House: The Architecture of Alfred Hitchcock*, 278–95. Rotterdam, The Netherlands: 010 Publishers, 2007.

Kipnis, Jeffrey. "A Conversation with Jacques Herzog." *El Croquis*, no. 84 (1997): 7–21.

Kraft, Kerstin. "Cutting Patterns." *form + zweck*, no. 15 (1998): 66–69. Originally published in Mentges, Gabriele, and Heide Nixdorff. *zeit.schnitte. Kulturelle Konstruktionen von Kleidung und Mode*. Dortmund, Germany: Editions Eberbach, 2001.

Le Corbusier. "The Decorative Art of Today." In *The Decorative Art of Today*. Translated by James I. Dunnet, 83–99. Cambridge, MA: The MIT Press, 1987.

Lichtenstein, Rachel, and Iain Sinclair. *Rodinsky's Room*. London: Granta Books, 1999.

Lilley, Ed. "The Name of the Boudoir." *Journal of the Society of Architectural Historians* 53, no. 2 (1994): 193–98.

Loos, Adolf. "The Principle of Cladding." In *Spoken Into The Void: Collected Essays 1897–1900*. Oppositions Books series. Translated by Jane O. Newman and John H. Smith, 66–69. Cambridge, MA: The MIT Press, 1982.

Lupton, Ellen. "Skin: New Design Organics." In *Skin: Surface, Substance, and Design*, 28–41. New York: Princeton Architectural Press, 2002.

McAnulty, Robert. "Body Troubles." In *Strategies in Architectural Thinking*. Edited by John Whiteman, Jeffrey Kipnis, and Richard Burdett, 180–97. Cambridge, MA: The MIT Press, 1992.

Meisenheimer, Wolfgang. "Of the Hollow Spaces in the Skin of the Architectural Body." *Daidalos*, no. 13 (1984): 103–11.

Mullins, Charlotte. "House 1993." In *Rachel Whiteread*, 50–57. London: Tate Publishing, 2004.

Pallasmaa, Juhani. "An Architecture of the Seven Senses." In *Questions of Perception: Phenomenology of Architecture*. Edited by Steven Holl, Juhani Pallasmaa, and Alberto Pérez-Gómez, 29–37. Tokyo: a+u, 1994.

Rybczynski, Witold. "Domesticity." In *Home: A Short History of an Idea*, 50–75, 236–37. New York: Viking Press, 1986.

Schouwenberg, Louise. "For the Love of Things." In *Hella Jongerius*, unpaginated. London and New York: Phaidon, 2003.

Scott-Clark, Catherine, and Adrian Levy. "The Amber Room: Introduction." In *The Amber Room: The Untold Story of the Greatest Hoax of the Twentieth Century*, 3–8. London: Atlantic Books, 2004.

Serres, Michel. "The Five Senses: Boxes." In *The Five Senses: A Philosophy of Mingled Bodies*. Translated by Margaret Sankey and Peter Cowley, 146–48. London: Continuum, 2008.

Siegel, Jeffrey. "Engineering the Indoor Environment." Department of Civil, Architectural and Environmental Engineering, The University of Texas at Austin, 2010.

Slome, Manon. *Tongue and Groove: Movable Sculpture*. New York: Chelsea Art Museum, 2006.

Smith, Trevor. "The Rules of Her Game: A-Z at Work and Play." In *Andrea Zittel: Critical Space*. Edited by Paola Morsiani and Trevor Smith, 36–43. Munich and New York: Prestel Verlag, 2005.

Terpak, Frances. "Théâtre de l'univers." In *Devices of Wonder: From the World in a Box to Images on a Screen*. Edited by Barbara Maria Stafford and Frances Terpak, 307–14. Los Angeles: Getty Research Institute, 2001.

Urbach, Henry. "Closets, Clothes, disClosure." *Assemblage*, no. 30 (1996): 62–73.

Veenis, Milena. "Consumption in East Germany: The Seduction and Betrayal of Things." *Journal of Material Culture* 4, no. 1 (1999): 84–90.

Von Drathen, Doris. "Places at the Zero Point." In *Rebecca Horn: Moon Mirror*, 41–6. Ostfildern-Ruit, Germany: Hatje Cantz Verlag, 2005.

Weinthal, Lois. "Corners and Darts." *Thresholds*, no. 22 (2001): 84–89.

Wenders, Wim. "Notebook on Clothes and Cities." In *The Act of Seeing: Essays and Conversations*, 81–92. London: Faber and Faber Ltd., 1997.

Westra, Hans. *Inside Anne Frank's House: An Illustrated Journey through Anne's World*. Translated by Epicycles/Amsterdam. Woodstock, NY: Overlook Duckworth, 2004.

Wigley, Mark. "Inside the Inside." In *The Architectural Unconscious: James Casebere + Glen Seator*. Edited by Joseph N. Newland, 16–23. Andover, MA: Addison Gallery of American Art, 2000.

Wyatt, Monica. "Space-Enfolding Breath." In *Architecture Studio: Cranbrook Academy of Art 1986–1993*. Edited by Dan Hoffman, 194–201. New York: Rizzoli International Publications, Inc., 1994.

Index